# Texas Natural History
## A Century of Change

# The Total Synthesis
## of Natural Products

VOLUME 4

Edited by

John ApSimon

*Department of Chemistry*
*Carleton University, Ottawa*

A WILEY-INTERSCIENCE PUBLICATION

JOHN WILEY & SONS, New York • Chichester • Brisbane • Toronto

*Library of Congress Cataloging in Publication Data:*

ApSimon, John.
  The total synthesis of natural products.

  Includes bibliographical references and index.
  1. Chemistry, Organic–Synthesis.  I. Title.
QD262.A68    547'.2    72-4075
ISBN  0-471-05460-7 (v. 4)

Printed in the United States of America

10  9  8  7  6  5  4  3  2  1

# Texas Natural History
## A Century of Change

### David J. Schmidly

Forewords by
**Andrew Sansom** &
**Robert J. Potts**

Afterword by
**Clyde Jones**

TEXAS TECH UNIVERSITY PRESS

This book was set in Cheltenham BT and New Century Schoolbook. The paper used in this book meets the minimum requirements of ANSI/NISO Z39.48-1992 (R1997). ∞

Design by Brandi Price

Library of Congress Cataloging-in-Publication Data
    Schmidly, David J., 1943-
      Texas natural history : a century of change / David J. Schmidly ; forewords by Andrew Sansom and Robert J. Potts ; afterword by Clyde Jones.
        p. cm.
     Includes bibliographical references (p. ).
     ISBN 0-89672-469-7 (cloth : alk. paper)
     1. Natural history—Texas. 2. Ecological surveys—Texas. I. Title.
     QH105.T4 S36 2002
     508.764—dc21
                  2001004909

02 03 04 05 06 07 08 09 10 / 9 8 7 6 5 4 3 2 1

Texas Tech University Press
Box 41037
Lubbock, Texas 79409-1037 USA

1-800-832-4042
ttup@ttu.edu
www.ttup.ttu.edu

Dedicated to the legacy of Vernon Bailey and William B. "Doc" Davis, pioneers of Texas mammalogy, and to my scientific colleagues, in appreciation of their contributions to Texas natural history

# Contents

# Forewords

Although our mythology leads us to think of Texas as a frontier kind of place—wild, pristine, and limitless—the fact is, everything has changed. In this significant work, my colleague David Schmidly has given a meaningful historical perspective of biological change on the Texas landscape. In this updated classic, Bailey's *Biological Survey of Texas*, Schmidly moves beyond taxonomy to give us an understanding of just how drastically humans can affect the landscape in a relatively short period of time.

Although Spanish cattle had undoubtedly begun to alter the vegetation on the South Texas Plains since the advent of Europeans on this part of the continent, most of Texas was biologically virgin when Austin's first boatload of colonists washed up at the mouth of the Brazos in 1822. Barely more than a half century later, Vernon Bailey reported a biota that had been irrevocably altered forever.

Schmidly puts Bailey in context and cross-references the original work with updated scientific nomenclature and current ranges and habitats of the mammals first described one hundred years ago. Changes on the landscape continue—particularly noteworthy is a continual decline in biological diversity. On the other hand, thanks mainly to the stewardship of private landowners in Texas, much of the countryside is in far better condition today than when Vernon Bailey first laid eyes on it.

Given these insights, *Texas Natural History: A Century of Change* is more than a comprehensive biological review of our state since the turn of the twentieth century. It is more than a tremendous resource to biologists and others interested in our natural history who would otherwise not have access to this information. It is more than an update.

David Schmidly has given us original interpretation and research based on sound scholarship that suggests at the turn of the twenty-first century how we can learn from both the mistakes and successes of the past and be better stewards.

Vernon Bailey and David Schmidly have shown us that the biological world in Texas is not static. It has changed and will continue to change.

Andrew Sansom
Former Executive Director
Texas Parks and Wildlife Department

Texas is still a legendary place. From the Pineywoods of East Texas to the mountains and deserts of the west, from the Great Plains in the north to the subtropical Rio Grande Valley, from the springs and rivers of the Hill Country flowing to the bays and estuaries of the Gulf of Mexico, few places can equal Texas's scope and diversity. Yet the natural Texas landscape shrinks every year.

Nature changes so gradually that people usually do not notice. It is a human tendency to assume that the way a landscape looks now is "normal" and the way it ought to look. A Chinese tallow forest on the Texas coast is assumed to be "natural" by most of the population and the cause of little concern. Even the relatively rapid ecological transformation of a coastal prairie into a scrub forest of exotic trees in a couple of decades seems very slow from a human perspective.

No one alive today remembers what Texas was like one hundred years ago. Texas is fortunate that the U.S. Congress funded extensive biological surveys at the turn of the twentieth century in this state. These surveys, conducted by dozens of people over several years, provide an invaluable insight on the Texas we inherited. Texas is also fortunate that David Schmidly cared enough about the state's natural history to find, compile, and publish the work of these biologists. Dr. Schmidly's efforts have greatly enhanced the understanding that professional and amateur ecologists have of this state.

*Texas Natural History: A Century of Change* provides a perspective that anyone interested in the natural world in Texas will find indispensable. To understand what we have today and what we want for tomorrow, we need to know what we had in the past. To understand who we are as Texans, we must understand what our ancestors encountered, for they depended on the land and water of this state in very immediate and direct ways.

It is a rare accomplishment that a book can both look to the past and point to the future as David Schmidly has with this work. This book provides a picture of the past that will inform our vision of the future. It illustrates how close we are to losing much of the natural diversity of Texas. The challenge for generations alive today is to ensure that we do not forsake our heritage in our rush to the future. Texas is still a legendary place; we must not lose our sense of place, the source of who we are as a state and as a people.

Robert J. Potts
Vice President and Director
South Central Division
Nature Conservancy

# Preface

Texas is a place where major life zones intermingle. The fauna and flora include elements characteristic of the southeastern forests, the southern tropics, the southwestern deserts, the western mountains, and the northern Great Plains, as well as marine life associated with the extensive coast. Because of this as well as its size and geographic location, Texas has the greatest wildlife heritage of any of the United States. There are more than 1,245 kinds of fish and wildlife in Texas, of which 126 occur nowhere else in the world (*Texas Environmental Almanac*, 2000). Texas's wildlife resources comprise 20 percent of the nation's total deer population, more than 65 percent of the waterfowl in the Central Flyway, and more than six hundred species and subspecies of birds. The state's fish and wildlife are major resources that provide Texans with important recreational, commercial, aesthetic, and scientific values.

The purpose of this book is to look back at the twentieth century and evaluate what has happened to the natural history of Texas during this period. For a variety of reasons, but mainly because of my own scientific expertise, I have chosen mammals as the vertebrate group to illustrate the major patterns of faunal change that have occurred in Texas during the twentieth century. Mammals were selected for study because of their diversity, varied life histories, representation of several feeding levels, and ultimate reliance on plants for food and shelter. Be-

cause of their diversity in body size, morphology, and life history strategies, there is every reason to believe that the same patterns described for mammals have been repeated on more or less the same scale for the other major groups of vertebrates in the state. Also, mammals are part of what conservationists refer to as the charismatic megafauna, meaning they attract public attention and often become the focus of conservation issues and controversies. Large mammals are particularly useful as focal species in the reserve design process because of their need for vast areas of protected lands, habitat connectivity, and, in the case of large carnivores, their roles in maintaining ecological integrity of natural communities.

The restoration of populations of large mammals is a major component of modern conservation strategy. It takes place as part of government programs to recover species listed under the U.S. Endangered Species Act and to restore populations of game and other species of special public interest. Many large mammals, including large carnivores and some large ungulates, appear to play ecologically pivotal or keystone roles in ecosystems. In some cases their decline appears to have led to imbalances in populations of other species, reduced native species richness, and impaired ecological functions. Viable populations of a full suite of large mammals native to a region are a strong indicator of ecological integrity.

Mammals constitute about 12 percent of the total diversity of terrestrial vertebrates (amphibians, reptiles, birds, and mammals) in Texas. With 144 terrestrial mammal species, Texas ranks behind California (163) and New Mexico (146) and slightly ahead of Arizona (139) in terms of mammalian diversity in the United States. The state harbors a large and significant portion of the North American mammal fauna—about 40 percent of the total fauna in the United States. But for two major groups of mammals, bats and carnivores, the Texas fauna includes three-quarters of the species that occur in the United States.

Another reason for the focus on mammals is that there is a good historical perspective about this component of the Texas fauna. From 1889 to 1905, a team of federal scientists from the U.S. Bureau of Biological Survey (forerunner of today's U.S. Fish and Wildlife Service) surveyed the flora and fauna of the state, emphasizing mammals as the target group. Vernon Bailey, chief field naturalist of the U.S. Biological Survey and director of the field efforts in Texas, was one of the leading mammalogists of his era, and he summarized the results of the survey in a 222-page publication titled the *Biological Survey of Texas*. The report was published in 1905 as No. 25 of the North American Fauna series. This publication constitutes the only comprehensive study of Texas natural history available from the turn of the twentieth century. The book, however, has been out of print for more than seventy-five years. Today, copies of the survey are exceedingly difficult to obtain, and most biologists in Texas do not have access to its vast wealth of historical information.

The records of the biological survey of Texas provide a virtual natural history picture of every region of the state as it existed a century ago. This information can now be utilized as baseline data to compare with the results of current natural history studies in the state to assess landscape and biotic change. The publication of a recent book by William B. Davis and myself, *The Mammals of Texas*, summarizes the current status of mammals and provides a context for understanding the modern mammal fauna in the state. By comparing the mammal fauna during Bailey's time with the fauna today, it is possible to make some general statements about past conditions and the extent of biological change in the twentieth century.

It would be a surprise to no one, of course, to be told that Texas has changed in the last one hundred years. After all, the population has grown from just three million in 1900 to more than twenty million today. In 1900, most of the population lived in rural areas, with farming and ranching being the primary occupations of the day. Today, the state is highly urbanized and industrialized, with less than one-fifth of the population living in rural areas. The impact of human population growth and urbanization on the landscapes and wildlife of Texas during the twentieth century has been dramatic. The changes in American society during this period have gradually switched from a rural/utilitarian background where hunting, fishing, and trapping were once more common, to a society where human contact with wildlife is minimal and largely passive.

The general public has difficulty with conservation issues because they have become so far removed from the land itself and have little or no concept of biotic mechanisms. Conservationists and scientists who study the natural world and how it has changed have a tendency to interpret and write about it from their own biological perspectives, experience, and background. Unfortunately, in many cases, these personal experiences do not include an appreciation of the "land ethic" and are limited to rather narrow snapshots of a few decades, which is too short a period of time to obtain a meaningful understanding of long-term biological change. We seldom have adequate information, such as we now have for Texas mammals, to build a picture of faunal change over the time-scale of a century.

I, too, write from the perspective of my personal biases. These were shaped by my background and experience growing up as a farm boy on a cotton farm in Hockley County, Texas, during the decade of the 1950s; by my academic training in zoology and mammalogy at Texas Tech University and the University of Illinois (1962–71); and by my professional scientific career spent as a member of the faculty at Texas A&M University (1972–96) and Texas Tech University (1996–present). All but three years of my life, more than a half-century, have been spent in Texas. I collected my first mammal on a field trip to the Big Bend region in 1963 and began a love affair with fieldwork and the study of mammals that continues to this day.

I was most fortunate to be able to start my professional academic career at a land-grant university (the Department of Wildlife and Fisheries Sciences at Texas A&M University). In that capacity I was afforded the opportunity to interact with zoologists, such as myself, as well as natural resource professionals. For six years (1986–92), I served as head of my academic department at Texas A&M, an experience which offered me the chance to interact with farmers, ranchers, commodity organizations, and state and federal agencies responsible for the management of natural resources, as well as professional zoologists and wildlife managers. While in this capacity, I learned much about the practical aspects of managing wildlife on private lands and I developed a deep and abiding appreciation for the role of the landowner in the conservation of natural resources. I also learned that although many landowners have a strong land ethic, they do not necessarily and automatically extend this ethical structure to embrace a conservation ethic.

Much of my career has been spent in the joint capacity of teacher-research scientist and academic administrator. Although administration has taken some days away from my fieldwork and day-to-day scientific involvement, it has given me a greater appreciation for strategic thinking, long-term planning, "bigger picture" perspectives, and the importance of teamwork and partnerships in accomplishing goals and objectives. At Texas Tech I have been able to shape an administration research agenda deeply committed to environmental and natural history issues in Texas as well as affiliate with the largest academic mammalogy program in the United States. In effect, it has given me the best of both worlds.

For the decade of the 1990s, I also have had the distinct pleasure to affiliate with and serve on the board of trustees of the Nature Conservancy (TNC) of Texas, most recently in the capacity as Chair of the Conservation Committee. TNC is a non-profit wildlife conservation organization, using science-based research and a cooperative approach to protect the unique diversity of animals and plants native to Texas. A principle called "community-based conservation" is the key element in TNC philosophy. Community-based conservation is the concept of working with local residents to protect our unique and irreplaceable natural heritage, while taking into account the values and economic needs of people. This approach seeks to demonstrate the value of conservation and build consensus for it in the communities where TNC works, understanding that without support from those communities, conservation would be impossible. In a practical sense, community-based conservation means working in partnership with neighbors, private landowners, businesses, and other conservation agencies to conserve ecologically significant land in ways that benefit communities. Educational and research opportunities; sharing of information and best practices; and methods of compatible agricultural, industrial, and ecotourism development are among the potential benefits of community-based conservation.

My work with TNC has convinced me that these goals are best achieved through building mutually beneficial alliances among a broad array of partners—business, government agencies, private landowners, and environmental groups. I have also come to believe that we can no longer think of protecting the environment and excluding people. What will work for the future—what we must do—is to include people in planning for conservation, so that environmental protection is not viewed as having come at their expense.

So it is with this background, experience, and perspective that I have compiled this book. I use the word compiled intentionally, as I have not written all its contents. Much of the book is devoted to a reprinting of Vernon Bailey's 1905 publication. In addition, though, I felt it was important to include some historical background about that survey as well as provide a modern interpretation of its scientific conclusions. Finally, because of my own work in mammalogy, I could not pass up the opportunity to compare my work on Texas mammals, and that of other scientists, with the interpretations of Bailey to understand how the mammal fauna of Texas has changed during the twentieth century and to offer my perspective about what the future might hold for conservation in the state.

This book is organized into seven chapters followed by an appendix of scientific names, which relates the nomenclature used in Bailey's era with that used by modern taxonomists, and a literature/reference section. The introductory chapter includes a brief history of the U.S. Bureau of Biological Survey, a description of the biological survey in Texas, and biographies of key people involved in the survey. The second chapter includes a reprinting of the original *Biological Survey of Texas* with reference to endnote numbers that refer to annotations pro-

vided in Chapter 3 of the book. Most of the annotations are about mammals, the focus of Bailey's book and my professional interest. Chapter 4 describes Texas's landscapes during the period of the biological survey as based on the descriptions and photographs taken by the federal agents. Chapter 5 provides a brief overview of the major landcover and land-use changes in Texas during the twentieth century following the completion of the biological survey. Chapter 6 presents my perspective on the major changes that have characterized the mammal fauna of Texas during the twentieth century. In the final chapter, I talk about my perspective of what likely will be in store for conservation in Texas in the twenty-first century.

I have made a conscientious decision not to annotate Bailey's section about the lizards and snakes of Texas. I am not a herpetologist and an expert in that field would be far better qualified to interpret change in that aspect of the Texas fauna. Only incidental observations and collections of lizards and snakes were made by the federal agents during the Texas survey. I noted with interest that the agents did not report collecting any frogs, toads, or salamanders during the survey. All their herpetological specimens were returned to the National Museum of Natural History in Washington, D.C. where they were identified by Dr. Leonhard Stejneger, who was curator of herpetology at that time. The collection of 353 specimens included thirty-one species of snakes and thirty-two species of lizards. The most recent checklist of reptiles for Texas (Dixon, 2000) includes seventy-one species of snakes and fifty-one species of lizards. So, the biological survey uncovered evidence for about half of the snakes and lizards that live in Texas today. The interested reader can determine the modern scientific name for each reptile reported by Bailey and relate the information provided by Bailey with the modern species accounts of Dixon (2000).

# Acknowledgments

My plan to reprint Vernon Bailey's 1905 publication, *Biological Survey of Texas*, began in the early 1990s when I visited the Smithsonian Institution Archives in Washington, D.C. and discovered that the original survey reports, field notebooks, and photographs from the survey were archived there. Almost immediately I approached the Nature Conservancy of Texas about sponsoring a project to copy these materials and place them in an archive in Texas, so they would be more accessible to Texas biologists and others interested in Texas natural history. Working with Director Robert Potts, it was decided that not only would we bring this material to Texas, but a computerized database of the reports and photographs would be created and an annotated reprint of the original book would be published.

Over the years, the project evolved into *Texas Natural History: A Century of Change*, and several agencies and foundations provided funding and support for this project. First and foremost I wish to thank the project sponsor, the Nature Conservancy of Texas, along with Director Robert Potts, Jeff Weigel, and other staff of the Nature Conservancy for their continued support and patience as the project faced numerous delays in its progress. The Robert and Helen Kleberg Foundation, the Wray Foundation, the Helen Jones Foundation, and the Plum Foundation provided the financial backing for the publication of this book, the creation of the database, and the museum exhibit of the same name. I would like to extend special thanks and appreciation to these foundations for their gracious financial assistance and their sincere interest in furthering the study of Texas natural history and conservation.

Individuals in Washington, D.C. who deserve mention and thanks for their assistance in locating and providing archival materials include William Cox of the Smithsonian Institution Archives and Al Gardner and Robert Fisher of the National Museum.

I also wish to thank Nick Parker and his students of the Texas Cooperative Fish and Wildlife Research Unit; Clyde Jones, Robert Bradley, Robert Baker, and Kent Rylander of Texas Tech University; David Riskind and several biologists of the Texas Parks and Wildlife Department; Beryl Simpson and Andrea Weeks of the University of Texas; James Dixon and Keith Arnold of Texas A&M University; Keir Sterling, Stan Casto, and numerous others for their help with biological and biographical data, graphics, and editorial review of the publication. So many friends and colleagues have had a hand in this project over the years that it would be impossible to mention everyone here by name, but please know that I sincerely appreciate the assistance and support provided by all of them.

My research associate of the past nine years, Lisa Bradley, has been instrumental in bringing this long-term project to fruition. With my time in recent years devoted primarily to academic administration, I would undoubtedly still be struggling to complete this book if it were not for Lisa's assistance in writing, editing, research, data entry, and graphics.

# Texas Natural History
### A Century of Change

# Introduction

Texas was very different at the turn of the twentieth century from what it is today. In 1900, the human population was less than three million (about eleven people per square mile), compared to more than twenty million today (about seventy-eight people per square mile) (*Texas Almanac*, 1904; U.S. Census Bureau, 2001). The most populous city at the time, San Antonio, had just 53,321 residents. More than 80 percent of the population lived in rural areas. Farming, ranching, and lumber production were the primary means of income for residents. Railroads and horses were the primary means of transportation. Vast areas in the western part of the state remained unsettled and relatively undisturbed. Common wildlife species included gray wolves, red wolves, black bear, black-footed ferrets, pronghorn, and other species that are now extinct, endangered, or severely reduced in distribution.

This was the Texas visited by Vernon Bailey, chief field naturalist for the U.S. Bureau of Biological Survey. From 1889 to 1905, Bailey and a crew of twelve federal field agents traversed the state, recording detailed field reports of the mammals, birds, and plants they encountered and describing the topography, land use, and climate of each place visited. The

agents also collected and preserved plant and animal specimens and took photographs of the landscapes, plants, and animals they encountered. The purpose of these biological investigations was to thoroughly survey the flora and fauna of this vast state, to determine the distribution of its diverse plant and animal species, and to assess the economic relationship of birds and mammals to farming and ranching. In 1905, the *Biological Survey of Texas* was published as a summary of the thousands of pages of field notes, reports, documentation, and photographs generated by the efforts of Vernon Bailey and the other federal agents.

This introductory chapter includes a brief history of the U.S. Bureau of Biological Survey, a description of the biological survey efforts in Texas, biographies of key people involved in the Texas survey, and a discussion of contemporary mammalogists who also worked in the state at the time of C. Hart Merriam and Bailey.

## C. Hart Merriam and the U.S. Bureau of Biological Survey

The establishment in the late 1800s of the U.S. Bureau of Biological Survey can be attributed to the dedication and passion of one man, a young naturalist by the name of Clinton Hart Merriam (Fig. 1a, b). Merriam was later to become a leading biologist in the United States and is recognized today for his outstanding contributions to the fields of ornithology, mammalogy, and natural history research. For a detailed biography of Merriam and the full history of the U.S. Biological Survey, refer to the more comprehensive accounts of Keir Sterling (1974, 1989) and Jenks Cameron (1974).

Clinton Hart Merriam was born on December 5, 1855, and grew up on his family's rural estate in Locust Grove, New York, where he became fascinated by nature. In 1872, at the age of sixteen, he accompanied Spencer Fullerton Baird (author of *Mammals of North America*, 1859, and the first secretary of the Smithsonian Institution) on the Hayden Survey, an expedition into the Yellowstone region, as the expedition's naturalist. Merriam demonstrated a passion for collecting and a penchant for detailed record keeping even at this early date.

Merriam entered Yale's Sheffield Scientific School in the fall of 1874. In the same year, he wrote a manuscript that foreshadowed his later theories on life zones and geographic distribution of species, although it was never published. In 1877, at the age of twenty-two, Merriam published his first major work in natural history, "Review of the Birds of Connecticut, with remarks on their habits," which established his reputation as an authority in ornithology.

Merriam entered medical school at Columbia University in 1877 where he met Albert Kenrick (A. K.) Fisher, also an ornithologist. The two became lifelong friends and col-

Fig. 1. C. Hart Merriam as a young man (a, top) and in later life (b, bottom). a. Courtesy Biological Survey Unit, U.S. Geological Survey, Patuxent Wildlife Research Center, National Museum of Natural History. b. Courtesy Biological Survey Unit, U.S. Geological Survey, Patuxent Wildlife Research Center, National Museum of Natural History

leagues. After completing medical school in 1879, Merriam spent six years as a practicing physician but was never devoted to the field. Rather, he regarded his work as a doctor primarily as a source of income to support his true love of natural history study.

In 1883, Merriam and Fisher were instrumental in the formation of the American Ornithologists' Union (AOU). Merriam was appointed as chairman of the committee on the Migration of Birds, and he organized a network of twelve hundred volunteers throughout the United States and Canada to gather bird migration data. The resulting flood of data soon overwhelmed Merriam and his small group of volunteer assistants. On the advice of longtime friend and mentor Spencer Fullerton Baird, Merriam appealed to the federal government for aid.

The funding request presented to Congress suggested that farmers could benefit from a clearer understanding of the distribution, food habits, and economic impact of birds. In truth, the economic impact of birds on agriculture was of little interest to Merriam, but he was well aware that successful funding was more likely if the proposal was justified by its benefit to the agricultural interests of the nation. The bill passed Congress, and in 1885 the Division of Entomology of the U.S. Department of Agriculture became the Division of Entomology and Economic Ornithology. Merriam was appointed as economic ornithologist and was granted an annual research budget of $5,000.

Merriam's duties as ornithologist were described as "the study of the interrelation of birds and agriculture, an investigation of the food, habits, and migration of birds in relation to both insects and plants, and publishing reports thereon." Although Merriam's official staff in the first year consisted only of Fisher, whom Merriam had appointed as his assistant, and one clerk, Merriam soon had numerous volunteers sending in specimens for study. Among

the collectors was a young farm boy named Vernon Bailey, who contributed great volumes of specimens and so impressed Merriam that he was later hired as a special field agent.

In 1886, Merriam's budget was doubled to $10,000 and his duties were expanded to include the study of the economic importance of mammals to farmers and livestock raisers. The office was separated from that of entomology and retitled the Division of Economic Ornithology and Mammalogy. Although the purpose of the office remained the study of the economic relationships of birds and mammals to agriculture, Merriam's primary interests were with the collection and naming of species, the geographic distribution of birds and mammals, and the eventual completion of a national biological survey. He gradually guided the efforts of his division to these studies and subsequently met with great opposition from the Agriculture Committee of the House and other members of Congress who felt Merriam's work was not of practical value to the government or the public. Merriam, however, contended that one could not deal with the economic effects of birds and mammals without knowing precisely which birds or mammals one was dealing with.

Despite ongoing criticism that his division was not fulfilling its true mission of economic studies, Merriam continued to direct the research efforts of his staff primarily to the study of the geographic distribution of species and biological survey work. By the late 1890s, agricultural research was a minor role of the division. To better reflect its true role, the office was renamed the Division of Biological Survey in 1896, and in 1906 it was elevated to a bureau.

Among the research efforts Merriam directed were several state and regional biological surveys (Fig. 2). Merriam was fiercely dedicated to the field investigation method and developed the field method used by the biological survey teams. This involved sending out parties in the area to be studied to collect mammal,

Fig. 2. Vernon Bailey, C. Hart Merriam, T. S. Palmer, and A. K. Fisher during the biological survey of Death Valley, California, 1891. Courtesy National Archives, 22-WB-47Admin.-B1929

bird, reptile, amphibian, and plant specimens, taking thorough notes on the life history, numbers, distribution, and economic importance of the species observed and taking photographs of the regions studied (Sterling, 1978).

Merriam was dedicated to publishing the results of the bureau's varied lines of research. Many contributions appeared in the various series of the Department of Agriculture, such as technical bulletins, farmers' bulletins, yearbook articles, circulars, and the *Journal of Agricultural Research*. But the bureau had three sets of publications which were its own—the *North American Fauna* series, the Biological Survey bulletins, and the circulars of the Bureau of Biological Survey. During the first twenty years of the bureau (1885–1905), twenty-three *North American Fauna* were issued, as well as twenty-two bulletins and forty-eight circulars. The

most valuable and enduring was the *North American Fauna* series, which consisted primarily of regional reports of extensive natural history studies and technical monographs of groups of birds and mammals.

Gradually, from 1900 to 1910, the Bureau of Biological Survey was forced by demands from farmers and ranchers to devote increasing attention to the control of noxious and predatory animals. In addition, several actions by Congress during the same time transformed the mission of the agency from survey-oriented research to active management of wildlife resources and their habitats. The study of geographic distribution of species became a minor role of the bureau, and Merriam realized that his dream of a national biological survey would never come to pass. Frustrated by these events, Merriam retired as chief of the Bureau of Biological Survey in 1910, ending a government career of twenty-five years. Following his retirement, Merriam surprised his friends and former colleagues by dedicating himself to the study of the culture and vocabularies of the vanishing Indian tribes of California (Osgood, 1943). C. Hart Merriam died March 19, 1942, at the age of eighty-six.

Merriam's influence in the development of the field of mammalogy deserves mention. From 1885 to 1900, revolutionary changes in mammalogy took place largely as a result of research by Merriam and his biological survey colleagues. Within fifteen years, the number of known species and subspecies of American mammals nearly quadrupled. Merriam himself described no less than 660 new mammals; his mammal collection totaled 136,613 specimens, and his published writings included more than six hundred titles. He was a co-founder of the American Society of Mammalogists and served as its first president (1919–21). Merriam's dedication to training collectors, utilizing the most advanced methods of collection, carefully preserving specimens, taking extensive field notes, and publishing results set a standard for the field of mammalogy that is followed to this day.

One of Merriam's greatest contributions to mammalogy was the adoption of a technique he had learned from the study of birds—the idea of bringing together and studying in minute detail large series of specimens, all uniformly prepared, from every possible locality (Miller, 1929). This introduced the concept of local and geographic variation into the study of mammals and linked an understanding of mammalian variation with Darwin's theory of evolution. Toward this end, Merriam was greatly assisted by the development of the "Cyclone" mousetrap which was developed in the late 1880s and which revolutionized the collecting of small mammals. Using this new technology to collect mammals and applying the species

concept, Merriam and the federal agents obtained volumes of specimens, and they were able to begin mapping the geographical distribution of species.

The great collection of mammals brought together by the Bureau of Biological Survey was, from the beginning, cared for in the U.S. National Museum, one of the branches of the Smithsonian. To avoid scientific duplication, the National Museum directed its research efforts to the study of mammals outside of the United States (Miller, 1929). Gerrit S. Miller, Jr., came to the National Museum in 1898 from the Bureau of Biological Survey, and for forty years he cared for the mammal collection (Kellogg, 1946). From 1889 until 1943, the Division of Reptiles and Batrachians at the National Museum was supervised by Leonhard Stejneger, who assisted Bailey with the section on snakes and lizards in the Texas biological survey.

## The *Biological Survey of Texas*

One of C. H. Merriam's visions for the Bureau of Biological Survey was the completion of a nationwide biological survey. He focused his early efforts for this survey project, however, on the western states because they were the agricultural states, and there he could justify his survey projects to Congress by the benefit they would have to agricultural interests. One of the early states chosen for a survey project was Texas. This was justified by the need to study urgent economic problems such as the decimation of cotton crops by the boll weevil, the depletion of range forages by the millions of prairie dogs in the state, and the loss of sheep and goats to predation by coyotes and other large carnivores. Merriam's conviction that an understanding of the taxonomy and distribution of mammals was basic to providing solutions to economic problems of agriculture was the impetus for a program of basic research on mammalian systematics that continues to this day (Wilson and Eisenberg, 1990).

In truth, Merriam's desire to conduct a biological survey of Texas was motivated in large part by the fact that the state had such a wide variety of soil types, climates, and topography, and these factors resulted in diverse and abundant plant and wildlife resources. By nature of its geographic location in the south-central United States, Texas sits at the juncture of at least four major biomes: the deciduous forests of the southeast, the grasslands of the central plains, the deserts and mountains of the southwest, and the brushlands and tropical habitats of the south. The convergence of these ecological regions provides habitat for Texas's native terrestrial mammal and bird species, many of which reach their distributional limits in the state.

The diverse and abundant natural resources in Texas had been recognized by many early explorers and settlers who wrote excellent descriptions of Texas and its natural resources up to the mid-1800s (Weniger, 1984; 1997). These accounts describe an area teaming with vast herds of buffalo, pronghorn, deer and other game, filling the millions of acres of prairies, plains, and forests of the state with wildlife too plentiful for modern man to comprehend.

During the mid-1800s, however, the "taming" of Texas began in earnest. The last of the Native Americans in West Texas were killed or forced onto reservations by 1875, and the bison, once numbering an estimated sixty million, was already decimated in many areas by 1860. By the early 1880s less than two hundred bison remained.

In 1870, Texas was occupied by only 818,579 people (Texas Almanac, 1873). In 1871, a state government office titled the Bureau of Immigration of the State of Texas was created to encourage immigration from other states and foreign countries. As a result of the Bureau of Immigration's efforts and the rapid growth of railroads in the state, from 711 miles in 1870 to 11,294 miles in 1904, the population grew dramatically. An estimated four hundred thousand immigrants entered the state in 1876 alone. By the turn of the century, the population had grown to 3 8,710, an increase of 372 percent from . This dramatic rise in population a natural resources in many ways, as prairies, rangelands, forests, and wil rces were exploited or depleted by far hing, lumber production, predator c hunting.

The dramatic growth a during the 1870s and 1880s may ed an additional role in Merriam's o conduct a biological survey of th . In 1889, Merriam appointed Vernon Bailey to lead the investigation and to train new field agents as they joined the team. Field agents were often hired as temporary employees, but other agents were permanent employees of the bureau and were based in Washington, D.C. when not conducting field research (Fig. 3).

Much of the fieldwork was conducted in conjuncti rk in other states. Field agents woul rk in northern states during the summ s and move south during the fall, wint spring. However, all seasons of the epresented in the field data for Tex y efforts were conducted from 18 2, in 1894, and from 1899 to 19 ve field agents who worked 2,185 day ). Survey work took place at more an two hundred sites in all ten ecological regions of the state (Maps 1–2j).

At each site visited, the field agents prepared written reports describing the physiography of the region and annotated lists of the mammals, birds, and plants observed or collected. These reports were prepared in addition to an annual field journal for each agent, describing their day-to-day movements and activities, and a field catalog of all specimens collected (Figs. 4, 5). The agents also took more

Fig. 3. A. K. Fisher, E. W. Nelson, W. H. Osgood, and Vernon Bailey, working at the National Museum in Washington, D.C., early 1900s. Courtesy Biological Survey Unit, U.S. Geological Survey, Patuxent Wildlife Research Center, National Museum of Natural History.

than a thousand photographs of landscapes, habitats, plants, and animals from throughout the state.

During the 1901 survey of the Trans-Pecos region, Vernon Bailey and ornithologist Harry Church Oberholser were joined in the field by the famed wildlife artist, Louis Agassiz Fuertes. Fuertes produced some of his finest works during this trip. His portfolio, after four months in the field, included more than a hundred portraits of birds as well as a number of mammals and reptiles (Fig. 6a–f).

The working conditions for the field agents were primitive at best, and arduous or even life threatening, at worst. The agents usually traveled from Washington, D.C. to the scheduled first stop by train, using vouchers provided by the bureau to pay for their train fare. Once in

Texas, however, virtually all the agents' day-to-day living expenses were paid out of their own pockets, from a salary that averaged only $100 per month. The agents would hire a local to serve as their "camp man," who would cook for them and set up their camps in the field (Fig. 7). They would also rent horses, mules, and wagons, as needed, and purchase all their food and other supplies from a local town, then set out to the field to observe and collect data and specimens. Their stay in any one locality would range from one day to two weeks or more.

At most localities, the field agents would set up camp and travel on foot or by horseback as they collected specimens and recorded their observations (Fig. 8). The agents often befriended the local landowners and were usually welcomed to collect specimens and to camp on

Table 1. Man-days[1] in Texas by each survey contributor

| | 1889 | 1890 | 1891 | 1892 | 1894 | 1899 | 1900 | 1901 | 1902 | 1903 | 1904 | 1905 | 1906 | **Total** |
|---|---|---|---|---|---|---|---|---|---|---|---|---|---|---|
| Bailey | 25 | 39 | 0 | 28 | 0 | 58 | 45 | 94 | 88 | 0 | 47 | 0 | ! | 425 |
| Bray | 0 | 0 | 0 | 0 | 0 | 50 | 0 | 0 | 0 | 0 | 0 | 0 | 0 | 50 |
| Cary | 0 | 0 | 0 | 0 | 0 | 0 | 0 | 0 | 119 | 0 | 0 | 0 | 0 | 119 |
| Donald | 0 | 0 | 0 | 0 | 0 | 0 | 0 | 0 | 19 | 0 | 0 | 0 | 0 | 19 |
| Dutcher | 0 | 0 | 0 | 27 | 0 | 0 | 0 | 0 | 0 | 0 | 0 | 0 | 0 | 27 |
| Fisher | 0 | 0 | 0 | 0 | 6 | 0 | 0 | 0 | 0 | 0 | 0 | 0 | 0 | 6 |
| Gaut | 0 | 0 | 0 | 0 | 0 | 0 | 0 | 0 | 0 | 135 | 10 | 106 | 0 | 251 |
| Hollister | 0 | 0 | 0 | 0 | 0 | 0 | 0 | 0 | 86 | 0 | 0 | 0 | 0 | 86 |
| Howell | 0 | 0 | 0 | 0 | 0 | 0 | 0 | 0 | 0 | 51 | 0 | 114 | 36 | 201 |
| Lloyd | 0 | 176 | 233 | 87 | 0 | 0 | 0 | 0 | 0 | 0 | 0 | 0 | 0 | 496 |
| Loring | 0 | 0 | 0 | 0 | 108 | 0 | 0 | 0 | 0 | 0 | 0 | 0 | 0 | 108 |
| Oberholser | 0 | 0 | 0 | 0 | 0 | 0 | 150 | 123 | 124 | 0 | 0 | 0 | 0 | 397 |
| Total | 25 | 215 | 233 | 142 | 114 | 108 | 195 | 217 | 436 | 186 | 57 | 220 | 37 | **2185** |

[1]Total days from beginning to end of each trip—includes days collecting as well as days traveling between sites, writing reports, and so forth.

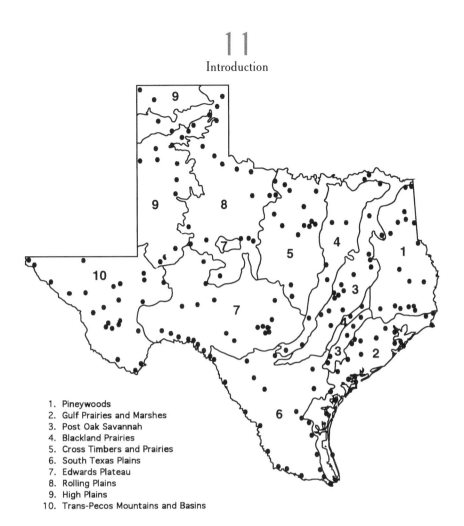

1. Pineywoods
2. Gulf Prairies and Marshes
3. Post Oak Savannah
4. Blackland Prairies
5. Cross Timbers and Prairies
6. South Texas Plains
7. Edwards Plateau
8. Rolling Plains
9. High Plains
10. Trans-Pecos Mountains and Basins

Map 1. The ecological regions of Texas and localities visited (●) by federal agents during the biological survey of Texas, 1889–1905

the property. Occasionally they were fortunate enough to be invited to supper and to stay in the landowner's home or barn for the night. More often than not, however, the field conditions for the agents were rigorous, and the field diaries contain accounts of being caught in raging flood waters, becoming isolated in areas without food or water, losing horses and pack mules, suffering from the extreme heat, and becoming ill without a doctor or medicine available.

Following are selections of accounts from field diaries of the agents. These accounts provide a vivid picture of the hardships these men endured as well as their unwavering dedication to hard work and their passion for natural history study.

Vernon Bailey, Finley's Ranch
(14 miles west of Ft. Davis).

January 13, 1890. Twenty-two degrees at sunrise, clear and still. Coldest morning of the winter so far. Took a horse and started over the mountains to see the country on the north side and visit the ranches and get bear skulls. Went up the canyon about 3 miles and then climbed the right side and crossed the divide where it is 7,270 feet, measured by W. H. Cameron of Waco. Followed an old government road down the canyon on the other side and reached Mr. Perkins' ranch at 1 p.m. This is about as high as Finley's— 6,000 feet. Was welcomed by four hounds and the rest of the family. After dinner went farther down the canyon and killed a *Lepus sylvaticus* [= *Sylvilagus floridanus*]. Saw a *Spermophilus grammurus* [= *Spermophilus variegatus*]. Birds and plants are about

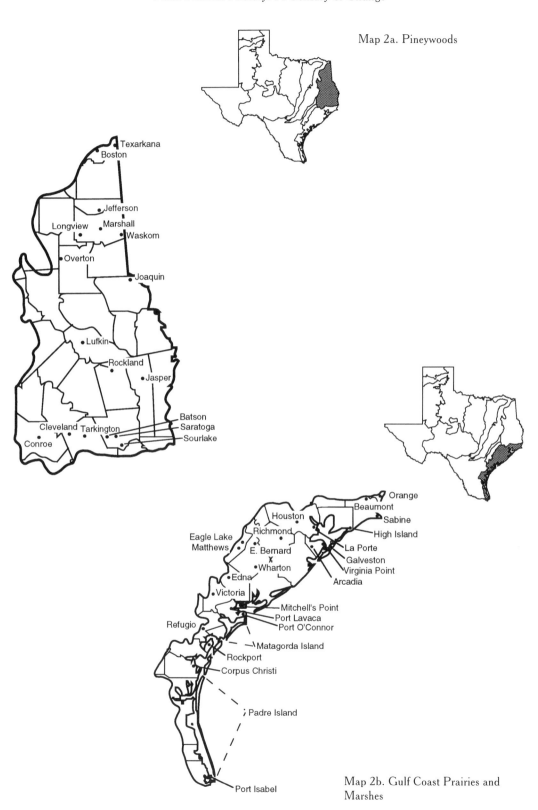

Map 2a. Pineywoods

Texarkana
Boston

Jefferson

Longview  Marshall
Waskom

Overton

Joaquin

Lufkin

Rockland

Jasper

Batson
Cleveland  Tarkington  Saratoga
Sourlake
Conroe

Orange
Beaumont
Houston  Sabine
Richmond  High Island
Eagle Lake
Matthews  E. Bernard  La Porte
Wharton  Galveston
Virginia Point
Edna  Arcadia

Victoria

Mitchell's Point
Port Lavaca
Port O'Connor
Refugio

Matagorda Island
Rockport
Corpus Christi

Padre Island

Port Isabel

Map 2b. Gulf Coast Prairies and
Marshes

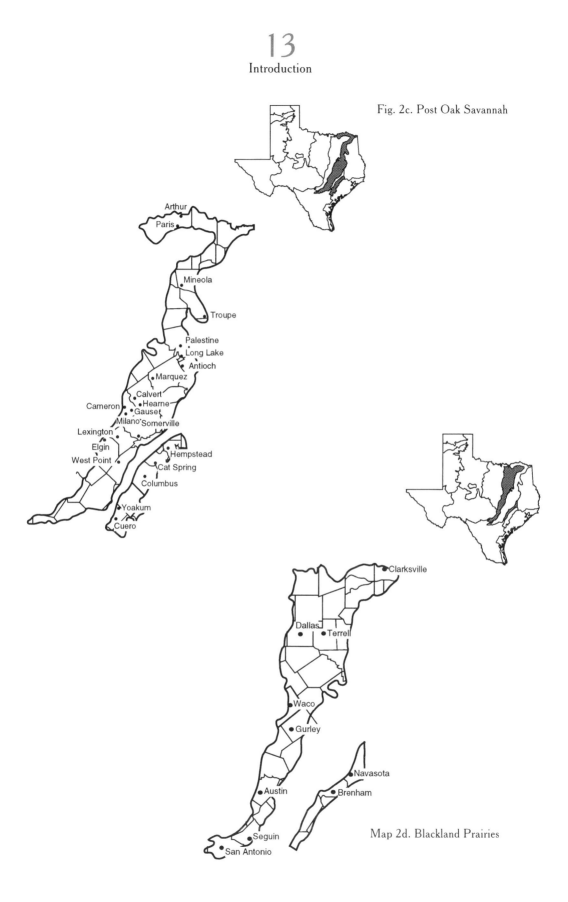

Fig. 2c. Post Oak Savannah

Arthur
Paris

Mineola

Troupe

Palestine
Long Lake
Antioch

Marquez

Calvert
Hearne
Gauset
Cameron
Milano Somerville
Lexington
Elgin
West Point
Hempstead
Cat Spring
Columbus

Yoakum
Cuero

Clarksville

Dallas
Terrell

Waco

Gurley

Navasota
Austin
Brenham

Seguin
San Antonio

Map 2d. Blackland Prairies

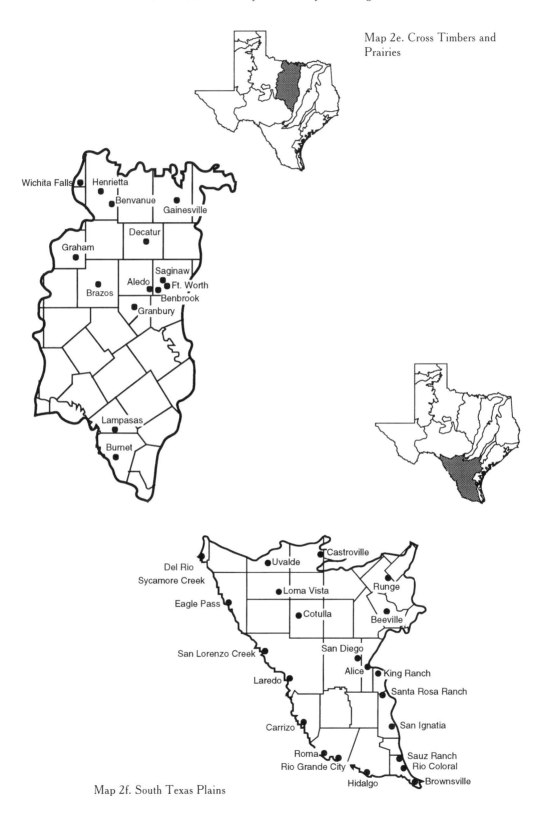

Map 2e. Cross Timbers and Prairies

Wichita Falls • Henrietta
• Benvanue
Gainesville •

Decatur •

Graham •

Saginaw •
Aledo • • Ft. Worth
Brazos • Benbrook -
Granbury •

Lampasas •

Burnet •

Map 2f. South Texas Plains

Castroville •
Del Rio • Uvalde
Sycamore Creek
Runge •
Loma Vista •
Eagle Pass • Beeville •
Cotulla •

San Lorenzo Creek • San Diego •
Alice • • King Ranch
Laredo • Santa Rosa Ranch

Carrizo • San Ignatia •

Sauz Ranch
Roma • Rio Coloral
Rio Grande City • Brownsville •
Hidalgo •

Map 2g. Edwards Plateau

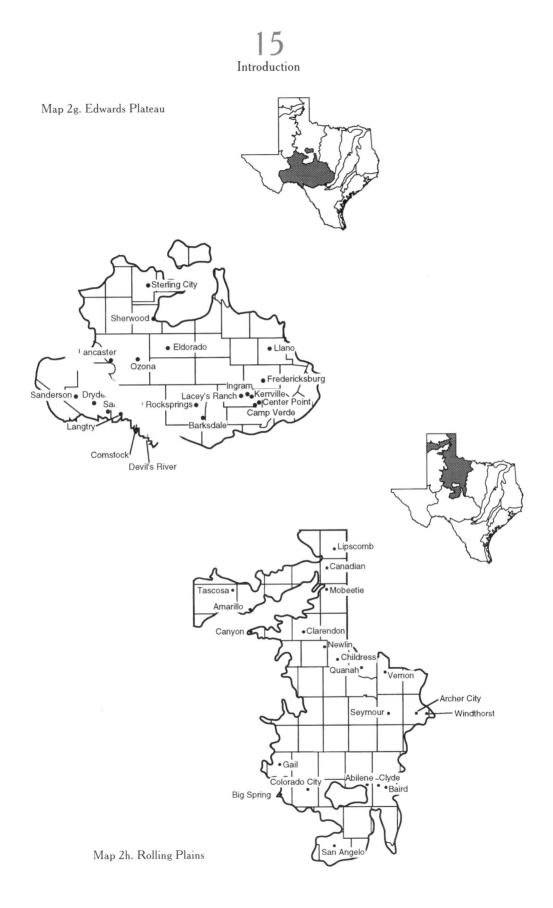

Map 2h. Rolling Plains

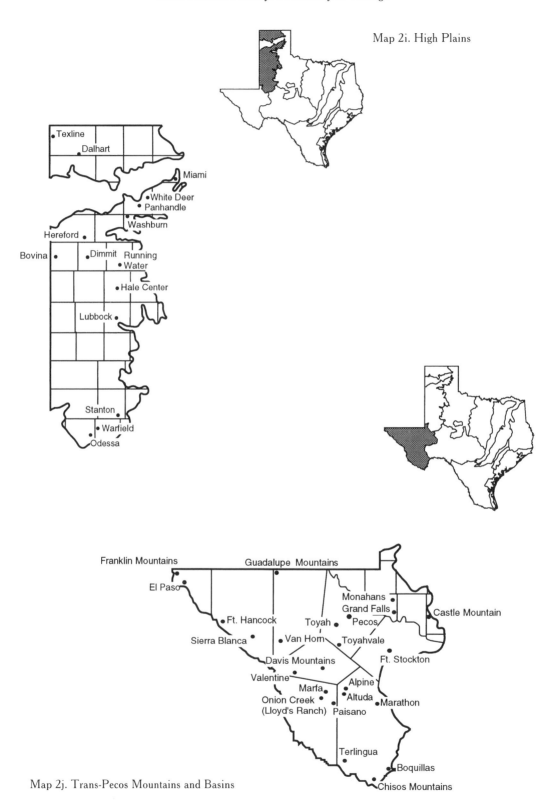

Map 2i. High Plains

- Texline
- Dalhart
- Miami
- White Deer
- Panhandle
- Washburn
- Hereford
- Bovina
- Dimmit
- Running Water
- Hale Center
- Lubbock
- Stanton
- Warfield
- Odessa

Map 2j. Trans-Pecos Mountains and Basins

- Franklin Mountains
- Guadalupe Mountains
- El Paso
- Monahans
- Grand Falls
- Castle Mountain
- Ft. Hancock
- Toyah
- Pecos
- Sierra Blanca
- Van Horn
- Toyahvale
- Davis Mountains
- Ft. Stockton
- Valentine
- Alpine
- Marfa
- Altuda
- Onion Creek (Lloyd's Ranch)
- Paisano
- Marathon
- Terlingua
- Boquillas
- Chisos Mountains

Fig. 4. A typical night's capture of small rodents in Cyclone traps. Courtesy National Archives, 22-WB-50-B15515

Fig. 5. A sampling of rodents captured in Cyclone traps and snap traps, Seguin, Guadalupe County, 1904. Courtesy National Archives, 22-WB-62-7225

Fig. 6. A portfolio of mammal sketches by Louis Agassiz Fuertes: cottontail rabbit, jackrabbit, pocket mice, skunk. Courtesy Philadelphia Academy of Natural Sciences

Fig. 7. U.S. Bureau of Biological Survey field agents at a typical field camp. Courtesy Biological Survey Unit, U.S. Geological Survey, Patuxent Wildlife Research Center, National Museum of Natural History

Fig. 8. Field agents on horseback, near the entrance to one of the Painted Caves, Val Verde County, Texas, 1901. Courtesy National Archives, 22-WB-30-2790

the same as at Finley's. *Pinus flexilis* and the narrow-leaved oak grow on the north side of the mountains high up. The canyons are brushy and deep. The north side of Livermore Peak is a perpendicular face of granite that looks to be 500 feet or more. In evening went fox hunting with three boys and five hounds. It was windy and dry and the dogs could not keep a trail and caught nothing. They ran two tracks for some time and made lots of music. We followed up and down the mountains over broken rocks and nearly broke our necks. It was dark and cold. Staid [sic] out till 1:30 a.m. It paid me well for the work just to hear the dogs among the rocks. We couldn't tell which was dogs and which echo.

January 14. Couldn't get any bear skulls at Perkins'. They had killed a number but a long way from home and did not bring in the skulls of but one and the boys smashed it. Could not induce Mr. Perkins to take a cent for my board. Said no one ever paid a cent for staying under his roof. They are tough but generous and intelligent people as are most of the ranch men. Mr. Perkins told me where I could find a panther skull at a ranch 9 miles west of there, Mr. Kerr's, so I started to follow his directions up one canyon and down another. Killed a *Spermophilus grammurus* and saw another. They were in a sheltered place in the canyon where the sun shone and it was warm; were feeding under juniper trees. The one killed had its cheek pouch full of juniper berries and was very fat, though not an adult. Saw no new birds or much game of any kind. Went over a divide and down another canyon, came to Mr. Kerr's ranch about 2 p.m. Found the bones of two *Felis* [= *Puma*] and got the skull of one and the upper part of skull and the tail bone and scapula of the other. They had the skin of one, but Mr. Kerr was not at home and I could not get it. It was in fine pelage, of a grayish brown and has the nose and claws and tail all on. Both the panthers were said to be female. Found a bear's skull, which is of a female that had two cubs. Went down the canyon a mile farther to Mr. Kirksey's after a bear skull that was said to be there, but couldn't find it. Came back into Mill Creek Canyon and then over the main divide home. The sun went down while I was eight miles from home with a mountain to cross and trail over the top. By good luck I did not get lost and reached Mr. Finley's at 8 o'clock. Rather enjoyed the trip, saw much country, got some good specimens, and met several pleasant people.

William Lloyd, Eagle Pass.

October 21, 1890. Caught one usual *Neotoma*, owing to sharp norther (first of season) blowing up about midnight and continuing with considerable force all day making all bird life and animals quiescent. Saw three Audubon's warblers and put out 18 traps principally for *Sigmodon*.

October 22. Norther still continued but with diminished severity. Caught nothing in traps, but two coon traps set and several Cyclone carried off. Sharp frost, first of year. A few birds about but principally cactus wrens, mockingbirds and *Melanerpes*.

October 23. See a rat in afternoon and putting out a trap startled an immense frog and trying to secure it put my hands on a large rattlesnake coiled up. I was within two feet of it [for] over ten minutes [while] arranging the trap. Put my foot on it and caught it by neck and brought it back to camp. Bat flying along ground in night, medium size, first seen since 11th. Slight frost but so hot in middle of day that a rabbit was blown by blowflies in an hour after it was killed. Find large block of petrified wood, pine?

October 24. The trap put out yesterday by rat hole caught an *Onychomys*. A ranchman to whom I showed it said he had lived there six years and it was the first mouse he had seen. Saw flock of *Parus atricristatus* and wounded one but could not secure it. Also saw a lone long-billed curlew, and even a sandhill crane grazing on prairie. Caught three more rats and coyotes ran away with two Cyclone and one Climax, and two steel had fragments of lips and claws, one of a possum and the other a *Neotoma*. Into Eagle Pass and crossed river to Piedras Negras. Find a strict quarantine is established (small pox) rendering it out of question to collect on other side without delay and bother. Moved south of Eagle Pass about six miles.

Vernon Bailey, Paris, Texas.

June 11, 1892. Took the 10:45 train west to Blossom, then to Reno and then to Paris, where I stopped and set traps and shot bats in evening. Shot three *Atalpha noveboracensis* [= *Lasiurus borealis*] and three *Vesperus* [= *Eptesicus*]. Caught nothing in my traps at Clarksville and do not expect to here. The soil is hard and baked. Most of the country is grassy prairie or fields. Perhaps half timbered. Timber and prairie alternate from Clarksville to here. The large mounds extend most of the way from Clarksville to Paris. Got a set of four eggs of the Scissor-tail Flycatcher and saw the bird alive for the first time. A hot day.

June 12. Sunday, a hot day, 88 degrees in my room. Don't feel well.

June 13. Took up my traps, they had not been touched. Shot scissortails and a *Chondestes* and made up skins. Failed to get a *Sturnella*. Was sick all night and am now so weak I can hardly stand up. My eyes begin to turn yellow so I know it is only jaundice. Could hardly drag myself around to get my traps. Saved a few plants. Will take the 6 p.m. train northward. Another hot day. Left Paris at 6 p.m. and went to Arthur, 15 miles north at crossing of the Red River and stopped. Shot at bats but got none. All clay land from Paris to Arthur, some fields of cotton, oats, corn, castor plant, etc. Most of the way in uncleared scrub oak land. Arthur is composed of six or eight little houses on the bank of the Red River. A crew of men are building a saw mill.

Vernon Bailey, Chisos Mountains.

June 8, 1901. Fuertes and I took our saddle horses and went around the south side of the mountain into the big gulch leading up from the south into the big canyon that cuts nearly through the mountains. Left our horses at an old sheep camp at 5,500 feet and climbed up the gulch west of us past the obelisque-like pinnacle around the base of Mt. Emory and turning south again up onto the big, forested ridge that joins the southernmost spur of the mountains. On reaching the top of this ridge the aneroid read 6,200 feet (probably 300 feet too low as it works slowly) and Mt. Emory just across the gulch to the northwest appears at least 500 feet higher. As the climb up had taken six hours and it was 7 p.m. when we reached the top we concluded not to return tonight so found a sheltering rock, made a bed of pine boughs and grass and gathered wood for a fire and camped, comfortable but hungry. . . .

June 9. The night was cool and we had to keep the fire burning to keep warm enough to sleep, but passed a comfortable night. Hunted an hour or so before starting down the mountain and then shot birds on the way down. Reached the horses at 11 a.m. and camp at 2 p.m., tired and hungry. Had only two biscuits for lunch yesterday and nothing to eat since for 26 hours, but were fortunate in finding plenty of water. Got a good lot of birds but no mammals except old skull of a bear and a deer. Found a fine old hound lying on our saddle blankets near the horses and glad to see us. Had evidently got lost so we took him to camp.

Louis Agassiz Fuertes (from a letter written to his family), Chisos Mountains.

May 29, 1901. Your letter of the 21st came over with Bailey from Boquillas last night, and as we are going to send a lot of stuff over this evening I will just send along a little note to tell you that we are all right, in good health and happiness, having replenished our larder which for the last day or two has been without coffee, baking powder, or condensed milk.

Well, I got the hawk, and had an adventure in the bargain by virtue of which I spent a delightful hour in a hole 400 feet up a 600 foot cliff till Oberholser could get to camp and back with a rope, on which to continue my journey. The bird [a zone-tailed hawk] is a Texas record, and one of the very few U.S. records, so that when I had at last shot him, after three days straight of hunting him, it would never have done to let the splendid thing rot just because he fell over a cliff down in the canyon. I don't think I was in any danger any of the time, for when I found myself unable to go any further because of a boulder that was lodged in the fissure above me, and also at least unwilling to go down, I got O[berholser] to go for a rope. Then I sat in my comfortable hole, sang to a superb echo for a while, watched lizards and ravens and got rested for an hour, and came out all right, and the bird had by that time earned his record. I painted him fresh that afternoon, and am mighty glad of it, for all his lovely plum bloom has gone, in the skin, and he is still splendid, but nearly dead black, instead of like a rich ripe black plum.

The culmination of the survey was Bailey's 1905 publication, *Biological Survey of Texas*, which is reprinted in its entirety in Chapter 2. The report on the birds of Texas, to be authored by H. C. Oberholser, was too lengthy to include in the survey publication and was to be published separately. Oberholser continued to edit and revise the manuscript, however, and it was to remain unpublished until 1974, eleven years after his death (Oberholser, 1974). The information gleaned from the botanical reports and plant collections made during the survey appeared in a number of early publications about the vegetation and plant communities of Texas (e.g., Bray, 1906). Over the years the specimens obtained during the Texas survey have been used in hundreds, if not thousands, of publications about Texas natural history.

Biographies of the Federal Field Agents

During the early years of the U.S. Bureau of Biological Survey, the appropriations were small and the personnel limited in numbers, but the outstanding interest of the members of the staff and their devotion to duty enabled them to make noteworthy advancements in the field of science and to place the bureau in the foremost ranks of the world's scientific organizations engaged in wildlife research at the time. The field agents who participated in the Texas survey included some individuals who would go on to distinguish themselves scientifically—people such as Vernon Bailey, William Bray, A. K. Fisher, Ned Hollister, A. H. Howell, and Harry Oberholser, as well as some of the lesser known agents who made only limited scientific contributions such as Merritt Cary, Gordon Donald, Basil Dutcher, James Gaut, William Lloyd, John Loring, and Clark Streator. Nonetheless, this latter group of individuals still made enormous contributions to the specimen collections and physiographic descriptions.

**Vernon Orlando Bailey**

Vernon Orlando Bailey (Fig. 9a, b) was born June 21, 1864, in Manchester, Michigan. At the age of six, he moved with his pioneer parents to a farm in Elk River, Minnesota. It was there that Bailey's interest in nature began. He began collecting birds, mammals, and reptiles, and he learned the art of taxidermy from a small book on the subject and a great deal of experimentation. In the beginning, he collected specimens primarily by trapping, and many of the trapping methods he used were of his own design. At age eleven, his father gave him his first gun—a long-barreled, 16-gauge, muzzle-loading shotgun that was longer than he was tall (Kofalk, unpub. manuscript). Bailey soon filled a room of his parents' home with preserved specimens.

Bailey developed a particular interest in shrews and devised a method for trapping them easily, but he was at a loss as to the proper identification of the various species he was collecting. Bailey was advised by an acquaintance to contact C. H. Merriam, whose reputation had already reached Minnesota, which he did in 1884. Bailey was eager for scientific information, and so he wrote Merriam asking if he would identify animals if prepared specimens were sent to him. Merriam not only agreed but also offered to buy specimens from Bailey of the different species found in Minnesota. The prices he offered seemed fabulous to the young farm boy—twenty-five cents apiece for mice and shrews and a dollar for woodchucks and skunks. He soon had a box packed for shipment, which Merriam received eagerly, and thus began a life-long relationship that eventually would culminate with Bailey's marriage to Merriam's sister, Florence.

The following excerpt is an example of Vernon Bailey's early correspondence with Merriam:

Fig. 9. Vernon Bailey as a young man (a, left) and in 1905, the year of publication of the *Biological Survey of Texas* (b, right). a. Courtesy Biological Survey Unit, U.S. Geological Survey, Patuxent Wildlife Research Center, National Museum of Natural History. b. Courtesy Library of Congress, LC-USZ62-058826

I wrote him and received a prompt and courteous reply, offering to identify any specimens that he could and also asking if I would collect certain things for him that he needed. This I was more than glad to do and supplied Dr. Merriam with series of specimens of each of the different kinds of shrews, mice, and small mammals that I was finding. At first he wanted to purchase all the shrews I could get, but when the number ran into hundreds, he put a limit on the number of each kind that he would need. He also wanted to buy skulls of many of the larger mammals, including those trapped for fur, such as muskrat, mink, otter and foxes. Of these he wanted all he could get, but when I sent him the first lot, including a hundred muskrat skulls nicely cleaned and labeled, he said that would be enough muskrats for the present, but continued to take other species in moderate numbers. My greatest interest now was in hearing from Dr. Merriam and getting names of different animals that I was sending him, and, more important, getting his criticism and suggestions in regard to preparing specimens. Dr. Merriam

took the greatest pains in correcting errors in my methods, giving careful directions for taking measurements, labeling, cataloguing, and keeping notes on all mammals collected. He wanted information on habits and abundance and many factors relating to the lives of the mammals, and I was able to furnish him much information that was of use to him, while he was giving me the training that I needed for natural history work.

In May, 1887, Merriam hired Bailey as the first field agent of the Division of Economic Ornithology and Mammalogy. His official salary was $40 per month, but Merriam personally supplemented this by an additional $10 per month (Sterling, 1978). Bailey's first field experience lasted from May through November and took him from Minnesota, throughout the Dakota Territory, and into Montana. In November, Merriam asked Bailey to remain in the field and move on to Texas, but Bailey elected to return home to Elk River. Bailey came from a close and loving family, and being away from his family for the first time in his life, for a period of six months, had proven difficult for him and his family. Bailey's continued refusal to make the trip to Texas did not please Merriam, but Merriam did not want to officially remove Bailey from the payroll. Bailey was put on an official leave of absence without pay, effective from December 1 to the following June 1. In the summer of 1888, Bailey once again set out for a season of field work, a pattern that would continue almost without change for the next forty-five years.

Bailey's first season of field work in Texas began in December, 1889, in El Paso. Bailey worked at several localities in the Trans-Pecos and began moving eastward to Langtry and Del Rio. At Del Rio, however, Bailey became quite ill, and in February, 1890, he abruptly returned home to Elk River to recuperate.

Bailey had quickly become a key figure in the field for Merriam, and in 1890 he gained the title of chief field naturalist. Bailey was given the primary responsibility for training new field investigators and supervising the parties of field agents conducting biological survey work throughout the western United States.

Bailey returned to Texas in 1892. He spent more than two months surveying the flora and fauna from Clarksville in northeastern Texas to Canadian in the Panhandle region. His third trip, from April through June of 1899, began in Galveston and continued northwestward through Central Texas and into the Panhandle region. Additional trips took place in 1900, 1901, 1902, and 1904. In total, Bailey spent 425 days surveying Texas before publishing his report in 1905. Bailey's collecting trips thoroughly traversed the state and included work in every ecological region.

In 1899, Bailey married Florence Merriam, C. Hart Merriam's younger sister. Florence Merriam Bailey was a prominent ornithologist

and often accompanied her brother and her husband in the field, assisting in the identification of birds during survey trips (Fig. 10). The Baileys took their first field trip together in 1900 in Texas, traveling by train to Texarkana and on to Corpus Christi where they started on a 360-mile wagon trip across the prairies to the Mexican line, camping on the King Ranch and other places in route (Kofalk, 1989). It was during this trip that Florence Bailey became aware of the slaughter of thousands of water birds for the millinery trade, a practice she was determined to stop (Doughty, 1983). She reported her findings to Witmer Stone who commented on the problem in a 1901 article published in the *Auk*.

During his career, Bailey conducted biological surveys of Texas, New Mexico, North Dakota, and Oregon, and studies of the mammals of several national parks. He contributed more than thirteen thousand mammal specimens to the biological survey collections, a large number of them new species. A bibliography of his work contains 244 titles. He authored six of the most significant *North American Fauna* publications, numbers 17, 25, 35, 39, 49, and 53 (see literature cited for complete citations).

Bailey was particularly concerned with the humane treatment of animals and was a pioneer in the development of new live traps. He designed and perfected the trap widely used in beaver restocking efforts as well as the "foothold" trap and received recognition from the American Humane Association for his efforts. Bailey was a founding member of the American Society of Mammalogists and president of that organization from 1933 to 1935. He also served as president of the Biological Society of Washington and was an active member in numerous other wildlife and conservation societies.

Bailey retired from the bureau in 1933, after forty-six years of service, but remained active as a consultant and collaborator on special projects. He was planning a new expedition to

Fig. 10. Florence Merriam Bailey, wife to Vernon Bailey and sister to C. Hart Merriam, conducting field research in the Guadalupe Mountains, New Mexico. Courtesy American Heritage Center, University of Wyoming

Texas at the time of his death, April 20, 1942, at the age of seventy-seven (Zahniser, 1942).

**William Bray**

William Bray was born September 19, 1865, in Burnside, Illinois. He received his Ph.D. ("Vegetation of Western Texas") in botany from the University of Chicago in 1898. Bray was a professor of botany at the University of Texas, Austin, from 1897 to 1907, where he organized the Botany Department and became its first head. He served as a collaborator with the U.S. Forest Service from 1899 to 1909.

Bray contributed thirty-one plant and physiography reports to the biological survey of Texas over a fifty-day period in 1899, during which time he traveled from the Gulf Coast region through the central and northwestern part of the state. In 1907, Bray left Texas and went to Syracuse University where he spent the remainder of his career in various administrative positions until retiring in 1943. Bray passed away May 25, 1953, in Syracuse, New York.

**Merritt Cary**

Merritt Cary (Fig. 11) was born in Nebraska in 1880. He joined the bureau in 1902. Cary worked in Texas from June through October, 1902, for a total of 119 days in the field. During that time he prepared 31 survey reports and collected 255 mammal specimens. His travels began near Kerrville and continued westward into the Trans-Pecos region, then northeastward through Abilene, and ended in Tarrant County.

During his career, Cary participated in fieldwork in many of the western states and in central and northern Canada. His most important

Fig. 11. Merritt Cary in Canada, 1903. Courtesy National Archives, 22-WB-46-B6585

works were a biological survey and list of the mammals of Colorado (*North American Fauna* No. 33, 1911) and the life zones of Wyoming (*North American Fauna* No. 42, 1917) (Henderson and Preble, 1935). He resigned in 1917 because of ill health and died not long afterward in 1918.

### Gordon Donald

Gordon Donald worked in Texas from July through September of 1902. He first met up with Bailey at Howard Lacey's ranch in July and apparently traveled with Bailey for a few weeks until he sent him to Devils River to collect. Donald surveyed the area from Paisano through Valentine and Fort Hancock. From there Donald traveled with Merritt Cary eastward through Pecos, Monahans, Warfield, and Abilene. Donald contributed 131 mammals, 17 birds, and 5 reptiles to the collections of the biological survey. Nothing else is known about this gentleman. It appears that he was only temporarily employed by the bureau, and his activities before and after the summer of 1902 are unknown.

### Basil Hicks Dutcher

Basil Hicks Dutcher (Fig. 12) was born December 3, 1871, in Bergen Point, New Jersey. Dutcher became interested in natural history while a young boy, and he accompanied his father, William Dutcher, an ornithologist, on frequent collecting trips (Hume, 1942). In 1890, at the age of nineteen, Dutcher was appointed by Merriam as a temporary field agent to participate in a biological survey of Idaho. In

Fig. 12. Basil Hicks Dutcher, date unknown. Courtesy Library of Congress, LC-USZ62-073584

Fig. 13. Albert Kenrick Fisher at Fort Huachuca, Arizona, 1892. Courtesy Library of Congress

1891, Dutcher became a member of the bureau's Death Valley Expedition, involving a biological survey of southern California, southern Nevada, and parts of Utah and Arizona. In 1892, Dutcher was appointed to the Texas survey for his third and final summer of fieldwork for the bureau. Dutcher spent twenty-seven days at four localities in Texas (Stanton, Colorado City, Brazos, and Saginaw) during August and September. He collected fifty-six mammal specimens and prepared sixteen survey reports during that time.

After graduating from the College of Physicians and Surgeons, New York, in 1895, Dutcher joined the U.S. Army as an assistant surgeon with the rank of 1st lieutenant. He served for twenty-five years, and retired from active service in 1920 as a colonel. He died January 16, 1922, at the age of fifty.

## Albert Kenrick Fisher

Albert Kenrick Fisher (Fig. 13) was born March 21, 1856, in Sing Sing (now Ossining), New York. In 1879, Fisher received his M.D. from Columbia University. In 1885, C. Hart Merriam, a friend and fellow ornithologist, hired Fisher as his assistant in the new Division of Economic Ornithology and Entomology. Fisher's only contributions to the biological survey of Texas consisted of a six-day visit to Colorado City and El Paso in 1894. Fisher was promoted to assistant biologist in 1896 and assistant chief of the Bureau of Biological Survey in 1902. In 1906, Fisher was placed in charge of economic investigations, and he served in this capacity until his retirement from the bureau in 1931. He passed away at the age of ninety-two on June 12, 1948, in Washington, D.C.

Fig. 14. Louis Agassiz Fuertes at a century plant in the Big Bend of Texas, 1901. Courtesy National Archives, 22-WB-30-3658

During his career, Fisher participated in the Death Valley Expedition (1891), the Harriman Expedition to Alaska (1899), and biological surveys of several western states from 1892 to 1898. Among the most important of Fisher's 160-plus publications were *Ornithology of the Death Valley Expedition of 1891* and *Hawks and Owls of the United States* (1893). Fisher was a founding member of the AOU and served as its president from 1914 to 1917.

### Louis Agassiz Fuertes

Louis Agassiz Fuertes (Fig. 14) was born February 7, 1874, in Ithaca, New York. Fuertes was fascinated by nature from early childhood and collected all types of specimens, alive and dead. He was introduced at a young age to the works of John James Audubon and soon began drawing birds himself. His first painting of a bird "from the flesh" was at the age of fourteen. His early insistence on working from live or freshly killed specimens, rather than preserved specimens, led him to actively collect birds and to become skilled at observing bird behavior as well as mimicking bird calls. In 1896, while a senior at Cornell University, Fuertes attended his first meeting of the AOU. A collection of Fuertes's paintings had been displayed at the previous year's AOU Congress. At the 1896 meeting, Elliott Coues, one of the foremost ornithologists of the day and a mentor of Fuertes, introduced Fuertes to the scientific community as a young artist "on whom the mantle of John James Audubon has fallen" (Peck, 1982). C. Hart Merriam was at that meeting and was among the many members of the scientific community who were impressed by the young Fuertes and his obvious talent. He immediately began commissioning works from Fuertes for the publications of the Division of Economic Ornithology and Mammalogy. In that same year Fuertes also illustrated the book *A-Birding on a Bronco* by Florence Merriam. In 1899, Merriam recommended that Fuertes be invited to join the Harriman Expedition to Alaska. Fuertes's genial personality and commitment to hard work made him a welcome member of any expedition, and for the remainder of his life he was seldom without an invitation to travel.

In 1901, Fuertes joined Vernon Bailey and H. C. Oberholser for a four-month survey of the Trans-Pecos region of Texas. Fuertes found the experience exhilarating, for he was able to study a wider variety of birds than on any previous trip. He produced hundreds of bird portraits, as well as paintings and sketches of a number of mammals, a whip scorpion, and several lizards. Most of his works from that trip were purchased by the government for $20–30 each.

Fig. 15. James Gaut, preparing specimens at camp, 1904. Courtesy Biological Survey Unit, U.S. Geological Survey, Patuxent Wildlife Research Center, National Museum of Natural History

Fuertes continued to travel and paint, with major expeditions to the Bahamas, Mexico, Colombia, and Abyssinia (in eastern Africa). During his thirty-year career, Fuertes illustrated more than thirty-five books and approximately fifty educational leaflets, handbooks, and bulletins. He was also a regular contributor to more than a dozen popular and scholarly journals. Recognized as one of America's greatest ornithological artists, Fuertes is celebrated at at least seven institutions that hold major collections of his work. Fuertes was killed at age fifty-three when his car was struck by a train in Unadilla, New York, on August 22, 1927.

**James Gaut**

James Gaut (Fig. 15), who had been acquainted with several of the more active natu-

ralists about Washington, D.C., worked as a scientist for the survey collecting specimens and performing other tasks (Henderson and Preble, 1935). His mammal field notes indicate that he collected more than 3,860 mammals at least from November 2, 1896, to January 25, 1906. Gaut collected mammals in many areas of North America, including Virginia, Maryland, California, New Mexico, Texas, Oklahoma Territory, and Colorado.

Gaut's efforts in Texas began with a trip from February to June of 1903, from the Franklin Mountains (El Paso County) to Del Rio and then Alpine. He briefly visited the state in June and October of 1904, then conducted work in southeastern Texas westward to Langtry and Samuels from February to June, 1905. He spent a total of 251 days in Texas, prepar-

Fig. 16. Ned Hollister, 1908. Courtesy Library of Congress, LC-USZ62-073596

the bureau, including Vernon Bailey. In 1902, Bailey hired Hollister as a temporary field agent to assist him in the Texas survey. Hollister spent eighty-six days in the state during that year and collected in the Pineywoods, the Edwards Plateau, and the Trans-Pecos region. Hollister contributed sixteen survey reports and 119 mammal specimens to the survey. The following year, Hollister was again hired for a temporary position to accompany Wilfred Osgood to Alaska. He was finally appointed to a permanent position with the Bureau of Biological Survey in 1904 and participated in biological surveys of New Mexico, British Columbia, Washington, Oregon, California, Nevada, Louisiana, and Arizona. From 1910 to 1916, Hollister served as assistant curator of mammals at the U.S. National Museum. Hollister was hired as the superintendent of the National Zoological Park in 1916 and served in this position until his death on November 3, 1924, at the age of forty-seven.

Hollister's contributions to the bureau's collections totaled 3,625 mammals and 1,509 birds, including the type specimens for 26 mammals. He named 162 new mammals and published more than 150 titles. Hollister was involved in the formation of the American Society of Mammalogists and served as the first editor of the *Journal of Mammalogy*.

ing thirty-five survey reports, numerous bird specimens, and more than seven hundred mammal specimens. Gaut resigned from the Bureau in 1906 and died in an automobile accident in 1914 at the age of thirty-five.

## Ned Hollister

Ned Hollister (Fig. 16) was born in Delavan, Wisconsin, on November 26, 1876. Self-taught in nature studies at an early age, Hollister took part in private studies in zoology from 1896 to 1901. His first scientific paper was published when he was just sixteen and included data collected from the time he was twelve years old (Osgood, 1925). Hollister began voluntarily contributing specimens to the Bureau of Biological Survey in 1892. In 1901, Hollister visited the Smithsonian and the National Museum and met several key figures of

## Arthur Holmes Howell

Arthur Holmes Howell (Fig. 17) was born May 3, 1872, in Lake Grove, New York. With only a public school education, Howell was a self-taught naturalist. He was first employed by the Bureau of Biological Survey in 1895, when he served his apprenticeship in northern Montana with Vernon Bailey. During his tenure with the bureau he conducted survey work in Alabama, Alaska, Arkansas, Florida, Georgia, Illinois, Kentucky, Louisiana, Missouri, Montana, New Mexico, North Carolina, and Texas.

Fig. 17. Arthur Holmes Howell, 1903. Courtesy Library of Congress

Fig. 18. William Lloyd, 1929. Courtesy Library of Congress, LC-USZ62-58589

Howell's work in Texas began with a two-month visit to the northern Panhandle in 1903. He returned in 1905 for a thorough four-month survey of an area extending from Falls County southward to Aransas County, and from Waller County westward to Medina County. Survey results from a third visit in 1906 were not included in the 1905 publication. Howell's three visits to the state totaled more than two hundred days of fieldwork in eight ecological regions. He contributed 48 reports, 180 mammal specimens, and 76 photographs to the efforts of the Texas survey.

Howell worked for the Bureau of Biological Survey until his death July 10, 1940. During his career he published works on the birds of Arkansas and Florida and the mammals of Alabama, as well as a large number of monographic revisions of mammalian genera, including harvest mice (genus *Reithrodontomys)* and flying squirrels (genus *Glaucomys)*.

### William Lloyd

William Lloyd (Fig. 18) was born in 1854 of English parents in Cork, Ireland, and immigrated to the United States in 1876 (Casto, 1992). In 1881, Lloyd met John A. Loomis, owner of the Silvercliffe Ranch near Paint Rock, Concho County, and Lloyd was invited to join Loomis and two of his ranch hands on a hunt in Zavala County (Loomis, 1982). It was on this hunting trip that Lloyd's interest in ornithology began. Upon returning from that hunting trip, Lloyd was employed as a sheep herder on the Loomis ranch for two years and during that time spent many hours studying birds and educating himself about natural history from the books and journals in the ranch library. In 1885, Lloyd was elected an associate member of the AOU and in 1887 published an annotated list of birds of the Concho Valley. Lloyd spent much of 1887 collecting birds for George B. Sennett, a businessman, conservationist, and ornithologist who devoted much of his life to collecting birds in Texas and Mexico (Maxwell, 1979b). Lloyd was then hired by Frederick Godman of the British Museum of Natural History to collect birds in Mexico from 1888 to 1889. In July, 1889, Godman discharged Lloyd, and he returned to his ranch in Marfa.

Lloyd was an acquaintance of C. H. Merriam's as a fellow member of the AOU. In 1890, Merriam sent Bailey instructions to meet Lloyd at his ranch near Marfa for a collecting trip, with Lloyd as a protégé and prospective field agent. A letter from Bailey to his family explained that "Merriam says Lloyd can't make good skins and can't trap but wants me to show him all I can and get him started at it" (Kofalk, unpub. manuscript).

Apparently, Bailey's training was successful, and Lloyd was hired as a field agent on July 1, 1890. His travels took him from his home near Marfa southeastward along the Rio Grande to Laredo and ended there December 26. In May of 1891, Lloyd resumed his travels beginning at Laredo and continuing southward to Brownsville and then northward along the Gulf Coast to Houston, where he ended his work for the survey in March of 1892. Lloyd's total of 496 days in the field exceeded even Bailey's efforts in Texas prior to the 1905 publication. Lloyd's work took him into four ecological regions, but most of his efforts were in the Gulf Prairies and Marshes and South Texas Plains regions. He contributed fifty-one survey reports and 1,181 mammal specimens to the bureau's collection.

After 1892, little is known about William Lloyd's life, but he apparently never again worked as a naturalist. By 1898, Lloyd had

Fig. 19. John Alden Loring, 1913. Courtesy Library of Congress, LC-USZ62-073590

moved to New Orleans where he owned a store and dealt in old books, coins, and stamps. Lloyd died in New Orleans in October, 1937 (Geiser, 1956).

**John Alden Loring**

John Alden Loring (Fig. 19) was born March 6, 1871, in Cleveland, Ohio. He served as a field agent with the Bureau of Biological Survey from 1892 to 1897. Noted for being a most enthusiastic collector, Loring worked in many of the western states and in central Canada. His fieldwork in Texas involved 108 days, from January to May, 1894. He traveled from El Paso southward to Brownsville and Hidalgo, then proceeded northward, collecting from Arcadia on the Gulf Coast through eastern Texas to Fort Worth, then westward to Tascosa in the Panhandle. He contributed nineteen survey reports and more than three hundred mammal specimens to the survey.

From 1897 to 1901, Loring served as curator of animals at the New York Zoological Park. While conducting fieldwork in Europe for the National Museum, Loring broke all previous records by collecting and preserving the skins of 913 mammals and birds in 63 days (Palmer, 1954). Loring was a participant in the Smithsonian-Roosevelt Scientific Expedition to Africa, 1909–10.

Loring's publication record contains primarily popular articles and nature books for children, including *Young Folks' Nature Field Book*. Loring died May 8, 1947, in Osweego, New York, at the age of seventy-six.

### Harry Church Oberholser

Harry Church Oberholser (Fig. 20) was born June 25, 1870, in Brooklyn, New York. He entered Columbia University in 1888 but was compelled to withdraw in 1891 because of poor health. In later years he received the B.A. and M.S. (1914) and the Ph.D. (1916) from George Washington University.

In 1895 Oberholser was appointed as an ornithological clerk in the Division of Economic Ornithology. He was promoted to assistant biologist in 1914, biologist in 1924, and senior biologist in 1928. He retired from the government in 1941 at the age of seventy-one but served as curator of ornithology at the Cleveland Museum of Natural History until 1947. Throughout his forty-six-year government career, his primary duty was the identification of birds; in later years he was often called as an expert witness to identify evidence in trials for alleged violations of federal game laws. He conducted fieldwork in many states but most notably in the Southwest. Oberholser published nearly nine hundred papers during his career and was a member of forty scientific and conservation organizations.

Fig. 20. Harry Church Oberholser, 1939. Courtesy Library of Congress, LC-USZ62-117490

Oberholser's lifelong interest in the birds of Texas began with his first biological survey trip with Vernon Bailey in 1900, a five-month survey of portions of the Gulf Coast, South Texas, and northern Texas at Henrietta. Oberholser returned for four months in 1901, when he traveled from San Angelo westward into the Trans-Pecos region and northward to the Panhandle. In 1902, Oberholser surveyed the eastern third of the state for four months. His survey efforts during those three years, a total of 397 days in the state, took him to every ecological region. Oberholser contributed 118 survey reports, 276 mammal specimens, and 710 photographs of landscapes, wildlife, and habitats to the survey.

The ornithological data gathered during Oberholser's survey trips were originally to be published as part of the *Biological Survey of Texas*, but the report soon grew too lengthy, and it was decided that a separate report on the birds would be published. However, Oberholser's work continued to grow in length, and remain unpublished through the years, as he continuously strove to update and expand the information to satisfy himself that it was suitable for release. In 1941, when Oberholser retired from government service, the manuscript had grown to over three million words. Eventually, the University of Texas Press acquired funding from a private source to publish *The Bird Life of Texas*. They assigned an editor, Edgar B. Kincaid, Jr., to assist Oberholser with the task of reducing the manuscript from three million to one million words. Oberholser continued to work on the book until shortly before his death on December 25, 1963, at the age of ninety-three. Mr. Kincaid completed the editing of the book, and *The Bird Life of Texas* was finally published as a two-volume set in 1974.

Fig. 21. Clark Streator, 1930. Courtesy National Archives, 22-WB-46-B4414M

### Clark Perkins Streator

Clark Perkins Streator (Fig. 21) was born in Ohio in 1866. In the early 1880s, Streator traveled extensively in the West Indies collecting birds for ornithologist Charles B. Cory. About 1890, he collected in British Columbia for the American Museum of Natural History. In later years, Streator collected in Mexico with E. W. Nelson and E. A. Goldman and in several western states, including Idaho, Colorado, California, Nevada, and Texas. Streator was considered an authority on the mammals of California and had visited the type localities for almost every mammal species in the state (Palmer, 1954).

Streator's contributions to the *Biological Survey of Texas* were limited to travel with William Lloyd during November and December, 1890, in Maverick and Webb Counties. Streator contributed fifty-eight mammals, eleven birds, and two snakes to the survey collection during this trip, including the type specimen for *Cratogeomys castanops angusticeps* from Eagle Pass.

Streator died at Santa Cruz, California, on November 28, 1952, at the age of eighty-six.

### Local Naturalists

Bailey and the field agents relied heavily on local naturalists and landowners while conducting the survey. Bailey was particularly fond of an Englishman, Howard Lacey, who owned a ranch near Kerrville in the Hill Country of Central Texas. Also, H. P. Attwater from San Antonio made numerous trips to secure important specimens when the field agents were not in the state. Both Lacey and Attwater made significant contributions to Texas natural history and brief biographies are included for them.

Fig. 22. Howard Lacey's ranch near Kerrville, Kerr County, 1906. (In this and all subsequent landscape figures, county designations reflect current county boundaries.) Courtesy National Archives, 22-WB-30-9048

## Howard George Lacey

Howard George Lacey was born at Wareham, Dorset, England, on April 15, 1856. At the age of twenty-six he emigrated to the United States and settled in the Texas Hill Country on a ranch on Turtle Creek, about ten miles from Kerrville (Fig. 22). He made his livelihood by raising horses, cattle, and Angora goats, but he was very interested in natural history and soon became an authority on the fauna and flora of Central Texas (Palmer, 1954). He maintained correspondence with naturalists in various parts of the country and welcomed many to his ranch to conduct natural history studies, including Vernon Bailey and other members of the Bureau of Biological Survey.

In his field diary of May 7, 1892, after spending several days with Lacey, Bailey wrote: "We were sorry to say good-bye to Mr. Lacey who has treated us with the greatest hospitality and helped us in many ways with our work. He is one of the best specimens of a typical, whole-hearted, generous Englishman I have met. He has a good ranch but does not give much time to farming or business. Collects butterflies and knows birds and mammals well . . ."

Lacey collected many natural history specimens himself and donated a number of them to the collections of the biological survey and National Museum. In recognition of his contributions to natural history research, three taxa of small mammals were named for him (*Peromyscus pectoralis laceianus, P. boylei laceyi,*

Fig. 23. Henry Philemon Attwater. Courtesy Library of Congress, LC-USZ62-073594

and *Reithrodontomys laceyi*). In 1919 Lacey sold his central Texas ranch and returned to England, where he died March 5, 1929.

### Henry Philemon (H. P.) Attwater

Henry Philemon (H. P.) Attwater (Fig. 23) was born in London, England, April 28, 1854. In 1873 he emigrated to Ontario, Canada, where he engaged in farming and bee-keeping. Attwater soon became interested in natural history. During 1884 he made a trip to Bexar County, Texas, to collect specimens. Attwater was employed in 1884 and 1885 to prepare and exhibit natural history specimens in the Texas pavilion at the New Orleans World's Fair (Casto, 1999).

In 1889 Attwater moved to San Antonio, Texas. He soon became an authority on the natural products and resources of the state and conducted experiments in agriculture and horticulture. In 1900, he was appointed agricultural

and industrial agent of the Southern Pacific Railroad and relocated to Houston. He continued to expand his natural history collections and contributed numerous specimens to museums, including the U.S. National Museum and the American Museum of Natural History (Palmer, 1954). He was always eager to assist anyone who needed information or material that he could provide. He was devoted to the protection of birds and other wildlife and he had an important influence on the development of wildlife conservation laws in the state. The Attwater's greater prairie chicken (*Tympanuchus cupido attwateri*) and several small mammals are named in his honor, in recognition of his major contributions as a scientist and conservationist.

H. P. Attwater passed away September 25, 1931, at his home in Houston.

### Farmers, Ranchers, and Woodsmen

Local farmers, ranchers, and woodsmen contributed much to the wildlife information base in the Texas survey. For example, Ab Carter, a farmer and woodsman from Tarkington Prairie in Liberty County in the southeastern part of the state, provided Bailey with information about the demise of bear populations in that area (Figs. 24, 25). According to Carter, he and a neighbor personally had a hand in killing 182 bear within a ten-mile radius of their ranches over a two-year period.

Likewise, Mr. C. O. Finley, a rancher from Ft. Davis in the Davis Mountains of West Texas (Fig. 26), provided Merriam and Bailey with the following detailed account of the killing of the only grizzly bear ever shot in Texas.

"The Davis Mountain Silvertip,"
by C. O. Finley, Pecos, Texas.

I have been asked to write the true story of a bear hunt on which the only grizzly bear had ever been killed in Texas.

Fig. 24. Ab Carter, hog raiser and bear hunter, near a bear-gnawed tree, Tarkington, Liberty County, 1904. Courtesy National Archives, 22-WB-51-7236

Never an oath was heard nor a bottle of whiskey came to our camps.

Our party usually ran from forty to seventy-five people. Men, women, and children, and they ran from young untried hands to old tried and true bear dogs. We had from 100 to 150 saddle horses and always took three or four old time chuck wagons and plenty of good Mexican cooks, as good ones as ever cooked a meal around a campfire and they always keep plenty of warm grub to eat. We always had two day horse wranglers and two night hawks, as they were called, to herd our horses, day and night. In the morning the old cooks would be up early and have us a good hot breakfast ready before daylight, so we were always ready when our night hawks brought our horses up near camp by the time it was light enough for us to see how to rope our horses for the days ride. Such a good time we had roping and saddling our horses. All horses those days were not pets and every morning before we could get saddled and out of camp, some would be pitching with their saddles and some with their riders, and very often some "old boy" would get pitched off and his horses would have to be caught. When everyone was ready, which was never later than sunup and pretty cold in October and November in the mountains, someone would blow their horn and off we would go to the mountains, which was bear heaven.

We hardly ever failed to get a bear and sometimes three or four during the day. And every day or so some one would get lost from the bear chase and kill a deer or two. While this was all good sport, especially if you got in the chase and got to the killing of the bear (which was sometimes up a tree or a cave, or out in the open) it was awfully hard on the horses and men, who rode hard and reckless in that rough country trying to follow and keep up with the hounds.

When we got in to camp of an evening, horses, men and dogs were usually all in, but a well cooked meal, a little rest and a few cups of coffee, and we were ready for a good talk and a prayer by one of our ministers. We would then clear us off a spot of ground and dance the old square dances for an hour or so, as we always had musicians and plenty of music in the camp. Then off to bed and a good night's rest in our tents and on our old camp beds, and early the next morning we were ready for another days hunt. Some days we had

As a prelude to this story, I will give a brief history of the beginning of what turned out to be an annual bear hunt by a number of the old pioneer ranchmen in the Davis Mountains.

In the early Nineties, some seven or eight families of us, the Means, Evans, Marleys, Jones, Mayfields, Finleys, and a number of others, all met at what is known by all of the people in the Davis Mountains as the Rock Pile, near Saw Tooth Mountain and one of the most beautiful spots for camping in the Davis Mountains. Here we met several years prior to the noted year that we killed the old grizzly. In addition to our own families we always had a number of friends from over a good part of Texas that would come from Fort Worth, Dallas, San Antonio and other parts to spend a week with us on our hunts. We also invited one or two ministers every year to our camp, which was as clean and free of bad language as was possible.

Fig. 25. Ab Carter's house at Tarkington, Liberty County, 1904. Courtesy American Heritage Center, University of Wyoming

Fig. 26. C. O. Finley's ranch, Davis Mountains, Jeff Davis County, 1890s. Courtesy Museum of the Big Bend, Sul Ross State University

fine luck and other days our luck was not so good. These hunts were made up of old men, young men, women and children old enough to ride. The women and children would stay as long as possible, but not often did they get in a chase after a bear and see him killed, but would drop out and a few of the older men would drop back to take care of them and see that they got back to camp. It was always uncertain which way a bear would run or how far. If he was fat he would probably not run over a mile or two, but would climb a tree, but if he was poor he was always hard to stop and sometimes would get away entirely. When we found an old poor bear and failed to stop him, we always lost some of our dogs and they would not get in for sometimes a day or so, all footsore and almost starved.

Well, I started this story to tell you of the jolliest old days ever spent by our party or any other parties in the Davis Mountains, which was in the fall of 1900. On the 29th day of October, we met at our old campground at the Rock Pile, about 75 of us, just as we had each year before, with every one feeling good. The horses were fat and the dogs in good shape and we all anticipated a good time, and we had it. We spent the first four days with just fairly good luck, getting a bear or two and some blacktail deer each day. On the third day of November, which was our fifth days hunt, we all left camp as usual about sunup and all went together that morning right into the mountains. We traveled some eight or ten miles crossing up near the head of what is known as Saw Mill Canyon just north of Livermore Peak, and on southeast over into the head of Limpia Canyon. This is the canyon that part of Fort Davis is on and in going from the head of Saw Mill Canyon through the mountain over into Limpia Canyon, there is a gap that was always called Bridge Spring Gap. Well, all of our party, some thirty or forty people, went on through the gap, we dropped back behind and turned south up the side of the mountain, topped out and rode along the top, parallel with the balance of our party and the dogs, who were going down Limpia Canyon. All the country is very rough. Full of canyons, bluffs, and lot of timber from shin oak thickets to pines fifty feet high. Well, when John Means and I got out on top, we were possibly a mile or more from the balance of the party. We heard a dog yelp and then another and pretty soon the whole pack was running and yelping and the dogs and Means all rode up on a four year old fat cow that had been killed

up on the side of the mountain and then drug down to the hill about 100 yards into a big thicket and part of her had been eaten. Well by that time the dogs had started the old bears trail and when the bear heard the dogs, he pulled out from where he was bedded up near the cow he had killed, and ran out of the canyon south across the mountain and crossed out on top just ahead of John Means and myself, so we rode like drunk Indians to keep up in hearing of the dogs.

Just after we had crossed their trail in behind them, John looked around to the right and said "Otie, I see the old devil." He had gotten out on an open spot and stopped. Then we switched around some brush and rocks to where we could get a shot at him but when we came out to where we could get a shot, the old bear was gone and there set four dogs, the only dogs out of the whole pack that would run his trail. Well, we muched [sic] them a little and got them to go on and we got back on our horses and followed them about a mile and a half further on over some very rough canyons and down into the head of Merrill Canyon. There the old bear had stopped again. Means and I had ridden as far as we could and had to leave our horses and walk down the mountainside to where we heard the dogs barking. When we got about a quarter of a mile where they had stopped the old bear, we met the four dogs all coming back, trailing along one just behind the other to meet us. Well, we muched [sic] them up again and got them to go back to where they had stopped the bear, which was down in a deep bushy rough canyon. We located him standing with his head toward us in the brush with the dogs standing off barking. When we got down to within about 125 yards of him, we sat down, side by side, on a small bluff of rocks with our little short saddle guns, 30-30, and began pumping lead into him. We evidently hit him with our first shots as he began to pitch and bellow like a wild bull, and made a dash in the brush at all the dogs, but only succeeded in catching one old blue speckled bob-tailed hound that belonged to Bill Jones and the bear tore the dogs jaws and neck up so bad that we had to kill the old fellow. He failed to catch the other dogs as they were younger and could get out of his way. He then came back and stopped exactly in the same place he was in when we shot our first shots. We did not lose any time shooting four more shots each into him and he just melted down on his old belly. We did not know yet what we had, but knew he was an extra big bear. We took a little round and got about one hundred feet above him on the canyon and stopped to see if he was sure enough dead. While we were standing there, Means raised up his gun and said "Otie, hadn't I better put one in his old head? He looks awfully big." And I said, "No, lets don't tear his head up, as he looks awfully big and some of us might want to keep it." So about that time a little black and tan hound that belong to Joe Marley walked up and caught the bear by some hair and shook him a little, then we knew the old bear was dead, so we went down to him. When we got down we discovered the gray tips of his hair. John yelled like a Comanche and threw his hat as high in the air as he could and said, "Otie, we have got a grizzly." To say we were an excited pair is putting it very lightly. Well, we turned him over and opened him up and removed his entrails then turned him back to drain good and went back up the mountainside out on top to where we had left our horses and blew and blew our horns and finally got eight more men to come to us. The party was scattered out over the mountains trying to locate the dogs and bear. We went back to the old bear with the eight men but he was so large there was no way to take him back to camp, so we took his hide off and left his feet and head on the hide and put the hide across the biggest stoutest horse we had, and lit out for camp, with the man who had been riding the horse riding behind another man. We could not go straight through the mountains to camp and lead this horse with such a load, as we had estimated the old bear to weigh at least 800 pounds, so his hide and feet would weigh 400 or 500 pounds. We had to go around and out of the mountains on the west side and out by my ranch. The horse that was carrying the hide had the thumps and almost had lockjaw so we had to turn him loose and get a pair of little Spanish mules and an old buck board I had at the ranch to carry our hide on to camp. All this was about 20 miles from where we had killed the bear. It was about 9 o'clock that night when ten of us with our three hounds got into camp with our kill. All worn out and hungry, not having had anything to eat since before daylight that morning. You can imagine how good those old cooks and their old dutch ovens filled with good warm camp grub and that black coffee looked to us.

When we had unsaddled and turned our tired and worn out ponies loose and had unloaded and stretched the old bear hide over a big rock, we were the most excited bunch of people ever seen. Everybody was talking, some asking questions and some telling their story of what had happened and how it all happened. We had all seen a lot of this kind of thing for a good many years, but this was the biggest days hunting that had ever been pulled off in the Davis Mountains.

The next morning we cut off his feet and found that he only had three claws on one of his front feet and one on the other. George Evans, John Means, and I kept three of them and took them to El Paso and had them plainly mounted for watch fobs, and the fourth we gave to a good friend of ours by the name of Tat Hulling who ranched at that time back north of Kent on the Delaware, but who has since died, but his widow still lives in El Paso. Mr. Means and Mr. Evans always wore their bear claws for watch fobs, just as they were mounted, but they were so big and heavy that I did not like to wear mine so I had a pin put on it for Mrs. Finley to wear and she wears a pin different from any other woman.

The hide we sent to San Antonio and had it nicely dressed and gave it to Mr. L. S. Thorn, who at that time, was the General Superintendent of this western district of the T & P Railroad, who was a good friend of ours, as we all shipped a good many cattle over his road those days from Van Horn and Kent.

The head I kept Mr. Means from shooting into, I took home and put it in an old big wash pot and boiled all the meat off of it and scraped it and cleaned it up good and hung it over our front door outside and never did expect anything to be done with it other then to be seen and admired by all guests. However, that winter, a young man from the biological department of Washington came to the Davis Mountains to collect specimens of all kinds of varmints and fowls that grew in the mountains and came to our ranch and asked to stay. Mrs. Finley let him stay and during the winter he heard us talking about our past fall bear hunt and saw the bears head hanging out over the door, and when he went back to Washington the next spring, he related the story to the departments heads and they wrote me and asked me to send it to them, which I did. After keeping it several months, they sent it back with several long names attached to it that we couldn't read, but pronounced it a real grizzly bear and that there was no history of one every having been found in Texas before. In about a year the department wrote me again and asked me to return it to them, which I did as they wanted to resurvey it. Then they wrote and asked to buy it for the Government stating that it was a very rare specimen and that they would forever preserve it and attach any record to it that we might want to keep with it. We tried to get them to send it to Dallas to be exhibited at the Fair but the Department said they kept it locked in a vault and were afraid to let it go. I have a nice letter from them which is attached hereto and will give an idea what it is and what they think of it in Washington.

In conclusion I must say a few more words about our hunts and our association with our neighboring ranchmen in the Davis Mountains. In all of our sports or meeting together, thanks to our mothers and wives, there was a spiritual side to it all that gave us the association of the most religious people and out of this group of old ranchmen and their families grew our little camp meeting, which originated from the mind of our beloved little preacher, Mr. Bloys, and a few of our old pioneer ranch mothers in 1890, and was and is called Bloys Campmeeting, and started with only a few people of all four denominations and which has continued as a union meeting from the beginning and has grown as a great many of you know to a regular attendance each year of about 3000 people and grows a little larger every year. Most of the original starters of the meeting have gone on to their reward but a few survivors have great faith in the present generation carrying this meeting on forever.

## Life Zones and Texas Vegetation

Determining and understanding the factors that governed the geographic distribution of birds and mammals was C. Hart Merriam's scientific passion and a major justification for his extensive fieldwork and biological surveys across the United States. His first theories on this question apparently were influenced by accounts he had read as a child of the zonal pattern of life in the Andes Mountains and by his own observations around his home near the Adirondacks in New York. Even from these early years, Merriam believed that the distri-

bution of species was determined by differences in temperature and humidity, with temperature during the breeding season being the most crucial factor. These beliefs formed the basis for Merriam's Life Zone Theory, first articulated in the 1890 *North American Fauna* publication based on Merriam's ecological studies of the San Francisco Mountain region of Arizona (Merriam, 1890b).

Merriam recognized four life zone belts, designating them the Canadian, Transition, Upper Austral, and Lower Austral, the boundaries of which coincided closely with isotherms (Merriam, 1894). Each of these zones was divided, at about the 100th meridian, into eastern humid and western arid faunal areas to indicate the secondary role played by moisture and vegetation. The 100th meridian practically bisects Texas, a fact that undoubtedly had much to do with Merriam's interest in conducting an extensive biological survey of the state. Texas, with its varied geography and vegetation types, including both arid and humid conditions, was a key state for verifying Merriam's hypotheses about plant and animal distributions.

Four of the transcontinental life zones are represented in Texas as broad bands stretching across the state or as encircling rings or caps on elevated peaks and mountain ranges in the far western part of the state (Map 3a). The life zones, divisions, and biotic regions listed for Texas include the following (Merriam, 1898b):

Lower Austral Zone
  Lower Sonoran Division
    Gulf Strip of Texas
    Austroriparian of Eastern Texas
    Grand and Black Prairies
    Coast Prairie
    Coast Marshes
    Beaches and Marshes
    Semiarid Lower Sonoran
    Extreme Arid Lower Sonoran

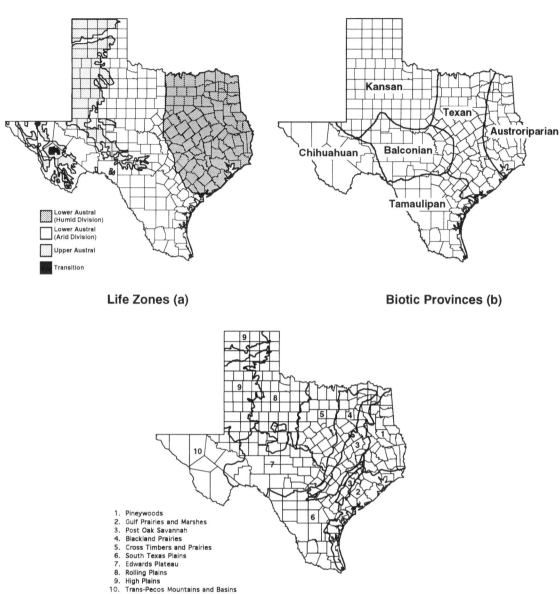

Map 3. The Life Zones (a), Biotic Provinces (b), and Ecological Regions (c) of Texas.

Upper Austral Zone
  Upper Sonoran Division
Transition Zone (upper slopes of the
  Guadalupe, Davis, and Chisos
  Mountains)
Canadian Zone (along northeast base of
  Mt. Livermore in the Davis Mountains)

Bailey often spoke of the Lower and Upper Sonoran as if they, too, were zones, but in reality they were only the arid subdivisions of the Lower and Upper Austral Zones, respectively. The humid divisions of these same zones were designated as the Austroriparian and the Carolinian, although only the former was represented in Texas. Bailey also recognized a number of unique biotic regions within the major zones and divisions. These regions were not formerly recognized in Merriam's life zone maps, but they were sufficiently unique to warrant distinction by Bailey.

Although useful in the local analysis of faunal origin, dispersal, and evolution, Merriam's efforts to explain the geographic distribution of birds and mammals based on temperature and humidity alone received acceptance for only a short period (Kendeigh, 1932). Investigations of biogeography by other scientists revealed flaws in Merriam's data and conclusions and demonstrated that many factors other than temperature and humidity played important roles in the geographic distribution of species (Shelford, 1932, 1945). His conclusions were considered too simplistic to explain the geographic distribution of birds and mammals in all cases. Under Merriam's system, the lower Rio Grande Valley, the eastern Panhandle, and the deserts of the Trans-Pecos are placed in the same life zone. Such diverse regions as Kerr County on the Edwards Plateau, the Hueco Mountains of the Trans-Pecos, and the High Plains of the Panhandle are placed together in another life zone. Such a system obviously is not descriptive of animal distribution and ecology in Texas and has limited meaning (Blair, 1950).

Texas was divided into biotic provinces by Lee Dice (1943), who mapped the general distribution of the biotic provinces in the United States. In 1950, Frank Blair, an ecologist from the University of Texas, mapped and described the biotic provinces in Texas (Map 3b). A biotic province is defined as a considerable and continuous geographic area, characterized by the occurrence of one or more ecological associations that differ, at least in proportional area covered, from the associations of adjacent provinces. In general, biotic provinces are characterized also by peculiarities of vegetative type, ecological climax, flora, fauna, climate, physiogra-

phy, and soil. The utility of biotic provinces has proven far more useful in describing the fauna and flora of Texas than Merriam's life zones.

Most biologists working in Texas today use ten vegetational regions in referring to the distribution of plants and animals in the state (Map 3c). The delineation of these regions is based on the interaction of geology, soils, physiography, and climate (Table 2).

### Contemporary Mammalogists of Merriam and Bailey

During the time that Bailey and the federal agents worked in Texas, other naturalists were at work as well. Another government exploration was underway along the Mexican boundary and the region of the Rio Grande. Dr. Edgar A. Mearns, who had been stationed at three military posts on the Texas border, was detailed in 1892 by the War Department to act as medical officer for the International Boundary Commission. This commission had been established in the 1880s when the United States and Mexico signed a treaty providing for an international boundary survey to relocate the existing frontier line between the two countries. Mearns was assigned to the Commission as survey surgeon and naturalist. The scientific work involved a biological survey of the Mexican boundary region. Three years (1892–95) were spent in the survey of more than seven hundred miles of the boundary. Mearns and his assistants traversed the entire border, including all of Texas, collecting plants and animals and recording detailed natural history information.

In 1907, Mearns published *Mammals of the Mexican Boundary of the United States*, recording his observations and scientific information (Mearns, 1907). He contributed more than thirty thousand plant and animal specimens to the National Museum, including seven thousand mammals (Wilson and Eisenberg, 1990), and he described fourteen taxa of Texas

Table 2. Summary of the physical and climatic characteristics of the ecological regions of Texas.[1]

| | Million acres | Topography | Elevation (feet) | Annual precipitation (inches) | Frost-free days |
|---|---|---|---|---|---|
| Pineywoods | 15.8 | Nearly level to gently undulating | 200–700 | 40–56 | 235–265 |
| Gulf Prairies and Marshes | 10.0 | Nearly level | 0–250 | 26–56 | 245–320 |
| Post Oak Savannah | 6.85 | Nearly level to gently rolling | 300–800 | 30–45 | 235–280 |
| Blackland Prairies | 12.6 | Nearly level to rolling | 250–700 | 30–45 | 230–280 |
| Cross Timbers and Prairies | 15.3 | Gently rolling | 500–1500 | 25–35 | 230–280 |
| South Texas Plains | 20.9 | Nearly level to rolling | 0–1000 | 18–30 | 260–340 |
| Edwards Plateau | 25.45 | Deeply dissected hilly, stony plain | 1200–3000 | 12–32 | 220–260 |
| Rolling Plains | 24.0 | Nearly level to rolling | 1000–3000 | 18–28 | 185–235 |
| High Plains | 19.4 | Nearly level high plateau | 3000–4500 | 14–21 | 180–220 |
| Trans-Pecos | 17.95 | Mountain ranges, rough, rocky land, flat basins and plateaus | 2500–8751 | 8–18 | 220–245 |

[1]Reprinted from Hatch et al. (1990).

mammals from throughout the borderlands region. Many of the species he named have now been placed in synonymy with other taxa.

J. A. Allen was a contemporary of Merriam and Bailey who served as the curator of birds and mammals at the American Museum of Natural History in New York City. Allen purchased several private collections of mammals from South Texas, including Bexar County (Allen, 1896) and Aransas County (Allen, 1894). H. P. Attwater was well acquainted with Allen and provided him with specimens and descriptions of Texas mammals. Also, three well-known amateur ornithologists, George Sennett, F. B. Armstrong, and George Ragsdale, worked in Texas, and they also provided specimens to both Bailey and Allen. Allen was a prolific taxonomist, and he described fifteen taxa of mammals from Texas, but insofar as I am aware he never visited the state.

# Biological Survey of Texas, 1889–1905

Bailey's 1905 publication contained only a small part of the information generated by the survey. At the conclusion of the Texas survey, and after the publication was issued, all the accumulated materials were deposited in the Bird and Mammal Laboratory of the U.S. Department of Agriculture, the U.S. National Museum, the National Archives of the Smithsonian Institution in Washington, D.C., or the National Archives and Records Administration in College Park, Maryland. The archival materials included scientific specimens of birds, mammals, and reptiles; museum catalogs of the scientific specimens; field trip diaries describing the travels of the field agents; detailed biological reports of plants and animals observed; reports of significant biological events; physiographic reports of each place visited in Texas; special correspondence with landowners and field agents; and almost a thousand black-and-white photographs of Texas landscapes. These archival materials represent a detailed depiction of Texas natural history at the turn of the century.

By any measure possible, the biological survey was a huge success scientifically. More than five thousand scientific specimens were obtained by the federal agents during the period from the beginning of the survey until the publication of Bailey's book in 1905. These specimens included 353 reptiles and 4,820 mammals. Forty-nine taxa of mammals were described from the specimens obtained during the survey (Table 3). Nine were described directly in Bailey's 1905 work and the others in other outlets of the time, such as the proceedings of the Biological Society of Washington. C. Hart Merriam and Vernon Bailey described most of the taxa, and Bailey himself collected twenty of the type specimens. All but nine of the forty-nine mammals described are still recognized as valid species or subspecies in Texas today, which is a tribute to the taxonomic ability of the mammalogists working for the biological survey.

In 1992, a project was initiated to document all the archival natural history information from the Texas biological survey (Schmidly, 1998). The complete set of archives has now been deposited at the Southwest Collecti on, Texas Tech University. This collection of field reports, other material, and photographs provides a wealth of detailed information not included in the published book and never before available to biologists in Texas.

Table 3. List of mammalian taxa described from specimens collected during the biological survey of Texas (* indicates those taxa described in Bailey, 1905). Adapted from Poole and Schantz (1942), Miller and Kellogg (1955), and Hall (1981). (S) indicates taxa that have been placed in synonymy by modern taxonomists.

| Original Taxon | Type Locality | Collector (Date Collected) | Modern Taxonomic Designation |
|---|---|---|---|
| Didelphis marsupialis texensis (s) | Brownsville, Cameron County | F.B. Armstrong (4/13/1892) | Didelphis virginiana california |
| Tatu novemcinctum texanum*(s) | Brownsville, Cameron County | F.B. Armstrong (6/10/1892) | Dasypus novemcinctus mexicanus |
| Lepus pinetis robustus | Davis Mountains, Jeff Davis County | V. Bailey (1/6/1890) | Sylvilagus robustus |
| Eutamias cinereicollis canipes | Guadalupe Mountains, Hudspeth County | V. Bailey (8/24/1901) | Tamias canipes |
| Tamias interpres | El Paso, El Paso County | V. Bailey (12/10/1889) | Ammospermophilus interpres |
| Spermophilus spilosoma annectens | Padre Island, Cameron County | W. Lloyd (8/24/1891) | Spermophilus spilosoma annectens |
| Spermophilus spilosoma arens (s) | El Paso, El Paso County | A.K. Fisher (5/10/1894) | Spermophilus spilosoma canescens |
| Spermophilus spilosoma marginatus | Alpine, Brewster County | V. Bailey (7/5/1901) | Spermophilus spilosoma marginatus |
| Spermophilus tridecemlineatus texensis | Gainesville, Cooke County | G.H. Ragsdale (4/15/1886) | Spermophilus tridecemlineatus texensis |
| Glaucomys volans texensis | Sour Lake, Hardin County | J.H. Gaut (3/15/1905) | Glaucomys volans texensis |
| Thomomys aureus lachuguilla | El Paso, El Paso County | V. Bailey (9/24/1901) | Thomomys bottae lachuguilla |
| Thomomys baileyi | Sierra Blanca, El Paso County | V. Bailey (12/28/1889) | Thomomys bottae baileyi |
| Thomomys baileyi spatiosus | Alpine, Brewster County | V. Bailey (5/26/1900) | Thomomys bottae spatiosus |
| Thomomys bottae guadalupensis | McKittrick Canyon, Guadalupe Mtns. | V. Bailey (8/22/1901) | Thomomys bottae guadalupensis |
| Thomomys bottae pervarius | Lloyd Ranch, 35 mi S Marfa, Presidio County | V. Bailey (1/20/1890) | Thomomys bottae pervarius |
| Thomomys fulvus texensis | Head of Limpia Creek, Davis Mtns. | V. Bailey (1/7/1890) | Thomomys bottae texensis |
| Thomomys lachuguilla confinalis | 35 mi E Rock Springs, Edwards County | V. Bailey (7/11/1902) | Thomomys bottae confinalis |
| Geomys arenarius | El Paso, El Paso County | V. Bailey (12/14/1889) | Geomys arenarius |
| Geomys breviceps ammophilus (s) | Cuero, DeWitt County | V. Bailey (4/26/1899) | Geomys attwateri |
| Geomys breviceps attwateri | Rockport, Aransas County | H.H. Keays (11/18/1892) | Geomys attwateri |
| Geomys breviceps llanensis*(s) | Llano, Llano County | V. Bailey (5/15/1899) | Geomys texensis |
| Geomys breviceps sagittallis | Clear Creek, Galveston Bay | W. Lloyd (3/28/1892) | Geomys breviceps sagittalis |
| Geomys personatus | Padre Island, Cameron County | C.K. Worthen (4/11/1888) | Geomys personatus personatus |
| Geomys personatus fallax | Nueces Bay, Cameron County | W. Lloyd (11/30/1891) | Geomys personatus fallax |
| Geomys texensis* | Mason, Mason County | Ira B. Henry (12/17/1885) | Geomys texensis |
| Cratogeomys castanops angusticeps | Eagle Pass, Maverick County | C.P. Streator (11/11/1890) | Cratogeomys castanops angusticeps |
| Cratogeomys castanops perplanus | Tascosa, Oldham County | V. Bailey (6/5/1899) | Cratogeomys castanops perplanus |

| | | | |
|---|---|---|---|
| Perognathus paradoxus spilotus | G.H. Ragsdale (10/8/1886) | Brownsville, Cameron County | Chaetodipus hispidus spilotus |
| Dipodomys ambiguus | V. Bailey (12/13/1889) | Cummings Creek, Colorado County | Dipodomys merriami ambiguus |
| Dipodomys compactus | C.K. Worthen (4/3/1888) | Gainesville, Cooke County | Dipodomys compactus |
| Dipodomys elator | J.A. Loring (4/3/1894) | El Paso, El Paso County | Dipodomys elator |
| Liomys texensis | J.A. Loring (2/19/1894) | Padre Island, Cameron County | Liomys irroratus texensis |
| Castor canadensis texensis* | F. Brune (12/25/1900) | Henrietta, Clay County | Castor canadensis texensis |
| Reithrodontomys griseus* | H.P. Attwater (3/4/1897) | San Antonio, Bexar County | Reithrodontomys montanus griseus |
| Reithrodontomys merriami | W. Lloyd (3/15/1892) | near Alvin, Brazoria County | Reithrodontomys humulis merriami |
| Peromyscus boylei laceyi*(s) | H.P. Attwater (12/4/1897) | Turtle Creek, Kerr County | Peromyscus attwateri |
| Peromyscus pectoralis laceianus | V. Bailey (5/3/1899) | Turtle Creek, Kerr County | Peromyscus pectoralis laceianus |
| Peromyscus taylori subater* | W. Lloyd (2/25/1892) | Columbia, Brazoria County | Baiomys taylori subater |
| Onychomys longipes | W. Lloyd (3/11/1883) | Concho County | Onychomys leucogaster longipes |
| Sigmodon ochrognathus | V. Bailey (6/13/1901) | Chisos Mountains, Brewster County | Sigmodon ochrognathus |
| Microtus mexicanus guadalupensis | V. Bailey (8/21/1901) | Guadalupe Mountains, Hudspeth County | Microtus mexicanus guadalupensis |
| Canis nebracensis texensis* | J.M. Priour (12/14/1901) | 45 mi SW Corpus Christi, Nueces County | Canis latrans texensis |
| Ursus horriaeus texensis (s) | C.O. Finley (11/2/1890) | Davis Mountains, Jeff Davis County | Ursus arctos horribilis |
| Lutra canadensis texensis (s) | B.V. Lilly (3/-/1908) | 20 mi W Angleton, Brazoria County | Lontra canadensis lataxina |
| Spilogale leucoparia | Ira B. Henry (12/2/1885) | Mason, Mason County | Spilogale gracilis leucoparia |
| Conepatus leuconotus texensis | F. B. Armstrong (8/20/1892) | Brownsville, Cameron County | Conepatus leuconotus texensis |
| Conepatus mesoleucus mearnsi | Ira B. Henry (2/20/1886) | Mason, Mason County | Conepatus mesoleucus mearnsi |
| Conepatus mesoleucus telmalestes* | J. H. Gaut (3/17/1905) | 7 mi NE Sour Lake, Hardin County | Conepatus mesoleucus telmalestes |
| Ovis canadensis texianus (s) | V. Bailey (9/2/1902) | Guadalupe Mountains, Hudspeth County | Ovis canadensis mexicanus |

The scientific names of plants and animals have changed substantially since Bailey's publication. This is a result of new collections and specimens, as well as modern taxonomic revisions. Consequently, many of the plants and animals that Bailey lists from Texas appear today under different scientific names. The current scientific and common names for all plants and animals mentioned in the *Biological Survey of Texas* are provided in the Appendix and discussed throughout the text.

Documenting and understanding the changes in Texas's diverse and unique biota depends on reliable data about the flora and fauna of the region before it was negatively affected by humans. The availability of Bailey's 1905 publication, together with the discovery of its complete archives, gives a virtual natural history picture of every region of the state as it existed a century ago. This information provides crucial baseline data to compare with the results of current biological surveys and to assess landscape and biotic change information useful to land managers and others seeking to improve land and ecosystem management. This chapter includes a reprinting of the *Biological Survey of Texas*, with numerical annotations marked with endnotes that are explained in the next chapter.

The following reprint of the *Biological Survey of Texas* is a faithful reproduction of the original book, with only a few minor exceptions:

- The Index, found on pages 21–222 of the original publication, has not been reprinted. The Index for *Texas Natural History: A Century of Change* (pages 513–534) includes all the items indexed in the original publication.
- The Frontispiece of the original publication, designated as Plate I, was an over-sized color map of the Life Zones of Texas. That map has been recreated as a black-and-white line drawing and can be found in Chapter 1, Map 3a.
- The remaining Plates (II–XVI) have been reproduced and can be found as a group in the midsection of the *Biological Survey of Texas* reprint.

U. S. DEPARTMENT OF AGRICULTURE

BIOLOGICAL SURVEY

# NORTH AMERICAN FAUNA

## No. 25

[Actual date of publication, October 24, 1905]

## BIOLOGICAL SURVEY OF TEXAS

LIFE ZONES, with Characteristic Species of Mammals, Birds, Reptiles, and Plants
REPTILES, with Notes on Distribution
MAMMALS, with Notes on Distribution, Habits, and Economic Importance

BY

### VERNON BAILEY
CHIEF FIELD NATURALIST

Prepared under the direction of

### Dr. C. HART MERRIAM
CHIEF OF BIOLOGICAL SURVEY

WASHINGTON
GOVERNMENT PRINTING OFFICE

1905

LETTER OF TRANSMITTAL.

U. S. DEPARTMENT OF AGRICULTURE,
BIOLOGICAL SURVEY,
*Washington, D. C., July 10, 1905.*

SIR: I have the honor to forward herewith, for publication as North American Fauna No. 25, a report on the results of a biological survey of Texas, by Vernon Bailey. The report consists of three sections: The first characterizes the life zones and defines the distribution areas of the State; these are mapped in detail and are accompanied by practical suggestions as to their adaptation to agricultural uses. The second comprises a brief report on the snakes and lizards, adding considerably to previous knowledge of the distribution of these groups. The third consists of a report on the mammals of the State, and contains much of a practical nature on distribution, habits, and economic relations of the several species.

The maps and illustrations are essential to the clearness and brevity of the report.

C. HART MERRIAM,
*Chief, Biological Survey.*

Hon. JAMES WILSON,
*Secretary of Agriculture.*

3

## CONTENTS.

# ILLUSTRATIONS.

## PLATES.

## TEXT FIGURES.

8                                    ILLUSTRATIONS.

No. 25.     NORTH AMERICAN FAUNA.     Oct., 1905.

# BIOLOGICAL SURVEY OF TEXAS.

By Vernon Bailey.

## INTRODUCTION.

For a number of years the Biological Survey has been collecting information and specimens bearing on the natural history of Texas. Some of the results are here brought together in a discussion of the life zones and their subdivisions and a report on the mammals and reptiles of the State. The original plan included also a report on the birds of Texas, by H. C. Oberholser, but the present paper has grown to such proportions that the bird report will be published separately.

Much of the field work has been carried on in connection with that in adjacent regions, and on several occasions it has been possible to continue parties in the field until late in the season or throughout the winter by moving them southward into Texas in the fall, or to begin work there early in the spring before the season had opened sufficiently for operations farther north. Hence, while the Texas work has the appearance of being desultory and scattered, the ground in reality has been covered with great economy of time and labor. Part of the field work has been carried on in connection with special studies of urgent economic problems, as the prairie dog, coyote, and boll weevil pests, and throughout all of it the economic status of birds and mammals has received special attention. The distribution of mammals, birds, reptiles, and plants, so far as they have an important bearing on the extent and boundaries of faunal areas, has been studied in detail in the field, and in the case of most species a sufficient number of specimens has been collected to show the variation due to climatic differences. Of many of the larger game mammals, and especially of the deer, bear, and panther, it has not been possible to secure enough material to satisfactorily establish the present geographic limits of the species and subspecies, but it is greatly to be hoped that the growing interest in natural history will inspire local hunters and residents of the country to send specimens of these vanishing forms to the National Museum before it is too late. Many important problems can be solved only by aid from local naturalists or other intelligent residents of the State. The skull that is left in the woods or thrown away would often aid in solving one of these problems.

## PERSONNEL OF BIOLOGICAL SURVEY WORK IN TEXAS.

In carrying on the field work in Texas the writer was assisted at different times by the following regular or temporary field naturalists of the Biological Survey: William Lloyd, Clark P. Streator, William L. Bray, Harry C. Oberholser, N. Hollister, Merritt Cary, Gordon Donald, Arthur H. Howell, and James H. Gaut.

Several local naturalists and collectors have added materially to the results of the work in Texas, and among these thanks are especially due to Mr. H. P. Attwater and Mr. Howard Lacey.

Extensive collections of mammals, birds, reptiles, batrachians, crustaceans, mollusks, and plants have been made from localities practically covering the State, and the field reports of the collectors contain a mine of important facts on habits, distribution, correlation, and economic importance of species. Much of this material has already been published by the Biological Survey in the form of bulletins and papers on economic subjects, and much still remains for use in future papers.

## ACKNOWLEDGMENTS.

To Dr. C. Hart Merriam, under whose direction the work was planned and carried out, I am indebted for the use of his private collection of mammals deposited in the United States National Museum. To Mr. F. W. True, curator, and Mr. Gerrit S. Miller, jr., assistant curator of mammals in the National Museum, I am indebted for the use of the museum collection; also to Dr. J. A. Allen, curator of birds and mammals in the American Museum of Natural History; Mr. Outram Bangs, curator of mammals in the Museum of Comparative Anatomy; and Mr. Witmer Stone, curator of birds and mammals in the Philadelphia Academy of Sciences, for the loan of types and topotypes of mammals from the collections under their supervision

## NEW SPECIES OF MAMMALS.

A number of new species of plants, reptiles, birds, and mammals has been found in the Texas collection. Most of these have been described and named by various specialists, but descriptions of a few previously undescribed mammals are included in the present report. They are as follows:

### FAUNA AND FLORA OF TEXAS IN RELATION TO LIFE ZONES AND MINOR DISTRIBUTION AREAS.

The fauna and flora of Texas are wonderfully rich and varied, not only in abundance of individuals and species, but in the number of genera, families, and orders, some of which do not occur in any other part of the United States. This richness is due, not so much to the enormous extent of the State, as to its varied physical and climatic conditions, for it embraces areas of abundant humidity and extreme aridity, of dense forest and extensive plain, of low coast prairies and rugged mountains. Besides stretching across the aerial pathway of north and south migrating birds and bats, it lies at the threshold of the Tropics and claims a large contingent of Mexican species. On the east it includes the fauna and flora of the lower Mississippi Valley, with most of the species ranging to the Atlantic coast, and on the west reaches far into the desert region of highly specialized forms, while in the middle portion it is traversed by a wide tongue of the more northern fauna and flora of the Great Plains. In the west several mountain masses reach an altitude of 8,000 feet, with peaks rising to 8,500 and 9,500 feet. This range of altitude, together with the great extent of latitude, suffices to include within the State the full width of three of the principal life zones, Lower Austral, Upper Austral, and Transition, each with its characteristic series of plants and animals. In the Lower Rio Grande and Gulf Coast region there is, moreover, a slight overlapping of tropical species, accompanying the almost tropical climate, while high up in the Guadalupe, Davis, and Chisos mountains are mere traces of Canadian zone species.

The agricultural and commercial interests of the State are as varied as the climatic conditions on which they largely depend, and when mapped they are found in many cases closely to correspond with the areas of distribution of certain species of native plants and animals. In other words, various agricultural industries are being slowly developed by endless and costly experiment along the same lines that the native species have followed in the course of adaptation to their environment. Thus the lumbering industries of the State are prescribed by the distribution of certain species of trees. On the other hand, successful stock raising depends in part on the absence of forests and the abundance of certain grasses, and in part on the absence of certain disease-conveying parasites. Several varieties of wheat are successfully raised over a limited area near the upper edge of humid Lower Sonoran zone, but most of the State lies below the belt of small grains. Rice and sugar cane are standard crops of the semitropical coast region, and cotton is the staple for the whole Lower Sonoran zone, wherever the rainfall is sufficient to mature the crop or water is available for irrigation. Parts of the State are peculiarly adapted to the production of early fruits and winter vegetables for the northern market, but these industries are as yet more or less restricted by inadequate facilities for quick transportation.

The division of the State into wheat, cotton, and stock-raising districts is no matter of accident, nor is it a matter of choice on the part of those engaged in the various industries. While usually there is no room for doubt in the middle of each area as to the crop it is best adapted to, there is always a question along the boundaries. For instance, where does the successful production of cotton yield to that of wheat? Nature in her processes avoids sharp lines and hard-and-fast rules, but usually gives reliable averages. Even after a season of copious rainfall in a valley clothed with cactus and scrubby mesquite trees, the experienced ranchman knows better than to plow and plant with the idea that the following season will be similar; but from the character of the vegetation and of the animals present he may not only learn approximately the average amount of rainfall, but also the life zone in which he is located, with its average range of temperature and many of the crops best adapted to it. While much has been done and much more will be done to overcome arid conditions and to convert the now almost worthless desert soil into the most productive in the State, the normal conditions limiting life zones can not be materially overcome, nor can they be safely ignored. The attempt to raise cotton in Upper Sonoran zone results only in failure and loss, but enough of this zone lies within the State to produce, with the water available for irrigation, an abundance of the finest apples, as well as many other fruits and crops not adapted to lower zones.

The primary object of the present report is a careful definition of the ranges of native species of plants and animals and a correlation of these ranges into well-defined areas of distribution. In 'Life Zones and Crop Zones of the United States' Doctor Merriam has given, with as much detail as the data collected to 1898 would allow, the adaptation of various crops to the zones and their subdivisions, and has clearly set forth the practical application of the knowledge

of faunal areas to agriculture. Under the heading 'Relations of the
Biological Survey to Practical Agriculture,' he says:[a]

The Biological Survey aims to define and map the natural agricultural belts
of the United States, to ascertain what products of the soil can and what can
not be grown successfully in each, to guide the farmer in the intelligent introduction of foreign crops, and to point out his friends and his enemies among
the native birds and mammals, thereby helping him to utilize the beneficial
and ward off the harmful. *   *   *   *

The farmers of the United States spend vast sums of money each year in
trying to find out whether a particular fruit, vegetable, or cereal will or will
not thrive in localities where it has not been tested. Most of these experiments
result in disappointment and pecuniary loss. It makes little difference whether
the crop experimented with comes from the remotest parts of the earth or from
a neighboring State, the result is essentially the same, for the main cost is the
labor of cultivation and the use of the land.  If the crop happens to be one
that requires a period of years for the test, the loss from its failure is propor-
tionately great.

The cause of failure in the great majority of cases is climatic unfitness.
The quantity, distribution, or interrelation of heat and moisture may be at
fault. Thus, while the total quantity of heat may be adequate, the moisture
may be inadequate, or the moisture may be adequate and the heat inadequate,
or the quantities of heat and moisture may be too great or too small with
respect to one another or to the time of year, and so on. What the farmer
wants to know is *how to tell in advance* whether the climatic conditions on his
own farm are fit or unfit for the particular crop he has in view, and what crops
he can raise with reasonable certainty. It requires no argument to show that
the answers to these questions would be worth in the aggregate hundreds of
thousands of dollars yearly to the American farmer. The Biological Survey
aims to furnish these answers.

Agricultural colleges, experiment stations and substations, horti-
culturists, and countless farmers are working out the details of these
problems in different parts of the country and constantly pushing
their experiments into new regions. As a crop becomes an established success in one locality, a study of the zone map will show over
what adjoining country it can be profitably extended. For instance,
Roswell, N. Mex., where apple raising has proved a great financial
success, is situated at the junction of Upper and Lower Sonoran
zones, or in a mixed belt of overlapping of the two, at the western
edge of the Staked Plains. By tracing this lower border of Upper
Sonoran zone around the southern arm and along the eastern edge
of the Staked Plains, a belt approximately 1,000 miles long of the
same zonal level and climatic conditions is found, lying within the
State of Texas. This is largely undeveloped agricultural land, but
a considerable part of it can be irrigated, and there is every reason to
believe that it will be found perfectly adapted to the varieties of
apples that thrive in the Pecos Valley at Roswell. The Staked

---

[a] Life Zones and Crop Zones of the United States, by C. Hart Merriam.
Bul. 10, U. S. Dept. Agr., Div. Biol. Survey, pp. 9, 12, 1898.

Plains, lying within this belt, are pure Upper Sonoran, the real home of most of the standard varieties of apples. Other northern crops, both cereals and fruits, have proved a success along this southern projection of Upper Sonoran zone, but have not been introduced as systematically as the advantages of its position seem to warrant. To quote again from Life Zones and Crop Zones, page 15, under the heading "Special value of narrow extensions of faunas," Doctor Merriam says:

> In looking at the map of the life zones it will be seen that nearly all of the belts and areas send out long arms, which penetrate far into the heart of adjoining areas. When such arms occupy suitable soils in thickly inhabited regions, so that their products may be conveniently marketed, they are of more than ordinary value, for the greater the distance from its area of principal production a crop can be made to succeed the higher price it will command. Hence, farms favorably situated in northern prolongations or islands of southern zones, or in southern prolongations or islands of northern zones, should be worth considerably more per acre than those situated within normal parts of the same zones. The obvious reason is that by growing particular crops at points remote from the usual sources of supply, and at the same time conveniently near a market, the cost of transportation is greatly reduced and the profit correspondingly increased.

Since the publication of Doctor Merriam's zone map, detailed work in Texas has enabled me to make minor corrections and to establish the zone boundaries with more precision than has been possible heretofore.

### TROPICAL ELEMENT OF THE LOWER RIO GRANDE REGION.

Until recent years more thorough biological collecting had been done in the Lower Rio Grande region than in any other part of Texas, with the result of giving a somewhat exaggerated impression of the tropical element found there. Later and more systematic field work over the State, together with the extensive investigations of Nelson and Goldman in Mexico, have shown that the Texas mammals of tropical groups—as the armadillo, ocelot, jaguar, red and gray cats, and spiny pocket mouse—elsewhere range through Lower Sonoran zone, or at least its Tamaulipan subdivision, while a more critical study of these groups, based on the rapidly increasing amount of material, has resulted in every case in the specific or subspecific separation of the Texas forms. The single specimen of *Nasua,* apparently of a tropical species, from Brownsville may have been imported, and if this is so not a strictly tropical mammal reaches the border of Texas.

The close proximity to the Tropics is shown most pronouncedly by the birds of the Lower Rio Grande region. A considerable number of species, mainly tropical in distribution, reach southern Texas, where some breed regularly, while others are more or less regular visitors.

BIRDS OF MAINLY TROPICAL RANGE WHICH EXTEND INTO SOUTHERN TEXAS.

*Columbus dominicus brachypterus.*
*Phalacrocorax vigua mexicanus.*
*Fregata aquila.*
*Nomonyx dominicus.*
*Dendrocygna autumnalis.*
*Guara alba.*
*Mycteria americana.*
*Ajaia ajaja.*
*Jacana spinosa.*
*Ortalis vetula maccalli.*
*Leptotila fulviventris brachyptera.*
*Columba flavirostris.*
*Melopelia leucoptera.*
*Scardafella inca.*
*Elanus leucurus.*
*Parabuteo unicinctus harrisi.*
*Buteo abbreviatus.*
*Buteo albicaudatus sennetti.*
*Urubitinga anthracina.*
*Falco fusco-caerulescens.*

*Polyborus cheriway.*
*Glaucidium phalaenoides.*
*Crotophaga sulcirostris.*
*Ceryle torquata.*
*Ceryle americana septentrionalis.*
*Nyctidromus albicollis merrilli.*
*Amizilis tzacatl.*
*Amizilis cerviniventris chalconota.*
*Tyrannus melancholicus couchi.*
*Pitangus derbianus.*
*Myiarchus mexicanus.*
*Pyrocephalus rubineus mexicanus.*
*Ornithion imberbe.*
*Tangavius aeneus involucratus.*
*Agelaius phoeniceus richmondi.*
*Megaquiscalus major macrourus.*
*Arremonops rufivirgatus.*
*Sporophila morelleti.*
*Vireo flavoviridis.*
*Geothlypis poliocephala.*

A few species of reptiles supposed to be of tropical origin enter southern Texas, but the task of verifying the records and determining ranges has not been undertaken in connection with the present work.

In the case of plants, as of mammals, the tropical element of southern Texas has been overestimated. A number of species of genera that are mainly tropical extend into the Lower Rio Grande region, but very few species of known tropical range. The Texas palm (*Inodes texana* Cook)[a] is found in limited numbers in the Brownsville region, but apparently nothing is known of its southern extension or zonal significance. So with other supposedly tropical forms the southern limits and zonal position have not been satisfactorily determined, but evidently no purely tropical species holds an important place in the flora of the Lower Rio Grande region. This absence or scarcity of tropical plants is fully accounted for by Professor Bray in the Botanical Gazette for August, 1901 (p. 102), as follows:

A record of sixteen years at Brownsville showed a minimum temperature of 18° (the minimum in February, 1899, was 12°) and five years without frost. At Indianola a record of fifteen years showed a minimum of 15° and four years without frost. Probably a freeze severe enough to kill tropical woody vegetation occurs in periods of ten to twelve years. The fatal temperature for tropical plants in this region is that due to northers, which bring abnormally low temperatures suddenly, and not infrequently during the growth season.

[a] *Sabal mexicana* Mart. of Sargent, Coulter, and Small.

A striking example of the fatal effects of a 'norther' was witnessed over the coast region of Texas from Galveston to Port Lavaca in the spring of 1899, following the extremely cold wave of the
preceding February, when the abundant huisache trees were killed
to the ground. In the Brownsville region, however, as I found in
the following spring, these trees had escaped, but all of the bananas
had been killed. Under such climatic conditions tropical species could
hardly be expected to persist, and it is not surprising that the preponderating species of plants and mammals are those characteristic
of Lower Sonoran zone. Nor is it surprising that tropical species of
birds, with their greater freedom of motion, should overlap the
limits of their zone slightly beyond the more stationary groups.

Bananas offer a good illustration of the partial success of a tropical
fruit in this region. During a period of warm years they thrive and
even bear fruit, but only to be killed by the first hard freeze. Even
at Brownsville they require artificial protection to insure their living
through the winter. Oranges in like manner are a partial success,
but an assured success only where artificial protection can be afforded
during the winter.

## LOWER AUSTRAL ZONE.

By far the greater part of Texas, including all but the Staked
Plains with their northern and southern extensions and the mountain
elevations in the western part of the State, lies within the Lower
Austral, or cotton-producing zone, the subdivisions of which within
the limits of the State equal, if they do not exceed, in practical
importance the more restricted intrusions of other transcontinental
zones. The most important of these subdivisions of Lower Austral
are the narrow Gulf strip, with semitropical climate, and the
Austroriparian, or humid eastern, and Lower Sonoran, or arid western, areas, which divide the zone in Texas into approximately equal
parts.

### GULF STRIP OF TEXAS.

A comparatively narrow strip of country bordering the Gulf coast
of Texas is characterized by a limited number of species of unques-
tioned tropical affinities, ranging as extensions from Mexico or
Florida part or all of the way along the Gulf coast, but not extending
back over the rest of Lower Austral zone. While associated with a
preponderance of characteristic Lower Austral species, they mark a
border of modified climatic conditions too important to be ignored.
This strip has been mapped as a semitropical or Gulf strip of the
Lower Austral zone, of which it is merely a subdivision.

In mammals the best representatives of a mainly tropical group
(subgenus *Baiomys*) are the little *Peromyscus taylori* and its sub-

species *subater,* which inhabit the coast prairies from Brownsville to Galveston. Among birds the caracara, a bird of wide tropical range, is common in the coast region of Texas as far east as Port Lavaca, while the jackdaws—the great-tailed and boat-tailed grackles—of the genus *Megaquiscalus,* extend in one form or the other from the tropics of eastern Mexico along the Gulf coast to Florida, and breed abundantly along the whole Texas coast region.

FIG. 1.—Distribution area of huisache (*Vachellia farnesiana*).

In plants some of the species marking the Gulf strip extend into the tropical regions of Mexico or Florida, while others are limited to some part of this narrow strip. As stated by Professor Bray,[a] the outlines of the strip are approximately indicated in Texas by the range of *Vachellia* (=*Acacia*) *farnesiana* and *Parkinsonia aculeata,* both species of partly tropical range, and to these I should add *Daubentonia longifolia* (*Sesban cavanillesii*) and *Lantana camara* as equally important, while others of less extensive range in Texas are

---

[a] Botanical Gazette, August, 1901, 103.

*Castela nicholsonii, Amyris parvifolia, Karwinskia humboldtiana, lbervillea lindheimeri, Castalia elegans, Yucca treculeana, Manfreda maculosa, Tillandsia baileyi, Jatropha macrorhiza* and *multifida, Malpighia glabra*, and *Solanum triquetrum*. It is worthy of note that none of these plants enter the swamp and timber country to any extent.

AUSTRORIPARIAN OF EASTERN TEXAS.

The eastern part of Texas, west to approximately the ninety-eighth meridian, agrees very closely in climate, physiography, and the bulk of its species of plants and animals with the lower Mississippi Valley. Except for the strip of coast prairie, and farther north the areas known as the Black Prairie and Grand Prairie,[a] it is largely a forested region, comprising both deciduous and coniferous trees and inhabited by forest species of birds and mammals.

While a rich though only half-developed agricultural region devoted mainly to cotton, corn, fruits, and vegetables, it still comprises extensive areas of native forest and uninhabited cypress swamps. Most of the numerous streams have wide bottom lands subject to occasional floods, from which they derive a deep rich soil especially adapted to luxuriant forest growth. These rich bottoms are largely grown up to sweet gum, sour gum, various oaks, swamp hickory, sycamore, willow, holly, and magnolia, while along the streams and in swamps and shallow lagoons the cypress, tupelo gums, and palmettoes are often the characteristic growth. Where interlaced with vines these bottom-land forests are almost impenetrable thickets. The uplands and ridges are usually more openly forested with deciduous trees, such as oaks, hickories, dogwood, and sassafras, or often densely covered with one or more of the three species of pines which furnish most of the lumber of the State. Of these *Pinus taeda* and *echinata* are distributed over the State as far west as Houston, Hockley, Trinity, and Palestine in about equal abundance. The longleaf pine (*Pinus palustris*) occupies the southeastern part of the State, and where untouched by ax or fire forms miles of dense forest of the cleanest, most uniform, and symmetrical body of pine to be found on the continent, excelling the yellow pine forests of Arizona and California in the close array of graceful trunks.

In eastern Texas many species stop short of filling the whole humid area, and when their ranges are carefully mapped are found to be absent from, or in fewer cases to be restricted to, some of the following nonforested sections: The Grand and Black prairies of the Fort Worth and Dallas region; the coast prairie; coast marshes; islands and beaches.

---

[a] Physical Geog. of the Texas Region. R. T. Hill, U. S. Geol. Survey, Topographic Atlas, p. 13, 1900.

### GRAND AND BLACK PRAIRIES.

The Grand and Black prairies, lying parallel, with only the narrow strip of Lower Cross Timbers between, extend from near Austin north in a broad strip to the Red River bottoms and east to Paris, forming an extensive area over which trees and forest species are mainly restricted to narrow stream bottoms. The rich black 'waxland' soil of these prairies is almost proof against burrowing rodents, which penetrate the region only along some sandy stream bottoms, while the open country tempts jack rabbits, coyotes, and other plains species eastward slightly beyond their usual bounds. Few, if any, species are restricted to these prairies, however, and the effect on distribution is mainly negative.

Here and there island strips of rich soiled grassy prairie occur in the timbered region farther east, becoming smaller and less frequent as they recede from the Black Prairie and Grand Prairie, and in some cases these islands are inhabited by a few plains species of birds, mammals, and reptiles nearly to the eastern edge of the State. Such an example is Nevils Prairie, near Antioch, where N. Hollister found scissor-tailed flycatchers, jack rabbits, and horned toads.

### COAST PRAIRIE.

Over a wide strip of level coast prairie, extending along the Gulf from western Louisiana to San Antonio Bay and irregularly beyond, the timber is restricted to relatively narrow strips in the river bottoms, while the greater part of the surface is characterized by a rich growth of grass and many flowering plants. Spreading live oaks, loaded with Spanish moss, border the prairies or grow in scattered motts over them. In addition to the strictly shore species and those of the salt marshes which occasionally range over it or follow up the rivers to the limits of the open country, a few species of birds and mammals are characteristic of these coast prairies.

The most characteristic mammals are *Didelphis v. pigra, Peromyscus taylori* and *subater, Oryzomys palustris, Reithrodontomys aurantius, R. merriami, Sigmodon h. texianus, Microtus ludovicianus, Geomys sagittalis, Lepus merriami,* and *Spilogale indianola,* and of these *Peromyscus taylori* and *subater, Microtus ludovicianus,* and *Geomys sagittalis* are, so far as known, restricted to it.

The characteristic breeding birds of the coast prairies are *Tympanuchus attwateri, Otocoris a. giraudi, Megaquiscalus major* and *macrourus, Ammodramus m. sennetti, Coturniculus s. bimaculatus,* and *Geothlypis t. brachidactyla.*

Among its flowering plants *Baptisia, Oenothera, Meriolix, Hartmannia, Monarda, Coreopsis, Ratibida, Grindelia, Callirhoe, Eustoma,* and *Hymenocallis* are conspicuous genera, with numerous species, while such low shrubs as *Daubentonia longifolia, Vachellia farnesiana, Morella cerifera, Ascyrum,* and low willows are found here and there in favorable localities.

### COAST MARSHES.

Extensive marshes border the Gulf shore irregularly as far west as Port Lavaca, and recur at intervals, mainly near the mouths of the streams, to the Rio Grande. These brackish, sedgy, tide-washed marshes are inhabited by rice rats, rails, water snakes, and great numbers of crustaceans. They are favorite resorts also for numerous migrating waders and water birds.

### BEACHES AND ISLANDS.

The Gulf beaches and low islands offshore have a largely maritime fauna, the most striking feature of which is the abundance of shore birds, pelicans, cormorants, gulls, and terns. Not until the long reef-like bar of Padre Island is reached do we find any restricted forms of island mammals, and here only two—*Perodipus compactus* and *Geomys personatus.*

The following species and subspecies of mammals, breeding birds, reptiles, and plants occur more or less commonly in the Austroriparian or humid subdivision of Lower Austral zone in eastern Texas, but rarely, if at all, in the arid western subdivision of the zone. None of the lists are complete.

### MAMMALS OF EASTERN TEXAS AUSTRORIPARIAN.

| | |
|---|---|
| *Didelphis virginiana.* | *Lepus aquaticus.* |
| *Didelphis virginiana pigra.* | *Lepus aquaticus attwateri.* |
| *Sciuropterus volans querceti.* | *Felis* (sp.?) (panther). |
| *Sciurus ludovicianus.* | *Lynx rufus texensis.* |
| *Sciurus carolinensis.* | *Canis ater.* |
| *Citellus tridecemlineatus texensis.* | *Vulpes fulvus.* |
| *Peromyscus gossypinus.* | *Urocyon cinereoargenteus floridanus.* |
| *Peromyscus leucopus.* | *Ursus luteolus.* |
| *Peromyscus taylori subater.* | *Procyon lotor.* |
| *Oryzomys palustris.* | *Lutra (canadensis?).* |
| *Reithrodontomys aurantius.* | *Lutreola lutreocephala.* |
| *Reithrodontomys merriami.* | *Spilogale indianola.* |
| *Neotoma floridana rubida.* | *Mephitis mesomelas.* |
| *Sigmodon hispidus texensis.* | *Conepatus mesoleucus telmalestes.* |
| *Microtus pinetorum auricularis.* | *Scalopus aquaticus.* |
| *Microtus ludovicianus.* | *Blarina brevicauda carolinensis.* |
| *Castor canadensis texensis.* | *Blarina parva.* |
| *Geomys breviceps.* | *Nycticeius humeralis.* |
| *Geomys sagittalis.* | *Lasiurus borealis.* |
| *Perognathus hispidus spilotus.* | *Lasiurus borealis seminolus.* |
| *Lepus floridanus alacer.* | *Pipistrellus subflavus.* |

### BIRDS BREEDING IN EASTERN TEXAS AUSTRORIPARIAN.

*Hydranassa tricolor ruficollis.*
*Florida caerulea.*
*Colinus virginianus.*
*Tympanuchus americanus.*
*Tympanuchus americanus attwateri.*
*Meleagris gallopavo silvestris.*
*Elanoides forficatus.*
*Buteo lineatus.*
*Falco sparverius.*
*Syrnium v. helveolum.*
*Bubo virginianus.*
*Megascops asio.*
*Campephilus principalis.*
*Dryobates pubescens.*
*Dryobates villosus auduboni.*
*Dryobates borealis.*
*Ceophloeus pileatus.*
*Melanerpes erythrocephalus.*
*Centurus carolinus.*
*Colaptes auratus.*
*Antrostomus carolinensis.*
*Chordeiles (virginianus?).*
*Chordeiles virginianus chapmani.*
*Trochilus colubris.*
*Coccyzus americanus.*
*Tyrannus tyrannus.*
*Myiarchus crinitus.*
*Contopus virens.*
*Empidonax virescens.*
*Cyanocitta cristata.*
*Agelaius phoeniceus.*
*Agelaius phoeniceus floridanus.*
*Icterus galbula.*

*Quiscalus quiscula aeneus.*
*Megaquiscalus major.*
*Spizella socialis.*
*Spizella pusilla.*
*Peucaea aestivalis bachmani.*
*Cardinalis cardinalis.*
*Guiraca caerulea.*
*Cyanospiza cyanea.*
*Piranga rubra.*
*Vireo olivaceus.*
*Vireo noveboracensis.*
*Vireo flavifrons.*
*Mniotilta varia.*
*Protonotaria citrea.*
*Dendroica dominica albilora.*
*Dendroica vigorsi.*
*Geothlypis trichas brachidactyla.*
*Geothlypis formosa.*
*Icteria virens.*
*Wilsonia mitrata.*
*Mimus polyglottos.*
*Galeoscoptes carolinensis.*
*Thryothorus ludovicianus.*
*Sitta carolinensis.*
*Sitta pusilla.*
*Baeolophus bicolor.*
*Parus carolinensis agilis.*
*Polioptila caerulea.*
*Hylocichla mustelina.*
*Sialia sialis.*

### A FEW OF THE LIZARDS AND SNAKES OF EASTERN TEXAS.

*Lizards.*

*Anolis carolinensis.*
*Phrynosoma cornutum* (local form).
*Ophisaurus ventralis.*

*Cnemidophorus sexlineatus.*
*Leiolopisma laterale.*
*Eumeces quinquelineatus.*

*Snakes.*

*Opheodrys aestivus.*
*Callopeltis obsoletus.*
*Lampropeltis getula holbrooki.*
*Natrix clarkii.*
*Natrix fasciata transversa.*
*Storeria dekayi.*
*Eutainia proxima.*

*Tropidoclonium lineatum.*
*Tantilla gracilis.*
*Elaps fulvius.*
*Agkistrodon piscivorus.*
*Agkistrodon contortrix.*
*Crotalus horridus.*

PLANTS CHARACTERISTIC OF HUMID EASTERN IN DISTINCTION FROM ARID WESTERN
TEXAS.

*Pinus taeda.*
*Pinus palustris.*
*Pinus echinata.*
*Taxodium distichum.*
*Juniperus virginiana.*
*Liquidambar styraciflua.*
*Nyssa sylvatica.*
*Nyssa aquatica.*
*Platanus occidentalis.*
*Magnolia faetida.*
*Magnolia virginiana.*
*Tilia leptophylla.*
*Acer drummondi.*
*Acer rubrum.*
*Hicoria ovata.*
*Hicoria alba.*
*Hicoria glabra.*
*Hicoria aquatica.*
*Juglans nigra.*
*Castanea pumila.*
*Carpinus caroliniana.*
*Ostrya virginiana.*
*Betula nigra.*
*Quercus phellos.*
*Quercus nigra.*
*Quercus marylandica.*
*Quercus digitata.*
*Quercus rubra.*
*Quercus virginiana.*
*Quercus acuminata.*
*Quercus macrocarpa.*
*Quercus lyrata.*
*Quercus minor.*
*Quercus alba.*
*Populus deltoides.*
*Salix (nigra?).*
*Ulmus americana.*
*Ulmus fulva.*
*Ulmus alata.*
*Toxylon pomiferum.*
*Celtis mississippiensis.*
*Asimina triloba.*
*Diospyros virginiana.*
*Sassafras sassafras.*
*Cynoxylon floridum.*

*Crataegus spathulata.*
*Crataegus texana.*
*Persea borbonia.*
*Leitneria floridana.*
*Ilex opaca.*
*Ilex decidua.*
*Ilex vomitoria.*
*Ilex lucida.*
*Morus rubra.*
*Gleditsia tricanthos.*
*Gleditsia aquatica.*
*Fagara clavaherculis.*
*Aralia spinosa.*
*Viburnum rufotomentosum.*
*Viburnum molle.*
*Viburnum (nudum?).*
*Callicarpa americana.*
*Cyrilla racemiflora.*
*Vaccinium* sp.——?
*Morella crispa.*
*Azalea* sp.——?
*Schmaltzia lanceolata.*
*Schmaltzia copallina.*
*Rhus radicans.*
*Cephalanthus occidentalis.*
*Rhamnus caroliniana.*
*Hamamelis virginiana.*
*Vitis* sp.——?
*Smilax laurifolia.*
*Smilax (renifolia?).*
*Smilax pumila.*
*Gelsemium sempervirens.*
*Bignonia crucigera.*
*Campsis radicans.*
*Bradleia* (wisteria).
*Passiflora incarnata.*
*Rubus (trivialis?).*
*Rubus (procumbens?).*
*Yucca louisianensis.*
*Yucca arkansana.*
*Sabal adiantinum.*
*Arundinaria macrosperma.*
*Dendropogon usneoides.*
*Mitchella repens.*
*Sphagnum* sp.——?

For crops of the Austroriparian faunal area of the United States see Life Zones and Crop Zones, page 46, under the headings 'Cereals,' 'Fruits,' 'Nuts,' and 'Miscellaneous.' Only a part of the crops listed are adapted to the east Texas region, however, while other varieties have been introduced since the preparation of these lists.

LOWER SONORAN OF WESTERN TEXAS.

In Texas the annual rainfall decreases gradually from about 50 inches in the eastern part of the State to about 10 inches in the extreme western part. While the extremes are so great and there is no abrupt change from eastern humid to western arid, there is still a well-defined division between the two regions, approximately where the annual rainfall diminishes to below 30 inches, or near the ninety-eighth meridian. By combining the limits of range of eastern and western species of mammals, birds, reptiles, and plants an average line of change can be traced across the State, beginning on the north at the ninety-eighth meridian, just east of Henrietta, and running south to Lampasas, Austin, Cuero, and Port Lavaca. This line conforms in a general way to the eastern limit of the mesquite, which more nearly than any other tree or shrub fills the whole of the arid Lower Sonoran zone. While scattering outlying mesquite trees are found farther east, the line is intended to mark the eastern edge of their abundance, or the transition from eastern prairie and timber country to the region dominated by the mesquite and associated plants.[a]

West of this line the region may be again subdivided into semiarid, or region of mesquite and abundant grass, stretching west to the Pecos Valley and from the northern Panhandle to the mouth of the Rio Grande, and extreme arid, or region of creosote bush and scanty grass, lying mainly between the Pecos and Rio Grande.

SEMIARID LOWER SONORAN.

The semiarid region is largely mesquite plains, varying from open grassy plains with scattered mesquite bushes to a miniature forest of mesquite trees, in places densely filled in with other thorny bushes and cactus, as along its southern stream valleys and over much of the plains of the Lower Rio Grande. Scattered oaks and other scrubby timber growth characterize the higher, rougher parts of the region, and narrow strips of tall timber are found along some of its streams. Toward the coast, flower-strewn grassy prairies extend irregularly nearly across the southern part of the State, forming a broken westerly extension of the more continuous eastern coast prairie. West of Matagorda Bay this prairie is mainly crowded

---

[a] The Mesophytic plant region of eastern Texas and the Xerophytic of western Texas of Coulter and Bray. (See Plant Relations, by John M. Coulter, pp. 168, 193, 230, 1899, and Ecological Relations of Vegetation of Western Texas, by William L. Bray, Botanical Gazette, XXXII, p. 111, 1901.)

back from the coast by dense thickets, consisting of mesquite, huisache, and numerous thorny shrubs mixed with cactus, or of miles of live-oak brush, in places only knee high; again, in dense jungles 10 or 20 feet high, in patches, strips, or isolated oak 'motts.' In Cameron County the oak motts occur as widely scattered islands on the prairie, and are usually made up of a few gnarled old trees. Along the stream bottoms and on the low coast flats the chaparral is especially dense and in places almost impenetrable from the abundance of cactus and thorny branches that interlace over the trails. The bulk of this chaparral is composed of common arid Lower Sonoran shrubs, such as *Momesia pallida, Zizyphus obtusifolia, Condalia obovata, Koeberlinia spinosa, Opuntia engelmanni, O. lepticaulis,* and other associated species, which in this semiarid region of rich soil grow with unusual vigor. Many other widely distributed species, such as *Parkinsonia aculeata, Vachellia farnesiana, Tillandsia recurvata,* and *Manfreda maculosa,* range through it, while a few others are peculiar to it or barely extend into it from farther south.

As Padre Island lies within this semiarid division, and is sufficiently large and isolated to provide a habitat for a few species of mammals, the following brief description by William Lloyd, who traveled its whole length in November, 1891, is of interest:

Padre Island is about 90 miles long, and at the south end runs out to a point, the last 10 miles of which is not over a mile wide, while for the last 5 miles it is only 300 or 400 yards wide. Its central and greater breadth is nearly 4 miles, including about two-thirds of the distance a muddy flat so soft that one sinks in it over 3 inches. From here it tapers again to its north extremity, which is about 300 yards wide. It is divided from the mainland by the Laguna Madre, which is only about a mile wide from Point Isabel and 2 miles wide opposite Arroyo Coloral. Here, however, the water is 8 to 10 feet deep in the channels. Farther north at the noted wagon crossing, about 15 miles south of Corpus Christi, near the north end of the island, the channel is 7 miles wide, with the water $4\frac{1}{2}$ to 5 feet deep at its ordinary elevation, although south winds raise it very rapidly so as to be impassable. The main island is surrounded by a network of smaller islands, with Mustang Island at the north end separated from it by a channel a mile wide. The drift or wrack and floating timbers on the Gulf side are rapidly embedded in the restless sand and form a nucleus for the sand dunes which stretch along the beach and form the backbone of the island. Beyond them are smaller mounds with some little vegetation, and at their feet lie sandy fields of grass, broken by numerous salt-water lakes where the sea has washed in from time to time.

The island has no arborescent growth worth noticing, with the exception of a shin-oak, which extends from the north end for about a mile and continues on sandy hills on the lagoon side for 5 or 6 miles farther. This is usually 6 inches to 18 inches high, but there are trees, perhaps a different species, 6 to 8 feet high. As this oak is always loaded with acorns, even now it is the favorite wintering ground of birds such as wood ibis, whooping and sand-hill cranes. Wild celery abounds also in the lagoon and attracts great numbers of ducks of various species.

A few willows, presumably *Salix nigra,* grow at the settlement and at one point north of it, and a few patches of buttonbush, *Cephalanthus occidentalis,* were observed, also a few stunted 'huisache,' *Acacia farnesiana,* and crab grass, cockleburr, and wild grapes. These are all on the north and center of the island, south of which grow salt grass and various waxy and creeping plants.

Strange to say, neither hackberry, mesquite, nor Mexican persimmon, though abundant on the adjacent mainland, have succeeded in obtaining a footing anywhere, and two straggling prickly pears (*Opuntia engelmanni*) were the sole representatives of the cactus family. Although palmetto and banana stumps wash ashore in great numbers, none were seen growing.

Gales cover the Gulf side of the island with debris that must come from the districts of Tampico or Vera Cruz. An iguana was taken a short time since on the island, and at least three species of snakes, including the rattlesnake, occur there. Deer and coyotes have been seen by several parties swimming or wading across to and from the island and mainland.

FIG. 2.—Distribution area of creosote bush (*Covillea tridentata*)

### EXTREME ARID LOWER SONORAN.

The extreme arid section of the arid Lower Sonoran zone of Texas includes the Pecos Valley and the Rio Grande Valley south to about Eagle Pass and all the country between the two valleys except the several mountain masses that rise as somewhat less arid Upper Sonoran and Transition zone islands. It has an irregular annual rainfall of 10 to 20 inches, and a half-barren soil, rich and mellow in the valleys, stony and baked on the mesas. It is subject to long, scorching drought, but after a single heavy rainfall bursts into verdure and bloom with a sudden brilliancy seen only in the desert. Its most characteristic shrub is the evergreen creosote bush, the range of which defines its extent better than any other plant, but its most conspicuous vegetation consists of yuccas, agaves, sotol, cactus, fouquiera, allthorn, and mesquite. Its mammals are mainly the species of the whole arid Lower Sonoran, but a few of these extend farther west without extending farther east than the Pecos Valley, among which are the following species:

| | |
|---|---|
| *Odocoileus hemionus canus.* | *Perodipus ordi.* |
| *Ammospermophilus interpres.* | *Dipodomys merriami.* |
| *Citellus spilosoma arens.* | *Dipodomys merriami ambiguus.* |
| *Onychomys torridus.* | *Geomys arenarius.* |
| *Peromyscus leucopus texanus.* | *Thomomys aureus lachuguilla.* |
| *Peromyscus sonoriensis blandus.* | *Canis mearnsi.* |
| *Peromyscus eremicus.* | *Vulpes macrotis neomexicanus.* |
| *Perognathus penicillatus eremicus.* | *Myotis californicus.* |
| *Perognathus intermedius.* | *Myotis yumanensis.* |
| *Perognathus nelsoni.* | *Pipistrellus hesperus.* |
| *Perognathus nelsoni canescens.* | *Corynorhinus macrotis pallescens.* |
| *Perognathus flavus.* | *Antrozous pallidus.* |
| *Perognathus merriami gilvus.* | *Promops californicus.* |

Including these somewhat mixed elements of semiarid, half open plains, strips of low prairie, dense cactus, thorny chaparral, and the more barren region of extreme aridity, under the heading of "Lower Sonoran Zone," we have in Texas an area which covers a little more than half of the State, and includes by far the largest number of species of mammals, birds, reptiles, and plants common to any subdivision in the State. It is characterized by the following species, some of which fill the subdivision and are restricted to it, while many more are restricted to definite areas within its limits, and still others range beyond through one or more of the other zones. Few of the species, however, extend through both arid and humid divisions of the zone without undergoing at least a subspecific change.

MAMMALS OF LOWER SONORAN OF WESTERN TEXAS.

| | |
|---|---|
| *Tatu novemcinctum texanum.* | *Citellus variegatus couchi.* |
| *Didelphis marsupialis texensis.* | *Citellus buckleyi.* |
| *Tayassu angulatum.* | *Citellus mexicanus parvidens.* |
| *Odocoileus virginianus texanus.* | *Citellus spilosoma major.* |
| *Odocoileus hemionus canus.* | *Citellus s. arens.* |
| *Sciurus ludovicianus limitis.* | *Citellus s. annectens.* |
| *Ammospermophilus interpres.* | *Onychomys torridus.* |

*Onychomys longipes.*
*Peromyscus leucopus texanus.*
*Peromyscus leucopus mearnsi.*
*Peromyscus michiganensis pallescens.*
*Peromyscus sonoriensis blandus.*
*Peromyscus eremicus.*
*Peromyscus attwateri.*
*Peromyscus taylori.*
*Oryzomys aquaticus.*
*Reithrodontomys intermedius.*
*Reithrodontomys megalotis.*
*Reithrodontomys griseus.*
*Neotoma micropus.*
*Sigmodon hispidus berlandieri.*
*Fiber zibethicus ripensis.*
*Castor canadensis frondator.*
*Liomys texensis.*
*Perognathus hispidus.*
*Perognathus penicillatus eremicus.*
*Perognathus intermedius.*
*Perognathus nelsoni.*
*Perognathus nelsoni canescens.*
*Perognathus flavus.*
*Perognathus merriami.*
*Perognathus merriami gilvus.*
*Perodipus ordi.*
*Perodipus sennetti.*
*Perodipus compactus.*
*Dipodomys spectabilis.*
*Dipodomys elator.*
*Dipodomys merriami.*
*Dipodomys merriami ambiguus.*
*Geomys breviceps attwateri.*
*Geomys breviceps llanensis.*
*Geomys arenarius.*
*Geomys texensis.*
*Geomys personatus.*
*Geomys personatus fallax.*
*Cratogeomys castanops.*
*Thomomys aureus lachuguilla.*

*Thomomys perditus.*
*Lepus merriami.*
*Lepus texianus.*
*Lepus arizonae minor.*
*Lepus floridanus chapmani.*
*Felis onca hernandezi.*
*Felis hippolestes aztecus.*
*Felis pardalis limitis.*
*Felis cacomitli.*
*Lynx texensis.*
*Canis rufus.*
*Canis nebracensis texensis.*
*Canis microdon.*
*Canis mearnsi.*
*Vulpes macrotis neomexicanus.*
*Urocyon cinereoargenteus scotti.*
*Bassariscus astutus flavus.*
*Taxidea taxus berlandieri.*
*Procyon lotor mexicanus.*
*Nasua narica (yucatanica?).*
*Putorius frenatus.*
*Putorius neomexicanus.*
*Spilogale leucoparia.*
*Mephitis mesomelas varians.*
*Conepatus mesoleucus mearnsi.*
*Conepatus leuconotus texensis.*
*Scalopus texensis.*
*Notiosorex crawfordi.*
*Blarina berlandieri.*
*Myotis velifer.*
*Myotis californicus.*
*Myotis incautus.*
*Myotis yumanensis.*
*Pipistrellus hesperus.*
*Dasypterus intermedius.*
*Antrozous pallidus.*
*Corynorhinus macrotis pallescens.*
*Nyctinomus mexicanus.*
*Promops californicus.*
*Mormoops megalophylla senicula.*

### BREEDING BIRDS OF LOWER SONORAN OF WESTERN TEXAS.

*Colinus virginianus texanus.*
*Callipepla squamata.*
*Callipepla squamata castanogastris.*
*Lophortyx gambeli.*
*Meleagris gallopavo intermedia.*
*Leptotila fulviventris brachyptera.*
*Melopelia leucoptera.*
*Columbigallina passerina pallescens.*
*Scardafella inca.*
*Elanus leucurus.*
*Parabuteo unicinctus harrisi.*
*Buteo borealis calurus.*

*Buteo abbreviatus.*
*Buteo albicaudatus sennetti.*
*Buteo swainsoni.*
*Urubitinga anthracina.*
*Falco mexicanus.*
*Falco fusco-caerulescens.*
*Falco sparverius phalaena.*
*Polyborus cheriway.*
*Syrnium varium helveolum.*
*Megascops asio mccalli.*
*Bubo virginianus pallescens.*
*Speotyto cunicularia hypogaea.*

Micropallas whitneyi.
Crotophaga sulcirostris.
Geococcyx californianus.
Coccyzus americanus occidentalis.
Ceryle americana septentrionalis.
Dryobates scalaris bairdi.
Centurus aurifrons.
Phalaenoptilus nuttalli.
Nyctidromus albicollis merrilli.
Chordeiles acutipennis texensis.
Amizilis cerviniventris chalconota.
Tyrannus vociferans.
Myiarchus cinerascens.
Sayornis saya.
Sayornis nigricans.
Pyrocephalus rubineus mexicanus.
Xanthoura luxuosa glaucescens.
Corvus corax sinuatus.
Corvus cryptoleucus.
Molothrus ater obscurus.
Tangavius aeneus involucratus.
Sturnella magna hoopesi.
Icterus auduboni.
Icterus cucullatus sennetti.
Icterus parisorum.
Icterus bullocki.
Megaquiscalus major macrourus.
Carpodacus mexicanus frontalis.
Astragalinus psaltria.
Amphispiza bilineata.
Amphispiza b. deserticola.

Peucaea cassini.
Aimophila ruficeps eremoeca.
Arremonops rufivirgata.
Cardinalis cardinalis canicaudus.
Pyrrhuloxia sinuata.
Pyrrhuloxia s. texana.
Guiraca caerulea lazula.
Cyanospiza versicolor.
Piranga rubra cooperi.
Phainopepla nitens.
Lanius ludovicianus excubitorides.
Vireo atricapillus.
Vireo belli medius.
Vireo b. arizonae.
Vireo noveboracensis micrus.
Dendroica aestiva sonorana.
Dendroica chrysoparia.
Icteria virens longicauda.
Mimus polyglottos leucopterus.
Toxostoma longirostre sennetti.
Toxostoma curvirostre.
Heleodytes brunneicapillus couesi.
Salpinctes obsoletus.
Catherpes mexicanus albifrons.
Thryomanes bewicki cryptus.
Thryomanes b. leucogaster.
Baeolophus atricristatus.
Auriparus flaviceps.
Polioptila caerulea obscura.
Polioptila plumbea.

REPTILES OF LOWER SONORAN.

*Lizards.*

Crotaphytus reticulatus.
Crotaphytus wislizenii.
Holbrookia texana.
Holbrookia propinqua.
Holbrookia maculata.
Holbrookia m. lacerata.
Sceloporus clarkii.
Sceloporus spinosus floridanus.
Sceloporus consobrinus.

Sceloporus dispar.
Sceloporus merriami.
Phrynosoma cornutum.
Phrynosoma modestum.
Coleonyx brevis.
Ophisaurus ventralis.
Cnemidophorus tessellatus.
Cnemidophorus perplexus.
Cnemidophorus gularis.

*Snakes*

Diadophis regalis.
Heterodon nasicus.
Bascanion flagellum.
Bascanion ornatum.
Drymobius margaritiferus.
Callopeltis obsoletus.
Drymarchon corais melanurus.
Rhinocheilus leconti.

Natrix fasciata transversa.
Eutainia elegans marciana.
Eutainia proxima.
Tantilla gracilis.
Elaps fulvius.
Agkistrodon piscivorus.
Crotalus atrox.

CONSPICUOUS PLANTS OF LOWER SONORAN.

*Prosopis glandulosa.*
*Prosopis pubescens.*
*Acacia constricta.*
*Acacia tortuosa.*
*Acacia roemeriana.*
*Acacia schottii.*
*Acacia wrightii.*
*Acacia amentacea.*
*Acacia berlandieri.*
*Vachellia farnesiana.*
*Leucaena retusa.*
*Mimosa emoryana.*
*Mimosa lindheimeri.*
*Mimosa borealis.*
*Mimosa fragrans.*
*Parkinsonia aculeata.*
*Cercidium floridanum.*
*Cercidium texanum.*
*Eysenhardtia amorphoides.*
*Sophora secundiflora.*
*Parosela frutescens.*
*Parosela formosa.*
*Juglans rupestris.*
*Celtis helleri.*
*Momesia pallida.*
*Chilopsis linearis.*
*Ehretia eliptica.*
*Koeberlinia spinosa.*
*Adelia angustifolia.*
*Adelia neomexicana.*
*Fraxinus greggii.*
*Porlieria angustifolia.*
*Covillea tridentata.*
*Schmaltzia microphylla.*
*Schmaltzia mexicana.*
*Schmaltzia virens.*
*Nicotiana glauca.*
*Brayodendron texanum.*
*Berberis trifoliata.*
*Zizyphus obtusifolia.*
*Zizyphus lycioides.*
*Condalia obovata.*

*Condalia spathulata.*
*Lycium berlandieri.*
*Lycium pallidum.*
*Leucophyllum texanum.*
*Leucophyllum minus.*
*Krameria canescens.*
*Fouquiera splendens.*
*Aloysia ligustrina.*
*Tecoma stans.*
*Ephedra antisyphilitica.*
*Ephedra trifurcata.*
*Croton torreyanus.*
*Bernardia myricaefolia*
*Euphorbia antisyphilitica.*
*Mozinna spathulata.*
*Baccharis (salicina?).*
*Baccharis (glutinosa?).*
*Flourensia cernua.*
*Agave lecheguilla.*
*Hechtia texensis.*
*Tillandsia recurvata.*
*Tillandsia baileyi.*
*Yucca macrocarpa.*
*Yucca treculeana.*
*Yucca radiosa.*
*Yucca rostrata.*
*Yucca rupicola.*
*Samuela faxoniana.*
*Samuela carnerosana.*
*Hesperaloe parviflora.*
*Opuntia lindheimeri.*
*Opuntia engelmanni.*
*Opuntia leptocaulis.*
*Cereus paucispinus.*
*Cereus enneacanthus.*
*Cereus stramineus.*
*Echinocactus horizonthalonius.*
*Echinocactus hamatocanthus.*
*Echinocactus wislizeni.*
*Echinocactus wrighti.*
*Cactus heyderi.*

For crops adapted to Lower Sonoran, see Life Zones and Crop Zones, pages 42—45, under heading "Crops of the Lower Sonoran Faunal Area," where under "Cereals," "Fruits," "Nuts," and "Miscellaneous" are listed the varieties that have proved a success in other parts of the area. Although many of these have not been tested in the Texas region, and while varieties other than those listed have proved successful, the list will be found helpful in selecting varieties for experiments.

Some practical suggestions may be derived also from the native species of plants, as in the case of *Schmaltzia mexicana,* variously known as *Rhus mexicana* and *Pistacia mexicana,* and related to the *Pistacia vera* of the Mediterranean region, from which the pistachio of commerce is obtained. In places in the canyons of the Rio Grande this large shrub grows in profusion, suggesting that the real *pistachio* also might succeed here.

One of the conspicuous plants often dominant over much of the

3          FIG. 3.—Distribution area of lecheguilla (*Agave lecheguilla*).

extreme arid Lower Sonoran zone of western Texas is a little century plant (*Agave lecheguilla*), best known by its Mexican name of 'lecheguilla.' Its rigid leaves are about a foot long, well armed with marginal hooks and stout terminal spines, which effectually protect them from the attacks of grazing animals. Even the hardy burros and hungry goats refrain from eating them, and pick their way cautiously among their dagger points. But within each leaf is a bundle of smooth, strong fibers suitable for the manufacture of brushes, matting, coarse twine, and rope. These plants grow in greatest abundance over limestone and lava mesas and steep rocky slopes that can never be irrigated and are often too steep and rough for grazing, even if the scanty grass were not crowded out by the cactus and agaves. Here, over thousands of square miles of the most worthless part of the desert, is a crop, not only offering in its leaf fibers a profitable industry awaiting development, but also suggesting that other species of agaves, yielding fiber of still more valuable quality, can be successfully introduced into this region—a region that now lies unimproved and almost uninhabited while hundreds of thousands of dollars worth of agave fibers are annually imported from Mexico.

In the Davis and Chisos and Guadalupe mountains the large *Agave wislizeni* and *applanata,* the mescal plants of the Mescalero Apaches, offer a nutritious food that might well find place on our tables as a delicacy. They grow over the barest and roughest slopes, not only yielding in the starchy caudex a rich store of food, but in the beautiful flowers a quantity of delicious honey equaled by few other plants. A single plant during its flowering period of about a month bears from one to two thousand flowers, each yielding nearly half a teaspoonful of honey. That the country is well adapted to bees is evidenced by numerous and extensive bee caves in the rocks, by bee trees, and by the success of domestic swarms. The numerous leguminous shrubs—acacias, mimosas, and mesquites, several species of the 'bee bush' (*Lippia* and *Goniostachyum*), and the abundant flowers of numerous species of Compositae—all yield rich stores of honey. In semiarid gulches where the native black-fruited Texan persimmon (*Brayodendron texanum*) bears an abundance of its almost worthless fruit it is probable that varieties of the delicious Japanese persimmon would thrive.

Other plants besides grass and cactus are important as food for stock or are of service to man. The sotol (*Dasylirion texanum*), with its double-edged saw-bladed leaves and stout caudex, when split open so that the inner starchy heart can be reached, yields a large amount of hearty food for stock. The plant is widely distributed over most of the region west of the Pecos and Devil rivers, and is most abundant over the barest and stoniest slopes. Like most desert plants, it is of slow growth, and its greatest value has been in tiding stock over periods of scarcity. Sotol cutting becomes an important business with sheep and cattle men when a dry summer is followed by a winter of bare pastures.

The value of the mesquite and screw bean (*Prosopis glandulosa* and *pubescens*) to stockmen and ranchers of western Texas can hardly be overestimated. Over much of the arid and semiarid region of the State they yield fuel, fence posts, and building material for the ranch, and also shade, shelter, and food for stock. The common mesquite, though barely reaching the dignity of a tree and often dwarfed to a mere shrub, is the only available timber over thousands of square miles. The wood is heavy, strong, and durable. The feathery foliage, while so thin that grass grows under the trees, affords a welcome shade to man and beast. The fragrant, honey-laden, catkinlike flowers blossom quickly, and in warm weather after a good rain a crop of long bean pods will mature and ripen with

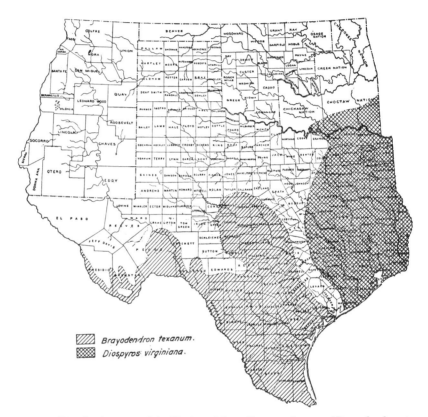

*Brayodendron texanum.*

*Diospyros virginiana.*

4    Fig. 4.—Distribution area of the black and the yellow persimmons (*Brayodendron texanum* and *Diospyros virginiana*).

little regard to season. Often two crops a year mature if rains come at proper intervals. The sugary pods serve to fatten cattle, horses, mules, burros, sheep, and goats. The small, hard beans pass through animals and seed new ground, so that the spread and increase of the mesquite has been a notable result of stock raising. The use of the sweet, nutritious pods as food by both Indians and early settlers seems to have been mainly given up, but the actual food value of the pods needs no better demonstration than is afforded by the condition of animals feeding on them.

A much neglected product of the mesquite is the gum which exudes from the branches and can be gathered in large quantities. Apparently, it has all the qualities of gum arabic, the gum of closely related Old World acacias, and needs only introduction to a market to become of commercial value.

The seeds and pods of other leguminous shrubs, the acorns of several species of oaks, and the sugary berries of the alligator-barked juniper also are of considerable value in special areas as feed for stock or poultry.

### UPPER AUSTRAL ZONE, UPPER SONORAN DIVISION.

East of the Pecos Valley, Upper Sonoran zone covers most of the Panhandle, the Staked Plains and the narrower secondary plain, or Edwards Plateau, running south as far as Rock Springs, as well as the tops and cold slopes of the ridges and bottoms of shaded gulches breaking down from the edge of these plains. West of the Pecos Valley it covers the foothills and lower slopes of the mountains, extending on southwest slopes nearly or quite to the tops of most of the peaks, but on the northeast slopes of the Guadalupe, Davis, and Chisos mountains giving place to Transition zone at about 6,000 feet. On such steep, arid slopes as these mountains present to the sun's rays the difference of zone level on opposite sides is often 2,000 or 3,000 feet, increasing with the steepness and barrenness of the slope. Over the mountains and rough country the zone is marked by a scattered growth of nut pines, junipers, and oaks, but over the plains, where short grass is the principal vegetation, its limits are often best determined by the absence of mesquite and other shrubs of the surrounding Lower Sonoran zone. Some of its most characteristic plants in the mountain region are *Pinus edulis* and *cembroides*, *Juniperus pachyphloea*, *monosperma*, and *flaccida*, *Quercus grisea* and *emoryi*, *Adolphia infesta*, *Nolina texana*, *Mimosa biuncifera*, *Cercocarpus parvifolius*, *Garrya lindheimeri*, *Fallugia paradoxa*, *Yucca baccata*, *Agave wislizeni* and *applanata*, while those on the plains, aside from grasses, are *Asclepias latifolia* and *speciosa*, *Laciniaria punctata*, several species of *Psoralea* and *Astragalus*, *Polygala alba*, *Yucca glauca*, and *Opuntia cymochila*.

In the mountains and rough country Upper Sonoran zone is especially characterized by the occurrence in the breeding season of birds such as *Cyrtonyx mearnsi*, *Coeligena clemenciae*, *Calothorax lucifer*, *Aphelocoma couchi*, *cyanotis*, and *texana*, *Pipilo mesoleucus*, *Vireo plumbeus* and *stephensi*, and *Psaltriparus plumbeus* and *lloydi;* and on the plains by such breeding species as *Podasocys montanus*, *Numenius longirostris*, *Chordeiles henryi*, *Pooecetes confinis*, and *Otocoris leucolaema*.

In the mountains and rough country some of the most characteristic mammals of Upper Sonoran zone are *Ovis mexicana, Odocoileus couesi* and *canus, Citellus grammurus* and *couchi, Peromyscus rowleyi, attwateri,* and *laceyi, Neotoma attwateri* and *albigula,* and on the plains *Antilocapra americana, Odocoileus macrourus, Cynomys ludovicianus, Citellus pallidus, Onychomys pallescens, Perognathus paradoxus* and *copei, Perodipus richardsoni, Lepus melanotis, Vulpes velox, Putorius nigripes.*

Including both plains and mountain slopes, the Upper Sonoran zone in Texas is characterized by the following species:

### MAMMALS OF UPPER SONORAN.

*Ovis mexicanus.*
*Antilocapra americana.*
*Odocoileus couesi.*
*Odocoileus virginianus macrourus.*
*Citellus variegatus grammurus.*
*Citellus v. couchi.*
*Citellus tridecemlineatus pallidus.*
*Citellus spilosoma marginatus.*
*Cynomys ludovicianus.*
*Onychomys leucogaster pallescens.*
*Peromyscus sonoriensis.*
*Peromyscus rowleyi.*
*Peromyscus attwateri.*
*Peromyscus boylei laceyi.*
*Neotoma attwateri.*
*Neotoma albigula.*
*Thomomys baileyi.*
*Perognathus flavescens copei.*

*Perognathus hispidus paradoxus.*
*Perodipus richardsoni.*
*Lepus texianus melanotis.*
*Lepus arizonae minor* (mainly Lower Sonoran).
*Lepus pinetis robustus* (mainly Transition).
*Felis hippolestes aztecus.*
*Lynx baileyi.*
*Canis griseus.*
*Canis nebracensis.*
*Vulpes velox.*
*Urocyon cinereoargenteus scotti* (also Lower Sonoran).
*Putorius nigripes.*
*Spilogale interrupta.*
*Mephitis mesomelas varians.*
*Taxidea taxus berlandieri.*

### BIRDS OF UPPER SONORAN.

*Numenius longirostris.*
*Podasocys montanus.*
*Cyrtonyx montezumae mearnsi.*
*Accipiter cooperi.*
*Chordeiles virginianus henryi.*
*Calothorax lucifer.*
*Coeligena clemenciae.*
*Trochilus alexandri.*
*Phalaenoptilus nuttalli.*
*Aeronautes melanoleucus.*
*Tyrannus verticalis.*
*Otocoris alpestris leucolaema.*
*Aphelocoma woodhousei.*
*Aphelocoma cyanotis.*
*Aphelocoma texana.*
*Aphelocoma sieberi couchi.*

*Cyanocephalus cyanocephalus.*
*Icterus bullocki.*
*Sturnella magna neglecta.*
*Carpodacus mexicanus frontalis.*
*Spizella socialis arizonae.*
*Aimophila ruficeps scotti.*
*Pipilo fuscus mesoleucus.*
*Cyanospiza amoena.*
*Zamelodia melanocephala.*
*Ampelis cedrorum.*
*Vireo solitarius plumbeus.*
*Vireo gilvus swainsoni.*
*Troglodytes aëdon aztecus.*
*Baeolophus inornatus griseus.*
*Psaltriparus plumbeus.*
*Psaltriparus melanotis lloydi.*

### LIZARDS AND SNAKES OF UPPER SONORAN.

*Lizards.*

Crotaphytus collaris.
Crotaphytus c. baileyi.
Uta ornata.
Sceloporus torquatus poinsettii.
Sceloporus consobrinus.

Phrynosoma hernandesi.
Gerrhonotus liocephalus infernalis.
Eumeces guttulatus.
Eumeces obsoletus.
Eumeces brevilineatus.

*Snakes.*

Diadophis regalis.
Heterodon nasicus.
Liopeltis vernalis.
Bascanion flagellum.
Pituophis sayi.

Chionactis episcopus isozonus.
Eutainia cyrtopsis.
Crotalus molossus.
Crotalus lepidus.
Crotalus confluentis.

### PLANTS OF UPPER SONORAN PLAINS.

Asclepias latifolia.
Asclepias tuberosa.
Polygala alba.
Laciniaria punctata.
Yucca glauca.
Yucca stricta.
Opuntia davisi.
Opuntia macrorhiza.
Cactus missouriensis.
Artemisia filifolia.
Ratibida columnaris.
Helianthus annuus.
Helianthus petiolaris.
Gutierrezia sarothrae.

Mentzelia nuda.
Astragalus molissimus.
Astragalus caryocarpus.
Psoralea linearifolia.
Psoralea digitata.
Parosela enneandra.
Acuan illinoensis.
Amorpha canescens.
Hoffmanseggia jamesi.
Petalostemon purpureus.
Ipomea leptophylla.
Merolix intermedia.
Linum rigidum.
Verbena stricta.

### PLANTS OF UPPER SONORAN MOUNTAINS AND FOOTHILLS.

Pinus edulis.
Pinus cembroides.
Juniperus pachyphloea.
Juniperus flaccida.
Juniperus monosperma.
Juniperus sabinoides.
Quercus grisea.
Quereus emoryi.
Quereus undulata.
Quercus texana.
Celtis reticulata.
Morus microphylla.
Adolphia infesta.

Mimosa biuncifera.
Cercocarpus parvifolius.
Garrya lindheimeri.
Garrya wrightii.
Philadelphus microphyllus.
Schmaltzia trilobata.
Arbutus xalapensis.
Cercis occidentalis.
Fallugia paradoxa.
Agave wislizeni.
Agave applanata.
Yucca baccata.
Nolina microcarpa.

The two long strips of Upper Sonoran zone lying east and west of the Pecos Valley at the present time are largely devoted to grazing, to which they are peculiarly adapted, but the time will come when they will be in part reclaimed for agriculture or horticulture, and the advantage of their position in adaptation to crops not grown in surrounding Lower Sonoran zone will be recognized. While grazing will long continue to be the chief industry, the introduction of successful crops will be of the greatest advantage to the stockmen. Most of the region is semiarid, with only sufficient rainfall for a good stand of native grasses, but by intelligent methods of handling the soil, deep plowing, dust mulch, and a system of cross-furrowing to utilize all the water that falls on sloping areas many kinds of fruits and other crops will thrive without irrigation. Where irrigation is possible, however, as it is in many places along streams or by means of water storage, artesian wells, or pumping, the returns will, of course, be far more certain and abundant.

For lists of cereals, fruits, nuts, and miscellaneous crops adapted to Upper Sonoran zone see Life Zones and Crop Zones, pages 37–40. This is preeminently the zone of standard varieties of apples and of many other fruits and grains. It is the only zone of any extent in Texas adapted to the sugar beet for the manufacture of sugar.

### TRANSITION ZONE.

The Transition is the most restricted and broken of any zone within the State, being confined to the Chisos, Davis, and Guadalupe mountains from about 6,000 feet on northeast slopes to the tops of the ranges, while between these mountains it is divided by wide strips of Upper Sonoran zone. It is well marked in each of these ranges by its most characteristic tree—the yellow pine (*Pinus ponderosa*)—but in each is characterized by a different combination of plants and animals. Although the home of the wild potato (*Solanum t. boreale*), it is too rough for extensive agriculture and is important mainly for its timber and for the hidden sources of streams that break out at lower levels.

In the Guadalupe Mountains the Transition zone mammals are:

*Odocoileus (hemionus?).*          *Thomomys fulvus.*
*Eutamias cinereicollis canipes.*    *Lepus pinetis robustus.*
*Neotoma mexicana.*                *Ursus (americanus?).*
*Microtus mexicanus guadalupensis.*

In the Davis Mountains:

*Odocoileus* sp.——?          *Lepus pinetis robustus.*
*Neotoma mexicana.*          *Ursus americanus ambliceps.*
*Thomomys fulvus texensis.*    *Ursus horribilis horriaeus.*
*Erethizon* sp.——?            *Vespertilio fuscus.*

In the Chisos Mountains:

*Odocoileus couesi.*          *Lepus pinetis robustus.*
*Neotoma (mexicana?).*        *Ursus a. ambliceps.*
*Sigmodon ochrognathus.*      *Vespertilio fuscus.*

The lists of breeding birds of the Transition zone show little variation in the Guadalupe, Davis, and Chisos mountains, and more thorough collecting high up in these ranges would doubtless show a still closer similarity of species.

The following species are common to all three ranges:

*Cyrtonyx montezumae mearnsi.*
*Columba fasciata.*
*Melanerpes formicivorus.*
*Trochilus alexandri.*
*Selasphorus platycercus.*

*Pipilo maculatus megalonyx.*
*Vireo solitarius plumbeus.*
*Piranga hepatica.*
*Sitta carolinensis nelsoni.*

The following species occur and probably breed in the Guadalupe Mountain Transition:

*Meleagris gallopavo merriami.*
*Syrnium occidentale.*
*Megascops flammeolus.*
*Dryobates villosus hyloscopus.*
*Selasphorus rufus.*
*Aimophila ruficeps scotti.*
*Junco dorsalis.*

*Helminthophila celata orestera.*
*Dendroica auduboni.*
*Dendroica graciae.*
*Sitta pygmaea.*
*Hylocichla guttata auduboni?*
*Merula migratoria propinqua.*

The following occur in both the Guadalupe and Davis Mountain Transition:

*Colaptes cafer collaris.*
*Cyanocitta stelleri diademata.*
*Piranga ludoviciana.*

*Parus gambeli.*
*Sialia mexicana bairdi.*

The following species occur in both the Guadalupe and Chisos mountains, but were not observed in the Davis Mountains:

*Antrostomus macromystax.*
*Nuttallornis borealis.*
*Contopus richardsoni.*

*Empidonax difficilis.*
*Wilsonia pusilla pileolata.*

The following were found in the Chisos Mountains only:

*Aphelocoma sieberi couchi.*
*Loxia curvirostra stricklandi.*

*Oreospiza chlorura.*
*Vireo huttoni stephensi.*

In the Davis Mountains a single *Asyndesmas torquatus* was seen. Most of these birds are Rocky Mountain forms, some of which reach their southern breeding limits in one of these groups of mountains; others range south into Mexico along this chain of Transition zone islands, while still others are more particularly southern and western forms that in one or more of the ranges reach approximately their northeastern limits.

The Transition zone plants of the Guadalupe Mountains are:

*Pinus ponderosa.*
*Pinus flexilis.*
*Pseudotsuga mucronata.*
*Acer grandidentatum.*
*Ostrya baileyi.*
*Quercus acuminata.*
*Quercus novomexicana.*
*Quercus grisea* (dwarf form).
*Quereus fendleri.*
*Quercus undulata.*

*Prunus (serotina?).*
*Amelanchier alnifolia.*
*Rhamnus purshiana.*
*Ceanothus greggii.*
*Robinia neomexicana.*
*Berberis repens.*
*Symphoricarpos (longiflorus?).*
*Solanum tuberosum boreale.*
*Linum perenne.*
*Oxalis violacea* or var.

Of the Davis Mountains:

*Pinus ponderosa.*
*Pinus flexilis.*
*Acer grandidentatum.*
*Quercus leucophylla.*
*Quercus novomexicana.*
*Quercus grisea* (dwarf form).

*Quercus emoryi* (dwarf form).
*Prunus serotina acutifolia.*
*Rhamnus purshiana.*
*Symphoricarpos (longiflorus?).*
*Solanum tuberosum boreale.*

Of the Chisos Mountains:

*Pinus ponderosa.*
*Pseudotsuga mucronata.*
*Cupressus arizonica.*
*Acer grandidentum.*
*Quercus grisea.*

*Quercus emoryi.*
*Quercus texana.*
*Prunus s. acutifolia.*
*Rhamnus purshiana.*
*Symphoricarpos (longiflorus?).*

The Transition area is so restricted in Texas as to be of comparatively little agricultural importance, especially as it lies within the arid section of the zone. Its greatest value, aside from its native timber, will be found in its adaptation to the culture of northern fruits, varieties of apples, pears, cherries, plums, grapes, and berries that will never prove successful elsewhere in the State.

For list of fruits that have been grown successfully in arid Transition zone in western Montana, eastern Washington and Oregon, and in parts of Idaho and Utah, see Life Zones and Crop Zones, pages 25–27.

## CANADIAN ZONE.

In the Davis Mountains a thicket of *Populus tremuloides* along the northeast base of a high cliff near Livermore Peak indicates a mere trace of Canadian zone, while a single specimen of the hoary bat, shot as it came down one of the gulches near the northeast base of Livermore Peak, July 10, strongly suggests that this Canadian zone species was on its breeding ground. *Nuttallornis borealis* and *Loxia curvirostra stricklandi* seen in the Chisos Mountains in June were probably breeding there, while *Nuttallornis borealis* and immature *Junco dorsalis,* observed in the Guadalupe Mountains in August, may or may not have been migrants.

## REPORT ON THE BIOLOGICAL SURVEY COLLECTION OF LIZARDS AND SNAKES FROM TEXAS.

The Biological Survey collection of reptiles in the United States National Museum contains 353 specimens from Texas, including 102 specimens and 31 species of snakes from 81 localities, 252 specimens and 32 species of lizards from 167 localities. No attempt has been made to identify or include the turtles and batrachians. The material has been gathered by the field assistants of the Survey as opportunity offered in connection with other work, but none of the collectors has made a specialty of reptiles. Until a systematic field study of these groups is taken up, we can not expect to know much of the distribution and habits of the species; but so much that is vague, erroneous, and misleading has been published, especially in regard to the Texas region, that it seems doubly important to put on record all definite localities from which specimens have been positively identified. Every specimen in the present collection is fully labeled with exact locality, including altitude in the case of most specimens from the mountains, date, name of collector, and in many cases notes on habitat. Only a knowledge of the country is requisite to enable each specimen to be referred to its proper zone. Of some species there are specimens from enough localities to determine with considerable accuracy their range and zonal position in the State, but of many others the few records will be useful mainly in future works of broader scope.

But few of the collectors' field notes on reptiles, when unaccompanied by specimens, have been made use of owing to the danger of confusing closely related species, and when such notes are used they are carefully distinguished. In a few cases the records of specimens in the United States National Museum collection from localities of peculiar importance are given separately. References to published records usually are avoided.

To Dr. Leonhard Stejneger I am greatly indebted for identification of the specimens. With the aid of his assistant, Mr. Richard G. Paine, I was able to simplify his task in many cases by making preliminary determinations.[a]

### Anolis carolinensis Cuvier.   Carolina Chameleon.

This little chameleon-like lizard is represented in the collection by specimens from Waskom, Joaquin, Sour Lake, and Columbia, and I have seen it in abundance at Jefferson and Timpson, but never in the western half of Texas.

### Crotaphytus collaris (Say).   Ring-necked Lizard.

Specimens of this beautiful lizard from Wichita Falls, Henrietta, Miami, Gail, Castle Mountains, Fort Lancaster, Fredericksburg, and Rock Springs, Tex., and from Roswell and Santa Rosa, N. Mex., carry the range of the species over the middle plains region of Texas, the region lying between the Pecos River and the eastern timbered

---

[a]Additional specimens identified by Mr. Paine and myself during Doctor Stejneger's absence are as follows: From Sour Lake, *Crotalus horridus, Callopeltis obsoletus, Agkistrodon contortrix, Storeria dekayi, Sceloporus consobrinus, Anolis carolinensis;* from Hempstead, *Tropidoclonium lineatum;* from Seguin, *Eutainia elegans marciana* and *Sceloporus spinosus floridanus;* from Washburn, *Heterodon nasicus* and *Liopeltis vernalis,* and from Cleveland, *Elaps fulvius.*

country. The above localities lie near the junction of Upper and Lower Sonoran zones, but this lizard inhabits at least a part of both zones. Fourteen out of the 15 specimens referred to *collaris* have the single row of interorbital plates. One specimen from Miami has two full rows of interorbitals, but with the large supraoculars and blunt nose of *collaris.*

### Crotaphytus collaris baileyi Stejneger.

Nine specimens of *Crotaphytus* from eight localities are referred by Doctor Stejneger to *baileyi.* They are from Comstock, Alpine, Paisano, Chisos Mountains (west base), Davis Mountains (east base), Toyah, 70 miles north of Toyah, Tex., and one from the east base of Guadalupe Mountains, west of Carlsbad, N. Mex. These localities are near the junction of Upper and Lower Sonoran zones. Five of the nine specimens from Comstock, Paisano, and Chisos Mountains and two from the Davis Mountains are typical *baileyi*, with two full rows of interocular plates, small supraoculars, and relatively narrow muzzle. The specimen from Alpine has the interoculars joined in a single row, but otherwise possesses the characters of *baileyi.* The specimen from the Guadalupe Mountains and the two from Toyah and 70 miles north of Toyah have the interoculars joined in a single row and other characters intermediate between *baileyi* and *collaris.* Considering the close relationship and evident intergradation of the two forms, it seems best to follow Witmer Stone in placing *baileyi* as a subspecies of *collaris.*[a]

### Crotaphytus reticulatus Baird.

Lloyd collected a specimen of this rare and apparently very locally distributed lizard at Rio Grande City, Tex., May 28, 1891.

### Crotaphytus wislizenii Baird & Girard. Leopard Lizard.

A fine, large individual of this big, spotted lizard was shot near Boquillas, in the Great Bend of the Rio Grande, by McClure Surber, and Cary and Hollister each collected a specimen near Toyahvale, in the Pecos Valley. The species is not common and occurs only in the low, hot valleys of extreme arid Lower Sonoran zone.

### Holbrookia texana Troschel.

This most brilliantly colored of the Texas lizards is represented by 11 specimens from the following nine localities: Fort Stockton, Adams, Toyahvale, Pecos River (5 miles west of Sheffield), Davis Mountains (east base), Boquillas, McKinney Spring (60 miles south of Marathon), Comstock, and Benbrook. It is a common and conspicuous species over all the hot, bare Lower Sonoran desert of western Texas and as far up the Pecos Valley as Santa Rosa, N. Mex.

[a] Proc. Acad. Nat. Sci. Phila., 1903, 30.

This species is so similar in both general appearance and habits to *Callisaurus draconoides,* the 'gridiron-tailed lizard' of the Death Valley country, that I never noticed the difference between them until Doctor Merriam pointed it out in a beautiful colored study of *Holbrookia texana* made by Fuertes in western Texas. Few animals possess more wonderful protective markings than these bar-tailed lizards. As they dash away, well up on their legs, with tail curled over the back, exposing their brightly colored sides and the black and white barred lower surface of the tail, they are strikingly conspicuous, until, stopping suddenly, they flatten themselves on the ground, when the speckled back blends into the earth colors and the lizards are lost to view.

**Holbrookia propinqua** B. & G.   Long-tailed Holbrookia.

There are 15 specimens of this slender-tailed Holbrookia from five localities in southern Texas: Brownsville, Sauz Ranch, Santa Rosa Ranch and Padre Island in Cameron County, and King's Ranch in Nueces County.

**Holbrookia maculata** Girard.   Spotted-sided Holbrookia.

The collection contains 19 specimens of this little, short-tailed lizard from the following eight localities in Texas: Mouth of Devils River, Fort Stockton, Fort Davis, Alpine, Paisano, Dimmitt (45 miles south), Henrietta, and Amarillo, places lying some in Upper and some in Lower Sonoran zones of the arid and the semiarid regions. Apparently the species has not been taken south of Devils River and San Antonio.

**Holbrookia maculata lacerata** Cope.   Spotted-tailed Holbrookia.

One specimen of the spotted-tailed lizard from Cotulla, two from 15 miles west of Japonica, and one from 25 miles southwest of Sherwood considerably extend the southern and western range of the species. Apparently it belongs to Lower Sonoran zone.

**Uta stansburiana** B. & G.

Specimens of this little lizard from El Paso, Pecos City, and Fort Stockton carry its range across the extremely arid part of Lower Sonoran zone in western Texas and mark the eastern limit of a widely distributed species.

**Uta ornata** B. & G.

Twelve specimens of this little lizard are from the following localities in western Texas: Mouth of Pecos, Langtry, Ingram, Chisos Mountains, Altuda, Paisano, and Fort Davis. The Chisos Mountain specimen was taken at 6,000 feet, and the four Fort Davis specimens at approximately 5,700 feet, in the midst of Upper Sonoran zone. Altuda, Paisano, and Ingram are at the lower edge of the zone, while

Langtry and mouth of Pecos, as well as the type locality of the species, Devils River, are just below the edge in Lower Sonoran. However, enough Upper Sonoran species of plants cling to the cold walls of side canyons in the Langtry, Pecos, and Devils River country to account for the presence of such rock-dwelling species, and I am inclined to consider the range of this lizard as strictly Upper Sonoran, at least in Texas. If all the southern Arizona and California records of the species are correct, it is certainly Lower Sonoran in that region.

### Sceloporus torquatus poinsettii (B. & G.).

This splendid, big, scaly rock lizard is represented in the collection by 14 specimens from the following localities in western Texas: Japonica, East Painted Cave, Marathon (50 miles south), Chisos Mountains (6,000 feet), Paisano, Davis Mountains (5,700 feet), Fort Stockton, Castle Mountains, near Toyah, and Guadalupe Mountains (south end of Dog Canyon, at about 6,700 feet). The species ranges throughout the width of Upper Sonoran zone, but in many places comes well into Lower Sonoran, as at Toyah and Fort Stockton.

### Sceloporus clarkii B. & G.

The collection contains but 4 Texas specimens of this big scaly lizard—3 from Boquillas and 1 from Langtry. Both localities are on the Rio Grande, in extremely arid Lower Sonoran zone.

### Sceloporus spinosus floridanus (Baird).

Eighteen specimens of this medium-sized *Sceloporus* from southern Texas come from the following localities: Seguin, Ingram, Brownsville, Rio Grande City, Lomita Ranch (6 miles north of Hidalgo), Devils River, Langtry, and Pecos River (50 miles from mouth), which carry its range across the State in Lower Sonoran zone.

### Sceloporus consobrinus B. & G.

Six localities in Texas are represented by the 8 specimens of this medium-sized *Sceloporus:* Joaquin, Sour Lake, Kerrville (Lacey's Ranch), Santa Rosa (Cameron County), Langtry, and Fort Davis. The range of the species apparently covers nearly the whole State where there are trees, in both Upper and Lower Sonoran zones.

### Sceloporus dispar B. & G.

Lloyd collected 5 specimens of this little slender *Sceloporus* at Lomita Ranch, 6 miles north of Hidalgo, in June, 1891.

### Sceloporus merriami Stejneger.

This beautiful little *Sceloporus,* which Doctor Stejneger has just described as new,[a] is represented by 5 specimens, 2 from the East

---

[a] Proc. Biol. Soc. Washington, XVIII, p. 17, Feb. 5, 1904.

Painted Cave, near the Rio Grande, a mile below the mouth of the Pecos; 1 from Comstock; 1 from the Pecos River Canyon, 55 miles northwest of Comstock, and 1 from Boquillas, in the Great Bend of the Rio Grande. Apparently the species is confined to the rocky walls of the Canyons of the Rio Grande and Pecos rivers.

**Phrynosoma cornutum** (Harlan).   Horned Toad.

This commonest and longest-horned species of the Texas horned toads is represented by specimens from El Paso, Grand Canyon of Rio Grande, Alpine, Altuda, Valentine, Davis Mountains (east base), Toyahvale (20 miles southeast), Fort Stockton, Fort Lancaster, Painted Caves, Carrizo, Roma, Rio Grande City, Sauz Ranch (Cameron County), King's Ranch (Nueces County), Corpus Christi, Center Point, Llano, Dimmitt, Henrietta, and Tascosa, and from Antioch and Virginia Point in eastern Texas, a series of localities covering at least the whole arid Lower Sonoran zone of the State and extending irregularly into the humid eastern division. Considerable variation however, appears within this range. The three specimens from Virginia Point and one from Antioch are much darker than any of the others, with sharply marked face bars and gray, thickly spotted bellies, while those of the upper Rio Grande Valley, El Paso, and Rio Grande Canyon are the lightest and brightest colored of all, with narrow face bars and white bellies. The transition from these extremes is gradual across the State, but the dark individuals from the eastern localities, the gray ones from the grassy plains, the strongly marked ones from the Pecos Valley, and the paler specimens from the Rio Grande Valley, indicate color forms comparable with the subspecies of horned larks found breeding in regions of corresponding differentiation.

**Phrynosoma hernandesi** (Girard).

This rusty-brown horned toad with short, stubby horns is represented in the collection by a single specimen from Texas, collected at about 7,000 feet altitude in the southern end of the Guadalupe Mountains. Farther north it is abundant in Upper Sonoran and Transition zones.

**Phrynosoma modestum** Girard.

*Anota modesta* of Cope and others.

Specimens of this little gray, short-horned horned toad from the west base of the Davis Mountains, 40 miles south of Alpine, 20 miles northwest of Toyah, Salt Valley, at west base of Guadalupe Mountains, and Big Springs carry the range of the species well over the arid region of western Texas in a series of localities where Upper and Lower Sonoran species are more or less mixed. Apparently the species belongs to Lower Sonoran zone and extends to its extreme upper limit.

A specimen from the west base of the Davis Mountains is rusty brown instead of ashy gray, like those from other localities, a peculiarity of coloration agreeing with the brown *Crotalus lepidus* from this lava soil region.

**Coleonyx brevis** Stejneger.   Gecko.

A single specimen of this odd little brown and yellow lizard was collected by Merritt Cary at Sheffield, August 9, 1902.

**Ophisaurus ventralis** Linn.   Glass Snake.

The glass snake is represented by two specimens from Texas, one collected by Lloyd near Santa Rosa, Cameron County, and the other by H. P. Attwater and W. H. Rawson, 3 miles north of Kerrville. These localities help to fix a western limit for this legless lizard of the Lower Sonoran zone of the Southeastern States.

**Gerrhonotus liocephalus infernalis** (Baird).

A single specimen of this glassy smooth lizard was collected in the Chisos Mountains at approximately 6,000 feet altitude in Upper Sonoran zone. It was nosing about in the dry leaves under scrub oaks on the mountain side in the manner peculiar to the individuals of the genus.

**Cnemidophorus tessellatus** (Say).   Whip-tailed Lizard.

This species is represented by specimens from Boquillas, Langtry, Fort Stockton (35 and 45 miles west), Castle Mountains, Monahans, and Van Horn, all of which localities lie in the extremely arid Lower Sonoran zone of western Texas. They mark the eastern limit of the known range of the species.

**Cnemidophorus perplexus** B. & G.

Two specimens of this species were collected by Cary, one at Pecos and one 4 miles west of Adams, in Pecos County. Both localities are in Lower Sonoran zone.

**Cnemidophorus sexlineatus** (Linn).

The collection contains specimens of this eastern species of the whip-tailed lizard from Waskom, Long Lake, Nacogdoches, Henrietta, Canadian, and Padre Island.

**Cnemidophorus gularis** B. & G.

This seems to be the commonest and most widely distributed of the whip-tailed lizards in Texas. There are specimens from Brownsville, Lomita Ranch (Hidalgo County), Rio Grande City, Roma, Carrizo, Cotulla, San Diego, near Alice, Corpus Christi, Cuero, Kerrville, Fort Lancaster, Fort Stockton, Devils River (near mouth), Comstock, Painted Caves, Paisano, and Marfa, and up the Pecos Valley in New Mexico to Santa Rosa and Ribera. Among these localities Ribera is the only one fairly out of Lower Sonoran zone.

### Leiolopisma laterale (Say).

Specimens of this little slender Eumeces-like lizard from Waskom, in northeastern Texas, and from Velasco, near Columbia and near the mouth of Navidad River in southeastern Texas, do not extend the range of the species, which apparently covers all the eastern part of the State.

### Eumeces quinquelineatus (Linn).

Hollister obtained a specimen of this species at Joaquin, near the eastern boundary of Texas.

### Eumeces guttulatus (Hallowell).   Skink.

Cary collected a specimen of this little skink at the east base of the Davis Mountains, 20 miles southwest of Toyahvale, at about 5,000 feet, and I took one at 6,800 feet in the south end of the Guadalupe Mountains, well toward the upper edge of Upper Sonoran zone.

### Eumeces obsoletus (B. & G.).   Skink.

A specimen of this larger skink was collected in the southern end of the Guadalupe Mountains, at 6,800 feet, in the same locality with the little *guttulatus*.

### Eumeces brevilineatus Cope.

Lloyd collected a single specimen at Paisano "in a damp fernery at 5,300 feet." Cope records it from Helotes Creek (the type locality), on the front line of hills 20 miles northwest of San Antonio, and from near Fort Concho (across the river from San Angelo).[a] While these localities lie at the upper edge of Lower Sonoran zone the species, if an inhabitant of damp gulches, may well belong to Upper Sonoran.

### Diadophis regalis B. & G.   Ring Snake.

A specimen of this little spotted-bellied snake was collected in the Chisos Mountains at 5,000 feet, June 3, 1901. The two previously recorded localities for Texas—Fort Davis and Eagle Springs[b]—are both close to 5,000 feet and, like the Chisos Mountain locality, at the edge of Upper and Lower Sonoran zones.

### Heterodon nasicus B. & G.   Hog-nosed Snake.

Specimens of the hog-nosed snake from Cameron County (El Haboncillo), Sycamore Creek, North Llano River, Washburn, and Amarillo carry its range over the whole north and south length of the State through Lower and Upper Sonoran zones in the semiarid region. It is not a common or conspicuous species, and with the exception of the specimens collected, I have not seen it in Texas.

---

[a] Ann. Rep. U. S. Nat. Mus. for 1898 (1900), p. 665.
[b] Ibid., p. 745

**Heterodon platirhinos** Latreille.    Blow Snake.

A single immature specimen collected by Lloyd, at Matagorda, does not add much to our knowledge of the range of the species, which apparently covers eastern Texas and reaches west to the Pecos and Devils rivers. All the Texas records are from Lower Sonoran zone, but farther east the species also ranges across at least Upper Sonoran.

**Opheodrys aestivus** (Linn.).    Rough Green Snake.

The little green snake is represented by 3 specimens from Corpus Christi, Kerrville, and Rock Springs. From a range over the whole eastern or humid division of Lower Sonoran zone the species apparently reaches in Texas its western limit. It does not enter the plains region nor the arid region except where brushy gulches enable it to cross the rough country south of the lower arm of the Staked Plains. The specimens from near Kerrville and Rock Springs were taken in gulches with such vegetation as pecan, sycamore, elm, black cherry, oak, and abundant underbrush.

**Liopeltis vernalis** De Kay.    Smooth Green Snake.

A specimen of the little smooth green snake was collected at Washburn by Gaut in July, 1904.

**Bascanion flagellum** Shaw.    Whip Snake.

The coach whip or whip snake is represented in the collection by specimens from Matagorda, Matagorda Peninsula, Padre Island, and the Chisos Mountains, and by a flat skin from Devils River. While apparently distributed over the whole State, the species is most abundant, or at least most frequently seen, in the half brushy, half open arid region, where it is one of the commonest snakes.

**Bascanion ornatum** B. & G.

Two specimens of this rare species were collected in Texas, one at the head of Devils River, by Cary, the other on the Rio Grande, 8 miles south of Comstock, by Hollister, both in July, 1902. Hollister wrote on the back of the label of his specimen, "Up in bushes."

Cope records the species from two localities only, "Western Texas" and "Howard Springs, Texas."[a]

**Drymobius margaritiferus** (Schlegel).

Lloyd collected a single specimen of this species at Brownsville on July 17, 1891.

**Callopeltis obsoletus** (Say).    Pilot Snake; Mountain Black Snake.

A specimen was collected by Lloyd, near the mouth of the Nueces, November 21, 1891, and another by Gaut, near Sour Lake, April 1, 1905.

[a] Ann. Rep. U. S. Nat. Mus. for 1898 (1900), p. 814.

**Drymarchon corais melanurus** Dum. & Bibr.

Lloyd collected a specimen of this Mexican black snake at Brownsville, July 6, 1891.

**Pituophis sayi** (Schlegel).    Prairie Bull Snake.

The prairie bull snake is represented in the collection by 3 specimens from Gail, Comstock (20 miles north), and Paisano, and by a flat skin from the head of Dog Canyon, in the southern Guadalupe Mountains. It is common over at least middle and northern Texas in Lower and Upper Sonoran zones. In a prairie-dog town near Gail I killed an unusually large individual, measuring 7 feet 8 inches in length. It was about 3 inches in diameter—large enough to have readily swallowed a full-grown prairie dog. Near Rock Springs a smaller individual was found in the act of swallowing a freshly killed squirrel (*Citellus m. parvidens*).

**Lampropeltis getula holbrooki** Stejneger.    King Snake.

Lloyd collected two specimens at Matagorda in January and February, 1892, and I collected one at Arthur in June of the same year.

**Rhinocheilus lecontei** B. & G.

A single specimen of this beautiful yellow and black ringed snake was collected about 30 miles west of Rock Springs, where a tongue of Lower Sonoran runs up into the Upper Sonoran plains. If the published records can be trusted, the species ranges over the whole arid Lower Sonoran zone of Texas.

**Chionactis episcopus isozonus** Cope.

A single specimen of this little, bright-colored, pink and black ringed snake was collected in the Chisos Mountains at about 6,000 feet altitude, in Upper Sonoran zone.

**Natrix fasciata transversa** (Hallowell).    Water Snake.

Specimens from Lipscomb, the Nueces River (near mouth), mouth of Devils River, the Pecos River (55 miles northwest of Comstock), and from Carlsbad, N. Mex., together with previously published records, indicate for the species a range in most of the rivers of the western half of Texas, excepting the Rio Grande. Lipscomb is apparently the only locality where the species has been found outside of pure Lower Sonoran, and this is just at the edge of the zone.

**Natrix clarkii** (B. & G.).    Striped Water Snake.

A specimen of the striped water snake was collected by J. D. Mitchel at Carancahua Bay, Calhoun County, Tex., in January, 1892, and the National Museum collection contains 5 specimens from Indianola, including the type, and one specimen from Galveston.

The following letter from Mr. Mitchel accompanied the specimen and 8 of the well-developed embryos:

This snake was captured with 3 others in a salt marsh on Carrancahua Bay, Calhoun County. It took to the salt water freely. One had 4 small mullets in its stomach, another some fiddler crabs. The other inclosure is part of the womb of one of the snakes, showing embryos. She had 4 on one side and 10 on the other, 14 in all.

### Storeria dekayi Holbrook.

Lloyd collected a specimen of this little brown snake at Barnard Creek, west of Columbia, March 4, 1892, and Gaut collected one at Sour Lake, March 14, 1905.

### Eutainia elegans marciana (B. & G.).   Garter Snake.

There are specimens of this plain little striped snake from Browns-ville, Santa Rosa Ranch (Cameron County), Corpus Christi, Victoria, Seguin, Sycamore Creek, Devils River, Paisano, and Boquillas. It is the common garter snake of the whole arid Lower Sonoran zone of western Texas, apparently reaching its eastern limit at Victoria.

### Eutainia proxima (Say).   Spotted Garter Snake.

The collection contains 12 specimens of this garter snake from Brownsville, Lomita Ranch (Hidalgo County), Sycamore Creek, Corpus Christi, and San Antonio River, near San Antonio. The species apparently has a wide range, including most of Texas.

### Eutainia cyrtopsis Kennicott.

One specimen of this beautiful garter snake with black nuchal spots was taken in the Davis Mountains, July 12, 1901, at about 5,700 feet, in Upper Sonoran zone.

### Tropidoclonium lineatum Hallowell.

Gaut collected a specimen of this little striped snake at Hemp-stead, February 28, 1905.

### Tantilla gracilis B. & G.

I collected a specimen of this tiny brown snake at Lacey's Ranch, near Kerrville, May 5, 1899. The species has been recorded from va-rious localities in eastern and southern Texas in Lower Sonoran zone.

### Elaps fulvius (Linn.).   Coral Snake.

Four specimens of the coral snake from Brownsville, Corpus Christi, Cleveland, and Kerrville nearly double the list of definite localities for the State. Cope records the species from Indianola, San Diego, Fort Clark, and Hempstead, but his records for Cameron County, Rio Grande, and Rio Pecos are too indefinite for practical purposes in outlining distribution. A live specimen sent to Doctor Stejneger from Beaumont, December 4, 1903, carries the range of the species nearly across the State in both humid and arid Lower Sonoran zones, but the Cleveland and Beaumont specimens are much darker and richer in coloration than those from farther west.

Fortunately this is not a common species in Texas. I have found it but once in the State. From its beautiful colors and harmless appearance it is likely to be handled carelessly, and its bite is dangerous.

**Agkistrodon piscivorus** (Lacépède).    Cottonmouth; Water Moccasin.

A single specimen of the water moccasin, collected by William Lloyd at the mouth of Devils River, September 24, 1890, slightly extends the known range of the species. (Indianola and Eagle Pass are the westernmost records given by Cope.[a]) A specimen collected in the Big Thicket of Liberty County was lost, but I could not have been mistaken in its identity.

**Agkistrodon contortrix** (Linn.)    Copperhead.

A specimen of the copperhead collected by H. P. Attwater near San Antonio and three others collected near Kerrville, Arthur, and Sour Lake help to fill out the range of the species in the State. Cope records it from Cook County, Sabinal, and between Indianola and San Antonio.[b] All of these localities are in Lower Austral zone.

**Sistrurus catenatus consors** (B. & G.).    Massasauga.

There is a single specimen of the massasauga in the Biological Survey collection, from Santa Rosa, Cameron County, Tex., collected by Lloyd in 1891.

**Crotalus horridus** Linn.    Eastern Rattlesnake.

Gaut collected a specimen of this rattlesnake in the Big Thicket, 8 miles northeast of Sour Lake, April 1, 1905.

**Crotalus atrox** B. & G.    Western Diamond Rattler.

This, the largest of the Texas rattlesnakes, ranges throughout at least the arid part of Lower Sonoran zone of Texas. In the collection there are specimens from Corpus Christi, Japonica, Devils River, Comstock, Sycamore Creek, Eagle Pass, Langtry, and Boquillas, and from as far up the Pecos Valley as Santa Rosa, N. Mex. Mr. Cary also saved a flat skin from Pecos, Tex., and Doctor Fisher one from Colorado, Tex. Specimens recorded by Cope[c] from Indianola, San Antonio, and Brazos River apparently mark the eastern border of the known range of the species. I have never found it in eastern Texas.

Throughout its Texas range this is the commonest rattlesnake.

---

[a]Ann. Rep. U. S. Nat. Mus. for 1898 (1900), p. 1135.
[b]Ibid., pp. 1137 and 1138.
[c]Ibid., p. 1166.

While it is often reported as excessively abundant, I have never found more than a dozen individuals in a season's field work of four or five months in its favorite haunts. Over most of the range we do not see more than an average of one or two in a month's field work. On an 18-days' camping and collecting trip—April 24 to May 11, 1900—from Corpus Christi to Brownsville and return, we saw only five rattlesnakes, where we had been led to expect hundreds; and in this region of dense cactus beds and thorny thickets they find perfect protection and probably reach their maximum abundance. Specimens from extreme southern Texas are reported by the residents as reaching a length of 11 to 13 feet; but the largest specimen I have seen alive measured only 50 inches in length.

### Crotalus confluentus Say.   Plains Rattlesnake.

This small, dull-colored rattlesnake is represented in the Biological Survey collection from Texas by one specimen from Amarillo, on the Staked Plains, in Upper Sonoran zone. I am familiar with the species on Upper Sonoran plains of New Mexico and Nebraska, but have not found it elsewhere in Texas. The specimen collected by Captain Pope (No. 4962, U. S. N. M.), and labeled "Pecos River, Texas," has not even a date by which to locate the place where obtained; but as it is well known that Captain Pope's specimens from the top of the Staked Plains on the east and from the Guadalupe Mountains on the west were labeled "Pecos River," this record can have no zonal significance. The specimen recorded by Cope[a] from San Antonio, Tex., is entered in the Museum catalogue as collected "between San Antonio and El Paso," and the one recorded from Rio San Pedro (Devils River) is catalogued from "between Ash Creek and Rio San Pedro." Mr. Brown's record for Pecos[b], based on a specimen collected by Meyenberg, can not, as Mr. Brown admits, be used for "minute zone work," as Meyenberg's specimens, while said to have been collected somewhere "within a day's journey by team of Pecos," may have come from much farther away. In 1902, at a place 75 miles northwest of Pecos, I met one of his men bringing in a wagonload of live animals, among them numerous snakes and lizards which had been collected along the base of the Guadalupe Mountains, mainly in Upper Sonoran zone, but probably also in Transition. As these specimens apparently were sent out as collected at Pecos, in Lower Sonoran zone, the difficulty of using Meyenberg's material for zonal work is apparent.

### Crotalus molossus B. & G.

This is the common rattlesnake of the Guadalupe Mountains in Upper Sonoran zone on both sides of the Texas and New Mexico line.

---

[a] Ann. Rep. U. S. Nat. Mus. for 1898 (1900), p. 1172.
[b] Proc. Acad. Nat. Sci. Phila., 1903, p. 551.

Specimens were collected near the edge of Transition zone on the east and west slopes of the mountains at 6,300 and 6,800 feet, but I assume that the species belongs to Upper Sonoran. A flat skin collected by Cary at a point 25 miles west of Sheffield is apparently this species.

We found this snake in August, 1901, in the gulches high up on the range. It is pugnacious, quick to sound its rattle and throw itself on the defensive. Because of its prevailing color of olive green, we always referred to it in the field as the "green rattlesnake."

### Crotalus lepidus Kennicott.

Five specimens of this little rattlesnake from western Texas, the mouth of the Pecos, Paisano, Chisos Mountains, and Davis Mountains, indicate a range confined to the most arid and rocky part of the State in both Upper and Lower Sonoran zones. The specimen from the mouth of the Pecos was in Lower Sonoran zone on the gray limestone ledges at the east end of the High Bridge. In color it is pale ashen gray, with the pattern faintly indicated in dusky lines. The color has not changed materially in the alcoholic specimen from that of the live animal collected May 20, 1900, when I called it the 'white rattlesnake' to distinguish it from anything previously known to me. Mr. Cary reports several seen on limestone ledges along the Pecos Canyon at Howard Creek and Sheffield, all of which were whitish in color like the lime rock on which they were found. One specimen from the Chisos Mountains at about 6,000 feet, one from Paisano, and two from 5,700 feet in the Davis Mountains, were all taken in Upper Sonoran zone. Others were seen in both the Chisos and Davis mountains at similar altitudes, but none lower. All of these specimens in life or when freshly killed, and the others seen but not collected, were dark rusty brown with a pinkish tinge, heavily marked with velvety black crossbars. The brown has faded considerably in the alcoholic specimens, as shown by comparison with a careful color study of the fresh snake made in the field by L. A. Fuertes.

These little brown rattlers were fairly common about our camp near the head of Limpia Creek, in the Davis Mountains. On the dark brown lava soil they were very inconspicuous, and they had a way of suddenly springing up between our feet that made us slightly nervous.

### REPORT ON THE MAMMALS OF TEXAS.

The following report on the mammals of Texas is based mainly on my own field notes and those of the other members of the Biological Survey who have worked in the State, supplemented by records from local naturalists and ranchmen.

52          NORTH AMERICAN FAUNA.          [No. 25.

5   **Tatu novemcinctum texanum** subsp. nov.   Texas Armadillo.

Type from Brownsville, Tex., No. $\frac{3\,4\,3\,5\,2}{4\,6\,4\,3\,8}$ ♂ ad., U. S. Nat. Mus., Biological Survey Coll. Collected by F. B. Armstrong, June 10, 1902; original No. 4.

*General characters.*—Similar to *mexicanum* from Colima, but with relatively heavier dentition, larger and more acutely triangular lachrymal bone, and with larger epidermal plates on forehead and wrists.

*Measurements of type.*—Total length, 800; tail, 370; hind foot, 100. Skull of type: Basal length, 81; occipito-nasal length, 100; nasals, 36; greatest zygomatic breadth, 43; mastoid breadth, 29; alveolar length of upper molar series, 27; of lower molar series, 27.

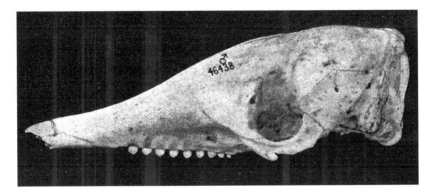

FIG. 5.—Skull of armadillo (*Tatu novemcinctum texanum*) from Brownsville, Texas. (Natural size.)

*Specimens examined.*—Brownsville, 12; El Blanco, near Hidalgo, 1; Corpus Christi, 2; Nueces Bay, 1 skull; Kerrville, 2 skulls.[a]

Armadillos are common in southern Texas from the Lower Rio Grande to Matagorda Bay, the mouth of the Pecos, and north to Llano. A few are reported farther up the Pecos Valley, at old Fort Lancaster, Grand Falls, and Loving County, and one from 22 miles north of Stanton, while a specimen in the National Museum is labeled "Breckenridge." They have been taken in Burnet County and at Austin and Elgin, and reported from Inez, Seguin, Columbus, Navasota, and as far east as Antioch on Nevils Prairie. The belief is

---

[a] A series of 9 specimens, collected at Colima, Mex., by Nelson and Goldman, agrees in respect to the small quadrate lachrymal and light dentition with the excellent figure of a skull of *Tatusia mexicana* (Pl. II, fig. 3) in Gray's Hand List of the Edentate, Thick-Skinned, and Ruminant Mammals in the British Museum. As no locality more definite than Mexico is assigned to either the type of *Dasypus novemcinctus* var. *mexicanus* Peters or the specimen figured by Gray, the type locality may be fixed by considering the Colima specimens typical. The exact relationship between *mexicanum* and *novemcinctum*, of Brazil, remains to be worked out.

general that they are spreading eastward and northward, but whether this belief is founded on a real extension of range or on an increase in numbers throughout an established range is not entirely settled by the data at hand.

In 1890 Streator reported armadillos as rare on Raglans Ranch, 32 miles southeast of Eagle Pass, where two had been taken within ten years. In 1891 Lloyd reported them as common north of Brownsville and "much sought after for eating purposes." One taken at La Hacienda, 10 miles southeast of Hidalgo, he says, "was very tender, without any gamy smell," and he adds, "they eat small coleoptera and ants, greater quantities of the latter." He says that a cowboy saw an armadillo near the center of Padre Island, and at Nueces Bay he reported finding the remains of one and traces where others had been digging.

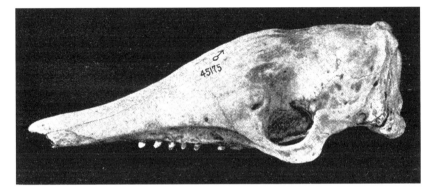

FIG. 6.—Skull of armadillo (*Tatu novemcinctum mexicanum*) from Colima, Mexico. (Natural size.)

In 1900 Oberholser reported them at Port Lavaca as not common, though occurring on the rivers at the head of Matagorda Bay and in the timber along small creeks west of there; at O'Connorport as not found except several miles back in the country, where quite rare; at Beeville as common at a little distance from town and frequently brought in by the Mexicans; at San Diego as common, living chiefly in timber along creeks and in chaparral about ponds; at Laredo as rare immediately south of town, but said to be common in places toward the north; at Cotulla as abundant, inhabiting principally the timber along the Nueces; at Uvalde as occasionally found along the Nueces; at Rock Springs as tolerably common in places. In 1901 he reported them at Fort Lancaster as said on good authority to occur on Independence Creek, 25 miles down the Pecos; at Langtry and the Pecos High Bridge as rare, but said to be occasionally found along the river; at Del Rio as reported to be common along the Rio Grande; at Comstock as rare. In 1902 he reported armadillos of occasional occurrence at Austin, where one was taken a few years ago, and as rare at Elgin, where there are well-authenticated instances of their capture along some of the creeks.

Near Antioch, Houston County, in 1902, Hollister obtained two records of the capture of armadillos on Nevils Prairie, the last about 1899, where one wandered into a smokehouse and was caught and kept alive for some time. Cary in his reports for 1902 records the capture of an armadillo by John Hutto, a sheep man living 22 miles north of Stanton, in 1892. Mr. Finnegan, the hotel proprietor at Stanton, saw the animal at the time. At Monahans Cary was told by Landlord Holman that armadillo shells were rarely found in the sandhills, but that he had seen a specimen killed at Grand Falls in 1899. In February, 1902, Mr. Royal H. Wright, of Carlsbad, N. Mex., wrote me that he had picked up an old armadillo shell in Loving County, Tex., close to the New Mexico line. At Llano, in 1899, I was told that armadillos were frequently killed around there or brought into town alive. In 1904 a few armadillos were reported at Seguin, and Mr. Samuel Neel told me that a few years ago he had found one in the garden under the vines of his cowpeas. At Columbus Mr. Henry Mathee told me of two armadillos killed there during the fall of 1904, and Mr. J. F. Leyendeker wrote me that one was taken near Frelsburg. At Navasota Mr. Charles Hardesty told me of one caught near there during the summer of 1904. In a letter of June 4, 1904, Mr. H. P. Attwater furnishes the following note:

> When in Port Lavaca last week I obtained some notes in regard to armadillos which may be of interest. Mr. J. M. Boquet, a very intelligent and reliable ranchman, says that these animals were first noticed in Calhoun County in 1886 or about that year; that they are now very common, and that he has no doubt there are hundreds of them in the county to-day. He says their favorite resort on the prairie ranches is in the long Cherokee-rose hedges, which have been grown in many parts of that and adjoining counties as a wind-break in winter for cattle. During the last few years since armadillos have become so common in the southwest and south central Texas I see baskets made of armadillo skins or shells in the curio stores at San Antonio and other places. The legs are cut off and the tail fastened to the mouth, forming the handle of the basket. At a curio shop in San Antonio two or three days ago I was informed that they sold for about $1.50 to $2 each.

The armadillos are strictly Lower Sonoran, but in the rough country between Rock Springs and Kerrville they range fairly into the edge of Upper Sonoran Zone. As a rule they do not extend east of the semiarid or mesquite region, nor to any extent into the extremely arid region west of the Pecos, but occupy approximately the semiarid Lower Sonoran region of Texas, north to near latitude 33°. They are partial to low, dense cover of coarse grass, thorny thickets, cactus patches, and scrub oaks, under which they make numerous burrows and trails, or root about in the leaves and mold, where they enjoy comparative safety under the double protection of leafy screen and armor plate. But they thrive best in a rocky country, especially where limestone ledges offer numerous caves and crevices of various sizes, from which they can select strongholds that will admit no larger animal. Almost every rock-walled gulch along the head-waters of Guadalupe River has one or more dens with smoothly worn doorways from which much traveled trails lead away through the bushes or to little muddy springs, where tiny hoof-like tracks and the corrugated washboard prints of ridged armor suggest that the arma-

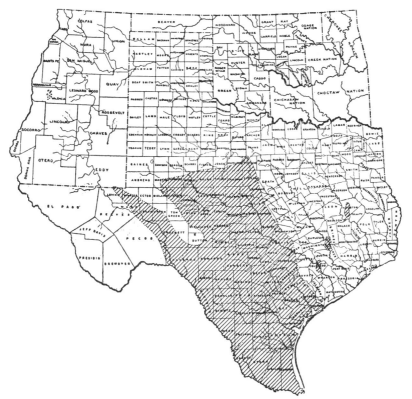

Fig. 7.—Distribution area of armadillo (*Tatu novemcinctum texanum*).

dillos not only dig and nose about in the soft ooze for their insect food, but, pig-like, enjoy also a cooling mud bath. Other trails lead along rocky shelves, up the sides of gulches, and away from thicket to thicket, and are easily followed sometimes for half a mile till they branch and scatter or connect with cattle trails, where the rope-like prints of dragging, horny tails are visible among the dusty cow tracks. Late in the afternoon one occasionally meets an armadillo trotting vigorously along a trail on his stumpy little feet, his tail dragging after him in a useless sort of way as he hurries nervously across the open spaces and stops in the thickets to nose about under the leaves in search of dainties from the fragrant soil. At such times the long, pointed nose seems to be the keenest organ of sense. The little eyes, half the time buried in rustling leaves, rarely detect an object not close by and in motion. I have followed one of these preoccupied little animals for half an hour, often within 20 or 30 feet, moving only when it was rustling in the leaves, and watching its motions without being discovered or creating alarm. Hunters say that if you stand still the armadillos will sometimes bump against your feet without discovering you, so short sighted are they and so intent on their own business. But when alarmed, they get over the ground with a rush that is surprisingly rapid considering their turtle-like build. If the first rush does not carry them to cover and an enemy overtakes them, they curl up in an ironclad ball that is not easily uncurled. In autumn, during the deer hunting months, when the young of the year are full grown, they are especially numerous and particularly obnoxious to the still hunters, who repeatedly mistake their rustling in the leaves for the noise of feet of bigger game. Where a dozen or twenty armadillos are met in a day's hunting, as sometimes happens, and possibly no deer are seen, the nervous strain and disappointment on the part of the hunter sometimes result in serious consequences to the innocent armadillo.

The excrement of the armadillos found scattered along the trails in the form of clay marbles and with the texture of baked mud gives some clue to the food habits of the animals. Careful examination shows only the remains of insects, mainly ants and a few small beetles, embedded in a heavy matrix of earthy matter.

6  **Didelphis virginiana** Kerr.   Virginia Opossum.

Specimens of opossums examined from northern and middle Texas, Gainesville, Vernon, Brazos, Mason, and Kerrville, have the light-gray coat, white ear tips, and comparatively short tail of *virginiana*. To the west the species does not extend much beyond the one hundredth meridian, except along some of the stream valleys, up which it reaches as far as San Angelo, Colorado, and Tascosa. I have seen no specimens from extreme eastern Texas, except from near the coast, where they are referable to *pigra*.

The Virginia opossums are more or less abundant throughout their range, and live mainly in the woods and brush along streams. In the daytime they sleep in hollow trees or logs, in holes in the ground, or merely curled up in the brush or weeds or sometimes on a large branch of a tree, and if disturbed appear stupid and dazed. At night they prowl about in search of food, and, not being epicureans, usually find it in abundance. They are especially fond of chickens and eggs and do considerable mischief in the henhouse. They will eat any kind of meat, even when it is old and stale, and often persist in getting into traps baited for more desirable game. Through the summer they feed extensively on fruit, and are usually lean and rangy. In the fall they become very fat and by many are then considered a great delicacy. Their importance as food and game animals and the value of their fur make up for the inconsiderable losses they now and then occasion poultry raisers. Winter skins in prime fur are quoted at 55 to 60 cents, and they usually constitute a large share of the fur harvest of local trappers.

**Didelphis v. pigra** Bangs.    Florida Opossum.

Specimens of the opossum from the coast region of Texas east of Matagorda Bay are generally a little darker than typical *virginiana,* with more dusky about the face. While not typical, they are nearer to *pigra* than to *virginiana,*[a] from which there is no sharp line of separation. They are merely the darker southern form inhabiting Florida and the South Atlantic and Gulf coast region, with habits modified by local conditions and environment. On the coast prairies of southeastern Texas they live much in the open, wandering along the margins of ponds and bayous, sleeping under fallen grass or low bushes and feeding extensively on crawfish and other small crustaceans. In the stomach of one taken near Galveston I found a horned toad and bird's feathers, besides the meat used for trap bait.

Gaut found them abundant in the Big Thicket northeast of Sour Lake, where he caught them in a line of traps set along Black Creek in the timber. He reports two females, caught March 18, carrying in the pouches young apparently four or five days old, one with five young, the other with six. He found the stomachs of two individuals filled with crawfish, one full of carrion of a dead hog, and in another traces of maggots and carrion.

**Didelphis marsupialis texensis** Allen.    Texas Opossum.

This subspecies of a widely distributed Mexican form is easily distinguished from both *virginiana* and *pigra* by its longer and blacker tail, the wholly black ears of adults, and by its dichromatism, about half of the individuals being entirely black instead of light gray. It inhabits the southern part of Texas, from Brownsville to Nueces Bay and San Antonio, and up the Rio Grande to Del Rio and the mouth of the Pecos. Doctor Allen, in his monograph of the genus *Didelphis,* considers the species distinct from *virginiana* and records specimens of both from San Antonio.[b]

---

[a]Doctor Allen refers these coast specimens rather doubtfully to *virginiana* (Bul. Am. Mus. Nat. Hist., XIV, 166, 1901), but all, with possibly one exception, seem to me nearer to *pigra.*

[b] Bul. Am. Mus. Nat. Hist., Vol. XIV, 149—188, June 15, 1901.

The habits of this opossum are peculiar only in so far as they have been modified to adapt it to the country in which it lives, a more or less open region of mesquite, brush, and cactus, with few hollow logs or stumps. For home and shelter the animals depend largely on burrows, which apparently they dig for themselves. In setting traps where fresh earth was being brought out of the burrow or out of several of a group of burrows each night, hoping to get a badger or armadillo, I have on several occasions been disappointed to find in my trap next morning only an old black opossum.

A female caught at Del Rio January 30, 1890, had nine tiny young in her pouch, each clinging to one of the slender teats and grasping the moist, crinkled, brown hair of the pouch lining with all four of its little hands. If forcibly pulled loose they would immediately regain their hold, the only instinct of their embryonic life being to hold on tight and get nourishment. They were too small to noticeably distend the pouch, and I discovered them only in preparing the specimen on the following day. I then noticed that the nine teats, arranged in two semicircular rows with one in the center, were not the full set. The anterior pair were functionless, but as the mother was not fully grown these probably would have developed with the next and larger litter of young. While in the trap this female showed no disposition to fight or defend herself, but an old male caught a day or two later fought viciously, growling and biting anything that came within reach, actually cutting deep gashes in the hard-wood stock of my gun. Another female, caught by James H. Gaut at the mouth of Sycamore Creek, 12 miles east of Del Rio, June 1, 1903, was carrying six very small young in the pouch.

7   **Tayassu angulatum** (Cope).   Texas Peccary; Javeline; Musk Hog.

Peccaries are still more or less common in southern Texas and along the Rio Grande to above the mouth of the Pecos, thence up the east side of the Pecos Valley into the unsettled sandhill region of southeastern New Mexico, and east along the broken edge of the plains to San Angelo and Kerrville, and along the coast to Corpus Christi. A few may remain here and there still farther east and north, where they once ranged, but they have been pretty thoroughly driven out by the settlement of the country, and are now merely clinging to existence in regions of deep rocky canyons or dense thorny cactus and chaparral and in an uninhabited waste of sand dunes. They are extremely wary, depending for protection mainly on caves in the rocks and impenetrable cover, and so may be able to hold their own for a few years longer. They are usually hunted with dogs and horses, as it is almost impossible to discover or get near them in any other way. The cowboys occasionally rope one, but claim that many good horses are ruined by being ridden over boars, which never fail to cut and gash the horses' legs in a dangerous manner.

In October, 1904, I was told that a half-grown peccary in the San Pedro Park, at San Antonio, had been captured in Nueces County within a month.

The following reports by Merritt Cary were made in September, 1902:

The peccary is common in Castle Mountains and on sand ridges northwest of there. Along Castle Gap I went into several caves beneath the rim rock

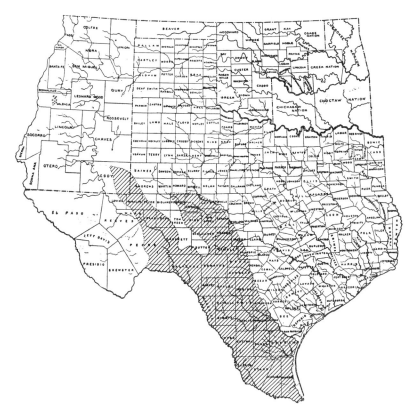

FIG. 8.—Distribution area of peccary (*Tayassu angulatum*).

and found the ground all tramped up by them, where they had evidently made their dens.

A peccary was killed 2 miles northeast of Odessa about September 1, 1902, but was very thin and evidently a wanderer. The animals are said to be common in the western portion of Gaines County.

Peccaries range throughout the sand along the Texas Pacific Railroad west to about Quito station and east rarely as far as Odessa. North they follow the sand belt well up into New Mexico, according to report, while to the south their range is continuous through the Castle Mountains and down the valley of the Pecos. From what I could learn, their center of abundance in the sand belt is some 10 to 15 miles north of Monahans, where the 'shinrick' is densest, and their principal food, the acorns, most plentiful. They are said to hide

60                         NORTH AMERICAN FAUNA.                    [No. 25.

in the 'cats-claw' (*Acacia*) during the day and range out into the sand hills for acorns at night or in cloudy weather. One was killed while we were at Hawkins's ranch, but the hide and skull were spoiled before we could secure them. Several peccaries have been killed at San Angelo in years past.

8  **Cervus merriami** Nelson.   Merriam Elk.

There are no wild elk to-day in the State of Texas, but years ago, as several old ranchmen have told me, they ranged south to the southern part of the Guadalupe Mountains, across the Texas line. I could not get an actual record of one killed in Texas, or nearer than 6 or 8 miles north of the line, but as they were common to within a few years in the Sacramento Mountains, only 75 miles farther north, I am inclined to credit the rather indefinite reports of their former occurrence in this part of Texas. Specimens of horns and a part of a skull from the Sacramento Mountains indicate that the species was very similar to and probably identical with the Arizona elk described by E. W. Nelson who has aided me in making the comparisons.

In his field report for May, 1904, from the Wichita Mountains, Oklahoma, Gaut says:

> Mr. A. T. Hopkins, of Lawton, killed an elk in 1881 on Rainy Mountain, about 40 miles west of Lawton. This apparently is the last specimen recorded from that region. Several antlers have been picked up within the last few years on Rainy Mountain, a high ridge about 12 miles west of Mount Scott, and Mr. O. F. Morrisey, the forest ranger, informed me that he frequently runs across elk antlers while on his rides through the reserve.

In 1852 elk were reported[a] by Captain Marcy from the Wichita Mountains, Indian Territory, and if they ever were common there they would naturally at times have strayed across the interval of less than 50 miles to the border of northern Texas. This report may have led to the inclusion of 'moose' with the game of Texas in Mary Austin Holley's History of Texas, 1836, but it is by no means certain. The particular form of elk which inhabited the Wichita Mountains will probably never be known, although it may have been referable to *C. canadensis*.

That northern Texas is well adapted to elk is shown by the perfect condition in 1902 of a herd of nine owned by Mr. Charles Goodnight, of Goodnight, Tex.

9  **Odocoileus virginianus texanus** Mearns.   Texas White-tailed Deer.

Specimens of the white-tailed deer from Corpus Christi, Kerr County, Rock Springs, and Langtry agree with the type and topotypes of *texanus* from Fort Clark, and indicate for this form a wide range over the semiarid part of southern and middle Texas, but do not in any way define the limits of its range. In the open and arid

---

[a] Explorations of Red River of Louisiana, p. 186, 1854.

region west of the Pecos white-tailed deer are rare. The skull of an old buck from San Elizario, on the Rio Grande, just below El Paso, has abnormally large molars and large audital bullae, and can only provisionally be referred to *texanus*. The few once inhabiting the Davis and Guadalupe Mountains have been almost exterminated, and they may have been the little *couesi* instead of *texanus*. Excepting a part of the Trans-Pecos region and, possibly, the open top of the Staked Plains, the whole of Texas is or has been occupied by some form of the white-tailed deer.[a]

A few imperfect specimens from Liberty, Hardin, and Jasper counties in extreme eastern Texas are apparently *texanus,* but more and better specimens from this region may show that they are nearer to *virginianus*. They certainly are not the large, dark *louisianae,* which, from geographical considerations alone, they might be supposed to be. In the Big Thicket region of Liberty and Hardin counties deer are still common, owing to the dense forest and the tangle of vines, briers, palmettoes, and canes which afford them almost impenetrable cover. They are now hunted mainly with hounds, but formerly when more abundant night hunting with a headlight was the favorite method, and deer were wantonly slaughtered in great numbers. One hunter told me that he had no idea how many deer he had killed for their skins, but that in the fall of 1886 he remembered selling 69 skins of deer, the carcasses of which were left in the woods. Even at the present time the law in this region is rarely enforced, and deer are killed without regard to season. With the natural advantages offered by extensive tracts of unoccupied forest and swamp land, dense cover, and abundance of acorns and other food, deer with some slight protection would soon become abundant again.

A collection of about 350 pairs of deer horns at Rock Springs is especially interesting, as all the horns came from deer killed in the vicinity, which is near the type locality of *texanus,* and consequently show the local variation. As usual in a large collection, there are some abnormal sets, and a number of very small sets which seem to be of either young or imperfectly developed individuals and not of the little Sonora deer. Through the courtesy of Mr. Fleischer I obtained photographs of a large number of the horns. It is to be hoped that the collection will eventually find its way to some museum, where it would be of considerable scientific interest.

At the edge of the little town of Rock Springs Doctor Richardson had six tame deer in a small inclosure—a 3-year-old buck, a 2-year-old doe, and four yearling does. They were all in the red coat when

---

[a] The group of white-tailed deer is sadly in need of revision, but the material at hand is too scanty for final conclusions in regard to the several described forms.

examined July 15, 1902, and the nearly grown horns of the buck were in full soft velvet. All these deer were perfectly tame, and would push and crowd the Doctor as he fed them bran from a basin. Bran and hay constituted their main food. Though in good health and spirits they were thin, and I urged the Doctor to give them some of their natural food—the leaves of live-oak brush, acorns, mesquite and other bean pods.

On many of the large ranches between Corpus Christi and Browns-ville, where the oak and mesquite thickets are interspersed with prai-rie and grassy openings, deer find ideal conditions, with abundant food and cover. The nature of the ground is such as to protect them from wolves and other natural enemies; but it is well suited to either hunting on horseback or still hunting, which, if freely allowed, would soon exterminate them. With protection, however, they in-crease rapidly, and in many places are abundant. Fresh tracks were common in the trails and even along the stage road in places, and the ranchmen usually know where to find a deer when needed. Similar conditions are reported over most of southern Texas, al-though varying greatly on the different ranches. From Kerrville west to Devils River and the Rio Grande deer are more or less abundant, both in the half-open mesquite valleys and over the rough juniper and oak-covered ridges. On certain large ranches they are still numerous, while on others they have become extremely scarce and would be entirely exterminated but for the recruits from sur-rounding and better protected ranches. Some of the ranchmen do not consider it worth while to protect the deer, while others leave the matter to indifferent foremen or else allow so much hunting by their friends that few of the animals escape. But such indifference is unusual. Almost every ranch gate we passed through bore the sign "Posted."

In spite of the protection of State laws and ranch owners there are still remote sections of rough, uncontrolled range where every year hunters kill wagonloads of deer for the market, or worse, kill the deer for the hides only, leaving the carcasses to rot. I was told that in the winter of 1901-2 hundreds of deer skins were brought out of the country west of Kerrville.

No part of the United States affords more perfect conditions for deer than southern Texas, and all that is required for their mainte-nance and rapid increase is efficient protection. In the past this has not been provided by the game laws; and the fact that the deer have not been wantonly destroyed over the entire region is due to the practical, business-like methods of the large ranch owners, who con-trol the hunting on their ranges, and would as soon think of depleting their herds of cattle as the game under their control. On some of the larger ranches mounted rangers are regularly employed to ride over the country and protect both stock and game, and to see that fences are kept up and that there is no hunting. But usually this is an important part of the business of the regular cowboys. As a practical business proposition the protection of deer can not be urged too strongly. Their presence on the range does not interfere with the cattle and horses. The deer rarely, if ever, eat grass or any forage plant eaten by horses and cattle, but live on the leaves and twigs of bushes, seeds, pods, and flowers of a great variety of plants, including acorns and the pods of the numerous kinds of bean bushes.

Opposition to private control of game was never more groundless than in this open country where without such control the deer would long ago have been exterminated over extensive areas where they are now common.

### Odocoileus macrourus? (virginianus) (Rafinesque).   Plains White-tailed Deer.

Two specimens of white-tailed deer from the sandhills 20 miles north of Monahans, and 3 from Beaver Creek where it crosses the Texas and Oklahoma line at the north edge of the Panhandle, can not be referred to *texanus* or *virginianus*. On geographic grounds they should be *macrourus,* described from the "plains of the Kansas River," so provisionally, at least, I refer them to this form.[a]

The two specimens from north of Monahans are fully adult. A doe, collected September 18, is in the pale yellow summer coat with traces of the fall 'blue coat' showing through, and a large buck taken November 12 is in full, fresh winter pelage. These specimens are larger than corresponding sexes of typical *texanus,* with relatively heavier, wider skulls. The doe is apparently lighter and brighter colored, with no trace of black on the tips of the ears, and the buck is much lighter colored around the face and ears than strictly comparable specimens of *texanus.* The three specimens in the United States National Museum collection from Beaver Creek, collected by Hornaday in 1889, are in faded, late winter pelage, very pale and yellowish. The three imperfect skulls without horns from the same locality agree in a general way with the Monahans skulls.

In September, 1902, Merritt Cary reported the white-tailed deer as common in the sandhill region south and north of Monahans, and as feeding principally on the acorns of the little shin oak which covers this region. At Canadian, in the northeast corner of the Panhandle, in July, 1903, A. H. Howell reported white-tailed deer as occurring

[a] At present I do not know of a specimen of the white-tail deer from the Plains near enough to the type locality of *macrourus* to be safely assumed to be typical of that form, and until typical specimens are obtained the status of the form must remain somewhat in doubt.

in small numbers in the brushy bottoms; and in July, 1904, Gaut reported them as common in the region about Mobeetie.

| 11 | **Odocoileus couesi** Coues and Yarrow.   Sonora Deer.

This little deer is the smallest of the white-tailed group found in the United States, an old buck rarely being estimated at over 100 pounds, while the does are variously estimated at from 50 to 75 pounds. The horns are small and closely curved in, with usually three or four points to a beam; the ears are considerably larger than in specimens of *texanus* weighing nearly twice as much. The young, after losing the spots, are light yellowish brown until after the change to the gray coat, which apparently takes place with the fall molt of the third year. The adults, after about two and a half years old, are light gray at all seasons, without black on ears or tail.

The species is widely distributed through the desert mountains of southern Arizona and northern Mexico and probably reaches its eastern limit in the Chisos Mountains of western Texas. Here these little deer range from 5,000 feet at the upper edge of Lower Sonoran zone through Upper Sonoran and Transition to the top of the mountains at 9,000 feet. They are closely associated with the oaks, junipers, and nut pines, and depend much on the cover of brush and timber. During the day they are usually found lying under a low, branching juniper tree or in a thicket of oak brush, and when started are more often heard bounding over the rocks than seen in the open. They are most numerous on the plateau top of the mountains, at 8,500 feet, where a steep 3,000-foot slope protects them from most hunters and where the sweet acorns of the little gray oak are abundant. Between rains the only water on this plateau is held in the rock basins, but it is usually ample for the needs of the deer. A few springs around the base of the mountains are permanent and always accessible in case of drought. The deer on the plateau are so little disturbed that they are often seen feeding or wandering about during the day. While sweeping the slopes with a field glass I often located deer and watched them without arousing their suspicion. At 11 o'clock one warm day I watched three does come down from an open sunny hillside and select cool beds in the shade of bushes along a deep gulch. At another time I watched a doe and two yearling fawns feed until they were satisfied and then scatter to make their beds under different trees on an open grassy slope. On several occasions, by moonlight, the flash of their white tails at close quarters was seen with startling effect, the gray bodies being quite invisible.

The food of the deer in June consisted mainly of leaves, flowers, green seeds, and capsules or pods of a great variety, of shrubs and plants, including the leaves of the little gray oak (*Quercus grisea*),

Fig. 1.—Cypress Swamp, near Jefferson.

Fig. 2.—Mixed Swamp Timber near Jefferson, Eastern Texas.

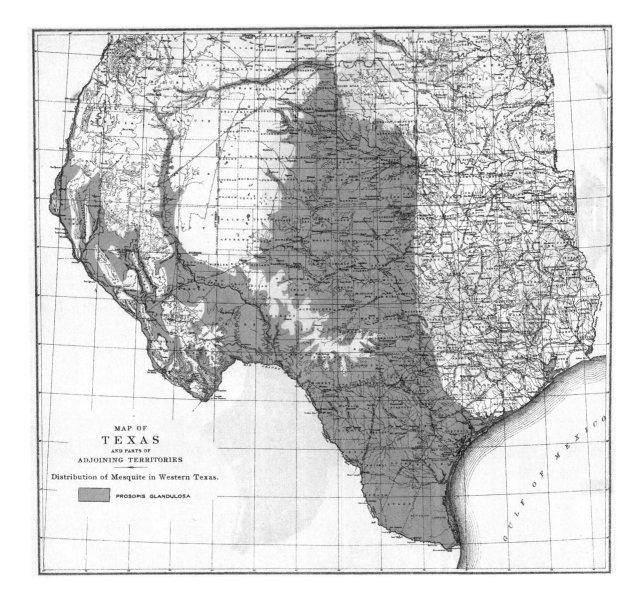

MAP OF
TEXAS
AND PARTS OF
ADJOINING TERRITORIES

Distribution of Mesquite in Western Texas.

PROSOPIS GLANDULOSA

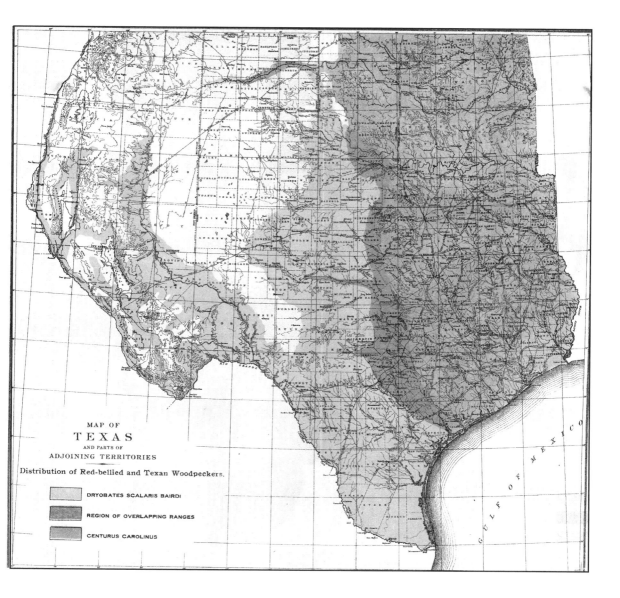

MAP OF
## TEXAS
AND PARTS OF
ADJOINING TERRITORIES

Distribution of Red-bellied and Texan Woodpeckers.

DRYOBATES SCALARIS BAIRDI

REGION OF OVERLAPPING RANGES

CENTURUS CAROLINUS

Fig. 1.—Ocotillo (Fouquiera splendens) and Creosote Bush
(Covillea tridentata).

Fig. 2.—Desert Vegetation of Great Bend Region.

Fig. 1.—Lecheguilla with Flowers and Fruit.

Fig. 2.—Lecheguilla (Agave lecheguilla) new Boquillas, Great Bend of
Rio Grande.

Agave wislinzeni in Flower, Davis Mountains. Hummingbird
at Flower Cluster on Left.

Fig. 1.—Sotol on Mesa near Comstock.

Fig. 2.—Sotol After the Leaves are Burned Off.

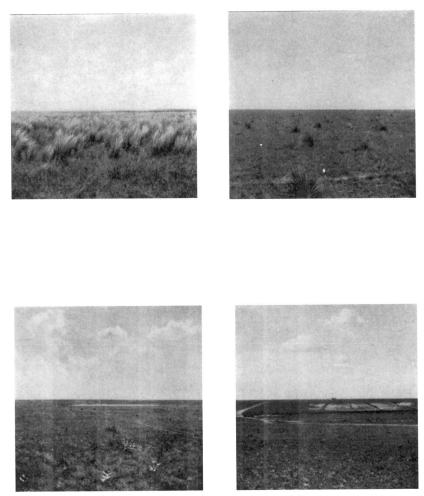

Views on Staked Plains near Hereford and Dimmitt.

Fig. 1.—Transition Zone Timber of Guadalupe Mountains.

Fig. 2.—Head of Dog Canyon, Guadalupe Mountains.

Transition Zone Timber of CHisos Mountains (Approximately 6,500 Feet).

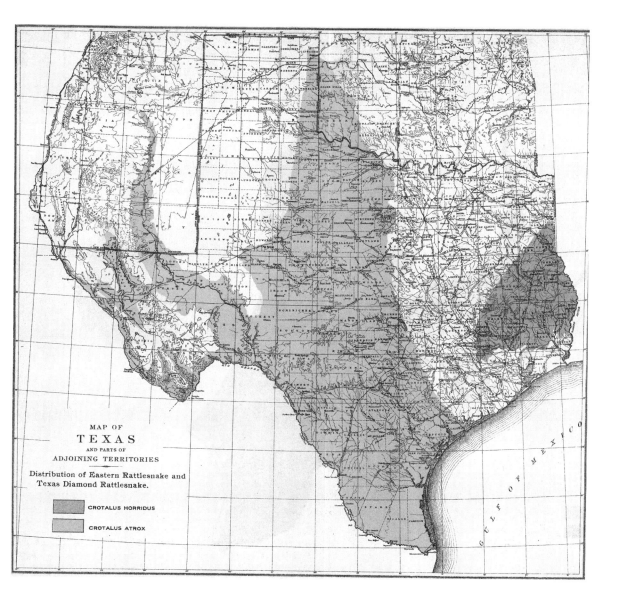

MAP OF
# TEXAS
AND PARTS OF
## ADJOINING TERRITORIES

Distribution of Eastern Rattlesnake and
Texas Diamond Rattlesnake.

CROTALUS HORRIDUS

CROTALUS ATROX

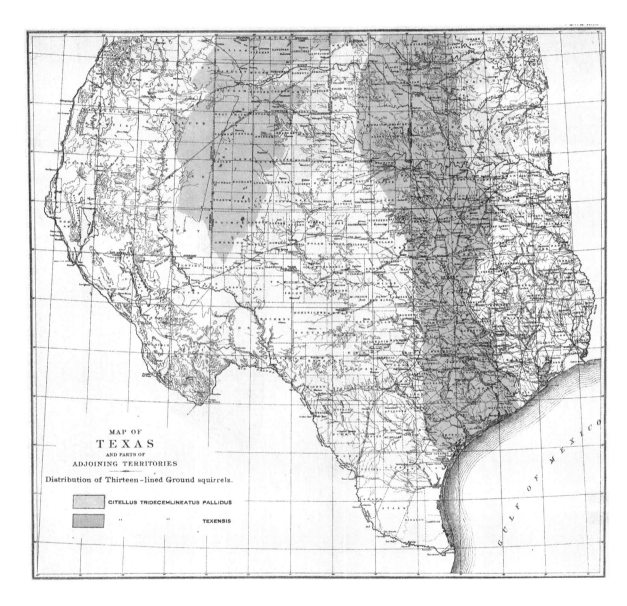

MAP OF
TEXAS
AND PARTS OF
ADJOINING TERRITORIES

Distribution of Thirteen-lined Ground squirrels.

CITELLUS TRIDECEMLINEATUS PALLIDUS

"        "        TEXENSIS

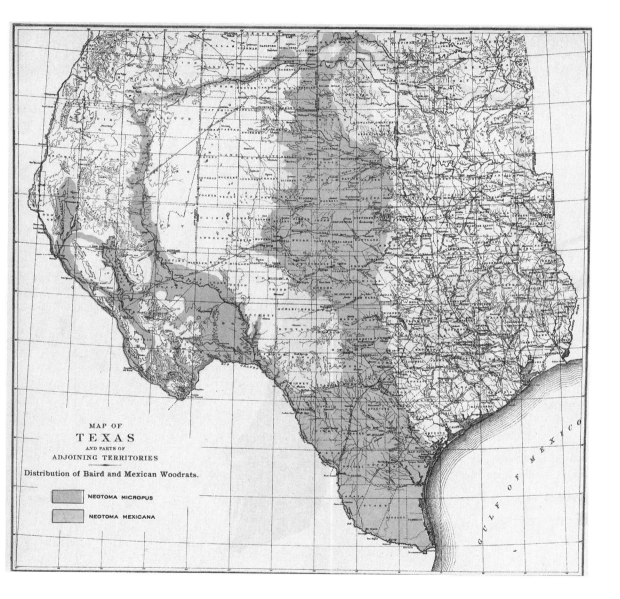

MAP OF
# TEXAS
AND PARTS OF
ADJOINING TERRITORIES

Distribution of Baird and Mexican Woodrats.

NEOTOMA MICROPUS

NEOTOMA MEXICANA

Head of Plateau Wild-cat (*Lynx baileyi*).

Civet Cat; Bassariscus (*Bassariscus Astutus flavus*).

leaves and wide, flat pods of several bean bushes (*Acacia roemeriana* and others), leaves and berries of sumac (*Schmaltzia microphylla*), leaves and capsules of a large *Pentstemon,* and flowers and stems of bear grass (*Nolina lindheimeriana*). The prints of the deer's teeth were often found on the half-eaten green stalks of the century plant (*Agave wislizeni*). Much-used trails and abundance of winter 'sign' among the oaks showed that acorns were the great attraction during fall and winter. No trace of grass could be found in any of the three stomachs examined.

**Odocoileus hemionus canus** Merriam. Gray Mule-deer.

12

Two skins (with skulls) of mule-deer and 8 skulls (or horns with parts of skulls) from the region about Samuels, Langtry, and the

FIG. 9.—Yearling buck of gray mule-deer, Langtry, Texas.

mouth of the Pecos River, a head and horns from Alpine, and a few old horns from the Chisos Mountains agree in a general way with the type and topotypes of *canus*. The skins show the same light gray color, and the skulls are small, the forehead flat, and the horns usually low and widespreading. I have seen no specimens from the northern end of the Staked Plains, but should expect the deer in this region to be *hemionus*. A skull of an old buck from the Guadalupe Mountains north of the Texas line in the collection of Royal H. Wright is not of the *canus* type; and a very large buck that I saw at 8,500 feet on the side of Guadalupe Peak was of the full size of *hemionus*. In the outlying desert ridges west and south of these mountains, where the deer are most abundant, the country is typical of the Lower Sonoran desert region inhabited by *canus*.

The mule-deer is still more or less common in many parts of western Texas, in the Guadalupe, Diablo, Franklin, Davis, Santiago, and Chisos mountains, and eastward to Devils River and the rough country along the east side of the Pecos River as far as Fort Lancaster and the Castle Mountains. A few are found in the deep canyons and gulches cutting into the edges of the northern part of the Staked Plains as far east as Washburn and Mobeetie, but it is much more probable that these range from the Rocky Mountains through the extremely rough country along the south side of the Canadian River than that they have a continuous range southward to meet those of the lower Pecos country. Still, it is not improbable that they range, or have ranged in the past, all along the east escarpment of the Staked Plains. None were found in the timbered part of the Chisos Mountains, but they were common in the barren foothills and outlying desert ranges at long distances from any known water. In the Guadalupe Mountains the same distribution was conspicuous, the mule-deer being far more numerous in the barren foothills on the west side of the range where no water has been found than in the high central timbered part. The deer apparently can go for a long time without water, getting an occasional supply from the rock basins after each rain, or, in cases of long drought, possibly making journeys of 20 or 30 miles to permanent springs. It is commonly believed by ranchmen and hunters, and on good grounds, that these deer can live indefinitely without water, getting all the moisture required from juicy plants. They eat the green stalks of the big century plants (*Agave wislizeni* and *applanata*) and paw open the cabbage-like caudex of the sotol (*Dasylirion texanum*) for its starchy and juicy center. Sheep are often herded on green feed for from three days to a month without water, and where there is snow, dew, or rain, for a much longer time. It is not strange that in a country where most of the springs are utilized for ranch use the deer should adapt themselves to desert conditions, especially as they offer them the greatest possible protection. In this open country, however, they are entirely at the mercy of hunters and unless protected by laws strictly enforced will be exterminated as soon as the country is settled.

At Langtry, in March and April, 1903, Gaut reported deer as "very plentiful a few years ago," and said:

I visited the localities where old hunters claimed to have seen large numbers a few years back, and it is safe to say the large numbers are not there now. A young buck and a very large doe were seen. The heads of small rough canyons seem to be their favorite feeding grounds, and at this time of year they seem to feed to a great extent on the blossoms of *Yucca macrocarpa* and *Dasylirion texanum*.

At Mobeetie in 1904 Gaut was told by Mr. Long, a thirty-two-year resident of the locality, that the only mule-deer he could remember having seen in that country was killed in 1896. In the Franklin Mountains in February, 1903, Gaut reported a few mule-deer, but said they were scarce and very wild. On February 12 he saw the track of a small buck at 4,500 feet altitude on the east slope of the mountains about 10 miles north of El Paso.

**Antilocapra americana** (Ord). Antelope.                    13

In traveling by wagon from Ringgold Barracks to Corpus Christi in December, 1852, Bartlett found abundance of antelope on the plains of southern Texas. On January 1, 1853, he says of the prairie:

> Thousands of deer and antelope were scattered over it. Never before had we seen such numbers. Droves of mustangs also appeared. The deer and antelope were usually grazing in herds of from ten to fifty, and as we approached they leisurely trotted off to a short distance and again stopped. We shot none, for I was desirous of reaching Corpus Christi before night.[a]

A few antelope still remain, scattered over the plains of western Texas, mainly west of the one hundredth meridian.

In 1899 they were frequently seen along the stage road 30 miles south of Colorado City and 10 miles north of Sterling, and were said to be common near Gail. Thirty miles north of Gail I saw three antelope and the tracks of others, and along the road to Lubbock the next day saw several more small bunches and many tracks. A few were reported near Tascosa, while from the train I counted 32, singly or in little bunches, scattered over the prairie from Canyon, Tex., to Portales, N. Mex.

In 1900 ranchmen told me that a few still remained on the prairies west of Alice, where they were once numerous; a few were reported to Oberholser 40 miles northwest of San Diego, a few 20 miles west and a few 25 miles southwest of Cotulla, a small herd 30 to 40 miles northwest of Rock Springs, and another small herd 35 miles northwest and another 50 miles southwest of Henrietta; while they were said to have entirely disappeared within a few years from the country about Laredo and from the big valley in which Alpine is located.

In 1901 a bunch of about a dozen antelope was reported near Bone Spring, 50 miles south of Marathon. Oberholser reported them as fairly common in bunches of 3 to 6 between Sherwood and Fort Lancaster, as occasionally seen in the open country a little north of Cornstock and Langtry, and as common on the plains about Hereford and Mobeetie. In 1890 they were common about Sierra Blanca and Marfa and the base of the Davis Mountains, but in 1901 these bands mainly had disappeared, as they had also from most of the open, uncontrolled stock range in that section.

[a] Bartlett's Personal Narrative, Vol. II, 526, 1854.

In 1902 a few were said to be still found on the open plains north of Rock Springs, and a few on the plains between Valentine and the Davis Mountains, where Mr. John Finley reported 3 in his pasture. At Van Horn within a few years they had disappeared from the valley near the station, but a few were still found in the region farther back from the railroad. At Sierra Blanca, August 3, I saw 3 young antelope which had just been brought in and picketed near the station. Late in August, Hollister and I saw a fine old buck and tracks of a few others on the high plateau at the south end of the Guadalupe Mountains, and on October 2, Hollister saw two small bunches near the railroad between Dalhart and Texline. In crossing the Staked Plains in September I saw from the train 5 antelope near Hereford and 9 near Canyon City, and Mr. Goodnight told me that about 30, which until the previous year had been protected in his pasture, had escaped to neighboring ranches. Cary obtained reports from resident ranchmen of a few on the mesas 15 miles east of Sheffield, of others a short distance to the northeast of Ozona, of a few to the west of Fort Stockton and in the vicinity of Grand Falls, and of others on the east and west sides of the Castle Mountains. He reported them as occasionally seen in the vicinity of Odessa, as common 25 to 50 miles north of Stanton and in smaller numbers 10 or 20 miles south of that place, and as occurring 15 miles north of Abilene, in Jones County. He reported also a bunch of 10 or 12 on the plains 10 miles northwest of Clyde, and a number in the vicinity of Pecos City, but mainly in fenced pastures, where the stockmen protected them and strictly prohibited hunting.

In August, 1903, Howell saw a bunch of 8 or 9 antelope on the prairie 15 miles west of Texline. In February of the same year Gaut reported a few in the valley east of the Franklin Mountains and was informed by Mr. Thomas Robinson, foreman of a large cattle ranch, that these antelope were being protected in one of the ranch pastures.

In 1904 Gaut reported antelope as still common on the plains near Washburn.

It is greatly to be hoped that the Texas State law prohibiting the killing of antelope for a period of five years will be extended indefinitely, as without it both the antelope in the open range and those on the big fenced ranches will soon be exterminated. In no other part of America, with the exception of the Yellowstone and a few private parks, can antelope be expected to last many years, and it is to be hoped for the credit of the State and nation that Texas will protect them for all time.

**Bison bison** (Linn.). Buffalo; American Bison.

Buffalo once ranged over almost the whole of the present State of Texas, and were exceedingly numerous from the coast prairies north over the prairies and plains of the middle part of the State. They were slowly driven back until in 1870 their range, as defined by Doctor Allen,[a] was limited to the plains of the northwestern part of the State. In the next five years they were mostly killed or driven back to the top of the Llano Estacado, where a few remained in the northwest corner of the Pan Handle until 1889, when W. T. Hornaday estimated their number at 25.[b] In 1901 Oberholser was informed by local ranchmen that the last buffalo were seen in 1889 in the Devils River country, and that a few were seen 20 miles north of the mouth of the Pecos the same year. In 1903 Gaut found well-preserved skulls and skeletons of two bulls and a cow in a shallow cave about 10 miles east of Langtry, and saved the skulls for specimens.

In 1894 numerous reports were published in the local Texas papers and copied in Forest and Stream and other journals, describing a herd of buffalo variously estimated at from 30 to 60 head in Valverde County, near the Rio Grande. Later this herd was supposed to have crossed the river and disappeared in Mexico. These reports were shown by Mr. H. P. Attwater to be wholly fictitious.[c] Again, in 1897, a herd of about 80 was reported from Presidio County and the Great Bend of the Rio Grande. In 1901 I could find no one in the Great Bend country who had ever heard of buffalo in that region, nor could I find any evidence to indicate that they ever inhabited the extremely rough and arid country along that part of the Rio Grande Valley.

In 1902 Cary made the following report from Monahans, in the sand-hill region east of Pecos:

Landlord Holman, of the Monahan Hotel, who is an old-timer here, informs me that the last buffalo in the sand-hill region was killed in the winter of 1885 by a professional hunter, George Cansey, who is credited with having killed more buffalo than any other man in Texas. In the fall and summer of 1884 Cansey killed several near the southeast corner of New Mexico, and finally, in January, 1885, while riding to Midland, came up with the last two remaining animals, a cow and calf, near the Water Holes. Cansey shot the cow and roped the calf, which he finally turned over to Mr. C. C. Slaughter, of Fort Worth, who eventually had it killed for a large barbecue. From the same source I learned that the last bull buffalo in the San Angelo region was killed in the fall of 1883, in the southern part of Green County, by a Mr. Mertz, of San Angelo.

At Stanton, Cary says:

I heard from a number of reliable sources that Will Work, who lived at Marienfeld (now Stanton) in the early eighties, killed several buffalo near the New Mexico line, in the western part of Gaines County, Tex., in the winter of 1885.

---

[a] The American Bison, Living and Extinct; J. A. Allen. Geol. Survey of Kentucky, Vol. I, pt. 2, 1876.
[b] Extermination of the American Bison. W. T. Hornaday, Rept. U. S. Nat. Mus. 1889.
[c] Dr. J. A. Allen in Bul. Am. Mus. Nat. Hist., VIII, p. 53, April 22, 1896.

In 1899, while crossing the top of the Staked Plains from Gail to Amarillo and Tascosa, I found a few old, much-weathered buffalo horns, but the bones had mostly disappeared. In places the old deeply worn trails leading to water holes were a conspicuous feature of the plains, but where not kept open by range cattle they were heavily sodded over. Farther west on the slope, toward the Pecos River, the outcropping layers of soft limestone are deeply furrowed by hundreds of parallel trails trending toward the river valley. These are the last traces of the wild buffalo in Texas. The well-known herd of Mr. Charles Goodnight, at Goodnight, Tex., numbered in September, 1902, about 50 full-blooded buffalo and 70 crosses of various grades with polled angus cattle. The buffalo are in good condition, quiet and contented, breed freely, and are very hardy. The cows bear only full-blooded calves, and the crosses are made from buffalo bulls to polled angus cows, and then from these half-bloods to three-quarters and seven-eighths buffalo and to three-quarter polled angus, which last cross Mr. Goodnight believes gives promise of establishing a very superior grade of cattle.

15   **Ovis mexicanus** Merriam.   Mexican Bighorn; Mountain Sheep.

Two 5-year-old rams and one 4-year-old from the southern end of the Guadalupe Mountains, Texas, and one 7-year-old ram from the mountains north of Van Horn agree in almost every detail of character with the type and topotypes of *Ovis mexicanus*[a] from Santa Maria, Chihuahua. They are older and a little larger than the type, and serve to accentuate some of the characters of the species.

Mountain sheep inhabit the Upper Sonoran and Transition zones of the desert ranges of extreme western Texas. They are found in the Guadalupe Mountains. A few have been killed in the Eagle and Corozones mountains and on the northwest side of the Chisos Mountains. They come into the Grand Canyon of the Rio Grande mainly from the Mexican side. Mr. R. T. Hill reports specimens killed in the Diablo Mountains, 25 miles north of Van Horn. The sheep are by no means confined to isolated mountain ranges. In several valleys I saw tracks where they had crossed from one range to another through open Lower Sonoran country. In this way they easily wander from range to range over a wide expanse of country in western Texas, and might be considered to have an almost or quite continuous distribution between the Guadalupe Mountains and the desert ranges of Chihuahua. Most of the ranges are steep, extremely rugged, and barren, with deep canyons and high cliffs. Here the sheep find ideal homes on the open slopes of terraced lime rock or jagged crests of old lava dikes, and, thanks to the arid and inaccessible nature of the country, they have held their own against the few hunters of the

---

[a] *Ovis mexicanus* Merriam, Proc. Biol. Soc. Wash., XIV, 29, Apr. 5, 1901.

region. An old resident of one of the canyons, who has supplied his table with wild mutton for many years, considers them fully as numerous now as fifteen years ago. He has seen as many as 30 in a herd, but says they usually go in small bunches of 3 to 10, sometimes all rams and sometimes all ewes and lambs, but usually in mixed bunches. They come down the sides of the canyon in sight of the ranch, and are shot only when needed.

While sweeping the slopes with the glass one evening near our camp in one of the big canyons opening into the Guadalupe Mountains, I located three sheep halfway up the face of the rocky slope, 1,000 feet above me. To the unaided eye they were invisible among the ledges and broken rocks, whose colors they matched to perfection, but through the glass they were conspicuous as they moved about feeding and climbing over the rocks. There were an old ram, a young ram, and a ewe. It was too near dark to make the long roundabout climb necessary to reach them, so I returned to camp and early the following morning started my camp man up the slope to the spot, while I went back up the canyon to get beyond them if they should run up the ridge. As I swept the slopes with the glass I heard a shot up where the sheep had been the evening before, and soon locating the hunter, watched him shoot two of them, while three others which were above climbed the cliff and finally disappeared over the crest of the canyon wall. The three that escaped were not much alarmed by the shooting. They jumped from rock to rock, pausing to look and listen, and turned back in one place to find a better way of retreat. They made some long leaps to reach the ledges above, but made no mistakes in their footing. Their motions were deliberate, and there was a moment's pause before each bound. I was amazed at the strength of the old ram, as, slowly lifting his massive horns, he flung himself with apparent ease to the rock above. The two lighter animals followed more nimbly, but with less show of power and without the splendid bearing of their leader, who often paused with head high in the air to watch the hunter below or to plan his way up the next cliff. While from below they seemed to be mounting the face of a steep cliff, I found later that it was not difficult to follow where they had gone.

It was interesting to note that these sheep had remained almost exactly where they were seen the night before. The two others may have joined them during the night, but more likely were all the time somewhere near, either lying down or hidden by the rocks.

The stomachs of the two sheep killed were full of freshly eaten and half-chewed vegetation, and most of the plants composing the contents were easily recognized by the stems, leaves, and fruit. The leaves, twigs, and carpels of *Cercocarpus parvifolius* formed a large part of the contents, while the leaves, twigs, and seed pods of *Phila-*

*delphus microphyllus* were present in less abundance. The seeds, stems, and leaves of the common wild onion of the mountain slopes were abundant and conspicuous in the mass, giving it a strong odor, while the black onion seeds, still unbroken and often in the capsules, were especially noticeable. A few bits of stems and leaves of grass were found in each of the stomachs, but they formed probably not over 2 per cent of the total mass.

Both of these sheep were in good condition, and the meat was tender, juicy, and delicious, with no strong or unpleasant taste. While it lacked the peculiar gamy flavor of venison, it came as near equaling it in quality as the meat of any game I know.

On August 22, in another range in which the bighorns were reported, I left the ranch accompanied by an old resident hunter. Riding hard up one gulch and down another we were soon 10 miles back in the mountains in a canyon with steep terraced walls rising from 1,000 to 2,000 feet above the open bottom. As we crossed the bottom a band of 12 or 15 mountain sheep bounded from the farther edge and started up the rocky slope in a long line of conspicuous bobbing white rumps led by three magnificent old rams. They had a quarter of a mile start, but in a very short time our hard-hoofed little horses had covered the stony gulch bottom and landed us at the base of the rocky slope within 250 yards of the sheep, which, having gained a point of sharp rocks above and feeling more secure, stopped to look down. As the king of the bunch suddenly paused on a sharp point and with a ponderous swing of his heavy horns turned to face us, my little 32-20 sounded weak and ineffective and only served to make him seek a higher ledge. But at the more spirited crack of the old ranchman's 30-30 the next in line, a buck with almost as heavy horns, rolled off the cliff with a broken neck and came sliding and tumbling to the base of the rocks a hundred feet below. The rest had scampered around the point of rocks, and as they came out again farther up and climbed cliff after cliff that from our base level seemed smooth and sheer a few more shots were wasted at long range. The herd divided and passed around both sides of the high peak. Following both trails for a mile or so to see if any of the sheep had been wounded, I found that I could go wherever they had gone. The cliffs were not so steep or so smooth as they had looked from below. In one place the animals had followed a narrow shelf above a sheer drop of 300 feet. Although they had jumped from point to point, striking their feet within an inch of the edge, I could not resist the impulse to lean close to the wall and keep my feet as far from the edge as the narrow shelf, which in places was not a foot wide, would allow. But some of the rocks crossed sloped at a steep angle, and the sheep had made daring jumps from rocky point to sloping surface, where their lives depended on their sure-footedness. The farther I followed the more I admired their skill and nerve. I asked my companion if he had ever known sheep to go where a man could not. He said he thought that they would sometimes make longer leaps down a sheer ledge than a man could attempt with safety, but that otherwise a man could go where they could.

I was especially interested in examining the feet of the old ram we had secured, and was struck first of all by the difference between the front and the hind feet—the front being fully twice as large as the hind, much squarer in form, with deeper, heavier cushioned heels, and lighter and less worn dewclaws. As the hind quarters of the sheep are light and fully two-thirds of the animal's weight comes over the front feet, this difference in size is not surprising. The greater wear of the hind dewclaws is easily accounted for by their constant use in holding back as the sheep goes down hill. While the points and edges of the hoofs are of the hardest horn, the deep, rounded heels are soft and elastic—veritable rubber heels—with a semihorny covering over a copious mass of tough, elastic, almost bloodless and nerveless tissue. While fresh, before the specimen is dried, these cushioned heels may be indented slightly with the thumb. It is easy to see how they would fit and cling to the smooth surface of a sloping rock where wholly hard hoofs like those of a horse would slip, just as you can turn your back to a steep slope of glacier-polished granite and walk up it on the palms of your hands where you can not take one step with the roughest hobnailed shoes. The dewclaws are also heavily cushioned beneath, but have fairly hard, horny points—mere movable, boneless knots. Among other peculiarities noticed in the fresh specimen were the pads of the breast and the knee, where the skin had developed to an almost cartilaginous shield over a quarter of an inch thick and so hard that it was not easily cut through with a sharp knife. The whole sternum and front of the knees were thus protected, and for very evident reasons. The beds where the sheep had been lying were found on rocky or stony shelves, usually above a sharp cliff and below a high wall of rocks sometimes on a bare surface of rock and almost always with at least a foundation of rough stones. If possible the sheep paw out a slight hollow, but they do this apparently more to make an approximately level bed than for the sake of the softness of the little loose dust they can scrape up among the stones. The hair is worn short over the knee and the breast pads, but the skin is unscratched either by rocks or thorns.

The legs of the sheep secured were filled, especially below the knee, with cactus and agave thorns that had gone through the skin and broken off in spikes half an inch to an inch long and lodged against the bone or the inner surface of the skin. A large share of these thorns were the terminal spikes from the leaf blades of *Agave lecheguilla,* which grows in great abundance over the hot slopes of the mountains, and which the horses avoid with even greater care than they do the numerous species of cactus.

The glandular disks under the eyes of this ram were more conspicuous than in any other specimen I have ever examined, probably on account of his mature age, which his horns showed to be 6 or 7 years. The gland is an elevated rim of thickened, black, scantily haired skin, with a depressed center, and measures about an inch across. It stands out prominently on the surface, and appears from the flesh side of the skin as well as from the front as a round thick pad. It has an oily or waxy secretion and a rank, sheepy odor.

In color the old rams were decidedly darker than the ewes and younger members of the herd, but all blended with astonishing harmony into the browned, rusty, old, weathered limestone of their chosen hillsides. Even the soiled white rump patches were just the color of freshly broken faces on the rocks seen here and there over the slopes. As the band of sheep sprang away up the slope the white rump patches were so conspicuous that I could not believe at first that the animals were not antelope; but higher up, as they stopped among the rocks to face us, they could easily have been mistaken for a group of rocks. As they appeared again farther away on the ridge beyond the gulch, the bobbing, white rump patches were conspicuous signal marks so long as the animals were running away from us, but when they turned their forms were completely lost in the background.

These sheep did not appear to run very fast, but probably few animals save the panther can catch them in a race over the rocks. A few days later, while hunting panther in these same hills, it was demonstrated that deerhounds can not catch nor tire out the sheep over their own trails, although my companion claimed that they were not very swift runners on open ground.

The meat of our 7-year-old ram was rather tough and dry, but without any bad flavor. The people at the ranch where I was staying, who had eaten young sheep, considered the meat superior to venison. Although shot at 4 p.m., our sheep had a full stomach and must have been feeding for an hour or two. His teeth were imperfect. One or two molars were missing in the lower jaw, and, as a result, the contents of his stomach were rather coarse, and many of the plants were easily recognized. Over half of the contents was composed of the green stems of *Ephedra trifurcata,* which I at first mistook for grass, but which could not be mistaken on careful examination. The stems, leaves, and flowers of *Tecoma stans,* a beautiful yellow-flowered bush, were conspicuous, as also were the leaves, stems, and berries of *Garrya wrighti.* A few twigs with leaves and fruit pods of *Pentstemon* were found, and a quantity of ripe fruit of *Opuntia engelmanni,* including the chewed-up pulp and seeds of at least half a dozen of the large pear-shaped berries. Some other leaves and stems were found that I could not recognize, but a careful search failed to reveal a trace of grass in the stomach. Part of these plants are Lower and part Upper Sonoran species, and the sheep seem to inhabit the two zones freely. The cold slopes and upper benches of the mountains are Upper Sonoran, however, and probably are to be considered the animals' real home. Transition zone does not occur in this range.

It is with some hesitation that I make public these facts as to the abundance, distribution, and habits of mountain sheep in western Texas, and only in the hope that a full knowledge of the conditions and the importance of protective measures may result in the salvation instead of extermination of the species. It would not be difficult for a single persistent hunter to kill every mountain sheep in western Texas if unrestrained. Not only should the animals be protected by law, but the law should be made effective by an appreciation on the part of residents of the country of the importance of preserving for all time these splendid animals.

**Sciurus ludovicianus**[a] Custis.    Western Fox Squirrel; Louisiana Fox    16
    Squirrel.

In eastern Texas the fox squirrels are large and richly colored like those of Louisiana, and a small proportion of their numbers are melanistic. Of 7 specimens taken at Arthur one was almost black, and the hunter with me said that among 14 squirrels killed on a previous hunt 4 were black or very dark. Hollister saw a black squirrel at Antioch and reported many at Rockland. A few black individuals among many of the others were reported at Tarkington. To the west the animals grade without any abrupt change into the smaller, paler colored *limitis*. Specimens from Gainesville and Matagorda county, while intermediate, are in size and color nearer to *ludovicianus* than to typical *limitis*.

Fox squirrels are reported by Loring, Oberholser, and Hollister as more or less common at Texarkana, Waskom, Joaquin, Antioch, Long Lake, Troup, Milano, Brenham, Rockland, Conroe, Jasper, near Beaumont and Sour Lake; and I have found them at Tarkington, Lib-

---

[a] If a type locality can be established for *Sciurus rufiventer* E. Geoffroy (Cat. Mus. Hist. Nat., 1803, p. 174) within the range of the form known since 1800 as *Sciurus ludovicianus* Custis, or if the type specimen sent to Geoffroy by Michaux from America can be identified as the Louisiana form, it will become necessary to revert to the name *rufiventer*. Meanwhile I prefer to use a long-established name in preference to one three years older, the application of which is still open to question.

erty, Richmond, Cuero, Jefferson, Gainesville, and Arthur. Others reported from Elgin, Austin, Decatur, Brazos, and Wichita Falls are probably intermediate between *ludovicianus* and *limitis*.

At Arthur in northeastern Texas, and in the Big Thicket region of southeastern Texas, they inhabit the hickory and oak covered ridges, and leave the dense river bottoms and swamps entirely to the gray squirrels; but farther west in the more open country they inhabit both the timbered river bottoms and the oak ridges. They live

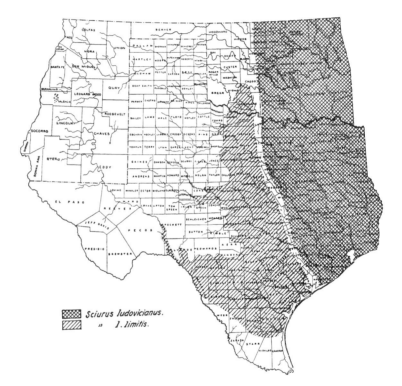

FIG. 10—Distribution areas of fox squirrels (*Sciurus ludovicianus* and *S. l. limitis*).

mainly in hollow trees, but also make bulky nests of leaves and twigs out on the branches. When alarmed these squirrels run to the nearest hollow tree or up the first tree with branches leading to one, and are soon safely hidden inside, but if they do not reach some safe retreat they are so skillful at hiding that they often escape the hunter by keeping on the farther side of trunk and branch. Their food consists mainly of nuts and acorns, but fruit, berries, and lichens also are eaten. When feeding on nuts their flesh has a delicious nutty flavor.

**Sciurus ludovicianus limitis** Baird.    Texas Fox Squirrel.

## 17

*Sciurus texianus* Allen, Bul. Am. Mus. Nat. Hist., XVI, p. 166, 1902. (Not of Bachman, 1838.)[a]

The Texas fox squirrel differs from the Louisiana animal in smaller size and paler coloration. So far as I can learn, it is never black. It inhabits the semiarid part of the Lower Sonoran zone, on the west reaching the canyon of the Pecos, the Rio Grande at the mouth of Devils River and at Del Rio, and farther south, extending across into Coahuila and Nuevo Leon, Mexico. To the east it grades into *ludovicianus,* but specimens from the mouth of the Nueces River, San Antonio, Seguin, Brownwood, and Henrietta are referable to *limitis.* There are specimens from Devils River, Del Rio, Rock Springs, Japonica, Ingram, Kerr County, San Antonio, San Antonio River in Victoria County, near the mouth of Nueces River, Cotulla, Mason, San Angelo, Brownwood, Henrietta, and Vernon; and Oberholser reports a few 12 miles north of San Diego and in the Pecos Valley near Fort Lancaster.

In this half-forested mesquite region the little fox squirrels inhabit the timber along the streams, where the pecan, hickory, oak, and little walnut trees furnish their favorite food and a few hollow trees afford protection, but nowhere within their range do they get the deep shade of the forests farther east. Wherever the pecan tree is found along the streams from Kerrville to the Rio Grande they are abundant. Specimens were collected on the Guadalupe at Ingram and Japonica, on the Hackberry near Rock Springs, and on Devils River. A few were seen on ridges between rivers, but they keep mainly to the bottoms. They are closely associated with the pecan tree, in the branches or hollow trunks of which they build their nests, living mainly on its nuts, and rarely wandering away from its shade. Along the Devils River, where these magnificent old trees reach their greatest perfection and form a miniature forest overarching the river with their spreading branches and shading its cool banks for miles, the little fox squirrels abound. Their leafy stick nests are common among the branches, but their safe retreats are the numerous hollows in the gnarled old trunks, the openings of which have been

---

[a] In using the name *texianus* in place of *limitis* for the little pale west Texas fox squirrel Doctor Allen seems to ignore Bachman's excellent description (P. Z. S., 1838, 87) and to base his decision on the fact that one of the specimens mentioned by Bachman was said to have come from Mexico, one from Texas, and one from southwestern Louisiana. It is necessary only to read Bachman's description, with specimens of both species in hand, to be convinced that it applies strictly to the large dark-colored *ludovicianus* and not to the little pale *limitis.* His measurements are the maximum for *ludovicianus.* I find nothing to indicate that Bachman had ever seen *limitis,* unless it be his statement that a specimen of an apparently undescribed species seen in the Museum at Paris was said to have been received from Mexico.

worn smooth by ages of use as doorways. Usually, however, no protection is needed beyond their quick ear for detecting an approaching footstep, their natural skill at hiding on the farther side of a trunk or branch, and their rapid retreat among the branches from tree to tree.

Late in July we found the squirrels beginning to cut off many of the green pecan nuts, apparently just to test if they were nearly ripe.

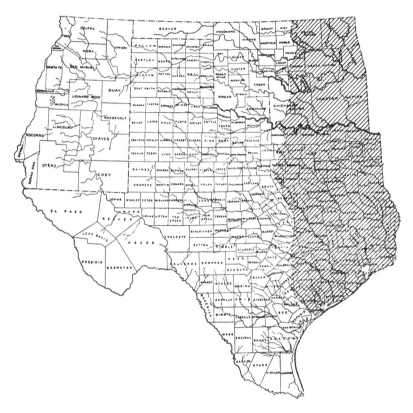

Fig. 11.—Distribution area of gray squirrel (*Sciurus carolinensis*).

The last year's crop of nuts was probably exhausted, as the squirrels were feeding on various other things. Along the Guadalupe River, July 4 to 7, they were eating seeds of the cypress cones, and had their hands and lips covered with pitch, while the ground was strewn with half-eaten cones. It was then too early for them to begin barking much, but a few soft barks of warning were heard near our camp on Devils River late in July.

**Sciurus carolinensis** Gmelin. Gray Squirrel.

Gray squirrels inhabit the timbered region of eastern Texas as far west as the mouth of the Colorado, Cuero, Austin, and Brazos.

18

Specimens examined from the mouth of the Colorado, Sour Lake, Liberty, Long Lake, Jasper, Troup, Arthur, and Joaquin are almost typical *carolinensis,* which seems to have a continuous range from the Atlantic coast west through Lower Sonoran zone to its extreme western limit in central Texas. Gray squirrels are reported from Texarkana, Jefferson, Waskom, Antioch, Long Lake, Jasper, Conroe, Rockland, Tarkington, Saratoga, near Beaumont, Brenham, Aledo, and Benbrook, and except along the western edge of their range are usually said to be common or abundant.

They seem to prefer the tall timber of the river bottoms and not to extend west into the lower and more open woods. At Arthur I found them abundant on the flats of the Red River, but found none on the upland ridges, where the fox squirrels were common. The two species seemed to keep entirely apart, and old hunters claim that the gray squirrels choose their ground and keep the fox squirrels away from it. In the Big Thicket of Hardin and Liberty counties, in November and December of 1904, the grays were numerous throughout the heavy timber and dense swamps of the bottoms, while the few fox squirrels were found in scattered groves along the edge of Tarkington and Liberty prairies. Acorns and nuts furnish abundance of food and countless hollow trees offer safe retreats. The squirrels also build numerous branch nests of twigs or Spanish moss or a mixture of the two. The perfect blending of the pelage of a gray squirrel with the gray moss which loads the branches of the trees saves many a squirrel from the hunter.

### Sciurus fremonti lychnuchus Stone & Rehn.   Pine Squirrel.          19

Several people in the Guadalupe Mountains claimed to have seen a small, dark-colored tree squirrel, which they said was very rare. I failed to find any traces of it, however, although the timber and country are well adapted to squirrels. Pine squirrels are common in the Sacramento Mountains, a little farther north, and it is not improbable that a few may find their way south along the crest of the range and across the Texas line.

### Sciuropterus volans querceti Bangs.   Florida Flying Squirrel.          20

Texas specimens from Texarkana, Gainesville, Troup, and Tarkington agree perfectly with the Florida subspecies and differ from typical *volans* in slightly darker coloration, dusky instead of whitish toes of the hind feet, and in slenderer nasals and muzzle and larger audital bullae.

Flying squirrels are reported from numerous localities over eastern Texas, where they seem to be fairly common and to have a continuous distribution throughout the forested region. The westernmost records are from Elgin, where Oberholser reported the species as tolerably common; and from Aledo and Benbrook (just west of Fort Worth), where Cary saw a stuffed specimen which came from that place, and was told of a family of 8 taken in 1901 from a hole in an elm a mile west of Aledo. They have been reported from Guadalupe River, Richmond, Brenham, Long Lake, Antioch, Rockland, Saratoga, Sour Lake, Conroe, Jasper, Waskom, Jefferson, and Texarkana.

Flying squirrels are among the most strictly nocturnal of mammals and are rarely noted except by timber cutters, who see them

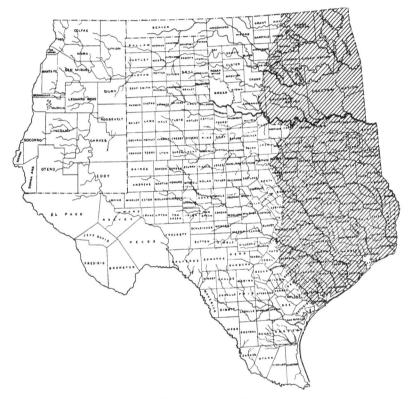

FIG. 12.—Distribution area of flying squirrel (*Sciuropterus volucella querceti*).

flying from their nests in falling trees. While every wood chopper in the east Texas region is familiar with them, it is difficult to get specimens. They are not easily trapped and often live in hollows in the large trees, where pounding with an ax does not start them from their nests. While hunting in the Big Thicket of Liberty and Hardin counties I often heard their fine, whistling squeak from the branches over my head at night, and occasionally the rustle of their feet on the bark of a tree close to the trail I was following.

At Mike Griffin's place, 8 miles northeast of Sour Lake, Gaut was shown a dead pine out in the field where flying squirrels were said to live in a deserted woodpecker's hole. By pounding on the base of the tree two flying squirrels were driven out and secured. A few days later two more were driven out of the same tree and secured, and again a few days later two more, making in all six specimens from one woodpecker's nest.

### Eutamias cinereicollis canipes Bailey.    Gray-footed Chipmunk.    21

The gray-footed chipmunks are common in Transition zone throughout the Guadalupe Mountains, from 7,000 feet in Dog Canyon and 6,000 feet in Timber Canyon up to at least 8,500 feet and probably to the top of the peaks at 9,500 feet, at which altitude they are common in the Sacramento Mountains a little farther north. While none were found in the lower part of the range, between the Guadalupes and the Sacramentos, they seem to be identical in the two ranges and may easily have a continuous distribution between. In the Sacramento Mountains they occupy the whole width of both the Transition and Canadian zones. In the Guadalupe Mountains they range from the lower edge of the Transition zone upward with the yellow pine and Douglas spruce, but in September they are more closely associated with the shrubby oaks, several species of which are abundant over the upper slopes of the mountains. They were occasionally seen in the densest timber, but more often in the open oak scrub, gathering the little sweet acorns in the tops of the bushes, or sitting on logs or rocks eating them. Both logs and rocks were covered with acorn shells. Occasionally these chipmunks were seen in the lower branches of a tree, but when alarmed they always ran to the ground and disappeared among rocks, logs, or brush. They were very shy, and in the thick cover it was difficult to get specimens. Their light 'chipper' was often heard from the bushes, and on a few occasions I heard their low 'chuck-chuck-chuck,' repeated slowly from a log or rock or the low branch of a tree, but it always ceased as soon as danger was suspected.

### Ammospermophilus interpres (Merriam).    Texas Antelope Squirrel.    22

The Texas antelope squirrel is common along the Rio Grande from El Paso to the mouth of the Pecos, but less common up the Pecos Valley to the Castle Mountains and in the country between the Rio Grande and Pecos valleys in Texas. Specimens collected at El Paso, Boquillas, Pecos High Bridge, Fort Lancaster, Castle Mountains, south end of Guadalupe Mountains, and Sierra Blanca carry the range of the species over the extremely rough and arid Lower Sonoran region of western Texas, but indicate a very irregular range along the course of canyons and the foothills of barren, desert mountains. In fact the presence of canyons, bare cliffs, and rocks, with which the species is closely associated, seems to be the determining factor of its range within its zone.

Near El Paso and in the Great Bend of the Rio Grande, near Boquillas, these little squirrels live along the steep banks of the river or in the narrow side gulches that cut back into the barren mesas. Along the Pecos Canyon they are found on the rock shelves of the canyon walls; and around the Castle and Guadalupe mountains, and

FIG. 13.—Distribution area of Texas antelope squirrel (*Ammospermophilus interpres*).

at Sierra Blanca they occur in rocky gulches or along low cliffs. They burrow under the edge of a bowlder or around the base of a bunch of bushes or cactus, and are usually seen either running from bush to bush, sitting on a point of rock, or running over the rocks with their short, bushy tails curled tight over their rumps. Sometimes they climb to the top of a cactus or low bush, apparently in search of food, but at the first alarm they rush for a burrow or the nearest rocks.

Near Boquillas in May the half-grown young were out with the others getting their own food from the various seeds and fruits, and climbing the acacia and mesquite bushes to secure the ripening bean pods, which were found scattered in abundance about their burrows. The stomach of one shot in September in the Castle Mountains by Gordon Donald was full of the fruit of *Opuntia engelmanni,* which Cary, who examined the specimen, thinks must have been the squirrel's steady diet for some time, as its flesh was tinted throughout with the purple color of the fruit.

In autumn these little fellows become very fat and probably hibernate during the coldest weather. At El Paso in December, 1889, I found them out on warm days, although very lazy and sluggish. They were then feeding on various seeds, including those of the creosote bush. They were in the beautiful long silky winter fur, very different from the short, harsh summer coat. Along the east base of the Franklin Mountains, in February, 1903, Gaut found them running about in a drizzling rain when the temperature was close to freezing.

**Citellus variegatus couchi** (Baird).    Couch Rock Squirrel.                    23

These black-headed, or often entirely black, rock squirrels are common throughout the Chisos and Davis mountains and along the canyons of the Rio Grande, Pecos, and Devils rivers. While varying in color in the gray phase from entirely dark gray to the usual gray back and black head or crown, no specimens I have seen show the combination of black back and gray rump of *buckleyi,* nor the light gray head and shoulders of *grammurus.* A specimen collected at Boquillas and one on the Rio Grande near Comstock are entirely black, exactly like Baird's type of *couchi.* Several other entirely black individuals have been seen along the Rio Grande and near the month of the Pecos in company with the gray ones, while seven entirely black specimens collected at Santa Catarina, Mexico, the type locality of *couchi*, by Nelson and Goldman, seem to prove complete dichromatism for the species.

In the Davis and Chisos mountains the rock squirrels range with the oaks and junipers in canyons and over rocky slopes throughout the Upper Sonoran zone; while along the river canyons they are confined to the Lower Sonoran zone with the modifying influence of canyon walls and narrow gulches. Along the canyons they are usually found sitting on the prominent points of rocks, and their loud whistle often reverberates from side to side. When alarmed they disappear among the rocks or climb to the tops of the tallest cliffs. In the mountains they live mainly among the rocks, cliffs, and ledges, but range out among the oaks and junipers for food. They climb the trees for acorns and berries, but when surprised in the branches they always rush to the ground and scamper away to the nearest rock pile or burrow. During early summer they feed extensively on the old juniper berries and acorns of the previous year, digging for them under the trees and in many places keeping the ground well stirred. By the middle of July they begin on the nearly matured acorns of one of the black oaks (*Quercus emoryi*) and also on the new crop of juniper berries (*Juniperus pachyphlœa*). Some of those shot were feeding largely on green foliage, the leaves of clover and various plants, and along the Rio Grande mainly on the juicy fruit of *Opuntia engelmanni*. None of those taken in summer were very fat, but in January, 1890, in the Davis Mountains, I found them excessively so. They were then keeping very quiet and came out of their rocky dens only on warm days.

24 **Citellus variegatus buckleyi** (Slack). Black-backed Rock Squirrel.

This, the handsomest of the rock squirrels, with glossy black head and shoulders, inhabits a restricted area in the rough and semiarid mesquite country along the eastern slope of the southern arm of the Staked Plains, from Mason and Llano to a little west of Austin and San Antonio, and again west to Kerrville and the head of the Nueces River. Specimens examined from Mason, Llano, near Austin, near Kerrville, Japonica, and Rock Springs (39 in all) do not vary to any great extent, except that in a few the black extends over the back to base of tail.

Along the upper branches of the Guadalupe and Nueces rivers these squirrels are common in rocky places. I saw them near Ingram and collected specimens near Japonica and on Hackberry Creek near Rock Springs, while the ranchmen reported them as common in all rocky gulches throughout this strip of rough country. West of Rock Springs we did not find any trace of rock squirrels, there being no suitable country, until *couchi* was found in the lower part of Devils River Canyon. Apparently the open divide between the headwaters of the Nueces and the headwaters of the streams flowing into the Rio Grande separates the ranges of *buckleyi* and *couchi* with a neutral strip in which neither occurs. Near Camp Verde, in Kerr County, Cary found them common in the rocky cliffs, where he secured specimens, and was told by the ranchmen that the squirrels had a habit of appearing in considerable numbers on the cliff just before a storm. They did this with such regularity that the ranchmen depended on it as a sure sign of rain.

Mr. J. H. Tallichet, of Austin, sent a specimen from Bull Creek, Travis County, and wrote, under date of September 18, 1893:

I send to you by this mail a specimen of the spermophile which occurs in this part of the State. * * * The specimen is an immature male which I killed while camping last year. His cheek pouches were filled with corn and melon seeds. These rock squirrels live in the debris at the foot of the canyon walls and are very wary. Full-grown specimens are nearly as large as tree squirrels and are eaten by the country people.

In habits *buckleyi* is a true rock squirrel, and is never seen at any great distance from cliffs or broken ledges. At Llano I found one pair near a cliff living in a hollow oak tree which they entered by holes in the branches 15 or 20 feet from the ground. They climbed the tree and disappeared—as quickly as any tree squirrel could have done—and did not show themselves at the openings for half an hour. Generally, however, the squirrels are found sitting on the rocks doing picket duty, ready at the slightest alarm to slide noiselessly over the edge of a rock into a burrow, under a bowlder, or into a break in the cliff. They are exceedingly shy and have to be stalked as carefully as an antelope. By the middle of May the half-grown young are out caring for themselves and feeding in the same manner as the adults.

Piles of acorn shells near the burrows indicate that acorns, when obtainable, are the principal food of the squirrels, which in summer, however, feed mainly on flowers, fruit, and green vegetation. The stomach of one examined contained mostly pulp of green cactus fruit (*Opuntia engelmanni*), together with parts of the big yellow cactus flower, while several of these flowers with the green berry attached were found on the rocks where the squirrels were in the habit of sitting. The stomach of another was filled with the white starchy pulp from the base of young leaves of *Yucca stricta*. Most of the yucca plants near the dens of the squirrels had part of their leaves cut out, and on examination I found the base of these leaves tender, sweet, and starchy, with a rather pleasant flavor. Another individual had the stems and leaves of a little stonecrop in its pouches. Flowers seemed to be a rather common food, and the contents of the stomachs often showed spots of red, yellow, and blue from the various species eaten. A squirrel shot on Hackberry Creek at the edge of a little corn field July 14 had its cheeks stuffed full of green corn, and the field showed many ragged ears.

Most of the squirrels collected in May were lean and muscular, but one that happened to be in good condition proved as good eating as any tree squirrel, while the young of the year were always tender and delicious.

25

### Citellus variegatus grammurus (Say).   Rock Squirrel.

The rock squirrels of the southern Guadalupe Mountains and the Franklin Mountains near El Paso, Tex., are typical *grammurus,* with light gray head and shoulders. In the Guadalupe Mountains they are common, together with the junipers and oaks, from 4,000 to 7,000 feet throughout the Upper Sonoran zone. They usually live along the rocky canyons, but are sometimes seen in the open woods, where they climb the trees for the sweet berries of *Juniperus pachyphlœa* and the little acorns of the gray oak, or dig acorns of the previous year from the ground under the trees. Down in the foothill canyons we found them feeding on cactus fruit (*Opuntia engelmanni* and *Cereus stramineus*) and walnuts (*Juglans rupestris*). One specimen shot in Dark Canyon had thirteen of these little walnuts of the size of small cherries in its cheeks and a lot of cactus fruit in its stomach. They are shy and usually silent, but when danger threatens, their loud, vibrant whistle rings back and forth from the canyon walls.

26    **Citellus mexicanus parvidens** (Mearns).   Rio Grande Ground Squirrel.

The Rio Grande ground squirrels show no important geographic variation over a wide range in western Texas. Specimens from Brownsville are a little larger than typical individuals, and those from Altuda are of minimum size. They inhabit approximately the whole mesquite region or arid Lower Sonoran zone of Texas; are common at Brownsville, Rockport, Mason, Colorado, and Gail, in the Pecos Valley north to Roswell, and westward to the Rio Grande and beyond. Wherever the scrubby mesquite tree grows their burrows are sure to be found under its shade, or, if in the open, near enough to it for them to feed on the sweet pods, pieces of which are often seen scattered around their holes. They are strictly 'ground squirrels,' and climb only into low bushes for seeds and fruit, and depend entirely on their burrows for protection. Like most of the smaller ground squirrels of the arid regions, they usually burrow under the edge of a cactus or some low, thorny bush, where they obtain shade and the protection of thorny cover. They apparently do not hibernate, but during the cold weather have the unsquirrel-like habit of closing their burrows and remaining inside. I have caught them in these closed burrows at Del Rio in January and at Dryden on the 9th of May, when my traps were set, as I supposed, for pocket gophers or moles. Also near Rock Springs in July I found closed burrows that I attributed to this species. The habit of closing the entrance of the burrow is unusual in the squirrel family, but may probably be accounted for as a protection against enemies, and especially snakes. Near Rock Springs I took a half-grown squirrel from a bull snake which had killed and just begun to swallow it.

Like other members of the genus, these ground squirrels feed on seeds, grain, fruit, green foliage, lizards, and numerous insects, and often gather around gardens and grain fields, where they do considerable damage in spring by digging up corn, melons, beans, and various sprouting seeds, and, in summer and fall, by feeding on the ripening grain. Specimens examined at Roswell, N. Mex., in June were feeding on about equal proportions of seeds and insects.

27    **Citellus tridecemlineatus texensis** (Merriam).   Texas Ground Squirrel.

This southernmost form of the 13-striped ground squirrel occupies a narrow strip of half prairie country through the middle part of

Texas, where the timber and plains intermingle—from Gainesville and Vernon on the north to Richmond and Port Lavaca on the south. Apparently its range is more or less broken and scattered, although the animal is common in places. A little colony was found at Richmond, and Oberholser saw a mounted specimen at Port Lavaca, said to have been killed near the town, where they were reported as occurring.[a]

In habits, voice, and general appearance they do not differ much from *tridecemlineatus*. They live in the open grassy prairies or around fields and depend on their burrows for shelter and their striped brown coats for protection. They feed largely on grasshoppers and other insects, together with seeds, grain, fruit, green herbage, and flowers.

### Citellus tridecemlineatus pallidus (Allen). Pale Ground Squirrel. 28

The little, pale striped ground squirrel is common in Upper Sonoran zone over the top of the Staked Plains, where it is often seen running through the short grass or standing erect and stake-like at the edge of its burrow. A number of specimens collected in August at Washburn had been feeding mainly on grasshoppers, which were abundant over the plains. A few other insects were noted in the stomachs examined, and one of the spermophiles had been eating the fruit of the small prickly pear (*Opuntia macrorhiza?*), the seeds of which were stored away in his pouches.

### Citellus spilosoma major (Merriam). Large Spotted Ground Squirrel. 29

The spotted spermophiles from Lipscomb, Canadian, Miami, Mobeetie, Colorado, Pecos City, and Monahans, Tex., and Carlsbad, Roswell, and Santa Rosa, N. Mex., agree in their large size and coarse, indistinct spotting with *major* from Albuquerque, N. Mex., but show slight variation with almost every change of soil and surroundings. The foregoing localities, which completely surround the Staked Plains, lie near the junction of Upper and Lower Sonoran zones, but as the species ranges north to Las Animas and Greeley, Colo., it apparently belongs to Upper Sonoran.

These quiet, shy, inconspicuous little ground squirrels live in burrows under the edge of clumps of bushes or on open, grassy plains. Their fine, trilling whistle is often heard from behind a bush or weed patch. I have found their stomachs full of grasshoppers and beetles and their pouches full of seeds of sand bur (*Cenchrus tribuloides*), and have seen little heaps of the empty bur shells scattered about

---

[a] Two specimens recorded by Doctor Allen from Bee County, Tex. (Bul. Am. Mus. Nat. Hist., III, p. 223, 1890), as *Spermophilus tridecemlineatus,* eight years before *texensis* was described, I assume to be referable to this form.

their burrows. Usually they are not sufficiently numerous in agricultural regions to do serious damage in the grain fields.

**Citellus spilosoma marginatus** (Bailey).    Brown Ground Squirrel.

This little brown, sharply spotted ground squirrel is apparently an Upper Sonoran form, living on the dark lava soil of the Davis Mountain plateau. The type was caught in the open valley near Alpine, and others were seen on the mesa at Fort Davis and along the east base of the mountains. Specimens from Valentine, Presidio County, Van Horn, and Toyahvale are referred to the species, though not all are typical. The Toyahvale specimens show some of the characters of *major*.

In no part of their range have we found these spermophiles common, but like other members of the group they are inconspicuous, shy little fellows, rarely heard or seen. They burrow in the open or under the edge of a bush or cactus and usually keep close to their homes. They often live under the dense, spinescent bushes of *Microrhamnus,* which is common in this region.

30  **Citellus spilosoma arens** (Bailey).    Spotted Sand Squirrel.

These little sand-colored ground squirrels are common in the open part of the valley bottom below the town of El Paso, where they make their burrows in the sand banks among scattered bushes of *Atriplex*, *Suaeda*, and mesquite, with little protection from the glaring light and scorching heat of summer. Their coloration is wonderfully protective, and being shy little animals and not very abundant they are rarely seen unless located by their fine bird-like whistle. They seem sensitive to a slight degree of cold and apparently hibernate early in winter, for I could find no trace of them in December about the same holes where I had caught them the previous July. Doctor Fisher found them common in May, but says that a windy day kept them in their burrows.

31  **Citellus spilosoma annectens** (Merriam).    Padre Island Ground Squirrel.

A number of specimens, including the type of *annectens,* were taken by William Lloyd near the two ends of Padre Island, and others by H. P. Attwater on Mustang Island.[a] In August, 1891, Lloyd says they were abundant, but in November, when the island was again visited, only one was seen. Apparently they were keeping mainly in their burrows. He reported them also from the mouth of the Rio Grande and at Rio Grande City, but secured only one specimen on the mainland—on the sandy beach at the mouth of the Rio Grande. He says that they seem to live in the crab burrows and are very shy, but their call note, similar to that of a grass finch, is occasionally heard.

---

[a] Bul. Am. Mus. Nat. Hist., VI, p. 182, 1894.

**Cynomys ludovicianus** (Ord).    Prairie Dog.                    32

The prairie dogs inhabit an area comprising more than one-third of the State of Texas. Their range extends from Henrietta, Fort Belknap, Baird, and Mason west almost to the Rio Grande, north over the Staked Plains and the Pan Handle region, and south to the head draws of Devils River, to 10 miles south of Marathon and 25 miles south of Marfa. While to the northward inhabiting mainly Upper Sonoran zone, in Texas they extend well into the upper edge

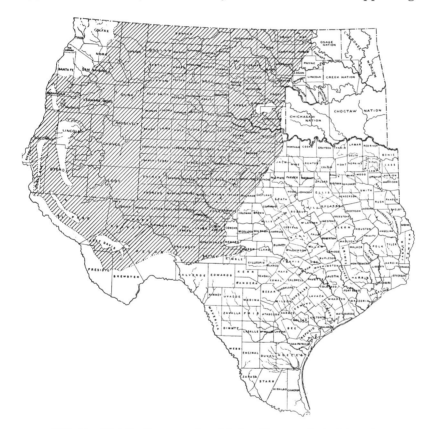

FIG. 14.—Distribution area of prairie dog (*Cynomys ludovicianus*).

of Lower Sonoran. So far as I can learn, they are not found in the immediate valley of the Rio Grande or nearer to the river than Sierra Blanca, except one little colony 2 miles east of Fort Bliss, nor do they occur elsewhere in the Lower Sonoran zone much beyond the scattered traces of Upper Sonoran species of plants. Normally they belong to Upper Sonoran zone, but their strong tendency to expansion carries them slightly beyond its bounds. In the Davis Mountains they range up to 5,800 feet in an open valley on Limpia Creek at a point where the first yellow pines appear, while on the main ridge of the Guadalupe Mountains and in Dog Canyon, which is named for them, they straggle up to 6,900 feet, or to the very upper limit of the Upper Sonoran zone. Usually they are found in scattered colonies or 'dog towns,' varying in extent from a few acres to a few square miles, but over an extensive area lying just east of the Staked Plains they cover the whole country in an almost continuous and thickly inhabited dog town, extending from San Angelo north to Clarendon in a strip approximately 100 miles wide by 250 miles long. Adding to this area of about 25,000 square miles the other areas occupied by them, they cover approximately 90,000 square miles of the State, wholly within the grazing district. It has been roughly estimated that the 25,000 square mile colony contains 400,000,000 prairie dogs.[a] If the remaining 65,000 square miles of their scattered range in the State contains, as seems probable, an equal number, the State of Texas supports 800,000,000 prairie dogs. According to the formula for determining the relative amount of food consumed by animals of different sizes (Yearbook Department of Agriculture, 1901, p. 258), this number of prairie dogs would require as much grass as 3,125,000 cattle.

In many places the prairie dogs are increasing and spreading over new territory, but on most of the ranches they are kept down by the use of poison or bisulphid of carbon, or, better, by a combination of the two. As a Texas cattle ranch usually covers from 10,000 to 100,000 acres, the expense of destroying the prairie dogs in the most economical manner often means an outlay of several thousand dollars to begin with and a considerable sum each year to keep them down.[b]

The increase of prairie dogs is plainly due to the destruction of their natural enemies, badgers, coyotes, foxes, ferrets, hawks, eagles, owls, and snakes, many of which are destroyed wantonly.

The prairie dog is a plump, short-eared, short-legged, short-tailed little animal of the squirrel family, cleanly in habits, good-natured, and eminently social in disposition. If there are only a dozen in a big valley they will be located on an acre of ground where they can visit back and forth among the burrows, play or fight, and take turns in standing guard. If there are thousands of them their burrows will be found close together over the plain to the edge of the 'dog town,' beyond which none will be seen for perhaps 10 or 20 miles. On a trip from San Angelo north over the Staked Plains we were with them for weeks, both in the region of their continuous range and among

---

[a] Yearbook U. S. Department of Agriculture, 1901. p. 258.

[b] For methods of destroying prairie dogs see 'The Prairie Dog of the Great Plains,' by C. Hart Merriam (Yearbook U. S. Department of Agriculture, 1901, pp. 257-270), and 'Destroying Prairie Dogs and Pocket Gophers,' by D. E. Lantz (Bul. 116, Experiment Station, Kansas State Agricultural College, Manhattan, Kans.).

scattered colonies. In places they were comparatively tame, and would sometimes let us drive within 20 feet, and even then they would not go entirely down their burrows. From a distance they could be seen watching us. A few were always sitting on top of their mounds barking an alarm, but on our nearer approach all scampered for the nearest burrows, while those farther ahead took up the alarm. When once half within the funnel-shaped entrance of the burrow the courage of the prairie dog revives, and with hands braced across the doorway, and with erect, flipping tail, the animal keeps up a steady barking at the intruder, sinking lower and lower, until finally with a quick dive, a shrill chatter, and a farewell twinkle of the tail, it vanishes down the hole. Frequently when you reach the burrow the animal can still be heard sputtering and chuckling deep down in the earth, and when once driven into its hole it does not soon reappear. It takes no little patience to await an hour or more the reappearance of the little black eye that cautiously peeps over the rim to see if the coast is clear.

Promptly with the rising sun the prairie dogs come out for their breakfasts, at which time a 'dog town' is as animated as any metropolis, but with the setting sun they retire to their burrows. Breakfast lasts for a good share of the day, with intermissions for work and play and a good long midday nap. There are always burrows to be dug deeper or new ones to be started, rims to be built higher, and in damp weather the crater-like mounds to be molded. Immediately after a shower, often before the last drops have fallen, the prairie dogs are out scraping up damp earth on the rim around the burrow and pressing the funnel-shaped inside into proper form with their stubby noses. In this way an effectual dike, sometimes a foot or two in height, is formed around the entrance of the burrow. But during a cloud-burst I have stood in a dog town and seen all of the burrows with rims not over 6 inches high fill with water; and in the track of an unusually violent downpour have seen the bodies of dozens of drowned prairie dogs scattered along the gulches.

The food of the prairie dog is mainly grass. Not only are the leaves and stems eaten, but the roots are dug up until the circles of bare ground around the burrows become wider and wider. Many other plants, some seeds, and a few insects are eaten, but to a less extent than grass. After a long season of drought or a succession of dry years it often happens that every green thing is exterminated in a prairie-dog town and the animals are forced to move on to new pastures. In a dry season I have ridden over long stretches of barren and deserted dog towns; and, again, after a year of abundant rain, have found this same ground growing up to worthless weeds, or, if to grass, only to the equally worthless foxtail.

In autumn the prairie dogs become fat, but in Texas they do not regularly hibernate as they do to some extent in the North. If their fur should become fashionable, or roast prairie dog an epicurean dish, the problem of keeping them in check would be settled, and there is no reason, save their name, for not counting them, properly prepared and cooked, a delicacy. While owing their name to a chirping or 'barking' note of warning, they are in reality a big, plump, burrowing squirrel of irreproachable habits as regards food and cleanliness. An old stage driver expressed the idea in graphic words one day: "If them things was called by their right name there would not be one left in this country. They are just as good as squirrel and I don't believe they are any relation to dogs."

33   **Mus musculus** Linn.   House Mouse.

Common house mice are found practically over all the settled part of Texas, even at most of the isolated ranches at a distance from railroads and towns. They were caught at deserted adobe cabins in the Great Bend of the Rio Grande, 100 miles south of the Southern Pacific Railroad. They are by no means confined to houses and outbuildings, but over much of the country have become established in the fields, meadows, hedgerows, and weed patches, from which they collect in the stacks of hay and grain, and are ready to attack each crop as it matures.

34   **Mus norvegicus** Erxl.   Wharf Rat.[a] Brown Rat.

Wharf rats are common in most of the towns of Texas and on some of the ranches, but they are not so generally distributed in thinly settled regions as the house mouse, nor do they take so readily to the fields and country. In the years 1889 and 1890 there were reports of swarms of rats overrunning parts of the State, but the species are uncertain, nor is it known whether the wharf rat was one of them. At Seguin, Guadalupe County, in November, 1904, I found wharf rats in great abundance around farm buildings and along fences and weedy borders of fields, wherever sufficient cover was offered. Their runways and burrows resembled those of the cotton rats, but were larger and did not extend so far out from cover. Along the edge of a cornfield numerous cobs were scattered under the fence, where the corn had been eaten off. In Mr. Neel's tomato patch the ripe tomatoes were being rapidly devoured, and I caught a rat in the midst of the patch by using a ripe tomato for bait.

---

[a] *Mus rattus* Linn. Black Rat. A black rat collected by Lloyd at Brownsville proves to be a melanistic *Mus norvegicus,* closely resembling *M. rattus* in color. I find no specimens or records of the latter species from Texas, but as it is found farther east and west it undoubtedly will be taken in the State.

**Mus alexandrinus** Geoffroy. Roof Rat.  35

Two specimens of the roof rat, caught in July, 1902, on the Guadalupe River, at Ingram, Kerr County, constitute, so far as I can learn, the second record of the species for the State. It seemed strange to find this exotic mammal, which is usually found near the coast, so far in the interior of a thinly settled country, but the explanation is simple. The Guadalupe River is subject to violent floods, sometimes rising suddenly to 50 feet above low water. The enormous heaps of drift rubbish deposited along the bottoms and in the branches of trees have evidently furnished a highway for the distribution of the rats from the coast up the river. The two individuals secured were living in these drift heaps and were caught in traps set for *Neotoma attwateri*. One was caught on the ground at the edge of a drift heap; the other on a pole reaching across from one heap to another. A specimen reported by H. P. Attwater in 1894 was caught on a boat that made trips between St. Charles Peninsula and Rockport, and was said to have been on the boat about a year.[a]

**Onychomys longipes** Merriam. Texas Grasshopper Mouse.  36

This large dull-colored form of the grasshopper mouse occupies the semiarid Lower Sonoran zone of southern Texas, and, so far as known at present, reaches its eastern limit at Rockport, its northern limit at San Angelo, and its western limit at Comstock and Sycamore Creek, and extends south of Brownsville into Mexico. As it occupies so much of the brushy, half-open cactus and mesquite country, its apparent absence from the region of San Antonio and Austin and north to the Red River on the east side of the Staked Plains is probably due to the fact that this strip of country has not been thoroughly worked. Unlike most species of *Onychomys, longipes* inhabits weedy, grassy, brushy land, and specimens are found in the woods as well as the open. It is strictly nocturnal, and its shrill little whistle is often heard not far from our camp fires in the evening.

**Onychomys leucogaster pallescens** Merriam. Pale Grasshopper Mouse.

Throughout most of its range this pale, plains form of the grasshopper mouse is found in the Upper Sonoran zone and crowding into the edge of both Transition and Lower Sonoran. In Texas it extends over the Staked Plains, meeting or overlapping the range of *torridus* in the Pecos Valley at Monahans and Fort Lancaster, Tex., and Carlsbad, N. Mex. Specimens examined from Lipscomb, Texline, Miami, Mobeetie, Washburn, Amarillo, and Hereford are fairly typical *pallescens,* and one specimen from Fort Lancaster, not fully adult, is referable to *pallescens* rather than *longipes*.

At Texline, Howell caught a series of 12 specimens in the valley of a small dry creek, where he found that they preferred sandy soil

[a] Bul. Am. Mus. Nat. Hist., VI, p. 174, 1894.

with a good growth of sagebrush (*Artemisia filifolia*). They make few holes, though two were taken at the mouths of small burrows. A turtle ate the head of one specimen and a rattlesnake tried to swallow another, but was prevented by the trap.

Throughout a wide range these little animals live on the short-grass plains or in the sagebrush country, and are caught at all sorts of burrows, an old badger, prairie-dog, or spermophile hole being a favorite resort, probably on account of the insects to be found within. They are strictly nocturnal, and while never seen by daylight, their long-drawn, fine whistle is often heard in the grass between dusk and early dawn. The morning round of a line of traps usually reveals one or more specimens that have been attracted by the oatmeal bait, and just as often shows some half-eaten *Perognathus, Peromyscus,* kangaroo rat, or other small rodent that happened to be in the trap when this forager came along. The *Onychomys* stomachs usually contain, besides finely chewed seeds and grain, an interesting assortment of grasshoppers, crickets, beetles, scorpions, and small insects, and occasionally parts of a lizard or mouse.

37  **Onychomys torridus** (Coues).   Arizona Grasshopper Mouse.

> *Onychomys torridus arenicola* Mearns. Proc. U. S. Nat. Mus., XIX, Advance Sheet, May 25, 1896, p. 3. Type from El Paso.[a]

These little long-tailed grasshopper mice occupy the arid Lower Sonoran zone of western Texas from El Paso to near the mouth of the Pecos, and up the Pecos Valley to old Fort Lancaster and Mona-hans, and Carlsbad, N. Mex. They are found on the open, barren mesas among stones and cactus and the characteristic desert vegetation, or in the sandy mesquite bottoms of the Rio Grande and Pecos rivers. Like all the genus they are strictly nocturnal, and while prowling about at night get into traps set at the burrows of various other mammals. About all that we know of their habits is gained from examination of their stomachs, which usually contain, besides a small portion of seeds or grain, a larger share of scorpions, grasshoppers, crickets, beetles, and various other insects.

38/39  **Peromyscus leucopus** (Rafinesque).   White-footed Mouse.

The dark-colored *Peromyscus* from the coast region of south-eastern Texas, while not quite typical *leucopus,* seems to be nearer to it than to *mearnsi.* There are specimens from near Alvin, near Galveston, Velasco, Elliott, Arcadia, Matagorda, Deming Station, and east Carancahua Creek. To the west apparently it grades into

---

[a] Specimens in the Biological Survey collection from El Paso, Sierra Blanca, Marfa, and Alpine do not differ so far as I can see from the type of *torridus* and from specimens taken around the type locality, when corresponding pelages are compared. It is a little, dark, richly colored species, becoming pale in late winter and spring. Neither in the dimensions nor in the skulls can I find any character by which to recognize the subspecies *arenicola.*

*mearnsi,* while immature specimens from Gainesville, Decatur, and Benbrook suggest intergradation with the same form.

Lloyd reports these mice at Deming Bridge, Matagorda County, "as found only where a quantity of brush had been cut down to fill a gap in the road." Near Matagorda he says "they live in trees, both in nests in the moss and in hollows in the roots." At Velasco he records one from "edge of creek" and another from "edge of old field." At Austin Bayou, near Alvin, he collected an old female containing 4 fully grown embryos, March 17, 1892. Beyond these fragmentary notes by Lloyd nothing is known of the habits of the species in this region, where apparently it inhabits the timbered and brushy bottoms with the palmetto and Spanish moss.

**Peromyscus leucopus texanus** (Woodhouse).   Texas White-footed     40
   Mouse.

> *Peromyscus tornillo* Mearns. Proc. U. S. Nat. Mus., Vol. XVIII, Advance Sheet,
>    March 25, 1896, p. 3. Type from Rio Grande 6 miles above El Paso, Tex.

This is a common species over the arid Lower Sonoran zone of western Texas from El Paso to Del Rio, Rock Springs, and Fort Lancaster. To the south it grades into *mearnsi.* Specimens from Del Rio, Rock Springs, and San Antonio are not typical of either animal, but combine enough of the characters of both to be considered fairly intermediate. A series of 11 specimens from Lipscomb, 4 from Canadian, 2 from Miami, and 3 from Mobeetie, on the plains of the northern Panhandle, and one from Henrietta, while not typical *texanus,* can be referred to it better than to *leucopus.*

In this arid region these mice take the place of *leucopus* and other members of the *leucopus* group, to which they belong. They have the general habits of the group and in places live among rocks, but more often on the weedy and brushy bottoms under rubbish or dense vegetation, where they are often the most abundant mammal. At El Paso and Juarez, Loring says: "Common on both sides of the river. They were caught in traps set at holes and in the brush along irrigation ditches and baited with oatmeal and small pieces of meat." At Sierra Blanca I found them only in an old *Neotoma* house in a bunch of yuccas in the open valley, while *eremicus* occupied the nearest cliffs and the little *blandus* lived out on the open plain. At Fort Lancaster Oberholser reported them as "abundant in the chaparral," and at Langtry as "not common." The two specimens taken at Langtry were caught under logs and among dead leaves and rubbish near water in a deep side canyon. At Del Rio I found them common in holes in the creek bank, under thick brush, and in old houses; and Gaut collected two specimens "in high grass along the main irrigation ditch west of town."

At Lipscomb Howell took specimens only "in brushy places along the creek bottoms." At Canadian he caught one "in the grass along an irrigation ditch" and another "in a deserted cabin." At Miami he caught two "in the rocky bluffs near town and one on the sandy bottoms," and at Mobeetie others "along the sandy creek bottoms in traps set for *Perognathus* and *Perodipus.*"

Like other members of the genus, they are strictly nocturnal, and during the day keep safely within their burrows in the ground or in some other dark retreat. As a result they are almost never seen alive except when they get their tails instead of their necks in our traps. Very little is known of the habits of this species.

### Peromyscus leucopus mearnsi (Allen).    Mearns White-footed Mouse.

*Peromyscus canus* Mearns. Proc. U. S. Nat. Mus., Vol. XVIII, Advance Sheet, March 25, 1896, p. 3. Type from Fort Clark, Tex.

The Mearns white-footed mouse ranges over southern Texas from Brownsville north to Eagle Pass, Fort Clark, and San Antonio, and east to Rockport, grading into *leucopus* on the east and *texanus* along its northern boundary. There is certainly not room for an intermediate form between *texanus* and *mearnsi,* which *canus* proves to be.

The region inhabited by *mearnsi* is semiarid chaparral and cactus plains in Lower Sonoran zone. At Brownsville, the type locality of the species, Lloyd collected a large series of specimens and reported the species as "very common out to the sand belt." He also caught a few on Padre Island and around Nueces Bay. Another series was collected at Brownsville by Loring, who says of the mice: "Quite common. Found in the willows along the river bank and under logs and brush near the overflows. Several were caught in traps baited with meat." At Hidalgo, Loring says: "They were taken in traps baited with oatmeal and set by hedge fences, cactus beds, and underbrush." In writing of specimens obtained at San Lorenzo Creek and Santa Tomas, Lloyd says: "They prefer an arid region where grass is scant among the cactus." At Corpus Christi the mice were very scarce, and I caught but one in a long line of traps. It was at a hole in the bank just back of the beach. At Beeville Oberholser reports them as "evidently not very common, as all my trapping failed to reveal more than a single individual." At San Diego he says: "This animal does not appear to be more than tolerably common. It lives only in the damp thickets bordering the ponds and water holes in the chaparral; at least my trapping in all kinds of situations failed to reveal its presence anywhere else."

41    **Peromyscus michiganensis pallescens** Allen.    Little Pale Peromyscus.

This pale little mouse is represented in the collection by 9 specimens collected at San Antonio and one from near Alice. The one from Alice was collected by Lloyd 12 miles southwest of the town on open prairie. San Antonio specimens were caught by H. P. Attwater in traps set for harvest mice around brush piles.[a]

**Peromyscus sonoriensis** (Le Conte).　Sonoran Peromyscus.　42

A few specimens of this little *Peromyscus* from Washburn, Tex., seem to be nearer to typical *sonoriensis* than to any of the subspecies in the group. One specimen was caught at a tiny burrow on the short-grass plains, miles from any cover that would conceal even a mouse, and others were caught on the prairie at the edges of fields.

**Peromyscus sonoriensis blandus** Osgood.　Frosted Peromyscus.　43

This pale, silky-haired little mouse is common in western Texas over the rough and arid region between the Pecos and Rio Grande valleys. There are specimens from the Franklin Mountains (15 miles north of El Paso), Sierra Blanca, Valentine, Onion Creek (Presidio County), and Bone Spring (53 miles south of Marathon). All the above localities are in rough country near the junction of Upper and Lower Sonoran zones, where more or less mixture of the two occurs, so that the zonal range of the species is not perfectly determined by them.

Although in a rough country, broadly speaking, these white-footed mice inhabit the smooth spots in the bottoms of open valleys. At Sierra Blanca they were on the broad flats southeast of the station, where the principal vegetation was low, scattered, composite shrubs (*Gutierrezia microcephala?* and *Crassina grandiflora*), among which they burrowed in the mellow soil, and the seeds of which furnished in winter a large share of their food. So far as their own genus was concerned, they held this ground by themselves, the larger *P. texanus* being caught in an old woodrat's nest under a yucca and the long-tailed *P. eremicus* in the nearest cliff of tilted rocks. At Onion Creek they were found living in holes in the soft, level ground of the creek valley, where none of the other species of *Peromyscus* were taken. At Valentine, out in the middle of a big open valley, I caught one of these little fellows under the doorstep of the house where I boarded, on the edge of town, and near Bone Spring, 50 miles south of Marathon, I caught another under a mesquite out in the open valley.

**Peromyscus gossypinus** (Le Conte).　Pine Woods Peromyscus.　44

Specimens of this large, dark-colored *Peromyscus* from Texarkana, Jefferson, Long Lake, Joaquin, Jasper, and Sour Lake, indicate an

---

[a] Bul. Am. Mus. Nat. Hist., VIII,, p. 64, 1896.

extensive range for the species over the timbered region of eastern Texas.

Apparently it is not an abundant species anywhere in this region, and much trapping is necessary to procure a few specimens. At Jefferson Hollister caught two in the woods near Big Cypress Creek, and at Joaquin one under a log on heavily timbered creek bottoms. Oberholser caught one in a canebrake along the Red River at Texarkana, one in heavy woods on the edge of McCracken Lake, near Long Lake, in Anderson County, and several in a cabin and one along a stream in the woods north of Jasper. In the heart of the Big Thicket, 7 miles northeast of Sour Lake, I caught several in and around old tumbledown buildings, and Gaut caught them around old logs and stumps in the woods.

45  **Peromyscus boylei rowleyi** (Allen).   Rowley Peromyscus.

> *Peromyscus boylii penicillatus* Mearns. Proc. U. S. Nat Mus., Vol. XIX, Advance Sheet, May 25, 1896, p. 2. Type from El Paso.

A large series of this big, long-tailed *Peromyscus* from the Franklin and Organ mountains is typical *rowleyi,* as apparently are also six other specimens taken in Dog and McKittrick canyons in the Guadalupe Mountains. In this region and farther north they range throughout Upper Sonoran zone, being closely associated with junipers and nut pines, as well as with rocks and cliffs. In places they follow the cliffs slightly below the junipers, but only where canyon walls offer especially favorable haunts. In the Guadalupe Mountains they range to the upper limits of junipers, where the yellow pines begin on dry, hot slopes at 7,800 feet, and down in the northeast gulches near Carlsbad at the east base of the mountain slope at 3,100 feet. While usually found along cliffs or among rocks, they are often common among junipers, nut pines, and oaks at considerable distance from any rocks. In such places they live in hollow trees or logs or take advantage of any convenient cover. I have occasionally found them curled up in a soft nest in a hollow tree, and have often found a nest that I attributed to this species in a knothole or under a loose layer of bark. At one of our camps on top of the Guadalupe Mountains, in a beautiful orchard-like park of junipers, one took possession of the camp wagon and made its nest among boxes and sacks.

The food of these mice consists largely of juniper berries, or at least the seeds of juniper berries, of which there is usually an abundant supply at all times of the year, but acorns and pine nuts are eaten while they last. The empty shells of seeds and nuts and acorns show the favorite feeding grounds to be under the hollow base or low spreading branches of a juniper.

**Peromyscus boylei laceyi**[a] subsp. nov.    Lacey Peromyscus.                46

> Type from Turtle Creek, Kerr County, Tex. Adult male, No. 92746, U. S.
> National Museum, Biological Survey Coll. Collected by H. P. Attwater, Dec.
> 4, 1897. No. 1372, X Catalogue.

*General characters.*—Size and proportions about as in *rowleyi,* to which it is most nearly related. Color decidedly darker; under surface of tail more grayish.

*Color.*—Adults in winter pelage dull, dark ochraceous, brightening on sides; ankle and upper surface of long hairy tail blackish; lower surface of tail, dusky gray; belly and feet, pure white. Summer pelage, brighter in the rufescent phase; paler in the gray phase; lower surface of tail less grayish.

*Skull* with interpterygoid fossa generally narrower than in either *boylei* or *rowleyi.*

*Measurements.*— Type not measured in the flesh, but the hind foot measures 24 when dry. Average of four topotypes: Total length, 188; tail vertebrae, 97; hind foot, 23.2.

*Skull of type.*—Total length, 28; basioccipital length, 23.3; nasals, 10; zygomatic breadth, 14; width of braincase, 13; mastoid breadth, 12; alveolar length of upper molar series, 4.

This big rufescent species of the group of long-tailed *Peromyscus* inhabits the Upper Sonoran, rocky, juniper-covered hills of Kerr and Edwards counties, the Davis Mountains, and the Chinati Mountains. Specimens from Turtle Creek and Ingram, Rock Springs, the Davis Mountains, Paisano, and the Chinati Mountains show some variation, but may all be included under one name. Three specimens from Ozona and one from Big Springs, at the edge of the plains, are very pale. From *attwateri,* the only similar species with which they are associated, *laceyi* may be easily distinguished by larger size, darker color, black ankle and heel, and gray underside of tail, as also by good cranial characters.

At Lacey's ranch, near Kerrville, I caught them in cliffs and gulches with *attwateri,* without noting any difference in habits or habitat of the two species. At Rock Springs and in the Davis Mountains also they occur with *attwateri,* and apparently have very similar habits. They are largely cliff dwellers, but live also in open woods, on oak and juniper covered ridges, and in brushy gulches. In the central part of the Davis Mountains they were the only species of *Peromyscus* that we found at 5,500 to 6,500 feet in the basalt cliffs and over the timbered slopes, but down near the east base of the mountains Cary caught one specimen in the same cliff with an *attwateri.* Lloyd caught them among the rocks at Paisano and in the

---

[a] Named for Mr. Howard Lacey, at whose ranch the specimens were taken.

Chinati Mountains, 35 miles south of Marfa. At Ozona and Big Springs they were taken in cliffs in the comparatively open country.

47    **Peromyscus attwateri** Allen.    Attwater Peromyscus.

The Attwater peromyscus inhabits the cliffs around the edges of the lower arm of the Staked Plains from Big Springs, Llano, Austin, and Kerrville, west to Comstock and Langtry, and up the Pecos Valley to Fort Lancaster and Sheffield, the cliff and canyon country along the Rio Grande, and at least the lower slopes of the Davis and Chisos mountains, and extends westward into Mexico. Most of these localities are so near the edge of Upper and Lower Sonoran zones that the species might belong to either, except that among the cliffs and canyons it probably gets the cooler temperature of the higher zone.

At Howard Lacey's ranch, near Kerrville, where the type of the species was collected in 1895 by H. P. Attwater, I found these animals abundant in 1899, and caught them in crevices along the cliffs, under logs in the woods, and under fallen grass and weeds on the creek bank in the bottom of the gulch. At Ingram, also near Kerrville, Cary and I caught them in the rocks along the bluffs and under the heaps of flood drift on the river bottoms. At Camp Verde Cary caught a few under rocks and logs. One was taken on the crest of a juniper ridge near Rock Springs; Gordon Donald took one in the cliffs near Devils River Station, and N. Hollister caught a series in a little canyon near Comstock and one in the cliffs of the Rio Grande Canyon 8 miles south of Comstock. Lloyd caught one at the Painted Caves and Gaut collected 12 specimens in the canyons around Langtry. Oberholser caught 5 among the rocks at Fort Lancaster. Cary and Hollister found them in the cliffs along the Pecos Canyon as far up as Sheffield, and Cary took one individual of this species, together with *laceyi,* in a canyon at the east base of the Davis Mountains. In the Chisos Mountains a few were taken in Upper Sonoran zone from 6,000 to 7,000 feet. A small series taken among the rocks at Llano is typical *attwateri,* but a series of 13 specimens collected in the cliffs near Austin, where Oberholser reported them as the commonest small mammal of the locality, is not typical.

48    **Peromyscus eremicus** (Baird).    Desert Peromyscus.

*Peromyscus eremicus arenarius* Mearns. Proc. U. S. Nat. Mus., XIX, Advance Sheet, May 25, 1896, p. 2. Type from El Paso, Tex.

This wide-ranging desert species inhabits the arid Lower Sonoran zone of western Texas from the Pecos Valley to El Paso. Specimens from Comstock and vicinity and from Carlsbad (Eddy), N. Mex., mark the eastern limit of its known range. There are specimens in the Biological Survey collection also from El Paso, Franklin Mountains, Sierra Blanca, Presidio County, Boquillas, Terlingua, 20 miles south of Marathon, Langtry, Painted Caves, and 65 miles northwest of Toyah. The slight variation in specimens from Texas localities does not warrant separation from typical *eremicus* of Fort Yuma, Cal.

At El Paso the species is common in the cliffs just back of town, and at Sierra Blanca two were caught in a cliff near the station. At Lloyd's ranch, in Presidio County, 30 miles south of Marfa, it was common in the cliffs, and a few were taken in cliffs at Terlingua, Boquillas, 20 miles south of Marathon, at Comstock, and along the canyons of the Rio Grande at Langtry and Painted Caves. At Carlsbad, N. Mex., it occupied a limestone cliff near the river with *rowleyi,* which belongs to the zone above, and in this same cliff I caught both *Neotoma micropus* and *albigula,* belonging, respectively, to Lower and Upper Sonoran zones. Of the habits of the desert peromyscus little is known save what our traps reveal of its choice of homes on the dusty rock shelves of cliffs and caverns, where lines of tiny footprints lead to and from cracks and small openings in the rocks. I have never known of its being found away from rocks, and this peculiar habitat may have some connection with the wholly naked sole of the foot.

### Peromyscus taylori (Thomas).    Taylor Baiomys.    49

Specimens of this tiny, short-tailed *Peromyscus* from Brownsville, Beeville, and San Antonio do not show any appreciable variation, and are assumed to be typical *taylori,* as they come from both north and south of San Diego, the type locality of the species.

At Brownsville Loring reported them as "common in weeds and brush and along fences in meadows and a few in small willows near the river;" but Lloyd found them "only in open fields and meadows, where they have very small, round holes." At Beeville Oberholser caught one "at the edge of a clump of *Opuntia engelmanni* in the chaparral." H. P. Attwater collected a series of specimens at Watson's ranch, 15 miles south of San Antonio, and furnished the following interesting notes on their habits:

The specimens sent were taken under a pile of dry weeds and rubbish in an orchard, where the two nests sent were also found. There were several others with them which escaped. The two specimens taken in March were kept alive till May 29. They were fed on sugar-cane seed, oats, corn, and bran. They used to drink water when I put it in the cage, but appeared to do just as well without it. * * *

One of the nests sent was found by Mr. Watson while digging up a small pecan tree in the river bottom near his ranch. The nest was about a foot below the surface of the ground, among the roots of the tree, and several passages led down into the ground below the nest. In one of these holes a number of pecan nuts were found. The nest contained an old female and three half-grown young.[a]

### Peromyscus taylori subater subsp. nov.    Dusky Baiomys.

Type from Bernard Creek near Columbia, Brazoria County, Tex. No. $\frac{3\ 2\ 6\ 1\ 6}{4\ 4\ 5\ 3\ 9}$ ♀ ad., U. S. Survey Nat. Mus., Biological Coll. Collected by Wm. Lloyd Feb. 25, 1892. Original No. 1122.

*Characters.*—Size and proportions of *P. taylori,* but much darker colored. Upper parts blackish or sooty gray, belly buffy.

*Measurements of type.*—Total length, 91; tail, 37; hind foot, 15. Average of 7 topotypes: Total length, 95; tail, 39; hind foot, 14.8.

*Skull of type.*—Basal length, 14.8; nasals, 6.3; zygomatic breadth, 10; mastoid breadth, 8.4; alveolar length of upper molar series, 3.

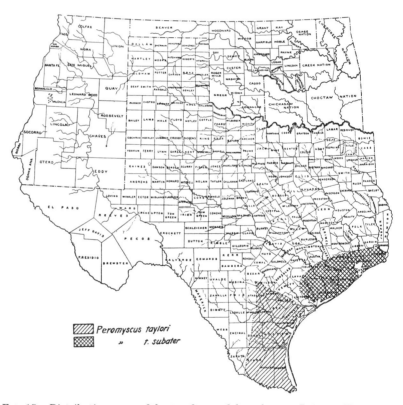

FIG. 15.—Distribution areas of the two forms of the subgenus *Baiomys* (*Peromyscus taylori* and *subater*).

This dusky form of the little *Baiomys* inhabits the coast prairies of Texas east of Matagorda Bay. Specimens from Matagorda, Matagorda Peninsula, Bernard Creek (12 miles west of Columbia), Richmond,

[a] Allen, Mammals of Bexar County, Tex. Bul. Am. Mus. Nat. Hist., VIII, p. 66, 1896.

Virginia Point, Alvin, and Sour Lake are referred to it, although the Matagorda specimens are a little grayer and evidently tend toward *taylori.*

At Virginia Point on the mainland opposite Galveston, I caught two of these little mice in a grassy orchard at a ranch on the broad prairie. They were trapped in the grass-covered runways of sigmodons. At Richmond these mice were fairly common under the rich carpet of grass on the open prairie. Their tiny runways, leading from one little burrow to another, wound about over the surface of the ground among the plant stems and indicated habits so similar to those of *Microtus* that at first I thought I had discovered traces of a diminutive species of that genus. At Sour Lake Hollister collected one specimen "on the open prairie." On Matagorda Peninsula Lloyd found these mice living under logs near the Gulf shore where he collected both old and young. One young, about two weeks old, was found in a nest under a log February 11. In another nest two young were found, and an old female taken the same day contained two fully developed embryos. On the mainland near Matagorda Lloyd "caught them in the long grass skirting the edges of fields," and a nest containing three young was plowed up in the field February 2.

**Oryzomys palustris** (Harlan).    Rice Rat.                                  50

> *Oryzomys palustris texensis* Allen, Bul. Am. Mus. Nat. Hist., VI, p. 177, May 31, 1894. Type from Rockport, Aransas County, Texas.

The rice rats inhabit the coast marshes of Texas as far south as Corpus Christi and a little reef near the north end of Padre Island. Apparently they have not been found farther from the coast than Wharton County, some 40 miles up the Colorado River, and they seem to be common only in the salt marshes. At Port Lavaca, Oberholser says, "they are common in the tall grass bordering the bayous and are apparently confined to such places. The ground where they live is quite wet, but still out of reach of ordinary tides, though the whole area was flooded during part of my stay. The runways are not covered and not plain, though there are usually fresh signs at intervals." On Matagorda Island he says the rice rats are "tolerably common in the tufts of coarse grass bordering bayous, making conspicuous covered runways where the grass is thickly matted, but are not found more than a short distance back from the bayous." At Matagorda Bay, Lloyd says, "they occur along the shore of the bay and also on Selkirk Island and Peninsula, where they were found in the high, rank grass near the shore;" and at Nueces Bay, he says, "they are common out in the low grass on the marshes, where they take to water readily. Several were found drowned while held down by my traps. On a small island reef about 100 yards off the north end of Padre Island they were found in patches of marsh 'cranberry.' Two of their round cup-shaped nests, composed of fine rootlets, were found under old boards." At Virginia Point, opposite Galveston, I caught them in runways under the grass and rushes along the edge of the salt marsh. At that time, in April, they were rather scarce, but the people say that occasionally they become very numerous, especially in and around the rice fields.

51 **Oryzomys aquaticus** Allen. Rio Grande Rice Rat.

This species is known only from the vicinity of Brownsville, near the mouth of the Rio Grande.

Loring reported it as common in grassy spots in the mesquite brush.

52 **Reithrodontomys intermedius** Allen. Rio Grande Harvest Mouse.

*Reithrodontomys laceyi*[a] Allen, Bul. Am. Mus. Nat. Hist., VIII. p. 235, Nov. 21, 1896. Type from Watson's ranch, 15 miles south of San Antonio, Tex.

This long-tailed harvest mouse inhabits the Lower Sonoran zone of southern Texas from Brownsville to Corpus Christi, San Antonio, Kerr County, and Del Rio, and extends south into Mexico.

At Brownsville Loring reported that he caught several specimens of this species in traps baited with meat and set among small willows, weeds, and high grass near the river. At Del Rio I caught them at little burrows on the brushy flats, and near Kerrville found them common around fields and in weedy places generally and caught them at burrows and runways under the fallen grass. Lloyd reported one found on Padre Island in an old cow's horn, and two dead ones in an old barrel. Between Laredo and Rio Grande City he reported two as living in old nests of the cactus wren, and near Corpus Christi he found one in a nest in a catsclaw bush. In April, 1900, I found what looked like an old verdin's nest in a bush of *Momesia pallida* near Corpus Christi. The nest was about 4 feet from the ground, a globular structure of grass, lichen, and short gray moss (*Tillandsia recurvata*), with a small opening at one side. As I touched the side, two black eyes appeared at the doorway, but after watching me for a moment were withdrawn. At a slight shake of the

---

[a] Specimens of *Reithrodontomys laceyi* from San Antonio and Kerr County agree perfectly with specimens of comparable age and pelage from Brownsville, Matamoras, and Santa Tomas, and I see no way but to consider them typical *intermedius*. The slightly smaller and grayer specimens are evidently young of the year. The difference in size indicated by Mr. Attwater's measurements does not appear in comparison of skulls or hind feet and may be due to a slight difference in the methods of measurement. My own measurements of Kerrville specimens and Goldman's of his Matamoras specimens agree almost to a millimeter. While all of the small series of topotypes of *laceyi* can be matched from the large series of *intermedius* from Brownsville, there are none in as bright summer pelage as some specimens in the Brownsville series.

bush, out popped a trim little long-tailed harvest mouse, which sat undecided on the branch for a moment and then ran gracefully along branches and stems from one bush to another and finally down to the ground, where it disappeared in the tall grass. On examining the nest I found a firm base, evidently an old bird's nest that had been arched over with a substantial roof which left an opening at the side only large enough for my finger. It was neither a verdin's nor a cactus wren's nest, and evidently had been built or remodeled by the present tenant. When I returned the next day, the mouse was at home, but so sleepy that I merely disturbed him enough to make him come out and sit for a moment on the branch, after which I withdrew and let him go back to finish his nap. Further search revealed two more similar but old and unoccupied nests in the bushes near by, but no trace of runway, burrow, or other signs of the mice on the damp sticky soil beneath. A good line of traps set among the bushes and under the adjoining prairie grass remained untouched until the bait grew moldy. Even at the base of the bush under the occupied nest nothing was caught in several days' trapping and after a trip of two weeks I returned to find the little fellow still occupying his nest.

Along the Medina River 15 miles south of San Antonio, Mr. H. P. Attwater says he occasionally came across these mice in 1889 and 1890 while hunting for birds' nests. He says they were found singly in the daytime in little round nests made of grass and placed in the lower branches of small trees.[a]

**Reithrodontomys aurantius** Allen. Louisiana Harvest Mouse.                          53

This largest and richest colored of the Texas harvest mice inhabits eastern Texas, and extends along the coast region as far west as Matagorda Bay, and in the interior north to Hempstead, Nacogdoches, Joaquin, and Texarkana. There is every reason to suppose that it inhabits the whole of eastern humid Texas, as usually it is not an abundant or easily captured species and is often overlooked by collectors. At Texarkana Oberholser caught one and reported the species as rare about thickets on the edge of cleared ground. Hollister caught several at Joaquin on grassy ground along the railroad and at the edge of a cotton field, and at Sour Lake a few in tall grass at the edge of the woods. At Hempstead Gaut caught them in brushy woods between cultivated fields. In southern Louisiana I found them in runways among weeds and tall grass on low ground at Iowa Station, and caught one in a trap where an *Oryzomys* was caught the preceding night. In Matagorda County, Lloyd reported

---

[a] Mammals of Bexar County, Tex., J. A. Allen, Bul. Am. Mus. Nat. Hist., VIII, pp. 66-67, 1896. For further interesting notes on habits of this harvest mouse in Bexar County by H. P. Attwater, see also page 236, same volume.

them under old logs and in low brush, where numerous nests were seen with holes leading into the ground beside them. He called this species the "tree mouse," but does not speak of any nests in bushes or anywhere except on the ground. At Hempstead, Gaut caught a few in traps set at the bases of trees in a brier thicket between two cultivated fields, and in the Big Thicket, northeast of Sour Lake, he reports it as the most abundant mouse, living under the dead grass wherever there was dry ground.

54  **Reithrodontomys megalotis** (Baird).   Big-eared Harvest Mouse.

This pale, desert harvest mouse comes into western Texas between the Rio Grande and the Pecos, as shown by specimens from Fort Stockton, Pecos City, Alpine, and the southern parts of the Guadalupe and the Franklin mountains.

Cary secured a single specimen on the grassy plain 25 miles west of Fort Stockton, and another under matted grass near a flowing well at Pecos City, but was unable to catch any more in either locality. Gaut caught one in a patch of high grass about two miles north of Alpine, and another on a grassy flat in the foothills of the Franklin Mountains, 15 miles north of El Paso, at 4,400 feet. One was caught in a *Microtus* runway at 8,400 feet altitude on top of the ridge at the head of Dog Canyon in the Guadalupe Mountains. It was among grass, shin oak, and other low brush, and in a most unexpected locality for a *Reithrodontomys*. No other specimens were secured, although considerable trapping was done in the vicinity.

55  **Reithrodontomys merriami** Allen.   Merriam Harvest Mouse.

This little dusky harvest mouse, the smallest species in the State, inhabits the coast prairies of southeastern Texas west to Richmond, but apparently is nowhere common. Near Richmond I caught two under the grass on the open prairie in the same runways where *Peromyscus taylori subater* was caught. Both of these specimens while in the traps were eaten by some other mouse, so that only the skull of one and the ragged skin of the other could be saved. At Austin Bayou, Lloyd caught the species in "rank grass on the prairie," and at Lafayette, La., R. J. Thompson caught one in "tall meadow grass on the prairie."

56  **Reithrodontomys griseus** sp. nov.   Little Gray Harvest Mouse.

Type from San Antonio, Tex., No. 87852, ♂ ad., U. S. Nat. Mus., Biological Survey Coll. Collected March 4, 1897, by H. P. Attwater. Collector's number 1068 (X Catalogue No. 371).

*General characters.*—Size small, tail short and sharply bicolor; color buffy gray with indistinct dorsal streak of dusky; brain case short and wide.

*Color.*—Upper parts dark buffy gray, darkened especially along the dorsal line with black tipped hairs; ear with a large black spot on upper outer surface and another on lower inner; feet and whole lower parts white; tail white with a narrow blackish line above.

*Cranial characters.*—Compared with that of *merriami,* the geographically nearest neighbor in the group, the skull is larger with relatively lower, shorter, wider brain case, and flattened instead of circular foramen magnum, smaller bullae, and wider basioccipital. From *albescens* it differs as from *merriami* in relatively shorter, wider brain case.

*Measurements.*—Type: Total length, 120; tail vertebrae, 56; hind foot, 14.5 (15 measured dry). Average of six adult males from type locality measured by H. P. Attwater: Total length, 114; tail vertebrae, 55; hind foot, 14.6.

*Skull of type.*—Occipitonasal length, 19.2; basal length, 16; nasals, 7; zygomatic breadth, 10.4; mastoid breadth, 9; greatest breadth of brain case, 9.8; interorbital constriction, 3.

*Distribution.*—Specimens examined from San Antonio, Mason, San Angelo, Clyde, and Gainesville, Tex., indicate a rather unusual distribution along the eastern edge of the plains. At San Angelo, Oberholser caught one at a hole in the grassy margin of a cultivated field; at Clyde, Cary caught one in a patch of sand burs in the corner of a sandy cotton field. Another specimen was taken at Gainesville on open prairie, but in all of these localities they seemed to be extremely scarce.

*Remarks.*—The present species holds its characters with surprisingly little variation over an extensive area from San Antonio north to southeastern Nebraska, where, if it grades into *albescens* as seems probable, it must do so entirely between London and Neligh in that State. The smaller, darker *merriami* shows no variation throughout a wide range over the coast prairies of Texas and Louisiana, and if it grades into *griseus* the complete transition must occur between Richmond and San Antonio.

**Neotoma floridana rubida** Bangs.    Swamp Wood Rat.

The common wood rats throughout the Big Thicket of eastern Texas are typical *rubida* of southern Louisiana, while a specimen from Texarkana possibly indicates a shading toward *baileyi.* The Big Thicket is a continuation of southern Louisiana swamp country, extending into Texas from the lower Sabine west to the San Jacinto and marking the western limit of range of many species. Wood rats are well known to settlers throughout its extent. They are reported from near Cleveland and Tarkington in Liberty County and at Bragg and Saratoga in Hardin County, and I found them common in the thickest woods and around old deserted buildings near Dan Griffin's place, 7 miles northeast of Sour Lake. The first one secured was in a house of its own building at the base of an old dead pine. It had piled up pine bark and pieces of rotten wood around the base of the tree to a height of 2 feet, and in the cavities in this mound had made several soft nests of grass and bark fiber. There was a nest also in an old hollow log close by and several holes under a rotten stump not far away. As I tore the house to pieces in search of its builder a gray squirrel ran out of the first nest of grass and bark near the top and rushed up the old dead pine. As I uncovered deeper chambers one was found well filled with white-oak acorns and berries of the cat brier, and a cache of green leaves was safely stored away under a shelf of pine bark. The rat was found in a chamber deeper down near the bottom of the house. When finally uncovered it ran to the hollow log near by, then to the holes under the stump, then back to the house before I got a shot at it. It proved to be an old female, as were two others caught the next night under an old log in an equally dense part of the thicket. No trace of the rats was found except under the protecting cover of dense timber, brush, or vine tangle, or in hollow logs, trees, or old buildings. An old log house where hay was stored was apparently well stocked with them, judging from the stick piles under the floor, tracks in the ashes of the old fireplace, piles of characteristic pellets in the corners, and a familiar wood-rat odor pervading the air. More or less evidence of their presence was noticed in other old buildings.

In the thicket near Saratoga the Flower boys told me that a wild cat (*Lynx*) killed a short time before had been opened and its stomach found to be full of wood rats. The abundance of wild cats and barred owls throughout the Big Thicket probably accounts for the habit of the wood rats of choosing the most impenetrable cover.

At Houma, La., near the type locality of the species, I found these wood rats common in the woods and swamps. Some of the houses were built at the bases of hollow trees, over old logs, or under thick brush mats, but just as commonly they were placed in the lower branches of trees or in vines 10 to 30 feet from the ground. Those in the branches were usually in a fork or on a large limb close to the body of a tree, or in a thick tangle of branchlets and connected with the ground by numerous vines, while those suspended in the vines were globular stick masses from 1 to 4 feet in diameter, worked in among a lot of ascending vine stems or into a snarl of vine branches and resembling magpies' nests. Slender sticks, twigs, and pieces of bark and gray moss formed the main body of these elevated houses, while a hole at one side afforded entrance to the soft nest of bark fiber and moss within. By shaking and jerking the vines I drove the rat out of one of these houses and watched him climb up the vines and branches to near the top of the medium-sized tree, probably 60 feet from the ground. He climbed readily, but not with squirrel-like freedom and speed, and avoided the trunk of the tree. Another that I shook out of a house at the base of a small tree climbed up the vines to the top of the tree, some 20 feet from the ground, but I have never seen one climb the trunk of a large tree. No doubt, however, they could climb a rough-barked trunk. Several of the houses located on the ground were examined and in each was found at least one nest of fine bark or moss in a chamber near the ground. No holes could be found entering the ground below the houses, probably owing to the dampness of the soil, which may also account for the elevated houses in this region. Some stick piles and nests were found in hollow logs, and on the ground inside the shell of an old hollow sycamore stub, that measured $10\frac{1}{2}$ feet across, the rats had built a good-sized house against the wall. Several holes entered the sides of this house, and superficial examination located one snug nest in a back corner. Well-marked trails sometimes were found leading through grass and weeds from one house to another or from a house to the nearest log, tree, or brush heap.

**Neotoma floridana baileyi** Merriam.    Nebraska Wood Rat.                    58

This northernmost form of the *floridana* group of wood rats barely gets into northern Texas. Two specimens in the Merriam collection from Gainesville, Cook County, are best referred to it, although they are a shade darker in color and in this respect intermediate between *baileyi* and *rubida.* As a larger series of specimens from across the line in the Wichita Mountains, Oklahoma, is more nearly typical *baileyi,* it seems necessary to refer the Gainesville specimens also to this species.

*Neotoma baileyi* is a large, pale, bicolor-tailed form of the *floridana* group, extending up the wooded river valleys across the plains country from Texas to northern Nebraska. At Gainesville Mr. G. H. Ragsdale secured a few of the wood rats in wooded ravines, but said they were very scarce. In the Wichita Mountains Gaut found them common from the bases to the tops of the ridges. In the timber along Medicine Creek he occasionally found them in hollow logs or about the overhanging roots of a tree at the edge of a steep creek bank, in houses made of sticks, leaves, bones, and cow chips. Up the steeper slopes of the ridges they were more numerous among the rocks and in crevices of the bluffs. At Valentine, Nebr., where the timber is restricted to the canyons, these rats inhabit the cliffs and caves along the canyon walls, and forage in the brush and timber along the sides and bottoms of the canyons. In fact, over most of the range of the species cliffs, caves, and cut banks furnish the favorite homes. At Marble Cave, Stone County, Mo., I found their tracks in the deepest recesses of the great cave, but found the animals and their stick

houses more common under the shelving limestone ledges along the
sides of the ravines. Three or four of those collected were cooked at
the ranch where I was staying, and we all pronounced them better
than gray squirrels. The meat was very tender and of good flavor,
with no trace of the external musky odor peculiar to wood rats.

**Neotoma floridana attwateri** Mearns.    Attwater Wood Rat.

On the juniper ridges of the southern arm of the Staked Plains
this big buffy-brown wood rat, which appears to be an Upper
Sonoran form of the *floridana* group, lives in a rocky, half-forested
region. It makes its house sometimes among the rocks, piling up its
rubbish in a broken cliff, rock pile, or old stone wall, and sometimes
in the woods at the base of a tree, under a brush pile, in some old
cabin, or along the river in heaps of flood drift.

In company with Mr. Howard Lacey, on his ranch in Kerr County,
I uncovered one of the houses in the corner of an old log cabin where
the rats had built up a pile of rubbish among the fallen logs and
boards. As the material was removed the rat ran out of the nest
into a hollow log, where he was easily caught. The nest on the
ground under the rubbish pile was a bulky mass of soft juniper bark,
with an opening at the side. Above it the spaces between logs and
boards were filled with several bushels of rubbish, including a large
number of cactus thorns. A quantity of green leaves of walnut and
some pieces of green cactus stems were found near the nest, while
scattered acorn and walnut shells, juniper berries, and cactus capsules showed part of the menu of the occupant.

Mr. H. P. Attwater, who first collected this species, tore down
numbers of the houses and found nests in underground burrows as
well as in the rubbish piles. He says:

> In one of the underground passages at the nest on the oak ridge were found
> stored away about three dozen bunches of wild grapes; also many acorns and
> black haws. In another nest in the cedar brake were about two dozen small
> mushrooms, partly dry and shriveled. All the heaps in the cedar brakes con-
> tained large stores of cedar berries, most of them with the outside pulp eaten
> off and the seeds eaten out. When the very small size of the seed is taken into
> consideration, it is surprising what an immense amount of work is necessary
> before enough can be obtained for a meal, as probably a thousand would be
> required. One nest contained shells of nuts of the Mexican buckeye (*Ungnadia
> speciosa*), although these nuts are reputed to be poisonous.[a]

Near Ingram, in the valley of the Guadalupe River, a few of
these wood rats were caught in the cliffs and rocks bordering the
river valley, but they were more common under the great heaps of
driftwood and rubbish along the river bottoms. The Guadalupe, like
many of the Texas rivers, is subject to floods, and in a sudden rise of
sometimes 50 feet great quantities of driftwood are washed into the

---

[a] Bul. Am. Mus. Nat. Hist., 1896, pp. 61-62.

bottoms and left wherever the trees are close enough to hold it. In places among the old cypress trees tons of this driftwood lie in heaps like haystacks, and in and under these the wood rats find ideal homes. They make holes and runways through the heaps, and hollow out cavities for their nests inside. Often instead of making runways they traverse the logs from one heap to another. A favorite place for a nest is in the drift lodged in vines and branches of trees and reached by means of the vines or rough bark. The presence of the rats in these drift piles is easily detected by their peculiar musky odor. In spite of the odor, which apparently comes from the large gland along the skin of the belly, the flesh of the animals is delicious, of good flavor, white, tender, and more delicate than that of the squirrel.

**Neotoma micropus** Baird.　　Baird Wood Rat.[a]　　　　　　　　60

This large, light slaty-gray *Neotoma* inhabits the arid mesquite country of the western half of Texas and the adjoining parts of Mexico, and extends north up the Pecos Valley in New Mexico to at least Santa Rosa, and from central Texas northward across western Oklahoma. Specimens examined from Rockport, San Antonio, Brazos, Seymour, Henrietta, Mobeetie, and Lipscomb mark approximately the eastern limit of the species in the State, as at present known. Judging by the characteristic houses which I found abundant near Wichita Falls, the species ranges east to the western edge of the Upper Cross Timbers, while a few old houses at Tascosa and Logan indicate a continuous range with the low mesquite up the Canadian River and across to Santa Rosa on the Pecos, thus completely encircling the Staked Plains. It is the most abundant and widely distributed of the Texas wood rats. It lives mainly in the half open country and builds houses under mesquites, acacias, zizyphus, allthorn, yuccas, cactus, or anything else sufficiently thorny to prove an effectual protection against its enemies. Rarely it lives among rocks. The favorite building site, however, is in and around a bunch of the big flat blades of the prickly pear (*Opuntia engelmanni*), where the stack of rubbish—cow chips, sticks, bark, leaves, stones, bones, pieces of metal, dishes, leather, rags, or any other available material, well salted with bits of cactus and other thorny things—is often built into a dome 4 or 5 feet high. An allthorn bush is another choice building site, and when the house is largely composed of its rigid angular thorns, well mixed with cactus, a more

[a] The name of black wood rat applied to this species by Professor Baird is as much of a misnomer as its specific name *micropus*. As the species is one of the palest of the genus, I have thought best to change its name to Baird Wood rat. The name 'rat' leads many people to associate with the wharf rats— filthy animals introduced from the Old World and naturalized around our stables and cellars—the wood rats, which belong to a different genus, are natives of America, and animals of exemplary and extremely interesting habits.

bristling and formidable combination can hardly be imagined. Most of the houses, wherever located, are so well protected with thorns that they are rarely molested by the larger mammals, not even by the tough-hided badger. But how the rats can run over these houses and along the trails strewn with cactus spines and never show a scratch on the bare, pink and white soles of their feet is a mystery. One or more nests placed in cavities of the house or in the ground beneath, and entered by openings through the sides or under the edges of the mass of rubbish, are well protected not only from outside enemies, but from occasional violent storms and the glaring heat of the sun. Usually these nests are slight structures of leaves and grass, always kept neat and clean when in use, and quite free from scattered remains of food and excrement. Well-worn trails lead under the brush from one house to another, or away to feeding grounds, or to neighboring rock piles, for the rats seem to be of a social disposition, several usually living together and apparently doing much visiting.

Their food consists of a great variety of green vegetation, especially the juicy flesh of cactus, but mainly of seeds, nuts, and fruit. Cactus fruit and the sweet pods of the mesquite bean are extensively eaten; also acorns, nuts, and any kind of grain within their reach.

At times the wood rats become exceedingly numerous, and their houses appear in every nook and corner of brush, thicket, and cactus patch, while the animals crowd into fields and about ranch buildings, and do some mischief even in a thinly settled stock country. But at such times they attract great numbers of hawks, owls, and other enemies, and after a year or two of unusual abundance they decrease to, and sometimes below, their normal numbers. I have seen a *Parabuteo u. harrisi* come out from under the mesquite with one of this species in its claws, and have found the skulls of large numbers of the rats in and around the nest of this hawk, as well as their flesh and fur in the crop of the bird. The skulls are among the commonest bones recognized in pellets under the cliffs where the great horned owls roost. Being both diurnal and nocturnal, these rats are subject to the attacks of both hawks and owls. Coyotes, foxes, and wild cats catch them whenever opportunity offers, and especially when they are numerous enough to be frequently encountered away from their houses. Snakes are apparently still more deadly enemies, as they enter the holes and houses of the rats and swallow the occupants. Rattlesnakes, bullsnakes, blacksnakes, and whipsnakes are often found in and around the rat houses, and at Comstock, Lloyd opened a rattlesnake and found a wood rat in its stomach. Under ordinary conditions these wood rats are of little economic importance, and will never prove to be a serious pest unless as a result of the destruction of their natural enemies.

                    MAMMALS.

Cary found this species abundant at Monahans, and says:

They usually have their nests in mesquite or zizyphus thickets, but frequently take up their abode in the abandoned burrows of *Dipodomys spectabilis,* where thorny branches in the mouth of the burrow give notice of their presence. Their stores usually consist of mesquite beans. They proved a veritable nuisance by continually getting into our small traps and running off with them. They took a number also of our traps home. So commonly was this done that on missing a trap Donald and I would go to the nearest rat house, where we were almost certain to find it. The people at Monahans, and in fact throughout the region, call them chicken rats on account of their supposed fondness for young chickens.

**Neotoma albigula** Hartley.    White-throated Wood Rat.    61

This wood rat extends into Texas from the west, reaching its eastern limit along the eastern edge of the Staked Plains at Llano, near

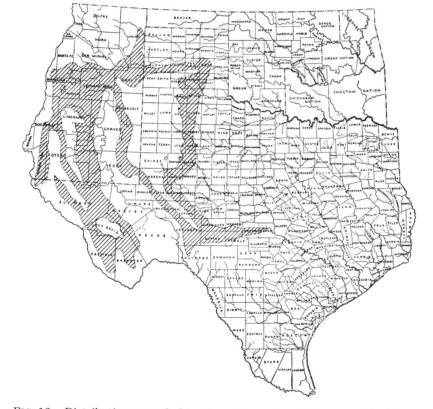

FIG. 16.—Distribution area of white-throated wood rat (*Neotoma albigula*).

Colorado, and in a canyon near Washburn. It apparently belongs to Upper Sonoran zone, but along cliffs and rocky gulches extends into the upper edge of Lower Sonoran, and so slightly overlaps the range of the larger and grayer *micropus*. Both species occur side by side at El Paso, Sierra Blanca, Kent, Stanton, and Colorado, and in Presidio County, Tex., and at Carlsbad, N. Mex., but each retains its distinctive characters and habits, *micropus* living mainly in its stick houses in the brush, and *albigula* always keeping among the rocks along cliffs and gulches. In a few cases I have caught *micropus* in the rocks, but have never found *albigula* away from them. Being a cliff dweller, its houses are largely provided by nature, and a few sticks, chips, and stones piled among the rocks in addition are often all that seems to be required, but sometimes these accumulations of rubbish in a favorite and long-inhabited den amount to 20 or 30 bushels. The doorways are usually plainly indicated by scattered remains of food and various unmistakable signs. A strong musky odor characteristic of the genus is the usual indication that the dens are inhabited.

I have never known this species to become very abundant or very troublesome. It sometimes enters houses and barns located near the rocks and does a little mischief, but is easily caught in traps. Along its native cliffs and canyon walls it is the especial prey of *Lynx, Urocyon,* and *Bassariscus,* which, with the owls, keep its ranks thinned until in many places few are left.

The remains of food scattered about the dens show a varied taste for fruit, seeds, and green things, and usually include pieces of cactus stems and fruit, mesquite, acacia, and other leguminous pods, juniper berries, acorns, and various seeds, green foliage, and flowers.

62  **Neotoma mexicana** Baird.   Mexican Wood Rat.

This little dark-colored wood rat is the smallest of the species occurring in Texas, and, being mainly a Transition zone animal, has but a limited distribution in the State. It is common in the upper parts of the Davis and Guadalupe mountains, and probably occurs also high up in the Chisos Mountains, where we found old signs but failed to get specimens. In the Davis and Guadalupe mountains it lives in the rocks and cliffs where the junipers and yellow pines are mixed, and also ranges to the very tops of the mountains, where Transition species predominate. In habits it does not differ materially from *albigula,* or any of the rock-dwelling species. Its food seems to be largely acorns and the sweet berries of *Juniperus pachyphlœa.*

63  **Sigmodon hispidus texianus** (Aud. & Bach.).   Texas Cotton Rat.

The cotton rats of the eastern half of Texas, while lacking the rich brown color of true *hispidus* of the Atlantic coast, are distinctly darker and more brownish gray than those of western Texas. Specimens from Gainesville, Vernon, Richmond (on the west bank of the

OCT., 1905.]                    MAMMALS.                    115

Brazos), Sour Lake, Port Lavaca, Seguin, and San Antonio are fairly typical, although they become slightly paler at San Antonio. Along the Gulf coast and lower Rio Grande they become still paler without reaching the extreme of the light gray *berlandieri*.

Although not often seen the cotton rats are usually common, and at times they become excessively numerous, living under cover of tall grass and weeds, in meadows, around the edges of fields, and along the banks of streams and ditches. They live in bulky nests of grass

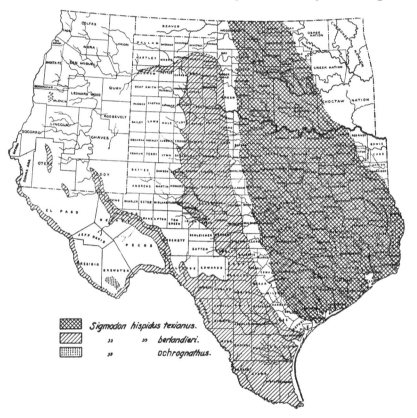

FIG. 17.—Distribution areas of cotton rats (genus *Sigmodon*).

on the surface or in underground burrows, and make numerous long runways under cover of fallen grass and dense vegetation. Apparently they breed rapidly. Gaut records a female containing 8 embryos. For food they cut the green stems of grass and various plants along their runways—eating stems, leaves, and seeds—and along the edges of grain fields they gather to feed on both green and ripening grain. The amount of damage they do depends on their abundance and the kind of crop attacked.

Near Seguin, in November, 1904, I found the cotton rats numerous around fields, in grass patches, under brush heaps and fallen weeds, in the mesquite woods, and in fact everywhere that any cover or concealment could be found. Thickets of thorny chaparral and bunches of cactus offered the most perfect protection, and even at midday the animals often were seen running about under the prickly pear. A network of their runways covers the surface of the ground and connects the numerous burrows wherever protecting cover is offered. Along the edges of cotton fields they are especially numerous, and the runways opening into the fields are often fairly lined with cotton that has been pulled from the bolls and dragged under cover where the seeds can be eaten in safety. Some cotton minus its seeds is also found scattered over the ground near the edges of fields where the animals are abundant, and a smaller amount is carried away for nests. The loss of cotton is not great in any one field, but considered over the entire range of this group of cotton rats, which coincides in a general way with the cotton-producing area of the United States and Mexico, it is considerable.

A simple and effective remedy would be to clean out the borders of fields by burning the weeds, grass, and rubbish accumulating along the fences year after year as a harbor for various rodent and insect pests and a perennial source of supply of weed seeds. If these borders were burned yearly, mowed and raked, treated with oil or chemicals to prevent weed growth, closely pastured, or thoroughly cultivated, the hawks and owls would quickly dispose of the rodents, which would then have no protecting cover. Marsh hawks are abundant and constantly skim over the fields, frequently diving into the grass. Harris hawks sit on the mesquite trees and telegraph poles watching the ground below; sparrow hawks sit on the fence posts, and barred owls are heard hooting every evening from the moss laden live oaks. There is no lack of enemies eager to prey on the rodents, and no simpler way of reducing the number of such pests than by the aid of their natural enemies.

As is the case with rabbits, and many other species of rodents, the abundance of the cotton rats varies greatly with the different localities during the same year, and with different years in the same locality. At times they are extremely scarce over extensive areas, and again so numerous as to suggest the plagues of voles that from time to time have overrun parts of Europe. Mr. H. P. Attwater describes one of their invasions, and the enemies that attacked them, as follows:

In the year 1889, Sigmodons appeared suddenly in this [Bexar] county in great numbers, and were known as "tramp rats." Where they came from, or from which direction, I have been unable to find out. Thousands first appeared about the 1st of May, and were heard from in all the region for many miles around San Antonio. They were most numerous in the high, dry parts of the country, and were not noticed in the lowlands along the rivers. They were very numerous all through the "chaparral," and made their nests with the wood rats (*Neotoma*) in the bunches of *Opuntia,* with a network of runways leading in every direction, through which they were often seen running in the daytime. They seemed to agree with the wood rats, but in the oat stacks and around the ranch buildings the common brown rats fought, killed, and ate them. Mr. Watson's boys killed over 100 in one afternoon in a brush fence, and for several months their cat used to bring in from 6 to 12 every night. He says that on one occasion, when the rats were thickest, they counted 38 which this cat in one night had piled up in the wood box for the amusement of her kittens.

The "tramp rats" played particular havoc with all kinds of grain crops, and corn in particular, but they were not good climbers, and consequently the ears on leaning stalks suffered most. Some farmers lost half their corn crop, and in some instances small patches were entirely destroyed.

During the winter of 1889 and 1890 marsh hawks were very numerous, no doubt attracted by the rats. The hawks were seen skimming over the fields in the daytime chasing the "tramps." In 1890 and 1891 short-eared owls, on their way north in the month of March, stopped over to attend to the Sigmodons; in other years I have not noticed these owls during migration. Weasels and little striped skunks were much more common than usual in 1890 and 1891, which I attribute to the same cause. Rattlesnakes and other snakes were seldom seen abroad, and when disturbed in their retreats were found gorged with cotton rats. The large skunks and coyotes hunted them, and dogs, generally in the habit of killing rats and mice and shaking them, also ate them.

The bulk of these rats stayed for about eighteen months. After the crops were gathered in 1890 they began to get scarce, and gradually disappeared during 1891. Whether they died out or "tramped" out I am unable to say, but I am inclined to think many of them migrated. Old settlers say they remember a similar invasion about the year 1854.[a]

### Sigmodon hispidus berlandieri Baird.   Berlandier Cotton Rat.   64

*Sigmodon hispidus pallidus* Mearns, Proc. U. S. Nat. Mus., XX. Advance Sheet, March 15, 1897, p. 4. Type from 6 miles above El Paso, Tex.

This pale-gray form of the cotton rat inhabits the desert region of eastern Mexico and western Texas along the Rio Grande and Pecos valleys. East of the Pecos Valley it grades into *texianus* so gradually that no dividing line can be drawn.

The habits of this species do not differ from those of *texianus,* except in so far as modified by the character of the arid desert country in which it lives. The rats find suitable food and cover mainly along the more fertile stream valleys or in the irrigated sections, where they usually live under the fallen grass, canes, weeds, or brush, and they eagerly gather in fields of growing grain or alfalfa. Their burrows often perforate the banks of creeks and irrigation ditches, but their nests are found also on the surface of the ground, scattered through the fields and over the level bottoms.

[a] Quoted by J. A. Allen, Mammals of Bexar County, Tex.: Bul. Am. Mus. Nat Hist, Vol. VIII, pp. 62-64, 1896.

An old female, taken at Carlsbad, N. Mex., September 9, 1901, contained 11 nearly matured embryos, which is probably an unusual number, as the old one had but 10 mammae—inguinal $\frac{1}{1}$, abdominal $\frac{2}{2}$, pectoral $\frac{2}{2}$. The front pair were between the arms, almost on the throat. Another specimen had 8 mammae.

FIG. 18.—Cotton rat (dead) and nest in Johnson grass, Pecos Valley.

Besides grass, grain, and alfalfa, a few grasshoppers were found in the stomachs of the specimens examined at Carlsbad.

65    **Sigmodon ochrognathus** Bailey.    Chisos Mountain Cotton Rat.

These little yellow-nosed sigmodons are abundant in grassy parks among the oaks, nut pines, and junipers over the top of the Chisos Mountain plateau at 8,000 feet altitude. They live in numerous burrows and runways under short grass and feed on the stems of grass and various small plants. They are mainly diurnal, and we often saw them running along their little roadways in the daytime, while our traps were rarely disturbed at night. On June 13, 1901, besides young of several ages, two females were caught, one of which contained four small and the other four large embryos. Some old grass nests were found on the surface of the ground, but these apparently were winter nests. The runways all led to fresh burrows in the ground, which were at least the summer homes of the sigmodons.

As the country around the Chisos Mountains is a hot, Lower Sonoran desert, the species seems to be entirely isolated on top of the mountains. Its nearest relatives are on similar isolated ranges in Mexico.

**Microtus mexicanus guadalupensis** Bailey.   Guadalupe Vole.                    66

These little, short-tailed, snuff-brown voles are common over the brushy or grassy slopes of the Guadalupe Mountains from 7,800 to 8,500 feet in Transition zone. Unlike most species of *Microtus,* neither the presence of water nor moist nor grassy ground is required for their homes. In the head of McKittrick Canyon they live in the dry grassy parks and open places in the woods, where their runways, burrows, and old winter nests are abundant under the tall grass and weeds. Higher up on open ridges their runways wind about among stones and leaves under the shin oak and other low bushes of the driest mountain slopes, and sometimes well into the edge of the woods. The runways are distinct, well-worn little roads leading from burrows to feeding grounds or to other burrows. The summer homes seem to be entirely under ground, but unused grass nests found here and there on the surface appear to have been built for winter use under the snow. Green vegetation seems to be the principal food of this vole, and little, clean-cut sections of grass and various plant stems are found scattered along the runways on the feeding grounds.

Several old females, caught late in August, contained embryos, and at the same time young of various ages were caught in the traps.

**Microtus ludovicianus** Bailey.   Louisiana Vole.                    67

At Sour Lake, in southeastern Texas, Hollister secured a single specimen of this little vole, previously known only from Calcasieu Parish, La. It was caught in a brush patch at the edge of the prairie in company with the cotton rat. The prairie about Sour Lake is very similar to that just east of Lake Charles, La., where I found these little voles fairly numerous, living in the peculiar, flat mounds that are scattered over the low, damp prairie, and making their runways through the grass from one to another. Some of the mounds were perforated with a dozen or more of the little round holes, from each of which a smooth trail led away. A colony of a dozen or less of the voles, in some cases all adults, in others both adults and half-grown young, was usually occupying a mound. One female taken April 8 contained three well-developed embryos, and several others taken on the same date were giving milk. As usual in the females of this subgenus (*Pedomys*) the mammae were uniformly inguinal $\frac{2}{2}$, pectoral $\frac{1}{1}$. A few winter nests of grass were found on the surface of the ground where the standing grass had burned off, but the breeding nests apparently were all in the burrows below the surface.

Fire had recently run over most of the prairie and left the burrows exposed and the trails sharply defined over the blackened ground, but as the animals were caught as readily over the burned area as in the standing grass, the burrows are evidently a safe retreat in case of fire.

The stomachs of those caught contained only green vegetation, and along the runways grass and various small plants had been cut for food. As rice is the principal crop over these low prairies and as the ground is flooded while the rice is growing, this little vole is not likely to do serious damage.

68    **Microtus pinetorum auricularis** Bailey.    Bluegrass Vole.

Two specimens from Jefferson, in northeastern Texas, prove to be nearest to this form of the subgenus *Pitymys,* although differing slightly in the more elongated skull and larger bullae. They were caught about a mile south of town at the edge of a swampy run under a tangle of old grass and blackberry bushes. Most of their numerous runways, nests, and burrows were unused at the time the specimens were taken (June 12, 1902), which would indicate that previously the occupants had been much more numerous. There were none of the surface ridges which are usually found marking the tunnels of *pinetorum* and allied species, probably owing to the ample cover of vegetation which hid their runways. Neat, little grass nests were found here and there on the surface of the ground under the leaves along the trails, and burrows entered the ground at frequent intervals. A few bits of grass and tender plant stems were the only traces of food noticed along the runways.

A flat skin and smashed skull, apparently of this subspecies, sent in 1895 to the Department from Baron Springs, near Fredericksburg, Tex., by Fritz Grosse, formed the only previous record of the subgenus from Texas, although it ranges over the southeastern United States and reappears in Vera Cruz, Mexico.

69    **Fiber zibethicus** (Linn.).    Muskrat.

Nine specimens of the muskrat from Lipscomb and three from Canadian fail to show any cranial characters that will separate them from typical *zibethicus,* assuming that New York, Massachusetts, and Minnesota specimens are typical; but size and cranial characters separate them widely from their near neighbors, *ripensis,* of the Pecos Valley. The pelage of these 12 specimens, which were collected June 25 to July 16, is worn, faded, and very pale, while the more northern specimens, collected in fall, winter, and spring, are comparatively fresh and dark. I have seen, however, equally pale summer specimens at Elk River, Minnesota.

Lipscomb and Canadian are practically at the junction of Upper and Lower Sonoran zones, and apparently mark the extreme southern limit of range of *zibethicus.* At Canadian, Howell reports muskrats as "numerous at Clear Creek, living in the fish ponds and irrigation ditches, where they cause considerable trouble by tunneling into the banks and thus releasing the water." At Lipscomb he says:

They are found in small numbers in nearly all the small grassy creeks throughout this region. I secured two on Cottonwood Creek, 5 miles east of here, and a man who went fishing there a few days later saw three more. He approached near enough to one, which was feeding on the bank, to hit it with his fishing pole, and after it had retreated into a hole in the bank he prodded it until it came out and swam away. I set traps at this place later, but caught nothing. In a creek known as First Creek, flowing into Wolf Creek from the north 15 miles west of Lipscomb, I found the muskrats really abundant, the local conditions being peculiarly favorable for them. This stream consists of a series of wide and deep holes, with abundance of marsh grass growing on their borders, and partially filled with a flowering water plant (*Batrachium divaricatum*) upon which the muskrats feed. Their trails could be seen leading in every direction through this mass of floating vegetation, and one could hardly walk a half mile along the creek at any time of day without seeing one or more of the rats. Their favorite feeding times are about sundown and sunrise, and at these times I sometimes saw eight or ten in a short distance. They swim out from the bank into the water plant, and rest quietly on the surface while they feed. Several which I shot had the flowers of this plant in their mouths. These rats do not build nests, as their eastern cousins do, but live entirely in holes in the banks, entering either below or just at the surface of the water. When alarmed they dive and take refuge in one of these hidden retreats. When I first began to hunt them they were much less wary than after several had been killed, and if one were to sit quietly on the bank they would feed and move about unconcernedly. I secured seven in two evenings' hunting, besides wounding several which got away. I failed to catch any in traps, except one, which got away with the trap. I was told that they are common for miles up this stream, and, if so, there must be hundreds of them. (June 19 to July 10, 1903.)

**Fiber zibethicus ripensis** Bailey.    Pecos River Muskrat.          70

This small, dull-colored muskrat lives apparently in suitable places along the whole length of the Pecos River and on some of its tributaries, and along the Rio Grande near the mouth of the Pecos. In 1890 I found a few unmistakable muskrat tracks and signs on the banks of the Rio Grande near Del Rio, and ten years later again found their signs in the Pecos Canyon above the High Bridge. In 1902 Cary and Hollister collected a series of specimens at Fort Stockton, where they were common in the rushes along the banks of Comanche Creek, and Gaut collected a few higher up on the Pecos at Santa Rosa, N. Mex. They are common near Carlsbad (Eddy), N. Mex., in the river and irrigation canals, where their burrows enter the banks below the surface of the water and are high enough up for a dry nest chamber, often at a considerable distance from the brink. Grassy or tule-fringed banks are chosen, if possible, with the double advantage of cover and a supply of food close at hand. The muskrats are largely nocturnal, but usually come out of their burrows before dark and are sometimes seen swimming at midday. They bring up roots and stems of grass, sedges, and various aquatic plants, and after eating them on little shelves or niches in the bank, leave rejected and scattered parts behind that show the nature of the food. At the slightest alarm they dive with a splash and are seen no more, either coming up at some distant point or hiding under the banks or in their nests.

In several places their burrows were found in the banks of the large irrigation canals, where no doubt they cause some of the mysterious breaks that occur in the ditches.

71

### Castor canadensis texensis subsp. nov.    Texas Beaver.

> Type from Cummings Creek, Colorado County, Tex., No. 135744, U. S. Nat. Mus., Biological Survey Coll. Original number, 5139, X Catalogue. Made over from a mounted specimen purchased of A. Hambold, New Ulm, Tex. Caught in Cummings Creek by Florence Brune, Dec. 25, 1900, and kept alive until Jan. 10, 1901. Sex not indicated. Old and large.

*Characters.*—Coloration pale, as in *frondator,* possibly due in part to fading.

*Skull.*—Sagittal crest short and lateral ridges lyrate or spreading even in extreme old age; supraoccipital crest doubly curved, nasals long, spatulate, and tapering to narrow point posteriorly.

*Measurements.*—Type: Hind foot, measured dry, 174; naked portion of tail, measured dry, 265 long, 113 wide.

*Skull of type.*—Basal length, 136; nasals, 57; breadth of nasals, 30; zygomatic breadth, 107; interorbital breadth, 29; mastoid breadth, 67; alveolar length of upper molar series, 32.

*Specimens examined.*—Type, skin, and skull, and two skulls from Cypress Mills, Blanco County, farther up the Colorado River.

*Remarks.*—The characters shown by these three specimens are so well marked and uniform as to justify describing the subspecies, even on so scanty material. Whether the beaver of other streams north and south of the Colorado Valley of eastern Texas are the same can be settled only by specimens; but I have grouped the scattered notes and records for all but the Rio Grande and Pecos valleys of Texas under this form.

Beaver are still found in many of the streams of eastern Texas, especially in the larger rivers, where deep water and steep banks afford protection against relentless trapping. In 1892, at Arthur, in northeastern Texas, I was informed that they were fairly common along the Red River and that trappers caught a few each year. In 1902, at Texarkana, Oberholser was told that a few were still found in the Red River, and in 1901, at Mobeetie, was informed that they were common in Sweetwater Creek, a branch of the North Fork of the Red River. In 1903 Howell reported them as still common in the Sweetwater and Gage creeks not far from Mobeetie; also in the Wichita and Canadian rivers not far from Canadian. In the Colorado River a few were reported in 1892, by B. H. Dutcher, about 10 miles below Colorado City; again, in 1902, they were reported by Oberholser as rare near Austin and Elgin, while in 1892 Lloyd found trees girdled by them along the Colorado in Matagorda County. In 1901 Oberholser saw a skin that was brought into San Angelo, and was probably taken near there on the Concho, a branch of the Colorado. In 1902 he reported beaver in the Brazos as rare in the region of Brenham; in the Trinity River as occurring at Long Lake; in the Neches as occurring rarely in the river and bayous in the region of Beaumont, and as occurring in some of the larger streams about Jasper (probably branches of the Neches or Sabine). In 1899, at Lake Charles, La., I was told that trappers came down the Sabine River every winter, and among other furs brought some beaver. In the Big Thicket, in 1904, Dan Griffin told me that beaver were abundant a few years before in Village Creek, Polk County. In 1900 Oberholser was told of a colony of beaver 40 or 45 miles northwest of Uvalde, which would place them on the headwaters of the Nueces. In 1902 Mr. Gething, of Rock Springs, told me of a fine beaver skin that he bought the previous winter, which was obtained on the headwaters of the Rio Frio.

Through the kindness of Mr. Attwater, I am able to give the following interesting notes from his correspondence with Mr. J. F. Leyendeker, who writes from Frelsburg, Tex., under date of June 6, 1904:

I have your favor of the 3d instant and will cheerfully give you all the information at my command in regard to beavers in this section of Texas. I have heard of beavers and seen them in the Colorado River and Cummings Creek, a tributary of the Colorado River, which has its source near Giddings in Lee County, and empties into the Colorado River in the big bend about 2 miles nearly north of the town of Columbus. It is quite a large stream, with many deep-water holes or pools, sometimes over half a mile long and from a few to 10 or 12 feet deep.

The first beaver I ever saw was a very large male, weighing over 40 pounds, killed by my brother in said creek, in February or March, 1866. But few were noticed until after the big overflow of the Colorado River in 1869 and 1870, after which they were more numerous, especially where the creek passed through Mr. F. A. Brune's plantation, about 7 miles nearly north of Columbus. In this place there was quite a colony of the beavers, in fact so many that they did considerable damage to Mr. Brune's growing corn crop by cutting off the stalks, and I suppose using the ears as food. About six or seven years ago they constructed a dam across the creek, 40 or 50 feet long, in Mr. Brune's field, using blood weeds mostly and some other material for that purpose. This dam was perhaps a foot to 15 inches high, and strong and compact, but of course the first rise in the creek washed it away.

Mr. Emil Brune, a son of F. A. Brune, was here yesterday, and, after questioning him in regard to beavers, he said that he trapped six or seven, among these the one sent to San Antonio in January or February two years ago—he did not recollect the exact date. He also stated that while fishing he broke through into a beaver cave and there found four young beavers, which he carried home, but they soon died. I have been informed that there are still some beavers in Cummings Creek, near Mr. Justin Stein's place, a few miles nearly west of Frelsburg. It is also said that there are still some beavers in the Colorado River, near Mr. William Schulenburg's place, about 4 miles above the town of Columbus.

In 1872, while surveying land 18 miles above Fredericksburg, I found the beaver quite abundant in the Perdinales and White Oak creeks, and I have no doubt that some may be found there yet.

72  **Castor canadensis frondator** Mearns.   Broad-tailed Beaver.

Beaver are still found in many places along the Rio Grande, Pecos, and Devils rivers. In 1891 Lloyd reported them as common on the Mexican side of the Rio Grande 12 miles below Matamoras, and in 1900 at Brownsville I was told that a good many beaver were caught in the river above there every winter. In 1902 a fine specimen was taken by Goldman at Camargo, on the Mexican side of the river, and Mr. F. B. Armstrong told Mr. Nelson that the live beaver sent to the New York Zoological Gardens were caught in the Lower Rio Grande within 8 miles of the mouth. In the summer of 1901 we found fresh beaver 'sign' near Boquillas, in the Great Bend, and in the following winter trappers reported a good many beaver caught in the Rio Grande, Pecos, and Devils rivers, but stated that their numbers were rapidly decreasing. Still, one of these trappers assured me that he expected to make $500 on a trapping trip down the Rio Grande from Langtry to Brownsville the next winter, and was counting on getting $5 for each of his beaver skins.

In the winter of 1902-3 one trapper was reported to have caught 200 beaver on the Rio Grande between the Grand Canyon and Del Rio.

In the summer of 1902 I visited a beaver pond in the Pecos River Canyon, where apparently a good-sized family of beavers was living. This pond was a natural reservoir in a deep, sheer, walled side canyon, and was filled from the river in times of flood until it formed a deep lake a hundred yards wide and half a mile long, held in at the narrow outlet by a dam not over 30 feet long and at the time of my visit only 2 or 3 feet high. This pond—or lake, as it is called—with steep earth banks on one side, overhung by willow trees, with deep holes, big bowlders, and little islands, is an ideal spot for a beaver home. The willows furnish the principal food of the beaver, and have for ages, as shown by the old stumps and fallen timber along the shore, together with the freshly cut trees and gnawed bark and branches. The beaver often cut a tree so that it falls into the water, leaving the base anchored to the stump, and then at their leisure gnaw off the bark and cut the branches. Many trees fall inland, however, and in that case are abandoned, or else are well trimmed of branches and bark or cut into sections and carried away. The banks offer such good retreats that apparently no houses have been built around the lake, and at the time of my visit the river was high and the top of the dam was 2 feet under water. The photographs taken of the pond and its surroundings showed some of the cut trees, though little else of the beaver's work.

A beaver house near the head of Devils River was built on the bank of a deep rock-bottomed pond, where the clear, blue water spread out into a quiet little lake full of fish and margined in places with lily pads and willows. The house was placed on a rocky bank just above deep water and was mainly composed of old beaver cuttings— willow stems and branches cut to a convenient length for transportation. These were simply piled up in a mound some 8 or 10 feet wide and 3 or 4 feet high without mud or other filling, but when I tried to open a doorway to the nest I found them interlaced in a snarl that was not easily broken through. The house had the appearance of a big brush heap or a pile of driftwood on the bank, and might have been passed unnoticed save for its position and the gnawed ends of the sticks. Apparently it was either new or merely the summer house of one old beaver, and consequently was small and not substantially built. Its walls were so thin that as my shoes touched the rocky ledge at the back I distinctly heard the beaver get up and slide out of his nest into the water. As he left the house I caught a glimpse of him deep under the water, and for some time followed his course of travel by the line of bubbles that came to the surface as he swam up and down the lake or came back near the house to watch for a chance to return and finish his nap. At no time did he show himself at the surface, and the glimpses I had of him were at a depth of 6 or 8 feet, where he looked like a great fish dashing along with the speed of a racing boat. Quietly withdrawing, I returned at sundown to watch for his appearance. Just before reaching the house I saw a big head with short stubby ears rise quietly from the water near the middle of the lake and lie motionless for a few minutes and then move toward the bank a few rods below the house and disappear just before reaching it. A moment's stealthy creeping put me in the bushes close to the house, where I could watch the water, and after a few minutes the beaver again came to the surface with a stick in his mouth, apparently a willow root from under the bank. He swam leisurely around a big bowlder and then came directly toward me. When about a rod from shore his head went down and his round back rolled up as he dived to his submarine doorway. A moment later I heard him enter the house beside me. For fifteen minutes I could hear his big chisel teeth crunch, crunch through the wood and bark as he munched his evening meal. When the munching stopped there was another stir inside, followed by a gurgling of water from below. Then a line of bubbles spread out along the surface of the water for several rods from shore, and soon the familiar head rose to the surface. After remaining quiet for about a minute the beaver started back to the same feeding spot at the bank and again dived at the base of the willow tree. For about three minutes he remained below, and then came up again with food and started for the return trip to the house. As dusk was now deepening and as I fully realized the importance of securing a specimen from a river where no beaver had ever been collected, I dared not wait longer, but decided to shoot him with buckshot, as the light was far too dim for rifle sights. For fear of injuring his skull I aimed for his neck, which was deeper under water than I counted on. At the report a thundering splash told that he was not dead. A second later he leaped from the water close to my feet and at a single dash crossed a narrow point of land at the edge of his house and disappeared in the deep water, followed by a line of bubbles that shot up the pond. Such strength, such powerful bounds, and racehorse speed I had never dreamed of in the clumsy looking beaver. I had emptied my pockets of notebook and cash, to be ready to dive for the prize in case he sank, but I would as soon have jumped on a grizzly bear in his native gulch as this live beaver in the water. A little later a loud slap of his tail on the water far up the pond sounded like a "come on," and the old trappers tell me that this is really a fighting challenge. I waited until after dark without further developments, and then picked my way over the rocks for the long 2 miles back to camp. In the morning the old moon was still shining, and I was at the beaver house before day began to break, but there was no beaver either in the house or outside. He had moved, and probably had not returned to that part of the river since his fright. All that was left for me to do was to examine and photograph his house. With a good deal of difficulty I forced an opening through the stick wall so that I could put my arm in and feel the damp walls of the chamber, the big round hole where the water came just to the edge of his bed, and the bed of grass and weeds scattered over with peeled branchlets and roots of willow. No trace of other food was found. It was evident from the size of the house and the nest chamber that this was the bachelor quarters of an old beaver. Carefully closing the opening, I left the house as nearly as possible as I found it.

In talking with John Seawel, an old beaver trapper, I asked him why it would not pay to protect the beaver in a pond like that above the Pecos Bridge and let them multiply. The idea was not new to him, for he had talked it over with other trappers and all agreed that it was not worth trying, because they considered the beaver naturally ferocious, to a great extent solitary, and a slow breeder. Seawel says that two old beavers rarely live together in one house or even in one small pond; that they fight and chase away any newcomers; that if a family grows up and is undisturbed in a pond or a deep bend of the river, its members keep all others of the species away, and that they attack and kill any one of their number that is found in a trap or is sick or crippled. While he thinks that systematic breeding for fur is out of the question, he admits that the beaver should be protected all over the country, until the few that remain increase and restock the rivers. There are probably more beaver in the Rio Grande and Colorado rivers than in any other southern streams, and it is important that Mexico should cooperate with the United States in protection of the mammal that has played so important a part in the history of the development of the country.

**Liomys texensis** Merriam.    Spiny Pocket Rat.                    73

> *Heteromys alleni* Allen, Bul. Am. Mus. Nat. Hist., III, 1891, p. 268 (in part,
> specimens from Brownsville).

A large series of these little spiny pocket rats has been collected in the region about the mouth of the Rio Grande, at Brownsville, Matamoras, and Lomita.

Loring reports them at Brownsville as "common in the timber under logs and the roots of trees;" and Lloyd says they are "found at Lomita in the densest brush on the ridges forming the old banks of the river, and around old corrals." He adds:

> Their habit of throwing out a white clayey mound like the gophers attracts attention, and, although the mound may be a month old, by cleaning out a hole and putting a trap in it you will in time capture the occupant. The ordinary outlets are generally covered up by fallen leaves, which in some instances seem to have been placed there by the occupants. They are strictly nocturnal in their habits, and feed on the seeds of hackberry, mesquite, and various other shrubs. Young and old inhabit the burrows together.

**Geomys breviceps** Baird.    Louisiana Gopher.                    74

These little, dark-colored pocket gophers, usually known throughout their range as 'salamanders,' extend from Louisiana into eastern Texas, and, with considerable variation, westward to Navasota, Brenham, Milano, Peoria, Decatur, and Gainesville, or a little beyond the ninety-seventh meridian, thus inhabiting most of the eastern humid area of Texas, to the edge of the semiarid mesquite country, where they grade into a larger, paler form.

Their range is broken and irregular. Across sandy ridges their hills abound for miles, and then across miles of occasionally flooded bottom lands or wide stretches of black wax-land prairie they are entirely wanting. They live impartially in timber and open country, and are rarely found on clay or hard soil, but are most abundant on the sandiest and mellowest land. At the edge of flood lands they burrow mainly in the large flat mounds so characteristic of the region, and if not responsible for the construction of a certain class of these mounds, at least constantly add to them the earth brought up from below. Owing to the small size of these gophers, their scattered distribution and choice of poor, sandy soil for their most active work, there is comparatively little complaint of their mischief. In the heavier, better soil of cultivated fields they are not so common, and they throw out fewer and smaller mounds, but in pastures, potato fields, gardens, and orchards they sometimes do serious damage, besides leaving unsightly mounds over lawns and parks. They are easily trapped and there is no excuse for allowing them to injure crops or trees. A field once cleaned out will not be repopulated to any extent for several years, as the animals rarely travel except by extending their underground tunnels.

Like all species of the genus, they are strictly vegetarian in diet and cleanly in habits. Their flesh is sweeter, better flavored, and more delicate than that of squirrel or rabbit, and their small size is the only objection to their use as a table delicacy.

75 **Geomys breviceps sagittalis** Merriam. White-throated Pocket Gopher.

This white-throated form of the *breviceps* group seems to have a very local distribution on the coast prairie west of Galveston Bay. There are specimens from Clear Creek, Arcadia, and Virginia Point. I failed to find any trace of this gopher on Galveston Island or the point east of the bay at Bolivar. Along the Santa Fe Railroad from Virginia Point to Houston they are common most of the way over the prairie, where low mounds furnish favorite burrowing places. In certain localities they are numerous, and there are many complaints of the mischief they do, especially to orchards.

On the ranch of Mr. Lee Dick, at Virginia Point, they had entirely destroyed an orchard of 200 six-year old fig trees in bearing. Most of the dead trees had been piled up over the fence, where I examined them and found that all the small roots had been cut off, and in many cases the tap root where it was 2 or 3 inches in diameter. A few dead trees that were still standing were tipped over and the roots found in the same condition—all bearing the unmistakable marks of the teeth of the gopher. Five hundred dollars would be a small cash value to place on this lot of trees, and probably a dozen gophers had done the mischief. Mr. Dick had wasted a good deal of time trying to shoot them, but he had given up and said the people might as well move out and let the gophers have the country. I set nine No. 0 steel traps in this orchard patch, and a few hours later took out of them seven gophers. Not more than two or three remained in the field. The owner then acknowledged that with half a dozen traps a few hours' work might have freed his orchard of gophers, and that the loss of his trees was wholly unnecessary. His claim, moreover, that other gophers would soon come in from the surrounding prairie is true only to a very limited extent, and the immigration could be entirely prevented by trapping in the immediate vicinity of the field.

**Geomys breviceps attwateri** Merriam.　Attwater Pocket Gopher.　　76

This pocket gopher inhabits the islands and coast prairie between the mouth of the Colorado River and Nueces Bay and extends inland nearly to San Antonio. It is larger and lighter colored than typical *breviceps* and inhabits a decidedly more arid region.

Mr. H. P. Attwater has furnished the following interesting notes on their habits at Rockport:[a]

> The animals are very abundant all over the peninsula in Aransas County wherever the soil is sandy. There is hardly a foot of land that has not been 'plowed' several times over by gophers, and I believe the fertility of some sections has been greatly improved by them, by bringing the poorer soil up to the top. I have noticed that the richer the land the richer the gophers. Of course they do considerable damage to vegetable crops, especially to young fruit trees and cuttings just rooting. The samples sent you of mulberry trees cut by gophers were from the Faulkners' ranch, on St. Charles peninsula, in the eastern part of the county. Mr. Samuel Walker, the manager of the ranch, told me that he killed over 250 gophers in his young pear orchard between the 1st of March and April 15, 1893. This orchard was set out where sweet potatoes had grown the year before, and they came up again and covered the ground, and I think the potatoes attracted the gophers in the first place more than the pear trees.

**Geomys breviceps llanensis** subsp. nov.　Mesquite Plains Gopher.　　77

> Type from Llano, Tex., No. 97086, ♂ ad., U. S. Nat. Mus., Biological Survey Coll., May 15, 1899. Vernon Bailey. Original No. 6912.

*General characters.*—Similar to *breviceps,* but larger and lighter colored with more arched skull.

*Color.*—Upper parts light liver brown, in three of the females much darker, with dusky over the back; lower parts creamy or buffy white.

*Skull.*—Long and slender, with very narrow braincase and rostrum and small bullae as in *breviceps,* but with narrower and arched instead of convex interorbital region, nasals not sharply emarginate or abruptly constricted posteriorly; occiput sloping instead of abruptly truncate.

*Measurements.*—Type: Total length, 270; tail, 88; hind foot, 32. Adult male topotype: Total length, 270; tail, 82; hind foot, 32. Adult female: Total length, 230; tail, 74; hind foot, 30.

*Skull of type.*—Basal length, 44.3; zygomatic breadth, 29.6; mastoid breadth, 25; interorbital breadth, 6.3; breadth of muzzle at root of zygoma, 9; alveolar length of upper molar series, 8.5.

*Remarks.*—While closely resembling *texensis* externally and while the ranges of the two almost or quite meet it needs but a cursory examination of the skulls to show that this form has no connection with that species. It is a large, light-colored plains form of *brevi-*

---

[a] Merriam, N. Am. Fauna No. 8, p. 136, 1895.

*ceps* which follows up the river valleys from eastern Texas and becomes differentiated as it enters the open country. Specimens from Colorado, Stanton, Brazos, Childress, Vernon, Newlin, Canadian, Lipscomb, and Tascosa, Tex., are referable to it. Two females from Brazos are clearly intermediate between the present form and *breviceps.* In general contour of skull and especially in slender rostrum it resembles *phalax,* but in the slender audital bullae and small mastoids and consequent narrow base of skull it differs widely from that species.

So far as known at present the range of the form in Texas extends mainly along strips of sandy soil in the Llano, Colorado, Brazos, Red, and Canadian river valleys, in a region of scattered mesquite bushes, but does not reach the Staked Plains and rarely extends over the hard-soiled ridges between stream valleys. Gaut caught one gopher two miles south of Washburn, but could find no other trace of them in the country around there. At Lipscomb Howell says "they are plentiful both on the prairie and in the sandy bottoms. Their burrows are very difficult to open, as they are usually closed for a distance of about 18 inches below the surface, at which depth they take a horizontal direction."

Owing to their scattered distribution over a sparsely settled stock country, these gophers are at present of little economic importance, but as irrigation reclaims the mellow soil of these semiarid bottom lands they will constitute one of the problems to be dealt with by the farmers.

**78** **Geomys texensis** Merriam.    Texas Pocket Gopher.

This little, brown-backed, white-bellied gopher inhabits a few spots in central and western Texas. A series of 28 specimens in the Merriam collection from Mason, the type locality, indicates its abundance there, while a single specimen from each of two sandy patches along the Rio Grande, at Del Rio and at the mouth of Sycamore Creek, suggests a scattered distribution along this part of the Rio Grande Valley and a probable former extension of range up the Devils River and across to the head of the Llano as far as Mason. The country immediately north and south of its range has been pretty thoroughly worked without disclosing any species of *Geomys.* We succeeded in catching only *Cratogeomys* and *Thomomys* along Devils River, so at the present time the Mason and Rio Grande colonies seem to be widely isolated.

**79** **Geomys arenarius** Merriam.    Desert Pocket Gopher.

This gopher is common on both sides of the river at El Paso. Specimens have been taken at Las Cruces and Deming, N. Mex., and in 1902 Cary caught one that is almost typical *arenarius* in the sand hills near Monahans, Tex., at the east edge of the Pecos Valley.

This last locality can hardly be considered a part of the general range of the species, but probably marks a long isolated colony.

At El Paso gophers are common on the sandy river bottoms just below the town, where they throw up numerous and very large mounds of the mellow sand. I have never been able to find one in the irrigated orchards and fields, for there the water fills their burrows and drowns or drives them out. Loring reports them as especially abundant in railroad grades and banks of irrigation ditches at El Paso, and he caught seven in one day in the railroad grade a few miles north of Las Cruces, N. Mex. He says: "When pulled from their holes they hissed violently and when two were placed together they fought like bulldogs."

**Geomys personatus** True.  Padre Island Pocket Gopher.  80

This large, light-colored pocket gopher inhabits the central and northern part of Padre Island, a sandy belt along the mainland in Cameron County, and a sandy area near Carrizo, on the Rio Grande. Apparently it does not inhabit the lower Rio Grande Valley, as Lloyd did not find any trace of it between Carrizo and Brownsville nor between Brownsville and Sauz. On a trip from Corpus Christi to Brownsville I found its hills abundant across the sandy country between Olmos Creek and Sauz Ranch, but entirely wanting in the baked clay soil outside of these limits. At Carrizo Lloyd found them in only one patch of sandy soil, and there is nothing to show that they have a continuous range across from this point to Cameron County. On the light sandy soil and drifting dunes where these gophers abound there are no crops to be injured.

On Padre Island, Lloyd says:

> Their habits are in some respects peculiar, owing, perhaps, to the soft sand, that caves in on them, for they fill up their tunnels after throwing out the earth to a distance of 1 and sometimes 2 yards. They can not go very deep in the flats or they would reach water; in fact, the water filled some of the tunnels for about a foot until they curved upward.

**Geomys personatus fallax** Merriam.  Nueces Pocket Gopher.  81

Since this relatively small and dark subspecies of *personatus* was described I have been over its range pretty thoroughly and am convinced that it is an isolated and very local form, inhabiting the sandy strips near the coast between Nueces Bay and the Salt Lagoon at the mouth of San Fernando Creek and extending a short distance up the south side of the Nueces River. Except for very limited sandy strips along the coast and some of the stream shores the country is characterized by a tenacious black clay soil so sticky when wet and so hard when dry that no burrowing rodents inhabit it. From Corpus Christi west to San Fernando Creek we did not see any signs of gophers nor any soil that they could live in. Nueces Bay and the Nueces River, with its flood bottoms, cut off this range entirely from that of *attwateri* on the north, while the Laguna Madre, Salt Lagoon, and streams radiating from them separate as effectually the range from that of *personatus* on the south. Two females from Laredo agree more nearly with *fallax* than with any other form, but probably the range of this colony has no connection with that of *fallax* of the Nueces Bay region.

In the region of Corpus Christi the sandy soil is especially desirable for growing early vegetables, and the presence of the gophers is a source of much annoyance and considerable loss to the farmers.

82 **Geomys lutescens** Merriam.　Yellow Pocket Gopher.

Two specimens of barely adult females from near Texline agree with *lutescens* in external characters, but possess cranial characters that suggest the possibility of a local subspecies. Howell reported numerous burrows in a range of sand hills 15 miles east of Texline, where the two specimens were caught, but elsewhere in the region none were seen.

83 **Cratogeomys castanops** (Baird).　Chestnut-faced Pocket Gopher.

This, the largest of the Texas pocket gophers, with the single-grooved upper incisor, is common in Lower Sonoran zone and the edge of Upper Sonoran of western Texas from Eagle Pass, the headwaters of Devils River, Fort Lancaster, Big Springs, Hail Center, and Tascosa westward. A few are scattered here and there over the Staked Plains, but generally they inhabit valleys with fertile and mellow soil lower down, becoming very numerous and troublesome in some of the cultivated land. Their concentration on the best soil, together with the large size of their burrows and mounds, makes them one of the most injurious of the gopher family.

In habits they do not differ materially from the various species of *Geomys,* except in being more alert and possibly more diurnal. During the day they are often seen at the mouths of their burrows pushing out earth, at which times their comparatively large eyes are conspicuous, bright, and alert. They see a person much more quickly and at a greater distance than do most species of *Geomys* or *Thomomys,* and hence move about somewhat more freely at the entrance of the burrow. Still no protective measures are neglected, and the burrows are always promptly closed and packed with earth, sometimes for a distance of 2 or 3 feet back from the main tunnel. The mounds of these gophers often contain a bushel or more of earth, and when located in a meadow or alfalfa field they cover and destroy much of the crop, besides interfering with machinery in harvesting. The greatest damage caused by the gophers, however, is in cutting off roots, especially in such crops as alfalfa and garden vegetables, but most of all in the case of fruit trees. In many instances small orchards have been almost destroyed by a few gophers that could have been trapped with little trouble. They are so easily caught in steel traps that it would hardly pay to poison them except on a large ranch, though undoubtedly they could be poisoned in the same way as other gophers by dropping raisins, prunes, soaked corn, or small potatoes containing strychnine into the burrow and then closing the opening from above. On a cattle ranch in the foothills of the Davis Mountains I found where a couple of the gophers were working in dangerous proximity to the roots of a half dozen flourishing and fruit-laden peach trees growing near the windmill reservoir, while in the 3-acre patch of alfalfa just below, the hills of the animals were numerous. Under a neighboring cliff where a pair of horned owls had raised their young the same year I counted 20 skulls of *Cratogeomys* among bones of other rodents, but for fear these owls would catch the chickens one had been killed by the ranchmen and the others driven away.

**Thomomys fulvus** (Woodhouse).   Fulvous Pocket Gopher.     84

The pocket gophers from the Transition zone summit of the Guadalupe Mountains, while differing slightly from typical *fulvus,* do not seem to require separation from that wide ranging species. They are abundant over the timbered slopes of these mountains in Transition zone and often in places where the yellow pines are mixed with nut pines and junipers. They were common in the head of Dog Canyon, at 7,000 feet, the head of McKittrick Canyon, at 8,000 feet, and on top of the ridges, from 7,000 to 9,000 feet, and probably to the highest peaks, at 9,500 feet. There, as elsewhere, they inhabit partly forested slopes covered with abundant vegetation. They make endless tunnels and throw up numerous hills, often working among the rocks and constantly bringing to the surface the rich, mellow soil. In walking over the mountain slopes one's feet break into the burrows that honeycomb the soil beneath. The long, rope-like ridges of dry earth on the surface of the ground show where the gophers have worked in winter under the snow and filled snow tunnels with the earth brought up from below.

In mountain districts the gophers can do no possible harm, and besides their beneficial effect on the soil their underground tunnels catch and carry into the ground much of the water that would otherwise run off the surface and be lost.

**Thomomys fulvus texensis** Bailey.   Davis Mountain Pocket Gopher.

This little, dark-brown gopher inhabits the timbered part of the Davis Mountains in Transition zone and in at least the upper edge of   85
Upper Sonoran, ranging from about 5,000 feet up through the juniper and yellow-pine belts to the highest part of the mountains. The highest point where their mounds were seen was on the main

ridge of Mount Livermore, at about 8,200 feet. In the gulches they come down nearly to Fort Davis. In habits as well as general appearance and zonal position they are much like *fulvus,* living in a region of abundant vegetation and considerable rainfall and burrowing in the rich mold on stony mountain slopes or in open grassy parks. For a part of each year they live under the snow. The sides of the mountains are plowed over by them, and the mellow earth that is brought up from between the stones is washed down by the rains and deposited in the gulches below, where other gophers, with their endless underground tunnels, are mixing and stirring the soil and steadily improving it for cultivation. The service to man thus performed by these little animals is not to be lightly estimated.

In this region of extensive stock ranges and very limited agriculture the gopher will never prove a serious pest. The few that get into gardens and orchards are easily caught in traps, while those outside go on cultivating the soil without harming anything. With the larger *Cratogeomys* of the lower country, before mentioned, the case is different.

86  **Thomomys baileyi** Merriam.   Sierra Blanca Pocket Gopher.

This unique little gopher is known only from the specimens collected at Sierra Blanca on the open arid plain at the junction of Upper and Lower Sonoran zones. It is probably an Upper Sonoran species of the open country, as no trace of any *Thomomys* has been found in the big valley to the south and east, while its hills are common over the mesas and low mountains northeast of Sierra Blanca and north of Van Horn. Its characters do not suggest relationship with its nearest neighbor *lachuguilla* from the Lower Sonoran, Rio Grande Valley, or with any other of the surrounding species. It probably represents a long-isolated colony of very limited distribution.

87  **Thomomys aureus lachuguilla** Bailey.   Lachuguilla Gopher.

This little gopher inhabits the hottest and most arid part of western Texas. It lives on the barren mesas along the east side of the Rio Grande Valley, from El Paso to the Great Bend country, where the principal vegetation consists of scattered desert shrubs, cactus, yuccas, and agaves. Its little mounds are distributed over the baked and stony mesas, sometimes in long lines across barren strips, but usually grouped around the base of a bunch of cactus or a group of yuccas or agaves, the roots of which furnish it with both food and drink. The roots, stems, and leaves of apparently every plant encountered are eaten, but the favorite and principal food of the species is the tender, starchy caudex of the little *Agave lecheguilla,* a plant protected by sharp hooks and rigid spines from every outside attack, but wholly unprotected from below. The gophers burrow under and eat out the whole pineapple-like heart of the stem until the leaves and flower stalk dry up and topple over, while they burrow along to the next plant in their way, often leaving a long trail of dead agaves to mark their course. As the agave is extremely abundant and generally is considered a nuisance, the gophers are given credit for good work in destroying it, but if its fiber proves of value, as seems probable, the verdict in favor of the gopher must be reversed.

**Thomomys perditus** Merriam.    Little Gray Pocket Gopher.                    88

These little gray gophers are scattered sparingly over the high, stony mesa from Comstock to the Pecos High Bridge and Langtry, and still more sparingly to the head of Devils River. Farther east they do not seem to have a continuous range, but their hills were seen at points east and west of Rock Springs, and a specimen was taken on the high plain 35 miles east of Rock Springs, and another in the Castle Mountains in Crockett County.

The animals are not only scarce, but difficult to catch, as they live in scanty, stony soil where their little mounds are often mainly composed of stones instead of earth, while their tunnels become blocked by stones and are soon abandoned. Sometimes the doorways are left open apparently for lack of soil to close them, or because the gopher has abandoned the burrow in the hope of finding more favorable conditions elsewhere; sometimes they are merely blocked by two or three stones, but usually they are closed to a slight depth. The burrows do not extend far and the hills thrown up are few and small. Sometimes the old ones are almost obliterated before a fresh one is thrown up, and I have caught the gophers where the nearest hill appeared to be a month old.

Most of the food of the gopher is procured under ground from various roots, largely of yucca and sotol, or from the inside fleshy parts of cactus, *Cereus, Echinocactus,* and *Cactus,* which they burrow into and eat out from below. The roots and starchy base of a yucca or sotol will furnish food for an individual apparently for a week or more.

**Perognathus hispidus** Baird.    Hispid Pocket Mouse.                    89

This big pocket mouse is common in the more or less brushy part of the Lower Sonoran zone over southern Texas and the adjoining part of Mexico. In Texas it ranges from Brownsville north to O'Connorport, Cuero, Seguin, Llano, and probably, judging by immature specimens, to Brazos and Henrietta on the east, and to Del Rio on the west. It is less partial to open ground than most species of the genus, and is often caught in brushy or grassy places among the mesquite, at the edge of a thicket, along the fence at the edge of a field, on a weedy sand flat, or even in the midst of a corn or cotton field.

Some of the burrows suggest inch auger holes bored straight down into the ground, with no trace of earth that has been brought out; others are closed flush with the surface of the ground so as to be almost invisible, while others are closed 2 or 3 inches below the surface. At almost every den, however, there is a mound of earth that has been brought out of the burrows and heaped up, sometimes to the size of a gopher or mole hill, over the closed main entrance. This fact probably accounts for the absence of earth at other burrows that have been opened out from the main tunnel.

FIG. 19.—Pocket mice (*Perognathus hispidus*) caught in traps at Seguin, Texas.

At Seguin, in Guadalupe County, in November, 1904, I found these big pocket mice unusually abundant. Their characteristic inch auger holes and gopher-like mounds were found mainly along the edges of sandy fields, but also frequently in the middle of corn and cotton fields that had been thoroughly cultivated. Some of the mounds were 6 inches high and contained 6 or 8 quarts of earth, and were distinguished from gopher hills only by being solitary instead of in a series. By opening the burrow under these mounds I could catch the occupant at any time of day, but most of my specimens were caught at night in traps set at the open doorways or in artificial runways scraped with my foot along the ground near by. Sorghum seed proved the most attractive of the several kinds of bait tried.

Mr. Neel, the market gardener with whom I stayed, complained of great trouble in raising cantaloupes and green peas, because something dug up the seeds as fast as he could plant them. In the midst of his cantaloupe patch, where only four or five plants had survived, I found traces of these mice and caught two of the animals. A few others lived around the edge of the field, but a few nights' trapping would have cleared them all out and no doubt would have prevented further trouble.

Like others of the genus, these mice are mainly nocturnal and are rarely seen alive. The little that is known of their habits has been gathered by trapping them for specimens. At times they are readily caught in traps baited with rolled oats or various grains, and again they obstinately refuse to touch any kind of bait or to come near the traps. When caught they often have their cheek pockets stuffed full of the trap bait or of wild seeds.

They are active all winter and apparently never become very fat or show signs of hibernating.

**Perognathus hispidus paradoxus** Merriam.    Kansas Pocket Mouse.          90

This large, pale subspecies of the *Perognathus hispidus* group ranges over the open plains and desert country from South Dakota to Arizona, including northern and western Texas, south to Presidio County and Comstock and east to Rock Springs, Colorado, Mobeetie, and Lipscomb, mainly in Upper Sonoran zone. From the smaller and darker-colored *hispidus* on the south and from *spilotus* on the east the shading off is so gradual that no sharp line can be drawn between the ranges. Immature specimens from Brazos, Henrietta, and Tebo can not be positively referred to one rather than another of the three forms, and the Lipscomb specimens shade toward *spilotus*.

The habits of *paradoxus* do not differ from those of other forms of the group except as they have been modified to meet the conditions of plains and desert. In the Guadalupe Mountains I caught one in the head of Dog Canyon at 6,800 feet altitude, just below the edge of Transition zone, and at Amarillo, on the top of the Staked Plains, I caught one and found part of the skin of another at the entrance of a burrowing owl's nest in a prairie dog hole. The subspecies is common in the Pecos Valley, but apparently does not occur along the Rio Grande. Loring took one at Henrietta by the stone foundation of a bridge, and Oberholser another under a mesquite tree. At Mobeetie Oberholser caught one in the stone foundation of an old house. At Brazos Cary caught one in a cane field and another with corn in its pockets in a field of Johnson grass. One taken in January in Presidio County had its pockets full of *Convolvulus* seeds, and another at Smithville, S. Dak., in June had its pockets full of *Cymopterus* seeds. In the Castle Mountains Cary took one from the stomach of a rattlesnake, and near Texline Howell also found one in one of these snakes.

91    **Perognathus hispidus spilotus** Merriam.    Black-eared Pocket Mouse.

A specimen collected by Hollister at Jefferson not only extends the range of this group of pocket mice eastward almost across the State, but exhibits in an accentuated degree the characters of *spilotus,* described from Gainesville specimens. This record, with a few others, gives an extensive and logical range to what seems to be a fairly well-marked subspecies, which differs from typical *hispidus* in slightly darker and richer coloration, with more of a tendency to suffusion of yellow over the belly and along the top of the foot and the under surface of the tail, in larger and blacker spot on upper edge of ear, and in the extension of the nasals back to or beyond the posterior tips of premaxillae. Besides the Gainesville and Jefferson specimens, I should refer to the subspecies a richly colored flat skin from Long Point in the National Museum collection, a good skull from Saginaw, a few specimens from Ponca and Orlando, Okla., Red Fork, Ind. T., and an immature specimen from Garden Plain, Kans.

At Gainesville I caught two specimens on the edge of a pasture in rather tall prairie grass, but they, as well as all other rodents, were scarce on the black, hard soil of that region. At Jefferson they were fairly common, and Mr. Richard Crain told me that he often plowed them out, and that his cat frequently brought them to the house. I found a number of their characteristic burrows with fresh tracks around them, but could not coax the animals into my traps with any kind of bait. Hollister caught one in a trap set in a path running between a cotton field and the woods, but at Antioch he could not catch them, although the farmers there described the species accurately and said that at times they were common. One of the Gainesville specimens had seeds of a little Mimosa in its pockets, and another at Ponca had its pockets full of *Petalostemon* seeds.

92    **Perognathus penicillatus eremicus** Mearns.    Desert Brush-tailed
Pocket Mouse.

This desert pocket mouse inhabits the Lower Sonoran zone of extreme western Texas, ranging from El Paso east to Monahans, south to Boquillas, and westward into Mexico. There are Texas specimens from El Paso, Boquillas, east base of Chisos Mountains, 35 miles south of Marathon, Toyahvale, Pecos City, and Monahans.

At El Paso, in 1889, I caught this soft-haired species in the sandy bottoms below town and supposed that it had a different range from the spiny-rumped *intermedius* caught at the same time in the rocks above town; but later Doctor Fisher caught one on the gravelly mesa near El Paso, Cary caught one among the mesquites at Pecos City, and a number among the mesquites on a hard, limy ridge at Monahans. In the Boquillas and Great Bend region Oberholser and I found the species associated with *nelsoni* on sandy bottoms and among rocks of the cliffs bordering the Rio Grande, and around old stone cabins. While they are evidently partial to valley bottoms, the one essential for their burrows is a bit of mellow soil which may be found among broken bowlders or between thin strata of limestone, as well as on the sandy flats, or in the soft mesa soil that collects around the base of desert bushes. The little mounds that usually cover the entrances of their closed burrows are easily distinguishable from the work of any other species of the region except *intermedius* or *nelsoni*. They are often elongated or fan shaped, and stretch away to a distance of a foot or so from the point where the earth was brought up, as if pushed or kicked out, much like the mound or strip of dirt thrown out in front of the burrows of the smaller species of *Dipodomys*. The entrance of the burrow is usually but lightly closed and can be easily broken into with the finger. By breaking the crust above it the burrow may be followed for a considerable distance where it runs near the surface. As usual with pocket mice and kangaroo rats, there are several openings and radiating tunnels from the central cavities of the subterranean den, and while part of these are closed, there are generally concealed openings or some means of ready escape.

These mice, like the whole family, are mainly nocturnal, but can be caught in the daytime by opening a closed burrow and setting a trap inside, sometimes in a very short time after placing the trap. Usually they take rolled oats readily, and are easily caught in traps set around their burrows or in long furrows drawn in the sand, which they almost invariably follow till a trap is reached. When caught their cheek pockets are often full of rolled oats from the trap bait, or partly filled with seeds of various plants.

**Perognathus intermedius** Merriam.    Intermediate Pocket Mouse.

A large series of specimens from the El Paso region are almost typical *intermedius*. From *eremicus,* with which these pocket mice are associated, they are easily distinguished by the spinescent hairs of the rump and apparently by a difference of habitat. At El Paso, in 1889, I caught them only in the rocks in the foothills of the Franklin Mountains, and *eremicus* only on the sandy flats below town. In 1903 Gaut collected them in the eastern foothills of the Franklin Mountains up to 4,800 feet, and reported them as living around the rock slides and cliffs. While in other localities *eremicus* also has been taken among rocks, *intermedius* throughout its range is closely

93

associated with cliffs, canyons, rocky gulches, stone walls, or the edges of bowlders.

94  **Perognathus nelsoni** Merriam.   Nelson Pocket Mouse.

Specimens of this dark-colored form of brush-tailed pocket mouse from Boquillas, east base of Chisos Mountains, Alpine, and east base of Davis Mountains, carry the range of *nelsoni* from Mexico well into western Texas, where it overlaps the range of the superficially similar but quite distinct *eremicus*. At Boquillas and the east base of the Chisos Mountains, Oberholser and I caught the two species together along the cliffs, on sandy flats, and about old stone cabins. While the freshly caught animals were readily distinguished by the spinescent rump and dusky soles of *nelsoni*, no constant difference was found in habits or habitat of the two species. Near Alpine Lloyd caught one specimen at the base of a cliff; and at the east base of the Davis Mountains, at approximately 5,000 feet, Cary caught one under a pile of rocks.

95  **Perognathus nelsoni canescens** Merriam.   Gray Brush-tailed Pocket Mouse.

The gray pocket mouse is represented from Texas by 5 specimens from Comstock, 4 from Langtry, and 1 from Sheffield. Except for the slightly larger and more angular interparietal, they seem to be typical *canescens,* which was previously known only from the type locality, Jaral, Coahuila, Mexico.

Hollister caught one among the rocks in a small canyon near Comstock, several others along the edge of the Rio Grande Canyon a few miles south of there, and still another on a steep rocky slope near Sheffield; Gaut caught four in the vicinity of Langtry in small caves among the rocks of the river canyons.

Nothing is known of the habits of this pocket mouse save what can be gathered from the character of its habitat, an extremely hot and barren region with light-colored soil and gray limestone cliffs.

96  **Perognathus flavus** Baird.   Baird Pocket Mouse.

In Texas the Baird pocket mouse is common at El Paso, Sierra Blanca, Valentine, Alpine; and probably in the Pecos Valley, and in the northwest corner of the Panhandle, since it occurs just beyond the Texas line at Carlsbad (Eddy), N. Mex., and at Beaver River, Okla.

At El Paso these little yellow pocket mice were common in December, 1889, along the edges of the sandy valley bottom 2 miles below town, where little sand drifts were heaped up around the base of *Atriplex* and *Suaeda* bushes. Their burrows were usually in groups of three or four, under the edges of the bushes. The occupied ones were closed, and were discovered only by following the lines of tiny footprints across the bare patches of sand from bush to bush till they disappeared at little mounds of fresh earth that served as doors and blinds to the underground houses. By scraping away the earth a burrow big enough to admit my little finger was disclosed under each tiny mound. Traps baited with rolled oats set near the burrows and along the lines of tracks soon yielded a series of 8 specimens in the rich satiny winter coats—the daintiest, most exquisite of the rodents commonly classed as 'mice.' On chilly nights they did not move about much, but on mornings following a warm night their lines of tracks were abundant, and radiated from the burrows to the nearest patches of wild sunflower and pigweed, whose seeds seemed to furnish their favorite food. One specimen caught December 15 was apparently nursing young, or lately had been, as the teats contained milk.

At Valentine in August, 1902, I turned over a flat stone in the hotel yard and caught one of these little pocket mice as he jumped out of his burrow, and at Sierra Blanca in December, 1889, caught one at a hole in the mellow soil of the railroad bank. At Alpine Gaut caught one in an old gopher mound about 3 miles east of town.

**Perognathus merriami** Allen.   Merriam Pocket Mouse.                 97

This little dusky and yellow pocket mouse ranges over southern Texas from Padre Island and Brownsville north to Devils River, Austin, Mason, and southward into Mexico. Specimens from Devils River and Comstock are fairly intermediate between *merriami* and *gilvus,* as apparently are two specimens from Washburn, which would indicate that *merriami* ranges well up along the east side of the Staked Plains.

The species is common on sandy or mellow soil, more often among weeds and brush than in the open. Their little mounds of earth thrown out on two or three sides of a cactus, bunch of bushes, or flat rock mark the main entrances to their dens. These doorways are always closed during the day if the den is occupied, and when opened from without are usually promptly closed again from within. A careful search near the mounds will generally disclose several little round holes standing open, with no trace of earth thrown out, but with the openings often concealed under bushes or leaves. If you dig into the main burrow or stamp on the ground, a *Perognathus* will often dart out of one of these openings, or more often break through a thin crust of earth that covered a concealed exit and after a leap or two will sit trembling and blinking in the dazzling light of day. It is then so easily caught in the hands that many of our specimens are secured in this way. Most of these are young of the year, however, as apparently the adults are not so readily driven from their dens. When caught they do not offer to bite, but sometimes utter a fine squeak, and if held gently for a while soon cease struggling and seem to lose all fear. The light evidently hurts their eyes, and after blinking for a while they soon close them if held quietly in the hands or placed in an undisturbed position on the ground. While often abundant, these little mice are not easily caught in traps, and usually seem indifferent to any bait we use, frequently pushing the traps out of the way or turning them over when set near their burrows or in places where they run. Sometimes they can be caught by placing the trap where they have to step in it in going out of or into their burrows. Near Kerrville a number were caught in this way, while only one out of five had filled his pockets with the rolled oats used for trap bait. A couple were caught in traps baited with juniper berries, which seemed to be a favorite food. In a number of burrows I found juniper seeds or the empty shells from which the kernel had been eaten out through a little hole in one end. In some cases these berries must have been brought from a distance of 10 or 20 rods. In one den under a flat rock, where three tunnels, a foot to a foot and a half long, met in a nest chamber the size of my fist, there was a handful of fresh juniper seeds carefully cleaned of the outer pulp. As this was in May, and the occupant of the burrow was not a full-grown animal, this store was probably laid up for a rainy day rather than for a winter supply. At another burrow a lot of old moldy corn and bits of rubbish mixed with fresh earth were brought out, a little each night, as if in a general house cleaning, indicating that various seeds and grains are stored up in times of abundance. As the mice do not hibernate and as seeds of one kind or another are usually abundant, there is no need of laying up large stores of food.

**98**

### Perognathus merriami gilvus Osgood.    Dutcher Pocket Mouse.

The Dutcher pocket mouse inhabits the Pecos Valley from Carlsbad (Eddy), N. Mex., south to Langtry and the Painted Caves, eastward to Big Springs, and 20 miles east of Rock Springs, and westward to Van Horn and Presidio County; in other words its range coincides approximately with that of the creosote bush in all but the western corner of the extremely arid Lower Sonoran zone of western Texas. It overlaps the range of *flavus,* occurring with it at Carlsbad, and apparently overlaps also the range of *copei* in the country north of Monahans, from both of which it is quite distinct and easily distinguished. From *merriami,* of which it is a larger, lighter yellow subspecies, it shades off along the southern edge of the open and extremely arid region. Specimens from near Rock Springs, along Devils River, and near the mouth of the Pecos are more or less intermediate between the two forms.

In habits these pocket mice do not differ from *merriami* except in so far as they have become adapted to a more open and arid region.

At Langtry Oberholser found them common on the stony mesa, and at Fort Lancaster in the chaparral of the bottom of the Pecos Valley. At Monahans, Cary reported them as abundant in September throughout the sand dunes and as feeding extensively on the seeds of a low, shrubby *Baccharis*. In the dry and barren valley 6 miles south of Marathon I caught them in the baked soil among the scattered mesquite bushes and cactus, and 10 miles farther south found them fairly common in the still more arid and stony valley of Maravillas Creek. Their characteristic little burrows were found around the edges of stones, under bushes and cactus, and occasionally in open spots of bare ground, but the occupants refused to enter my traps or touch any bait. A few were dug out of their burrows and caught in our hands, and from these Mr. Fuertes was able to make some extremely lifelike studies. When first caught the little fellows were greatly frightened and struggled to escape, but never offered to use their teeth. After being held gently for a few minutes they seemed to forget their fear and would sit quietly on the open hand for a minute at a time, blinking sleepily in the unfamiliar glare of daylight. At a sudden motion they would bound away in long leaps, but soon stop, under a weed or bush. While sitting motionless with panting sides they could be easily recaptured by approaching cautiously and covering them quickly with the open hand.

**Perognathus flavescens copei** Rhoads.    Cope Pocket Mouse.        99

Three specimens taken by Gaut in July, 1904, at Mobeetie, the type locality of *copei,* possess characters which enable this form to be recognized as a bright-colored subspecies of *flavescens.* Two others taken by Cary in the sand hills 20 miles north of Monahans show slightly accentuated characters and, so far as known, mark the limit of its southern range. They suggest also that its range near the southeastern corner of New Mexico probably overlaps that of both *gilvus* and *flavus*.

The 3 Mobeetie specimens, 1 adult female and 2 young of the year, were caught at a den on the edge of a millet field in traps set by the closed entrances of two burrows on opposite sides of a sun-baked furrow. The millet in the field was about ready for harvesting and each of the animals had millet seed in its cheek pouches. A long line of traps yielded no more specimens, and as no other traces of the animal were found it is evident that the species is very scarce in this locality. The failure of several other collectors to procure topotypes of the species is a further compliment to the prowess of the rattlesnake from the stomach of which the type was taken by Professor Cope. (*Cf.* Proc. Acad. Nat. Sci., Phila., 1893, 405.)

**100**  **Perodipus ordi** (Woodhouse).   Ord Kangaroo Rat.

This little five-toed kangaroo rat is common in the Rio Grande Valley at El Paso and Fort Hancock, and a few specimens have been taken in a tributary valley of the Rio Grande at points 6 to 20 miles south of Marathon. A specimen from Kent, one from Toyahvale, and an imperfect one from Pecos seem to be almost typical *ordi,* while the larger, brighter-colored *richardsoni* is almost typical at Monahans, only 37 miles east of Pecos. The specimens at hand do not clearly prove intergradation in this region and the two forms have well-defined ranges which conform closely to Upper and Lower Sonoran zone limits.

*Perodipus ordi* is one of the few Lower Sonoran species of this mainly Upper Sonoran genus. In the extremely hot and arid valleys of western Texas it ranges over much of the same ground as *Dipodomys ambiguus,* which it closely resembles in habits as well as appearance. At El Paso I caught specimens on the sandy flats below the town under brush and cactus on the same ground and even at the same holes with *Dipodomys ambiguus.* At Deming, N. Mex., they were common in the sandy strips along the dry valley of the Rio Mimbres, where, in patches of scattered brush and weeds, they were feeding on seeds of wild sunflowers, *Parosela,* and other wild beans. Of ten adult females caught November 29 to December 6, four were giving milk. At the same time numbers of nearly full-grown young were caught, which would indicate either that two litters of young are raised in a season or that the breeding season is very irregular.

**101**  **Perodipus montanus richardsoni** (Allen).   Richardson Kangaroo Rat.

This largest and brightest colored of the four species of five-toed kangaroo rats inhabiting Texas comes into the State from the Upper Sonoran plains to the north, but instead of keeping to the hard-soiled, Upper Sonoran part of the Staked Plains it completely encircles them. It lives in the sandy stream valleys in the upper edge of the Lower Sonoran zone, but nowhere extends far enough down to be out of reach of Upper Sonoran plants. There are specimens in the Biological Survey collection from Texline, Lipscomb, Tascosa, Canadian, Mobeetie, Newlin, Vernon, Colorado, Stanton, and Monahans in Texas, and from Carlsbad, Roswell, Fort Sumner, and Santa Rosa, in the Pecos Valley, New Mexico. At Carlsbad and Monahans it meets the range of and occupies the same ground with *Dipodomys merriami.*

Throughout its range this species shows a marked partiality for sand, and from Nebraska to Texas fairly revels in the mellow soil of the yellow, shifting, naked drifts and dunes that the wind piles up along the edges of most of the river valleys.  It digs an apparently

unnecessary number of burrows, which it abandons to other less ener-
getic rodents or uses only as convenient resorts in case of sudden
danger. It scampers over the smooth surface with the apparent
enjoyment of rabbits on a crusted snow or boys on a skating pond,
and paired tracks of the long hind feet are found in the morning in
zigzag lines over the drifts, sometimes registering hops of a few
inches, again flying leaps of 4 to 6 feet, only to be wiped out each
day by the drifting sand and re-registered each night in varying form.
Through the weeds and grass of a sandy prairie or the standing grain
or scattered stubble of a wheat field the kangaroo rats make little
roads, either from burrow to burrow or radiating from burrows to the
feeding grounds, and always keep a clear track for retreat to doors
that usually are left wide open day and night. Many of the burrows
are single, but generally the home den has several openings, with
trails leading away from each. For the size of the animal the burrows are large, and in a mound or slope they go back horizontally,
so that in case of a hard rain the water runs out of instead of into
them. Even on level ground the holes enter as nearly horizontally
as possible, and sometimes run along for 10 or 15 feet without going
down a foot below the surface. If no sand bank offers the proper
angle, the burrow is usually placed under a bunch of cactus, a clump
of mesquite bushes, or under some shrub that affords protection as
well as a slight eminence to burrow into.

The food of this, as of other species of the genus, is almost entirely
seeds, including those of many grasses, various native plants, and
any of the small grains. These seeds are neatly shelled out and eaten
on the spot or carried in the ample cheek pouches to the dens to be
eaten at leisure. No matter how small the seed the shell is always
removed, and the contents of the very small stomach of the little
animal are always clean and free from indigestible particles. Often
the bottom of the burrow is covered with the shells of seeds, but
in the several dens examined I never found stores of seeds or grain.
Occasionally a little ripe grain is eaten, and a small amount of seed
wheat or other grain is dug up; but unless the animals become far
more numerous than usual the loss from their depredations is too
insignificant for serious consideration.

**Perodipus sennetti** (Allen).　Sennett Kangaroo Rat.　　　　　102

The type of *Perodipus sennetti* was labeled "near Brownsville,"
Cameron County, Tex., but the efforts of several collectors to pro-
cure topotypes have not resulted in specimens from nearer than the
Rio Coloral, 35 miles north of Brownsville. In reply to a letter
asking just where he collected the type of *Perodipus sennetti,* Mr.
Priour writes under date of February 22, 1903, that it was taken at

Santa Rosa stage station, 85 miles southwest of Corpus Christi. This is on the Alice and Brownsville stage road, near the northwest corner of Cameron County, 145 miles from Brownsville. From this point north to Santa Rosa, across 60 miles of mainly sandy prairie, the species is abundant, and a series of specimens from Sauz Ranch and Santa Rosa shows no variation in characters. A specimen recorded by Mr. Oldfield Thomas[a] from San Diego is shown by the skull measurements to be of this species, but whether collected by Mr. Taylor at San Diego or from the sandy country farther south is not stated. Oberholser found no trace of any kangaroo rat at San Diego. Mr. H. P. Attwater collected 5 specimens 18 miles south of San Antonio. Through the kindness of Dr. J. A. Allen I have examined two of these specimens, now in the American Museum of Natural History, and agree with him that they are typical *sennetti*. Mr. Attwater reported a female taken August 23, containing "two small embryos," and says: "These beautiful little animals appear to be quite common in the sandy black-oak region south of the Medina River in Bexar County. Their burrows seem to be most numerous in the poorest, sandy soil."[b]

Along the Alice and Brownsville stage road the burrows of the Sennett kangaroo rat are common in the yellow sand, sometimes remaining open during the day and sometimes being securely closed with earth. William Lloyd, who camped in this region, says:

> In the deep sand around the stage stations they soon learn what corn and oats are and become great robbers. They seem to enjoy the moonlight nights, skipping about, and on several occasions coming close up to my bed. A motion and they are ten steps away, crouched against the sand; then, if not noticed, they rise and continue their rambles. A lighted lantern seems to puzzle them, and leaving one on the ground to attract them I have caught two of the animals in my hands. At Santa Rosa, while out with the lantern, I saw one starting a burrow. It tried two or three places, presumably to find one sufficiently soft, and at last, apparently suited, pushed its nose in, and drawing its hind feet up close to its jaws, scratched vigorously and soon had made a good beginning to a burrow, when I caught it in my hands.

103  **Perodipus compactus** (True).    Padre Island Kangaroo Rat.

While closely resembling *sennetti* in cranial characters, *compactus*, even in its darkest color phase, differs from all the mainland forms of Texas in its light coloration, white-margined ears, usually white soles of feet, and mainly white under surface of tail. In the light phase it is unique in having the upper parts a pale ashy gray. In a series of 23 specimens there are 9 of the dark phase and 14 of the light, caught on the same ground by William Lloyd, who said that

---

[a] Proc. Zool. Soc. London. 1888. p. 446.
[b] Allen, Mammals of Bexar County, Tex., Bul. Am. Mus. Nat. Hist., VIII, 57, 1896.

while he found no difference in their habits he could tell them apart even by moonlight.

These kangaroo rats are probably common over the whole length of the 100-mile sand reef known as Padre Island, as Lloyd found them at both the north and south ends. He reported them as sometimes found in the level soil, but usually living in the sand dunes and always on the side away from the prevailing wind. He says:

> At the north end of the island, where most abundant, they close their burrows before daylight, throwing out several quarts of sand in a little mound like a small gopher hill and opening them again after dark. Their object in thus closing their doors is not very evident, as snakes and crabs are too few to bother them. I believe it must be to keep out the black carrion beetles that occupy every disused hole, and a species of pale sand grasshopper that lives in similar situations. Traps set in their burrows were usually covered up with sand, and most of the specimens were caught in the runways, where the prints of their two hind feet and the swish of their tails made unmistakable signs. They feed on the seed of a small sand plant like purslane, and take oatmeal readily as trap bait. After a violent storm their bodies are common objects among the wreckage along the shore, attracting the attention of the boatmen, who call them white rats.

**Dipodomys spectabilis** Merriam.    Large Kangaroo Rat.[a]

This beautiful, big kangaroo rat is common in the upper edge of the arid Lower Sonoran zone of extreme western Texas, east to the eastern edge of the Pecos Valley at Monahans and Odessa, and north and south along the Pecos Valley from Adams, Tex., to Santa Rosa, N. Mex. It apparently does not inhabit the lower half of the zone, as it extends neither into the Rio Grande Valley of Texas nor the Gila Valley of Arizona. I have not found it nearer to El Paso or the Rio Grande than Sierra Blanca, Tex., and Jarilla, N. Mex., on the east, and Deming, N. Mex., on the west. While ranging to the extreme upper edge of the zone, it does not enter Upper Sonoran to any extent. In Texas it is common at Sierra Blanca, Van Horn, Valentine, Kent, Toyah, Toyahvale, Adams, Pecos, Grand Falls, Castle Mountains (west base), Monahans, and Odessa; and Gaut collected one specimen at the east base of the Franklin Mountains, 10 miles north of El Paso.

Although strictly nocturnal animals and rarely seen alive, these kangaroo rats usually make their presence evident by conspicuous mounds scattered here and there over the barest and hardest of gravelly mesas, mounds as characteristic and unmistakable as muskrat houses or beaver dams, and as carefully planned and built for as definite a purpose—home and shelter. An old mound that has been inhabited for years is often 3 or 4 feet high and 10 or 12 feet wide, a

[a] It is to be regretted that the name 'kangaroo rat' has become firmly fixed to this group of beautiful Jerboa-like rodents, which are as unratlike as they are widely removed from the Marsupials.

dome-shaped pile of earth entered from the top and sides by a half dozen, or sometimes a dozen, big burrows that would easily accommodate a cottontail rabbit. Well-beaten paths lead away from each of these doorways to others or to neighboring mounds. Usually one or more of the doorways are closed each morning with earth behind the retiring inmates, probably to keep out rattlesnakes and other unwelcome guests. At night these earth doors are opened for use, and the best place to set a trap for the animal is in front of a closed, rather than an open, door. While all of the holes are used more or less at night, apparently only the closed ones are occupied in the daytime. All the fresh earth brought out of the burrows and much that is dug up outside is scraped back on to the mound, so that its size slowly increases with age. Inside, the burrows widen out into roomy chambers, some of which are close to the surface, while others are deep and at the ends or sides of winding burrows. In trying to walk over these mounds one is almost sure to break through knee deep into the chamber below.

While the kangaroo rats do not hibernate or store up great quantities of food, they carry considerable food into the burrows to be eaten probably during the day, as shown by deposits in their chambers, by the shells of seeds and grain brought outside during house cleaning or found scattered over their chamber floors, and by the presence of seeds in the fur-lined cheek pouches of individuals caught in traps. That the inmates of these mounds are not always asleep during the daytime can be proved by tapping or scratching at the entrance of the burrow and then listening for a response. A low drumming sound can usually be heard from deep underground, sometimes from two or three points. Apparently it is made as the similar drumming of the wood rats is known to be, by beating the soles of the hind feet rapidly on the ground, which produces a tiny, vibrating roar, and is used as a signal of alarm, call note, or challenge. The animals are social. Often three or four are caught in a mound, and the trails lead from one mound to another. The paired prints of the two long hind feet are fresh every morning in the trails and dusty roads, but I have never seen a print of the tiny hands which apparently are never used in locomotion. When caught in traps or in the hands, the animals struggle violently, but never make a sound or offer to bite. Like rabbits, they are gentle and timid and depend on flight and upon their burrows for protection.

**Dipodomys elator** Merriam.   Loring Kangaroo Rat.

Specimens of these kangaroo rats are known only from near Henrietta and a point 10 miles to the southwest, and from Chattanooga, Okla. Oberholser says:

> They are not common in the immediate vicinity of Henrietta, but seem to be of frequent occurrence from 20 to 30 miles to the southwest and most abun-

dant between 2 and 13 miles in this direction. The approximate limits of their range are from Henrietta about 4 miles north, 5 miles east, 22 miles south, 8 miles west, and about 43 miles southwest. They live, so far as determined, almost exclusively among the mesquites and make their holes around the roots of the mesquites and bunches of *Opuntia*. One of the specimens caught was found in the throat of a large rattlesnake that had swallowed it as far as the trap would permit.

Loring, who first caught these kangaroo rats at Henrietta, says:

At one set of holes the main entrance was closed every morning with dirt from the inside, and my traps were not touched. The hole was so small that I thought it might be a *Perognathus*, so got a pick and shovel and dug it out. The burrow branched from below and opened out at four different points. One of the rats was caught in a muddy pocket the size of my fist at the end of the main burrow, the other was covered with dirt in a sharp bend of the burrow, but escaped into another hole near by. The deepest and longest burrow ran about 3 feet underground. I did not find any grass or seeds in any of the burrows. Taking the rat that I had caught to a large field, I turned it loose. It sat for a minute, dazed by the sun, but when I poked it scampered off at such a lively rate that I could hardly keep up and could not see whether it used its fore feet or not. It was very quick and graceful. While jumping its tail was slightly curved up and was not used in any way to aid in its progress.

Near Chattanooga, Okla., some 50 miles northwest of Henrietta, Tex., Prof. D. E. Lantz collected a specimen and reported on the species as follows:

While not numerous, they seem to be well distributed in the vicinity of Chattanooga. Nearly all of the settlers with whom I talked were acquainted with them and informed me that they lived about the premises of their homes. Several were confident that they could capture one or more specimens for me, but only one was secured. This was killed by a farmer as he was walking across the prairie on a dark night with a lantern. It had been foraging in a Kafir corn field, and I found its pouches widely distended with grain. They contained 100 seeds of Kafir corn and 65 seeds of *Solanum rostratum*. In the vicinity of Chattanooga the animals are found on hard clay soils, and they seem to prefer the vicinity of houses, living under houses and outbuildings and in caves made for storing vegetables and other household supplies. They seem to be attracted by lanterns or other lights carried on dark nights.

Mr. Laurie, living in Chattanooga, has a cave back of his hardware store in which a pair of kangaroo rats had taken up their winter quarters. He purchased a couple of bushels of wheat to feed to his poultry and placed it in the cave. Some time later, when he wished to begin to use it, he found that it had all disappeared. Last spring he removed some boards which lined the lower part of the cave on the inside and found all of the wheat carefully stored away behind the boards by the kangaroo rats.

**Dipodomys merriami** Mearns.    Merriam Kangaroo Rat.               107

This little dull-colored kangaroo rat of the four-toed group ranges over most of the extremely arid Lower Sonoran zone of western Texas, except where it gives place to *ambiguus* in the immediate valley of the Rio Grande. Specimens from near Langtry and 6 miles south of Marathon, Fort Stockton, Toyahvale, Pecos, Monahans,

Kent, and Sierra Blanca, Tex., and from Carlsbad and Tularosa, N. Mex., are almost typical *merriami,* differing slightly in duller and darker coloration, the opposite extreme from *ambiguus.* The cranial characters throughout the group are extremely uniform.

The habitat of this species is mainly dry, half-barren mesas or open desert valleys, where the animals make their homes in baked and stony soil or less frequently in sandy patches. At Monahans Cary found them only on the hard soil of the valley and never among the sand dunes with *Perodipus richardsoni,* though at Marathon, Kent, Stockton, and Sierra Blanca they were caught in the same ground with *Perodipus ordi.* Except in choice of higher, rougher ground they seem not to differ in habits from *ambiguus.*

**Dipodomys merriami ambiguus** Merriam.   El Paso Kangaroo Rat.

This little four-toed kangaroo rat, differing from *merriami* in its brighter, more golden color, seems to be of very local distribution along the sandy bottom of the Rio Grande Valley from El Paso and Juarez south to Boquillas in the Great Bend country. A series of specimens from Sierra Blanca is intermediate and can be referred in part to this and in part to *merriami.*

In the Rio Grande Valley it does not differ much in range or habits from *Perodipus ordi,* which it resembles so closely externally that specimens can not be safely named without reference to the toes on the hind feet. In the flesh the two can be distinguished at a glance by the much slenderer feet and tail of the *Dipodomys.* On the sandy river bottoms just below El Paso, where I caught many specimens of the two genera on the same ground and sometimes at the same burrow, I could find no difference in habits or local habitat.

Their little burrows usually are under a bunch of mesquite, acacia, or creosote bushes or cactus, evidently for the sake of protection from enemies, or in order to get a little shade from the fierce heat of the sun's rays. Often their burrows enter from several sides of the bunch of bushes or cactus, and converge toward a common center, where they apparently meet below. Some of their doorways are usually closed during the day, while others are left open. Like all the genus, they are strictly nocturnal and at night feed on the ripe seeds of various plants or carry them into the burrows to be eaten at leisure. Often when caught in traps their cheek pouches are stuffed with seeds or with the rolled oats used for trap bait. Occasionally a bit of green leaf is found in the pockets, but I have seen only the fine white pulp of ripe seeds in their stomachs—no green foliage or anything that would seem to furnish moisture.

**Erethizon (epixanthum?)** Brandt.   Yellow-haired Porcupine.

The only specimen of porcupine I have seen from Texas was a badly stuffed skin and a fragment of skull brought me at Tascosa in

1899 by a ranchman who had killed the animal there the previous year. At Alpine in 1900 the ranchmen told me that porcupines were occasionally found there, and in the Davis Mountains in 1901 I found a bushel of their unmistakable signs in a cavity under the rocks, where a porcupine had evidently lived for a good part of the previous winter. As the Finleys, who have lived for many years in the Davis Mountains, had never seen nor heard of these animals, they are evidently not common there.

**Lepus merriami** Mearns.   Black-naped Jack Rabbit.                    109

The black-naped jack rabbits are common over southern Texas, from Brownsville north to the mouth of the Devils River, Fort Clark, and San Antonio, and east to Cuero, Port Lavaca, and Matagorda. They occur with *texianus* in the eastern part of their range and meet or overlap its range in the Devils River country.

In April, 1900, I found them common all the way from Corpus Christi to Brownsville, both on the prairies and in the mesquite and chaparral; and in April of the previous year, between Victoria and Port Lavaca, I counted from the train six that were so close that the black necks showed conspicuously and served to distinguish them from *texianus,* which also was seen along the road. In February, 1894, Loring reported them as common from Alice to Brownsville, as many as ten being seen in a bunch. In March, 1900, Oberholser reported them as numerous on the Thomas ranch, near Port Lavaca, inhabiting chiefly the open prairie, where they found cover under tall bunches of grass. In April and May of the same year he reported them at O'Connorport as only fairly common and very wild; at Beeville as common, living principally on the prairie and in the more open areas in the chaparral; in the immediate vicinity of town as very wild, but farther away, where not often hunted, as much less so; at San Diego as abundant in the more open portions of the chaparral; at Laredo as abundant all through the chaparral; at Cotulla as abundant in the chaparral and very tame, apparently living in the thick brush, although late in the afternoon frequenting the more open, grassy places, where sometimes as many as six or eight were seen together; at Uvalde as abundant and very tame, inhabiting the more open parts of the chaparral, particularly the area between town and the base of the hills to the northward; and at Rock Springs as common on some of the more open areas. On May 29 and 30, 1903, Gaut collected an old male and a 2-weeks-old young one near Del Rio, where he found jack rabbits scarce, although they were said to have been very numerous a short time previous. Only one other individual was seen in three weeks, although considerable time was devoted to hunting for them. Lloyd reported them, in 1891, as common on Padre Island and as generally found crouched in the short grass on the open sand.

Over most of their range the black-naped jack rabbits are sufficiently numerous to do considerable damage on farms and truck gardens, as they are fond of many cultivated plants. At Laredo, in April, Oberholser reported that a field of cantaloupes with vines 6 inches high was entirely ruined by them, and a similar field of watermelons was extensively damaged. As raising early vegetables and fruits has become an important industry in southern Texas, the abundance of the rabbits is a serious matter. Their consumption of range grasses in a region that is mainly devoted to stock raising is also a matter of considerable importance.

In general characters this species does not differ much from *texianus,* but in life the difference appears much greater than when specimens are compared. As the rabbit sits up at a distance or, with ears erect, runs across the prairie, the black nape contrasts sharply with the snowy white backs of the ears, and the black tail and rump stripe with the almost white hams and flanks. Near Cuero one jumped from beneath a low mesquite bush close to me and, after a few long leaps that were like flashlights of black and white, suddenly stopped and crouched, lowering the dull gray ears until their white surface rested on and wholly concealed the black neck; the tail was curled up till its black upper surface concealed the black rump stripe and left only the gray lower sides exposed, while at the same time the white hams and flanks close to the ground served to cut out shadow and obliterate form, so that the whole animal was transformed into a part of the great prairie.

This same rabbit, now made into a specimen, does not seem very different from *texianus,* except when the ears are raised to show the black neck; but alive and running, its specific characters might have been recognized at a distance of 40 rods.

110   **Lepus texianus** Waterhouse.[a]   Texas Jack Rabbit.

*Lepus texianus griseus* Mearns, Proc. U. S. Nat. Mus., XVIII, p. 562, 1896. Type from Fort Hancock, Tex.

The jack rabbits, except from extreme northern and southern Texas, can be referred to this form with gray or whitish nape and

---

[a] I find no grounds whatever for following Doctor Mearns (Bul. Am. Mus. Nat. Hist., II, p. 296, 1890) and Doctor Allen (Bul. Am. Mus. Nat. Hist., VI, p. 347, 1894) in restricting the name *texianus* to the Arizona jack rabbit. In Waterhouse's original description (Natural History of the Mammalia, II, p. 136, 1848) the only real characters mentioned which distinguish the Texas and the Arizona forms are in the fifth and sixth lines of the description on page 136, "throat and abdomen white; haunches and outer surface of legs gray; tarsus nearly white"—all of which applies to the Texas animal rather than to the Arizona form. The measurements, while evidently from a mounted specimen and of no real value, indicate the slightly smaller size of the Texas form.

light-gray flanks. They are common over the arid plains country of central and western Texas, south to Rock Springs and San Antonio, and from Austin and Brazos westward to Langtry and El Paso; and less common in the strips or islands of prairie country eastward nearly or quite across the State. A specimen collected by Hollister at Antioch, Houston County, is nearly typical *texianus.* A few jack rabbits, probably of the same species, are reported by Oberholser from the prairie near Boston, in the northeastern corner of the State, and a few from the coast prairie west of Beaumont. From residents of the country I have obtained reports of a few from Calcasieu Parish, in the southwest corner of Louisiana, and from the Texas prairies near Virginia Point and Richmond; and on the prairie near Houston, Cuero, and Port Lavaca have myself seen the rabbits close enough to be sure that they were not *merriami.* Specimens from San Antonio, Rockport, and Colorado City show a tendency toward *melanotis,* while others from Vernon and Henrietta can be referred to that subspecies, as can also those of the Panhandle country. In the Davis Mountains the jack rabbits ascend to the edge of the yellow pines, or completely through Upper Sonoran zone, where I have found them common in both July and January. In the Guadalupe Mountains they were common in August up to 7,000 feet on the open ridges, but the main part of their range in Texas lies in Lower Sonoran zone, in the arid part of which they are most abundant.

The abundance of the jack rabbits varies with different seasons and localities, but seems to have a wave-like sequence. After increasing for a few years until extremely numerous, they disappear rather suddenly, are unusually scarce for a few years, and then gradually increase again. This periodic change does not affect the whole country simultaneously, however, for at the same season the rabbits may fairly swarm in one valley and be scarce in another. In January, 1890, on a 30-mile trip from Marfa south to a ranch on Onion Creek, there was hardly a moment when jack rabbits were not in sight— sitting by the road or scurrying through the scattered brush of the desert. In places as many as 20 could be counted, and during December and February of the same winter they were almost as numerous about El Paso and Del Rio. I did not visit the Rio Grande Valley again for ten years, and then could not find one in the region about El Paso.

At Llano in May, 1899, they were numerous in spite of the 5-cent bounty that had been paid on 5,600 of them that year in the county. I often saw a dozen as I made the morning round to my traps, and many of these were limping about with great lumps on their backs and sides where the tapeworm larvae had developed under the skin. Along the wagon road from San Angelo to Colorado City, thence northwest to Gail and the eastern escarpment of the Staked Plains,

111

they were numerous, and in places where no rain had fallen that year and the vegetation was scant and dried up the jack rabbits had seconded the prairie dogs in eating the bark from the small mesquite bushes, from *Opuntia arborescens,* and a large part of the fleshy pads of *Opuntia engelmanni.*

The food of the jack rabbit consists mainly of grass and green vegetation, of which growing grain of all kinds, clover, and alfalfa are especial favorites. It has been estimated that five jack rabbits eat as much grass as one sheep.[a] Allowing one rabbit to the acre, which surely would not be overestimating their maximum abundance, the rabbits on a 1,000-acre ranch would consume as much grass as 200 sheep. That the rabbits are a serious drain on the grass supply of the stock range, especially in the more arid parts of the State, can not be denied. It is a question if they are not even more injurious than the prairie dog, as they cover about twice the area in the State that the prairie dog does, and instead of being in colonies and keeping to a definite locality they travel about freely, seeking cultivated fields, meadows, gardens, orchards, and the best pastures. They are as independent of water supply as any of the desert mammals, and in many of the valleys must go for months without water save what is obtained from their food.

For protection from their enemies the jack rabbits depend on protective coloration, the keenness of their ears and eyes, and the length of their legs, and all they ask of a coyote is a fair start and an open field. A greyhound will pick up one on a straight run, however, and foxhounds will often tire them out if there is moisture enough for good tracking. Coyotes, foxes, and wild cats catch them apparently with a quick bound in brushy places, leaving only patches of scattered fur and a few tracks to mark the spot next morning. Hawks, owls, and eagles prey extensively upon them. Their bones were among the commonest of those scattered over the ground under a great horned owl's nest on a cliff at the edge of the Davis Mountains and under a golden eagle's nest on a cliff near Marathon.

During the morning and evening hours jack rabbits may be seen loping along the trails to their feeding grounds, nibbling grass on the green patches, standing with ears erect, on the *qui vive,* or scurrying in alarm from real or fancied enemies. In the twilight they become almost invisible, and their highly protective coloration probably serves them better by night than by day, as they are then most active. During most of the day they sit in their forms, or merely crouch close to the ground under the edge of a bush or weed, or even in the open without other protection than the blending of their gray coats with

---

[a] 'Jack Rabbits of the United States,' by T. S. Palmer, Biological Survey, Bul. No. 8, p. 30, 1897.

the gray desert vegetation. When they bound away from the bare ground or short grass close to your feet, the surprise is greater than when they start from under a fuzzy-topped weed, though in both cases they may have been in plain view all the time. The only home they can claim for themselves and their young is the form, a slight depression scratched in the ground, usually under the shady side of a bush or weed. They can not endure the heat of the midday sun, and in hot weather always seek some shade. I have never known one to enter a burrow, though they could easily go down badger holes. The young are hidden in grass and weeds until large enough to escape their enemies by running, and they are such experts at hiding that they are rarely discovered.

Extermination of jack rabbits, even if practicable, is not desirable, as they have considerable value for game and food purposes, aside from the interest and pleasure of maintaining a reasonable number of our native animals. When in good condition their flesh is excellent, though usually not so tender as that of the cottontail or Belgian hare. The common prejudice against using them as food has been shown by Dr. T. S. Palmer to be entirely without foundation.[a]

**Lepus texianus melanotis** Mearns.    Kansas Jack Rabbit.                    112

Jack rabbits from Texline, Lipscomb, Canadian, Washburn, Henrietta, and Vernon, and apparently also an immature specimen from Saginaw, are almost typical *melanotis*. They are scarce over the northern part of the Staked Plains, and I have seen but a single specimen from that region and only a few individuals in life. One seen close to the train near Washburn September 22, 1902, had every appearance of being the brown-backed *melanotis* instead of the paler gray *texianus*. A few others reported from Tascosa, Hereford, Washburn, and Gainesville are probably *melanotis*. More specimens from eastern Texas may show closer affinities with *melanotis* than with *texianus,* as the few examined are to some extent intermediate between the two forms.

The habits of *melanotis* do not differ much from those of *texianus,* of which it is the plains and prairie representative. Instead of depending on low desert bushes for shade and concealment, the former usually hide in tall prairie grass, which habit may in some way account for their slightly shorter ears and smaller audital bullae and the browner coloration that constitute their principal subspecific characters.

They are generally less numerous than *texianus* or *merriami,* and consequently of less serious economic importance. They are also freer from parasites, and therefore more acceptable as game.

---

[a] See 'Jack Rabbits as Game,' in Jack Rabbits of the United States, by T. S. Palmer, Biol. Surv., Bul. 8, p. 71, 1897.

156                    NORTH AMERICAN FAUNA.                    [No. 25.

113    **Lepus floridanus alacer** Bangs.    Bangs Cottontail.

The cottontails of eastern Texas as far west as Port Lavaca and Gainesville are readily distinguished from *floridanus* by the small audital bullae, and from *chapmani* by the darker colors, in both of which characters they agree with *alacer* described by Outram Bangs, from Stilwell, Ind. T. The darkest specimens are from extreme eastern Texas, but to the westward the transition into the lighter, grayer *chapmani* takes place mainly along the line where timber and thick grass prairie change to mesquite plains.

The cottontails are common over practically all of eastern Texas, living in the densest timber and brush patches, in the open woods, in the rich prairie grass, or about fields and buildings. Where there are no dogs to chase them, their favorite home is under a house or other building. In the woods an old log, tree top, or brush heap usually protects them, though they are often found crouched in their forms under a bunch of briers, weeds, or bushes. On the prairie they often jump from under a tuft of overhanging grass and run to the nearest brush or weed patch for cover. They rarely find burrows to make use of and apparently never dig them.

Nowhere have I found them more than moderately common or in any way a serious pest. Their value as a food and game animal probably compensates for what little mischief they do in cutting off young fruit and forest trees, and for the small amount of grain and vegetables they injure in fields and gardens. If in places they become troublesome, it is easy to thin them out by hunting them with dogs, but usually the hawks and owls keep their numbers sufficiently reduced.

**Lepus floridanus chapmani** Allen.    Chapman Cottontail.

114    *Lepus floridanus caniclunis* Miller, Proc. Acad. Nat. Sci. Phila., p. 388, Oct. 5, 1899. From Fort Clark, Tex.

*Lepus simplicicanus* Miller, Proc. Biol. Soc. Wash.. XV, p. 81, Apr. 25, 1902. From Brownsville, Tex.

This small-eared cottontail ranges from Rockport, Brazos, Henrietta, Mobeetie, Canadian, and Lipscomb, westward to Stanton and Comstock, south to Brownsville in Texas, and across into Mexico. It is a small, pale-gray form of the *floridanus* group, amply covered by the name *chapmani,* given by Doctor Allen to Corpus Christi specimens. It is quite distinct from the long-eared cottontail (*Lepus arizonae minor),* with which it occurs at Stanton, Comstock, Del Rio, Fort Clark, and along a wide strip of country where the ranges of the two overlap. It inhabits the semiarid mesquite country of Lower Sonoran zone and usually is abundant throughout its range.

At Corpus Christi, and thence to Brownsville and Del Rio, these little rabbits live among the big bunches of prickly pear and in the thickets of mesquite and catsclaw, finding in the thorny cover the same protection that the wood rats and many other mammals do, and seeming to ignore the presence of thorns in and along their trails. One of their favorite resorts for a midday nap is in or among the big flat pads of a prickly pear, where they will stick to their form until fairly forced out. In the still more dense and thorny thickets of *Zizyphus* and *Momesia pallida* it is impossible to force them out. In the evening and morning hours they may be seen hopping around the edges of these thickets, where they are often comparatively tame, so confident are they of being able to dodge quickly into a safe retreat. In the country about Kerrville, and westward to Devils River, they are less common, and usually are found in the oak thickets or among junipers and scrub oaks, but the country does not seem to suit them as well as the more open mesquite region farther north at Llano, where they are abundant in the thickets of mesquite and *Zizyphus*. At Mobeetie, Miami, and Lipscomb, Howell found them inhabiting the brushy creek bottoms, and at Canadian both the brushy bottoms and the plum thickets over the sand hills. He says they were very wild, and that none were seen on the open country where the long-eared *minor* ranged.

I have never found these rabbits making use of burrows or of openings in the rocks.

Like all the cottontails, they are excellent food, and are usually free from grubs and other parasites. The young are especially delicious, and as white and tender as quail. Complaints are rarely made of the harm they occasionally do in orchards and gardens, as this seems to be compensated by their value as game.

**Lepus arizonae minor** Mearns.   Desert Cottontail.                    115

The long-eared desert cottontail can be distinguished from the short-eared *chapmani* by its much larger audital bullae with even more certainty than by its longer ears, and, as the two occur together over a wide stretch of country, this distinction is important. It is the common cottontail of western Texas, and extends from El Paso and along the Rio Grande east to Wichita Falls, Tebo, Colorado, San Angelo, Fort Clark, Cotulla, and San Diego, south to Rio Grande City, and north to Tascosa and Lipscomb. The eastern edge of its range overlaps the western edge of the range of *chapmani* in places for a distance of a hundred miles or more, where the two occur commonly together. While distributed mainly over the arid Lower Sonoran zone, it ranges into Upper Sonoran in the Davis and Guadalupe Mountains and on the Staked Plains, but perhaps not farther than a rabbit would wander in a few warm months.

Unlike *Lepus chapmani,* these cottontails are largely inhabitants of the plains and open country, caring little for cover when they can find prairie dog or badger holes for safe retreats. They are often most conspicuous and abundant in a half-deserted prairie-dog town in a barren valley, where they sit under a bush or weed until alarmed, when they rush to the nearest burrow and disappear, or stop, perhaps, at the edge to see if they are pursued.[a] Where there are no prairie-dog holes, badger holes are usually common throughout the range of this rabbit, and a large kangaroo rat burrow is often made use of in an emergency. Openings in and under rocks also are favorite retreats, and rabbits are usually common along the base of cliffs and in canyons and gulches where, besides the natural cavities among the rocks, they make use of burrows where skunks and badgers

FIG. 20.—Long-eared cottontail (*Lepus a. minor*) at badger hole under mesquite, Pecos Valley.

have dug out smaller rodents or made dens under big bowlders. Dense tangles of brush and impenetrable cactus patches also are resorted to for cover, but nowhere within the range of the species is there anything more nearly approaching real woods than scattered mesquite and junipers, with the exception of willows and cottonwoods on some of the river bottoms, which the cottontails seem to avoid. Like jack rabbits, they seem to feel more secure in the open country, where safety depends on keenness of sight and hearing and speed of foot.

---

[a] At Lipscomb and Canadian, Howell found them inhabiting old prairie-dog holes to such an extent that they were called by the ranchmen "prairie-dog rabbits" or "dog rabbits."

Over much of their range they are usually very abundant. While on the train going from Wichita Falls to Seymour, a distance of about 50 miles, I counted 16 of these rabbits, and from Wichita Falls to Childress, a distance of about 100 miles, I noted over 30. At Sycamore Creek in half an hour Lloyd counted 18, and in many places we found them equally numerous. Around ranches they are generally shot for food or chased away by dogs, so that there is little complaint of injury to crops. The amount of range grass consumed by them under ordinary circumstances can not be very great, but without natural enemies they would soon become so numerous as to be a serious pest.

They breed rapidly, but are preyed upon constantly by coyotes, foxes, wildcats, hawks, eagles, and owls. Under the nesting cliff of a great horned owl at the west base of the Davis Mountains parts of fully 100 skulls of this cottontail were found among other bones in the owl pellets.

As food these cottontails are equal to any rabbit and when young they are especially delicious. In camp they are often the only available fresh meat. As other game becomes scarce their importance as food and game will be greatly increased.

**Lepus arizonae baileyi** Merriam.   Plains Cottontail.                    116

Two specimens of cottontail from Texline and one from Buffalo Springs, 20 miles to the northeast of Texline, can be referred to *baileyi* better than to *minor* or *arizonae,* although not typical of either form. It is a question if the Lipscomb and Tascosa specimens referred to *minor* do not shade also toward *baileyi,* which appears to be an Upper Sonoran plains form of the *arizonae* group.

At Texline Howell says that these rabbits are numerous in the sagebrush draws near town. When started from the sagebrush (*Artemisia filifolia*), they usually make for the nearest rocks, or else run into a burrow. They are very wild, and if no cover offers quickly run out of sight.

**Lepus pinetis robustus** subsp. nov.   Mountain Cottontail.              117

Type from Davis Mountains, Texas, 6,000 feet altitude. No. $\frac{18262}{25165}$ ♀ ad., U.S. Nat. Mus., Biological Survey Coll. Collected Jan. 6, 1890, by Vernon Bailey. Original No. 873.

*General characters.*—Similar to *Lepus pinetis holzneri,* but larger, with relatively narrower braincase and conspicuously wider, more prominent postorbital processes.

*Color.*—Winter pelage: Crown and rump brownish gray, sides and rump light ashy gray, nape and exposed part of legs bright fawn color, lower parts white with buffy gray throat patch. The short summer pelage is not known.

*Cranial characters.*—Skull larger than in *pinetis* or *holzneri,* with relatively narrower braincase, slightly larger bullae, and conspicuously wider, more prominent postorbital processes.

*Measurements.*—Type specimen ♀ ad.: Total length, 460; tail vertebrae, 55; hind foot, 104; ear from notch (measured dry), 67. Average of 5 adults from western Texas: Total length, 458; tail vertebrae, 59; hind foot, 103.6; ear from notch, 68.

*Skull of type.*—Basal length, 60; nasals, 32; zygomatic breadth, 34; greatest breadth of braincase, 26.5; mastoid breadth, 25.5; interorbital breadth, 19.

*Remarks.*—This large brush rabbit needs comparison only with *pinetis* and *holzneri,* from both of which it differs enough to form a good subspecies, and from the range of which it is apparently entirely cut off by intervening valley country. From *arizonae* and its subspecies it is entirely distinct, differing widely in size and cranial characters and occupying the same ground in the lower part of its range. It is a Transition zone species, ranging from 6,000 to 8,000 feet in the Davis and Chisos mountains, rarely coming down the brushy slopes into Upper Sonoran zone. A specimen collected in midwinter in Presidio County was in the Upper Sonoran zone near the edge of the Chinati Mountains, at about 4,200 feet, where it may have wandered down along the brushy creek from a higher level.

It lives in brushy and timbered country and makes runways through the thickets, which, when started, it follows at a lively speed and with much noise. It is almost as large and heavy as the varying hare, and needs only to be seen or heard running to be distinguished from the light, slender *minor.* While many were seen or heard in the Davis and Chisos mountains, but few specimens were collected, owing to the difficulty of getting shots at them in the thickets. They seem to be entirely free from grubs and other parasites and are fine eating.

118 **Lepus aquaticus** Bachman.    Swamp Rabbit.

The swamp rabbits from near the coast of southeastern Texas agree in general appearance with *aquaticus,* in referring them to which species I follow Doctor Allen, although more specimens from this region, as well as more of typical *aquaticus,* are necessary to a final decision. Specimens examined: Selkirk Island, Matagorda County, 1; Bernard Creek (12 miles west of Columbia), 2; Austin Bayou (near Alvin), 1. Oberholser reported them as common in the moist woods near Beaumont, and Hollister found them "exceedingly numerous at Sour Lake, especially about the wooded islands." Lloyd reported them from Selkirk Island at the mouth of the Colorado River and in the salt marshes near Matagorda. My own acquaintance with the species has been in the Big Thicket of Hardin County, Tex., and in southern Louisiana, where they live in swamps, marshes, and low brushy woods near the bayous, making trails that often lead through shallow water. They usually jump from under old logs or tangles of briers and underbrush and go dashing off with a heavy thumping run, but usually with speed enough to escape the dogs. Fires are said sometimes to drive them out of the swamps and marshes by hundreds. In the Big Thicket in December, 1904, they were especially abundant under the dense growth of palmettoes and tangle of vines. At this season the ground was dry, but the quantity of large flattened pellets covering the tops of old logs suggested that during wet weather the rabbits spent much of their time on the logs.

Late in the following March Gaut found them abundant in this region during high water, and was informed by Mike Griffin, a hunter living on Black Creek, that they were great swimmers, and when chased by the dogs would invariably swim back and forth across the creeks. One female examined contained five embryos and two others were nursing young.

**Lepus aquaticus attwateri** Allen.    Attwater Swamp Rabbit.                          119

Swamp rabbits are common along the streams of eastern Texas as far west as Port Lavaca, San Antonio, Austin, and Gainesville. Specimens from Richmond, Antioch, Joaquin, Troup, and Gainesville are large and gray like typical *attwateri,* and can be referred to nothing else. They are reported as common in the swamps or bottom lands at Arthur, Texarkana, Jefferson, Waskom, Rockland, Brenham, and near Elgin. Those reported from Conroe and Jasper are probably nearer to *aquaticus.*

In habits these rabbits are similar to *aquaticus,* living in the timbered bottom lands along the rivers, often among the palmettoes, or in wet, half-swampy places in the woods. On the Brazos bottoms, near Richmond, I found them under old logs and brush in the densest woods, and at Troup, Loring reported them as hiding in fallen tree tops or under roots of trees and brush piles in low, swampy places. H. P. Attwater says:

> When frightened from their hiding places and chased by dogs they take refuge in hollow trees and in holes in the river bluffs. The dogs seem to have more difficulty in trailing them than they do the cottontails and jack rabbits, the swamp rabbits often eluding the hounds by taking to water. I have seen them on several occasions swimming across the river while the dogs were hunting for them on the other side.[a]

---

[a] Bul. Am. Mus. Nat. Hist., VII, p. 328, 1895.

162                    NORTH AMERICAN FAUNA.                    [No. 25.

120    **Felis hippolestes aztecus** Merriam.    Mexican Cougar; Mountain Lion; Panther.

The specimens of mountain lion from Texas available for determination of the species are few, and their status is unsatisfactory; but they indicate that at least the western part of the State is inhabited by *aztecus*. Two skulls of females from the Davis Mountains and one from Brownsville do not possess important specific characters, but they and a flat skin from the Davis Mountains and one from near Boquillas agree with *aztecus* more nearly than with any other species. A fine male seen in the San Pedro Park, at San Antonio, October 30, 1904, said to have come from Langtry, was in the light-gray coat of *aztecus,* and a nearly perfect skull of an old male from 20 miles north of Comstock shows the best-marked characters of that species.

In the rough and sparsely settled western part of the State mountain lions are still fairly common in certain sections, where they often lay a heavy tribute on colts, calves, and sheep. At Langtry Gaut reported them in 1903 as "quite common a few years ago, but now scarce," and adds: "One was shot in a pasture about half a mile from the station last winter, and an old hunter (Mr. E. B. Billings) at Samuels informs me that the stomach of one that he killed near Langtry a few years ago contained part of the foot of a raccoon and also some of the remains of a gray fox." Gaut reported a few panthers in the Franklin Mountains the same year, and said that he was shown a mule killed by one. The mule's neck showed deep gashes which had been cut by teeth and claws. Large numbers of colts were said to be killed every year in these mountains by panthers. Near Oakville, Live Oak County, Mr. F. A. Lockhart reported that a horse and two colts had been killed by a panther July 25, 1895, and that a hound was killed the next day by the same animal.

The rough desert ranges, full of canyons, cliffs, and caves, are the favorite haunts of the panthers, and will be their last strongholds, not only because of the advantages they offer for foraging but because of the protection they afford from hounds and hunters. In the desert mountains just north of Van Horn in August, 1902, a panther and I were mutually surprised at meeting in a narrow gulch, he evidently expecting a venison supper, and I, in my search for rock squirrels, discovering his big, round, yellow face between the rocks above me. I drew my sight a little too fine and caught the rock just under his chin with no more damage than to fill his eyes with rock dust and cause a quick retreat behind the crest of the ridge. I was scarcely more disappointed than was the ranchman in the next valley whose colts had been disappearing at frequent intervals. In the Davis Mountains these cougars have been hunted with hounds until scarce, but in the Santiago range, in the Chisos Mountains, and along the canyons of the Rio Grande and Pecos they are still common. A few are found even on the edges of the Staked Plains. On a ranch 22 miles north of Monahans Cary saw the skin of one that had been roped by a cowboy in July, 1902. It was a very large female, and was said to have measured 11 feet in total length. The size strongly suggests *hippolestes,* which it ought to be from geographic considerations.

The form inhabiting the timber and swamps of eastern Texas undoubtedly is different from either *aztecus* or *hippolestes,* but whether it is the Florida panther (*coryi*), the Adirondack panther (*couguar*), or something else, will remain doubtful until specimens are procured from the region. Baird speaks of the redness of a skin collected by Captain Marcy on the Brazos River (Pac. R. R. Rep., VIII, 84, 1857), but the skin can not now be found. An old female panther, which died in the National Zoological Park January 19, 1900, was caught August 12, 1892, when about two or three weeks old, near Memphis, Tex., in the Red River Valley, east of the Staked Plains. The skin of this animal, now in the National Museum collection, agrees fairly well with skins of *hippolestes,* but the skull does not agree with any of the skulls in the National Museum and shows peculiarities probably due to life-long confinement.

In most of eastern Texas panthers are reported as formerly common, but now as very rare or entirely extinct. Individuals have been killed, however, within a few years in the swamps not far from Jefferson in the northeastern part and Sour Lake in the southeastern part of the State. At Tarkington Prairie Mr. A. W. Carter says there were a few panthers when he was a boy in 1860, but he has not seen one since. In the Big Thicket of Hardin County a few panthers have been killed in past years, and Dan Griffin, who lives 7 miles northeast of Sour Lake, says a very large one occasionally passes his place. He saw its tracks in the winter of 1903-4.

**Felis onca hernandezi**[a] (Gray).   Jaguar.                              121

    *Felis onca* Baird, Mamm. N. Am., p. 86, 1857 (in part).

The jaguar, the largest of North American cats, once reported as common over southern Texas and as occupying nearly the whole of

---

[a] An adult male jaguar killed near Center City, Mills County, Tex., September 3, 1903, agrees very closely in color and markings with a skin of *Felis hernandezi* from near Mazatlan, Mexico. The ground color in the Texas skin is a shade yellower, and the spotting slightly coarser, but the difference is too slight for any important significance. Unfortunately there is no skull with the Mazatlan skin, but the Texas skull is scarcely distinguishable from comparable skulls of typical *onca* from Brazil.

Baird's detailed description of a skin from the Brazos River also agrees in a general way with this topotype skin from Mazatlan.

the eastern part of the State to Louisiana and north to the Red River, is now extremely rare. Occasionally there is a report that one has been killed, but in very few cases have the reports been substantiated by specimens. A skin from the Brazos River, Texas, without a date, but entered in the National Museum Catalogue in 1853 and described in detail by Professor Baird in the Mexican Boundary Survey (Vol. II, part 2, p. 6), seems to have disappeared. This specimen was obtained from J. M. Stanley, but no more definite locality was given than 'Brazos River.' The following note from H. P. Attwater was published by Doctor Allen in his list of mammals of Aransas County, Tex.[a] "Captain Bailey says he formerly owned a fine skin of a jaguar killed on the point of Live Oak Peninsula by J. J. Wealder and A. Reeves in 1858, but has not heard of any in this neighborhood since."

In reply to a request for detailed information relating to a mounted specimen of a jaguar mentioned in a previous letter, Mr. H. P. Attwater writes under date of June 4, 1904, as follows:

> Since writing I have been in San Antonio, and while there hunted up my friend Mr. Frank Toudouze, and from him obtained some information about the jaguar referred to in previous communication. Mr. Frank Toudouze, who is now living in San Antonio, remembers the circumstances very well, and tells me that the jaguar was killed by his brother, Henry Toudouze, and party of hunters, in 1879, about 10 miles south of Carrizo Springs, in Dimmit County, Tex. He tells me that it was a male, and even at that time considered a rare animal in that part of Texas. Mr. Henry Toudouze died a few years ago, but I have heard him tell about the killing of this particular animal many times, as well as hearing his father and brothers speak of it. When I came to Texas it was in Mr. Gustave Toudouze's (the old gentleman) collection, and he and I took it with other specimens to the New Orleans Exposition in 1884, as a part of the Texas Natural History Exhibit of which we had charge. At the close of the New Orleans Exposition it was brought with our collection back to San Antonio, and subsequently taken to Mexico by Mr. Frank Toudouze, who tells me that he sold it with the rest of the collection to the officials of the State Museum at Saltillo, State of Coahuila, and he says he has no doubt that the specimen is still there.

In 1902 Oberholser heard of a jaguar that was killed south of Jasper a few years before, and also obtained reports of the former occurrence of the species along the Neches River near Beaumont and in the timber south of Conroe. There have been several reports from different sources of one killed near the mouth of the Pecos in 1889, or near that date, and in 1901 Oberholser got a record of one killed south of Comstock "some years ago," but without a definite date. At Camp Verde, Cary was told by a Mr. Bonnell of a jaguar killed in 1880 at the head springs of the Nueces River, but this may have been the Toudouze specimen from Carrizo Springs.

---

[a] Bul. Am. Mus. Nat. Hist., VI, 198, 1894.

The skin and skull of a fine old male jaguar killed near Center City, Mills County, Tex., September 3, 1903, through the efforts of Mr. H. P. Attwater, the enthusiastic naturalist of Houston, Tex., have been secured and safely lodged in the National Museum. Through the courtesy of Mr. Gerrit S. Miller, Jr., assistant curator of mammals in the U.S. National Museum, the correspondence relating to the capture of the animal and the securing of the skin and skull for the museum has been placed at my disposal. The following extracts from this correspondence are of special interest.

In a letter of March 21, 1904, Mr. Attwater wrote to Mr. Miller:

> Last fall I heard that a jaguar had been killed near Goldthwaite, in Mills County, north of the Colorado River, in west central Texas, and wrote to parties in that section for particulars, but with poor satisfaction, so made up my mind to go there the first opportunity for the purpose of getting at the facts. I was so much engaged with my work that I was unable to spare time to do this until several weeks ago, but I am glad to say that I am now able to report very satisfactory results, and that I found the skull and hide still there, also ordered photographs (from the negative taken at the time), which have just come to hand. I take pleasure in sending you one with this letter, and later on will send you full particulars, with date of killing, etc., the most important of which I already have.

>       *       *       *       *       *       *       *

> In regard to the killing of the jaguar, I understood from Mr. Hudson, who skinned him, and from others, that they found it accidentally, and that they were hunting wildcats at the time they ran across him. I was told while I was there that another jaguar had been reported in the same locality after this one was killed, and it was supposed that there was a pair of them, but as far as I could find out nothing had been heard or seen of the other one for some time past. * * * In regard to how the jaguar came there, my idea is that it strayed there probably with its mate from the Rio Grande region, which it could easily have done by the route indicated on the inclosed map. The character of the country all along this route from the Rio Grande to Mills County is similar and not thickly inhabited, and I am inclined to think the animal made its way up the San Saba River and across the Colorado into Mills County. I took particular note of the country around Goldthwaite and in that part where the animal was killed it is rough with rocky ridges which they call 'mountains,' running parallel with the creeks and rivers, with uneven valley lands between the streams and the mountains. There is no tall timber, but the entire country is covered with a thick brush or chaparral, consisting chiefly of shin oak thickets known as the 'shinnery,' also sumac thickets and Spanish oak clumps with live oak trees scattered among them. On the lower flats there are considerable mesquite trees.

Later Mr. Attwater wrote as follows:

> I send you by express box containing the skin and skull of jaguar. * * * Miss Julia Kemp, the photographer in Goldthwaite, very kindly promised to write to the parties who killed the animal to get the data and other particulars for me. I herewith inclose you the correspondence, together with a letter she sent, received from Homer Brown, one of the parties in the "fight."

The following letter from Homer Brown was addressed to Miss Julia Kemp, March 20, 1904:

> Yours of 15th at hand. In regard to the jaguar, we killed him Thursday night, September 3. I will give some of the particulars. Henry Morris came to go hunting with me that night. I had a boy staying with me by the name of Johnnie Walton. We three took supper at my home and then started for the mountains, 3 miles southwest of Center City, where we started the jaguar just at dark. We ran him about 3 miles and treed him in a small Spanish oak. I shot him in the body with a Colt .45. He fell out of the tree and the hounds ran him about half a mile and bayed him. I stayed with him while Morris went to Center City after guns and ammunition. In about an hour and a half he came back and brought several men with him, so then the fight commenced. We had to ride into the shinnery and drive him out, and we got him killed just at 12 o'clock that night. We commenced the fight with ten hounds, but when we got him killed there were three dogs with him, and one of them wounded. He killed one dog and very nearly killed several others. He got hold of Bill Morris's horse and bit it so bad it died from the wounds. * * * The men in the chase were three of the house boys, Al and Joe Tangford, George Morris, Bill Morris, Thad Carter, Claud Scott, Henry Morris, Johnnie Walton, and myself. The jaguar measured 6 1/2 feet from tip to tip, 36 inches around chest, 26 inches around head, 21 inches around forearm, 9 inches across the bottom of foot; weight, 140 pounds.

## 122 Felis pardalis limitis Mearns. Ocelot; Leopard Cat.

*Felis pardalis* Baird, Mamm. N. Am., 87, 1857 (in part).

*Felis limitis* Mearns, Proc. Biol. Soc. Washington, XIV, p. 146, 1901.

The ocelots are still found in brushy or timbered country over southern Texas, as far north as Rock Springs and Kerrville, and up the Pecos Valley to the region of Fort Lancaster. One killed near the Alamo de Cesarae Ranch, in Brewster County, between Marfa and Terlingua, in 1903, was reported by Mr. G. K. Gilbert, and later its beautiful light-gray skin was purchased from Mrs. M. A. Bishop, of Valentine. This seems to be the westernmost record for the State. Farther east ocelots are still reported as very rare about Beaumont and Jasper, near the eastern line of the State, and farther north, near Waskom and Long Lake. Early records carried their range across into Louisiana and Arkansas, but it is doubtful if at the present time they are to be found in the United States beyond the limits of Texas. Most of the records are from hunters, ranchmen, or residents of the country, who know the animal by the name of ocelot or leopard cat, or describe it as a long-tailed, spotted cat the size of the lynx. In 1902 at Sour Lake Hollister reported "several so-called leopard cats killed near there," and says: "They are described as about the size of the wildcat but of a different build, spotted and with a long tail." Near Beaumont Oberholser reported them as occasionally killed in the woods along the Neches River. In Kerr County Mr. Moore, the sheriff, told me that he saw a beautiful skin of a large, long-tailed, spotted cat that was killed 10 miles south of Kerrville the latter part of June, 1902. At Rock Springs in July of the same year Mr. Gething told me that each year a few ocelot skins were brought into the store for sale. In his report from Sheffield Cary says: "I am informed that leopard cats are fairly common in the cedar brakes along the Pecos southeast of here." In 1899 Mr. Howard Lacey, the well-known naturalist of Kerr County, told me that he occasionally caught an ocelot while hunting with dogs for other game, and in January, 1903, he wrote of the species as follows:

The few that I have seen have all been found by the hounds, usually when we were hunting bear, and always in just the kind of country a bear would choose—the roughest, rockiest part of a dense cedar brake. Once on the head of the Frio River in November the hounds struck a hot trail and were just beginning to get off well together on it when a splendid male ocelot sprang into a large cedar close to us. Thinking the hounds might be on a bear trail I shot the cat at once, put him behind me on the saddle, and made after the hounds, that were getting off at a good pace. They ran about 2 miles and then treed a female ocelot in the bottom of a steep canyon. This we also shot and I think the two were together when we started them, and that they often go in pairs. They are not common here, but I fancy that they often rest in the trees and so escape the dogs.

They are heavier and more muscular than the bobcat, and our hounds, that always make short work of a bobcat, find the leopard cat 'a tough proposition.' Unlike the bobcat, they have the strong odor peculiar to the larger felines, and I never killed one without being reminded of the lion house at the London Zoo.

I have never had the luck to find any kittens, but a friend of mine ran a female into a cave with his hounds and killed her; then the dogs went into the cave and killed and brought out two kittens a few weeks old. This was in November. On another occasion he killed a female that in the course of a few days would have brought forth two kittens. Another of my neighbors killed a female and two kittens in a cave near here. This was also in November, and the kittens had not yet got their eyes open.

These cats do much damage to the stockmen, being especially fond of young pigs, kids, and lambs. They probably also kill fawns and turkeys, and, like many other cats, often hide what they can not eat under a heap of leaves.

### Felis cacomitli Baird (Berlandier MS.). Red and Gray Cat.                    123

1857. *Felis yaguarundi* Baird, Mamm. N. Am., 88, 1857. From Lower Rio Grande region; not *Felis yagouaroundi* Geoffroy, 1803, from Guiana. Gray phase.

1857. *Felis eyra* Baird, Mamm. N. Am., 88, 1857. From Lower Rio Grande region; not *Felis eyra* Fisch., 1815, from Paraguay. Red phase.

1859. *Felis cacomitli* Baird (Berlandier MS.), Report Mex. Boundary Survey, II, 12, 1859. From Matamoras, Mexico. Gray phase.

1901. *Felis apache* Mearns, Proc. Biol. Soc., Washington, XIV, 150, 1901. From Matamoras, Mexico. Red phase.

1902. *Felis cacomitli* Mearns, Proc. U. S. Nat. Museum, XXIV, 207, 1902. Gray phase.

A study of the specimens in the Biological Survey and U. S. National Museum collections, including five skins and skulls of the red cats and six of the gray from southern Texas and eastern Mexico, reveals no constant difference in cranial or external characters other than color. The striking coincidence of range and similarity of habits, as well as structure, of the red and gray cats strengthen the evidence tending to show that these supposedly distinct species present only another case of dichromatism, comparable to the black and cinnamon bear and the red and gray phases of the screech owl. A wide range of individual variation in size, shades of color, and in cranial characters is shown in the series of specimens examined. The type skull of *apache* shows the widest departure in characters, and especially in dwarfed size; but as the animal was captured when very young and kept in confinement throughout the rest of its life without becoming wholly domesticated, this may account for abnormal development.

Owing to lack of enough Central and South American specimens to show the relationship of *cacomitli,* through the several intervening forms, with typical *yagouaroundi* and *eyra,* it seems best for the present to treat this northernmost and relatively light-colored form as a species. When the relationships of the group are fully worked out it will doubtless stand as a subspecies of *yagouaroundi.*

The Biological Survey collection contains four specimens of the gray and one of the red cat from Brownsville, collected by F. B. Armstrong in 1891 and 1892, and a young one of the gray form collected by Lloyd, August 9, 1891. This quarter-grown young was reported as one of a litter of four caught by a boy and a dog in a 'resaca' near Brownsville. Lloyd also reported seeing one fresh and several dry hides of the gray cat in Brownsville, and mentioned two "ancient mounted specimens" of the red cat in Armstrong's collection there, but did not say where they originally came from. Since then Armstrong has sent to the National Zoological Park at Washington four of the red and two of the gray cats alive from the Lower Rio Grande region.

In a letter from Brownsville to Dr. Frank Baker, superintendent of the National Zoological Park, Armstrong writes:

Eyra and yaguarundi cats inhabit the densest thickets where the timber (mesquite) is not very high, but the underbrush—catsclaw and granjeno—is very thick and impenetrable for any large-sized animal. Their food is mice, rats, birds, and rabbits. Their slender bodies and agile movements enable them to capture their prey in the thickest of places. They climb trees, as I have shot them out of trees at night by 'shining their eyes' while deer hunting. I capture them by burying traps at intervals along the trails that run through these thick places. I don't think they have any regular time for breeding, as I have seen young in both summer and winter, born probably in August and March. They move around a good deal in daytime, as I have often seen them come down to a pond to drink at midday, and often see them dart through the brush in daytime. They are exceedingly hard to tame. Their habitat is from the Rio Grande, 40 miles north of here, as far as Tampico, Mexico. Beyond that I don't know.

A 'long-tailed yellow lynx' reported by John M. Priour from west of Corpus Christi in December, 1902, may have been this species. Mr. Priour thought it might be a partially albino ocelot. Apparently the same animal was seen there two years before by Dr. Adolph Huff, of San Antonio, who thought it might be a young panther.

**Lynx rufus texensis** Allen.   Texan Lynx.                          124

The large, dark, and usually much spotted and lined lynx of southern and eastern Texas ranges in Lower Sonoran zone north to at least Montague and Cooke counties and west to Kinney County. An immature specimen from Antioch and three skulls and six skins from Hardin and Liberty counties carry its range to near the eastern part of the State. More material may show that the form inhabits the whole Lower Sonoran zone of Texas, including the Pecos and Rio Grande valleys, and grades into *baileyi* or overlaps it in range in the Davis Mountains country. It is common over southern and eastern Texas and especially abundant in the dense chaparral of cactus and mesquite along brushy stream bottoms and in the timbered gulches where the lower arm of the Staked Plains breaks down into the low country, and in the swamp country farther east. At Port Lavaca Oberholser reports: "The wildcats are common in places away from town where there is sufficient cover, such as live-oak thickets and the great rose hedges. In the thickets they are not so difficult to hunt, but in the hedges they have almost impenetrable cover, and it is well-nigh impossible to reach them except by trapping." He says that at O'Connorport "a good many wildcats inhabit the thicker part of the oak brush, where they can be hunted only with dogs;" on Matagorda Island "they occur in the little chaparral that grows on the island;" and at Beeville "they are common in the denser portions of the chaparral, where specimens are frequently secured not far from town." From Corpus Christi to Brownsville in 1900 wildcats were common along streams and in the chaparral, where their tracks were abundant in the dusty trails and on the muddy margins of streams and pools, but where the cover was generally too dense and thorny to admit dogs or to allow any method of hunting save by traps or poison. Lloyd states in his report that along the lower Rio Grande and in Cameron County "most of the ranchmen will not allow the wildcats to be killed for fear their ranches will be overrun with wood rats, mice, and rabbits." Not only in this region, but farther north and east this fear has been realized many times in swarms of wood rats, cotton rats, and rabbits, but the services of such predatory mammals as wildcats, foxes, and coyotes are not always recognized by the ranchmen. I have found this lynx common at Uvalde, Devils River, Kerr County, and farther east at Seguin, but in no other locality so abundant as in the Big Thicket of

Liberty and Hardin counties. Here its tracks were seen in every muddy spot in roads and trails, and on damp mornings the dogs started one about as soon as they got into the thicket. The cat would rarely tree, but usually, rabbitlike, would run round and round in a limited circle in the thickest part of the swamp, depending on out-running or dodging the dogs. Cat hunting is a favorite sport in this region, and the hunters usually take stands in open spots and wait for the dogs to drive the game within shot. In one case I shot the cat in front of the hounds as it passed me for the third time. It did not seem tired or much alarmed, but easily kept out of sight of the dogs.

The stomach of this individual was full of venison that had not been perfectly fresh when eaten, probably from a deer that had been wounded by some hunters a week before. The hunter with me said he had examined the stomach of one not long before that was full of wood rats, and Gaut found wood rats in the stomach of one examined at Sour Lake. The food of this, like other species of lynx, consists mainly of rodents, rabbits, wood rats, ground squirrels, gophers, and mice, with a few birds, and occasionally some poultry. There are a few complaints of their killing sheep, young goats, and pigs.

**Lynx baileyi** Merriam.    Plateau Wildcat.

The lynx of the mountains and Staked Plains regions of western Texas, as shown by specimens from the Davis Mountains, and from near Alpine and Van Horn, and flat skins from Stanton and Odessa, is indistinguishable from *baileyi,* which seems to occupy at least the Upper Sonoran zone of Texas. An immature specimen from Pre-sidio County, a flat skin from the east base of the Chisos Mountains, and a flat skin labeled El Paso [?], are referred somewhat doubt-fully to this species, but good material from the Rio Grande Valley may change this decision.

The country occupied by this plateau wildcat is mainly open, arid, and rocky. Canyons, gulches, and cliffs are its favorite haunts and hunting grounds, while caves and clefts in the rocks furnish dens and safe retreats from which hunting excursions are made into the valleys and even to the edge of the plains. Fresh tracks are fre-quently seen where the cats have followed the lines of the cliffs, crept along narrow shelves of rock from one wood rat's den to another, or walked noiselessly in the dust under and around the great bowlders and broken talus at the base of a cliff where the cottontails hide. Most of the wildcat's hunting is done at night, but occasionally one is surprised at midday crossing a valley to another cliff or found toward evening getting an early supper. One shot among the rocks near Alpine just before sundown had already caught and eaten a wood rat, which made a good beginning for a meal. On the head of Onion

Creek, Presidio County, in January, 1890, while watching the hawks come into the cottonwoods to roost one evening at sundown, I saw a pair of bright eyes among the branches overhead and slowly traced out the almost invisible form of a wildcat flattened along a rough gray branch. I needed the specimen, so did not wait to see if hawks were the object of his hunt, but an empty stomach showed that he had met with no success.

Here and there in some rocky corners of the cliffs one finds elongated pellets of bones and fur, some freshly deposited, others old and bleached, and these throw important light on the food habits of the animal. Bits of fur, teeth, and jaws serve to identify many of the mammals that have been eaten, and usually disclose a great preponderance of rabbits and wood rats. Traces of many smaller rodents and a few bird feathers and bones are found, but no remains of food other than animal. The ranchmen complain of some poultry's being killed, and, still worse, a few sheep. This, with a few quail and other birds, is about all that stands against the account of the wildcat, with a much larger amount on the credit side.

Wildcats are not readily trapped, as they rarely follow the same trail twice or touch any kind of bait. A few are shot, and the cowboys occasionally rope one in the open, but they are most successfully hunted with dogs at night or early in the morning. When started, they quickly take to a tree or to the rocks, and are shot or driven out of the tree, or sometimes smoked out of the rocks.

**Canis griseus** Sabine.    Gray Wolf; Loafer; Lobo.                    126

The big, light-gray wolf, 'loafer,' or 'lobo' is still common over most of the plains and mountain country of western Texas, mainly west of the one hundredth meridian. As its range seems to extend into Lower Sonoran zone no farther than a wolf would naturally wander in a few nights, the animal seems to be restricted approximately to the Upper Sonoran and Transition zones in the State. The only Texas specimens which I have for comparison are a skull from the top of the Guadalupe Mountains, just south of the New Mexico line, and one from Monahans, east of the Pecos Valley, both of which agree with skulls of the Colorado and Wyoming animals, the skins examined by Merritt Cary from Monahans and 50 miles north of Stanton, on the southern end of the Staked Plains, and by myself from the Pecos Valley, and a live animal seen at Portales, N. Mex., all agree essentially with the fine series of Colorado, Wyoming, and Montana skins in the Biological Survey collection. Moreover, descriptions by the ranchmen over this region apply in every instance to the large, light-gray wolf, while along the southern edge of the plains almost all of the ranchmen distinguish between the red wolf or big coyote of the rough country and the larger, lighter-colored 'loafer' of the plains to the north. At Comstock, where special bounties are paid by sheep owners for the coyote and the common red wolf, the 'loafer' is unknown. A specimen killed 20 miles north of there on the higher plains in 1901 excited especial comment and raised the question whether or not the range of the gray wolf is being extended southward.

These wolves are most abundant in and about the Davis and Guadalupe mountains and over the Staked Plains and open country east of the Pecos River. Whether they are residents in the Pecos Valley or merely wanderers between the plains and the mountains is not easily determined, but I have no record of their breeding in the low part of the valley, while they are known to breed commonly in the high country on both sides. The present abundance of the species in any given place is not easily determined, as inferences are mainly drawn from the numbers killed, rather than the numbers left alive. Personally I have known of six or eight that were killed in 1901 and 1902 in the Davis Mountains, and a few in the Guadalupe Mountains and on the Staked Plains that were poisoned or dug out of their burrows. While my own observations have been limited, they aid in determining the accuracy of numerous other reports from resident hunters and ranchmen. These reports indicate that the wolves are not decreasing in numbers rapidly, if at all, in spite of those killed by ranchmen and by professional wolf hunters. On many of the large ranches a special bounty of $10, $20, or sometimes $50, is paid for every wolf killed. Several smaller ranches often combine to offer a large bounty in addition to that paid by the county, so that wolf hunting becomes a profitable business. In such cases there is a strong temptation for the hunters to save the breeding females and dig out the young each year for the bounty, thus making their business not only profitable but permanent. The hunters also bring wolves from a distance to the ranch paying the highest bounty. The bounty system offers dangerous temptations and has never proved effectual or even highly beneficial over any large area.[a]

To protect themselves from fraud and their stock from wolves many of the large ranch owners employ wolf hunters by the month and pay them well to keep the wolves and other noxious animals from their range. On the whole, when skilled hunters can be procured, this seems by far the most economical and satisfactory method.

When opportunity offers, the 'loafer' not only kills sheep but often kills a large number, apparently for the pleasure of killing. His regular and most serious depredations, however, are on the scattered

---

[a] Extermination of Noxious Animals by Bounties, T. S. Palmer, Yearbook U. S. Department of Agriculture, 1896, p. 55.

and unguarded cattle of the range. Two or three wolves usually hunt together and sometimes pull down a steer, but most of their meat is procured from yearlings or cows. Occasionally a colt is killed, but not often. Where two or three wolves take up their residence on a ranch and kill one or more head of cattle almost every day, the ranchmen become so seriously alarmed that they frequently offer a reward of $50 or $100 apiece for the scalps. In his report from Monahans, Merritt Cary writes:

I secured a skull of a very large female lobo wolf, which was killed on Hawkins's ranch in March, 1902, by Hugh Campbell. The skin when stretched on the side of the house is said to have measured 8 feet 4 inches from nose to end of tail, and was turned in to the Stockmen's Association, which paid Campbell $50 bounty on the animal. This female wolf was the mate to 'Big Foot,' a famous wolf throughout the region, whose track is always recognized by an extremely large right forefoot. On the second day of my stay at Hawkins's ranch Campbell and I got on the trail of 'Big Foot' and another wolf, which had crossed our own trail within two hours. Although on the trail for four hours we got no sight of them, nor did we find where they had killed any calves. There is a standing reward of $75 for 'Big Foot' by the Stockmen's Association; but although persistently hunted and trapped for a half dozen years, and thoroughly known to every cowboy in the region, the wily old wolf still retains his freedom, spurning poisoned baits, even disdaining to touch any meat not freshly killed by himself.

From Lipscomb, July, 1903, Howell reports: "Gray wolves occur in small numbers in this county, and a few cattle have recently been killed by them."

In disposition the 'loafer' is quite different from the coyote, lacking its cunning and assurance in the vicinity of man, and showing greater intelligence in the wild state and a better disposition when tamed. A half-grown 'loafer' that I found playing about the hotel at Portales, a little town on the edge of the Staked Plains, was like a big, good-natured puppy, full of fun and play, but soon became fighting angry if roughly handled. Although running at liberty over the town, he had never tried his puppy teeth on the chickens and pigs around him. He was the only survivor of a litter of seven, dug out of a burrow before their eyes were open. The others died, but 'Sampson' was nursed on a bottle for seventeen days—until his eyes opened. When I saw him in June he already gave promise of becoming a good-sized 'loafer.' He had a powerful voice and always responded to music with a doleful howl.

**Canis (ater?)** Richardson.  Black Wolf.

The black wolf is reported from a few localities in the timbered region of eastern Texas, but in most cases as "common years ago, now very rare or quite extinct." The more numerous reports of a "large gray wolf" or "timber wolf" in the same region merely indicate variation in color, and show that only a minority of the individuals are entirely black. Presumably they all are of the same species. Apparently there is not extant a Texas skin or skull of this wolf to show whether or not it is the same species as the one in Florida, and it is greatly to be hoped that specimens will find their way to the National Museum before the species becomes entirely extinct.

Audubon, who had more experience with these wolves in their wild state and original abundance than any naturalist will ever have again, considered the black wolf of eastern Texas, Louisiana, southern Missouri, Kentucky, North Carolina, and Florida as one species, and carefully distinguished it from the "red wolf" of southern Texas and the white or gray wolf of the plains.[a]

128 **Canis rufus** Aud. and Bach.   Texan Red Wolf.

Since his work on the coyotes in 1897, Doctor Merriam has made special effort to procure specimens of the large coyote or small wolf of southern Texas. As a result there are at the present time fourteen skulls and four skins of this wolf in the Survey collection from Columbus, Corpus Christi, O'Connorport, Port Lavaca, Kerr County, Edwards County, and Laredo, in addition to two skulls in the National Museum, one from Fort Richardson, Jack County, Tex., and one from Matamoras, Mexico. Based on these specimens and the field reports of the Biological Survey a definite range can be assigned the species, covering the whole of southern Texas north to the mouth of the Pecos and the mouth of the Colorado, and still farther north along the strip of mesquite country east of the plains, approximately covering the semiarid part of the Lower Sonoran zone. As yet there are no specimens to show whether these wolves extend into the more arid region west of the Pecos. While apparently nowhere overlapping the range of the larger, lighter-colored 'lobo' or 'loafer' of the plains, they take its place to the south and east as soon as the plains break down and the scrub oak and mesquite country begins, but their whole range is shared with the coyote. The ranchmen invariably distinguish between them and coyotes, and with good reason, for the wolves kill young cattle, goats, and colts with as much regularity as the coyotes kill sheep. While paying a bounty of $1 or $2 for coyotes, the ranchmen usually pay $10 or $20 for red wolves.

129 **Canis nebracensis** Merriam.   Plains Coyote.

Five coyote skulls from Canadian and three from Sherwood, Tex., and three from Clayton and two from 30 miles southeast of Carlsbad, N. Mex., agree with typical *nebracensis* skulls from Johnstown, Nebr.; while a flat skin from Monahans is as pale as the type of

[a] Aud. and Bach., Quad. N. Am., II, pp. 130-131 and 243, 1851.

*nebracensis*. This gives to the species a perfectly logical range over the Panhandle and Llano Estacado, or the open Upper Sonoran plains of Texas, but specimens from many more localities are needed before its full range can be accurately outlined. At Lipscomb, in the northeast corner of the Panhandle, Howell reported coyotes July 10, 1903, as "common at some seasons." At Canadian, where five old skulls were secured at Simpson's ranch on Clear Creek, he reported them as "killed here in winter in some numbers;" and at Texline he stated that they were "fairly common in this region," and added that "two were seen during my stay (August 1-8), and another was killed at Buffalo Springs."

In crossing the summit of the Staked Plains I have often seen the coyotes, both from the train and from our camp wagon, and night after night from our camp fires have heard their long quavering howls. But when seen they were always just out of rifle range. They were not afraid, and in this open, level country have little reason for fear.

### Canis nebracensis texensis[a] subsp. nov.    Texas Coyote.                    130

> Type from 45 miles southwest of Corpus Christi, Tex., ♂ young adult, No. 116277, U. S. Nat. Mus., Biological Survey Coll. Collected by J. M. Priour, Dec. 14, 1901. Original No. 3478, X catalogue.

*General characters.*—Similar to *C. nebracensis,* but darker and brighter colored and with lighter dentition. Smaller, brighter, and more fulvous than *latrans;* almost as richly colored as *ochropus,* but without the large ears of that species. Not in the same group as *microdon, mearnsi,* and *estor.*

*Color.*—Fresh winter pelage buffy gray, heavily clouded with black, becoming clear, bright, fulvous on legs, ears, and nose, and whitish on throat and belly; a strong line of black down front of foreleg. Summer pelage duller and darker.

*Skull.*—Slightly slenderer than in *nebracensis,* with conspicuously lighter dentition, narrower molars and carnassials.

*Measurements of type.*—Total length, 1,143; tail vertebrae, 355 (measured by collector); hind foot, 180 (measured from dry skin). Skull of type: Basal length, 169; greatest length of nasals, 67; zygomatic breadth, 94; mastoid breadth, 61; interorbital breadth, 30; length of crown of upper carnassial tooth, 19.8.

The Texas coyote is more or less common over at least middle and

---

[a] In his Revision of the Coyotes, published in the Proc. Biol. Soc. Wash., XI, 26, 1897, Doctor Merriam referred this coyote provisionally to *frustror,* of which the half-grown type was then the only available specimen. A series of topotypes of *frustror* secured since at Red Fork, Ind. T., shows it to be a widely different species, more nearly related to *Canis rufus.* The coyote of southern Texas is thus left without a name, and its nearest relative proves to be the pale *nebracensis* of the more northern plains.

southern Texas and apparently eastward on strips of prairie as far as Gainesville and Richmond. There are vague reports of a small wolf occurring farther east on the coast prairie even to the border of Louisiana, but specimens are needed before these reports can be associated with definite species. East of the semiarid mesquite region coyotes are rare and probably mere stragglers. True to their name of prairie wolf, they do not enter the timbered country to any extent, although at home in the scrub oak, juniper, mesquite, and chaparral, as well as over the open prairies of the southern part of the State. In the extreme southern part of the State their range is slightly overlapped by that of the little *microdon,* and in the extreme western part by that of *mearnsi,* while specimens from the northern Pan Handle country and Staked Plains are nearer to *nebracensis.*

In spite of the enmity of man, in spite of traps, poison, gun, and dogs, the coyote over most of his old range fairly holds his own. Combining with the cunning and suspicion of the fox a speed and endurance that almost insures his safety from ordinary hounds, he has little to fear except an occasional long-range shot or the traps and poison of the professional coyote hunter.

On many of the large ranches men are employed by the month to kill the coyotes, lobos, and panthers, and some of these men have attained such skill as to be able almost to extirpate the coyotes over a considerable area. But the coyotes are wanderers, and while they soon gather where food is abundant and easily procured, they quickly leave an inhospitable region for better hunting grounds. Civilization has little terror for them. I have heard them howling near many of the little towns and ranches, where they were attracted by the smell of freshly killed beef or by carcasses that were far from fresh, and near a ranch corral have found many dead coyotes poisoned at the carcass of a cow. After dark they show little fear of the ranch dogs, and sometimes seem even to invite a chase. In fact they not infrequently cross with the ranch dogs and produce hybrids with erect ears and wolfish appearance. I have seen several of these hybrids with characters that substantiated the statement that they were half coyote. At San Pedro Park, San Antonio, I was shown a 6-months-old cross between a coyote and shepherd dog, bred and born in the zoo. Except for being nearly black it had the general appearance of a coyote. It was kept chained in the open and was on friendly terms with the keeper.

About our camps the coyotes on rare occasions are surprisingly familiar, coming close to the camp wagon, especially if there is fresh meat in it, though usually paying their visits after dark. Sometimes the first man up in the morning gets a glimpse of one sneaking away or on rare occasions gets a good shot within easy range. Except during the breeding season, when they are very quiet, their frequent serenades are our regular camp music.

Within certain limits the credit and debit sheets of the coyote are well balanced. On the one hand, he kills many sheep and a few goats, some poultry, and considerable game. On the other hand, the bulk of his food the year round consists of rabbits, prairie dogs, ground squirrels, gophers, wood rats, mice, and all the small rodents that come in his way. An unusual increase of jack rabbits in any region is always followed by a corresponding influx of coyotes, which probably accounts in part for the often observed fact that in the years following their maximum abundance jack rabbits are unusually scarce.

At times the food of the coyote consists largely of fruit, including that of several species of cactus, juniper and forestiera berries, persimmons, and the sugary pods of mesquite; but in times of scarcity a piece of rawhide garnished with a few horned toads, lizards, and some horse manure suffices for a meal.

**Canis mearnsi** Merriam.    Mearns Coyote.                      131

Four good specimens, skins and skulls, of coyotes collected near El Paso late in February, 1903, by James H. Gaut are *mearnsi* in slightly worn and faded pelage. One skull from near the Texas and New Mexico line, in Salt Valley, at the west base of the Guadalupe Mountains, a good skin and skull from the same valley a little farther north, several specimens from the edge of Tularosa Valley, three old skulls from Sanderson, and two from Samuels, near the mouth of the Pecos, a skull from Grand Falls, in the Pecos Valley, and one from 30 miles southeast of Carlsbad, N. Mex., all belong to this slender, bright-colored desert form of the small-toothed coyotes. From the locality 30 miles southeast of Carlsbad, with the skull of an old male that is unmistakably *mearnsi,* were collected two skulls of *nebracensis,* while from Sanderson and Salt Valley there are skulls that I can refer only to *texensis.*

There is not yet material enough to show whether *mearnsi* grades into *microdon* farther south or into *estor* farther north, but it evidently overlaps the range of both *nebracensis* and *texensis.* Nor are there any specimens from the Davis Mountain plateau to show what form or forms occur there. *Canis mearnsi,* so far as known, is Lower Sonoran in range.

Coyotes are common throughout the extremely arid valleys of western Texas, including the Pecos and Rio Grande valleys south to their junction. Distance from water seems to have no effect on their abundance, although in this region they can hardly find a spot more than an easy night's journey, 20 or 30 miles, from open water. We find their tracks along every road and trail, and often see one of the animals loping across the valley or watching us from a ridge, and frequently hear them from our evening camp fires. At El Paso in 1889 I jumped one from under a creosote bush, where it was sleeping at midday, within rifle shot of the town, and at another time saw four together on the mesa half a mile out from the railroad station. At Fort Hancock Gordon Donald reported them in 1902 as very abundant, and said: "I heard them calling in the evenings, and the Mexicans had several young ones that they had caught in the vicinity. A ranchman told me that in the low foothills where his ranch was situated he saw two or three coyotes every day."

132   **Canis microdon** Merriam.   Small-toothed Coyote.

This little dark-colored coyote of the lower Rio Grande Valley overlaps the range of *texensis* in southern Texas. Specimens from Brownsville, Roma, and Alice show all that we know of its range in the State. These localities indicate that it is a chaparral rather than a prairie species, but there is nothing to prove that its habits are different from those of *texensis*.

133   **Vulpes fulvus** (Desm.).   Red Fox.

Apparently the red foxes are not natives of Texas,[a] but since their introduction they are becoming locally common, especially over the eastern half of the State. Oberholser obtained reports of their occurrence at Texarkana, Jasper, and Austin; Hollister, at Antioch, Rockland, and Sour Lake; and Cary, from Kerr County and along Howard Creek and the Pecos River. The following extract from a letter from Mr. T. H. Brown to Mr. H. P. Attwater is, as Doctor Allen says, a document of historic interest:[b]

I was the first to introduce 'red foxes' into this part of the State. We had exchanged our old-time native hounds, or, as they are usually called, 'pot lickers,' for the Walker dogs from Kentucky, and the gray foxes proved themselves no match for these dogs, only being able to run from twenty to forty-five minutes ahead of them. Having the dogs, it became necessary to get game that would give them a respectable race. Accordingly, in 1891, I imported from Kentucky and Tennessee 10 red foxes and placed them among the Bosque brakes, about 4 miles above where it empties into the Brazos River. They gradually scattered over a large area of country. The next spring (1892) I again brought in 23 more reds from the older States, planting 13 of them again among the Bosque brakes and 10 of them on White Rock Creek, on the east side of the Brazos River. These foxes afforded us some fine sport; but they, too,

---

[a] See Aud. & Bach., Quad. N. Am., II, 271, 1851.
[b] Extract of letter from T. H. Brown, Waco, Tex., in Bul. Am. Mus. Nat. Hist., VIII, p. 77, 1896.

gradually scattered, only a few remaining in the neighborhood of their adopted home, some wandering off through Bosque and Erath counties. The next spring I only succeeded in getting 2 reds from the East and planted these on the Bosque, and they remained and are still affording fine races. In the spring of 1895 I again planted 5 reds on the river near Lovers Leap, where the waters of all the Bosques mingle with the waters of the Brazos. Some of the bluffs here are 300 feet high and have a great many caves in them, and these last foxes seem well satisfied with their new home. Occasionally I hear of a red fox in various parts of this (McLennan) county, and I am satisfied that within a few years they will be as numerous here as in the old States.

I understand that Messrs. Eli and James Rosborough and Capt. T. H. Craig, all of Marshall, Harrison County, some ten or fifteen years since planted quite a number of reds in that, the eastern, part of the State, and occasionally they find them where they have located off some 20 or 30 miles from where originally turned loose.

Dr. John D. Rogers has, I think, during the spring of 1895, planted some 6 or 8 on his Brazos bottom farms in Brazos and Washington counties. I should suppose that in all there have been at least 100 red foxes imported and planted in the State.

**Vulpes velox** (Say).   Swift; Kit Fox.

134

So far as known the swift in Texas ranges only over the Upper Sonoran Staked Plains. It is reported at Tascosa and Washburn on the northern end of the plains and near Stanton and Midland at the southern end. In 1902 Cary secured five flat skins at Stanton, but says the ranchmen reported the swifts as scarce there in comparison with their numbers in former years. Most of these skins were secured by poison put out in winter, when the swifts were said to come to the poisoned bait generally the first night after it was put out, while the coyotes usually waited until later.

**Vulpes macrotis neomexicanus** Merriam.   New Mexico Desert Fox.

The little desert fox has been taken in the Rio Grande, Tularosa, and Pecos valleys just north of the Texas line, and one specimen was taken by James H. Gaut in Texas 10 miles north of El Paso. It is reported from as far south as the mouth of the Pecos. A flat skin brought in to the store at Sierra Blanca in December, 1889, had the characteristic large ear of the group, the ear measuring 78 mm. from crown. Apparently the range of the species corresponds in this region to that of *Dipodomys spectabilis* in the open desert valleys of the Lower Sonoran zone. It is by no means common in the region, and many of the ranchmen have never seen it, or else have never distinguished it from the common and much larger and darker-colored gray fox of the genus *Urocyon*.

135  **Urocyon cinereoargenteus scotti** Mearns.    Gray Fox.

*Urocyon cinereoargenteus texensis* Mearns,[a] Proc. U. S. Nat. Mus., XX,
Advance Sheet, January 12, 1897, p. 2.

The gray fox is common over all the western half of Texas, except
on the open plains. It is mainly an inhabitant of the timbered or
brushy country, living in hollow trees or logs, but preferably in
dens among the rocks. It lacks the cunning and swiftness of the red
fox, is easily caught in traps, and quickly overtaken by the hounds,
except where it can keep in dense cover. Often after a short run,
and sometimes at the very start, it trees or takes to its rock den,
where it is safe from the dogs; but if no such protection offers there

FIG. 21.—Gray fox (*Urocyon c. scotti*) in trap, Langtry, Texas.
(Photographed by Oberholser.)

is little hope for the fox. Even over rocks and in the brush I have
seen the hounds catch one in a 200-yard dash. With a good start,

---

[a] The original label on the type of *Urocyon c. texensis* reads: "Rio Bravo and
San Pedro. 1851. A. Schott." As is well known, Rio Bravo is synonymous
with Rio Grande, and at that time the Devils River was commonly known as
the San Pedro. (See Baird's Mammals of N. Am., p. 713, and Pacific R. R.
Rept., Vol. I, p. 110. Also see query after Eagle Pass in Mammals, Mex. Boundary Survey, Vol. II, pt. 2, p. 17.) This seems to necessitate changing the type
locality of *texensis* from 'near Eagle Pass' to the junction of the Devils River
with the Rio Grande, which, however, has no important bearing on the validity
of the species. In comparing the type of *texensis* and other specimens from
near the mouth of Devils River, Painted Caves, Langtry, San Diego, and the
Davis Mountains, in western Texas, with the type of *scotti* and with specimens
from all around the type locality—near Tucson, Fort Huachuca, Fort Bowie,
Chiricahua Mountains, and Fort Verde—I am unable to find any constant difference, either cranial or external, on which to recognize *texensis*.

however, one will lead the hounds a long chase over the roughest ground it can find, and if it does not make the mistake of climbing a tree, instead of taking to the rocks, it is pretty safe. Strange as it may seem, these foxes go up the trunk of a tree with almost cat-like ease. I have found them looking down at the dogs from 20 to 40 feet up in the branches of nut pines and live oaks, and have known of their climbing a yellow pine (*Pinus ponderosa*) where 20 feet of straight trunk over a foot in diameter intervened between the ground and the first branch. More often they take to a live oak or juniper, where the lower branches can be reached at a bound, and then, squirrel-like, hide in the swaying topmost branches. On the approach of the hunter they become anxious and seem to doubt the security of their position, sometimes making a flying leap to the ground. Stones and clubs will usually dislodge them from the tree top, but as they still have a good chance to escape the dogs and take to the rocks, it is a common and heartless practice to shoot them so as to break a leg and make escape impossible.

With his smaller but laterally flattened tail the gray fox certainly equals, if he does not surpass, the red fox in quickness of motion and skill at dodging the dogs. If uninjured, he will often strike the ground in the midst of the hounds and escape by a few quick bounds to right and left. Apparently it is only his small size that puts him at a disadvantage in a test of speed with the hounds or with his larger cousin, the red fox.

In choice of food the gray foxes are almost as omnivorous as the coon. Various fruits form the bulk of their food in summer and part of it in winter, while a great variety of small game, beetles, grasshoppers, maggots, mammals, birds, and some poultry fall a prey to them during the year. In June they were feeding extensively on berries of *Zizyphus obtusifolia* and *Adelia angustifolia* along the Rio Grande near Boquillas, while around the Davis Mountains in early August they were feeding mainly on the ripe fruit of *Opuntia engelmanni*. In December in the Davis Mountains and in September in the Guadalupe Mountains they were eating the sweet pulpy berries of *Juniperus pachyphloea,* which grow in great abundance in these ranges and in the Chisos Mountains. Mice, wood rats, ground squirrels, rabbits, and various other small rodents are eaten when obtainable, and, much to our annoyance, are often taken from our traps or carried away, trap and all. At Langtry, Gaut examined several stomachs, and in one found part of a mocking bird and in another a *Perognathus*. At most of the ranches there are enough dogs to keep the foxes at a respectful distance from the poultry; but they have a keen relish for chickens, and are often complained of in vigorous terms. Without data for positive statements it seems probable that the good done in destroying small rodents equals, if it does not exceed, the mischief done among poultry.

As a game animal this fox is holding its ground better than many more important species, and even from the sportsman's point of view needs little protection. The skin is of so little value for fur that it is rarely saved when the fox is killed.

**136**   **Urocyon cinereoargenteus floridanus** Rhoads.   Florida Gray Fox.

A nearly adult male gray fox from the Big Thicket, near Sour Lake, Tex., agrees with the Florida specimens in dark color, dusky legs, feet, and face, and in most of the cranial characters. The shorter, heavier muzzle is evidently due to slight immaturity. A flat skin from Tarkington Prairie is less dusky, and while probably shading toward *scotti,* more nearly resembles *ocythous.* A skull in the National Museum from Washington County, a little farther west, also shows some of the characters of *ocythous,* but is not typical of any form. While I have no hesitation in referring the Big Thicket *Urocyon* to *floridanus,* it is probable that this is not the only form inhabiting the eastern part of the State. Before final conclusions can be reached more specimens are needed, especially from farther north.

To show how generally the gray fox is distributed over eastern Texas the following localities are given from which it is reported as more or less common: Henrietta, Gainesville, Arthur, Texarkana, Waskom, Rockland, Jasper, Sour Lake, Tarkington Prairie, Evergreen, Hempstead, Matagorda, Washington, Antioch, and Long Lake. Those from Rockport and Brazos are likely to be nearer to *scotti.* My information in regard to the habits of the animal in this region has been received mainly from residents, who say that the foxes keep in the brush and timber, especially along the river bottoms, where the thickest growth is found. They are said to climb trees, and complaints of their killing poultry are more frequent than in the more open country farther west.

Near Sour Lake Gaut reports them as found mainly in the pine woods at the edge of the thicket, but as occasionally straying down into the densest part of the thicket, where he caught one on Black Creek, near Mike Griffin's place. The stomach of this individual contained a mass of crayfish.

**137**   **Bassariscus astutus flavus** Rhoads.   Civet Cat; Cacomistle.

The civet cat is common all over Texas except the open plains country of the western half from Brownsville, Corpus Christi, Seguin, Austin, Brownwood, and Grady westward. It has been reported east to Matagorda County, near the coast, and a specimen in the U. S. National Museum is labeled "Red River." One from Grady, Fisher

County, seems to be the northernmost authentic record for the State, but the species undoubtedly continues along the canyons and cliffs of the eastern edge of the Staked Plains to the Red and Canadian rivers.[a]

Although preeminently inhabitants of rocks, cliffs, and canyon walls, civet cats are common over the chaparral, mesquite, and cactus plains of southern Texas down to the very coast, a peculiarity of distribution shared by a number of other mammals which find in the thorny cover of dense patches of cactus and tangled thickets of chaparral ample protection and a greater abundance of small game than in the rocky haunts of the higher country. In habits they are catlike, mainly nocturnal and carnivorous. At night they prowl along the ledges of cliffs from cave to cave, leaving the prints of their little, round, catlike feet in the dry dust of the darkest corners, and helping themselves to a liberal share of the *Peromyscus* and *Neotoma* found in the traps of careless collectors. Usually, however, the small rodents are extremely scarce where the civet cats are at all common, and the wise collector scatters his small traps out over the valley until his steel traps have cleaned the cliffs of carnivorous species.

Owing to their nocturnal habits and the fastness of their rock dens, the civet cats are rarely seen in the wild state, but when tamed the ranchmen say they make affectionate pets and are better mousers than the domestic cat. A pair was caught in traps in one of the canyons of the Rio Grande and the male fought and screamed viciously as we approached, but the female was quiet and gentle. Even in the traps the animation and brightness of their faces were wonderful. The large ears, when directed forward, were in constant motion. The long, black, vibrating moustache, the striking black and light face markings, and, most of all, the big, soft, expressive eyes give a facial expression of unusual beauty and intelligence. L. A. Fuertes, who was with me when these two were caught, made a careful color study of the head of the male, which loses but little of its excellence in the black and white reproduction.

An old female caught near Boquillas May 27 contained three nearly

[a] The range of *Bassariscus* has been supposed to extend eastward to Arkansas (see Baird, Mammals of North America, p. 147), and a skin in the U. S. National Museum is labeled "Red River, Ark." On the remaining fragment of the original label of this specimen is only "Red River, Capt. Marcy." There is no date on the label, but the skin was entered in the Museum catalogue March 31, 1853. In 1852 Captain Marcy explored the headwaters of the Red River and in his report records *Bassariscus* from the "Cross Timbers," probably this same specimen. (See Exploration of the Red River of Louisiana, p. 186, 1854, by Capt. Randolph B. Marcy. Also, for route of Captain Marcy, see map opposite p. 36 of Annual Report of Wheeler Survey, Rept. Chief of Engineers for 1876, App. JJ.)

developed fetuses, which, with a litter of four young recorded by Mr. Clark from San Pedro River, would indicate small families.[a]

Most of the stomachs of *Bassariscus* examined have been found to contain the bones and hair of small rodents, which make up also most of the excrement found along ledges and in caves where the animals live. Fragments of a large centipede were found in the stomach of one caught by Gordon Donald on Devils River; and in other localities they have been reported as eating fruit. At Langtry, Gaut caught several in traps baited with meat.

**138** **Taxidea taxus berlandieri** Baird.   Mexican Badger.

The badger is generally distributed over the western half of Texas, but apparently is unknown in the eastern part of the State. Its eastern limit corresponds, in a general way, with the eastern edge of the mesquite country. Specimens have been taken as far east as Corpus Christi, San Antonio, and Mason, and there are records from Clyde, Henrietta, and Mobeetie. A significant fact is that the badger's eastern limit of range agrees closely with the eastern limits of the prairie dog and the Mexican ground squirrel. Its abundance depends mainly on food supply, reaching a maximum on the open plains in the prairie-dog country and decreasing slightly in the southern part of the State and in the mountains and rocky country of the extreme western part. But in speaking of badgers, abundance may mean one to a square mile, while with prairie dogs it may mean 10,000 to a square mile.

When food is scarce the badgers become great wanderers. Their short legs are fully compensated by their unusual strength and by their capacity for digging and fighting, that enable them to escape from most enemies. But with such abundance of food as is found in a populous prairie dog town, they waste little time in travel. They become fat and lazy; but as food grows scarce they start off again on their travels, sinking a house in the earth wherever sleeping time overtakes them.

The badger feeds mainly on small rodents, varied with grasshoppers, beetles, scorpions, lizards, or some larger animal found dead. It is accused of killing poultry, but the accusation is so rarely substantiated that it may well be ignored. Pocket gophers, kangaroo rats, wood rats, and various kinds of mice are always acceptable, but the badger lives mainly on prairie dogs and ground squirrels, which fall an easy prey. He often digs a dozen holes along the interminable tunnel of a pocket gopher and then gives up in disgust, but a fat spermophile or prairie dog at the bottom of its simple burrow is entirely at his disposal, nor does he have much trouble in digging it

---

[a] Baird, Mammals of North America, p. 147, 1857.

out. A few minutes' work with his powerful claws will unearth the spermophile, while by merely enlarging the prairie-dog hole about two diameters he enters its deepest chambers and is sure of a good square meal at the end. On a ranch in the Pecos Valley I found a badger living in an alfalfa field that had been overrun with prairie dogs. Every morning there was at least one new hole that he had enlarged, and while he may have secured two or three prairie dogs in some of the burrows he was evidently destroying at least one a day. This badger was needed for a specimen, and at the earnest solicitation of the ranch people, who were afraid he would kill their

FIG. 22.—Prairie-dog burrow enlarged by badger, Pecos valley.

poultry, I finally shot him as he came out about 4 o'clock one afternoon to get his supper. He had begun on a Swainson hawk that had been shot the day before. Otherwise his stomach was empty, but the lower part of his alimentary tract was full of wads of prairie-dog fur from his meal of the previous night. He was fat and had evidently been working all summer in that 20-acre field. The people had no reason to believe that he had ever killed any of their poultry, but they were afraid that he would. There were already two badger skins hanging in the tool house on this ranch, while a 20-acre field of alfalfa was rendered almost worthless by prairie dogs. When I tried to convince the owners that every badger on the ranch was worth $100 to them they only laughed. Some of the ranchmen, however, appreciate the services of the animal, but even then the temptation to try a shot at one at long range or to let the dogs catch one for a fight is often too great to be resisted. Dead badgers are frequently seen by the roadside with smashed skulls or bullet holes through them, and this most often in the heart of the prairie-dog country. When taken to task for their folly in destroying these valuable animals the ranchmen have usually stoutly denied the charge, saying that most of them were killed by emigrants and other 'tenderfeet.'

The cowboys, however, have a real grievance against the badgers, especially those who have been thrown from running horses that had inadvertently stepped in old and half-concealed holes. Such accidents are by no means rare, and sometimes they are fatal to both horse and rider. It is hardly surprising, therefore, that the cowboys look upon the badger as a legitimate target for their six-shooters. In a prairie-dog country, however, this is not a fair excuse, for prairie-dog holes are just as dangerous, and each badger helps to reduce the total number of pitfalls.

The rapid increase in the abundance of prairie dogs in certain parts of the State and their constant extension of range is unquestionably due in great measure, if not mainly, to the destruction of badgers. It seems unaccountable that the intelligent observations of ranch people should not result in a strong sentiment in favor of protecting badgers, but it must be remembered that without the support of protective laws nothing can be done to prevent the destruction of the animals by uninterested and irresponsible people.

**Ursus americanus Pallas.    Black Bear; Cinnamon Bear.**[a]

Specimens of the black bears collected in the Wichita Mountains, Oklahoma, prove to be *americanus,* and the bears reported from Mobeetie and near Washburn were undoubtedly the same. Others reported farther south from west of Austin and even to Kerrville may have been the same, also the bears from the Guadalupe Mountains, but as no specimens from these Texas localities have been seen the species can be admitted to the State list only provisionally.

At Washburn in 1892 I was told that there were a few black bears south of there in the canyon of the Prairie Dog Fork, and at Mobeetie in 1901 Oberholser reported them as "formerly common, now extinct." In 1902 Oberholser obtained a rather indefinite report at Austin that "a few bears were still to be found in the rough country west of there," and the same year at Kerrville I was told that bears

---

[a] As is well known, the black and cinnamon bears are merely dichromatic forms, or color phases of the same species, one cub of a litter often being black and another brown.

were becoming very scarce, but that one had been killed the previous year only 7 miles from there.

**Ursus americanus amblyceps** Baird.　New Mexico Black Bear.　　140

Black bears are still found in the timbered mountains of western Texas, where in a few restricted areas they are fairly common. A few specimens examined from the Davis and Chisos mountains can best be referred to *amblyceps,* but there are no specimens from the Guadalupe Mountains or from middle Texas to show where this form gives place to *americanus* on the north or to *luteolus* of the eastern part of the State. The records from Kerrville, west of Austin, Prairie Dog Fork, (near Washburn), and Mobeetie I am inclined to refer provisionally to *americanus.*

In July of 1902 a young black bear was caught by the section men on the railroad near Comstock, and a few were reported from the Pecos Canyon and vicinity. Bears were formerly abundant in this region, but apparently no specimen has been preserved to show what form ranged in the Pecos, Devils River, and Rio Grande country. On Onion Creek, 30 miles south of Marfa, in January, 1890, I picked up a skull from one of three bears killed near there in 1887. In June of 1901 black bears were common in the upper canyons of the Chisos Mountains, where fresh tracks of old and young were frequently seen and where there was an abundance of old 'sign' and turned-over stones. The old excrement was made up largely of acorns, juniper berries, and pine nuts, while the seeds of cactus fruit were noticed in the fresher deposits.

In the Davis Mountains black bears hold their own surprisingly well against unusual odds. In July, 1901, I found abundant 'sign,' fresh tracks, and turned-over stones along the crest of the higher ridges on the east slope of Mount Livermore, and again in August, 1902, found 'sign' equally abundant in the canyons on the west slopes. In following up a deep canyon west of the main peak on August 13 after a heavy rain of the previous day, I saw fresh tracks of bears of at least three different sizes—cubs, yearlings, and adults—and found numerous little diggings in the black mellow soil where roots or beetles had been unearthed, and many stones freshly turned over for the ants and beetles beneath them. In a side gulch a large buckthorn bush (*Rhamnus purshiana*) had been freshly torn up and half stripped of its ripening berries, while close by was a lot of fresh bear 'sign,' made up entirely of the skins and seeds of these berries. In other places on the east slope I found fresh 'sign,' composed mainly of the sugary berries of the checker-barked juniper (*J. pachyphloea*), and some that was older, largely composed of acorn shells.

In the southern part of the Guadalupe Mountains, on the upper slopes of almost inaccessible canyons, black and brown bears were common in 1901. In the head of McKittrick Canyon they had well-worn trails leading to and from their feeding grounds on the oak and juniper ridges and down the canyon to the upper water holes. In places along the sides of narrow, bowlder-strewn gulches the trails were series of big, deep tracks, where for ages each bear had stepped in the footprints of his predecessor. On the open slopes the trails spread out and were lost. On some of these slopes almost every loose stone had been turned over by bears in their search for insects, but at the time of my visit, in August, they were feeding mainly on the sweet acorns of several species of shin oak, berries of the checker-barked juniper, and, to a less extent, berries of *Berberis fremonti.* Some of the previous year's excrement contained shells of pine nuts (*Pinus edulis*), but this was the off year, when the nut pines did not bear.

Near one of the trails in the head of Dog Canyon in the Gaudalupe Mountains a Douglas spruce a foot in diameter had served for many years as a gnawing tree, while farther up the gulch a larger yellow pine was well blazed and deeply scarred by many old and a few new gashes of powerful teeth. In the Davis Mountains, on the ridge just north of Livermore, a yellow pine a foot and a half through had served as a bear register for apparently ten or twenty years. It was deeply scored on all sides from 4 to 6 feet from the ground, but on one side from 5 to 6 feet up, the bark had long been cut away and the dry weathered wood was splintered and gashed with deep grooves of various ages. Two fresh sets of tooth prints showed on opposite sides of the tree near the top of the ring, and one little bear had lately tried his teeth in the green bark about 4 feet from the ground. At the head of a gulch on the east side of Limpia Creek stood another big yellow pine that had been similarly treated, and on it, as on the others, the upper limit of reach was about 6 feet from the ground. Apparently the bear at each visit to one of these register trees had given but a single bite, leaving the marks of an opposing pair of canines.

In January of 1890 I learned that ten or twelve bears had been killed in the Davis Mountains the fall before, and the annual bear hunt of the ranchmen has become as firmly established an institution there as the annual camp meeting. In November a large crowd gathers with camp wagons, hounds, and saddle horses for a week's bear hunting. In 1900 ten bears were killed by the party, and in 1902 four were killed. Others are killed each year by local hunters.

At present the black bears do no serious damage to stock, and it is greatly to be hoped that their numbers will not be materially reduced.

141     **Ursus luteolus** Griffith.   Louisiana Bear.

The Louisiana bear formerly ranged over most of eastern Texas, and still is found in considerable numbers in the more extensive swamps and thickets. Skulls examined from Kountze,[a] Sour Lake, Tarkington, and Wharton have the long, low brain case and very large molars characterizing the species, while the skins are indistinguishable from those of *americanus* in the black phase.

The following reports of field naturalists for 1902 from scattered localities will give an idea of the present status of the bears over eastern Texas:

Texarkana:  Now very rare; one killed a few years ago.

Waskom:  Formerly common; now very rare.

Jefferson:  Very scarce; one killed near here a few years ago.

Antioch:  Formerly common; now extinct.

Rockland:  Now very rare or quite extinct.

Conroe:  A few still found in the 'big thicket' 15 miles south of here.

Beaumont:  A few still found in the forest northwest of here.

Brenham:  Formerly common along the Brazos; now extinct.

Elgin:  Formerly common; now rare or extinct.

Sour Lake:  Still common in the swamps near here; a few killed every year. An old one and two cubs seen during July.

At Richmond in 1899 I was informed that bears were still fairly common in the timbered bottoms along the Bernard River, 18 miles to the southwest, where in the fall one old trapper made a business of trapping them. At Seguin, in 1904, they were said to have been exterminated years ago, though formerly common.

The following reports, made in 1900 by Oberholser, probably also relate to this species:

Beeville:  Bears are still found on the Nueces, 20 miles west of here.

San Diego: One was seen a few years ago some 12 miles northwest of here.

Uvalde:  A few are still found in the canyon of the Nueces.

At Wharton in November, 1904, I secured the skull of a bear killed the previous year by a negro who said there were still a good many in the thicket near there. Mr. W. O. Victor also told me that he knew where several bears were living in the thicket, and that he hoped to kill some of them later in the season when they became fat. Mr. Victor has an apiary with a large number of hives located at several points in the dense woods and thickets bordering the Colorado River below Wharton, and the bears have caused him much trouble and considerable loss through their fondness for honey. During the past ten years he has killed eight or nine bears, mainly for the protection of his bees. Some of these were killed with set guns, some by trapping, and others in the hunt. One was shot at night by Mr. Victor

---

[a] The Biological Survey is indebted to Mr. J. B. Hooks, of Kountze, for the loan of one skull of this species and the presentation of another.

and two companions who were watching for it in the bee stand. When the men approached the bear after he was located, they could hear him whining and sniffling as if the bees were making it hot for him. This probably accounts for his letting them come near enough by moonlight for a fatal shot. This bee stand was about 3 miles from town and back from any settlement or ranch, and the bear had been feasting on honey for several nights before the mischief was discovered. Mr. Victor says about fifty swarms were destroyed, the hives turned over, part of the honey scooped out, and the bees scattered. In many cases the bear apparently became enraged at the stings and smashed the hives in retaliation. A photograph of this bear, taken the following morning, shows him stretched out among the overturned hives and gives some idea of the mischief he had done.

Mr. Victor says the bears in that region 'den up' for a little while during the coldest part of winter, or at least keep quiet in the densest thickets. He says they are invariably black, and he thinks the nose also is black.

In November, 1904, an old bear hunter, Ab Carter, living on the west edge of Tarkington Prairie, in Liberty County, told me that there were no bears at that time in Liberty County west of the Trinity River, but the active part taken by Mr. Carter in exterminating the bears in that locality makes his statements of peculiar interest. Forty-nine years ago he was born on the ranch he now owns, and his principal occupation, like that of his father, has been keeping hogs and killing bears. To a man with several hundred hogs running in the woods, bear killing was the most important part of the season's work, but it was not until about 1883 that the extermination of the bears began in earnest. At that time Mr. Carter and a neighbor each got a pack of good bear hounds and in the following two years they killed 182 bears, mainly within a radius of 10 miles from the ranches. This reduced the number of bears so that later not more than ten to twenty were killed annually up to 1900, when Mr. Carter killed the last two of the vicinity. Two years ago he killed the last of his bear dogs, and now keeps only hog and wolf dogs, while his hogs eat acorns in safety over 100 square miles of magnificent forest and dense thicket.

The number of hogs killed in a year could be only approximately estimated, but Mr. Carter thinks the bears sometimes got nearly half of the pigs and many of the hogs. Pigs were their favorite prey, and were easily caught, but the bears took anything they could get. One large 4-year-old boar was killed and partly eaten only a mile from the house.

As soon as acorns began to fall the bears would feed on them and let the hogs alone for a while, but during spring and summer pork was their principal food. The first berry to ripen in summer, Mr. Carter says, is on the 'grandaddy graybeard' bush (apparently *Ame-*

*lanchier),* of which the bears are very fond. Blackberries and huckleberries are abundant summer food for bears. Later the sour gum (*Nyssa sylvatica*) is a favorite food, and nearly every sour-gum tree in the woods has its top branches bent and twisted and its bark well clawed.

Mr. Carter went with me to an old pine 'measuring tree' in the woods that he said had been bitten deep into the wood about as high up as he could reach, but when we found the tree it was only a charred stump. Fire had destroyed all trace of the bear marks. Another small pine that we found had grown well out around the old bites that still showed plainly in the dead wood. Mr. Carter says cypress trees are sometimes bitten in the same way by bears, but less commonly than pines.

In the Big Thicket of Hardin County black bears were common in many parts of the thicket in December, 1904, but not so abundant as they were a few years ago. I had no trouble in starting one almost every day, but could not get a pack of dogs that would hold one till I could get to it. I had five good bear hounds, but each of the several bears that we started escaped. The bears in this region rarely tree for dogs, and unless the dogs keep one fighting on the ground he travels faster than a man can run through the jungle of palmettoes, brush, and vines. Horses are useless in the thicket.

While hunting I found numerous bear beds and old and fresh 'sign,' some composed of acorns, some of sour gum and other berries. We also saw half chewed acorns where the bears had been feeding. During summer the bears feed extensively on pigs belonging to the settlers, but in December both pigs and bears were rapidly fattening on the abundant acorn crop.

In several places in the heart of the Thicket I found cypress trees gnawed by the bears as high as they could reach, 6 to 7 feet from the ground, and I photographed two of these trees. One, which was about a foot in diameter, had been bitten lately and at different times previously for at least eight or ten years. Several large spots of wood were dead and bare of bark and full of old tooth prints. The other tree, over 2 feet in diameter, had been bitten for a longer time, probably fifty years, and the old dead wood was sunken 4 or 5 inches deep in the surrounding growth. The fresher bites were on new spots and some were made apparently the day before, as fresh mud had been rubbed against the trunk as high up as 4 feet. One old-field pine about 14 inches in diameter had been well bitten at the usual height, but in this region cypress seems to be the favorite biting tree, or 'measuring tree,' as called by the hunters. Several magnolia trees showed deep claw marks in the smooth, gray bark, and the rough bark of the sour gum is often clawed extensively, although the marks are indistinct. The bears are said to feed to some extent on magnolia berries and very extensively on the berries of the sour gum.

I have inquired of many hunters and find none who have ever seen a brown bear in this region. The nose is said to be brown in some and entirely black in others. The large old male, of which I secured the skull and incomplete skin, was said to have had a brown nose, as did the perfect skin of the female sent with it. Dan Griffin, who killed it, says it was the largest bear he ever saw. He thinks it would have weighed 400 pounds, although poor, and says that two men while skinning it had hard work to turn it over.

142   **Ursus horribilis horriaeus** Baird.   Sonora Grizzly.

The only specimen of grizzly bear that I have seen or heard of from Texas was killed in the Davis Mountains in October, 1890, by C. O. Finley and John Z. Means. The skull, which Mr. Finley has kindly sent me for comparison, proves to be that of a large and very old male of the Sonora grizzly, agreeing in all essential characters with Baird's type of *horriaeus* from southwestern New Mexico. The measurements of the skull are: Greatest length, 370; basal length, 310; zygomatic breadth, 220; mastoid breadth, 157; interorbital breadth, 71; postorbital breadth, 69. The claws on the front feet, Mr. Finley says, were about 3 1/2 inches long, and the color of the bear was brown with gray tips to the hairs. Its weight was estimated at 1,100 pounds, 'if it had been fat.' Mr. Finley says that this bear had killed a cow and eaten most of it in a gulch near the head of Limpia Creek, where the dogs took the trail. Out of a pack of fifty-two hounds only a few would follow the trail, although most of them were used to hunting black bear. These few followed rather reluctantly, and after a run of about 5 miles over rough country stopped the bear, which killed one of them before it was quieted by the rifles of Finley and Means. It took four men to put the skin, with head and feet attached, upon a horse for the return to camp.

143   **Nasua narica yucatanica**[a] Allen.   Nasua; Coati.

A specimen of this long-nosed, long-tailed, coon-like animal in the National Museum, collected in 1877 at Brownsville by the late Dr. J. C. Merrill, furnishes apparently the only record for the State. As nasuas occur over most of Mexico up to near the border of the United States, other records along the Rio Grande may be expected.

144   **Procyon lotor** (Linn.).   Raccoon; Coon.

The raccoon of eastern Texas, as represented by specimens from the coast region as far west as Matagorda and in the interior from Tex-

---

[a] Dr. J. A. Allen, in Bul. Am. Mus. Nat. Hist., XX, 53, 1904, identifies the Brownsville specimen as *Nasua narica yucatanica* Allen; it is possible, therefore, that this specimen may have been an imported animal that escaped from captivity.

arkana west to Kerrville and Mason, differs but little from typical *lotor* of the northeastern United States. The slightly larger size, wider muzzle, and usually heavier dentition show a tendency toward *mexicanus,* into which it grades to the west. The high frontals of specimens from the coast marshes of southeastern Texas suggest an approach to *elucus,* the Florida form, but in the light of the present material these coast specimens can best be referred to *lotor.*

Coons are abundant along the margins of streams, lakes, and bays, along the coast, in marshes, or around water holes, adapting their habits to almost any condition save that of dryness. In the timbered country hollow trees, hollow logs, cavities under old logs, or upturned roots provide them temporary homes in which to spend the day, and on the great salt marshes of the coast country masses of fallen grass and rushes provide dark cover, or hollow banks and windrows of drift stuff afford safe retreats, while the broken walls of rocky canyons and gulches toward the headwaters of the streams furnish the favorite, because the safest, dens. It is not uncommon for coons to leave the stream where they have been hunting and travel half a mile or a mile to dens in a cliff, though otherwise they are rarely found so far from water. They are mainly nocturnal, and every morning their unmistakable plantigrade tracks mark the shores of the streams, following the trails, logs, or mud flats, now in, now out of the water, often disappearing where the animals swam from point to point or from one side to the other of the stream in search of food. Often the coons follow the same line of travel again and again, until well-worn trails are formed along the margins of the streams or through the marsh grass. Along these trails scattered remains of food tell half the story of the coon's life. In places along the Guadalupe River, in Kerr County, almost every little point and island has its pile of mussel shells from which the mussels have been eaten, and every morning a few shells freshly scooped out are found on the piles until sometimes a bushel is accumulated. On the coast marshes the shells of crawfish are found scattered along the coon trails, while the excrement deposited here and there in well-chosen spots is made up largely of the indigestible parts of crustaceans mixed with a few scales and bones of fish and occasional traces of frogs and small mammals. As these marshes swarm with crawfish and small crabs, the coons have a perennial feast and naturally become numerous. On Matagorda Peninsula Lloyd reported them feeding on oysters as well as crabs and crawfish, and in the stomach of one caught near the mouth of the Colorado River he reported finding a meadow lark. In their selection of food coons are quite as omnivorous as bears, seeming to relish almost any kind of flesh, fruit, grain, nuts, and acorns. At Brazos they were reported by B. H. Dutcher as feeding on melons.

Their nightly raids on fields of green corn are too well known to need comment, and small fields of corn planted in or near the woods are sometimes almost destroyed, the ears being torn open and the corn eaten from the cob from the time of the early milk stage until ripe, and even after being cut and shocked.

In the Big Thicket coons are numerous along every stream and bayou, as shown by fresh tracks along roads and trails and in the muddy margins of ponds and water ways, and by skins drying under the sheds of almost every ranch. Their fur is the principal catch of most of the trappers and their abundance makes trapping fairly profitable in this region. During November and December they were feeding mainly on acorns, but were still eating crawfish, while the old shells of mussels, including the enormous pearl-bearing species (*Quadrula heros*) and the smaller thick-shelled *Quadrula forsheyi*, piled here and there along the banks of bayous, apparently marked the remains of summer feasts.

While watching for fox squirrels one morning in the heavily timbered bottoms I heard a scratching sound from an old cypress in the edge of the swamp near by, followed by a loud splash. A young coon less than half grown had fallen from the tree into the water. At the sound the old coon and two more young ones came out of a hollow some 30 feet up in the trunk and climbed down to near the bottom of the tree. They came down the tree slowly but steadily, head first, as a squirrel would have done, with the hind feet reversed and slightly divergent. When the old coon saw the young one climb out of the water upon the tree trunk she turned about and ascended the trunk, followed by the three young. The one that had fallen, besides being very wet, was slightly hurt, and climbed with difficulty. When halfway up he stopped on a limb to rest and began whimpering and crying. The mother had already reached the hole, but on hearing his cries turned about and climbed down to him. Taking a good hold of the back of his neck and placing him between her fore legs so that he, too, could climb she marched him up the tree and into the hollow.

**Procyon lotor mexicanus** Baird.    Mexican Raccoon.

Raccoons are common along every stream in Texas, and especially common along the coast and on the islands. Specimens from the Rio Grande, Pecos, and Devils River country are large and pale; they have a long tail and the more quadrate molars of *mexicanus* to which subspecies they are referred, although differing in having the narrower basioccipital and yellow nape of *lotor*.[a]

[a] It has been customary to refer specimens from western Texas to *hernandezi*, but a number of specimens of that species from the type region in Mexico, collected by Nelson and Goldman, prove to be quite different from the Texas animal.

In the northern part of the State the range of *mexicanus* is partly cut off from that of the smaller, darker coon of eastern Texas by the plains; but near the coast, where there is no break in the ranges, only an arbitrary division can be made between the two forms. Specimens from as far east as Corpus Christi can safely be referred to *mexicanus* and others from as far west as Matagorda to *lotor,* while specimens between, from Port Lavaca and Aransas County, can be referred as well to one as the other. Assuming, as seems necessary, that Baird's redescribing and correctly naming "*Procyon lotor* variete mexicaine" of St. Hilaire[a] fixes the type locality at Mazatlan, Mexico, the name *mexicanus* becomes available for the coon of western Texas, which, though not typical, is certainly nearer to this form in general characters, as well as in geographic position, than to any other.

In western Texas coons are closely restricted to the streams, and consequently are rare over the wide intervals of dry desert country between. Along the Rio Grande, Pecos, and Devils River valleys they are especially abundant, and their dens are almost invariably located in the broken walls of cliffs and canyons. In the low country toward the coast of southern Texas, where dense chaparral, cactus patches, and the tall grass of the salt marshes offer ample shelter and streams are not infrequent, they have a more continuous distribution. From Corpus Christi to Brownsville their tracks were seen along the shores of every stream and pond and were especially numerous near the coast, where the animals apparently lived on the little fiddler crabs (*Gelasimus pugilator?*), always found in abundance on the low, sandy soil. Lloyd reported hackberries (probably *Momesia pallida*) in the stomach of one caught at Corpus Christi. In the Pecos and Devils River canyons the heavy shells of one of the pearl-bearing mussels (*Lampsilis berlandieri*) are often found in piles along the banks of the streams, but the ripe fruits of the prickly pear (*Opuntia engelmanni*) and of the black persimmon (*Brayodendron texanum*) were their principal food in July and August. The sweet pods of mesquite were also eaten, and apparently some of the insipid berries of *Zizyphus, Condalia, Adelia, Lycium,* and *Momesia.*

**Lutra (canadensis?)** (Schreber).   Otter.                              145

Otters are not uncommon in the streams of eastern Texas, but, being unable to procure a specimen from any part of the State, I can only provisionally refer the species to *canadensis.* The only specimen that throws any light on the question is a fine old male collected at Tallulah, Madison County, in northeastern Louisiana, by W. E. Forbes and N. Hollister, which agrees in most characters with *canadensis* and shows no tendency toward intergradation with the Florida otter, *L. c. vaga.*

---

[a] Voyage de la Venus, Zoologie, p. 125, 1855.

In the Big Thicket of Liberty and Hardin counties otters are common, and a few are caught each year by the local trappers. During low water the black pools of the half-dry bayous, swarming with landlocked fish, are their favorite haunts. Oberholser obtained reports of otters at Mobeetie and along the Red River at Texarkana, and along the Neches and San Jacinto rivers near Beaumont and Conroe. Lloyd reported them from Palacio Creek, Matagorda County, and John M. Priour writes that they are found on the Colorado River in the region of Austin. None of our field men have ever heard of them along the Rio Grande or Pecos rivers, however, while several old trappers, long familiar with the Rio Grande, Pecos, and Devils rivers, have assured me that otters were never found along these streams. In addition to this evidence, Mr. W. H. Dodd, of Langtry, has told me that for many years in buying fur of the local trappers no skins or even reports of otters had come to his notice in that region. Along Big Cypress Bayou, below Jefferson, in northeastern Texas, Mr. Richard Crane told me in 1902 that otters were fairly common, and in fifteen years' hunting and fishing along this stream he had killed eight or ten, most of which he shot. One that came up near his boat and then dived, leaving its tail temptingly above water for a second, he caught by the tail, whereupon it promptly curled up and severely bit his legs and hands before he could kill it. He says $50 would not tempt him to catch another otter by the tail.

146 **Lutreola lutreocephala** (Harlan).    Large Brown Mink; Southeastern Mink.

Minks are common over approximately the eastern half of Texas, but apparently are unknown in the western part of the State.[a] The western limit of their range is roughly indicated by specimens from Gainesville, Brazos, and Mason, and by reports of occurrences near Austin and on the lower Guadalupe River.

I have examined specimens from Gainesville, Brazos, Mason, Navasota, Harris County, Matagorda, Tarkington Prairie, Rockland, Antioch, and Texarkana, but find no characters, cranial or external, by which to separate them from typical *lutreocephala* from Maryland and the District of Columbia.

Along most of the streams and bayous of the timbered country of eastern Texas, minks are so common as to form an important item in the catch of the local trappers. In fall and winter a few of their skins are usually found among the more numerous coon, opossum, and

---

[a] Cary obtained an indefinite report of 'mink' at Fort Stockton, in the Pecos Valley, but there is a possibility that the name may have been applied to some other animal.

skunk skins at trappers' camps or cabins, or in general merchandise or fur stores of the town. While usually closely associated with stream courses, where much of their food consists of fish, frogs, crustaceans, birds, and mice, minks are perfectly at home in the dry parts of woods and swamp, and even on the open prairie. At Navasota I caught one in woods near the river and another in a trap set in a cut bank gulch in the middle of a wide field. Both were attracted by bodies of birds that had been shot for specimens, and while in the traps had gorged themselves with the bait. At Tarkington Prairie minks are said to be much less common in the timber than on the open prairie, where myriads of birds roost at night in the long prairie grass, and crawfish chimneys thickly dot the margins of shallow ponds. Along the coast marshes the minks follow the shores of bayous and ditches, where their tracks usually may be found in the mud and sand, or range back over the wide expanse of marsh and prairie, where tall grass and drift heaps furnish ample cover. Over these marshes they feed extensively on crawfish and minnows, as shown by their excrement. One caught by Lloyd on Matagorda Peninsula had a freshly eaten cotton rat in its stomach.

The occasional losses from the raids of minks on the poultry yard in most cases can be prevented by a little care on the part of the farmer in providing roosting places out of reach of the prowling minks, if necessary, with tin-covered uprights. Minks are good climbers, and will sometimes climb to the top of a tall tree to escape the dogs, but they seem to hunt almost entirely on the ground. An ordinary poultry fence with fine wire mesh affords perfect protection, not only from minks, but from many other troublesome 'varmints.' The value of the mink's fur makes the animal of considerable economic importance, especially as it has proved its ability to hold its own in thickly settled districts. Its value as a destroyer of small rodents compensates in part, if not fully, for its depredations.

**Putorius nigripes** Aud. and Bach.   Black-footed Ferret.                147

The black-footed ferret has been reported from a number of localities in the prairie-dog country of Texas east and south of the Staked Plains. A very large weasel, described by B. H. Dutcher in 1893 at Stanton, may or may not have been of this species. Merritt Cary learned of one that was killed in 1894 at Seymour. J. A. Loring found an almost perfect skull of a fine adult at Childress on the house of a wood rat. A flat skin in the U. S. National Museum, labeled "Gainesville, Texas," probably came from some point west of there, as it is merely a rough hunter's skin, evidently not prepared by G. H. Ragsdale, whose name is on the label. If this were a bona fide record for Gainesville it would be the first from any point far out of the range of the prairie dog.

In September, 1902, Cary writes:

A number of black-footed ferrets are said to have been caught at the dog town south of the Stanton stock yard in past years, and every person questioned was familiar with the animal and could give a good description of it. Doctor Vance, living just north of town, saw one about a week before I arrived there and set a rude box trap at the hole in an attempt to capture the animal alive, but without success. A Mr. Williams, living at Fort Stockton, kept for a year or more a black-footed ferret which a Mexican caught in a trap set at an old adobe house on the edge of a dog town just north of the Pecos River at Grand Falls. It was described to me as built like a mink, with dark-brown feet and a bar across the face.

At Lipscomb, in July, 1903, A. H. Howell "saw the hide of one killed there the previous summer and was told of a den of them located near First Creek."

148    **Putorius frenatus** (Lichtenstein).    Bridled Weasel.

While never common, the bridled weasel seems to be generally distributed over the low country of southern Texas. There are specimens in the Biological Survey collection from Brownsville and near Hidalgo. Oberholser examined mounted specimens at San Diego, Beeville, and Port Lavaca. Lloyd reported the species from Corpus Christi, and Attwater from San Antonio.

149    **Putorius frenatus neomexicanus** Barber and Cockerell.    New Mexico
Bridled Weasel.

This species, so far as I know, is not positively known to occur in the State of Texas, but in the winter of 1889 I found the tracks of a weasel winding in and out of the *Dipodomys* and *Perodipus* holes in the sandy bottoms just below El Paso. A record of a weasel taken several years ago at Langtry (reported to Oberholser by W. H. Dodd, of that place) may have been of this species, and suggests a continuous range from the country of *frenatus* up the Rio Grande to the type locality of *neomexicanus* at Mesilla Valley, N. Mex.

150    **Spilogale leucoparia** Merriam.    Rio Grande Spotted Skunk.

This beautiful little spotted skunk, with broad white stripes, occupies the rough country bordering the southern arm of the Staked Plains from Mason and Waring to Langtry, Comstock, and Eagle Pass and farther south into Mexico. It is probably the form occupying also the rough country east and west of the Pecos Valley. In the Davis Mountains the ranchmen report a spotted skunk as common, and say that it climbs trees as readily as a squirrel. It is often treed by the dogs at night and shot from the branches by the hunters. Under the nest of a great horned owl in the face of a cliff at the west base of the Davis Mountains I found several jaws of these little skunks in the owl pellets. Throughout most of its known range it inhabits rocky gulches, cliffs, and canyons, or the brushy bottoms usual in such places.

**Spilogale interrupta** (Rafinesque).    Prairie Spotted Skunk.

This dark form of the spotted skunk, or spilogale, with the narrow white stripes, comes into Texas from the more northern plains, and is represented by specimens from Canadian, Gainesville, and Brazos. Beyond these localities there are no specimens to show the limits of its range in the State or to indicate whether it grades into the neighboring forms to the south. Though the little "spotted skunks," "hydrophobia cats," or "phoby cats" are reported from

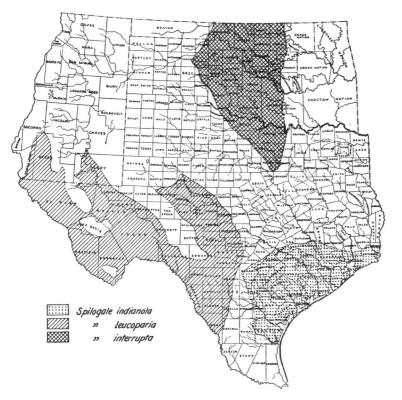

FIG. 23.—Distribution areas of spotted skunks (genus *Spilogale*).

almost every part of Texas, even including the top of the Staked Plains, there is still much to be learned of the range and relationships of the several forms inhabiting the State.

Although, broadly speaking, plains animals, these spilogales, like most species of the genus, take advantage of any cover in the way of bushes, tall grass, stream banks, or old buildings that the country offers. In Kansas I have caught them in burrows in the sandy soil, but whether the burrows were of their own digging or borrowed from spermophiles or other burrowing mammals I could not tell. At Canadian, Tex., one was caught in a No. 0 steel trap set in an old tumbledown shed in the corner of a field and baited with the bodies of birds that had been skinned for specimens. I had with me a bottle of bisulphid of carbon for experiments on prairie dogs. Thinking to try a new experiment, I scraped a hollow about 8 inches deep in the sand, and with a stick gently loosened the trap chain and slowly drew the little skunk to the hole. He tumbled in, thinking he had escaped, and curled up in the bottom. I then poured a couple of ounces of bisulphid on a bunch of grass and threw it into the hole, and after waiting five minutes found the skunk dead and perfectly free from unpleasant odor. This method of killing any of the skunks, when it becomes necessary to trap them around buildings, can safely be recommended.

152    **Spilogale indianola** Merriam.    Gulf Spotted Skunk.

This little spotted skunk inhabits the coast region of Texas from Corpus Christi to southwestern Louisiana and extends inland as far as Beeville, San Antonio, and Navasota. So far as known, it is mainly an animal of the cactus and chaparral patches of the open country. In the Big Thicket region I could get no reports of it east of Conroe, but at Navasota I found it common and caught two in traps in brushy places. At Beeville Oberholser caught one in a trap set in the runway of a wood rat. Of two specimens secured by Lloyd in Matagorda County one was taken in a group of burrows in a thicket on the prairie and the other in an old cotton gin. In the stomach of the former were found parts of a *Perognathus hispidus* and some crawfish. Near Corpus Christi I caught the animals in bunches of prickly pear and in wood-rat houses under the mesquites. At Virginia Point, on the prairie near Galveston, I shot and trapped them in the big bunches of cactus (*Opuntia engelmanni*) found here and there on the prairie. Such confidence had they in the protection of these thorny masses that one came out repeatedly, thrusting its head between the cactus blades to watch me with its keen little eyes, first at one window then at another, moving about freely among the thorns and refusing to enter its burrow even when I approached to within a few yards. Its motions were quick and alert, and its expression bright and weasel-like rather than skunk-like, which, added to its beautiful markings, made it a most attractive little animal. The burrows under the cactus and thorny huisache bushes were apparently dug by skunks, as no other burrowing animal near their size occurs there. The stomach and intestines of the specimens taken contained only shells and legs of a large brown beetle which swarmed about the houses at night. A few legs and wings of grasshoppers were found in the lower intestines of one individual.

153    **Mephitis mesomelas** Lichtenstein.    Louisiana Skunk.

The Louisiana skunk is common over the whole of eastern Texas and about as far west as Wichita Falls and Matagorda Bay. Specimens from O'Connorport are clearly intermediate between *mesomelas* and *varians,* as are also specimens from Wichita Falls. There is apparently no locality in Texas where skunks are not more or less common, and the transition from *mesomelas* to *varians,* while not abrupt, seems to follow approximately the line of transition from humid forest and prairie country to semiarid mesquite plains.

Skunks are generally less common over eastern than western Texas, owing probably to the more thickly inhabited country to the eastward, to the number of dogs kept at every little farm or cabin, and to the popular superstition that all skunks convey hydrophobia and should be destroyed whenever possible. There are undoubtedly authentic cases of rabies in skunks, as well as in other animals that have been inoculated with the disease, but there is no reason to suppose that they are any more subject to it than dogs or cats nor more dangerous to human beings when they do have it. On the other hand, they are among the most useful of the predatory mammals, destroying great numbers of small rodents, grasshoppers, beetles, and larvae, and should be protected, except in rare cases of mischief. There are a few complaints of their destroying poultry, but in most cases this mischief can be easily prevented.

At Virginia Point, on the prairie opposite Galveston, I trapped a skunk one morning in a bunch of cactus and by a bungling shot allowed it to discharge its odorous fluid. Being anxious to save the skin in spite of its odor, I sat down on a patch of dry sand to skin it, and in a few minutes a black shadow passed me on the ground. Looking up I saw not less than 50 turkey buzzards and black vultures beating up the wind in a long line straight toward me. They were flying low and keenly scanning the ground. Many came within 20 feet, apparently, before seeing me, and soon I was the center, though not the object of attraction, of the constantly increasing flock. As my work ended and I moved away they pounced on the carcass, and soon there was nothing but the large scent gland and its odor to mark the spot. Even the bones had mostly disappeared. This is but one of many similar instances in which turkey buzzards and vultures have quickly responded to the smell of a freshly killed skunk, although they usually leave a cleanly picked skeleton as well as the scent gland.

**Mephitis mesomelas varians** Gray.    Long-tailed Texas Skunk.

The long-tailed skunk ranges over western Texas from Brownsville to El Paso and east to Rockport, San Antonio, Mason, Brazos, Canadian, and Lipscomb, or approximately over the mesquite region and plains of Texas in both Upper and Lower Sonoran zones. Although generally distributed even over the top of the Staked Plains, these skunks are most abundant in the chaparral or brushy country, especially along bushy-bottomed, rocky walled gulches and in canyons, where to an abundance of food are added ample cover and the protection of numerous safe retreats. The sandy bottoms and dusty trails are almost invariably marked with their tiny, bear-like tracks, and they are frequently met with morning or evening racking along the trail on their way home or abroad. At night they often come into camp, and leave tracks in the ashes of the campfire or around the 'grub box,' but in years of camp life where they are common I have never know them, when unprovoked, to be discourteous or disagreeable. One morning in the Davis Mountains we noticed tracks and numerous little holes dug in search of beetles around our beds and among the frying pans and kettles. We had evidently camped on the favorite digging ground of this particular skunk and he had quietly put up with the inconvenience of our presence.

The skunks often acquire the habit of coming to camp for the discarded bodies of birds and mammals that have been skinned for specimens, but if their favorite foods—grasshoppers, cicadas, beetles, and grubworms—are abundant, it is difficult to entice them into traps with any kind of bait. Any small game that they can catch for themselves is welcome and they sometimes raid an unprotected chicken coop. I have found their stomachs filled with berries of zizyphus, and have noted the remains of cactus fruit, black persimmons, and small berries in the 'sign' along their favorite trails. But legs and shells of grasshoppers and beetles usually form the bulk of their 'sign.' One caught at Santa Tomas by Lloyd had just dined on a cotton rat, and in other places Lloyd reported them as feeding on wood rats. Occasionally they find our traps and eat the small rodents caught in them.

## Conepatus mesoleucus mearnsi Merriam.    Mearns Conepatus; Hognosed Skunk.

154

The white-backed or hognosed skunk is common over most of western Texas, from Kerrville, Mason, and Llano to the Rio Grande and beyond, and south to Dimmit County. Along Devils and Pecos rivers and the canyon country of the Rio Grande and in the Davis Mountains it is evidently the commonest skunk. It apparently has not been taken in the El Paso part of the Rio Grande Valley, but as it is found farther north, it undoubtedly occurs there also. Oberholser obtained a report of its rare occurrence at Austin, which is its easternmost record. Specimens reported by H. P. Attwater from San Antonio are probably of this species.[a]

The scarcity of specimens of *Conepatus* in collections is not due

[a] Allen, Mammals of Bexar County, Tex., in Bul. Am. Mus. Nat. Hist., VIII, 72, 1896.

entirely to the scarcity of the animals. In several localities where they were common and their long-clawed tracks and peculiar diggings were abundant and fresh every morning, I utterly failed to trap them, as they would not come near any kind of bait that I could offer; but in these localities their favorite food—a large brown beetle—was abundant. Near Boquillas, in the side canyons of the Rio Grande, the mellow sandy bottoms were pitted with little funnel-shaped holes about 2 inches deep where the animals had dug out the beetles, whose round holes perforated the ground on all sides like half-inch auger holes. One of the skunks shot by moonlight early in the evening on his digging ground had already filled his stomach with these crisp juicy beetles to the number of several hundred. In skinning him the next morning I was struck with the adaptability of his long naked nose to the work of probing the beetle holes. A sniff would probably show whether the beetle was at home and worth digging for or whether the hole was occupied by a tarantula. This and two other specimens, which I failed to shoot in such a way as to break their backs and prevent the discharge of their scent gland, curled up with their last gasp and drenched their bodies from head to tail with the reeking fluid, which differs neither in quantity nor strength from that of *Mephitis.* The repetition of this act by the two individuals indicates a habit not shared with the common skunk, which to its last breath tries to avoid soiling itself in using its weapon of defense. In general the habits of *Conepatus* and *Mephitis* are very similar even to a choice of the same brush patches and gulch bottoms for foraging ground. They must frequently meet, whether on friendly terms or otherwise.

Along Devils River in July *Conepatus* was common, but as usual was difficult to catch. One got into a trap set in a trail and another was shot by moonlight as it trotted through camp. They were feeding on beetles, grasshoppers, crickets, and the ripe fruit of the prickly pear (*Opuntia engelmanni*). Near Langtry Gaut caught an old female, March 24, which contained a single embryo that he thought would have been born a week later.

### Conepatus mesoleucus telmalestes subsp. nov.  Swamp Conepatus; White-backed Skunk.

155

Type from the Big Thicket, 7 miles northeast of Sour Lake, Tex., ♂ ad., No. 136551, U. S. Nat. Mus., Biological Survey Coll. Collected by James H. Gaut, March 17, 1905. Original No. 3485.

*General characters.*—Similar in general appearance to *Conepatus mesoleucus mearnsi,* skull usually slenderer, dentition lighter.

*Color.*—Whole upper parts and tail white, the white extending forward on forehead nearly to eyes; lower parts, sides, legs, and face black.

*Skull* of type elongated, with slender muzzle, narrow interorbital region and prominent mastoid processes; upper molar relatively long and narrow, upper and lower carnassials strikingly smaller than in comparable specimens of *mearnsi*.[a]

*Measurements of type.*—Total length, 625; tail vertebrae, 257; hind foot, 78. Of two female topotypes: Total length, 610; tail vertebrae,

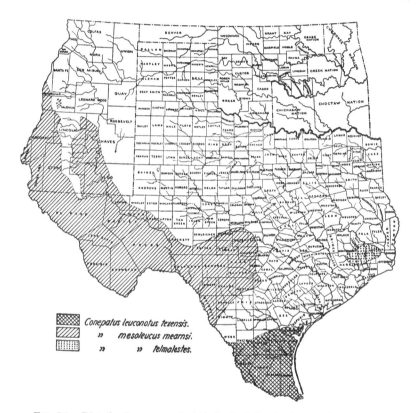

FIG. 24.—Distribution areas of white-backed skunks (genus *Conepatus*).

265; hind foot, 67; and total length, 676; tail vertebrae, 304; hind foot, 74.

*Skull of type.*—Basal length, 65.2; zygomatic breadth, 44.3; interorbital breadth, 22.3; postorbital constriction, 20; mastoid breadth, 40.3; alveolar length of upper molar series, 16.3.

Three skins and four skulls have been examined from the Big Thicket, 7 to 10 miles northeast of Sour Lake, in Hardin County, and one skin and two skulls from Tarkington Prairie, in Liberty County.

---

[a] The skull of a large male from Tarkington lacks the slender rostrum and narrow interorbital region, but agrees with the others in tooth characters and spreading mastoid processes.

At Saratoga, Kountze, and Cleveland the white-backed skunk is said to be the commonest species, and under a trapper's shed at a ranch on Tarkington Prairie in November, 1904, I saw eight or ten of their skins hanging up to dry with a smaller number of skins of *Mephitis mesomelas.* They were valued at 40 cents each, or less than half as much as the blacker skins of *Mephitis.*

Apparently no *Conepatus* are found in the country west of Liberty County until the range of *mearnsi* is reached near Austin, or that of the more widely different *texensis* at Rockport. The extension of range of the genus is less surprising than that a local form of a group so generally associated over a wide area with arid desert regions should be found restricted to the most humid and densely timbered corner of the State of Texas.

The residents of the Big Thicket country are familiar with these animals, which they call "white-back skunks" to distinguish them from the black-backed or two-striped *Mephitis.* I could not learn of any difference in habits or habitat of the two species. Gaut reports two females taken in April as nursing young, and with one of these he found two small young about a week old in a hollow stump. He also reports that the stomachs of three adults were filled with ground up insects—mostly beetles—with a few grubworms, large brown flies, and grasshoppers.

**Conepatus leuconotus texensis** Merriam.    Texas Conepatus.    156

From Brownsville, on the lower Rio Grande, this larger form of the white-backed skunk extends up the coast as far as Rockport and up the Rio Grande Valley to Laredo. Lloyd, who collected specimens at Brownsville and Laredo, reported them as rare. He also reported them as occurring occasionally on Padre Island and at Nueces Bay.

**Scalopus aquaticus** (Linn.). Eastern Mole.    157

One specimen from Joaquin and fifteen specimens from the Big Thicket, 7 miles northeast of Sour Lake, show no distinguishing characters when compared with a large series of typical *aquaticus* from Virginia, Maryland, and the District of Columbia. The slightly lighter color and larger molars indicate a shading toward *texanus,* but in so slight a degree as to be merely a suggestion.

The sandy pine ridges of eastern Texas, and even the mellow soil of the river bottoms and the low mounds above flood level, are crisscrossed by innumerable mole ridges, and dotted here and there with little heaps of yellow sand pushed up through the carpet of fallen leaves and pine needles. The moles are abundant, and save for the barriers of rivers have an almost unobstructed range west to the black wax land prairies. Their work is most conspicuous on the lightest, sandiest soil, which is kept so well stirred and plowed that in walking over it the feet constantly sink into the network of old burrows. In fields the freshly raised ridges can be traced for long distances. The moles are commonly accused of eating sweet potatoes, cutting the roots of fruit trees, and of doing other mischief, for most of which the pocket gopher or 'salamander' is responsible. The food of the moles consists almost entirely of insects, earthworms, and various other inhabitants of the soil, in pursuit of which the animals sometimes are troublesome by disturbing the roots of young plants and by marring the surface of lawns and parks with ridges and little mounds of earth. But all things considered the mole is too valuable an ally of the farmer to be destroyed.

**Scalopus aquaticus texanus** Allen.   Texas Mole.

So far as known, *Scalopus texanus* is found only in semiarid Lower Sonoran zone, from Cameron County north to Mason. Specimens examined from Rockport, Corpus Christi, Santa Rosa Ranch (near northwest corner of Cameron County), Padre Island (north end), and Mason, as apparently also two imperfect specimens from San Antonio and Long Point, while showing marked variation at every locality from which perfect specimens were secured, can all be referred to this form. While at each locality the specimens are surprisingly uniform in characters, and the variation is sufficient for recognition, a careful comparison of specimens indicates that the result of further subdivision would only be confusing. The physiography of the middle Gulf region of Texas tends to the isolation of all burrowing mammals. Some of the rivers with headwaters in sandstone and granite formations cut through wide plains of the most impervious, waxy soil, in which no mammal can burrow, and while some of these streams leave more or less continuous deposits of mellow, sandy soil along their courses, others carry their contributions to the coast, to be built into interrupted areas of sand flats, dunes, and islands, between which the rivers with their wide flood bottoms form as impassable barriers as the wide stretches of waxy prairie. In some cases the isolation is complete; in others, partial. While the general conditions are similar, locally they are more or less varied, and their effect on the burrowing mammals is analogous to that on mammals found on a series of oceanic islands.

In habits *texanus* does not differ from other species of the genus. At Corpus Christi it is common on the scattered patches of sandy soil, and common also over the sandy prairie for a distance of 65 miles, from near Santa Rosa to Sauz on the Alice and Brownsville stage road. Lloyd reported it as abundant on Padre Island. On the half-naked sands near the coast mole ridges are usually conspicuous, and the mounds, while less numerous, are often as large as those of the pocket gopher.

**Scalopus aquaticus intermedius** Elliot.  Plains Mole.  159

Two specimens of moles from Mobeetie and three from Lipscomb, while not typical *intermedius,* are nearer to it than to any other species. Externally they agree with topotypes from Alva, Okla., but the slender skulls indicate a distant connection with *aquaticus* farther east. One of the specimens from Mobeetie is tinged all over with a delicate purple, evidently from the root juice of a *Lithospermum.*

Howell reports that these moles are more or less abundant at Mobeetie, Miami, Canadian, and Lipscomb, where their runways are especially numerous in cultivated fields, among the sand hills, or on sandy bottoms, while a few were found on wet bottoms and on ground that was flooded in times of high water. At Tascosa in 1899 I found mole ridges common over the sandy river bottoms.

**[Sorex personatus** Geoffroy Saint Hilaire.  Common Eastern Shrew.  160

A specimen of this shrew, recorded by Mr. Oldfield Thomas[a] as received with the William Taylor collection from San Diego, Tex., is apparently the only record of a *Sorex* for the State. As numerous collectors have failed to find the species in the State, or anywhere within the life zone including San Diego and most of Texas, it seems probable that this specimen originally came from some other part of the country.]

**Notiosorex crawfordi** (Coues) (Baird MS.).  Crawford Shrew. Eared  161
Shrew.

*Notiosorex* differs from *Blarina* in having 28 instead of 32 teeth. *N. crawfordi* is larger than *B. parva* or *berlandieri,* with more conspicuous ears, and with tail about $2\frac{1}{2}$ instead of $1\frac{1}{2}$ times as long as hind foot.

This shrew was described from specimens collected at old Fort Bliss, 2 miles above El Paso, and additional specimens have since been collected at San Diego, Corpus Christi, and San Antonio. It has a wide range in the arid Lower Sonoran zone of Mexico, southern California, and Arizona, and so far as we know reaches its eastern limit near Corpus Christi and at San Antonio.

**Blarina brevicauda carolinensis** (Bach.).  Carolina Short-tailed Shrew.  162

A specimen of the Carolina short-tailed shrew from Joaquin and two from the Big Thicket, 8 miles northeast of Sour Lake, extend the range of this species from eastern Arkansas and western Mississippi into eastern Texas. Though these shrews are never abundant and are easily overlooked in collecting, they may yet be found over much of eastern Texas where the conditions are favorable. Hollister caught the Joaquin specimen in a runway under old grass on low ground at

---

[a] Proc. Zool. Soc. London, 1888, p. 443.

the edge of a cotton field about a mile east of town. It was half eaten while in the trap by some other animal, probably by one of its own species. Gaut caught the two Big Thicket specimens in traps set by old logs in the woods near Mike Griffin's place.

163    **Blarina parva** (Say).    Least Short-tailed Shrew.

This smallest of the United States species of short-tailed shrews has been taken at Gainesville, Hempstead, and Richmond. As throughout a wide range over the eastern United States it is a rare, or at least a rarely taken species, it may well be as common over a large part of eastern Texas as over the rest of its range.

The Gainesville specimens in the Merriam collection were taken by G. H. Ragsdale, but on the same ground in 1892 I was unable to find any trace of these animals save a few old runways under a carpet of fallen prairie grass. At Richmond in 1899, while trapping for *Sigmodon* on the big coast prairie, I caught one in its own little runway under the prairie grass. At Hempstead Gaut caught one in a trap set in the dry grass near a rain pool.

164    **Blarina berlandieri** Baird.    Rio Grande Short-tailed Shrew.

The Rio Grande *Blarina* is slightly larger and paler than *parva,* but very similar in general appearance. It was described from specimens collected at Matamoras, Mexico, and other specimens have been taken at Brownsville, San Diego, and Del Rio, Tex. Little is known of its habits, which apparently are similar to those of *parva.*

At Del Rio in February, 1890, I caught one in a *Sigmodon* runway on grassy bottoms of San Felipe Creek a couple of miles from the point where the creek joins the Rio Grande.[a]

165    **Myotis velifer** (J. A. Allen).    Cave Bat.

The four localities from which this little brown bat is known in Texas—the mouth of the Pecos, Langtry, New Braunfels, and San Antonio—when added to its wider range from Arizona to Missouri and south to southern Mexico, indicate that the species covers at least the western half of Texas. Specimens collected at mouth of Pecos by Lloyd, August 23 and September 4, 1890, and at Langtry by Gaut, March 29, 1893, indicate that it is a summer resident along the Rio Grande. Lloyd's specimens were "found in a cave tunnel," and Gaut's were taken in Pump Canyon, a deep box canyon near Langtry. I collected three adult males of this bat at Marble Cave, Mo., on June 28 and 30, 1892. One was caught in the cave 150 feet below the surface of the earth; the others were shot as they came out of the mouth

---

[a] This Del Rio specimen, which is typical *berlandieri,* was by some accident referred by Doctor Merriam to *parva,* although he had previously written the name *berlandieri* against it in the catalogue. (N. Am. Fauna, No. 10, p. 18, 1895—Revision of Shrews.)

of the cave in the evening. If this bat is habitually a cave dweller, the distribution of caves probably accounts for its somewhat erratic range.

**Myotis californicus** (Aud. and Bach.).    Little California Bat.    166

This tiny bright brown bat comes into the desert country of western Texas, but evidently is not very common. A single specimen collected at Paisano by Lloyd on July 21, and another that I shot at Peña Coloral, 5 miles south of Marathon, May 14, and one on Terlingua Creek, July 1, seem to furnish the only records for the State. The species is common in New Mexico just north of the Texas line. Five specimens—three males and two females—collected by James H. Gaut in the foothills on the east slope of the San Andreas Mountains, New Mexico, January 19 and 20, 1903, indicate that the bats are not only resident, but are active during winter months. At Santa Rosa, N. Mex., I found them common in May, and a female shot on the 29th contained one small embryo. On the wing they are scarcely distinguishable from *Pipistrellus hesperus,* but they are usually found in the open or among trees, while *hesperus* keeps mainly to the canyons and cliffs.

**Myotis incautus** (J. A. Allen).    House Bat.    167

Apparently the only known specimens of this bat are the five taken at San Antonio by Mr. H. P. Attwater, from which Doctor Allen described the species; seven collected by M. Cary and myself 15 miles west of Japonica, Kerr County; one collected at Langtry by James H. Gaut, and eight collected at Carlsbad, N. Mex. The San Antonio specimens were collected March 12 and October 10, which would suggest that they were migrants. The Japonica specimens were taken July 7 and 8, and were on their breeding ground, as probably were those taken at Carlsbad July 29 and September 17. A female collected in Pump Canyon, near Langtry, March 29, may have been either resident or migrant.

Little is known of the habits of this species. On the North Fork of the Guadalupe, west of Japonica, Cary and I found them early in the evening, flying up and down the rocky bed of the stream in great abundance, dipping to the water pools to drink and then zigzagging through the air in pursuit of insects. With a fairly good light, we secured seven of the bats after a few minutes' rapid shooting. The bats apparently came from the limestone cliffs both above and below the open space where we found them.

At the water tower 3 miles southwest of Carlsbad, where a large pool is formed from the pure mountain water pumped up to supply the town, these bats came in over the dry plain on the evening of July 29 from some limestone hills several miles away.

They were flying straight for the water pool without a crook or turn, and I shot four without missing, a rare occurrence in bat shooting. These were all females, but four taken on September 17 at the Bolles ranch, 6 miles south of Carlsbad, were all males. Three of these were shot in the evening as they flew about the house, and one was caught in the daytime in a corner of an outhouse.

In the original description of the species, based on a series of five specimens taken at San Antonio by Mr. Attwater, March 12 and October 10, Doctor Allen says: "It is a 'house' bat, all of the specimens having been taken in the house except one, which was caught in a barn."[a]

## 168    Myotis yumanensis (H. Allen).    Yuma Bat.

This little light-brown bat was not known from Texas until May 26, 1903, when Gaut found a breeding colony near Del Rio. He collected a series of eight adult females and one young, and says: "They were taken from a colony of bats, all the same species, in a shallow cave near the railroad about 10 miles west of Del Rio. When disturbed they flew about, the females each carrying a young one clinging to its breast. One of these young was obtained and prepared." It was very small, almost naked, and apparently its eyes were not yet open.

## 169    Pipistrellus hesperus (H. Allen).    Little Canyon Bat.

These tiny gray bats are easily recognized by their jet-black ears, tail, and wings. They come into arid Lower Sonoran zone of western Texas as far east as the Pecos Valley. There are specimens from El Paso, Chinati Mountains, Grand Canyon of Rio Grande, Terlingua Creek, Boquillas, points 15, 20, and 80 miles south of Marathon, Alpine, Paisano, Davis Mountains (east base), Sanderson, Pecos River (at mouth), and farther up the Pecos Valley from near Carlsbad and Santa Rosa, N. Mex.

These bats are usually the most abundant of the species where they occur, and they are, more than any other species I know, strictly canyon or cliff dwellers. They often follow up the canyons to the extreme limits of Lower Sonoran zone on the warm slopes where the surrounding country is entirely Upper Sonoran or even Transition, and the hotter, dryer, and barer the canyon the thicker these midgets swarm. They fly early, sometimes coming out on the shady side of a canyon before the last trace of sunlight has disappeared, but even with a fair amount of light they are not easily shot. Their flight is rapid and crooked, and the collector wastes more ammunition on them than on almost any other bat.

The Texas records for this species are all for summer, May 10 to

---

[a] Bul. Am. Mus. Nat. Hist., VIII, 239, 1896.

August 26, and breeding specimens are found throughout their range. A female collected 20 miles south of Marathon, May 10, contained two half-developed embryos, and two collected near Boquillas, May 23 and 24, each contained one large embryo. Another taken at Santa Rosa, N. Mex., May 27, contained two small embryos.

In specimens of this bat shot only a few minutes (twenty or thirty at most) after they began to fly in the evening, I have invariably found the stomachs stuffed full of freshly eaten insects—a fact which speaks well for their skill as flycatchers.

**Pipistrellus subflavus** (F. Cuvier).    Georgian Bat.                    170

Specimens of the Georgian bat from Clear Creek, in Galveston County, Long Lake, Brownsville, Devils River, Comstock, and Del Rio indicate a range over the eastern part of the State and as far west as the timber extends along streams in Lower Sonoran zone. The species has a wide range over the southeastern United States, and finds its western limits in Texas. The Brownsville specimen collected October 10, 1891, may have been a migrant, as may also have been those from Clear Creek, taken on March 28. One from Devils River, collected July 23, and three from Long Lake, procured July 19 and 20, were undoubtedly on their breeding grounds, as were probably those from Del Rio, collected May 21 and 22, and one from Comstock, collected May 3.

**Vespertilio fuscus** Beauvois.    Large Brown Bat.                    171

Specimens of the brown bat from Jefferson, Sour Lake, the Brazos River, Grady, and the Davis and Chisos mountains carry the range of the species across Texas from east to west without defining any limits of range, but the species apparently has not been taken in the southern part of the State. The specimen collected by Hollister at Jefferson, June 14, may have been a late migrant, as the species is supposed not to breed in Lower Sonoran zone. One collected by Gaut near Sour Lake, March 17, was undoubtedly a migrant. The Brazos River specimen is an old alcoholic (No. 11217, U.S.N.M.), without date. The Davis and Chisos mountains specimens were in Transition zone, and probably on their breeding grounds. Both are males, and in both localities the species seemed to be common. The one from the Davis Mountains was shot by L. A. Fuertes on the evening of July 12 as it came down the gulch over our camp at 5,700 feet altitude. The Chisos Mountain specimen was shot by McClure Surber, June 9, at our camp in the gulch at 6,000 feet altitude, at the edge of Transition zone.

At Mr. C. O. Finley's ranch, at the west base of the Davis Mountains, I found two lower jaws of this bat among numerous other bones in pellets under the nest of a great horned owl.

172 **Lasiurus borealis** (Müller).   Red Bat.

The red bat is common over eastern Texas and westward to the lower Rio Grande, Devils River, and Wichita Falls. Specimens have been taken at Jefferson, Clarksville, Arthur, Paris, Waco, Tarkington Prairie, Wichita Falls, Camp Verde, Ingram, Nueces Bay, Corpus Christi, Brownsville, Fort Clark, and Devils River. Its western limit in the State apparently corresponds to the limit of essentially treeless plains. Being a tree bat and partial to the deep shade of bottom-land forests, it follows the stream courses into the plains as far as they carry timber.

The dates on Texas specimens, covering a period from March 19 to November 30, do not indicate whether the species is migratory or resident, or whether, if resident, it hibernates or is active during the winter months, but there is abundant proof that it breeds throughout its Texas range. A female shot at Clarksville June 10 contained two fully developed fetuses, as also another, shot the next evening at Paris. Two females shot at Paris June 11, and 3 at Arthur June 16, were all nursing young. In a large series of specimens collected by F. B. Armstrong at Brownsville there are 39 young, ranging in size from tiny, almost naked individuals a few days old to almost full-grown animals, and bearing dates from May 19 to July 25. Most of the very small young were taken in May, but one of the smallest is dated July 18. Adults were collected at Brownsville by Lloyd as late as September 10, at Corpus Christi November 13, and at San Patricio, near the mouth of the Nueces, November 30.

These bats are among the least difficult to collect, as they come out early in the evening and their flight is comparatively slow. In leafy woods they often come out soon after sundown, while there is still light enough to distinguish the species by its color, form, and flight. At Wichita Falls I shot one as it was flying about in the woods near the river in bright sunlight at about 4 p.m. In the big pecan grove near the head of Devils River they were very numerous in July.

173 **Lasiurus borealis seminolus** (Rhoads).   Florida Red Bat.

A single specimen of this rich mahogany-brown subspecies, recorded by Gerrit S. Miller, jr., from Brownsville[a] is the only record for Texas. It was killed September 8, 1891, and was probably a migrant from its usual summer range in the South Atlantic and Gulf States east of Texas. Upon all grounds of geographic distribution this bat should be a summer resident of eastern Texas, and it will probably be found there when this most neglected group of all our North American mammals becomes better known.

---

[a] N. Am. Fauna, No. 13, p. 109, 1897. Revision of N. Am. Bats of the Family Vespertilionidae, by Gerrit S. Miller, jr.

**Lasiurus cinereus** (Beauvois).   Hoary Bat.                         174

The hoary bat probably migrates over the whole of Texas, but it is known in the State only from nine specimens collected at Brownsville and one from the Davis Mountains. The seven available Brownsville specimens are dated October 23, November 16, December 20, January, May 7, and May 23, and probably are migrants. The Davis Mountain specimen was shot by L. A. Fuertes, July 10, 1891, at 5,700 feet altitude, in a gulch northeast of Mount Livermore. It is an adult male, and was shot early in the evening as it came down the gulch from the east side of the mountain.

**Dasypterus intermedius** H. Allen.   Yellow Bat.                     175

Specimens of this large, yellow, short-eared bat from Brownsville and the south end of Padre Island, Texas, and Matamoras, Mexico, furnish all that is known of the range of the species, a range covering scarcely 30 miles near the Gulf coast in the semiarid cactus and mesquite country of Lower Sonoran zone.

None of the collectors of this bat have written anything on its habits, but a male collected by Lloyd on Padre Island August 26, and a series of 57 males, females, and young collected by Armstrong at Brownsville from May 12 to August 4, show that this region is the breeding ground of the species. Females collected May 12, 14, and 19 contained each two large fetuses, and seven young collected June 7 to 17 are about half grown, while one taken July 16 is but little larger.

**Nycticeius humeralis** Rafinesque. Evening Bat.                      176

This little, dark brown bat has been taken over eastern and southern Texas at Paris, Arthur, Texarkana, Jefferson, Jasper, Hidalgo, Lomita Ranch, and Brownsville, at dates ranging from May 8 to August 19. At Texarkana Oberholser took two nearly full-grown young, June 23, and at Jasper three not fully adult specimens on August 18 and 19. At Brownsville a series of fifteen less than half-grown young was collected by F. B. Armstrong, June 1 to 12, and two about half-grown young on June 17 and 24. Twelve adults taken May 8 to June 17 were all females, but an apparently adult male was taken by Lloyd on July 23. It was "found hanging on mesquite."

At Texarkana Oberholser reports this species as "the common bat of the bottoms," and at Jasper as abundant. Near Jefferson Hollister shot two on the evening of June 13 at our camp in the timber by Big Cypress Creek, where bats apparently of this species were numerous.

177 **Corynorhinus macrotis pallescens** Miller.    Long-eared Bat.

A single specimen of this pale subspecies of the long-eared bat, collected by Lloyd in the "east" Painted Cave, September 5, 1890,[a] apparently forms the only record for Texas. From its wide range over Mexico and arid Lower Sonoran of southern California and Arizona, the species may be expected to inhabit at least a large part of western Texas. In the eastern part of the State its place would naturally be taken by the darker colored *macrotis,* which has not yet been recorded from Texas, but which breeds abundantly in southern Louisiana.

178 **Antrozous pallidus** (Le Conte).    Pale Bat.

This large, light-colored bat is common throughout the summer in arid Lower Sonoran zone of western Texas from Sycamore Creek, Devils River, and the Pecos Valley westward, and a single specimen was obtained at Tascosa, in the northwestern part of the Panhandle. The records cover a period from April 18 to October 11, but these limits are apparently dates of collectors' entering and leaving the region rather than of the migration of the bats. Still in the Rio Grande Valley enough winter work has been done to prove that the bats either migrate or hibernate during cold weather. That they breed in the region is amply proved by their remaining throughout the summer months, and by a female shot near Boquillas, May 28, and three females taken at Comstock May 11, each containing two large fetuses. Lloyd collected a half-grown young at Paisano, July 18.

During the day they hide in cracks of buildings, and probably also in cliffs, as they inhabit rocky country where there are no buildings. At Comstock, May 11, 1901, Oberholser found "eight or nine roosting behind the signboard of a store, and they were said to have been driven from a similar place at the railroad station." He secured five of these, which proved to be four females and one male. On July 24 and 25 of the following year Hollister caught seven more (four males and three females) from behind the signboard at the railroad station at Comstock. At Van Horn one came into my room in the evening of August 23, and was caught. Near Carlsbad, N. Mex., these bats were abundant around the house on the Bolles ranch in September, coming out of cracks in buildings early in the evening and flying softly around the house in the twilight before the smaller bats began to appear. During the day I often heard them squeaking behind the casings, and with a pair of forceps took five from behind a board. Of six specimens taken, three were males and three females. In this species I have never found a striking preponderance of either sex, probably because I have found them only in the breeding season.

---

[a] Probably the third cave, about a mile below the mouth of the Pecos.

Their flight is soft and noiseless, and, while rapid, it is not so quick and jerky as that of most bats. Their light color and large size render them unmistakable in the early evening; even the long, projecting ears can sometimes be distinguished as the bats fly over. An old female, previously mentioned as containing two fetuses, measured 345 mm. (approximately a foot) from tip to tip of wings while fresh.

**Nyctinomus mexicanus** Saussure.    Free-tailed Bat.

179

The free-tailed bat is the most abundant species over approximately the western half of Texas in arid Lower Sonoran zone. Its eastern limit of range, so far as known, agrees closely with the eastern limits of mesquite. There is a specimen in the U. S. National Museum collection labeled Indianola. The species is abundant at San Antonio, and I have examined specimens from Brazos, San Angelo, Kerrville, Ingram, Padre Island, Brownsville, Hidalgo, Eagle Pass, Del Rio, Comstock, mouth of Pecos, Langtry, Boquillas, Alpine, Davis Mountains, Fort Stockton, and up the Pecos Valley as far as Roswell, N. Mex. The abundant bats in the town of El Paso are probably of this species.

In at least a part of their Texas range these bats are not only resident, but active throughout the winter months. At Del Rio I found them abundant in January and February, 1889; Lloyd and Streator found them common at Eagle Pass in November, and Lloyd collected one on Padre Island November 11. At Brazos Cary found them as late as October 9, 1902, and says: " I shot twenty of these bats in a crack in the bridge where the Texas Pacific Railroad crosses the Brazos. The bats were in the cracks by hundreds." Most of his alcoholic specimens are very fat, which would suggest that later they might have hibernated. At San Angelo Oberholser reported the species April 2 to 4, 1901: "Abundant along the Concho, where one was taken. All the bats seen were apparently of this genus." At Fort Stockton, in August, Cary reports them as the "most abundant bat." At Alpine, July 5, they swarmed out of the adobe walls of empty houses in the evening until the town was full of them and their musky odor. A few were shot in the canyons of the Davis Mountains July 10, and their unmistakable odor was very noticeable among the old adobe walls at Fort Davis. At the ranch of Mr. Howard Lacey, near Kerrville, these bats were numerous May 1 to 7, 1899. Some were shot around the ranch buildings in the evening, and one of their roosting places was found in a crack under an overhanging rock of a high cliff. I heard them squeaking and apparently fighting in the crack. A few shots of the auxiliary brought sixteen of them to the ground, and examination showed these to be males and females in about equal numbers. The embryos in these females were just beginning to enlarge noticeably, but a female shot at Boquillas May 28 contained a half-developed embryo. On a hot May evening in San Antonio I have watched a stream of these bats fly from under the cornice of the old adobe hotel, making the hot air heavy with their odor. They are partial to towns and adobe houses. At Del Rio, in January and February, 1889, they were excessively numerous. At dusk the air seemed full of them, and several people told me that their houses were so infested with bats that no one would rent them. On visiting one of these vacant houses in the evening I found bats pouring out of cracks and holes in the boards that covered the adobe walls. There was an incessant squeaking and scratching as they climbed over the inner surface of the boards and fought and pushed each other at the narrow places of exit. The noise could be heard across the street. I stood at a knothole and caught them as they came out one at a time, until I had nine in my hands, but by the time I had dispatched these the others were all out and on the wing. My specimens were covered with lice and redolent with a peculiar rank, musky odor that did not leave my hands for a couple of days. The odor is like that of the house mouse, only much stronger, and it is often noticeable as you walk along the sidewalk past some of the bat-infested houses.

**180**   **Promops californicus** (Merriam).   Bonnet Bat.

A single specimen of this large bat, collected at Langtry, Tex., March 8, 1903, by James H. Gaut, adds the species to the Texas fauna and extends its range from the southern parts of Arizona and California. Gaut says it was caught in the pump house at the bottom of Pump Canyon, near Langtry.

**181**   **Mormoops megalophylla senicula** Rehn.   Rehn Bat.

The only specimen of this Mexican and West Indian bat recorded from the United States was taken by Dr. E. A. Mearns at Fort Clark, Tex., December 3, 1897. Doctor Mearns says:

A lady called me to her house to see a 'very remarkable bat' which had attached itself to the inner side of a door-screen. I found this bat very much alive, at a season when all other bats of the locality were dormant or had migrated. No other bats were seen until the following March, when the common *Nyctinomus* reappeared in the usual abundance.[a]

[a] Proc. Biol. Soc. Wash. XIII, p. 166, 1900.

# Annotations to the *Biological Survey of Texas*

This chapter includes annotated comments corresponding to the numerical endnote designations placed in the margin of Bailey's reprinted work in Chapter 2. The annotations are intended to update the scientific nomenclature and taxonomy of each mammal and provide notes regarding changes in distributions, abundance, and conservation status of mammals in Texas since the turn of the twentieth century. A few comments also are included about some of the plant distributions in the survey publication.

The mammal survey by the federal biologists was comprehensive; Bailey documented 121 of the 144 native terrestrial species of mammals (about 84 percent) that occur in Texas today. The only group he failed to document accurately was bats (16 of 33 species), which is not surprising given that modern bat-detection techniques were not available at that time. The remaining seven undocumented species represent mammals with very confined ranges in geographically remote portions of the state. Forty-nine new taxa were described from material collected during the survey, including nine in the 1905 publication (see Table 3, Chapter 2).

The comments written about each species and subspecies of mammal are based on my own experience of studying Texas mammals in conjunction with the published scientific literature about this subject. Unless mentioned otherwise the scientific documentation for the accounts was compiled from the following publications: Taylor and Davis (1947); Davis (1960, 1966, and 1974); Davis and Schmidly (1994); Dalquest and Horner (1984); Hall (1981); Schmidly (1977, 1983, 1984a, 1984b, and 1991); Jones and Jones (1992); and Jones, J. K. Jr. et al. (1988). The application of scientific names for mammals follows Manning and Jones (1998) unless noted otherwise.

## Annotations

1. *Acacia farnesiana* is a valid scientific name but this species does not occur in Texas. The Texas species is named A. *smallii* by modern plant taxonomists. The current distribution of huisache is depicted in Map 4.

2. The current distribution of creosote bush in Texas is depicted in Map 5.

3. The current distribution of *Agave lechuguilla* is depicted in Map 6.

Large-scale production of agave fibers was never attempted in Texas. By the 1920s and 1930s synthetic fibers had become widely avail-

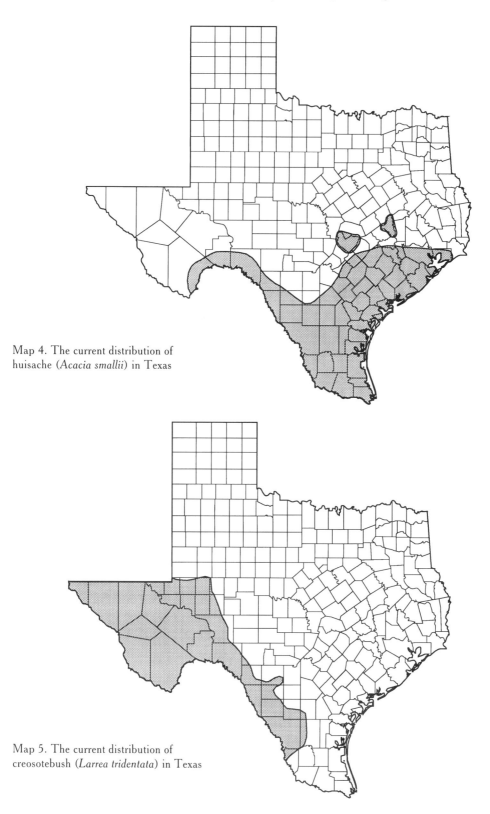

Map 4. The current distribution of
huisache (*Acacia smallii*) in Texas

Map 5. The current distribution of
creosotebush (*Larrea tridentata*) in Texas

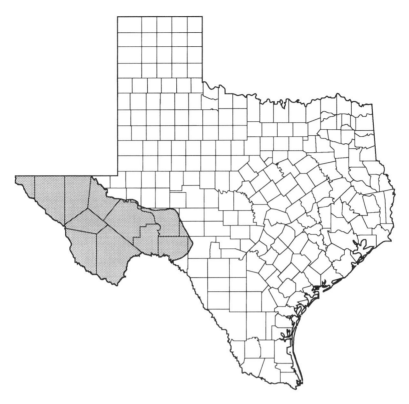

Map 6. The current distribution of lechuguilla (*Agave lechuguilla*) in Texas

able and replaced natural fibers for most uses. Agave is still harvested in Mexico, however, for production of fiber, various beverages, including tequilla, and other products.

4. Both the black and yellow persimmons are currently included in the same genus, *Diospyros* (*D. texana* and *D. virginiana*). The current distribution for the two species is depicted in Map 7.

5. Although Bailey classified *Tatu novemcinctum texanum* as distinct from *T. n. mexicanum*, modern taxonomists consider these to be synonymous and recognize the current name of *Dasypus novemcinctus mexicanus* for the nine-banded armadillo in Texas. The range of the armadillo has expanded northward and eastward considerably since the time of the biological survey (for a complete discussion of the status of this species in Texas, see Chapter

6). The species is less common in the western part of its range in Texas, where it is mostly found along creeks and river terraces. Although not known in Bailey's time, reproduction in the armadillo is marked by the unusual phenomenon of specific polyembryony, which results in the normal formation of identical quadruplets.

6. The range of the opossum has expanded westward considerably since the time of the survey, and recent records (Hollander and Hogan, 1992) show that its range now encompasses all the state with the exception of the most xeric areas of the Trans-Pecos. Range extensions have occurred primarily along streams and rivers, where woody vegetation has permitted the opossum to penetrate the otherwise treeless grasslands and deserts of western Texas. Modern taxonomists classify the opossum into two subspecies, *Didelphis virginiana pigra* in

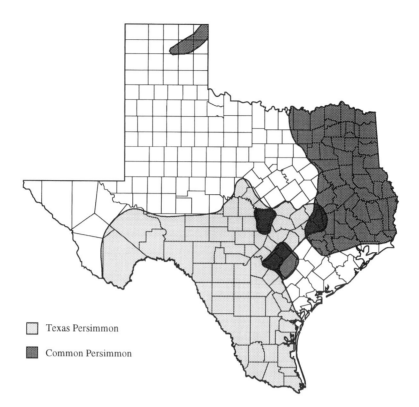

Map 7. The current distribution of Texas persimmon (*Diospyros texana*) and common persimmon (*Diospyros virginiana*) in Texas. The more heavily shaded areas represent areas of overlap or sympatry between the two species.

the south and southeast, and *D. v. virginiana* in northern and Central Texas. The name *D. marsupialis texensis* has been changed to *D. v. californica* and its application is restricted to opossums occurring in Central America (see Gardner, 1973). The specimens discussed here as *D. marsupialis texensis* are today recognized as *D. v. pigra*.

7. The name *Tayassu angulatum* has been changed to *Pecari tajacu*, and the subspecies in Texas is *P. t. angulatus*. Interestingly, Bailey and the federal agents did not collect or observe peccaries in the Big Bend or the Davis Mountains, places where they are common today. It appears the range of this species has declined in the east and north and expanded to the west during this century. An introduced population occurs along the Red River in Wilbarger and surrounding counties (Dalquest and Horner, 1984). Map 8 depicts the current range of the peccary in Texas.

8. Modern taxonomists classify Merriam's elk as a subspecies, *Cervus elaphus merriami*, but it was extinct by the time of the biological survey. There have been reintroductions but not of the native subspecies. For a discussion, see Chapter 6.

9. The spelling of *texanus* has been changed to *texana*. The subspecies *Odocoileus virginianus texana* occurs naturally throughout most of the state and has been stocked in the northeastern region of Texas where *O. v. macroura* once occurred and along the Gulf coast where *O. v. mcilhennyi* once existed. With the exception of *O. v. carminis*, the Carmen Mountain Whitetail, which occurs in

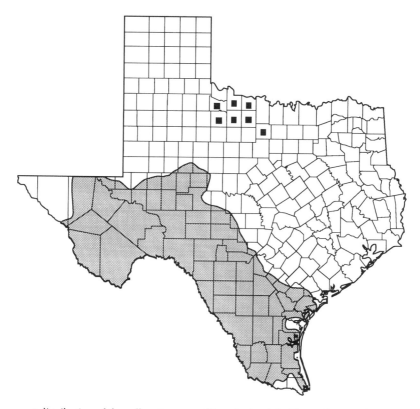

Map 8. The current distribution of the collared peccary (*Pecari tajacu*) in Texas. Squares (■) indicate counties with introduced populations.

the higher elevations of the isolated mountain tops in the Big Bend region, it is virtually impossible to distinguish subspecies of white-tailed deer in Texas because of the massive introductions and movements of animals from location to location across the state the latter half of the twentieth century. The specimen discussed here from El Paso County is now believed to have been brought in by hunters or other persons traveling through the area.

10. Modern taxonomists would refer specimens from Monahans and the High Plains to the subspecies *texana* (Hall, 1981). The spelling of *macrourus* has been changed to *macroura*, a subspecies which once occurred in the extreme northeastern corner of the state.

11. Modern taxonomists restrict the use of the name *couesi* to a subspecies, *Odocoileus virginianus couesi*, that occurs in Arizona, western New Mexico, and Mexico. The specimens Bailey described from the Chisos Mountains are now recognized as *O. v. carminis*. This subspecies is represented by a small, isolated population in the Chisos Mountains, where it is well protected within the borders of Big Bend National Park and by populations from the Rosillos, Christmas, Chinati, and Davis Mountains in the Trans-Pecos (Krausman et al., 1978).

12. The name *Odocoileus hemionus canus* has been changed to *O. h. crooki*, and this is the only subspecies of mule deer recognized in Texas today. *O. h. hemionus* occurs north and west of Texas. Although mule deer are not nearly as numerous in Texas as white-tailed deer, they do represent an important big game

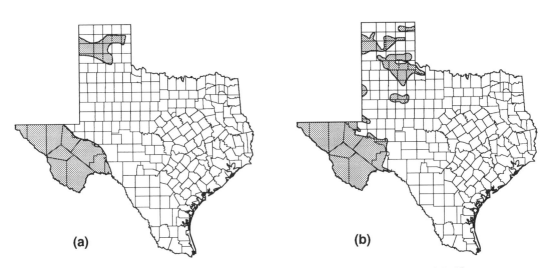

(a)                                      (b)

Map 9. The historic (a) and current (b) distribution of the mule deer (*Odocoileus hemionus*) in Texas

resource in the Trans-Pecos and Panhandle areas. Populations are now fairly stable but experience periodic declines because of natural mortality factors such as predation, disease, and weather. In 1998 the estimated mule deer population in Texas was 144,000 animals, and an estimated 4,300 were harvested in 1997. It is interesting to note that Vernon Bailey's 1890 mammal report for the Davis Mountains includes a comment that white-tailed deer and mule deer may be producing hybrids in this area. It is now common knowledge that these two species do in fact interbreed and produce hybrid offspring (Carr et al., 1986). However, the production of first generation hybrids between free-ranging populations of the two species of deer appears to be a rare event (Ballinger et al., 1992), although a relatively high proportion of backcross individuals have been documented (Cathey et al., 1998). Map 9 depicts the historic and current distribution of mule deer in Texas.

13. See Chapter 6 for a discussion of the decline and recovery of the pronghorn in Texas. Two subspecies of pronghorn occur in Texas today, *Antilocapra americana americana* in the Panhandle and *A. a. mexicana* in western

and Central Texas, although reintroductions, beginning in the late 1930s, to augment a declining population may have altered this situation. Map 10 depicts the historic and current distribution of pronghorn in Texas.

14. The name *Bison bison* has reverted to the original name, *Bos bison*. The subspecies is *B. b. bison*. Most of the bison had been exterminated in Texas by the time the biological survey was started in the late 1880s (see Chapter 6 for a discussion).

15. The bighorn or mountain sheep of Texas is recognized as a subspecies, *Ovis canadensis mexicana*. Bighorn sheep were still wide ranging over many parts of Trans-Pecos Texas during the time of the biological survey. For a discussion of their demise and reintroductions, see Chapter 6. Map 11 depicts the historic and current distribution of the bighorn sheep in Texas.

16. All the fox squirrels in Texas and the United States are now recognized as a single species, *Sciurus niger*, with ten distinct subspecies of which three occur in Texas. The three subspecies of the fox squirrel in Texas are *S. n. ludovicianus* in the east, *S. n. limitis* in most of the western part of the species' range in the

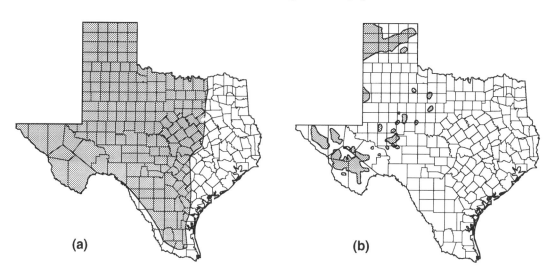

Map 10. The historic (a) and current (b) distribution of the pronghorn (*Antilocapra americana*) in Texas

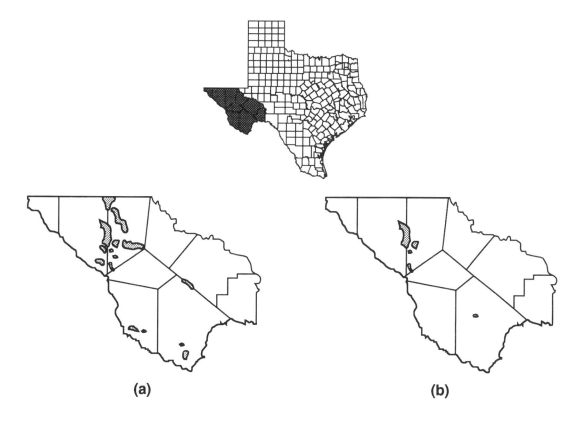

Map 11. The historic (a) and current (b) distribution of the bighorn sheep (*Ovis canadensis*) in Texas. All current populations are of a different subspecies and were introduced into the state. No native bighorns exist in Texas today.

state, and *S. n. rufiventer* from the Canadian River drainage and adjacent areas of northwestern and extreme North-Central Texas. See Chapter 6 for a discussion of the status of this species in Texas.

17. This squirrel is now classified as *Sciurus niger limitis*.

18. Gray squirrels, or cat squirrels as they are sometimes called locally, are among the most important game animals in eastern Texas. Prior to 1910, these squirrels were abundant over the entire region where suitable habitat was found. The last eighty-five years, however, have witnessed a drastic reduction of suitable habitat as a result of detrimental land-use practices, such as logging of hardwoods, practices of timber stand improvement and establishment of pine plantations, overgrazing by domestic livestock, flooding of bottomland habitats through reservoir impoundments on major streams and rivers, and drainage of lowland bottomlands. Their future will depend on the acreage remaining in hardwood forests, the lengths of timber rotations, the species composition of hardwood stands, and the abundance of mast supplies and dens.

Where gray and fox squirrels occur together in eastern Texas, gray squirrels prefer the poorly drained types of forest cover in the hardwood timber along the larger creeks and rivers. Fox squirrels prefer the upland creeks and well-drained bottomlands generally found along the smaller creeks and in the upland pine and hardwood timber. There is evidence to suggest that fox squirrels may be increasing in abundance at the expense of gray squirrels. The drainage of lowland bottomlands seems to result in a reduction of the number of gray squirrels and an increase in the number of fox squirrels. Gray squirrels have been introduced in many places in Texas outside of their natural range. For example, they are now common in Lubbock in the northwestern part of the state (see Chapter 6 for a discussion).

19. Current taxonomy recognizes the pine or red squirrel from New Mexico as *Tamiasciurus hudsonicus lychnuchus*. Despite the speculation by Bailey, this squirrel has never been documented in the Guadalupe Mountains or any other place in Texas.

20. Modern taxonomists now refer to *Sciuropterus volans querceti* as *Glaucomys volans querceti* and restrict this name to a subspecies that occurs in Florida and southeastern Georgia. The subspecies of flying squirrel that occurs in Texas, *G. v. texensis*, was described by A. H. Howell (1915) on the basis of specimens collected during the biological survey by J. H. Gaut on March 15, 1905, at seven miles northeast of Sour Lake, Hardin County, in the Big Thicket (Howell, 1918). The status of this species is difficult to predict as we enter the twenty-first century.

21. *Eutamias cinereicollis canipes* is now classified as *Tamias canipes canipes* (Nadler et al., 1977; Levenson et al., 1985). Bailey described this taxon on the basis of specimens collected from 7000 feet in Dog Canyon in the Guadalupe Mountains on August 24, 1902. These chipmunks are most numerous in coniferous forests where fallen logs, in which they often build their nests, are common. Subsequent to the biological survey, populations of the gray-footed chipmunk have been documented from the Sierra Diablo Mountains in southwestern Culberson County. In a survey of the mammals of Guadalupe Mountains National Park, Hugh Genoways and associates (1979) obtained nine specimens of the gray-footed chipmunk near The Bowl and in Upper Dog Canyon at the higher elevations of the park. Thus, the status of the species appears to be good within the protected confines of the national park.

22. The Texas antelope squirrel was described as *Tamias interpres* by C. Hart Merriam in 1890 on the basis of specimens collected by Vernon Bailey at El Paso on December 10, 1889 (Merriam, 1890a). Bailey is the first au-

Map 12. The predicted current distribution of the Texas antelope squirrel (*Ammospermophilus interpres*) in Texas. This distribution map is based on the known range of the species and the available appropriate habitat for the species.

thor credited with the application of the name *Ammospermophilus interpres* for these squirrels. This species is more widely distributed in western Texas than depicted by Bailey's map. It occurs throughout the Trans-Pecos region (and not just adjacent to the drainages of the Rio Grande and the Pecos River), extending eastward to Reagan, Crockett, and Val Verde Counties (Map 12). These ground squirrels inhabit rocky foothill terrain, characterized by shrub desert habitat. Despite the speculation by Bailey, it is now known that these squirrels do not hibernate and are active throughout the year. In fact, they are one of the few small mammals active during the day in the hot summer months of the Big Bend.

23. For several decades, taxonomists referred all the ground squirrels to the genus *Citellus*, until Bryant (1945) provided the justification for the application of the name *Spermophilus* for all these squirrels. Thus, the name *C. variegatus couchi* has been changed to *S. v. couchi*, which is used in reference to specimens from the Big Bend region of Texas. Rock squirrels tend to be found in the lower life zones from the pine-oak forests down into the desert. They occupy broken, usually rocky terrain, and are common in rocky hillsides and along arroyos. They are quite common and have adapted well to human encroachment.

24. The name *Citellus variegatus buckleyi* has been changed to *Spermophilus variegatus buckleyi*, and it refers to populations from the

Hill Country in South-Central Texas. Rock squirrels show considerable variation in color, ranging from specimens that are light gray to dark gray to entirely black. Specimens of the subspecies *buckleyi* from the Edwards Plateau show a large preponderance of entirely black individuals which is why Bailey applied the common name "black-backed rock squirrel" to this taxa. Specimens from the far western Edwards Plateau in Crockett and Val Verde Counties have been referred to the subspecies *S. v. grammurus* (Goetze, 1998) along with populations from the Davis and Guadalupe Mountains and from El Paso County in West Texas (Hall, 1981). The taxonomy of rock squirrels is badly in need of revision, prompting some modern taxonomists to suggest that all rock squirrels in West Texas should be referred to a single subspecies, *S. v. grammurus* (Jones and Jones, 1992).

25. The name *Citellus variegatus grammurus* has been changed to *Spermophilus variegatus grammurus*, and it refers to those rock squirrels from the western part of Texas.

26. The name *Citellus mexicanus parvidens* has been changed to *Spermophilus mexicanus parvidens*. Edgar Mearns (1896), who led the biological survey of the United States–Mexican boundary area (see Chapter 1), described this subspecies on the basis of specimens collected at Fort Clark in Kinney County on March 21, 1893.

27. The name *Citellus tridecemlineatus texensis* has been changed to *Spermophilus tridecemlineatus texensis*. C. Hart Merriam described this subspecies in 1898 on the basis of specimens sent to the biological survey by a Mr. G. H. Ragsdale from Gainesville in Cooke County (Merriam, 1898a). Ragsdale, who obtained the specimens on April 15, 1886, wrote journal articles about natural history in Cooke County, and he did much to popularize natural history through his contributions to the local newspapers. The subspecies *texensis* has be-

come rare in the prairies which extend through the middle part of the state as those areas have become encroached by brush and chaparral.

28. The name *Citellus tridecemlineatus pallidus* has been changed to *Spermophilus tridecemlineatus pallidus* and refers to a subspecies restricted to the north-central region of the United States. The specimens recorded by Bailey in the Panhandle are today recognized as *S. t. arenicola*. The ranges of the two subspecies, *arenicola* and *texensis*, are not as disjunct as indicated by Bailey (Map 13). Specimens of *texensis* have been recorded from Hardeman and Foard Counties along the Red River, and *arenicola* is known from Hemphill, Wheeler, and Motley Counties in the Panhandle. This is a widely occurring and common ground squirrel throughout the Texas Panhandle (Jones, J. K. Jr. et al., 1988).

29. The spotted ground squirrels are now classified as *Spermophilus spilosoma*. Although Bailey recognized four subspecies in the state, only three are considered valid today: *S. s. annectens* in the southern part of the state, *S. s. canescens* in far western Trans-Pecos, and *S. s. marginatus* in the remainder of the range. The specimens identified by Bailey as *Citellus spilosoma major* are now classified as *S. s. marginatus*. This species remains in good shape throughout its range in Texas.

30. Bailey (1902) described the subspecies *arens* on the basis of specimens collected by him in El Paso, but he later placed this form in synonymy of the subspecies *canescens* (Bailey, 1932).

31. The subspecies *annectens* was described by C. Hart Merriam in 1893 on the basis of specimens collected by William Lloyd on Padre Island (Merriam, 1893). Populations remain common on the island today.

32. Bailey did not refer Texas populations of the prairie dog to subspecies. Today, however, two subspecies are known in the state: *Cynomys ludovicianus arizonensis* in the

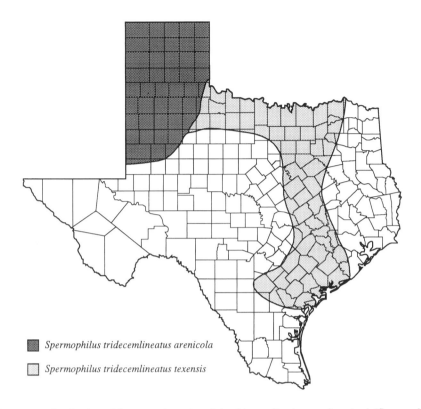

Map 13. The current distribution of the two subspecies of the thirteen-lined ground squirrel (*Spermophilus tridecemlineatus*) in Texas

Trans-Pecos and *C. l. ludovicianus* elsewhere (Hall, 1981). The large concentrations of prairie dogs described by Bailey, such as between San Angelo and Clarendon, are things of the past in Texas. Land conversion to agriculture and the extensive use of poisons to kill the animals have considerably reduced their former range and numbers. Past state law, since repealed, required a landowner to destroy all prairie dogs on his property. The result is a scarcity of prairie dog towns today. In the northern Panhandle, prairie dogs have been observed at numerous localities on rangelands, but these colonies rarely number more than a few hundred individuals. The decline in prairie dogs has been so dramatic during the past few decades that the National Wildlife Federation has petitioned the United States Fish and Wildlife Service (USFWS) to list the species as threatened or endangered (see Chapter 6).

33. Although not native to Texas, the house mouse has become widespread and occurs either as a commensal—those living in buildings and farm structures—or feral animal throughout the state. We have learned much about this introduced rodent since the time of Vernon Bailey. Commensal populations differ from feral ones in having longer tails and darker coloration, and social behavior differs between the two types. Commensal house mice live in small groups dominated by an adult male that does most of the mating of females in the group. The group occupies a defended home area from which casual immigrants are excluded. Wild or feral house mice do not occur in rigidly structured colonies but instead live within a home

range in a manner that is typical of native rodents.

34. The scientific name of the wharf or brown rat (now commonly known as the Norway rat), *Mus norvegicus*, has been changed to *Rattus norvegicus*. Likewise, the scientific name for the roof rat, or black rat, is now *Rattus rattus* instead of *Mus alexandrinus* as listed by Bailey. Roof rats are largely commensal and live in close association with man. They seldom become established as feral animals as do the Norway rats. As noted by Bailey, the wharf or Norway rat seems to be more common in Texas. A more recent immigrant to the United States, it is larger and more aggressive and appears to be supplanting the roof rat in many parts of the country.

35. Members of the genus *Rattus* can be mistaken for the native pack rat of the genus *Neotoma*. However, the introduced animals have a nearly naked, scaly tail (rather than a well-haired, usually bicolored tail), and they are grayish or dark-colored ventrally, rather than white. Black rats are darker in color than Norway rats and have a tail that is longer than the head and body rather than shorter.

36. Modern taxonomists now recognize three subspecies of the northern grasshopper mouse, *Onychomys leucogaster*, in Texas: *O. l. albescens* in El Paso and Hudspeth Counties; *O. l. articeps* in the Panhandle and adjacent areas to the east, south to Crockett and Pecos Counties; and *O. l. longipes* from Tom Green and Terrell Counties southward to the Rio Grande and southeastward to Nueces County. The taxa *longipes*, referred to by Bailey as the Texas grasshopper mouse, was described by C. Hart Merriam in 1889 on the basis of a specimen collected in Concho County on March 11, 1887, by William Lloyd. Subsequently, Ned Hollister (1913) designated *longipes* as a subspecies of the more wide-ranging species *O. leucogaster*. The name *O. l. pallescens*, which Bailey applied to grasshopper mice from the

Panhandle and northern Texas, applies now to populations occurring in New Mexico, Arizona, Colorado, and Utah, and Texas specimens are referred to *O. l. articeps*. The conservation status of grasshopper mice is good throughout their range in Texas.

37. The scientific name *Onychomys torridus*, as used by Bailey, is no longer applicable to populations of grasshopper mice from western Texas. Recent genetic work revealed that two "cryptic" species had been included under the name *O. torridus* and the populations occurring in Texas are now classified as *O. arenicola*. The application of the name *torridus* now applies to populations occurring from southwestern New Mexico westward (Hinesley, 1979). The type specimen of *arenicola* was collected by E. A. Mearns along the Rio Grande about 6 miles above El Paso in El Paso County on February 29, 1892. Hence, the common name, Mearns's grasshopper mouse, is applied to this species. It is in good shape throughout its range in Texas.

38. Deer mice of the genus *Peromyscus* are the most taxonomically diverse and complex group of rodents in Texas. Not until Wilford Osgood published his classic taxonomic revision of the group in 1909 was it possible to make much sense of the confusion surrounding this widespread genus of rodents. At the time Bailey wrote his accounts of deer mice, there were 130 nominal species and more than sixty subspecies ascribed to the genus. Bailey recognized seven species and nine subspecies of deer mice in the state. Osgood reduced the number of valid species to forty-three and raised the number of subspecies to one hundred. Osgood recognized seven species and ten subspecies in Texas, but the application of scientific names changed substantially from those used by Bailey. Today, nine species and sixteen subspecies of deer mice are recognized from Texas. All but four of these were recorded in the state by the biological survey field agents.

39. The white-footed mouse has a state-wide distribution, and it is the most common and widespread of all the species of *Peromyscus* in Texas. The subspecies are: *P. leucopus leucopus* in the eastern one-third of the state, *P. l. texanus* in Central Texas (west to Brewster, Terrell, and Val Verde Counties), and *P. l. tornillo* in the Panhandle and much of the Trans-Pecos. The subspecies *mearnsi*, which is mentioned by Bailey, was described by J. A. Allen in 1891 on the basis of specimens from Brownsville in Cameron County, but it was placed in synonymy of *texanus* by Wilford Osgood in his 1909 revision of the genus.

Two chromosomal races of *P. leucopus*, designated southwestern and northeastern, have been identified in the south-central United States (Baker et al., 1983). The two races, which divide in the ecotone between the Great Plains Grassland and Eastern Deciduous Forest biomes in Oklahoma (Stangl, 1986), are genetically distinct (Nelson et al., 1987) and reflect a major genetic division of the species. Interestingly, the ranges of the two races do not correspond to the classical subspecific boundaries for *P. leucopus*. So far, only one of the races, the southwestern one, has been documented in Texas, although no specimens have been examined from the woodlands of extreme eastern Texas, where the northeastern race might be expected to occur (Stangl and Baker, 1984).

40. *Peromyscus leucopus texanus* is now restricted in distribution to Central Texas. Specimens from Lipscomb in the Panhandle are referred to the subspecies *P. l. tornillo* by modern taxonomists.

41. *Peromyscus michiganensis pallescens* is now classified as *P. maniculatus pallescens* (Osgood, 1909). The loss of native grassland habitat in the central part of Texas presents a major concern for the future of this subspecies. I have attempted without success to collect this species at several localities where it was previously known.

42. *Peromyscus sonoriensis* is now classified as *P. maniculatus sonoriensis*, but this subspecies does not occur in Texas. Populations of deer mice from the Texas Panhandle are now referred to *P. m. luteus* (Judd, 1970). This subspecies is not nearly as common nor as broadly distributed as its larger congener, *P. leucopus* (Jones, J. K. Jr. et al., 1988).

43. *Peromyscus sonoriensis blandus* is now classified as *P. maniculatus blandus*. This taxon is still common throughout its range in Texas which encompasses the Trans-Pecos and areas immediately to the east of the Pecos River.

44. The cotton mouse, *Peromyscus gossypinus*, is the most common rodent in the woods of the Big Thicket in southeast Texas. The subspecies in Texas is *P. g. megacephalus*.

45. The spelling of *boylei* has been changed to *boylii*. Bailey listed *Peromyscus boylii penicillatus* from El Paso as a synonym of *P. b. rowleyi*, and it remained as such until Vic Diersing (1976) demonstrated that the type specimen of *penicillatus* was actually a representative of another species of deer mouse, *P. difficilis*. Diersing and Donald Hoffmeister (1974) also documented that a specimen collected by Bailey on August 22, 1901, at McKittrick Canyon in the Guadalupe Mountains was a representative of the species *difficilis*. *P. difficilis* has recently been shown to comprise two cryptic species with the northern populations, including those from Texas, being referred to the species *P. nasutus* (Carleton, 1989). *P. nasutus* is now known to have a spotty distribution in far western Texas with specimens known from the Chinati, Chisos, Davis, Guadalupe, and Franklin Mountains (Bradley et al., 1999b). The conservation status of this species in Texas is uncertain.

46. Although Bailey classified specimens of this mouse as a new subspecies, *Peromyscus*

*boylei laceyi*, this assignment proved to be an error. In a paper he published in 1906, he wrote, "I gave the name *laceyi* to a mouse of the genus *Peromyscus* occurring in central Texas. Through a most unfortunate misconception the name was applied to the wrong one of the two species found together at the type locality, to the larger, darker colored form previously named *attwateri* by Dr. J. A. Allen. The smaller, paler animal is now for the first time described under the name *laceianus* as a subspecies of *pectoralis*, its nearest relative." Thus, the two species that Bailey collected at Lacey's Ranch on Turtle Creek were *P. attwateri* and *P. pectoralis*. Specimens of *laceyi* from the Davis Mountains, Paisano, and the Chinati Mountains are now referred to *P. b. rowleyi*. Specimens from Turtle Creek, Ingram, Rock Springs, Ozona, and Big Springs are referred to either *P. attwateri* or *P. pectoralis*. The two species, *attwateri* and *pectoralis*, occur sympatrically throughout the Hill Country of Texas (Goetze, 1998). *P. pectoralis* is one of the most common deer mice in Central and West Texas.

47. J. A. Allen, a contemporary mammalogist of Bailey who worked at the American Museum of Natural History in New York City, described *Peromyscus attwateri* in 1895 on the basis of specimens from Turtle Creek in Kerr County. Bailey (1906) subsequently arranged *attwateri* as a subspecies of *boylii*, an arrangement which Osgood followed when he revised the genus in 1909. On the basis of chromosomal and morphological differences, Schmidly (1973a) showed that *attwateri* was specifically distinct from both *boylii* and *pectoralis*. *P. attwateri* occurs in the central part of the state where it is one of the most common rodents in the juniper-breaks habitat. It is now commonly referred to as the Texas mouse, although its distribution also includes Oklahoma, Kansas, Missouri, and Arkansas. The species is common throughout its range.

48. Cactus mice, *Peromyscus eremicus*, are most commonly found on the bajadas and canyon bottoms of lowland desert areas. This species is common throughout its range in Texas. A recently published analysis of mitochrondial DNA in populations of *P. eremicus* from the Chihuahuan and Sonoran Deserts indicate these populations may represent recently diverged "cryptic" species (Walpole et al., 1997), although Riddle et al. (2000) argues against recognizing two distinct species.

49. The prevailing taxonomy at the time Bailey published this account was to include the pygmy mice in with the deer mice of the genus *Peromyscus*. However, the late Robert L. Packard, a mammalogist at Texas Tech University, split out the pygmy mice into a separate genus, *Baiomys*, in 1960 on the basis of a number of unique features of the skull, skeleton, and teeth. Two subspecies occur in Texas: *B. taylori subater*, which was described by Bailey himself on the basis of specimens from East Bernard in Brazoria County, and *B. t. taylori*, which had been described in 1887 on the basis of specimens collected at San Diego in Duval County. Since the early twentieth century, the subspecies *taylori* has consistently extended its range northward and eastward by invading the oak-hickory association, the blackland prairies, the cross-timbers, rolling plains, and the high plains (Map 14) (see Chapter 6 for a discussion). The subspecies *B. t. subater* remains restricted to extreme southeast Texas.

50. Bailey described the distribution of *Oryzomys palustris* as confined to the coastal marshes from Corpus Christi to Galveston and no further inland than forty miles. Today, the species has been recorded throughout the eastern part of Texas, west to Hunt and Lee Counties and then southward at least to Willacy County. Rice rats are common on the dikes and levees thrown up in the coastal marshes. Inland, they prefer wetlands, such as marshes and

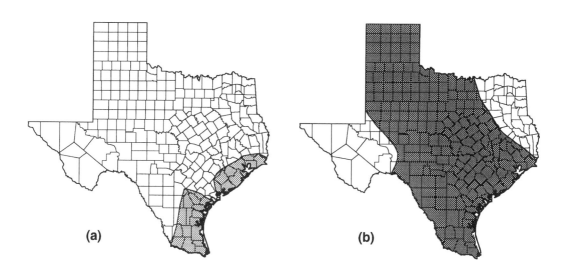

Map 14. The historic and current distribution of the northern pygmy mouse (*Baiomys taylori*) in Texas

moist meadows, but occasionally they live in forested areas. J. A. Allen described the subspecies *texensis* in 1894 on the basis of specimens collected by George B. Sennett, a well-known amateur ornithologist, who made extensive biological collections in South Texas during the 1880s and 1890s. This species is common over most of its range in Texas but the continued loss of wetlands habitat could place it in jeopardy in the future.

51. This rice rat is a seemingly rare, subtropical rodent of the Texas-Tamaulipas borderlands. It is now classified as a subspecies, *Oryzomys couesi aquaticus*, and it has been recorded from only two counties (Cameron and Hidalgo) in extreme South Texas (Benson and Gehlbach, 1979). Prior to 1996, the Coues' rice rat was listed in the Federal Register as a Category 2 species, and it is still listed as threatened by Texas Parks and Wildlife. Loss of habitat is the primary threat to this species. The resaca environment is declining in southern Texas, largely because of drainage for irrigated agriculture. Resacas bordered by cattail-bulrush marsh and subtropical woodland are essentially confined to the Cameron-Hidalgo County region.

52. The taxonomy of harvest mice (genus *Reithrodontomys*) in Texas has changed dramatically since Bailey's time. Bailey recognized five species in the genus from Texas, but today only four are considered valid. *R. intermedius* and *R. aurantius* are now classified as subspecies of the wide-ranging species, *R. fulvescens*, as is *R. laceyi* which Bailey regarded as indistinguishable from *intermedius*. Much of the taxonomic revisionary work on harvest mice was published by A. H. Howell (1914) who assisted Bailey with the Texas survey. Robert J. Russell (1953) noted the distinctness of *laceyi* and separated it from the other subspecies of *fulvescens*. The distribution of all taxa of *Reithrodontomys* in Texas differs from the description provided by Bailey. For example, the federal biologists during the Texas survey did not catch *R. fulvescens* in the Big Bend region or in West-Central Texas, nor did they record *R. megalotis* from the High Plains and Panhandle. *R. fulvescens*, *R. megalotis*, and *R. montanus* have now been documented in the Big Bend region of Texas,

and the former two species have been taken sympatrically at Big Bend Ranch State Park (Yancey et al., 1995a).

53. *Reithrodontomys fulvescens* occurs in eastern and Central Texas (west to Armstrong, Childress, and Wheeler Counties in the north) and in parts of the Trans-Pecos region. The subspecies are *R. f. aurantius*, in the eastern part of the state, *R. f. canus* in the eastern and southern Trans-Pecos, *R. f. intermedius* on the Rio Grande Plain and in adjacent areas of South Texas, and *R. f. laceyi* in the central part of the state. This species, throughout its range, prefers weedy or grassy habitats intermixed with shrubs, vines, and bushes. Undoubtedly, it has faired well since the turn of the century as mesquite and other brush have covered many areas of the state that were formerly prairie or grassland.

54. *Reithrodontomys megalotis* occurs in western Texas, from the Panhandle southward to the Trans-Pecos region. The subspecies are *R. m. aztecus* in the northern part of the range and *R. m. megalotis* to the south. These mice prefer grassy or weedy areas, especially in the vicinity of water. They appear to be in good shape over most of their range, although they are seldom captured in large numbers by mammalogists.

Yancey and Jones (1997) studied the dispersal of *R. fulvescens* and *R. megalotis* between the High Plains and Rolling Plains of Texas and found these two species have dispersed back and forth between these vegetative regions by making extensive use of the grassy habitats associated with a "railtrail" created when Texas Parks and Wildlife converted about 100 km of former railway into a hiking and horseback trail. This example of using man-made dispersal routes may be representative of the way other small mammals have dispersed across different vegetative regions during this century.

55. The taxa *merriami* and *griseus*, as understood by Bailey, are today regarded as subspecies of *Reithrodontomys humulis* and *R. montanus*, respectively. Both species are small with short tails as compared to *R. fulvescens* and *R. megalotis*. *R. montanus* is found in the western and central parts of the state, and *R. humulis* occurs in the eastern part of Texas. There is no evidence the two species intergrade, as speculated by Bailey, but they can be difficult to distinguish from one another. The distribution of both species is considerably more extensive than depicted by Bailey, but nowhere are they common.

56. Bailey did not record either *Reithrodontomys megalotis* or *R. montanus* (= *R. griseus*) from the Panhandle or High Plains region of Texas, a region where both of the species occur today (Choate, 1997). Map 15 depicts the current distribution of the two species and the counties which the federal agents surveyed at the turn of the century.

57. The eastern woodrat, *Neotoma floridana*, has been recorded from the eastern part of Texas, south to Victoria County, and westward to Edwards and Kerr Counties. Three subspecies are known from Texas, the same number recognized by Bailey, but different trinomial combinations apply to these populations today. *N. f. illinoensis*, described by A. H. Howell in 1910, is known in Texas on the basis of one specimen from Bowie County collected in 1902 by Oberholser. Bailey suggested this specimen might be a representative of the subspecies *baileyi*. The other subspecies are: *N. f. attwateri*, which is common in the northern and western parts of the range in the state, and *N. f. rubida*, in the southeast. *N. f. rubida* is the second most common rodent, aside from *Peromyscus gossypinus*, in the Big Thicket region of southeast Texas. It is especially abundant in flatland hardwood, flatland hardwood pine, and lower slope hardwood pine forests.

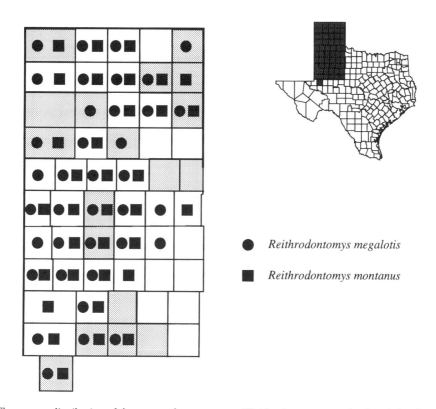

Map 15. The current distribution of the western harvest mouse (*Reithrodontomys megalotis*) and the plains harvest mouse (*Reithrodontomys montanus*) according to recent county specimen records from the Panhandle region of Texas. Shaded areas indicate counties surveyed by federal agents from 1889 to 1905, but no specimens of either species were obtained during the survey.

58. Modern authors (Hall, 1981) apply the name *Neotoma floridana baileyi* to woodrat populations from South Dakota and Nebraska. The specimens from Gainesville, discussed by Bailey, are classified by modern taxonomists as *N. f. attwateri*.

59. Modern taxonomists refer woodrats from the southern arm of the Staked Plains to the species *Neotoma micropus* and not *N. floridana attwateri* (Choate, 1997). The range of *N. f. attwateri* extends no farther west than a line extending from Wichita to Edwards Counties in the central part of the state.

60. Bailey's distribution map for *Neotoma micropus* shows it to be absent from the Llano Estacado and from the region extending southeastward to the western reaches of the Edwards Plateau. However, recent collecting has shown the species is actually common in these areas (Choate, 1997; Goetze, 1998). Both *N. micropus* and *N. floridana* occur in the western region of the Edwards Plateau and there is some evidence that the two species may hybridize with each other in this area (Birney, 1973), but this has not been proven conclusively. Map 16 depicts the distribution of *N. micropus* and *N. floridana*. *N. micropus* likely has been excluded from, or its numbers greatly reduced, in areas of intensive agricultural activity. Regular plowing, use of defoliants, and the absence of habi-

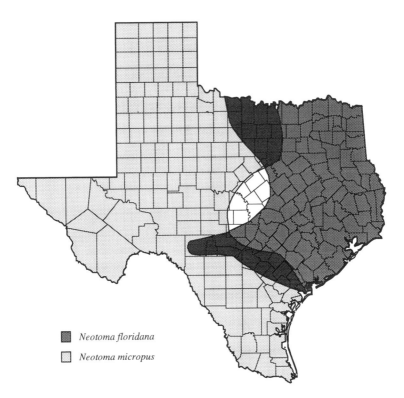

Map 16. The current distribution of the southern plains woodrat (*Neotoma micropus*) and the eastern woodrat (*Neotoma floridana*) in Texas. The more heavily shaded areas represent regions of overlap or sympatry.

tat in some areas leave little room for this rodent. Bailey describes this species as a serious pest in many places and this is true even today.

61. The distribution of the white-throated woodrat has changed little since the time of the biological survey. Populations have been discovered in extreme northern Texas, in North-Central Texas (Cottle, Hardeman, Foard, and Baylor Counties), and over most of the Edwards Plateau. As depicted by Bailey, this woodrat occurs in a variety of habitats in arid regions, but it is almost always associated with slopes and other rocky areas. Cody Edwards and his associates, using techniques of molecular biology, demonstrated a distinct genetic division between populations of this woodrat located east and west of the Rio Grande in New Mexico. According to these authors (Edwards

et al., 2000), those populations east of the Rio Grande represent a different species, *Neotoma leucodon*, from those west of the river, *N. albigula*. Using this logic, all Texas populations would be assigned to the species *N. leucodon*. Duke Rogers and I had previously assigned Texas populations of the white-throated woodrat to two subspecies. Following the new species assessment, the two subspecies in Texas would be *N. l. warreni*, from the extreme northern part of the Texas Panhandle, and *N. l. melas* from the remainder of the range. In 1954, Frank Blair referred specimens from the lava rocks in the mountains of the southern Trans-Pecos to a new melanistic race, which he designated as the subspecies *robusta* (Blair, 1954a), but Rogers and Schmidly (1981) included this population as a variant of the other

Texas subspecies. Some modern taxonomists (Manning and Jones, 1998), however, continue to recognize *robusta* as a distinct subspecies. There is a need for further study of the taxonomic assignment of Texas populations of the white-throated woodrat.

62. *Neotoma mexicana* is a small woodrat, which frequents rimrocks, canyon walls, and other rocky areas at mid to high elevations, and is known only from Trans-Pecos Texas, where it occurs in mountainous regions of Brewster, Culberson, Hudspeth, Jeff Davis, and Presidio Counties. Although he did not collect it there, Bailey speculated it would occur in the Chisos Mountains, and indeed that is the case. The subspecies in Texas is *N. m. mexicana*, and it is common throughout its range in Texas.

63. Cotton rats are more broadly distributed in Texas than Bailey ever envisioned. They are statewide in distribution, probably occurring in every county of the state. The two subspecies are the ones recognized by Bailey, *Sigmodon hispidus berlandieri*, which occurs from the Panhandle southward to the Trans-Pecos and the Rio Grande Plain, and *S. h. texianus* in the eastern and central parts of the state. Populations of cotton rats are cyclical and subject to extreme fluctuations in density. Incredible densities of this rat have been documented following several successive wet, rainy years and mild winters. H. P. Attwater referred to the huge outbreak of cotton rats around San Antonio in 1889 (Allen, 1896) and many other episodes have been documented in the twentieth century. Records reveal a severe outbreak statewide in 1919 (Davis and Schmidly, 1994), in McLennan County in 1928 (Strecker, 1929), statewide in the late 1930s and 1940s (Davis and Schmidly, 1994), throughout East Texas from 1958 to 1960 (Haines, 1963, 1971), and near Wichita Falls in 1961 (Dalquest and Horner, 1984). Interestingly, extreme outbreaks have not been reported in the past three decades. A variety of factors have been postulated by mammalogists to account for these cyclic fluctuations, including rainfall cycles, parasitism, and protracted periods of temperature extremes.

64. The subspecies *Sigmodon hispidus berlandieri* is much more broadly distributed today than indicated by Bailey. It occurs in virtually every county in West Texas, most likely having spread there along railroad and highway rights-of-way that provide suitable habitat for dispersal.

65. *Sigmodon ochrognathus*, the yellow-nosed cotton rat, is similar in appearance to *S. hispidus* but it differs in having a paler overall coloration and a distinctly orange or rusty snout. As discussed by Bailey, it is common at the higher elevations of the Chisos Mountains, and it has now been recorded from the Davis Mountains in Jeff Davis County, from Big Bend Ranch State Park in southern Presidio County (Yancey and Jones, 1996), the Elephant Mountain Wildlife Management area in Brewster County (Heaney et al., 1998), and from the Sierra Vieja in western Presidio County. Trapping evidence suggests this species is becoming more abundant and widespread throughout its range in the Trans-Pecos. Until recently, it was thought to be rare and restricted to montane habitat. But recent collecting shows it to occupy a number of non-montane habitats, albeit in small numbers.

66. During his professional career, Vernon Bailey was considered a leading authority on the taxonomy and life history of voles belonging to the genus *Microtus*, having written a taxonomic revision of the genus in 1900. *M. mexicanus* is a relict species with Rocky Mountain affinities, and it represents one of the unique taxa in Guadalupe Mountain National Park, the only place in Texas where it occurs. Collections of mammals made in the Guadalupe Mountains subsequent to the biological survey (Davis, 1940b; Davis and Robertson, 1944; Genoways et al., 1979) show this to be one of

the most common small mammals at the highest elevations of the park (above 1,920 meters elevation). Bailey described *M. m. guadalupensis* in 1902. As this taxon is currently understood, populations occurring in the Manzano, Capitan, and Sacramento Mountains in New Mexico are also included in it. The species remains in good shape in Texas within the confines of the national park.

67. *Microtus ludovicianus* is now regarded as a subspecies of a wide-ranging species, *M. ochrogaster*, and it is thought to be extinct throughout its range in Texas and Louisiana (for a discussion, see Chapter 6). The late J. Knox Jones Jr., his colleague Clyde Jones, and their students at Texas Tech University collected eight specimens of another subspecies of *M. ochrogaster*, *M. o. taylori*, from two counties (Hansford and Lipscomb) in the northern Panhandle (Jones, J. K. Jr. et al., 1988). A. H. Howell worked extensively in Lipscomb County in 1903, collecting twenty species of small mammals none of which were voles. The occurrence of *M. o. taylori* in Texas is almost certainly an invasion which occurred later in the twentieth century.

68. Although Bailey recorded *Microtus pinetorum* from only two counties in Texas (Bowie County in the far northeastern corner of the state and Gillespie County in the Hill Country), it has subsequently been reported from numerous places in the eastern and central parts of the state, but nowhere does it appear to be common within its range in Texas. Two subspecies are known from Texas, both of which were described by Bailey on the basis of specimens collected in other states, namely *M. p. auricularis* (type locality in Mississippi) in the southern part of the range in Texas and *M. p. nemoralis* (type locality in Oklahoma) to the north. Bailey assigned both of his specimens to the subspecies *auricularis*. Continued degradation of grassland habitats could have a major impact on this species in Texas.

69. The name *Fiber zibethicus* has been changed to *Ondatra zibethicus*. Bailey and the other field agents found muskrats to be abundant at the beginning of the century in the Canadian River drainage. Similarly, Blair (1954b) reported a dense population in the tule marshes of Moore and Bugby Creeks in Hutchinson County. J. Knox Jones Jr. and colleagues (1988), while conducting an extensive survey of the mammals of the northern Texas Panhandle during the 1980s, did not find any evidence of muskrats at the sites where they had been previously reported. The only recent specimens they obtained came from the shores of Lake Meredith. According to Clyde Jones (personal communication), most of the creeks are now dry and the tule marshes are greatly reduced in scope. See Chapter 6 for a discussion of the conservation status of muskrats in Texas.

70. Bailey did not attempt a subspecific assignment of the specimens from the Texas Panhandle, but he did assign the specimens from the Rio Grande and the Trans-Pecos to the subspecies *ripensis* which he had previously described in 1902. In addition to *ripensis*, the subspecies recognized today are *O. z. cinnamominus* along the Canadian River drainage and *O. z. rivalicius* on the Gulf Coastal Plain.

71. By the 1850s beavers were reduced to very low population numbers over a considerable part of Texas because of excessive annual harvests by trappers. However, these animals were able to survive on the remote streams of the upper and western Hill Country, along the Devil's River, along the edge of the Panhandle, and around El Paso (Weniger, 1997). By the early 1900s, the federal agents found them to be increasing in numbers and shortly thereafter strict harvest regulations were imposed and restocking of depleted populations became common practice. Today, beaver are found over most of the state where suitable aquatic habitat prevails.

72. The subspecies of beaver that occurs along the Rio Grande is now classified as *Castor canadensis mexicanus*. Bailey described this subspecies himself in 1913, making the following comments: "In my report on the mammals of Texas in 1905 I referred the beavers of the Rio Grande and Pecos rivers to *Castor canadensis frondater* Mearns. Since that time specimens have been collected at additional localities along the Rio Grande and its tributaries, and in working over the material in the Biological Survey Collection from New Mexico I find that the beavers of the Rio Grande drainage differ so markedly and constantly from those of the Colorado drainage that it becomes necessary to provide a name for them." (Bailey, 1913b).

73. These mice are now classified as *Liomys irroratus texensis* Merriam. The species is widely distributed across much of Mexico, but it occurs in the United States only in extreme South Texas. In addition to the specimens reported by Bailey from Brownsville in Cameron County, the species has now been collected in six other counties (Zapata, Jim Hogg, Starr, Hidalgo, Kenedy, and Willacy) in the lower Rio Grande Valley. This species is relatively abundant where it occurs in Texas.

74. Baird's pocket gopher has only recently been recognized as a distinct species. It was described in 1855 by Spencer Fullerton Baird on the basis of specimens from Louisiana, but Rollin Baker and Bryon Glass grouped it in 1951 as a subspecies of *Geomys bursarius*. Rodney Honeycutt and David Schmidly (1979) and Priscilla Tucker and David Schmidly (1981), using chromosomal characteristics, demonstrated the distinctness of *G. breviceps*.

75. Whereas Bailey refers only pocket gophers from the coastal prairies around the western edge of Galveston Bay to *Geomys breviceps sagittalis*, Rodney Honeycutt and David Schmidly (1979) have demonstrated that all populations of *Geomys* from East Texas should be referred to this subspecies. Bailey reported this gopher as common all the way from Virginia Point to Houston. Apparently, this is no longer true. Land clearing and land subsidience have removed many of the low mounds characteristic of the coastal prairie at the turn of the century. Hice and Schmidly (1999) found sign of gophers at Virginia Point, and they even collected a specimen near Hitchcock, but these burrowing rodents have completely disappeared around Clear Creek and toward Houston.

76. Following the previously mentioned work of Rodney Honeycutt, Priscilla Tucker, and David Schmidly, *Geomys attwateri* is now regarded as a distinct species from *G. breviceps*. The dividing line between them is approximately along the Brazos River from Waco to the coast. *G. breviceps* occurs east of the river and *G. attwateri* to the west. Small zones of range contact and overlap occur where land transfers from one side of the river to the other have occurred as a result of the river switching banks. C. Hart Merriam described *G. attwateri* in 1895, on the basis of specimens collected at Rockport in Aransas County, in honor of H. P. Attwater for his numerous contributions to early Texas mammalogy (Merriam, 1895). The species *G. attwateri* is monotypic and subspecies are not recognized by modern taxonomists. This gopher is locally common throughout its range in Texas.

77. *Geomys breviceps llanensis* is now regarded as conspecific with *G. texensis* and has been synonymized with that species. This conclusion is based on detailed genetic analysis conducted by Earl Zimmerman and his students at the University of North Texas (Block and Zimmerman, 1991). Modern taxonomists refer the specimens from Colorado, Stanton, Childress, Vernon, Newlin, Canadian, Lips-

comb, and Tascosa to *G. bursarius major*. Specimens from Brazos County are assigned to the taxa *G. breviceps sagittalis*.

78. C. Hart Merriam described *Geomys texensis* in 1895 on the basis of specimens from Mason in Mason County (Merriam, 1895). The subspecies *G. t. texensis* has been reported from McCulloch, San Saba, Kimble, Mason, Gillespie, Lampasas, and Llano Counties (Pitts et al., 1999). Recently, Smolen et al. (1993) described a new subspecies of *G. texensis*, *G. t. bakeri*, from the drainages of the Frio River in Uvalde, Zavala, and Medina Counties. Populations of *G. texensis* from Sycamore Creek and the Rio Grande are now extinct because of the flooding of their habitat when the Amistad Reservoir was created. This species is locally abundant and does not appear to be threatened.

79. *Geomys arenarius*, the desert pocket gopher, is known only from El Paso County. The specimen Bailey refers to from Ward County is now classified as *G. knoxjonesi* by modern taxonomists (Baker and Genoways, 1975). *G. arenarius* and *G. knoxjonesi* are cryptic species but research on mitochondrial DNA, ribosomal DNA, chromosomes, and allozymes by Robert Baker and his students at Texas Tech University indicates the two forms are genetically distinct (Baker et al., 1989; Bradley et al., 1991). *G. arenarius* remains common in El Paso County as well as several localities where it has been obtained in New Mexico, and *G. knoxjonesi* is locally common throughout its range as well.

Where the range of *G. knoxjonesi* contacts that of *G. bursarius major* in eastern New Mexico, the two taxa hybridize in a narrow hybrid zone (Baker et al., 1989; Pembleton and Baker, 1978). In an extensive study of this zone, Robert J. Baker and his students at Texas Tech found that *G. b. major* and *G. knoxjonesi* differed in diploid numbers, mitochondrial and ribosomal DNA, and allozyme systems. Baker et al. (1989) and Bradley et al. (1991) determined that both premating and postmating isolating mechanisms reduced gene exchange and resulted in hybrids that were either sterile or had reduced fertility, thus indicating the two taxa were behaving as good biological species. It is virtually impossible to distinguish the two on the basis of overall appearance and morphology.

80. *Geomys personatus*, the Texas pocket gopher, has a much more extensive range and complicated taxonomy than originally presented for the state by Bailey. The most recent taxonomic revision of the species recognized seven subspecies in Texas (Williams and Genoways, 1981). The subspecies *G. p. personatus* is restricted to Mustang and Padre Islands in Kleberg and Nueces Counties, and it does not extend more than halfway down Padre Island. It is common throughout this area.

81. The specimens from Laredo and Carrizo, referred to *Geomys personatus fallax* by Bailey, are representatives of a new subspecies, *G. p. davisi*, described by Williams and Genoways (1981) from western Webb and Zapata Counties. The remainder of the specimens available to Bailey are classified as *G. p. fallax* which was described by Merriam in 1895 on the basis of material collected by William Lloyd, a federal agent on the survey, from the south side of Nueces Bay in 1891.

82. J. Knox Jones Jr. and Clyde Jones of Texas Tech University (1988) referred the specimens collected by A. H. Howell from fifteen miles east of Texline to the subspecies *Geomys bursarius jugossicularis*. This gopher is common in the northern Panhandle of Texas.

83. Collections made by mammalogists since the biological survey have revealed that the yellow-faced pocket gopher, *Cratogeomys castanops*, has a broader distribution and many more subspecies than recognized in Texas by Bailey. Hollander (1990) conducted a taxonomic review of this species in the United States

and recognized seven subspecies in Texas. Interestingly, Bailey comments about a conspicuous absence of any species of gopher from the lower Rio Grande Valley. In 1977 Art Cleveland reported C. *castanops* from near the Rio Grande in Cameron County just across the river from Tamaulipas, Mexico. Cleveland observed numerous burrows southeast of Brownsville in 1976 but stated that no burrows had been observed at the same site in 1972. These observations suggest the possibility of a recent invasion by these gophers from the south side of the river. The population from Brownsville is assigned to the subspecies C. *c. tamaulipensis*. Bailey's specimens from Eagle Pass are now assigned to the subspecies C. *c. angusticeps*; those from Val Verde County to C. *c. clarkii*; and those from Big Spring, Stanton, and Tascosa to C. *c. parviceps*. This remains one of the most common pocket gophers throughout its range in Texas.

84. Some of the most fascinating problems in mammalian variation and geographic and ecological distribution are related to gopher taxonomy. The history of the nomenclature and taxonomic practice of species of the genus *Thomomys*, where 213 subspecies have been described in only one species, is probably the best example of this. Vernon Bailey was one of the leading authorities on the taxonomy of this species complex, authoring the first serious revision of this genus in 1915. Bailey recognized four species of *Thomomys* in Texas: the wide-ranging *T. fulvus* from the Guadalupe and Davis Mountains; *T. baileyi* from Sierra Blanca in Hudspeth County; *T. aureus* from El Paso to the Big Bend Country; and *T. perditus* from Comstock and the head of the Devil's River to the vicinity of Rock Springs. Modern taxonomists have grouped all these taxa into a single species, *T. bottae*, which occurs over much of Trans-Pecos Texas eastward across the Edwards Plateau, with eight recognized subspecies. Specimens from the Guadalupe Mountains are now recognized as a distinct subspecies, *T. b. guadalupensis*.

85. In 1902, Bailey described the small pocket gopher from the head of Limpia Creek at 5,500 feet in the Davis Mountains in Jeff Davis County, under the name *Thomomys fulvus texensis*. In 1934, Nelson and Goldman found evidence that *T. fulvus* and *T. bottae* intergrade and placed all forms formerly recognized as races of *fulvus* in the species *bottae*. The Davis Mountain gopher then became known as *T. b. texensis*. In 1939, Frank Blair described a new race, *T. b. limpiae*, from the mouth of Limpia Canyon, one mile north of Fort Davis. Thus, two subspecies are now recognized from the Limpia Creek drainage in the Davis Mountains, *T. b. texensis* at the higher elevations and *T. b. limpiae* in the foothills (Davis and Buecher, 1946). Interestingly, recent attempts by mammalogists to collect these gophers near the town of Fort Davis have proven futile (Clyde Jones, personal communication), raising the possibility that *T. b. limpiae* may now be extinct. There is some indication that *Cratogeomys* may be replacing *Thomomys* as a result of climate changes involving increased aridity. Reichman and Baker (1972) studied the distributional relationships of *Cratogeomys* and *Thomomys* from 1968 to 1970 along Limpia Creek in the Davis Mountains. As the area became drier, *Thomomys*, which occurred from near the stream bed to the foot of the rocky bluffs lining the canyon, moved closer to the stream, and *Cratogeomys* spread into the vacated areas. These distributional changes may be linked to a decrease in soil moisture and a subsequent increase in xerophytic plants. Both of these conditions would favor *Cratogeomys* over *Thomomys*.

86. Modern taxonomists regard *Thomomys baileyi* as a subspecies of *T. bottae*, and it is now extinct in Texas. See Chapter 6 for a discussion.

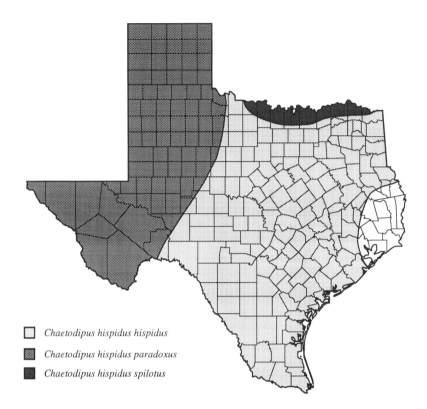

□ *Chaetodipus hispidus hispidus*

▨ *Chaetodipus hispidus paradoxus*

■ *Chaetodipus hispidus spilotus*

Map 17. The current distribution of the three subspecies of hispid pocket mouse (*Chaetodipus hispidus*) in Texas

87. The name *Thomomys aureus lachu-guilla* has been changed to *T. bottae lachuguilla*.

88. The name *Thomomys perditus* has been changed to *T. b. perditus* and applies to gophers that occur in Mexico. The specimens listed in the survey are today classified as *T. b. limitaris*.

89. Recent taxonomic studies (Hafner and Hafner, 1983) have shown that the hispid pocket mouse, along with all spiny-rumped pocket mice in Texas, should be included in a separate genus, *Chaetodipus*. Formerly included with *hispidus* in the *Perognathus* species group, the desert pocket mouse (*C. penicillatus*), rock pocket mouse (*C. intermedius*), and Nelson's pocket mouse (*C. nelsoni*) are now placed by taxonomists in the genus *Chaetodipus*. Bailey recognized three subspecies of *C. hispidus* in Texas, although their distribution in

the state has been rearranged by modern taxonomists. The subspecies are *C. h. hispidus* in the east, *C. h. paradoxus* in the western one-third of the state, and *C. h. spilotis* in a limited area of north Central Texas (type locality at Gainesville, Cooke County) (Map 17). The conservation status of the subspecies seems to be okay at the present time, but this is another species that could be impacted by the continued degradation of grassland habitats in Texas.

90. The name *Perognathus hispidus paradoxus* has been changed to *Chaetodipus hispidus paradoxus*, as explained in note 89.

91. The name *Perognathus hispidus spilotus* has been changed to *Chaetodipus hispidus spilotus*, as explained in note 89. This subspecies is widely distributed in eastern Oklahoma, Kansas, and Nebraska but only barely gets into Texas in the vicinity of Gainesville on the

Texas-Oklahoma border. The specimens from Jefferson mentioned by Bailey are today regarded as *C. h. hispidus*.

92. The desert pocket mouse (*Chaetodipus penicillatus*) is a small heteromyid rodent with a widespread distribution in the low desert areas of Trans-Pecos Texas. In a recent study of speciation in the desert pocket mouse, Lee et al. (1996) have shown that *C. penicillatus* should be divided into two species (*C. penicillatus*, a Sonoran Desert form, and *C. eremicus*, a Chihuahuan Desert form) on the basis of studies of allozymes, chromosomes, and mitochondrial DNA sequences. Thus, Texas specimens of this species are now classified as *C. eremicus*. This taxon was described by E. A. Mearns in 1898 on the basis of specimens from Fort Hancock in Hudspeth County, Texas. The desert pocket mouse typically is found on sandy or soft alluvial soils along stream bottoms, desert washes, and valleys. It is seldom found on gravelly soils or among rocks, a habitat preferred by the externally similar species, *C. intermedius* and *C. nelsoni*. Frank Yancey (1997) recorded all three of these species at Big Bend Ranch State Park in southern Presidio County.

93. *Chaetodipus intermedius* occupies the western portion of the Trans-Pecos region in El Paso, Hudspeth, Culberson, Jeff Davis, and Presidio Counties where it prefers rocky habitats and is closely associated with cliffs, canyons, rocky gulches, or the edges of boulders in deserts and lower grasslands. The eastern limits of the range of *intermedius* roughly follow the western boundary of the range of *C. nelsoni* which also occupies areas characterized by large rocks and boulders in the eastern two-thirds of the Trans-Pecos. This species, too, is common throughout its range in Texas.

94. *Chaetodipus nelsoni* is distinguished from *C. penicillatus* and *C. intermedius* in having numerous elongated, black-tipped spiny hairs on the rump that overreach the normal

guard hairs. The three species are difficult to distinguish even by trained taxonomists (Wilkins and Schmidly, 1979; Manning et al., 1996).

95. All specimens in Texas are referable to the subspecies, *Chaetodipus nelsoni canescens*, which is common throughout its range in the state.

96. Silky pocket mice of the genus *Perognathus* are very small pocket mice characterized by tan-, buff-, or salmon-colored upperparts contrasting with white underparts, by conspicuous buff-colored patches behind the ears, and by short tails that lack tufts of long hairs on their ends. There are three species of silky pocket mice in Texas, *P. flavus*, *P. merriami*, and *P. flavescens*, all of which remain common throughout their ranges in the state.

97. In 1892, J. A. Allen named *Perognathus merriami* on the basis of seventeen specimens from the vicinity of Brownsville, Texas. He compared this material with specimens of *P. flavus* from El Paso and concluded that they represented a distinct species. Mammalogists, including Bailey, followed his taxonomic arrangement for most of the twentieth century. Although Bailey comments that silky pocket mice do not hibernate, we now know they readily become torpid when stressed by low temperatures or by lack of food, and they may spend some time in torpor (Findley, 1987).

98. Bailey followed the taxonomic arrangement of W. H. Osgood who revised the genus *Perognathus* in 1900 (Osgood, 1900). Osgood named *P. merriami gilvus* based on three specimens from West Texas and four from New Mexico, and he noted the intermediacy of this subspecies to both *flavus* and *merriami*. Don Wilson (1973) used a detailed statistical analysis of skull measurements to confirm this interpretation, namely that the two taxa are conspecific, and he combined both under the name *P. flavus*. A subsequent study using genetic analyses has shown, however, that two species

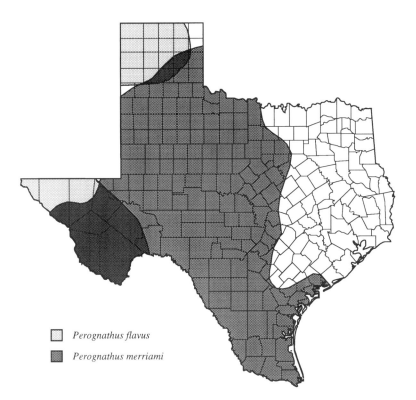

Map 18. The current distribution of the silky pocket mouse (*Perognathus flavus*) and Merriam's pocket mouse (*Perognathus merriami*) in Texas. The more heavily shaded areas represent regions of overlap or sympatry between the two species.

are indeed represented. Using karyology and allozyme studies, Lee and Engstrom (1991) have shown that, although the two taxa are highly similar morphologically, they do not appear to interbreed in areas of sympatry. Thus, in the central Trans-Pecos region and perhaps in the extreme northern panhandle region, these nearly identical species of pocket mice occur together but are reproductively isolated from each other. The distribution of the two species is essentially as described by Bailey (Map 18).

99. As discussed by Bailey, *Perognathus flavescens copei* occupies sandy soils with sparse vegetation in the Great Plains region of northwestern Texas. Its distribution today includes all the High Plains east to Wilbarger County and south to Midland and Ward Counties. In

1960, the late M. Raymond Lee captured a silky pocket mouse near El Paso, which he and J. Knox Jones Jr. identified as *P. apache*, a species thought to be closely related to *P. flavescens* (Jones and Lee, 1962). However, recent studies by Dan Williams (1978) have shown that *apache* and *flavescens* are conspecific, and the El Paso specimen is now considered to be a representative of a subspecies of *flavescens*, *P. f. melanotis*. There are no records of *P. flavescens* in the region of West Texas between El Paso and Ward Counties.

100. Bailey followed the conventional wisdom of the time in recognizing two genera of kangaroo rats: *Perodipus* for those taxa with five toes on the hind foot and *Dipodomys* for those species with four toes. However, in 1919

Joseph Grinnell showed that some of the four-toed *Dipodomys* had five toes on one hind foot and four on the other, and, consequently, he placed *Perodipus* as a synonym of *Dipodomys* which is the generic name now applied to all the kangaroo rats (Grinnell, 1919).

101. The subspecies of *Dipodomys ordii* have changed radically since Bailey published the biological survey (Baumgardner and Schmidly, 1981). The subspecies now recognized in Texas are: *D. o. medius* from the central Llano Estacado southward east of the Pecos River to Crane, Crockett, and Upton Counties, and east to Jones County (identified as *Perodipus montanus richardsoni* by Bailey); *D. o. obscurus* in the western, central, and southern parts of the Rio Grande Plain and in the southern Big Bend area (not recorded from these areas by Bailey); and *D. o. richardsoni* from the Panhandle and adjacent areas southward at least to Floyd County and east to Montague County (identified as *P. m. richardsoni* by Bailey). *D. ordii* is common throughout its range in Texas.

102. Bailey's conclusion that *Dipodomys sennetti* and *D. compactus* were separate species and distinct from *ordii* was followed until 1942 when William B. Davis observed close resemblances in external proportions and cranial features between *ordii* and *sennetti* and therefore concluded that they were only subspecies of one species (Davis, 1942). Davis further observed that the difference between *compactus* and *sennetti* was of approximately the same degree as that between *sennetti* and *ordii*. From this he concluded that all three taxa were subspecies of the one species *D. ordii*. The current taxonomic arrangement of kangaroo rat populations in South Texas is based on the work of Schmidly and Hendricks (1976) and Baumgardner and Schmidly (1981) who used karyotypes and features of the skull, analyzed with sophisticated statistical techniques, to show that *compactus* and *ordii* are distinct from one another and that they co-occur at the same lo-

cality without evidence of hybridization. These authors recognized *sennetti* as a subspecies of *D. compactus*, with the former occurring on the mainland and the latter on the barrier islands.

103. There are two species of kangaroo rats recognized today in South Texas: *Dipodomys compactus* with two subspecies, *D. c. compactus* on the barrier islands and *D. c. sennetti* on the adjacent mainland; and *D. ordii* with a single subspecies, *D. o. obscurus*, from the western two-thirds of the South Texas mainland. Both species remain common throughout their ranges in South Texas. With the exception of three specimens collected in 1900 by Oberholser at Cotulla, all the specimens obtained during the biological survey were of the species *D. compactus*. As noted by Bailey, island populations of *compactus* exhibit intrapopulational variation in color, characterized by distinct red and gray color phases.

104. Although not mentioned by Bailey, William Lloyd made a remarkable observation about the feeding behavior of kangaroo rats which to my knowledge has not been observed or noticed by other mammalogists. To quote from Lloyd's field itinerary about Padre Island:

But what did they [kangaroo rats] eat was the question! Dissection showed in some cases some animal matter, others were the sagebrush seeds. We went out each night with a lantern and could see them making strange antics, when at last we saw what they were doing — jumping up in the air and catching minute *Coleoptera*. We watched them several nights, having wondered why they always kept in the open sand and away from the brush but their madness had method in it.

105. The banner-tailed kangaroo rat has now been recorded from several counties in the southern part of the Llano Estacado. At the time of the biological survey, Texas specimens were not assigned to a subspecies, but in 1923 E. A. Goldman assigned them to the subspe-

cies *Dipodomys spectabilis baileyi*, named in honor of Vernon Bailey. This taxonomic assignment is still pertinent today. Bannertail kangaroo rats remain common throughout their range in Texas, but further degradation or loss of grassland habitat could severely impact them.

106. The only specimens of the Texas kangaroo rat captured during the biological survey were by Loring in 1894 and Oberholser in 1900 from Bellevue and Henrietta, respectively, in Clay County. Subsequently, the species has been reported from Montague County to the east and as far west in North-Central Texas as Motley and Cottle Counties, including Hardeman, Wichita, and Wilbarger Counties. See Chapter 6 for a discussion of the status of this species.

107. Bailey assigned specimens of *Dipodomys merriami* to two subspecies in Texas: *D. m. ambiguus* along the Rio Grande from El Paso to Boquillas in the Big Bend Country; and *D. m. merriami* over the remainder of the species range. Modern taxonomists (Lidicker, 1960) only recognize a single subspecies, *D. m. ambiguus*, in the state today. Federal field agents during the time of the biological survey did not collect this species on the Llano Estacado or in South Texas, but mammalogists have now collected it from the southwest sector of the Llano (Choate, 1997) and in Dimmit County in South Texas. This is one of the most common kangaroo rats in the state.

108. Bailey only found evidence of the porcupine in Texas from the Panhandle (Tascosa) and Trans-Pecos (Davis Mountains) regions. Today, the species has been documented from the entire western one-half of the state, east to Bosque County (Map 19). Thus, this is another example of a mammal that has expanded its range in Texas since the turn of the century (see Chapter 6 for a discussion).

109. Jackrabbits from southern and southeastern Texas are now classified as a subspecies, *Lepus californicus merriami*. Populations

in the southeastern part of the state have declined dramatically this century as a result of declining habitat.

110. Jackrabbits from the western Edwards Plateau and eastern Trans-Pecos are now classified as *Lepus californicus texianus*. This subspecies is common throughout its range in Texas.

111. Jackrabbit abundance varies in a cyclical pattern, with years of abundance being followed by years of scarcity. One period of particular abundance in Texas occurred in the 1920s, spurring ranchers and farmers to mount large campaigns to round up and destroy the jackrabbits. This estimate of five jackrabbits consuming as much grass as one sheep is an exaggeration. It is generally believed today that it takes eighteen jackrabbits to consume the same amount of range vegetation as one sheep, or 128 jackrabbits to consume the same vegetation as one cow. Jackrabbits tend to concentrate on pastures that are overgrazed by livestock; thus, a rancher should recognize an overabundance of jackrabbits as an indication that he has been overstocking his range. Ranchers should be aware that attempts to eliminate predators, ostensibly to protect their livestock, will often result in an increase in jackrabbits, and the subsequent damage the jackrabbits inflict on the range may be more detrimental to the rancher's livelihood than the occasional loss of a calf to a coyote. Today the jackrabbit generally is not considered a desirable food resource because they often carry disease and parasites.

112. The name *Lepus texianus melanotis* has been changed to *L. californicus melanotis*, a subspecies which occurs in the northern Panhandle of Texas where it is very abundant. An additional subspecies, *L. c. eremicus*, occurs in the El Paso area. Thus, the range of the black-tailed jackrabbit encompasses the entire state except for the forested Big Thicket area.

113. The name *Lepus floridanus alacer* has been changed to *Sylvilagus floridanus alacer*.

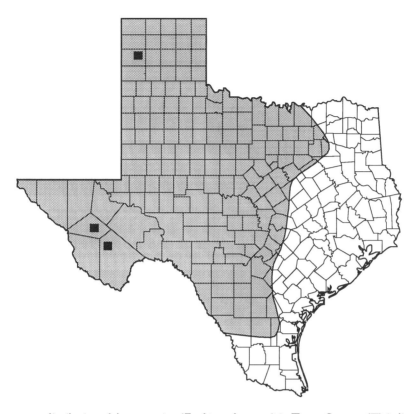

Map 19. The current distribution of the porcupine (*Erethizon dorsatum*) in Texas. Squares (■) indicate localities where Bailey (1905) recorded the species.

This species occurs statewide, with three subspecies recognized: *S. f. alacer* in eastern Texas, *S. f. chapmani* in the central and southern parts of the state, and *S. f. llanensis* on the Llano Estacado. This species is common throughout its range.

114. The name *Lepus floridanus chapmani* has been changed to *Sylvilagus floridanus chapmani*.

115. The name *Lepus arizonae minor* has been changed to *Sylvilagus audubonii minor*. *S. audubonii* occupies upland habitats in the western one-half of the state, and it is abundant throughout this region. *S. a. minor* is the subspecies occurring in the southern Trans-Pecos eastward to Val Verde County.

116. The name *Lepus arizonae baileyi* has been changed to *Sylvilagus audubonii baileyi*

but the application of this name is restricted to rabbits occurring in the northern plains states. The specimens from Texas, discussed by Bailey, are today classified as *S. a. neomexicanus*, which occurs in the northern part of the species' range in Texas, southward to Reeves and northern Brewster Counties. A third subspecies, *S. a. parvulus*, occurs from Llano County southward in South-Central Texas to the Rio Grande.

117. Originally described by Bailey as a distinct species, *robustus* maintained its specific rank until Hall (1951b) arranged it as a subspecies of the widespread eastern cottontail, *Sylvilagus floridanus*. Recently, Luis Ruedas (1998) from the University of New Mexico has studied the morphometrics of cottontails in the southwest and presented evidence that *robustus*

indeed is a distinct species based on distinct characters of the teeth. The known range of *S. robutus* includes the Guadalupe Mountains of Texas and New Mexico, the Chisos and Davis Mountains of Texas, and the Sierra de la Madera of Coahuila, Mexico. The Guadalupe and Chisos Mountains populations have been severely reduced and no specimens have been seen or collected from these areas in the past thirty years. Recently, mammalogists from Texas Tech University have obtained several specimens of *robustus* from the Davis Mountains, and it appears that a healthy population remains in this area. The species currently is not listed as threatened or endangered by the USFWS or Texas Parks and Wildlife Department (TPWD). Prior to 1996, it was listed as a potential Category 2 taxon.

118. The name *Lepus aquaticus* has been changed to *Sylvilagus aquaticus*.

119. The name *Lepus aquaticus attwateri* has been changed to *Sylvilagus aquaticus*. The swamp rabbit is a monotypic species and subspecies are not recognized. Historically, swamp rabbits are found in the eastern third of the state, west to a line from Cooke, Wise, and Palo Pinto Counties south to Brown County, thence to Travis and Bexar Counties, and then south to Aransas County on the coast. Recently, John Baccus and one of his students (1997) documented these rabbits at several locations along the major river systems in the Edwards Plateau. Optimum habitat in much of the swamp rabbit's range is shrinking with drainage of wetlands and clearing of hardwood forests, and consequently there is much concern about the future conservation status of this rabbit in Texas. In the Hill Country, they are threatened by habitat fragmentation.

120. The name *Felis hippolestes aztecus* has been changed to *F. concolor azteca*, and it refers to mountain lions from Arizona, New Mexico, and Mexico. The mountain lion of Texas is currently recognized as *F. c. stanle-*

*yana*. However, Manning and Jones (1998), in their official checklist of Texas mammals, have recommended the use of *Puma* as the correct genus. Thus, they refer to Texas mountain lions as *Puma concolor stanleyana*. Historically, mountain lions occurred in almost every kind of habitat throughout the state. Years of predator control efforts by livestock producers, however, have forced the remaining mountain lions into the more remote, thinly populated areas. See Chapter 6 for a discussion of the status of this species today.

121. The name *Felis onca hernandezi* has been changed to *Panthera onca hernandesii* and refers to the jaguar of western Mexico. The jaguar that once ranged through Texas is now classified as *P. o. veraecrucis*. This magnificent cat is now extinct in Texas (see Chapter 6 for a discussion).

122. The name *Felis pardalis limitis* has been changed to *Leopardus pardalis albescens*. The ocelot was still common over much of Texas during the time of the biological survey, but its range and numbers have now been greatly reduced in the state. It is listed as endangered by the USFWS, and it is now restricted to a few small, isolated patches of suitable habitat in three or four counties of the Rio Grande Plains. Michael Tewes, of the Caesar Kleberg Wildlife Research Institute in Kingsville, Texas, has been studying the ecology and conservation of ocelots in Texas. He has documented aspects of their biology and natural history, and he has developed a habitat conservation plan for this species.

123. The jaguarundi of southern Texas is now considered to be a subspecies and it is classified by modern taxonomists as *Herpailurus yagouroundi cacomitli*. Apparently, it still occurred in the Rio Grande Valley of South Texas at the time of the biological survey. Today, it is the rarest of all the native cats in Texas, occurring only in the brush country of extreme South Texas. As with the jaguar and

ocelot, predator control and habitat destruction have taken their toll on this species. The clearing of brushlands in the Rio Grande Valley has removed most of its habitat in Texas, and it is now regarded as endangered by the USFWS.

124. The bobcat, *Lynx rufus texensis*, is distributed statewide and prefers rocky habitats or thickets, depending on availability in the region. Unlike the other wild cats of Texas, the bobcat is highly adaptable and in most areas has coped well with the inroads of human settlement.

125. *Lynx baileyi* is now recognized as a subspecies, *L. rufus baileyi*, but this name is used in reference to bobcats occurring west of the continental divide in New Mexico. All bobcats in Texas, according to Schmidly and Read (1986), belong to the subspecies *L. r. texensis*.

126. At the time Bailey wrote the biological survey, the classification of doglike carnivores (genus *Canis*) was almost totally based on a typological species concept. Virtually every local population, including color variants, was regarded as a distinct species. Today, with the application of the modern biological species concept, which uses the criterion of reproductive connectedness among populations, the number of recognized species has been reduced dramatically. Thus, many of the species names used by Bailey are now placed in synonymy. The name *Canis griseus* is now synonymous with *C. lupus*.

Predator control and habitat destruction led to the extirpation of the gray wolf from Texas. The elimination of the wolf and other large predators over most of its former range released predator pressure on such big game as deer, which in part created a serious problem of overpopulation of deer in several localities in Texas. The gray wolf is regarded as endangered by the USFWS.

127. *Canis ater*, although considered a distinct species at the time of the survey, is today considered to have been a melanistic form of the gray wolf, *C. lupus*.

128. The historic distribution of the red wolf as described by Bailey was not totally accurate, according to modern accounts. The Laredo (Webb County) and Matamoras, Mexico, specimens are erroneous. This species did not occur in southern Texas except along the coast as far south as Kleberg County, nor did it occur as far west as the Pecos River. It appears that red wolves occurred primarily in the eastern half of Texas (Map 20). Their numbers and range quickly declined in the twentieth century, however, under pressure of intensive land use in the region (see Chapter 6 for a discussion of their status).

129. *Canis nebracensis* is a synonym for *C. latrans*. All coyotes in Texas, once considered to be many different species, are now recognized as subspecies of *C. latrans*. The coyote occurs statewide and is probably the most adaptable of all North American predators. Until the beginning of the twentieth century, coyotes did not generally occur in East Texas, where red wolves were common. With the eradication of red wolves, however, coyotes expanded their range to include that part of the state.

130. The name *Canis nebracensis texensis* has been changed to *C. latrans texensis*.

131. The name *Canis mearnsi* has been changed to *C. latrans mearnsi* and refers to a subspecies that ranges from New Mexico westward. The specimens from Texas are today classified as *C. l. texensis*.

132. The name *Canis microdon* has been changed to *C. latrans microdon*. This subspecies occurs just south of Texas in Mexico.

133. The red fox of Texas is today recognized as the subspecies *Vulpes vulpes fulva*. This introduced subspecies has done remarkably well in Texas, having expanded to cover most of the state except for the far western and southern regions.

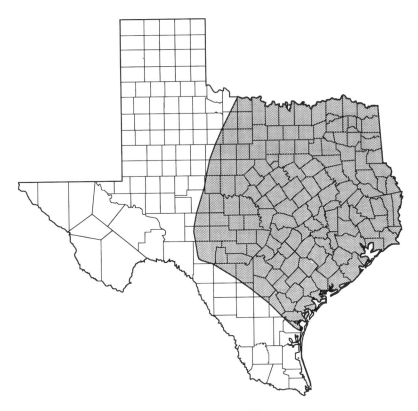

Map 20. The historic distribution of the red wolf (*Canis rufus*) in Texas

134. For most of the twentieth century, arid-land foxes have been regarded as comprising two similar but separate species, the swift fox (*Vulpes velox*) and the kit fox (*V. macrotis*). This was the arrangement used by Bailey. However, in a recent taxonomic study of these foxes using advanced morphometric and pro-tein-electrophoretic methods, Dragoo and colleagues (1990) concluded that these taxa are not sufficiently distinct to warrant separate species status. Thus, the two foxes are now grouped into a single species, *V. velox*, comprising two subspecies, *V. v. velox* from the Panhandle and adjacent areas and *V. v. macrotis* from the Trans-Pecos (Map 21). *V. macrotis neomexi-canus*, according to the new taxonomic arrangement, would be *V. v. macrotis*. These foxes are notoriously susceptible to trapping and poisoning. Consequently, they have been greatly re-duced or entirely eliminated in areas of their range where predator control campaigns have been carried out. *V. velox* is listed as a candidate species by the USFWS, and it is on the Texas Organization for Endangered Species (TOES) Watch List.

135. Gray foxes are widely distributed throughout Texas except the northern Panhandle region. The subspecies *Urocyon cin-ereoargenteus scotti* occurs in the western two-thirds of the state. The gray fox remains common throughout the state.

136. The subspecies *Urocyon cinereo-argenteus floridanus* occurs in eastern Texas. The gray fox is more common in eastern Texas than in the remainder of its range.

137. The distribution of *Bassariscus astutus flavus* is now known to be statewide, although it apparently is uncommon in the lower Rio

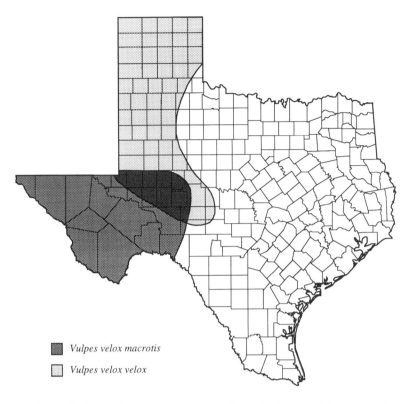

Vulpes velox macrotis

Vulpes velox velox

Map 21. The historic distribution of the two subspecies of swift fox (*Vulpes velox*) in Texas. The more heavily shaded area represents a geographic region of intergradation between the two subspecies.

Grande and Coastal Plains of southern Texas. The ringtail is an economically important furbearer on the Edwards Plateau but is less important elsewhere.

138. *Taxidea taxus berlandieri*, the badger, is now distributed throughout much of the state. Bailey commented on its absence in eastern Texas, but recent records suggest it has been extending its range eastward at least as far as the Navasota River bottom as a result of land-clearing operations. Although the range and numbers of prairie dogs have been greatly reduced since the time of the biological survey, badgers apparently tolerated this reduced food source well by relying more on ground squirrels and other rodents. The fact that their range is expanding supports the belief that badgers are quite adaptable, and in some areas their densities may be increasing.

139. The black bear once ranged across Texas except for the southernmost counties. Now it is extinct in Texas except for a few remnant populations in western and southern Texas. The last records of black bear in the Hill Country came from Kerr County in 1902 (reported by Bailey) and from near New Braunfels in Comal County in 1893 (reported by Davis, 1945a). On the basis of geographic probability, Bailey referred these Central Texas bears to the eastern race, *Ursus americanus americanus*. In 1938, Pierce Uzzell presented William B. Davis with a large, incomplete bear skull that he had found in a cave on the Bacon Ranch in the southern part of Edwards County

(Davis, 1945a). Davis compared the specimen with representatives of the subspecies of the black bear and concluded it was most like bears of Trans-Pecos Texas, New Mexico, and northern Coahuila, Mexico, currently known as *U. a. amblyceps.*

140. Black bears are sighted infrequently in western Texas, but a small, remnant population of *Ursus americanus amblyceps* still exists in the Chisos Mountains of Big Bend National Park and sightings have been on the increase in recent years. Studies suggest that there is a resident, breeding population in the park, perhaps augmented by bears dispersing from the nearby mountains of Mexico. There also have been recent sightings in the Davis Mountains around Alpine, and even in South Texas. Apparently, black bear populations have rebounded in northern Mexico and are beginning to crossover and disperse into Texas.

141. The black bear of eastern Texas is now considered a subspecies, *Ursus americanus luteolus,* of the more widespread continental species, *U. americanus.* Black bears are sighted very rarely in the wooded areas of eastern Texas and the only reports are of individuals that have wandered into the state from release sites in Louisiana. A resident population of the black bear no longer occurs in East Texas.

142. The grizzly bear is today recognized as a single species, *Ursus arctos,* and it is listed as threatened by the USFWS. The subspecies in Texas was *U. arctos horribilis,* and the grizzly bear reported by Bailey from the Davis Mountains remains the only available specimen of this species from Texas. The date of October, 1890, given by Bailey for the collection of the Davis Mountains grizzly is apparently an error. According to a written account of the hunt by C. O. Finley, who shot it, the bear was killed on November 3, 1900 (see Chapter 1). The records of the National Museum, however, give the date of collection for this specimen as November 2, 1899.

143. The name *Nasua narica yucatanica* has been changed to *N. nasua yucatanica.* This subspecies of coati does not occur in Texas, and the specimen discussed by Bailey may, indeed, have been introduced. *N. narica molaris* is the subspecies of coati that occurs in the extreme southern and southwestern areas of the state. Because of its erratic distribution and destruction of most of its habitat, the coati is listed as endangered by TPWD and it is on the TOES Watch List. However, available evidence suggests the coati was never as abundant in Texas as it is in southwestern Arizona.

144. The subspecies of the common raccoon in Texas are *Procyon lotor hirtus* in the Panhandle north of the Canadian River; *P. l. mexicanus* in the western part of the Trans-Pecos; and *P. l. fuscipes* throughout the remainder of the state. Thus, the specimens identified here by Bailey as *P. l. lotor* would today be recognized as *P. l. fuscipes.* Raccoons are common throughout the state, but they are seldom found far from water, which has an important influence upon their distribution.

145. The subspecies of river otter in Texas is *Lontra canadensis lataxina* Cuvier. The otter is presently known from about the eastern one-fourth of the state in major watersheds. For a discussion of its status, see Chapter 6.

146. The name *Lutreola lutreocephala* has been changed to *Mustela vison* and the subspecies in Texas is *M. v. mink.* This species occurs in the eastern one-half of the state and westward to the northern Panhandle in habitats near permanent water. It has declined in abundance this century with the decline in natural surface water and does not appear to be common anywhere in the state.

147. The name *Putorius nigripes* has been changed to *Mustela nigripes.* The black-footed ferret has been extirpated from Texas. Its historic range was roughly the northwestern third of the state including the Panhandle, much of the Trans-Pecos, and a considerable part of the

Rolling Plains region. This distribution corresponded with that of the ferret's principal prey, the black-tailed prairie dog. The black-footed ferret was extirpated primarily as a result of the destruction of the prairie dog towns (see Chapter 6 for a discussion).

148. The name *Putorius frenatus* has been changed to *Mustela frenata*. The long-tailed weasel probably occurs statewide, but it is scarce in most areas, especially in western and northern Texas. The decline in natural surface water in Texas may have prompted this decline as Hall (1951a) has suggested that the absence of water to drink may be a factor limiting distribution of long-tailed weasels. Five subspecies are now recognized in Texas: *M. f. neomexicana* occurs mostly west of the 100th meridian; *M. f. texensis* occurs in the central part of the state; *M. f. primulina* occurs in the extreme northeastern part of Texas; *M. f. arthuri* occurs in east-central and southeastern areas; and *M. f. frenata* occurs in the southern part of the state along the Gulf Coast and adjacent to Mexico (Hall, 1951).

149. The name *Putorius frenatus neomexicanus* has been changed to *Mustela frenata neomexicana*.

150. In his revision of the genus *Spilogale*, Richard Van Gelder (1959) suggested that the only differences between the eastern (*S. putorius*) and the western (*S. gracilis*) forms were size and color patterns. He therefore relegated *S. gracilis* as a subspecies of *S. putorius*. Thus, spotted skunks in Texas were treated as a single, wide-ranging species with four subspecies (designated *gracilis, leucoparia, interrupta, and putorius*). However, using reproductive data, Mead (1968a, b) found that the eastern and western spotted skunks in the United States were behaving as species. The western form exhibited a period of delayed implantation that was absent in the eastern form which meant their breeding seasons were separate and they were reproductively isolated. A recent molecular study of the spotted skunks by Dragoo et al. (1993) has corroborated these differences. So, in Texas today, there are two species of spotted skunks—*S. g. leucoparia* in the western part of the state and *S. p. interrupta* in the eastern part (Map 22). Populations of both species appear to be in decline, and there are serious concerns about their future in Texas. The name *S. leucoparia*, as used by Bailey, has been changed to *S. g. leucoparia*.

151. *Spilogale interrupta* is now recognized as a subspecies, *Spilogale putorius interrupta*. This subspecies was listed as Category 2 by the USFWS prior to 1996.

152. *Spilogale indianola* is now considered synonymous with the subspecies *Spilogale putorius interrupta*.

153. The striped skunk of eastern Texas is now recognized as the subspecies *Mephitis mephitis mesomelas*, whereas the western form is classified as *M. m. varians*. The combined range of the two subspecies covers the entire state, and this is unquestionably the most common skunk in Texas. An additional species of *Mephitis*, not obtained during the survey, is the hooded skunk, *M. macroura milleri*. This skunk is superficially similar to the striped skunk, but has longer, softer fur and a distinct ruff of longer hair on the upper neck. This is primarily a Mexican species that occurs in Texas in the Big Bend region and adjacent parts of the central Trans-Pecos, where it is relatively rare. Its status is unknown but there have been few sightings or specimens collected in recent years. Efforts should be made to monitor the status of the hooded skunk in the future.

154. *Conepatus mesoleucus mearnsi* ranges across southwestern, central, and southern Texas, and it remains relatively common throughout this region (Map 23).

155. This Big Thicket subspecies of the hog-nosed skunk is now thought to be extinct (see Chapter 6 for a discussion).

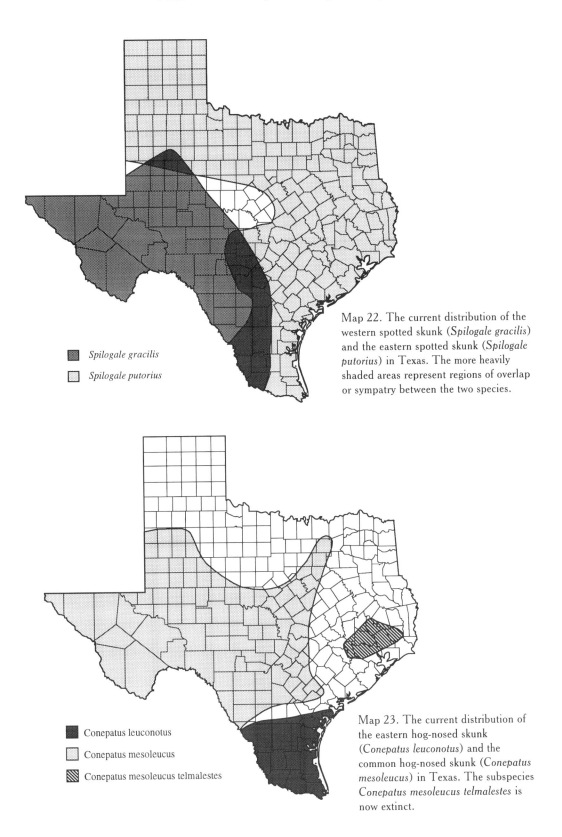

Map 22. The current distribution of the western spotted skunk (*Spilogale gracilis*) and the eastern spotted skunk (*Spilogale putorius*) in Texas. The more heavily shaded areas represent regions of overlap or sympatry between the two species.

*Spilogale gracilis*

*Spilogale putorius*

Map 23. The current distribution of the eastern hog-nosed skunk (*Conepatus leuconotus*) and the common hog-nosed skunk (*Conepatus mesoleucus*) in Texas. The subspecies *Conepatus mesoleucus telmalestes* is now extinct.

Conepatus leuconotus

Conepatus mesoleucus

Conepatus mesoleucus telmalestes

156. The eastern hog-nosed skunk of southern Texas is extremely rare and the population apparently has declined drastically in recent years (Map 23) (see Chapter 6 for a discussion). *Conepatus leuconotus texensis* was listed by the USFWS as a Category 1 species prior to 1996.

157. Five subspecies of *Scalopus aquaticus* are currently recognized in Texas (Yates and Schmidly, 1977). The distribution of moles encompasses the eastern two-thirds of the state and in the northern Panhandle extends to the New Mexico line along the Canadian River drainage. Moles remain very common in Texas wherever suitable soils exist.

158. *Scalopus aquaticus texanus* is an enigmatic race known only from Presidio County by a single specimen taken in 1887. The specimens Bailey discusses here from southern and Central Texas would probably be recognized today as *S. a. inflatus*, *S. a. alleni*, and possibly *S. a. cryptus*.

159. *Scalopus aquaticus intermedius* is now regarded as synonymous with the subspecies *S. aereus*, which is known from the Panhandle and extreme eastern Texas.

160. The name *Sorex personatus* has been changed to *S. cinereus*. As Bailey concluded, this species does not occur in Texas.

161. *Notiosorex crawfordi* is a relatively rare small shrew that occurs throughout the western and southern parts of Texas. Bailey did not record this species from northern Texas, but it is now known from throughout that part of the state.

162. *Blarina brevicauda carolinensis* has been elevated to specific status as *B. carolinensis* (Schmidly and Brown, 1979). Two subspecies, *B. c. carolinensis* and *B. c. minima*, occur in Texas. The range of this species is approximately the eastern one-fourth of the state. Another species of short-tailed shrew, *B. hylophaga*, has been discovered in Texas during the twentieth century (George et al., 1981). This

species is known from Montague County in northern Texas and from disjunct populations in southeast Texas (Aransas County on the Gulf Coast and Bastrop County in the Lost Pines region). Both species have been taken in near sympatry in Bastrop State Park near Bastrop, Texas (Baumgardner et al., 1992). *B. carolinensis* and *B. hylophaga* are cryptic species that are distinguishable from one another only by subtle morphometric differences and features of the karyotype (Stangl and Carr, 1997). The conservation status of both species in Texas in unknown, although it does not appear that either one is particularly common. There may be reason to have concern about the long-range conservation status of *B. hylophaga* (see Chapter 6).

163. The least shrew is currently classified as *Cryptotis parva*. The range of this species covers the eastern one-half of the state and the Panhandle, and it appears to be relatively common throughout this area. It is interesting to note that Bailey did not capture the least shrew in the Panhandle, despite extensive trapping efforts by the agents in that region (Map 24).

164. The subspecies of least shrew that occurs on the Rio Grande Plain is now recognized as *Cryptotis parva berlandieri*.

165. The cave myotis is a year-round resident of Texas, although it exhibits a varied seasonal distribution in the western two-thirds of the state. There are two subspecies in the state: *Myotis velifer incautus* in the Trans-Pecos, Edwards Plateau, and South Texas Plains region; and *M. v. magnamolaris* in the High Plains and Rolling Plains. The specimens discussed by Bailey were all *M. v. incautus*. This is one of the most abundant bats in Texas, roosting in caves and tunnels, rock fissures, manmade structures, and even in abandoned cliff swallow nests.

166. The California myotis, *Myotis californicus*, is a year-round resident of the Trans-Pecos, where it occurs in desert, grassland, and

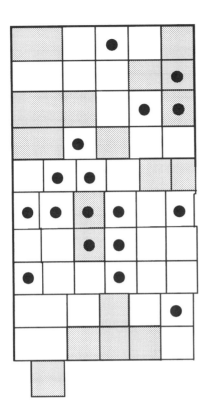

● *Cryptotis parva*

Map 24. The current distribution of the least shrew (*Cryptotis parva*) according to recent county specimen records from the Panhandle region of Texas. Shaded areas indicate counties surveyed by federal agents from 1889 to 1905, but no specimens of the species were obtained during the survey.

wooded habitats. One specimen has been recorded from Canyon in Randall County near the breaks of the Llano Estacado (Choate and Killibrew, 1991). This is one of the most common bats in the western part of Texas.

167. *Myotis incautus* is now regarded as a subspecies of *M. velifer*. It is the second most common bat, next to *Tadarida brasiliensis*, in the cave region of the Hill Country.

168. The Yuma myotis, *Myotis yumanensis*, is restricted in Texas to the southern Trans-Pecos and Rio Grande Valley where it inhabits desert, lowland habitats. Most specimens come from areas near the Rio Grande where the species appears to be common. Six other species of *Myotis* have been recorded in Texas since the biological survey, including the little brown myotis, *M. lucifugus;* southeastern myotis, *M. austroriparius;* northern myotis, *M. septentrionalis;* fringed myotis, *M. thysanodes;* long-

legged myotis, *M. volans;* and the western small-footed myotis, *M. ciliolabrum*. Most of these species are rare in Texas and have restricted distributions.

169. The western pipistrelle, *Pipistrellus hesperus*, is widely distributed in suitable rocky habitats from the Trans-Pecos region northward along the eastern escarpment of the Llano Estacado. This is one of the most common bats of the desert Southwest.

170. The common name of *Pipistrellus subflavus* is now the eastern pipistrelle. It occurs over the entire state except for far West Texas, but recent records from Big Bend Ranch State Park (Yancey, 1997) and the Davis Mountains (Clyde Jones, personal communication) in the Trans-Pecos suggest it is expanding its range westward. Two subspecies are now recognized in Texas: *P. s. subflavus* over most of the state (including Bailey's specimens from

Clear Creek, Long Lake, and Brownsville); and *P. s. clarus* from Val Verde County (Bailey's specimens from the Devil's River, Comstock, and Del Rio). The two subspecies were not delineated at the time of the Texas biological survey.

171. The big brown bat, with two recognized subspecies (*Eptesicus fuscus pallidus* and *E. f. fuscus*), has a disjunct distribution in Texas. The subspecies *fuscus* occurs in the eastern part of the state, and *pallidus* occurs in far North and West Texas. This species is a year-round resident and is common over most of its range in Texas.

172. The red bat occurs statewide but it is much more common in the eastern part of the state, where it is a year-round resident, than in the Trans-Pecos, where it occurs only in the summer. Another closely related species, *Lasiurus blossevilli*, has been recorded in Texas in the Sierra Vieja Mountains of Presidio County (Genoways and Baker, 1988), but none of the specimens secured by Bailey were representative of this bat.

173. The Seminole bat is now recognized as a distinct species, *Lasiurus seminolus*. This is a non-migratory species which occurs throughout the oak-hickory, pine-oak, and long-leaf pine forest regions of East Texas where its preferred roosting sites are in Spanish Moss. This species is locally abundant and does not appear to have declined substantially during the twentieth century. A recent record along the Devil's River suggests this species may be expanding its range in the state.

174. The hoary bat, *Lasiurus cinereus*, is a spring-fall migratory species that has been recorded seasonally in all vegetative regions of the state. In the Trans-Pecos, it is restricted to mountainous, wooded areas where it can be locally abundant.

175. The name *Dasypterus intermedius* has been changed to *Lasiurus intermedius*. It occurs primarily along the Gulf Coast in the Gulf

Prairies and Marshes region and also the South Texas Plains, but it does not appear to be common anywhere in its range. Texas specimens are referable to two subspecies, *L. i. floridanus* from Bexar and Travis Counties eastward and *L. i. intermedius* from San Patricio County southward. The specimens obtained by Bailey are of the subspecies *intermedius*.

Two other "cryptic" species of *Lasiurus*, *L. ega* and *L. xanthinus*, have been recorded in Texas since the biological survey. *L. ega* is known from the coastal region of South Texas and *L. xanthinus* from the Big Bend region (see Chapter 6). Both of these bats are rare and little is known about their status in Texas.

176. The evening bat, *Nycticeius humeralis*, is among the most common species of bats east of the 100th meridian in Texas. It is a year-round resident of the state, roosting in hollow trees and building attics. Recent captures of this species (Boyd et al., 1997; Dowler et al., 1999) west of the 100th meridian suggests it may be expanding its range to the west, much like the eastern pipistrelle.

177. *Corynorhinus macrotis pallescens* is now classified as *Plecotus townsendii pallescens*. This species occurs in suitable habitat (preferring caves and mine tunnels) in the western one-half of the state. *P. rafinesquii macrotis* is the current name for *P. macrotis*. Bailey was correct in predicting this species eventually would be found in Texas. It was first recorded in east Texas in 1965 (Michael and Birch, 1967), and specimens have now been recorded in a total of fifteen counties (Horner and Maxey, 1998). It is among the rarest bats in the state.

178. The range of the pallid bat, *Antrozous pallidus*, encompasses the western one-half of the state. There are two distinct subspecies, *A. p. bunkeri* in the northern Panhandle and *A. p. pallidus* in the western and southern parts of the range. Bailey and the federal agents obtained representatives of both of these subspecies.

Pallid bats are among the most abundant bats in the Trans-Pecos.

179. The name *Nyctinomus mexicanus* has been changed to *Tadarida brasiliensis*. There are two subspecies in Texas, *T. b. cynocephala* in the eastern fourth of the state and *T. b. mexicana* elsewhere. The Mexican freetail is probably the most common species of bat in Texas, reaching its greatest concentration in the caves of the Hill Country where summer populations may number between 10 to 20 million bats in each cave. The subspecies *cynocephala* roosts primarily in human structures and does not occur in such huge concentrations. The specimens obtained by Bailey were all of the subspecies *mexicana*.

180. *Promops californicus* is now classified as *Eumops perotis californicus*, the western mastiff bat. This is the largest, and one of the rarest, bats in the United States. Besides the specimen obtained by Gaut, individuals have been captured in Texas in the rugged, rocky canyon country from localities close to the Rio Grande in Presidio and Brewster Counties. This is a species that bears watching in this century.

181. *Mormoops megalophylla senicula* is considered a synonym of *M. m. megalophylla*. This species has the most distinctive facial ornamentation of any bat in Texas. Specimens have now been obtained in the Trans-Pecos, the southern escarpment of the Edwards Plateau, and extreme South Texas. At Big Bend Ranch State Park in Presidio County, this was one of the most common bats collected (Yancey, 1997). It is probably not as rare within its geographic range as previously thought.

# Texas Landscapes, 1889–1905

Texas's landscapes represent a microcosm of the rest of the United States. Grasslands stretch all the way from Canada down onto the High Plains and terminate at the prairies, marshes, and sandy beaches along our coastline. Coming in from the west, there is the grandeur of the mountain ranges and the desert which is bisected by the Rio Grande. On the east, the Big Thicket and Pineywoods represent the westernmost extension of the same forest that goes all the way to the Appalachians. To the south, there is the subtropical Rio Grande Valley and the brush country of southern Texas. These different landscapes converge in Central Texas where the country is broken and includes a mixture of grasslands, shrublands, and forests.

Bailey and the federal agents visited Texas during a time of intensive livestock use and severe drought in the western United States. The drought period of the 1880s continued over most of the West until about 1905. Until the late 1800s, the open range system dominated the cattle industry in Texas. Longhorn and "scrub" cattle roamed freely over the vast acres of rangeland in the western half of the state. By the turn of the century, however, the open range system had changed to a stock farming system,

largely as a result of the introduction of barbed-wire fencing and the utilization of drilled wells and windmills to produce water for stock. As the stock farming system gained prominence, longhorn and "scrub" cattle were replaced with blooded breeds such as Jerseys, Holsteins, and Herefords. Cattle production in the state increased dramatically, as well as the number of sheep and goats. It wasn't long before the overgrazing of Texas's vast rangelands became a serious problem (Fig. 27). Also, during this time Texas's grassland landscapes were subjected to rapid encroachment of cacti and woody plants, all associated with a decrease in prairie wildfires and the severe overstocking of rangelands (Lehman, 1969). A 1904 *Texas Almanac* article about the grasslands of Texas stated that what had been "one of the best stock ranges in . . . this country [is] so abused that today its capacity for sustaining livestock is very small in comparison with what it was 30 or even 20 years ago."

The turn of the century saw a change in Texas farming practices from predominately cotton farming to the concept of diversified farming. This change coincided with an increase in immigration of farmers from northern, grain-producing states which enormously in-

Fig. 27. Drought conditions and over-grazing by cattle and other livestock decimated the rangelands of Texas during the late nineteenth and early twentieth centuries. Courtesy The Southwest Collection, Texas Tech University

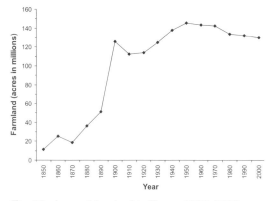

Fig. 28. Acres of farmland in Texas, 1850–2000

tions, helped to promote the idea of diversification. Although cotton farming continued to dominate agricultural production in the state, fruit, vegetable, and grain crops became profitable for landowners in many areas of the state less suitable for cotton production. From 1870 to 1900, cotton production increased 1000 percent, while wheat production increased 5200 percent, and oat production increased 3700 percent. Rice growing became an important industry in the coastal regions, as irrigated land in this area increased from 8,700 acres in 1899 to 235,000 acres in 1904. Rapid progress in irrigation was an important factor in the development of the arid and semi-arid regions of Texas, where irrigated land increased from 37,000 acres in 1899 to more than 100,000 acres in 1904.

creased the number of acres in farmland from 1880 to 1910 (Fig. 28). Also, the efforts of the Texas Agricultural Experiment Station, established in 1887 to conduct research into every phase of the state's crop and livestock opera-

Lumber production, primarily in the pine-oak forests of eastern Texas, was the leading industry in that region at the turn of the century and it was rapidly expanding and depleting the stands of virgin timber. The exploitation of these forests began in the early 1800s as settlers in the region viewed the trees as an impediment to settlement and agriculture. Lumbering became a dominant manufacturing concern in the region in the 1870s as the state's population began to grow and there was an increased demand for timber (Fig. 29). The ease of logging in the region, a climate conducive to year-round production, and technological improvements such as steam-powered sawmills and circular saws contributed to the growth of the lumber industry. At its peak in 1907, 2.25 billion board feet of lumber was produced in Texas. By 1926, at least 450 lumber mills were in operation in East Texas. The *Texas Almanac* for that year stated "at the present rate of lumber production, it is estimated that Texas within 9 or 10 years will have witnessed the passing of practically all of its virgin stand of timber and will be dependent largely upon timber products from the northwestern forests." The original area of Texas virgin forests had been estimated at 12 million acres. By 1926, 4.7 million acres had been converted to agriculture, 3.9 million acres had been cut over with little or no forest renewal, 1.9 million acres were in second growth timber, and only 1.5 million acres of virgin timber remained.

During the time of the biological survey, most of Texas's 3 million population resided in the eastern and upper coastal prairies of the state (Fig. 30). The far western and northwestern regions still were sparsely populated and for the most part remained as ranching country. Farming was just beginning to expand in these areas. Most Texans lived in rural areas and not in cities. Texas's largest city, San Antonio, had fewer than sixty thousand residents in 1900. Because people lived and earned a living on the

Fig. 29. Lumbering in East Texas, early 1900s. Courtesy East Texas Research Center, Steen Library, Stephen F. Austin State University

land, natural resources were under intensive use during this period. There were no federal or state parks or preserves to protect scenic places, and there was little public concern about the need for this.

## Texas Landscapes as Described by the Federal Agents

Bailey's 1905 publication included a description as well as a map of the life/crop zones of the state. The common faunal elements (primarily birds and mammals), together with the dominant plants and plant associations of each zone or important geographic region, were listed and augmented by a few photographs of landscapes and plant associations. For the most part, however, very few of the federal agents' extensive physiographic reports, landscape and habitat descriptions, or field trip itineraries

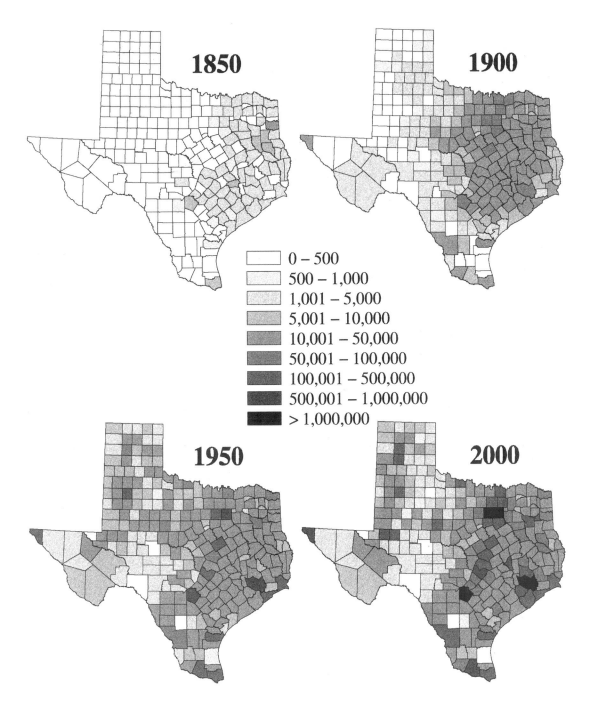

Fig. 30. Population expansion in Texas, 1850–2000

were included in the book. This chapter provides a description of Texas landscapes, selected from those reports and materials and supplemented with landscape photographs taken by the federal agents. These reports and photographs were selected to represent the ten ecological regions used by most biologists working in the state today (Map 3c; Table 2). Thus, they provide a modern perspective of Texas landscapes at the end of the nineteenth and beginning of the twentieth centuries. Biologists working in the state today do not use the life zone designations because of their limited utility (see Chapter 1).

Examination of the total portfolio of photographs reveals that profound changes to the landscape had already occurred prior to the time that Bailey and the other federal agents worked in Texas. With the exception of the High Plains and the northern parts of the Llano Estacado, most of the photos show remarkable impacts already by the beginning of the twentieth century. Vast expanses of native prairie that once covered parts of the state had already been turned under by the plow or overgrown by shrubs and woody plants. In fact, of all the community types represented in the photographs, the greatest adverse impacts appear to have been on grasslands.

The federal agents encountered a considerable amount of natural, free-flowing surface water throughout their travels across the state. Almost every photograph the federal agents took of a stream or river showed an abundance of natural, free-flowing surface water, which is not true of most of those places today. The federal agents were aware of, and collected at many of, the springs, and they liked to camp near springs because they provided a good source of drinking water. For example, Cary and Hollister in 1902 secured a series of Pecos River muskrats (*Ondatra zibethicus ripensis*) at Comanche Springs near Ft. Stockton (Fig. 31). Cary wrote the following description of the springs, which are dry today and no longer harbor muskrat, in 1902:

> Comanche Creek, a beautiful stream of clear water running some thirty miles in a northeasterly direction, has its source in some extremely large springs at Stockton, and is bordered with a heavy growth of tules. This stream is utilized for irrigation purposes by several ranchmen and some fine cornfields and alfalfa meadows were noted. Fine grassy meadows along this creek afford fine pasturage.

The field agents conducted fieldwork in all ten of the ecological regions of the state, with the greatest effort in the South Texas Plains and Trans-Pecos Mountains and Basins (19 percent of all field days in each region), Edwards Plateau (15 percent), and Gulf Prairies and Marshes (15 percent). Other regions ranked as follows: Pineywoods (9 percent), Rolling Plains (6 percent), Post Oak Savannah (5 percent), Cross Timbers and Prairies (5 percent), Blackland Prairies (4 percent), and High Plains (3 percent). The following descriptions, with accompanying photographs, of the landscapes and land-cover in the ten regions have been taken directly from the accounts of various field agents.

## Gulf Prairies and Marshes

Bailey and the federal agents found extensive marshlands and coastal prairies as they traversed the Gulf Strip along the coastline of Texas at the beginning of the twentieth century (Figs. 32–40). Bailey visited Galveston in 1899, prior to the great storm that killed more than five thousand people, but he did not collect there. He spent most of his time collecting at Virginia Point just across the bay from the city of Galveston and wrote the following account of traveling by train from Galveston to Houston across vast stretches of coastal grasslands and bottomland forests:

Fig. 31. Comanche Springs, Ft. Stockton, Pecos County, 1887. Courtesy Texas Parks and Wildlife Department

Virginia Point is the first station on the mainland north of Galveston. The station is only 5 miles from Galveston. The ranch where we stayed is 2 miles northeast of the station on open prairie only half a mile from the bay.

The country is all flat and open. Level prairie stretches away to the west and, at least as far as Houston, to the north. Generally it comes to the edge of the bay and terminates in a beach but in places great salt marshes border the shores. There is practically no native timber until Buffalo Bayou is reached near Houston. There are no hills or high ground of any kind. There are some low, marshy places over the prairie but generally the surface is level and flat save for the mounds scattered uniformly over it. Shell ridges have been thrown up along the shore in places but these are rarely over 4 or 5 feet above the surface of the shore and merely mark the combined efforts of high tides and storms. On Galveston Island are extensive sand dunes but I have seen none on the mainland shore.

The federal agents visited many places along the coast during their work in Texas, describing the coastal prairie and marshy habitats. William Lloyd wrote the following description of the country around Matagorda Peninsula (Matagorda County) in 1892:

The country east of the Nueces River along the coast and for 70 miles inland is generally a plain, bare of the slightest timber except along the river bottoms as far as the western edge of Jackson County, where commence copses of Live Oak usually in sharply defined areas. Further east one passes a Post Oak country around the two Caranchua Creeks and arrive at an interesting stream, the Tres Palacios, the western border of Matagorda County.

From here wide prairies stretch all over the county, low and often under water, a black loam, hog-wallow land it is generally termed, which is all of the same character except along the Bay shore where it is mixed with sand and intersected by pools of salt water.

Fig. 32. Shore of Galveston Bay, La Porte, Harris County, 1906. Courtesy National Archives, 22-WB-30-B9041

Fig. 33. Thicket of yaupon (*Ilex vomitorius*), High Island, Chambers County, 1907. Courtesy National Archives, 22-WB-40-B9908

Fig. 34. Mitchell's Point, Matagorda Peninsula, Calhoun County, 1900. Courtesy National Archives, 22-WB-40-B1257

Fig. 35. Open prairie near Port Lavaca, Calhoun County, 1900. Pools of water from recent rains. Courtesy National Archives, 22-WB-30-B1207

Fig. 36. Marsh by Big Chocolate Creek, near Port Lavaca, Calhoun County, 1900. Courtesy National Archives, 22-WB-30-1210

Fig. 37. Field of prickly pear (*Opuntia*) near Port Lavaca, Calhoun County, 1900. Courtesy National Archives, 22-WB-40-B1219

Fig. 38. Hedge of prairie rose (*Rosa setigera*) near Port Lavaca, Calhoun County, 1900. Courtesy National Archives, 22-WB-40-B1205

Fig. 39. Live oak chapparal and grassland near Port O'Connor, Calhoun County, 1900. Courtesy National Archives, 22-WB-41-B1300

Fig. 40. Clump of tall live oaks near Port O'Connor, Calhoun County, 1900. Courtesy National Archives, 22-WB-41-B1298

The Colorado River passes through the center of the district and is blocked up by a raft 9 or 10 miles long that reaches up to near Elliott's crossing and is increasing every year. As the river has many tributaries it is frequently swollen and yearly the water backs in increasing volume from against the raft, spreading over the surrounding low country for miles and will probably in time seek an outlet through Caney Creek which is supposed to be an old mouth of the Colorado.

The river itself is deep, far more than the Rio Grande at Brownsville, and at Elliott's about 100 feet wide and red-colored as its name implies, and carries so much silt with it, that, on account of the overflows, all the trees in the bottom are girdled to a height of about 10 feet choked and dead. Below the raft however it is different. The river is studded with islands some of large size but covered with so much dense undergrowth that they cannot be kept cleared.

The Peninsula, now an island or rather two, was separated from the mainland during a great storm in 1876, which also washed away Indianola. At that time it was well settled, over a hundred lives being lost on the Peninsula alone, the storm washing away two-thirds of the houses and cutting channels through it in four places two of which have since filled up, and covering the land from shore to shore with immense amount of drift; hundreds of logs over a hundred feet long and 2 to 5 feet in diameter. A few people stayed on when in 1886 came a second storm wiping off both the last vestige of a dwelling in Indianola and everything—people, stock, houses—from the peninsula, leaving a few ruined houses standing, and leaving the place to the mammals, which flourished untouched so that some outfits with dogs captured this year 117 raccoons but also leaving the place without a vestige of fresh water.

Many of the former settlers, the remnant of which now live in Matagorda, state it had 3 rows of sand hills some 40 to 50 feet in height but that the storms leveled them. They are now only to be seen as one small continuous elevation of shifting sand about five feet high.

Live Oak Creek, as suggested by its name, near the east border of the County and Brazoria County, is also the east boundary of the Matagorda plain, and is the last body of open land in Texas (except Houston prairie), all east of the creek being timbered densely.

Mankind has modified the topography of the County in one respect. It, the County, is well settled and has been so for seventy years and all of the river land has been cut into small pastures about a mile square in each, so wild animals were quickly exterminated, the finishing touch being the Scalp Law that came into effect last year.

Along the coast at Port Lavaca (Calhoun County), Harry Oberholser wrote the following description of the countryside in March of 1900:

Port Lavaca is situated on the west shore of the northwest area of Matagorda Bay, some ten or twelve miles south of the head of this bay, and about 25 miles from the Gulf of Mexico. The town lies on a bluff some 18 or 19 feet above the sea, and, excepting towards the bay, is on all sides surrounded by almost perfectly level grassy prairies which extend for many miles, and in which the principal interruptions are two small creeks some few miles south and west of Port Lavaca. These creeks have cut down several feet from the level of the country, forming rather broad shallow valleys; the water, however, runs only in the wet season. There are a few small ponds on the prairie, most of which are dry in the summer, but while they contain water, particularly during spring and fall, are favorite resorts for water birds and waders. The entire region is so nearly flat that large areas are flooded after a heavy fall of rain. There is comparatively little marshy land along the shore of the bay near Port Lavaca, since the bluffs extend, though less in height, nearly all the way from some distance north of the town, south to O'Connorport; and the only marshes lie at the entrances to a few small creeks and bayous. The opposite side of this part of Matagorda Bay is much the same in general appearance as is the vicinity of Port Lavaca. The environs of Port Lavaca are evidently part of an extensive alluvial plain, and the surface soil is, for some distance about the town, a very heavy black clay which in the hot sun bakes hard and cracks; farther to the west and south, however, it is much more sandy.

A belt of chaparral more or less dense, extends somewhat interruptedly from a distance south of town, northward along the bay shore to near Victoria, thence eastward to south of Inez and thence down along the east side of the northwest area of the bay. On the Port Lavaca side this chaparral belt is composed largely of *Acacia farnesiana* [= *Acacia smallii*], *Condalia obovata*, *Zizyphus obtusifolius*, *Berberis trifoliata*, and *Opuntia engelmanni;* but on the opposite shore there is a considerable infusion of *Prosopis juliflora* [= *Prosopis glandulosa*], due no doubt to the fact it has not been cut off, as I am assured has been the case about Port Lavaca. On this east side of the bay, on Mitchell's Point, there is a tract of elm woods, and here occur *Tillandsia usneoides* and *Phoradendron flavescens* [= *Phoradendron tomentosum*], which also were not found elsewhere near Port Lavaca. No timber grows near this locality except a narrow fringe along portions of the larger creek some miles west of town. The greater part of the prairie is practically without shrubby vegetation, except for such places as the Thomas Ranch, some seven or eight miles southwest of Port Lavaca, where hedges of *Rosa setigera* have been planted as windbreaks for cattle. These hedges have grown so rank that they threaten to appropriate much more of the prairie than was intended, and are from ten to twenty feet in height, and from ten to thirty feet in thickness. On this same ranch there is a considerable area of live oak brush, two to twelve feet in height, and in places very dense. Some of the less ephemeral ponds support a considerable growth of *Sesbania cavanillesii*.

Oberholser visited O'Connorport (now known as Port O'Connor), near Port Lavaca, in 1900 and wrote the following report describing the countryside:

O'Connorport is situated at Alligator Head, the point of land forming the southern extremity of the western shore of Matagorda Bay, and is almost due north of the northeastern end of Matagorda Island. The land about here is a sandy gently rolling prairie, only a few feet above sea level. Properly speaking, there are no streams, though the entire country is more or less intersected by shallow washes, through which water runs only after rains, and which lead usually into bayous. These bayous in some cases extend a considerable distance into the land from the bay, the largest of them being Powderhorn Bayou, about 9 miles north of Alligator Head and near the site of the former town of Indianola. There are a few small and more or less ephemeral ponds scattered over the prairie. The shore of the bay is bordered by a low bluff, at places only a foot or two in height, but increasing northward. The south shore, facing the bayous that separate the mainland from Matagorda Island, is bordered by extensive tide flats, the favorite feeding place of thousands of shore birds. The bay proper is itself very shallow, the slope from shore being for a long distance exceedingly slight, a condition similar to that existing at Port Lavaca.

With the exception of portions of the land lying along the shore, and frequent areas, more or less extensive, scattered throughout the region, the entire face of the country is covered with a dense growth of live oak brush. This grows to the height of twelve or fifteen feet on many of the small low mounds which are a curious feature of portions of this region, forming thus conspicuous clumps rising above the level of their surroundings. Other than this live oak growth there is little shrubby vegetation. Some *Opuntia* grows in the open places along the shore; and *Sesbania cavanillesii* is found in some of the ponds. At one place some twelve miles west of the settlement there is considerable *Persea borbonia* and *Balodendron arboreum* [= *Vaccinium arboreum*].

The federal agents worked extensively in the Semiarid Lower Sonoran region of south Texas, along with the interface of the South Texas Plains and Gulf Prairies and Marshes vegetation regions, which they generally characterized as a mesquite plain. William Lloyd provided the following description of the Nueces County area in 1891:

This county lies due north of Cameron and has for its boundary the great sandy area that runs up from the Laguna Madre touching the Rio Grande between Carrizo and Laredo. It is well watered in the maps but with exception of a swift, deep little treeless creek called the Santa Gertrudis, it has no other running water than the Nueces River that divides it from San Patricio County on the north. This river, noted as being a paradise for hunters for the last twenty years, is well-wooded and deep and runs into Nueces Bay, a deep long inlet of Corpus Christi Bay. The country from Santa Rosa to Alice on the north and to Banquete is all prairie, broken by a few sandy elevations, and sparsely covered with mesquite. A peninsula

jutting into Nueces Bay and another from Portland are flats full of swamps and saltwater lakes. A large saltwater reach also forms the mouth of the Oso on the Laguna Madre.

A large portion of the southern part of the county, especially near the mouth of the Nueces and along the Laguna Madre, is still covered with a dense scrubby jungle almost impassable that if not continually kept cleared will encroach on all sides and gives considerable shelter to the smaller mammals.

The soil is rich black loam mixed with layers of sand around Corpus and seems to offer the most inviting field for the operations of thousands of *Geomys* and it is hard to say how many *Scalops* [= *Scalopus*]. When the country was unsettled they worked under disadvantages but now they have increased largely and every ploughed field or additional clearing only adds an extra foothold for them which they are not slow to avail themselves of.

South winds prevail and though snowstorms do occur they are so rare as not to militate against the general mildness of the atmosphere which is now in the luxuriant growth of vegetable life.

In extreme South Texas, Bailey and the agents encountered tall stands of native sabal palm forests (*Sabal mexicana*) and dense forests of cedar elm and Texas ebony stretched along the Rio Grande from its delta in the Gulf of Mexico inland to Brownsville and beyond for several kilometers. This area was characterized by thick woods of mesquite, willow, huisache, and retama in the resacas, and the resacas still flooded once or twice a year after heavy rains. William Lloyd wrote the following description of the resaca habitat when he visited Brownsville in 1891:

The Rio Grande from about 10 miles north of Brownsville to its mouth is characterized by its numerous outlets, "resacas," that act as drainage channels for the river whenever it has an overflow which is always in the Fall, September and October. This overplus forms numerous lagoons which generally last all the year though of lessening extent; and, as the waters evaporate they become brackish and even in a few instances decidedly or entirely salty. They are the breeding homes of many of the waders and even of some of the sea-birds.

After passing Brownsville the river is so winding that a straight line drawn to its mouth would cross about equal parts of Texas and Mexican territory and the channel changes every season in half a dozen or so places keeping the border owners of land in continuous tribulation.

All the country was a jungle along the river, but it is now so thickly settled, that most of it has long since been cleared, and the timber is now principally in occasional strips along the river, with exception of the Palmetto and smaller brush-covered hills on the Mexican side.

Reaching to the edge of the river, or separated from it by the strips of timber already referred to, is a wide plain sometimes covered with small brush, or with coarse grama grass and still further south is a soft sandy expanse covered with a rank bunch grass. Alkali flats occur devoid of the slightest vegetation or life, except crabs, beds of mollusks, and grasshoppers and the birds that prey on them or a traveling jackrabbit or coyote. The bare level is occasionally relieved by sand dunes 30 to 50 feet high, which however are always shifting and changing.

The ground, generally speaking, away from the red clayey soil of the river is a rich black loam free from rocks or pebbles of any kind, in fact there is not a rock bluff or cliff in the whole locality. The temperature for the summer months is 95–98 but outside towns is always modified by the sea breeze. On the Mexican side of the river the sand does not commence until one reaches Bagdad, that once was a considerable settlement but now, like Clarksville which was on Texas side at the mouth, has been totally swept away by the sea and river combined overflow. The flats also in Mexico are studded with a series of detached low elevations covered with brush and are veritable oases in the desert around. They are usually covered with mesquite, chaparral, yuccas and cacti.

Padre Island is about 100 miles long and most of the lower half about 2 miles broad. It is a simple collection of sand dunes without any timber whatever on the Pt. Isabel end though there is said to be huisache etc. near the Corpus Christi end where the island is 4 miles broad. On the sea side there is no life except sea birds and crab as the strong wind blowing on shore keeps the sand particles in perpetual agitation preventing any vegetation from taking root. On the lagoon side (Laguna Madre) is a strip of soft beach about a mile wide in its usual distance, and like the sea-beach destitute of everything. All animal life is in the middle division where the north side of the hills are all covered with grass and low vegetation.

Of the immediate area around Brownsville, in Cameron and Starr Counties, Lloyd wrote the following description in 1891:

The principal trees of the Lower Rio Grande Valley to a point some few leagues north of Brownsville are the Hackberry, Elm, Ash, Mesquite, Huisache, and Mulberry. The Ebony have increased in size and, though not reaching the same dimensions as on the Rio de San Juan, still are a most important tree with its hard wood and deep shade. The only Cypress in the region under consideration are some in a pasture a little south of Rio Grande City and a few Anacua near Brownsville. Retama, Lignum, Vital, the Colima and Palo Brazil are common along the lagunas, and Coma (a well known fruit) are scattered amongst the chaparral. Two *Koeberlinias* occur on the edge of the region subject to flood and Willow generally along the river and are used (one species) for basket making. The Palmetto, referred to by Major Emory, has only a few specimens standing south of Santa Maria, then none occur until the tropical fauna of Brownsville is reached; they have been used for thatching jacals and now for making sombreros.

A few Yucca of large size—the Maquez—both planted and in a wild state, and the prickly pear which line all the belt beyond the valley of the river with a few *Echinocactus* and one species of *Mammillaria* are the sole representatives of the cactus family.

Sunflowers grow up in rank patches filling all the dry lagunas until they are leveled by another rise, and wild ipecac is abundant in the southern part of the district.

Corn fields are continuous for nearly the whole length of the river, with a few patches of cotton. Sugar has been tried but now abandoned.

A wild blackberry ripening in May and June is also abundant in the lower part of the region.

Texas has some of the longest barrier islands in the world, beginning with Galveston Island in the north and continuing southward to

Matagorda, San Jose, Mustang, and Padre Islands. During the biological survey, one or more of the federal agents visited all these islands except for Mustang and San Jose.

Harry Oberholser visited Matagorda Island in 1900. His survey report describes the physiography and vegetation of the island, and he made a list of the birds, reptiles, and mammals he observed. According to his field trip report,

Matagorda, or Saluria, Island is a low strip of land, some 40 miles long and from half a mile to about four miles wide, extending southwestward along the coast of Texas from the entrance of Matagorda Bay to beyond San Antonio Bay. It encloses San Antonio Bay and the various lagoons which connect this with Matagorda Bay. The northwestern end was the only portion visited, but the island is practically the same throughout its entire length. Viewed from the top of the lighthouse it is seen to consist of a few parallel ridges running lengthwise, with broad though slight depressions between, the highest parts of the land being only a few feet above the sea. Along the Gulf shore is a series of sand dunes, some of them from ten to fifteen feet in height. The inner shore of the island is bordered by broad, bare sand flats, some of them covered at ordinary high tide, others only occasionally under water. Between these tide flats, which are, it may be noted, favorite resorts for water birds and waders of all kinds, between these and the sand dunes lies the main portion of the island, covered for the most part with grass, and suitable for grazing. The soil here is a sandy loam so much like that of the neighboring mainland as to suggest the idea that this island was once a part of the mainland, rather than of marine origin, or at least is not of very recent formation.

There is little chaparral on Matagorda Island, a few small groves of *Prosopis juliflora* being about the only approach to such. *Tamarix gallica* is about the only other shrubby vegetation that is at all common, this growing principally on the sand dunes or along their inner border. Many of the sand dunes are to a greater or less extent covered with a growth of wiry grass. Matagorda Peninsula, which separates the bay from the Gulf, and of which Matagorda Island is an interrupted continuation, has according to information obtained, considerable more chaparral than the island, besides being more sandy.

William Lloyd traversed all Padre Island by foot in November of 1891. His account of that trip was one of the few intact physiographic reports that Bailey included in the 1905 publication.

## South Texas Plains

The agents worked at several sites throughout the plains region of southern Texas (Figs. 41–49) and along the Rio Grande throughout the Texas-Mexico borderland region. William Lloyd wrote the following account of the area around Eagle Pass (Maverick County) in 1890:

The country round Eagle Pass is a mesquite flat, sometimes rising into small elevations and everywhere cut into deep ravines, which though often only 10 feet across are several hundred yards long. The soil near the Rio Grande is composed of fine sand and principally overgrown with thistles, burrs, sunflowers, and crabgrass. It has a depth of over 20 feet, before one reaches the limestone strata below, and on the river changes into soft red clay, which gives the water its muddy color. There are also a few mesquite growing along the banks, with here and there a large hackberry, a mulberry, a few pecans, with an occasional wild china. Elm Creek, S of Eagle Pass about 4 miles, is, as its name denotes, bordered with some fine elms for the last mile or two of its course where it is one continuous pool of spring water. Fossil wood is abundant here in large pieces with the bark well defined and, in Eagle Pass, I saw 6 fossilized nuts that appeared pinon from this region. Mineral Paint, red, is also common and there is a large coal mine in the immediate neighborhood.

South of Eagle Pass opposite to the Rio Chiquito which empties a volume of clear blue-green water into the Rio Grande, of same extent as Sycamore Creek, were once large plantations of corn, etc. The river has been exceptionally high this year and has washed away all vestiges of crops and covered everything with an extra layer of sand one foot high. Here, all the country south to Laredo, there is no water whatever, except that of the River and the hills are covered with small brush instead of mesquite and often are almost entirely bare, but by the river the Bermuda grass has already

Fig. 41. Texas bluebonnets near Beeville, Bee County, 1900. Courtesy National Archives, 22-WB-41-B1321

Fig. 42. Edge of live oak and post oak forest near Beeville, Bee County, 1900. Courtesy National Archives, 22-WB-41-B1315

Fig. 43. Grassy opening in chaparral, Cotulla, LaSalle County, 1900. Courtesy National Archives, 22-WB-41-1424

Fig. 44. Hedgehog cactus and chaparral, San Diego, Duval County, 1900. Courtesy National Archives, 22-WB-40-B1354

Fig. 45. San Diego Creek, near San Diego, Duval County, 1900.Courtesy National Archives, 22-WB-40-B1365

Fig. 46. Yucca in chapparal, fifteen miles below Laredo, Webb County, 1900. Courtesy National Archives, 22-WB-40-B1419

Fig. 47. Looking north up Rio Grande from fifteen miles below Laredo, Webb County, 1900. Courtesy National Archives, 22-WB-41-B1381

Fig. 48. Chaparral composed entirely of creosotebush, below Laredo, Webb County, 1900. Courtesy National Archives, 22-WB-41-B1408

Fig. 49. Palm grove near Brownsville, Cameron County, 1911. Courtesy National Archives, 22-WB-41-12922

shown itself above the top of the sand and will in time probably cover the whole region.

In that same year, in November and December, Lloyd traveled from Eagle Pass to Laredo with Clark Streator and wrote the following account of the countryside:

The country all lies at a low altitude, the Rio Grande falling about 200 ft in the 120 or 130 miles from Eagle Pass south to Laredo. The country, on the Texas side, is as a rule with few hills or elevations over 40 or 50 feet, though the Rio Grande valley proper, is bordered by a chain of hills running continuously parallel with the river and from 1/4 to 1 miles from it of perhaps 100 ft. high. The only elevation in the country is "Las dos Hermanos," two circular hills of red sandstone and gravel of 600 feet high, and to the W and S one can see the blue ridges toward Monterey. Water is the great want beyond the Rio Grande which is practically worthless for collecting near it, owing to the great September floods.

Sous Creek, which meanders through the country and has a few willow on it, flows through a shrubless, treeless plain, and did not seem to have any sign of animal life whatever, owing perhaps to the countless bands of sheep and goats that go to the few water holes for water and have trampled all herbage and soil into a dusty mass.

San Lorenzo Creek has also a few pools of stagnant water and no doubt at times owing to the thick belt of timber, is tenanted by mammals that can feed on acorns, but this year the crop together with the pecans and hackberries have failed.

Santa Isabel has a few pools of saline water near its mouth, and is undrinkable, but mammals seems to like it, and it was by this creek, with its peculiar salty grasses, that we were most successful.

Most of the hills and a large proportion of the low lands are so gravelly as to render it hopeless to expect any mammals, as they avoid such places keeping to the fine sand which are found in places in the river bottom, and along the NE border of Webb County, and also in the cactus flats that, as yet, are not choked up with rank grass and small mesquite.

For the last 60 miles the road and country, from the Rio Grande E and S are broken by barrancas of little depth, in which the rain floods have twisted into all sorts of shapes. They are of soft earth and are utterly devoid of animal life.

Oberholser worked around the city of Laredo in April and May of 1900 and wrote the following description of the area:

Laredo is situated on the Rio Grande, about 200 miles from its mouth; and is in the neighborhood of 400 feet above the level of the sea. Behind the city, and some distance back from the river rise broken hills, between which and the stream the country is comparatively level. Farther down the hills approach in places much nearer the river. In fact, the whole region is a succession of hills and valleys, very little of which, except that close to ranch houses and a considerable area just north of Laredo, is under any kind of cultivation. The Rio Grande here runs for the most part between nearly vertical banks of varying height and where not too steep covered at least to some extent with trees or bushes. At Laredo the river bed is possibly a third or a half mile wide, and much of it is bare except at high water; but lower down it narrows in places to 100 or 150 yards, and is usually there all under water. The river is a swift, muddy, treacherous stream, and where narrow, rises of fifty feet in vertical measurement are not unusual. Its banks are sometimes pure sand, sometimes cliffs of solid rock. The hills in this region are usually rocky, almost always gravelly or stony, but the depressions between them are commonly sandy, and frequently cut into deep arroyos by the heavy and violent rains. These arroyos are of course most numerous in the vicinity of the river, and are there a conspicuous feature of the landscape.

This entire region is covered with chaparral, somewhat scattering and stunted on many of the stony hills, but rank and dense on most of the lower areas. The most abundant shrubs composing this growth are *Prosopis juliflora, Lippia ligustrina, Larrea mexicana* [= *Larrea tridentata*], *Leucaena pulverulenta, Diospyros texana, Condalia obovata, Zizyphus obtusifolius, Koeberlinia spinosa, Leucophyllum texanum,* and *Opuntia engelmanni;* the first two of which occur much less commonly on the hills. *Acacia farnesiana* is not of frequent occurrence but is found in some of the arroyos. *Parkinsonia aculeata* (now in bloom), *Celtis occidentalis* and *Ulmus crassifolia* grow commonly along the river banks; where also the mesquite most flourishes, attaining sometimes great size, 45 feet in height, with a diameter at base of over three feet, the largest one measured being 3 feet, 1-1/2 inches through.

In May and June of 1891, Lloyd traveled along the Rio Grande Valley from Laredo to Rio Grande City, in Webb and Starr Counties, and wrote the following description of the countryside:

The country from Laredo to Rio Grande City is a country differing widely from that to the north of it—principally in the wide river valleys which are entirely wanting above that place.

Above, the Rio Grande runs in a deep channel carved out of the reddish clay and alluvial soil which line its banks, and which add to the dirty look of the water and which always carries a large amount of soil in solution (a bucketful yielding about half an inch). It is nearly an average width all the way from Laredo 80 to 100 yards and is rarely approachable owing to its high banks, except at the mouth of its numerous arroyos (dry) which, like the river are for the most part entirely treeless. The road in many places passes through belts of fine sand, one north of Carrizo being about 20 miles in extent from north to south. This soil is the only part of the region under consideration that is rich in mammals such as armadillo, badger and gopher, but the great dearth of water in all the region renders it practically inaccessible at least with a wagon. There is no water whatever from Laredo south with exception of the wells at the Mexican ranches that lie away from the road, until after leaving Roma and approaching Rio Grande City, where after a continued rainfall are large depressions in the land that become veritable lakes and last quite a while, until they change into marshes. These lakes may perhaps be a continuation of the great chain that extend from the Nueces in Zavalla County and are supposed to touch the Rio Grande below Laredo. Some are of large extent, one said to be 40 miles around, and as I mentioned some time before, are almost entirely unknown.

## Edwards Plateau

The Edwards Plateau had already undergone extensive landscape and habitat change by the time Bailey and agents arrived in the area (Goetze, 1998). Before European settlement, the vegetation of the region was about half forest and half grassland. By the time Bailey and the federal agents worked there, most of the area was heavily overgrazed by cattle, goats, and sheep, and most of the grasses had been depleted and replaced by less desirable woody shrubs. Bailey and the agents visited twenty-one different places in this region including locations such as Kerrville, Llano, Austin, Fredericksburg, and Rock Springs, as well as several locations along the Mexican border (Figs. 50–61). While visiting Howard Lacey's Ranch, twelve miles east of Kerrville, Bailey wrote the following report in May of 1899:

The ranch of Howard Lacey, where we have worked for a week, is on a little branch of Turtle Creek, 12 miles west of Kerrville. The altitude of Kerrville is 1750 feet, of Lacey's Ranch approximately 2000 feet. The country is exceedingly rough and deeply eroded through horizontal layers of limestone. The surface lies in flat topped mesas extending back and becoming wider toward the source of drainage; in steep, terraced or cliffy slopes; and in narrow-bottomed stream valleys. The highest mesas are 300 or 400 feet above the stream valleys. There are some rocky canyons and numerous sheer walls and cliffs. As usual in limestone formations the cliffs are much broken and full of cracks and caverns. Most of the land is too rough and stony for cultivation, though the flat parts of the valleys are very mellow and fertile. The soil is mostly clay and very sticky when wet. Springs and streams are abundant and the water is generally good.

The country is mostly covered with scrubby timber which becomes dense and of considerable size in the canyon and gulches and scattered and dwarfed on the mesas. There are many open strips and bare or grassy slopes, and the flat valley land is now mostly cultivated. The characteristic vegetation of the mesa tops is juniper, shin oak, bastard oak, blackjack, mimosa, acacia, a few species of *Opuntia*, and *Yucca*. The canyons and gulches are characterized by the turkey oak (*Q. texana*), bastard oak (*Q. durandii = Quercus sinuata*), walnut, pecan, elms, *Celtis*, basswood, benzoin bushes, *Cornus*, viburnum, black cherry, *Rhamnus*, and grape and *Smilax* vines. The open valleys are especially characterized by live oaks (*Q. virginiana*), a few scattered junipers, some yuccas and cactus, mimosa bushes, and along the streams sycamores and willows.

The physical features are unusually varied and offer conditions suitable to an extensive flora and fauna. The mesa tops are almost arid, the canyons and gulches are damp and cold or hot according to slope and form, while the open valleys are warm and fertile. Birds and mammals are unusually numerous in both species and individuals.

Most of the good land is occupied by small farms. Corn, wheat, sorghum cane, some cotton, garden vegetables, and fruit are raised. Hogs, sheep, goats, and cattle are pastured on the rough land. Stock raising is evidently the main industry of the region.

In June of 1900, Oberholser penned the following description of the landscapes around Rock Springs in Edwards County:

Rock Springs lies on the divide between the Nueces and Llano Rivers, about 50 miles east of Devil's River, and is about 2300 feet above sea level. The entire surrounding country is more or less uneven, though not hilly, this being due to the many shallow valleys that have been cut down from the general level. The name Rock Springs does not convey an accurate impression, for there are no springs about the town, and although it lies at the ultimate sources of the Nueces River, these streams are merely channels for surface water after rains, the real canyons not beginning for ten or twelve miles to the southward. There are in this vicinity a few vegetation-choked ponds, usually dry in the summer, but while they contain water are resorts for various birds. The whole region is exceedingly rocky, and the soil, except for occasional somewhat sandy flats, is black and heavy. Very little of the land is under any kind of cultivation.

With the exception of frequent, though not often extensive, open grassy areas, the entire face of the country is covered with a growth of live oak brush, this being the predominant vegetation. Other common

Fig. 50. Hills along Pecos River near Ft. Lancaster, Crockett County, 1901. Courtesy National Archives, 22-WB-30-B2726

Fig. 51 (below). Looking up valley of Pecos River near Ft. Lancaster, Crockett County, 1901. Courtesy National Archives, 22-WB-30-2722

Fig. 52. Oak-juniper countryside near Kerrville, Kerr County, 1906. Courtesy National Archives, 22-WB-30-9045

Fig. 53. Oak-covered hills near Kerrville, Kerr County, 1906. Courtesy National Archives, 22-WB-30-9044

Fig. 54. Field of flowers near Rock Springs, Edwards County, 1900. Courtesy National Archives, 22-WB-41-B1482

Fig. 55. Chaparral near Rock Springs, Edwards County, 1900. Courtesy National Archives, 22-WB-41-B1475

Fig. 56. Looking up Nueces River near Barksdale, Edwards County, 1900. Courtesy National Archives, 22-WB-30-1496

Fig. 57. Hills just north of Barksdale, Edwards County, 1900. Courtesy National Archives, 22-WB-30-1497

Fig. 58. Pond in side canyon along Rio Grande, near Langtry, Val Verde County, 1901. Courtesy National Archives, 22-WB-30-B2748

Fig. 59. Pecos High Bridge from east side, Pecos River, Val Verde County, 1901. Courtesy National Archives, 22-WB-30-2779

Fig. 60. Looking down
Pecos Canyon from Pecos
High Bridge, Val Verde
County, 1901. Courtesy
National Archives,
22-WB-30-2778

Fig. 61. Large spring near
Del Rio, Val Verde County,
1901. Courtesy
National Archives,
22-WB-30-2795

components of this chaparral are two species of *Acacia*, *Xanthoxylum pterota* [= *Zanthoxylum fagara*], *Berberis trifoliata*, and *Zizyphus obtusifolius*. Occasional patches of *Prosopis juliflora* occur, but it does not appear to grow among the live oaks. Scattered throughout the live oak chaparral there are frequent live oak trees, as well as a few *Celtis occidentalis*, and some *Juniperus*. *Centaurea americana* and a species of lupine are very abundant.

Along the Rio Grande, J. H. Gaut visited Del Rio in May–June, 1903, and wrote the following physiographic report:

Del Rio, Texas, a flourishing town, with a population about four thousand, is situated near the Rio Grande in the southwestern part of the state. To the east, west, and south are rich farming districts, intersected throughout by numerous irrigating ditches, which are supplied with water from a group of springs about a mile northeast. Valuable crops are raised of which Johnson grass hay and corn seem to predominate.

Toward the southeast and west, the land is one gradual slope to the Rio Grande—a distance of about three miles. The soil is a sandy substance. Where the land is left in its natural state and the plant life is not disturbed by cultivation, *Prosopis juliflora*, *Opuntia engelmanni*, *Eysenhardtia amorphoides*, and *Artemisia ludoviciana* are found on the higher ground while low down in the vegas or made land *Nicotiana glauca*, *Fraxinus velutina*, *Salix*, *Melia azedarach* appear to flourish. The latter together with sunflowers are extremely abundant close to the water. North of Del Rio the surrounding country is of a gravelly mesa nature, connecting to the sandy river land by means of stony slopes and shallow arroyos. On these slopes live *Karwinskia humboltiana*, *Guaiacum angustifolia*, *Dalea formosa*, *Acacia amentacea*, *Microrhamnus ericoides* [= *Condalia ericoides*], and *Lycium berlandieri*, while in the arroyos are *Brayodendron* and *Prosopis juliflora*. On the vast stony mesa country and flats, *Leucophyllum texanum* and *Karwinskia humboltiana* are the most abundant species of plants, while the following are numerous: *Koeberlinia spinosa*, *Larrea mexicana*, *Macrorhamnus ericoides*, *Berberis trifoliolata*, *Opuntia engelmanni*, and *Dalea formosa*.

About two miles west of Del Rio is a small stream called Cienegas Creek, running south, which empties into the Rio Grande. Another stream, San Felipe Creek, quite a large affair, runs through a section of the town and eventually empties into the river about three miles south, while about twelve miles east of the town is another stream called Sycamore Creek, which empties into the river. Along the two latter streams are many pecan and hackberry trees, some of which grow to be enormous and afford fine shade from the heat of the sun.

This season has been very wet about Del Rio, hence therefore the weeds are very dense in the low places.

Two months earlier Gaut had visited Langtry (Val Verde County) about a hundred miles upriver from Del Rio and wrote the following description:

Langtry, a small place situated close to the Rio Grande in southwestern Texas, is reached by the G.H.S.A. Railway. The surrounding country on all sides, for many miles, is very rough, a rolling aspect with deep rocky canyons. Some of these canyons are so deep and rocky in places, that for miles on either side they are inaccessible except by means of ropes. The most characteristic of this is Pump Canyon, a short walk west of the town. In this gorge are several large springs from which the railway company secures water to supply its engines, and the inhabitants of the town. Due south the Rio Grande has formed another deep gorge which is accessible at intervals by means of benches.

Low down, just above the level of the river, are small sandy "vegas" or flats on which *Baccharis glutinosa* predominates over all other plant life. However, *Nicotiana glauca* and *Fraxinus velutina* and *Prosopis juliflora* are quite numerous. On the benches high up *Opuntia engelmanni*, *Selaginella lepidophylla*, *Karwinskia humboltiana*, *Euphorbia antisyphilitica*, *Dalea formosa*, *Guaiacum angustifolia* are plentiful, while *Leucophyllum texanum*, *Agave lechuguilla* and *Fouquieria splendens* are rather numerous. In the beds of the canyons, *Sophora secundiflora*, *Karwinskia humboltiana*, and *Fraxinus velutina* and *Prosopis juliflora* are found among the rocks and gravel. Along the slopes are found *Opuntia engelmanni*, *Echino-*

*cactus longihamatus, Cereus enneacanthus, Fouquieria splendens, Brayodendron* and *Guaiacum angustifolia.* On the gravelly hillsides in places *Agave lechuguilla* form a regular network and hinder the traveling of animals considerably. *Opuntia engelmanni* seems to flourish in such places, as well as *Dalea formosa, Acacia amentacea, Dasylirion texanum, Macrorhamnus ericoides, Lycium berlandieri, Leucophyllum texanum, Larrea mexicana, Mortonia scabrella, Echinocereus pectinatus, Echinocactus texensis, Echinocactus horizonthalonius, Cereus paucispinus.*

About ten miles west of Langtry, a vast flat country is found. Here may be seen *Larrea mexicana, Prosopis juliflora, Lycium berlandieri, Koeberlinia spinosa, Flourensia cernua,* and *Mammillaria heyderi.*

Along the western edge of the Edwards Plateau, in the region of the Concho Valley and Stockton Plateau, it is evident that by the end of the nineteenth century, woody species had increased in density and had begun to appear on the once near-treeless grasslands. Small mesquite began to appear widespread on the plains, although some areas remained largely shrubless. They also saw scrub oak and junipers on the hillsides where observers forty to fifty years earlier had not noted its presence (Maxwell, 1979a).

Bailey traveled through the Concho Valley in May, 1899. He described the vegetation from San Angelo to Big Spring, through the North Concho Valley: "San Angelo is an open, mesquite plain in the genuinely arid region. There are great stretches of smooth surfaces with only short grass and little desert plants, but much of the country is covered with a scattered growth of small mesquites." Between San Angelo and Sterling City he noted: "Mostly mesquite plains with short grass and scattered shrubs of *Lyssium, Condylia, Zizyphus, Acacias, Berberis, Mimosa, Cactus,* and *Yuccas.* The first buttes are near Water Valley where we had dinner and the next set near Sterling. These buttes seem to be covered with shin oak and some have juniper on them." William Bray

accompanied Bailey on this trip and elaborated on the butte slopes around Sterling City:

On three sides of Sterling City, plus or minus three miles (4.8 km) distant are buttes covered by oak scrub and *Juniperus.* The slope leading up these buttes is . . . very thin soiled with the flora listed at San Angelo . . . , including *Microrhamnus ericoides* (javelina bush). North of Sterling six miles (9.6 km) the road to Colorado City crosses a part of one of the buttes where the characteristic *Q. undulatus* (Mohr's scrub oak) and *Juniperus occidentalis* [= *Juniperus pinchotii*] (redberry juniper) occur abundantly. Beyond this lies a flat mesquite plain extending some 20 miles (32 km), having occasional *Opuntia arborescens* [= *Opuntia imbricata*] (tree cholla) and wide stretches of needle grass.

Harry Oberholser traveled from San Angelo to Ozona, following Spring Creek, in April, 1901. He described this region as follows:

San Angelo lies in west central Texas, close to the junction of the North and South Concho Creeks which together form the Concho River. These streams have in many places cut down considerably below the level of the country, and their banks are in many places rocky and precipitous. The country is generally rolling immediately about the town, though some miles away in various directions rise rocky hills. Close to the town much of the land is under cultivation, but farther away it is covered with a growth of low chaparral. This is composed chiefly of *Prosopis juliflora, Opuntia engelmanni, Acacia, Berberis trifoliata, Diospyros texana, Zizyphus obtusifolius,* and *Ephedra nevadensis.* There is a considerable fringe of timber along the streams, this composed chiefly of *Hicoria pecan* [= *Carya illinoiensis*], *Quercus,* and *Celtis occidentalis.*

To the southwest of San Angelo the country continues as a rolling chaparral-covered plain for several miles, then being interrupted by rocky hills covered with a growth of oak brush and low junipers. Beyond this the hills increase in number toward Sherwood, the valleys and mesas between them being covered with a growth of chaparral similar to that about San Angelo, the mesquite predominating in much of the level lower ground. Three streams drain this region, all of them similar in character; rocky, with low banks, and in many places with a fringe of timber. Spring Creek, which rises southwest of Sherwood, is fed by springs some six or eight miles from this town, and though the valley of the creek reaches for many miles farther southwest it is at even this season merely a dry bed. Near and beyond Sherwood the hills are less high and finally merge into the high plains to the southwest, the general level of this portion (Sherwood to 18 miles southwest) rising more rapidly than that farther to the northeast.

These high, almost level, grassy plains, evidently a southern extension of the Staked Plains, extend from about 20 to 45 miles southwest of Sherwood toward Ozona, broken only occasionally by shallow valleys. They are scarcely anywhere entirely free from shrubby growth, but in many places, particularly along the eastern side, are practically open, being only very sparingly dotted with *Prosopis juliflora* and a low species of *Acacia*, with an occasional bunch of *Opuntia*. Toward the western side, however, the brush increases in quantity, and in places forms a fairly dense chaparral. The only shrubby plants noted on the top of the plains are as follows, all but the first five being of uncommon occurrence: *Prosopis juliflora*, *Opuntia*, *Zizyphus obtusifolius*, *Acacia*, *Nolina texana*, *Ephedra nevadensis*, *Yucca g. stricta*, and *Berberis trifoliata*. On the stony slopes of the shallow valleys which cut the plains along their southwestern side there is much *Juniperus*, *Celtis occidentalis*, and *Diospyros texana*, with a few other shrubs unidentifiable at this season on account of lack of foliage.

West of these high plains toward the Pecos River the whole country is much cut up by deep canyons, with hills and sometimes high mesas between them. There are practically no running streams, the beds of all the canyons being entirely dry excepting after hard rains. These canyons have almost always steep rocky sides, having been scored out through almost always horizontal beds of limestone; and the appearance of most of the country is thus rocky and broken. Westward from Ozona, which lies a few miles beyond the high plains and not far from the head of one of the canyons, the vegetation is much the same as that on the northeastern side of the high plains. Many of the rocky slopes have an abundant growth of *Juniperus*, and the bottoms of the canyons are nearly always covered with chaparral consisting of the customary species. Between Ozona and Fort Lancaster the influence of the

Rio Grande—Pecos region is seen in the appearance of *Sophora secundiflora*, *Koeberlinia spinosa*, *Dasylirion texanum* and others.

## Trans-Pecos, Mountains and Basins

Bailey and the federal agents visited twenty-four sites in this vegetative region (Figs. 62–83). From their descriptions, the impact of over-grazing on the rangelands was evident, but the riparian habitats were relatively unaltered compared to today. Already, there was some evidence that stands of desert scrub were expanding at the expense of grassland habitat, and lumbering of the "islets" of coniferous and hardwood timber at the summits of desert mountains was underway, and free-standing natural water was rare throughout the region.

Bailey and his field party were the first to survey the Big Bend of Texas in what is known today as Big Bend National Park, having been established in 1944. In this region of diverse habitats and vegetation, varying from desert valleys and grassy plateaus to wooded mountain slopes, they discovered extensive plant and animal diversity. During the time of their visits, most of the land was native range in large holdings, typically used for livestock grazing (cattle, sheep, mixed cattle and sheep, and some Angora goats). Cultivated areas were confined largely to the irrigated valleys.

Bailey and Fuertes were particularly impressed with the magnificent canyons near where Terlingua Creek flowed into the Rio Grande. In his June 27, 1901, field trip itinerary Bailey wrote:

Fuertes and I walked down to mouth of canyon—2 miles from camp. Took photographs and explored it up 4 or 5 miles from the end. The river has cut its way down through about 1700 feet of stratified limestone as the rock rose slowly with a clean escarpment facing NE and a flat topped plateau dipping back to the SW. . . . There is not much talus at the bottom of the cliff and the walls are nearly vertical as also are the walls of the canyon. There is apparently no place

Fig. 62. Franklin Mountains, near Ft. Bliss, El Paso County, 1901. Courtesy National Archives, 22-WB-30-3776

Fig. 63. Looking over El Paso, El Paso County, and Juarez, Mexico, 1901. Courtesy National Archives, 22-WB-30-3787

Fig. 64. Looking up one of the main gulches at the head of Dog Canyon, Guadalupe Mountains, Culberson County, 1901. Courtesy National Archives, 22-WB-30-3759

Fig. 65. Gulch in head of Dog Canyon, Guadalupe Mountains, Culberson County, 1901. Ponderosa pine the typical tree. Courtesy National Archives, 22-WB-30-3764

Fig. 66. Sierra Blanca, Hudspeth County, 1901. Courtesy National Archives, 22-WB-30-3147

Fig. 67. Davis Mountains from east side of Toyahvale, Reeves County, 1901. Courtesy National Archives, 22-WB-30-3709

Fig. 68. Looking up Limpia Canyon from mouth of cave in cliff, Davis Mountains, Jeff Davis County, 1901. Courtesy National Archives, 22-WB-30-3136

Fig. 69. Ft. Davis, Jeff Davis County, 1901. Courtesy National Archives, 22-WB-30-3144

Fig. 70. Limpia Canyon, twenty miles below Ft. Davis, Jeff Davis County, 1901. Trees in bottom *Juglans rupestris* (walnut). Courtesy National Archives, 22-WB-30-3702

Fig. 71. Near lower end of Limpia Canyon, Jeff Davis County, 1901. Courtesy National Archives, 22-WB-30-3704

Fig. 72. Mouth of Tornillo Creek, Brewster County, 1901. Courtesy National Archives, 22-WB-30-B3617

Fig. 73. Looking down Rio Grande from above Boquillas, Brewster County, 1901 (now Big Bend National Park). Courtesy National Archives, 22-WB-30-B3615

Fig. 74. Badlands, east base Chisos Mountains, Brewster County, 1901 (now Big Bend National Park). Courtesy National Archives, 22-WB-30-3663

Fig. 75. South end of Santa Elena Canyon, Brewster County, 1901 (now Big Bend National Park). Courtesy National Archives, 22-WB-30-3015

Fig. 76. Lower entrance to Santa Elena Canyon, Brewster County, 1901 (now Big Bend National Park). National Archives, 22-WB-30-3016

Fig. 77. Looking up Santa Elena Canyon from terrace on south side, just above the mouth, Brewster County, 1901 (now Big Bend National Park). Courtesy National Archives, 22-WB-30-3669

Fig. 78. Primitive irrigation dam and ditch near mouth of Terlingua Creek, Brewster County, 1901 (now Big Bend National Park). Courtesy National Archives, 22-WB-30-3011

Fig. 79. Chisos Mountains, Brewster County, 1901 (now Big Bend National Park). Courtesy National Archives, 22-WB-30-B3548

Fig. 80. Chisos Mountains, Brewster County, 1901 (now Big Bend National Park). Camp in foreground. Courtesy National Archives, 22-WB-30-3651

Fig. 81. Looking up valley below Pine Canyon, Chisos Mountains, Brewster County, 1901 (now Big Bend National Park). Courtesy National Archives, 22-WB-30-2913

Fig. 82. Pena Colorado
Creek, near Marathon,
Brewster County, 1901.
Courtesy National Archives,
22-WB-30-2828

Fig. 83. Cottonwood grove
on Pena Colorado Creek, near
Marathon, Brewster County,
1901. Courtesy National
Archives, 22-WB-41-B2824

where either cliff or canyon wall can be climbed to the top without going 5 miles back from the river to get on the plateau or 5 or 6 miles up the canyon to climb the walls. From the escarpment the big open valley, mainly hot and barren desert, stretches away down the river and into the rough badland country toward the Chisos Mountains. Its bareness is relieved by the Mexican farms of corn, melons, etc. along the valley near the mouth of Terlingua Creek and by mesquites and cottonwoods along the river flats. The canyon is impressive on account of its sheer walls and narrowness—often apparently higher than wide and with walls leaning in as commonly as out. At present the river is low and we waded, swam, and climbed along shore up 4 or 5 miles into the canyon—to where the walls were lower—less sheer—not over 1000 feet. Next to the Grand Canyon of the Colorado it is the best I have seen—with its square walls it is far more impressive than the Yellowstone Canyon. One side is cold and shady, the other scorching hot. Springs come out of the banks. There are grand places to camp on sandy bars, in cool, deep caverns or under shadowy cliffs on little mesas.

The grandeur of this incredible place, known as Santa Elena Canyon, remains today, although some of the wildlife recorded by Bailey and Fuertes (e.g., bighorn sheep) no longer occur there. Scattered throughout the rugged topography of the Chihuahuan Desert in the Trans-Pecos are islandlike, forest-covered highlands. Some of these restricted projections rise only 1500 feet or so above the arid lowlands. Other mountain masses are higher, extending upward from the desert floor a thousand or so meters. These support montane habitats with luxuriant stands of oaks, pines, and sometimes firs, and other boreal growth. Bailey and the agents visited the most massive mountains along the Front Range, beginning with the Chisos Mountains near the Rio Grande and continuing northward to the Davis Mountains, in Jeff Davis County, and the Guadalupe Mountains on the Texas–New Mexico border.

Of the Chisos Mountains, which today constitute the heart of Big Bend National Park,

Bailey wrote the following description in June of 1901:

The Chisos Mountains are a small group of very old volcanoes pushed up through broken and tilted strata, then worn down until the hard, basaltic caves and old lava rims stand up as towers, pinnacles, cliffs and crests above the crumbling scattered debris of the lower slopes. Many of the old craters are almost obliterated by succeeding ones and by erosion but half a dozen large old rims may be traced for part of their circumference while many little craters, fairly well preserved, stand out from the main mass. As a result of their origin and age the mountains are extremely rough and steep and full of deep gulches, high cliffs and precipitous walls. A few old lava streams extend from them, one of the most conspicuous forming a plateau ridge toward the Rio Grande, but the lava flow seems not to have been extensive. The long axis of the group is east and west and a gap only 7000 feet high partly separates them into east and west groups. Our main camp is on the east slope of the eastern group, or rather in the central crater of the eastern part of the group at an altitude of 6000 feet, about 5 miles west of Rock Spring and more than 1000 feet higher. Half a mile above our camp a spring of good water comes out in the bed of the stream and a quarter of a mile farther up a pretty little water fall about 300 feet high trickles over the precipice. Below us the rugged amphitheater almost closes in, having only a narrow gap opening out over the valleys to the SE. Crossing the ridge just back of our camp one goes down into the long north and south canyon that partly separates the two groups and then either up the steep slope or around up the winding canyon that brings you into the east side of Mt. Emory or on top of the high, timber covered ridges south of Mt. Emory.

Mt. Emory (9000 feet) is a rather barren peak at the west end of the group, overlooking Terlingua and the Rio Grande Valley. From its sides the ridges extending east and south range from 8000 to 8500 feet high and form an extensive timber covered plateau, cut through by the central gulch. As this gulch slopes down to the north and then to the east it gives the coldest possible conditions and carries important species of trees and birds. The water in it is not permanent, or more important species, including mammals would be found in it.

In general the water of the mountains is scarce and ephemeral. Snow is said never to last long on the mountains. Sudden, violent rain and hail storms of short duration occur filling the pools and rock basins with water that sinks quickly into the stony slopes, not to reappear until some hard stratum brings it to the surface far out on the valley. The impervious rock bottom of the long gulch above keeps a little stream trickling over the falls back of our camp, only to be lost in the gravel below. There seems to be no permanent stream of any size. Little springs (aptly called "seeps") are found here and there over the lower slopes of the mountains. More of the accessible water is held in rock basins, where it stands from one shower to another unless they are far apart.

The soil of the mountains, where held on tops of the ridges or on the lower slopes, is a firm, red, volcanic soil of good fertility. Extensive slopes are bare masses of slide rock above the angle of stability.

From the foothills at 5500 to 6000 feet the mountains are generally covered with more or less open and scrubby timber to the tops. In the cool canyons it becomes more dense and on dryer slopes more scarce. Oaks, pines, and junipers are the dominant trees with cypress and Douglas spruce in one gulch. The giant century plant blooming over the lower slopes and common to the top of the mountains is a striking feature of the vegetation. The abundance of acorns, pine nuts, sweet juniper berries, and various beans attract many birds and mammals.

The main part of the mountain lies in Upper Sonoran zone. Lower Sonoran species reach to 5500 on the east and to 6000 on hot south slopes. Upper Sonoran species reach to the top of the mountains except on the cool north slopes and in cold gulches which carry mainly Transition forms. I find no trace of Canadian species of plants or animals.

Luxuriant grass covers almost the whole of the mountains and would make them important grazing country if water was more abundant. By digging wells, improving springs, and some piping all of the grass can easily be utilized and if not over stocked and killed out it will support much stock. There are one or two little ranches near the base of the mountains and other ranches for a distance of 50 miles draw their timber from them. In course of time every bit of timber on the mountains will be needed in the valleys and become valuable. The yellow pines, cypress (*Cupressus*), and junipers are all valuable timber to the ranchmen.

Of the Davis Mountains, situated along the Front Range about halfway between the Guadalupe Mountains to the north and the Chisos Mountains to the south, Bailey wrote the following description in July of 1901:

The Davis Mountains are a very old volcanic uplift. They stand as a group, not a range, with Mt. Livermore and a few other half basaltic cores rising as sharp peaks in the middle, but only a few hundred feet higher than the tops of the main ridges. The mountains owe their present form to ages of erosion that have cut deep gulches through the brown lava rock and left high ridges radiating from the center. As much of the rock is a roughly formed basalt, many of the gulches are canyons with cliff or pillared walls that become deeper toward the eastern edge of the mountains on account of the low base level of the Pecos Valley. The steeper ridges are bare, brown lava rock but in general they are covered with soil and a good growth of vegetation, grass, shrubs, and scrubby forest. From the east base the low, desert valley of the Pecos stretches out of sight, to the west the high, short grass plains come up to the edge of timber on the foothills. To the north and south low ridges reach away in the line of the axis of the Guadalupe and Ord and Santiago Mountains; which, with the Corrozone and Chisos Mountains make a somewhat continuous chain with the ranges of eastern Mexico (Coahuila).

Although a much eroded group of mountains, permanent water is scarce, especially in the central part. A few springs break out in the gulches and good wells are found at most of the ranches. Lower down in the canyons the streams are usually permanent for considerable distance, as we found in Limpia and Musquez canyons, but not with enough water to extend beyond the canyons except in time of rains. The rain comes in irregular showers that are quickly swallowed up in the stony soil and do not warrant a heavy growth of vegetation. Scrubby timber of oaks, junipers, and nut pine covers a great part of the mountains, with yellow pine and *monticola* (?) on the cold upper slopes. Generally the timber is open and scattered with grassy spaces intervening, but in many places it is filled up with dense scrub of brush and shrubby oaks. A shrubby form of *Quercus hypoleucoides* (402) forms extensive thickets. Maples, madrones, walnuts, and grapevines help to fill up the gulches. The big *Agave* grows on barren ridges along the top of Limpia Canyon and well up into the mountains.

With the exception of a few little farms in the canyons where small crops are raised the whole region is devoted to stock raising. The ranches are large with much rough country between for range and extensive areas where little stock ranges on account of scarcity of water. Much good grass has been utilized by means of reservoirs and wells and it is safe to say that all will be in course of time. The rains came late this year but at the present time grass is coming on fresh and green, though still short and with a fresh, spring appearance. The mountain plateau catches more rain than the lower country and is therefore a more productive stock region. It is also cooler and a desirable ranch country for its delightful climate.

Bailey was particularly impressed with the grandeur and magnificence of the Guadalupe Mountains where he described the Transition Life Zone in Texas and lamented the poor land use in the region. Guadalupe Mountains National Park was established by Congress in 1967 to preserve the fragile biological equilibrium between the fauna and flora of the Chihuahuan Desert in the lowlands and the Rocky Mountains at the higher elevations (Genoways and Baker, 1979).

Of the Guadalupe Mountains, Bailey wrote the following description in August of 1901:

The Guadalupe Mountains are approximately 100 miles long by 20 to 30 wide, the main ridges ranging from 7000 to 8500 feet and the peak reaching 9500. They lie half in New Mexico and half in Texas, the peak and highest part of the range lying south of the line. They are practically a southern continuation of the Sacramentos with only a low gap to cut them off. To the south they run toward the Davis Mountains but are separated from them by a wider gap. Each range forms a link in the chain, heading toward the mountains of eastern Mexico. The Davis Mountains are volcanic. The Guadalupes, like the Sacramentos, are of stratified limestone, faulted and abrupt on the west and dipping gradually toward the Pecos Valley on the east. The crest of the range is along the western edge. The north half is wider and plateau like while the part lying in Texas is narrower and deeply cut by canyons. South of Guadalupe Peak the range breaks down abruptly at the Point and straggles southward only as low ridges. The peak is given as 9500 feet high, which appears to be approximately correct. The ridge on the north side of McKitterick Canyon is 8600 feet (by the aneroid), that on the south side about 9000, and the peak, 10 miles farther south, still higher. North of the Texas-New Mexico line the crest of the range runs from 7000 to 8000 feet, apparently getting down to about 6000 near its northern end.

Water is scarce throughout the mountains and especially so on the higher parts and along the west slope. Rain falling on the open edges of tilted strata runs back toward the Pecos Valley. There is almost no permanent water except below 6000 feet in the canyons on the east slope. On top of the range the few ranches depend on artificial or natural tanks that are filled irregularly by the rains. There are no ranches on the west slope, owing to the difficulty of making tanks on the open edges of tilted strata, although the abundant grass and beautiful ranch valleys have tempted many such efforts. One little "seep spring" at the head of Dog Canyon furnishes a few buckets of water daily to a small mining camp and small natural tanks in the rocks hold water for some days after each rainstorm. A few springs occur in the big salt basin valley at the west base of the mountains.

An abundant growth of the best of forage grasses covers the mountains and valleys at their sides. From about 5800 feet on the east slope and 6500 feet on the west the mountains are covered with an almost continuous, but scattered growth of timber, mainly junipers, nut pines, and oaks. In cold canyons above 6000 and over all but the hot slopes above 7000 yellow pines and Douglas spruce are the common trees, with maples, hornbeam, and chestnut oak in the gulches. *Pinus monticola* is in the gulches from 7000 feet up and over open north slopes from 7800 feet up. Several species of live and deciduous oaks grow as low, round topped trees up to about 7000 feet, and several species of shin oaks grow in great abundance from 7000 feet to the top, forming extensive chaparral. The big *Agave applanata* is a conspicuous tree all over the mountains above 6000 feet, or at least up to 8600. *Yuccas, Dasylirion*, and cactuses grow over rocky slopes where they can crowd out other plants.

A conspicuous feature of the plateau top of the mountains is beautiful, grassy, park like, or orchard like, forests of scattered junipers, nut pines, and oaks. The trees being widely spaced take beautiful forms and the clean green sward below gives the effect of landscape gardens.

The only important industry of the mountains is stock raising, to which the country is admirably adapted in all but water supply. When proper reservoirs are built the number of cattle on the range can be doubled without over crowding. Snow lies but a few days at a time on most of the range and cattle get green grass all winter. In time of storms there is abundance of shelter in canyons and on warm slopes.

Some mines about the heads of Dog and McKitterick Canyons yield gold, silver, and copper in paying quantities but as the ore has to be hauled to Carlsbad (75 miles) and then shipped to El Paso there is little profit above cost of transportation and milling.

Bailey visited El Paso, a town of ten thousand inhabitants in far West Texas, in December of 1889 and wrote the following physiographic description of the area:

El Paso is on the east side of the Rio Grande just below where it has cut through a cross range of low mountains, leaving high rocky banks and a very rough country near the river. A mile or two back from the river the mountains are probably 1000 feet above the river on each side. They are rough and bare, of coarse granite and limestone, without timber or much other vegetation. Where there is a little soil over the rocks some yuccas, *Agaves*, cacti, *Fouquieria*, and a few scrubby shrubs grow. The foothills are pretty well covered with *Larrea mexicana*, *Fouquieria splendens*, cacti, and small bushes. Numerous deep cuts and washes have been worn from the high land down to the river, making a very uneven surface and leaving in places broad tables (mesas) between. On the east side of the river the mountains rise abruptly from the plain, which stretches from their base away east to the horizon. This is level, sandy and pebbly, and covered with the evergreen *Larrea mexicana*.

The flat river bottoms form a third well marked region. From one to several miles wide, they are hardly above high-water-mark, in places sandy and again of the hardest clay. Here and there are bare patches where nothing grows and the ground is crusted with

alkaline, but about half of the flats is covered with cottonwood timber and most of it with small brush, some mesquite and a number of saline plants, as *Atriplex*, *Salicornia*, saltgrass, and others. Several species of *Chenopodium* and wild sunflowers furnish food for the rodents as well as birds. Part of this flat land is irrigated and a variety of good crops raised. This season has been unusually dry and lack of water has been a disadvantage. A large canal for irrigation is being built along here now.

## High Plains

Probably no region of Texas has changed more since the time of the biological survey than has the Staked Plains or Llano Estacado region of the Texas High Plains. Bailey and the agents visited the area just prior to the time of major human settlement and agricultural development, and they were struck by the flatness of the land, its extensive grasslands, and the lack of water (Figs. 84–91). While traveling from Colorado City to Amarillo (via Gail, Lubbock, and Canyon) in 1899, Bailey wrote the following description of the region in one of his survey reports:

The escarpment of the real Llano Estacado begins just west of Gail but our road does not rise onto it for about 15 miles farther north. To the north the country rises slowly but steadily to Lubbock, Hail Center, Canyon, and Amarillo but appears as a flat plain, covered with short grass, free of bushes or trees, and mainly with no surface drainage. At Lake Tahoka, Lubbock, and Hail Center slight valleys open out to the east but most of the country drains into local depressions that are ponds after each rain and some permanent lakes. Most of the mesquites, thorn bushes, and cactus are left below the escarpment and soon disappear from the higher levels. Short grass and low prairie, or plains, plants cover the top of the plains and give the characteristic smooth carpet appearance to the region. The country is mostly fenced up in pastures of enormous extent, often containing several hundred square miles, and cattle are scattered over the whole region. Except on areas where there has been no rain for a long time the range is not overstocked and the grass is abundant.

Fig. 84. Sand hills fifteen miles east of Texline, Dallam County, 1903. Courtesy National Archives, 22-WB-60-B6184

Fig. 85. Prairie at Texline, Dallam County, 1903. Courtesy National Archives, 22-WB-54-B6186

Fig. 86. River bottom and buttes near Miami, Roberts County, 1903. Courtesy National Archives, 22-WB-30-B6172

Fig. 87. Town of Miami, Roberts County, 1903. Courtesy National Archives, 22-WB-30-B6173

Fig. 88. Sand Hills south of Dimmitt, Castro County, 1901. Courtesy National Archives, 22-WB-30-3157

Fig. 89. Staked Plains south of Dimmitt, Castro County, 1901. Courtesy National Archives, 22-WB-30-3156

Fig. 90. Tierra Blanca
Creek at Hereford, Deaf
Smith County, 1901.
Courtesy National Archives,
22-WB-30-3186

Fig. 91. Stock pond and
windmill on Staked Plains
south of Dimmitt, Castro
County, 1901. Courtesy
National Archives,
22-WB-30-3154

Farther to the north around Hereford (Deaf Smith County), at the northern extent of the Staked Plains, Oberholser wrote the following description of the countryside in 1901:

Hereford is located on the Staked Plains at an altitude of about 3800 feet, in the southeastern portion of Deaf Smith County, on the line of the Pecos Valley Railroad, about 45 miles southwest of Amarillo, Texas.

For long distances in any direction from the town the country is a level or slightly rolling grassy plain, at intervals interrupted by wide, scarcely abrupt, and usually not very deep grassy valleys, or "draws," as they are known in local parlance, which lead to the head waters of the Red River, but contain water only after heavy rains. Close to the south side of Hereford there is, however, a spring-fed creek, the Tierra Blanca, which for some fifteen miles is a running though sluggish stream. Along the sides of its broad grassy valley there are frequent outcrops of friable white limestone appearing in low isolated cliffs usually close to the present stream bed. The margins of this creek are overgrown with a dense mass of cattails and rushes, while on the cliffs occurs the nearest approach to a natural growth tree anywhere to be found—a few scrubby bushes of Celtis occidentalis. Scattered over the plain are numberless surface lakes, more or less ephemeral, and ranging from a hundred feet to half or three quarters of a mile across. Most of these have no growth in the water, but a few are filled with grass and rushes.

Some 45 miles to the south of Hereford the general evenness of the country is broken by an extensive area of low sand hills. Here the soil changes from the dark colored loam of the environs of Hereford to a pale sand which supports a much less dense growth of grass. The highest of these hills probably is not much over 30 feet above the plain; and all are usually covered with a growth of rank weeds and bushes of Rhus aromatica, with sometimes a few low trees of Celtis occidentalis. The trend of this range of sand hills seems to be about northeast to southwest, and beyond in the latter direction they become higher and less distinctive in character as the general face of the region becomes more rolling. After crossing them to the southeast the country more resembles that immediately about Hereford.

Among the low hills to the southwest and about 75 miles from Hereford are a number of salt, alkali lakes, some of them several miles in extent. Their beds are almost perfectly level and where exposed are encrusted with a heavy saline deposit. They are dry in seasons of drought, but at ordinary times contain some water. Immediately about the margins scarcely anything but salt grass flourishes but a few feet away the effect of the proximity of the salty ground is apparently lost. In the one visited, the water, even when the lake is full, can scarcely be anywhere more than a few feet in depth. Aside from herds of cattle, the only living animals seen about this lake were a few sandpipers, plovers, and swallows.

This entire region is apparently Upper Sonoran in its zonal affinities. The portion about Hereford is characterized by the absence of shrubby vegetation which begins to appear about 40 miles to the southward, in the shape of scattered bushes of Mimosa biuncifera, this increasing in amount to the southwest until it forms in many places a low chaparral. About 50 miles south of Hereford scattered scrubby bushes of Prosopis juliflora begin to be observable, and continue to occur along the road leading southwest.

To the north, Bailey and the agents documented landscapes at several places of the Texas Panhandle, including Lipscomb, Texline, Washburn, Tascosa, Canadian, Wheeler, and Amarillo. This was mostly cattle and ranching country, with few settlements, and the agents were impressed with the prairies in the region. A. H. Howell wrote the following description of the country around Lipscomb in 1903:

The country over this region is high rolling prairie, intersected by numerous streams. The soil on the higher portions is heavy and of a dark color, and supports a rich growth of grasses and an abundance of flowering plants. There are no shrubs or trees on the high prairie, with the exception of a few small patches of 'shin oak' about 3 miles north of Higgins. This is said to be the northern limit of this species. The soil in the creek bottoms and on some of the lower hillsides is sandy, and in such situations, sagebrush (Artemisia filifolia) flourishes in abundance, the wild plum (Prunus angustifolia) forms dense thickets, and 'skunk brush' (*Rhus trilobata*) covers many of the smaller dunes. The cottonwood grows sparingly along the streams, and to some extent in the 'draws' where the water is near the surface. It also joins with the elms (*Ulmus* sp.) and 'china trees' (*Sapindus marginatus*) [= *Sapindus saponaria*] to form groves of timber covering several acres. A few willows occur, mostly shrubby, though occasionally reaching the size of a tree.

There are no very high hills or deep canyons in this region. Most of the creeks are sandy and of small size. Wolf Creek, which flows east just north of Lipscomb, is the largest, and drains the whole region. It has cut a broad bed which is nearly dry at this season. The smaller creeks flowing into Wolf Creek contain more water than Wolf Creek. They run for short distances as narrow brooks through meadow grasses, then widen to form deep holes several hundred yards in length, containing fish, turtles, and water snakes. The most extensive creek I saw is the one known as First Creek, entering Wolf Creek from the north about 15 miles west of Lipscomb. This is broader than the others, and consists at this season of a series of wide, deep holes, separated from one another by meadowy stretches where the water has dried entirely out. A water plant (*Batrachium divaricatum*) [= *Ranunculus longirostris*] grows in abundance in most of these holes, and furnishes the staple article of food to the muskrats which here abound. In the region about this creek, numerous springs are found in the 'draws.' The sand bluffs along First Creek are higher and steeper than elsewhere in the region.

Similarly, Howell described the countryside around Canadian (Hemphill County) in the same year as follows:

Canadian is situated on the south bank of the Canadian River, which at this season is a very insignificant stream, but which in high water covers an area of half a mile in width.

The soil in the valley is very sandy, and supports only a scanty growth of sagebrush, wild plum bushes, 'skunk brush', various grasses and wild flowers, and a few cottonwood trees. The wind has piled the sand into curiously shaped hills on many of which there is no vegetation whatever.

In the bottoms, between the sandhills and the prairie which rises gradually from the valley, are numerous ponds, mud flats and meadows. Considerable hay is cut from the meadows, some of them being wet nearly all summer, others dry for most of the year. The sandhills described above are principally on the south shore of the river, at a point where the river makes a bend. On the north shore the conditions are somewhat different. The meadows are broader, and there are extensive marshy areas grown up to rushes. There are also good sized tracts of timber on this side, most of it on more or less swampy ground. The cottonwood is the prevailing tree, with a few elms, hackberries and willows. Shrubs noticed were *Cephalanthus occidentalis, Cornus asperifolia* [= *Cornus foemina*], *Prunus angustifolia.* Just back of the meadows the sandhills begin, the soil being of a more or less yellow color and grown over sparsely with sagebrush (*Artemisia filifolia*) and a few small shrubs.

Clear Creek flows into the Canadian from the north, and several fine ranches are located along its lower course, the water being used for irrigating the fields and gardens. I spent 4 days at Mr. Studer's ranch close to the river, and trapped in the sand hills and about the borders of the fields. Mesquite grows sparingly on the western slopes of some of the hills west of Canadian. The largest brush seen was about 10 feet high.

Vernon Bailey visited the area around Washburn (Armstrong County) in 1892 and wrote the following description of the region, which included Palo Duro Canyon:

Washburn is on the Staked Plains at an altitude of 3538 feet. There is nothing to break the smooth, even monotony of almost level prairie, meeting the horizon on all sides. There is no drainage, save the basin like depressions here and there over the prairie, and these so shallow as to appear, when dry, like their surroundings. The swells are so long and gradual as not to appear like ridges. A low, thick growth of grass covers the country, giving an almost velvety smoothness of surface. Here and there a thistle, an *Asclepias*, or *Euphorbia* rises a foot or so, but so scarce as to be hardly noticed. An occasional house, with windmill and fences, or cattle and horses grazing are all that break the monotony. The grass is becoming yellow and dry. During the heat of the day there is such a dancing of air that the ground can be seen for but a short distance and every object appears distorted.

The soil is a good mixture of clay and sand, but the rainfall is too slight to make farming a success. However, many crops are raised with considerable success. Most of the grain for use on the ranches and some vegetables are raised. Cattle and horses are the principal products.

Thirteen miles south of Washburn the Prairie Dog Fork of Red River flows through an abrupt canyon of about 1000 feet in depth. It is cut abruptly through the prairies like the canyon of Snake River, Idaho, and much of the way it does not drain the land back a mile from its edge. The sides of the canyon are argillaceous rock, clay, and sandstone, broken and rough. The top of the canyon is about a mile wide, the south side several hundred feet the highest. The bottom is sandy and smooth. The river bed is small and now almost dry.

The whole canyon is lined with trees, brush, and plants not found outside in the surrounding country, and furnishes the only timber for a long distance. Junipers are the most important and useful tree, being used for fence posts and fuel, and are very common along the sides of the canyon. A few cottonwoods grow along the bottom, also *Celtis* and Chinaberry tree. *Prosopis* fills the canyon and runs over an edge of prairie as also a little oak. *Lycium* is common, several species of *Rhus*, *Ptelea*, *Cercocarpus*, *Atriplex canescens*, 5 species of cactus, *Yucca angustifolia* [= *Yucca glauca*], *Artemisia* and others entirely new to me.

At Mobeetie (Wheeler County) along the eastern edge of the Panhandle, Oberholser in 1901 wrote the following description of the countryside:

Mobeetie, Wheeler County, lies in the extreme eastern portion of the region known as the "Panhandle." It is just below the top of the Staked Plains proper, and has an altitude of approximately 2400 feet. The general surface of the country is heavily rolling, with occasional areas of nearly level land. The two streams, Sweetwater Creek and its tributary Graham Creek, flow in broad shallow valleys, and have at some places low cut banks. The former is here a running stream, though shallow and of irregular volume; the latter is for the greater part dry, with water only in

deep holes. The soil in many places is very sandy, and there are many brush-covered sand hills in this vicinity.

This entire region is a grass country, and there are few uncovered areas. On large tracts, however, there is a dense growth of low live-oak brush (*Quercus undulata*) with not infrequent "mottes" of the same, this vegetation mostly confined to the sandy areas. Along the streams there is considerable timber, composed chiefly of *Populus monilifera* [= *Populus deltoides*], *Ulmus crassifolia*, *Salix nigra* and *Celtis occidentalis*. There are also in many places thickets containing much *Cephalanthus occidentalis*, *Cornus asperifolia*, *Vitis*, and *Prunus americana*. In other respects the flora of this locality is very similar to that about Hereford, Texas, and is essentially Upper Sonoran.

## Rolling Plains

To the east of the High Plains and Panhandle, the Rolling Plains represent a transitional grassland that progresses from the true tallgrass prairies in the east to the shortgrass prairies and desert grasslands to the west and southwest (Figs. 92–100). Originally the vegetation in this country was predominantly tall- and midgrasses. Massive cottonwoods lined the streams in the north, and pecans and walnuts were common in the south. Bailey and the agents spent some time in the Rolling Plains, especially the area that stretches today along Highway 287 from Childress to Vernon to Henrietta, as well as areas around the larger towns of Abilene and Wichita Falls.

Of the country around Abilene (Tebo, Clyde, and Baird), Merritt Cary wrote the following description in 1902:

The country is an immense prairie dog town extending north to the Red River, and nearly 100 miles to the south. There are rolling plains partly covered by mesquites. The mesquites grow quite high, and look more like trees with trunks than bushes. It is a farming country, where they grow hay, cotton, and a little corn.

Clyde is situated at the extreme eastern edge of the plains. It is a level country for the most part, and covered to a large extent by a dense growth of post oak. In

Fig. 92. Pond on prairie near Lipscomb, Lipscomb County, 1903. Courtesy National Archives, 22-WB-30-B6130

Fig. 93. First Creek, near Lipscomb, Lipscomb County, 1903. Home of *Ondatra zibethicus* (muskrat). Courtesy National Archives, 22-WB-30-B6143

Fig. 94. Studer's Ranch, near Canadian, Hemphill County, 1903. Irrigation ditch occupied by muskrat. Courtesy National Archives, 22-WB-30-B6166

Fig. 95. Sweetwater Creek near Mobeetie, Wheeler County, 1903. Courtesy National Archives, 22-WB-30-B6177

Fig. 96. Broken country along Little Wichita Creek, near Archer, Archer County, 1900. Courtesy National Archives, 22-WB-30-1535

Fig. 97. One mile south of San Angelo, Tom Green County, ford on South Concho Creek, 1901. Courtesy National Archives, 22-WB-30-B2667

Fig. 98. Hills west of San Angelo, Tom Green County, 1901. Courtesy National Archives, 22-WB-41-B2688

Fig. 99. Scattered brush near San Angelo, Tom Green County, 1901. Courtesy National Archives, 22-WB-41-B2662

Fig. 100. Town of San Angelo, Tom Green County, 1901. Courtesy National Archives, 22-WB-41-B2659

the immediate vicinity of the town there is an open plain upon which a colony of prairie dogs have their abode. This dense oak "shrub" extends west nearly ten miles where it merges into the open, mesquite plain. East of Clyde about three miles the level country comes to an end, and "breaks" down into a rocky, hilly country several hundred feet lower.

The principal shrubs in the vicinity of Clyde are *Forestiera*, *Zizyphus obtusifolia* (rare), *Prosopis juliflora* (rare), *Yucca stricta*, *Opuntia* sp., and *Celtis occidentalis*. *Eriogonum* and *Solanum rostratum* are found in sandy places.

Cotton is grown to a large extent at Clyde, and there are two gins. Cane is also grown. The country is thickly settled.

Baird is seven miles east of Clyde, in a rocky valley, surrounded by oak-covered hills. Shrubs noted here and not at Clyde are *Dalea formosa*, *Opuntia engelmanni*, *Opuntia leptocaulis*, *Acacia* sp., *Ulmus* sp. (smooth leaved). Other plants were *Grindelia* sp. and *Euphorbia maculata* [= *Chamoesyce maculata*]?

A fair amount of cotton is grown around Baird.

In 1892, Bailey described the physiography in the vicinity of Wichita Falls as follows:

From the western edge of the Upper Cross Timbers at Belcher west along the Ft. Worth and Denver Railroad to where it crosses the Prairie Dog Fork of Red River and from Wichita Falls to Seymour on the Brazos River the country is very similar. The characteristic features are gently rolling, dry plains with short grass and along the streams narrow strips of timber, and over much of the prairie shrubby mesquite— *Prosopis*.

Along the Wichita River at Wichita Falls there is an almost continuous belt of timber composed of cottonwoods, elms, *Celtis*, ash, and an occasional pecan tree. In places the belt is broken and no trees occur for some distance.

Southwest to the Brazos River at Seymour the prairie is mostly scattered over with mesquites and a *Lycium*, *Opuntia*, and *Yucca angustifolia*. I found no timber along the Brazos, save the upland trees of mesquite, *Xanthoxylum*, and cedar elm, though B.H. Dutcher writes me from Brazos (Palo Pinto Co.) that the Upper Cross Timbers extend 20 miles above there on the river.

North of the Wichita River after leaving the river valley there is more smooth prairie covered only with grass though an abundance of mesquites in valleys along the streams as far as the crossing of the Prairie Dog Fork of Red River where mesquite and *Artemisia* meet. At Clarendon there is some mesquite but *Artemisia* predominates.

The soil is a mixture of red clay and sand, usually baked hard, or when wet, muddy, except where the sand predominates as it does along the Brazos River and the Pease River and the Prairie Dog Fork of the Red River. Short grass (*gramma* and others) covers the whole region and furnishes good grazing. Stock raising is the chief industry. Farming is beginning to be carried on quite extensively, but crops have suffered much from drouth this year and are poor. Corn is small.

J. A. Loring penned this description of the physiography in the area between Henrietta and Childress in 1894:

Henrietta, Texas, is situated near the Wichita River just beyond the line of timber called "Cross-timber." It is a beautiful prairie country and fine for wheat raising. The soil is a reddish clay. The first mesquite trees seen in going west, were about two miles southwest of Henrietta, and the first cottonwood trees occurred there. Close to the Wichita River is a large tract of timber. Among the common trees found are *Ulmus americanus, Celtis mississippiensis*, sumac and oak. *Smilax rotundifolia* was very common. At Vernon, which is on the Pease River, the country is somewhat similar although there is more sand on the riverbanks, more cottonwoods, large tracts of mesquite. Here too, sagebrush was first found, on some small sandhills near the river.

Childress is on the open prairie like the two preceding towns. Just east of the village is an immense grove of mesquite, reaching for miles and miles, while to the north is a row of sandhills covered more or less with sagebrush, mesquite, and a species of yucca.

The Red River was a bed of dry sand when I reached Newlin, while on its banks was a row of sandhills covered with sagebrush and mesquite, while the surrounding country was open prairie.

## Cross Timbers and Prairies

Fingers of deciduous forest cross the prairie in northeastern Texas. This configuration, arranged on a north-south axis, creates alternating belts of grassland and forest known as the Cross Timbers (Figs. 101–106). The distinctive pattern of this vegetation became a milepost in the westward march across North America. Pioneers left the eastern deciduous forests and entered the prairie, but they encountered additional forested areas—the Cross Timbers—before reaching the grasslands that extended thereafter to the Rocky Mountains (Bolen, 1998). Bailey recognized the significance of the Cross Timbers as an area of faunal transition when he penned the following report:

Influence of the Cross Timbers
on the Texas Fauna

Among the many natural barriers to distribution of animal life, large and continuous bodies of timber are of no small importance. Where timber joins the prairie or open country it usually marks the limit of range of many species of animals, both those species inhabiting the timber and depending on it for protection and on its products for sustenance and likewise the species living on the prairies and subsisting on foods not found in the timber. A multitude of other causes might be brought up as influencing the range of different species of animals: different soils; the range and abundance of food plants; moisture; distance from water; climatic conditions; with birds, the manner of building nests; and with mammals, the kind of homes selected; not to mention the more general effects of latitude, and the great barriers of bodies of water and mountain ranges.

The distribution of timber itself depends so directly upon soil, moisture and climate that its effect on faunal areas may well be considered secondary but it is none the less real and evident.

In mapping the distribution of birds and mammals the boundary of the range of a species is often traced along the margin of a forest. Innumerable examples might be cited, but among them one strip of timber of

Fig. 101. Rolling prairie with artificial pond in distance, Henrietta, Clay County, 1900. Courtesy National Archives, 22-WB-30-1523

Fig. 102. Rocky hill eight miles east of Henrietta, Clay County, 1900. Courtesy National Archives, 22-WB-30-1527

Fig. 103. Little Wichita Creek,
near Henrietta, Clay County, 1900.
Courtesy National Archives,
22-WB-30-1538

Fig. 104. Brazos River,
near Graham, Young County,
1900. Courtesy National
Archives, 22-WB-30-1543

Fig. 105. Oak scrub near Granbury, Hood County. Courtesy National Archives, 22-WB-41-B2658

Fig. 106. Red River near Benvanue, Clay County, 1900. Courtesy National Archives, 22-WB-30-B1530

particular interest, namely the Upper Cross Timbers of Texas. This represents the lower Cross Timbers, this the Upper. The lower Cross Timbers covers a smaller area and is of less importance. Both are narrow strips of timber extending down from the Red River nearly to the center of the state. The adjoining and nearby surrounding country is prairie. East of the lower Cross Timbers and between the two is the black "waxland," a prairie of very rich and sticky soil. In the timbers the soil is sandy and the surface hilly. The timber does not occur along streams alone as I had supposed, but is continuous over hills and through valleys, apparently following the strips of sandy land. Oaks form the bulk of the timber, the commonest being *Quercus stellata, parvifolia, nigra, macrocarpa,* and *rubra.* Other common trees are *Ulmus alata* and *americana,* hickory, pecan, walnut, cottonwood, sycamore, hackberry, mulberry, redbud, persimmon, and of course many other species.

The Upper Cross Timbers join the Great Plains on the west and cut off the eastward extension of plains species, especially affecting the distribution of certain mammals.

After collecting on the prairie east of the lower Cross Timbers, Mr. Dutcher and I made somewhat thorough collections at different points on the strip of prairie between the two and then crossing to the western edge of the Upper Cross Timbers, we were able to determine with considerable accuracy what species passed through and what were brought to a stand by the timbers.

Fox squirrels, gray squirrels, and flying squirrels were, of course, restricted to the timbers. Prairie dogs are exceedingly numerous from the western edge of the Upper Cross Timbers westward but are not found east of them at any point in Texas. The little pocket mouse (*Perognathus flavus*) and the kangaroo rat (*Perodipus ordii*) were common west of the timbers but none were found on the east side. Two species of ground squirrels (*Spermophilus spilosoma* and S. *mexicana*) were found on the west side but not on the east. The cottontail rabbit (*Lepus sylvaticus*) [= *Sylvilagus floridanus*] was common over all eastern Texas and throughout the timbers, but on passing out upon the prairie west of the Upper Cross Timbers another smaller species (*Lepus nuttalli*) [= *Sylvilagus audubonii*] was met with great abundance.

Thus we found 6 species of mammals reaching their eastern limit along the western border of the upper Cross Timbers and 4 reaching their western limit at the edge of the plains bordering them on the west. Doubtless a more thorough search would add other species to this list. So far as the Upper Cross Timbers extend therefore they may be taken as the boundary of the Great Plains fauna.

## Blackland Prairies

Bailey and his agents encountered the Grand Prairie and the Blackland Prairies which lie in the transition area between the forests and grasslands of Texas (Figs. 107–108). They spent little time here probably because the landscape was already so altered that it held little promise of yielding wildlife. The main belt of the Blackland Prairie formed an essentially continuous north-south strip of grasslands from the Red River to Austin and south of San Antonio. The region was mainly a tallgrass prairie at the time of European settlement.

Of the area around Austin, William Bray wrote the following description in 1899:

The biological conditions in the vicinity of Austin are associated with three main structural features (1) the southeastern escarpment and deeply eroded edge of the plateau of the plains (2) the black prairie which joins the plains at the fault line extending from Austin northwestward, and southwest to San Antonio (3) the valley of the Colorado River which after emerging from its canyon in the hills, widens into a rather broad alluvial bottom. The first region embraces the vegetation of Kerrville and Lacey's ranch. The second presents an alternation of exposed chalk slopes or ridges or knolls with rich areas of deep black waxy soil. The flora of the former is conspicuously xerophytic of species found west and southwest. The latter being much richer is largely in cultivation and is attacked mainly by weeds, though a considerable indigenous element related to that of north central Texas and Indian Territory or to east Texas occurs. The valley of the Colorado possesses a flora much like that at West Point and Richmond but very much less luxuriant than the latter because of less rainfall.

Lying fifty to one hundred feet above the river about Austin are a series of gravelly clay terraces which offer the open texture favorable to "post oak"

Fig. 107. Bosque River near Waco, McLennan County, 1907. Courtesy National Archives, 22-WB-30-9886

Fig. 108. Bosque River near Waco, McLennan County, 1907. Courtesy National Archives, 22-WB-30-9883

formations, and according these areas are thickly covered by *Q. minor, Q. marilandica, Q. virginiana*, and other trees and shrubs in less abundance.

## Post Oak Savannah

The next vegetative region encountered by Bailey and the federal agents was the post-oak woodlands (Figs. 109–12). These woodlands, which occupy a narrow strip that is nowhere more than 60 miles wide, are located in the central part of eastern Texas and extend in a southwesterly direction, forming a peninsula surrounded by prairies. The topography is level to gently rolling and slopes gently from the northwest to the southeast. Vegetatively, the post oak region can best be described as an ecotone between the eastern deciduous forest and the tall-grass prairie. The area supports a stunted, open forest dotted with small tall-grass prairies. The dominant plants of the overstory are post oak and blackjack oak and to a lesser extent winged elm and black hickory. The land in the post oak region is used primarily for farming and ranching.

In 1902, as he traveled from Houston to Austin, Harry Oberholser penned the following description of the countryside through the southern reaches of the post oak country:

From Houston, which lies on the intermittently wooded coast plain, to within 5 miles of Hempstead, Texas, the country is principally open prairie, becoming more and more rolling. Hempstead is three or four miles east of the Brazos River, but not in its valley, and in a region of alternating oak woods and cultivated areas. There are here few running streams, though the dry watercourses are numerous, the surface of the land toward the river being much scored by them. The valley of the Brazos at this point is comparatively narrow, and nearly flat, and below its level the river channel has been cut with almost perpendicular banks twenty to forty feet high. The forest that undoubtedly once covered these bottom lands has been largely removed, and much of the land is in pasture or under cultivation.

West from Hempstead to Carmine the general face of the country is much the same, with exceptionally an area of rolling, unbroken, prairie such as exists south of Chappell Hill. On this prairie there are a few small springs, about which a tall rank grass, similar to *Nolina texana*, grows in profusion. So much of the region about Brenham is now in farms that the larger part of the timber left standing is along the streams. The country in the immediate vicinity of this town is more rolling than that about Hempstead, and to the northward a short distance becomes even somewhat rocky and broken.

The woodland of *Quercus marilandica* and *Q. minor* increases noticeably beyond Carmine, these two species making up by far the larger part of the arboreal vegetation. Between Ledbetter and Giddings much live-oak occurs, principally in mottes, but beyond the latter place it disappears. Beyond Giddings as far as Paige the country is more open, the post-oak and blackjack woods being replaced largely by mesquite chaparral; thence to Elgin the region is one of almost solid post and blackjack oak woods, with scattering areas of open mesquite chaparral in which *Opuntia engelmanni* occurs to some extent.

The country about Elgin is in general appearance much like that near Brenham—decidedly rolling, with frequent shallow narrow valleys cut by streams which run only during seasons of rain, and which are fringed by a growth of timber. The greater part of the land is either under direct cultivation, or in more or less grassy "pastures" grown up to *Prosopis juliflora, Zizyphus obtusifolius, Opuntia leptocaulis,* and *Opuntia engelmanni*—a characteristic assemblage indicating the predominance of arid Lower Sonoran influence, and marking rather definitely the eastern limit of this predominance.

Beyond Elgin toward Austin the country becomes more level, prairies preponderating, though mostly under cultivation.

In the post oaks between Austin and Bryan, and continuing to Waco, Oberholser in the same year wrote the following description:

From Austin to Round Rock there is practically no change in the aspect of the country, but farther eastward the prairies are more cultivated, the junipers disappear, and the mesquite becomes less abundant. Between Taylor and Thorndale, however, mesquite is numerous, as well as *Opuntia engelmanni* locally, but

Fig. 109. Live oaks and Spanish moss, Columbus, Colorado County, 1904. Courtesy National Archives, 22-WB-41-7228

Fig. 110. Live oaks on edge of cultivated field, Verhelle, DeWitt County, 1907. Courtesy National Archives, 22-WB-40-9892

Fig. 111. Guadalupe River, Verhelle, DeWitt County, 1907. Courtesy National Archives, 22-WB-30-9896

Fig. 112. Guadalupe River, near Cuero, DeWitt County, 1907. Courtesy National Archives, 22-WB-30-9894

beyond the latter place both are not common. East of Rockdale there are many areas of post oak woods, which increase as the Brazos is approached.

Gause is situated near the Brazos River, in the southeastern part of Milam County, about ten miles southeast of Hearne. From here to Waco, a distance of some 60 miles, the rolling uplands are partly woodland, partly prairie, and in many places largely under cultivation. The Brazos River, here a large stream, flows in a tortuous course between almost perpendicular earth banks some twenty or thirty feet in height. Its level valley is considerably below the surrounding country, and varies from one to ten miles in width. The bottom lands, though probably once largely if not entirely wooded, are now devoted principally to the raising of cotton and corn.

**Pineywoods**

The easternmost part of Texas, adjacent to the Louisiana border, is called the Pineywoods, an area where Bailey and the agents did a considerable amount of work, particularly in the southeastern part of the region known as the Big Thicket (Figs. 113–18). The Big Thicket forest is a mixture of evergreens, both conifers and hardwoods. Bailey provided the following description of the Big Thicket, writing in his 1904 report:

The Big Thicket of southeastern Texas is a well known and well defined area mainly within the counties of Montgomery, Liberty, Hardin, Tyler, Jasper, and Orange. From the Sabine River it extends 100 miles west, not as a solid body but following the flood lands, or "bottoms," of every river, creek, and bayou with endless branches that alternate with or surround strips or plots of open pine woods or grassy prairie. While the actual thicket does not cover more than about half of the area assigned to it, the thousand interlacing and connecting branches tie it together in a perfectly homogenous body so far as its influences effects the distribution of species of plants, mammals, birds, etc. Similar conditions prevail in a less marked degree along the river bottoms over most of the eastern half of Texas, so the boundaries of the Big Thicket are largely based on degree of density and abundance of species. Few if any species are restricted to it and its

greatest significance is as a last resort for such vanishing forms as *Ursus luteolus, Canis ater, Campephilus principalis*, etc.

The wide, flat river bottoms are frequently flooded and water left standing in shallow pools and basins. The general drainage is so slight that water often stands knee deep in the swamps during rainy seasons. As a result of abundance of moisture and rich alluvial soil a dense growth of palmettos, vines, and bushes fill in the base of the forest with an almost impenetrable jungle. Numerous vines several of them thorny help to make progress through the jungle slow and painful. The Big Thicket timber is mainly deciduous, save for the magnolia and holly. The pine timber is mainly in open woods on the adjoining higher and dryer ground, but in places the pines are scattered through dense portions of the thicket woods. The bald cypress and tupelo gum are restricted to the swampy ground, bayous or stream banks.

Any biologist who ever worked in the Big Thicket would appreciate this description. In 1974, Big Thicket National Preserve was established to protect the remaining biodiversity in this unique region.

Interestingly, prairies once were common where only trees now stand in East Texas. For presumably rational reasons, early settlers called many places in the southeast Texas forests "prairies," for example Tarkington Prairie in Liberty County where Bailey and the federal agents visited. Today, though plowed fields and mowed pastures abound, hardly a vestige of land remains that would not have trees if left alone (Truett and Lay, 1984). Vernon Bailey visited Sour Lake in Hardin County in 1902 and wrote the following survey report regarding his observations:

Sour Lake station lies about twenty miles west of Beaumont on the open prairie at an elevation of about 45 feet. The prairie at this point is dry and covered with a rich pasture grass, excellent for cattle grazing. Except for this grass there is very little vegetation on the prairie, but here and there are wooded "islands" with good timber—mostly oak of various species, black and sweet gum. There is a small sprinkling of short-

Fig. 113. Old cypress gnawed
by bear, Saratoga, Hardin County,
1904. Courtesy National Archives,
22-WB-51-7237

Fig. 114. Edge of clearing in Big Thicket
at Bragg, Hardin County, 1904. Courtesy
National Archives, 22-WB-41-7247

Fig. 115. Railroad cut,
Big Thicket at Bragg, Hardin
County, 1904. Courtesy
National Archives,
22-WB-41-7248

Fig. 116. Big Thicket near Dan Griffin's
place, Hardin County, 1904. Courtesy National
Archives, 22-WB-41-7249

Texas Landscapes, 1889–1905

Fig. 117. Pine woods near
Saratoga, Hardin County, 1904.
Courtesy National Archives,
22-WB-41-7244

Fig. 118. Tarkington Prairie,
Liberty County, 1904. Courtesy
National Archives, 22-WB-41-7242

leafed pines and one large "island" southeast from town is covered with a fine growth of long-leafed pine. In the lower country north and west of town a short ways there is an abundance of the small scrub "palmetto" and a few yuccas. To the north of Sour Lake lies the "big brush," a heavy thicket and almost wilderness. The country is very thinly settled but the recent discoveries of oil nearby and the value of the lands as rice fields as soon as properly irrigated are rapidly bringing numbers of people here. At points both east and west from the station are lower lands, in places marshy.

# Twentieth-Century Changes in Texas Landscapes and Land Uses

When Bailey and his crew of field agents began their survey work in Texas in the 1880s, the habitats and wildlife resources of the state were already dramatically changed from the conditions that had existed during the early days of exploration and settlement. Although it is beyond the scope of this book, Del Weniger (1984 and 1997) has written an excellent account about what Texas was like, including the lands, water, and animals up to 1860, just prior to the period of the biological survey. Robin Doughty (1983) also has written about environmental change and land-use practices in Texas during the nineteenth and twentieth centuries.

Comparison of old photographs taken by the survey field agents with modern landscapes from the same areas serve to document local landscape change, and from this evidence it is obvious that the landscapes of many sites have changed dramatically today. Some of the major changes are discussed briefly in this chapter, contrasting the conditions described and photographed by the federal agents with the opinions of land users, biologists, and conservation professionals regarding current conditions.

People have a tendency to view the natural world as static because so many important natural changes are slow and not obvious in our personal experiences over several decades or at the spatial scales we normally experience. The truth is that change is a normal part of the environment, a factor to which the components of all natural communities are more or less adapted. Variation in daily and seasonal weather changes, short- and long-term shifts in species composition, and climatic changes occur in nearly all communities, and natural communities rapidly adapt to such oscillations. However, changes caused by humans are often different from those to which natural communities are adapted, causing drastic alteration of land use and landscape patterns, including their inherent abiotic and biotic elements.

Humans have been significantly altering their environment for thousands of years. Arid and semiarid regions, such as those that characterize most of Texas, have been among the most fragile and susceptible to human alteration. Human disturbance in Texas prior to European colonization was minimal (Doughty, 1983), but the rapid population increases and the spread of people across the state throughout the nineteenth and twentieth centuries (see Fig. 30, Chapter 4) greatly accelerated landscape changes. Population growth presents a formidable challenge to conservationists because fish and wildlife resources and people share near identical needs for two critical commodities—water and land. The following discussion considers some of the factors resulting from population growth that have changed the face of Texas landscapes.

### Overview of Major Changes

**Land Conversion and Development**

During the twentieth century, land cover in Texas was altered principally by human activity, including farming and agriculture, ranching and raising of livestock, logging of forests, suppression of natural fire, and construction associated with expanding urbanization. Urban development, including both urban sprawl and development of vacation homes, has had a huge impact on the landscape of Texas. The Texas population has expanded from 3 million people in 1900 to more than 20 million in 2000, almost a 300 percent increase in one century (Fig. 119). Most of this growth occurred around major cities where 80 percent of Texans now live. Among the locations in Texas where "urbanization" has greatly altered the landscape, the Dallas–Fort Worth complex, the Austin to San Antonio corridor, the greater Houston area, and the Juarez–El Paso area are

probably the most intensive, but almost every region of the state has been severely impacted by urban development (Fig. 120).

The process of land conversion changed both land use and land cover. Land-cover changes represent differences in the area occupied by vegetative cover types or habitats through time. Land-use activities may alter the relative abundance of natural habitats and result in the establishment of new land-cover types. The introduction of new cover types can increase the variety of species by providing a greater diversity of habitats. Natural habitats, however, are often reduced by land conversion, leaving less area available for native species. Species that are not native, the so-called alien species, may gain a foothold and out-compete the native species. Also, the spatial patterns of habitat may be altered, resulting in the fragmentation of once continuous habitat. Finally, land-use activities may change the natural pattern of environmental variation by causing changes in natural disturbance events. In general, the chances of losing native animal and plant species and disrupting ecological functions increase when the patterns of natural habitats and disturbance are altered.

With urbanization and population expansion also came the need for dams, water diversions, and roads to support people's needs and facilitate their movements. Most changes in aquatic systems in Texas can be traced to the construction of dams, either for water storage or flood control, and to other developments on or near waterways, such as diversion structures and drainage of wetlands. Dam building and water diversions have significantly degraded most major rivers and coastal waterways.

**Misuse of Water**

Of all the water resources in Texas, rivers are by far the most seriously threatened. Rivers link our land and water ecosystems. The Texas landscape has been continuously sculptured by

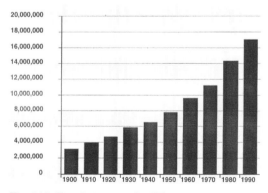

Fig. 119. Population growth of Texas, 1900–90.

Fig. 120. Urban development has greatly altered the landscapes of Texas during the last century.

the fifteen major river systems and more than eleven thousand named streams, very few of which are free-flowing today. All but four rivers eventually drain into one of the estuaries that form the Texas coast. Adequate stream flows and good water quality are essential to their health and the ecosystems they pass through. Every major river basin in Texas has been impounded and nearly six thousand small dams form a network of small reservoirs for livestock watering and soil stabilization. These impoundments have substantially altered our hardwood bottomland and riverine/streamside landscapes. Although there has been a reduction in flow in most springs and streams from perennial to intermittent, the total amount of water in the state is greater today because of the construction of thousands of tanks, large reservoirs, and man-made dams for irrigation, flood control, and water storage.

Texas originally had 281 major and historically significant springs, other than saline springs (Brune, 1975). These have been very important to Texas from the time of its first inhabitants. Many springs afforded stops on stagecoach routes, power for mills, water for medicinal treatment, municipal water supplies, and recreational parks. They also provided important habitat for many species of fish and wildlife. As many as sixty-three of the major springs have now completely failed and the water flow of many others has been severely reduced. A variety of factors caused the decline of spring flows. Clearing of forestland and heavy grazing of pastures in the late nineteenth and early twentieth centuries began to reduce recharge. The drilling of wells during this period greatly reduced the artesian pressure on springs. Heavy well pumping of underground water for irrigation, municipal, and industrial purposes during the twentieth century continued the decline and disappearance of our springs. Finally, the construction of surface reservoirs inundated some springs. In combination, these factors of surface impact, water diversion, groundwater depletion, and flow disruption have made, and are making, many springs endangered (Brune, 1975).

Natural flow regimes, which are a key element in maintaining Texas's diverse aquatic ecosystems, exhibit tremendous variability across Texas as a result of flash floods, seasonal periods of low flow, and extended periods of drought. Maintaining stable base flow is difficult because most water rights issued by the state do not contain provisions for instream flows and freshwater inflow maintenance. Today, most river basins in Texas are fully or over-appropriated and currently permitted diversions have the capacity to reduce stream flows significantly below levels necessary to maintain in-stream use.

Texas has seven major and three minor estuarine systems located along its Gulf coastline, and these are characterized by high biological productivity. Freshwater inflows are critical to the health of coastal estuaries. Most marine species are estuarine dependent during at least some portion of their life cycle, particularly the larval or juvenile stages. Water quality of freshwater inflows will become important as available freshwater inflows are likely to be more nutrient rich and subject to influences of non-point source pollution than at any time in the history of the state. As impervious cover increases in urban areas, the untreated runoff from streets and structures will eventually find its way to Texas's rivers and eventually to the state's estuarine environments.

**Suppression of Fire**

When Texas entered the Union, it was the largest prairie state, and fire was a major factor in shaping the landscape and land cover (Fig. 121). Today that is no longer true. Beginning in the nineteenth century and continuing throughout the twentieth century fire suppression has had a huge impact on the natural conditions throughout the state. The cessation of frequent natural surface fires in the late 1800s was because of reduced vegetation caused by intensive grazing by livestock. The initial suppression of natural surface fires by livestock grazing graded into the period of active fire suppression of all fires by land management agency personnel, shortly after the beginning of the twentieth century. Before fire suppression, Texas ecosystems were accustomed to frequent, low-severity wildfires that facilitated landscape and habitat diversity by providing opportunities for the establishment and maintenance of early successional species and communities. Under conditions of fire suppression, on the other hand, landscape complexity is made simpler, some early- and mid-successional plant communities are eliminated, shade-tolerant tree and shrub populations rapidly expand, and the importance of insects and pathogens is elevated. Without question, fire suppression over the past century has pervasively affected many Texas ecosystems.

**Invasion of Alien Plants**

Already by the turn of the twentieth century, alien plants had successfully invaded Texas landscapes. While working in the coastal prairies, Bailey and the agents photographed several landscapes in which McCartney's rose had been used to establish major hedgerows. But this was only the beginning, and by the end of the century, alien plants would be common all over the state.

Fig. 121. Natural fires were once common in Texas. During the twentieth century, fire suppression has negatively impacted many Texas ecosystems. Courtesy Carlton Britton, Texas Tech University

The salt cedar or tamarix (*Tamarix* spp.), in particular, has inflicted damage to our native landscapes and habitats. Tamarix was brought over from Eurasia and planted across the western United States by government agencies in the early 1900s for erosion control. It proved to be a vigorous invader of moist pastures, rangelands, and riparian habitats, having spread to almost every river, stream, creek, and wash in the arid southwest, infesting more than a million acres. It is of little forage value and provides no seed source for native species, and other than as nesting sites for some birds, it is not very valuable to wildlife. Even worse, this tree displaces native hardwoods and consumes tremendous amounts of water by filling riverbeds and sucking springs dry. Salt cedar has an extremely high rate of evapotranspiration. One plant alone may use two hundred gallons of water a day, more than the amount consumed by a

small family. Annual water losses often result in a substantial decline in water tables where it is abundant (Duncan et al., 1999), and the scaly leafed tree also adds large amounts of salt to the soil and river.

Since its introduction, salt cedar has proven to be very resilient and difficult to control, easily recovering from burning, efforts at mechanical control (root plowing, bulldozing, mowing, and shredding), and herbicide treatment. In 2000, government agencies launched a massive spraying effort, using the herbicide called Arsenal to control this water-hogging tree along the Pecos River in Texas. It will take years before the success of such an effort will be known.

One of the most striking examples of the rapid spread of salt cedar and its impact on local habitat change can be seen from photographs taken by the federal agents in the Big Bend region of the state. One of their photographs, taken at a working cattle ranch and farm near the mouth of Santa Elena Canyon, depicts open habitat and cottonwood trees along the river (see Fig. 75, Chapter 4). As this photograph shows, no salt cedar was present along the river. Today this region is covered with a dense stand of river cane and introduced salt cedar trees, with few native cottonwoods. Interestingly, river cane (*Phragmites* sp.) is also an alien grass and seems to have been well established in West Texas before the time of the biological survey.

A situation similar to that of salt cedar in the western part of the state exists along the upper Texas coast where the Chinese tallow tree (*Sapium sebiferum*) from Asia has proliferated substantially during the twentieth century. Chinese tallow is a deciduous woody tree, introduced into the United States some time between 1900 and 1910, that has now become established along the Atlantic and Gulf Coasts in floodplain forests, freshwater wetland basins, coastal prairie, abandoned rice fields, mixed bottomland hardwood forests, as well as disturbed sites (Conway et al., 1999). Its initial introduction into Texas, in and around Houston, was based on the economic potential of its seed oil, but it quickly expanded its distribution and now covers much of the coastal prairie from the Louisiana border to the semi-arid regions of South Texas near Kingsville. The invasion of Chinese tallow into coastal Texas has changed much of the region from coastal prairie to monotypic tallow woodlands, displacing native plant and wildlife species (Conway et al., 1999). This rapid-growing tree creates a sterile environment of dense thickets that have little or no value to wildlife. Conservationists battle Chinese tallow with herbicides, selective burning, and digging up seedlings, but none of these remedies is totally suitable for comprehensive control (Conway et al., 1999).

## Loss of Wetlands

Wetlands, hardwood bottomlands, and riparian areas have been impacted by land conversion and land use throughout Texas. Although wetlands comprise less than 5 percent of the state's total area, Texas has suffered significant losses of wetlands in the twentieth century (Tiner, 1984). Texas has two major types of wetlands: coastal wetlands, including marshes and estuaries; and inland terrestrial wetlands, including bottomland hardwoods, forests, shrubswamps, marshes and lakes in eastern Texas; springs and riparian vegetation in central Texas; playa lakes, saline lakes, and riparian habitats in western Texas; and ponds, potholes, and resacas in southern Texas. These interior wetlands account for 80 percent of the total wetland acreage in the state. It has been estimated that Texas has lost one-half of its coastal wetlands and 60 percent of its terrestrial wetlands in the past two hundred years (*Texas Environmental Almanac*, 2000). This trend continues today as much of the remaining acreage is being seriously degraded by saltwater intrusion because of construction of canals, channels, and drainage ditches; by land subsidence and groundwater depletion; by inadequate freshwater inflows because of upstream water projects (dams) and the alteration of natural hydrology; and by pollution from industry, shipping, and urbanization (Texas Parks and Wildlife Department, 1988). The wetlands associated with the playa lakes and prairie potholes of the High Plains and Panhandle have suffered from the dramatic lowering of the Ogallala aquifer and increased sedimentation as irrigated agriculture expanded in this region (Luo et al., 1997).

Forested wetlands in Texas are found primarily in the bottomland hardwoods of East Texas. Since the beginning of the twentieth century, Texas has lost up to 63 percent of its original bottomland forests due to reservoir development, timber clearing, and attendant land use changes (*Texas Environmental Almanac*, 2000). Large-scale loss and degradation of riparian landscapes throughout the state have resulted from the construction of impoundments; overgrazing by livestock, which has destabilized vegetation and resulted in arroyo cutting and gullying of the landscape; and the introduction of alien plants such as salt cedar and Russian olive. Old growth forests in the Big Thicket are believed to have declined between 85 and 98 percent just since 1960 (White et al., 1998).

### Encroachment of Brush

Since the turn of the twentieth century, brush and cacti have continued to cover many areas of the state that were formerly prairie or grassland. The spread of species such as mesquite, cedar, scrub oak, and prickly pear can be attributed primarily to overgrazing and the suppression of wildfires that had formerly so often swept the western plains (Lehman, 1969).

The two most obvious culprits in terms of the increase in woody plants are the spread of mesquite and juniper. Most early twentieth-century historical accounts published on mesquite in the southwestern United States contended that mesquite had spread into South Texas from Mexico (*Life* Magazine, 1952) and then into the southern plains (Bray 1906; Malin, 1953). However, early and mid-nineteenth-century sight descriptions of the South Texas Plains and the Rolling Plains indicated that large mesquite trees formed open groves on many different range sites, especially in low areas, along intermittent streams, and in river bottoms (Rappole et al., 1986; Maxwell, 1979a). Mesquite was definitely in many places in southern and western Texas, but the density and geographic extent were markedly less than in the mid twentieth century. The extent of mesquite increased by 1.3 million acres between 1948 and 1963, with a total of more than 56.7 million acres occupied by 1963 (Smith and Rechenthin, 1964).

The precise sites of juniper growth in the nineteenth century were difficult to determine. S. E. Wolff (1948) described the original red-berry juniper range site in western Texas as the fringes of mesas and bluffs. Dalton Ellis and Joseph Schuster (1968) studied dispersal of red-berry juniper on a butte in Garza County, Texas. In the mid nineteenth century, juniper were largely confined to the upper and mid-slopes on the north face. Significant lower slope spread did not begin until around 1876, with the greatest increase after 1900. Juniper was reported on approximately 19 million acres in Texas in 1948 (Wolff, 1948) and had increased to more than 21 million acres by 1963 (Smith and Rechenthin, 1964). The 1948 juniper coverage was considered to be four times greater than that occupied in 1848 (Wolff, 1948).

David Harris (1966) reviewed the possible causes for the increase in domination by woody plants. He concluded that two factors—suppression of grassland fires and the introduction of domestic livestock—were primarily responsible for initiating the "invasion" of mesquite on grass-dominated sites. Livestock production on ranches in western Texas was apparently heavy during the mid to late nineteenth century and later. Jennifer and Timothy Frey have demonstrated that railroads were a mechanism for the expanded distribution of mesquite through rapid and extensive movement of livestock in the late nineteenth and early twentieth centuries (Frey and Frey, 2000). Harris (1966) believed that suppression of fire was primarily responsible for initiating the invasion of juniper.

### Livestock Grazing

Widespread grazing of domestic livestock caused major cumulative effects on the ecology of Texas (Fig. 122). The extremely high historical stocking rates and concomitant over-

Fig. 122. Widespread grazing by domestic livestock has had a major impact on land cover in Texas. Courtesy The Southwest Collection, Texas Tech University

grazing led to significant alterations in the species composition of vegetation across the state. Cool-season grasses and other preferred forage species declined, while unpalatable weedy species, shrubs, and non-indigenous plants increased. The year-round, high-intensity grazing of open ranges that occurred in the past also led to marked reductions in herbaceous plant and litter cover. Overgrazing was also a major contributor to soil erosion, flooding, and arroyo cutting. Livestock grazing, together with fire suppression, both interacting with fluctuations in climate cycles, has had a major impact on land cover in Texas.

Range deterioration continued through the drought of the Dust Bowl era in the 1930s but has improved since. New understandings about how to manage rangelands have been discovered by range scientists, and land managers have developed a better understanding of stocking rates and rotational grazing systems. Although there are still many areas of the state in need of brush management and removal, the current status of our rangelands does indicate that range can be improved with good management and favorable climatic conditions (Box, 1990).

## Land Fragmentation

Habitat fragmentation is rapidly becoming the most serious threat to landscape integrity in Texas today (Fig. 123). Habitat fragmentation is a process by which stands of native vegetation become smaller and discontinuous because of the clearing of land for various purposes, such as agricultural, residential, or commercial use (Hobbs et al., 1993). The effects of habitat fragmentation on animals, plants,

Fig. 123. Agricultural and urban development have severely fragmented and reduced in size the remaining stands of natural habitat in Texas. Courtesy Michael Tewes

and their habitats are numerous, and the biological diversity of native species is almost always reduced. The effects vary depending on the size and shape of the remnant and the different abilities of species to move across land between remnants (Saunders et al., 1991). In general, the smaller the fragment, the higher the probability of extinction because of loss of genetic diversity, catastrophes, or an imbalance in relations of competing species, predators, and their prey (Soule et al., 1988; Soule and Mills, 1998).

As cities spread and urban dwellers seek land ownership outside the confines of city limits, land holdings exhibit accelerating fragmentation and those species which rely on large continuous tracts begin to decline. The land area of Texas is approximately 167 million acres, of which 144 million acres is considered rural "open-space." Thus, about 86 percent of the state's land area is rural land (Wilkins et al., 2000). Traditional land uses on these lands are primarily agricultural and timber production. It has been estimated that Texas has 133 million acres of wildlife habitat remaining (Texas Audubon Society, 1997).

A little-appreciated but important factor contributing to fragmentation has been the rapid change in land-tenure systems, especially during the latter half of the twentieth century (Sansom, 1995). Many parts of Texas are experiencing reductions in land ownership sizes. Landowner numbers are increasing while property size is decreasing (Map 25). This trend is largely because of a reduction in owner-operated farms and ranches; the rural property demands of a rapidly increasing urban population; and transfer of estates to a new generation of landowners.

# Number of Rural Land Owners

(% change 1987 - 1997)

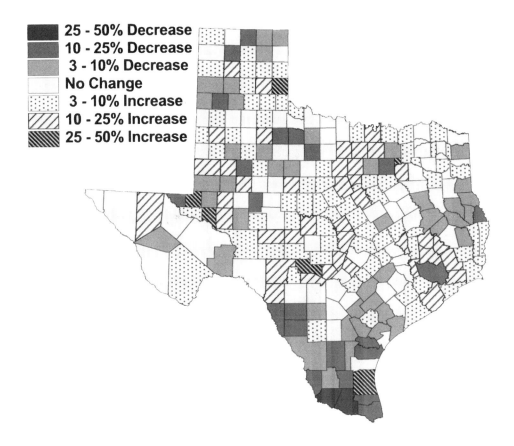

Map 25. Percent change in number of rural landowners, 1987–1997. A decline in the number of landowners indicates consolidation, whereas an increase in the number of landowners indicates fragmentation.

Discounting forestlands, Texas had approximately 181,000 farm ownerships in 1992 (National Agricultural Statistics Service, 1999). In the succeeding five years, that number increased by 7 percent to 194,000 farms, while average ownership size decreased from 725 to 676 acres. As a result, many rural areas, especially those near urban centers, are going through rapid transition in land ownership and use. Texas now leads all states in the loss of rural farming and ranching lands (Wilkins et al.,

2000). The annual rate of conversion from 1992 to 1997 nearly doubled from the previous ten years.

## Regional Landscape Change

The timing and sequence of land-use changes in Texas have varied among regions. Among the most altered places are the prairies and wetlands, the riparian and riverine ecosystems, and the rangelands of the Edwards Plateau,

Rolling Plains, the South Texas Plains, and the Texas Panhandle (Sansom, 1995), but no place in the state has remained immune from human impact.

**Borderlands**

One region of the state warrants special attention insofar as wildlife habitats and wildlife diversity are concerned. This is the borderland region between Texas and Mexico, which stretches for 1,250 river miles along the Rio Grande from the Gulf to El Paso (Gehlbach, 1981). Bailey and the federal agents worked at several places along the Texas-Mexico border, but it was Edgar Mearns, the naturalist and surgeon on the second U.S.-Mexico boundary survey, who wrote a detailed account of the mammals of the region in 1907.

More recently, Fred Gehlbach (1981) and Peter Steinhart (1994) have published modern accounts of the natural history of the borderlands, including its many unique species and habitats and the human impacts in the region. Earlier in the century, over-grazing, compounded by short-term climatic cycles, exacerbated man-made vegetative changes, but more recently, irrigation, industrial development, and an increase in urban populations have put a different face on the human presence in the Borderlands.

According to the non-profit watchdog group American Rivers, the Rio Grande ranks as the nation's seventh most endangered river. Massive water diversions and proposed flood control projects have substantially changed the river's character. Diversions from municipal and agricultural use already claim nearly 95 percent of the Rio Grande's average annual flow to such an extent that long stretches of the river are now dry (American Rivers, 2000). Channelization and flood control measures have altered the river channel and its banks, and reservoir construction and inundation have flooded hundreds of acres of riparian and canyon habitats.

Pollution problems along the entire length of the Rio Grande include hazardous waste dumps, municipal and industrial effluent, irrigation return flows, and municipal runoff.

The upper Rio Grande essentially stops at El Paso, where the river is entirely diverted from its channel for human use. Where the river is dry, sediments and vegetation have clogged the channel. The river does not begin to flow again until approximately 250 miles downstream at the confluence with the Rio Conchos near Presidio. The Conchos supplies the Rio Grande with two-thirds of its flow below that point, although Granero Dam on the Rio Conchos in Chihuahua, Mexico, greatly restricts water flow into the Rio Grande at certain times of the year.

The Rio Grande corridor provides essential wildlife habitat to numerous species as it traverses the Chihuahuan Desert region. Many wildlife species depend on surface water to survive. In addition, flowing water and associated riparian habitats act as vital dispersal corridors for many species and, conversely, as effective distributional barriers for other species. Species abundance and composition have been altered as some species have undergone local extinctions, other species have changed their distributional limits, and new species have invaded the region. Clyde Jones and I summarized the twentieth-century changes in mammals and mammalian habitats along the Rio Grande/Río Bravo from Fort Quitman to Amistad reservoir (Schmidly and Jones, 2000).

The southern part of Texas along the Rio Grande, known as the Tamaulipan Brushland or Lower Rio Grande Valley, has been especially altered since the time of the biological survey. Dense brush in this unique ecosystem provides food, nest sites, and cover for many wildlife species, including a large number of neotropical origin. The most important human-caused components of environmental change have been water diversion and flood control, brushland clearing, human population increases, contaminants, and continued dredging of the Intracoastal Waterway in Laguna Madre (Rappole et al., 1986; Chapman et al., 1998). Particularly significant have been the conversion of native brushland and riparian woodlands to agricultural uses and the subsequent large-scale fragmentation of remaining native habitats. Since the 1920s, more than 95 percent of the original native brushland has been converted to agricultural or urban use, and more than 90 percent of the riparian habitat along the Rio Grande has been cleared. Brush clearing, pesticide use, and irrigation practices associated with agriculture have been intensive (Jahrsdoerfer and Leslie, 1988). Water development, both for flood control and municipal use, has resulted in extensive clearing of brush, alteration of riparian habitats, and changes in water flow in the Rio Grande. Population increases and associated urban expansion have resulted in brush clearing and increased pollution. Industrialization has degraded water quality. Brushland habitats have been converted to rangeland with herbicides, mechanical clearing, and fire.

The natural habitats of the Lower Rio Grande Valley virtually disappeared in the twentieth century. The Lower Rio Grande Valley was a densely vegetated, sometimes marshy, woodland—a wet oasis in the middle of a long dry stretch of scrub country. Good riparian and gallery woodlands extended upriver—in fact, where conditions allowed, all the way into the deep canyon country of the Big Bend. Much of the delta was a diverse mix of grasslands, brushlands, marshy habitats, and riparian woodlands and gallery forests. By 1937, the extent of the sabal palm forest was confined to a limited area near the Rio Grande in and around Brownsville (Leonard et al., 1991). Since 1937, clearing for agriculture destroyed most of the palms except for the grove on the Rabb Ranch which was purchased by the Audubon Society in

1975 and for the Southmost Ranch Tract purchased by the Nature Conservancy of Texas in 1999. These are the last remnants of the relatively extensive riparian woodland forest. The resaca environment has been declining also, largely because of drainage for irrigated agriculture.

Conserving and managing wildlife in the borderlands region requires close collaboration and coordination with Mexico. While the picture is often grim, conservation efforts on both sides of the border are gaining momentum as preserves are developed and damaged habitat reclaimed. In the United States, private and federal agencies such as the Nature Conservancy and the U.S. Fish and Wildlife Service are working to acquire land and nurture the recovery of endangered species.

### Texas Gulf Coast

Of all the areas in Texas, the historical coastal prairie, which extends from Mexico all the way to the Louisiana border, has seen the greatest industrial development since World War II. The prominent features of this region include: the prairies, which in many places include small depressional wetlands but which are now largely fragmented by agricultural and urban development; coastal marshes, which are mostly tidal but also include both isolated and transitional fresh and intermediate marshes; bays and lagunas, which support extensive seagrass beds, tidal flats, and reef complexes; barrier islands; and forested riparian corridors, mottes, and dense brushy habitat.

The coastal area of Texas is home to some 4.6 million people (plus a good number of "winter Texans") and this number continues to grow. Houston is the nation's fourth largest city and Harris County is the nation's second most populated county. The world's second largest petrochemical complex and some of the nation's busiest port facilities are also located along the coast. Conspicuous human-induced impacts are therefore numerous. Urbanization and other industrial developments have eliminated habitats; water and air pollution are significant problems; natural fire has been all but eliminated; and agriculture has altered most of the native prairies, substantial acreage of marsh, and much of the forested and brush habitats. The growing population has often over-utilized its water supply and over-harvested its fishery. Hydrological modifications are substantial. Reservoir construction has robbed the rivers of their sediments, and jetties and navigation channels have disrupted long-shore transport, exacerbating erosion and subsidence problems. Freshwater inflows have been reduced and the Gulf Intracoastal Waterway and other dredging, irrigation, and flood control projects have had a huge influence on historical water circulation patterns. Wildlife habitat in this region has been greatly impacted by the loss of wetlands, land subsidence, degradation of coastal grasslands, and habitat fragmentation associated with urban and suburban expansion.

Although highly impacted, the coastal system remains quite productive for a wide variety of fish and wildlife species. The near coastal forests are critically important for the nation's songbird resource as the vast majority of these species utilize this habitat during their trans-Gulf/circum-Gulf migrations. The forested habitats in the region are world famous for the spring "fallouts" when twenty or more species might be seen in a single tree at one time. A number of rare species of animals and plants occur across the variety of habitats along the Texas coast. All the critically endangered Attwater's prairie chickens and almost all the wintering whooping cranes are completely dependent on coastal habitats in Texas. The native brush habitats of the lower coast make up the northeast range of the ocelot. Recovery of all these species is highly (and in some cases entirely) dependent on habitat conservation and restoration activities in the region.

## The Hill Country

The eastern edge of the Edwards Plateau or the Hill Country in the vicinity of Austin and San Antonio, because of the incredible human population growth, is an area where major conservation problems have developed as a result of human impacts during the twentieth century. Throughout the twentieth century, ashe juniper has increased its distribution across the Edwards Plateau because of a reduction in wildfires across the region. Increasing demands for water by metropolitan areas in the Balcones Fault Zone and by agricultural and industrial enterprises have caused water flow to be reduced in many springs and rivers, and it has severely depleted the Edwards Aquifer. Several species of animals and plants have suffered from a loss of forest and riparian habitats, degradation of karst (cavernous) habitats, and water quality impacts.

The Hill Country has also been subjected to severe land and habitat fragmentation. Only tiny remnants of the native landscape survive today, and the average tract size in many counties has dropped in this generation alone from thousands of acres to fewer than two hundred. These areas, which once provided large blocks of land for wildlife habitat and outdoor recreation, now consist of tiny plots of introduced vegetation that cannot sustain the native wildlife.

## The Chihuahuan Desert and the Trans-Pecos

Human impact has been expanding in the Chihuahuan Desert region of West Texas. Grazing pressure was severe in this region during the time Bailey and the agents worked there and this initiated a desertification process that continues today. The region includes a mixture of semidesert grasslands, intermixed with desert shrubs and surrounding island mountains of pine-oak-juniper woodlands. Even though livestock numbers in these areas have stabilized well below historical levels, these are marginal grazing habitats, and the combination of reduced fire frequency and continued topsoil erosion has sustained a land-cover decline in which much of the remaining grassland is being converted to desert shrubland (Bogan, 1998). Semidesert grasslands in good condition in western Texas are rare today. Rollin Baker (1988) predicted the following environmental changes for the Chihuahuan Desert region as a whole: reduction in surface and ground water; alteration of riparian habitats; arid lands in ever-larger sectors irrigated for crop production; natural forage subjected to grazing by larger numbers of domestic livestock; stands of desert scrub expanded at the expense of already limited grassland habitat; islets of coniferous and hardwood timber at the summits of desert mountains subjected to lumbering; and introduction of noxious plants and animals.

Sadly, air pollution has begun to impact the deserts and mountains of the Trans-Pecos. A large coal-burning power plant in Mexico, known as Carbon II, is located 125 miles southeast of Big Bend National Park. At peak periods of operation, and under certain climatic conditions, the smoke generated by this plant has degraded visibility by up to 60 percent in Big Bend National Park and the effects also have been noticed at McDonald Observatory in the Davis Mountains (Bartlett, 1995). There is some concern that this air pollution could also impact rainfall patterns in the region. Daniel Rosenfeld (2000), an atmospheric scientist at Hebrew University of Jerusalem, has published research that demonstrates that air pollution can spread hundreds of miles downwind of a large industry's plume of pollution and can alter clouds and natural precipitation. Even remote, protected national parks are no longer immune to the impacts of modern society.

## The Great Plains Region (High Plains and Rolling Plains)

Since the High Plains was settled late in the nineteenth century, virtually all lands have been disturbed by cultivation or overgrazing. Changes in the native vegetation have been substantial. Even the playa lakes have been impacted with the advent of extensive irrigation that has lowered the water table and removed most of the natural springs which once existed in the region. Bailey was absolutely correct in predicting that the High Plains would, with irrigation, become a major agricultural area. Today, more than one-third of the total crop production in Texas, and more than one-third of the cotton raised in the state, occurs in this region. Almost 80 percent of the region now consists of agricultural fields, a stark contrast from the days of the biological survey when there were very few farms or towns in this area.

There are approximately thirty thousand playa wetlands in the southern High Plains region (Osterkamp and Wood, 1987). A playa is a relatively small wetland with a closed watershed (Luo et al., 1997). These wetlands provide critical ecological and societal benefits for the region, serving as recharge sites for the underlying Ogallala aquifer, water storage during flood events, irrigation water for crops, and water for livestock as well as vital wildlife habitat. During the twentieth century almost all the land area surrounding the playas was either cultivated or subjected to grazing by livestock. Consequently, they have lost volume through sediment deposition and unless the problems of soil erosion are reversed it has been estimated that sediments could fill all cropland playas in another ninety-five years (Luo et al., 1997).

In the latter two decades of the century, a portion of the region has been converted from agriculture back to productive grassland habitat, primarily through the Conservation Reserve Program (CRP). This initiative deserves special mention as it represents an example of a government program that has been good for private landowners and, in turn, has produced positive environmental benefits.

The CRP was established by the U.S. Department of Agriculture in 1985 as a land reclamation program. The primary objective is to conserve and improve soil and water resources by taking highly erodible land out of crop production and establishing suitable vegetative cover in its place (Food Security Act of 1985). Throughout the southern High Plains, under the supervision of the Soil Conservation Service, landowners have established grasslands, either of native or introduced grasses, on previous cropland. One year after planting, these sites are either sprayed with an herbicide or mowed to facilitate establishment of grasses. After establishment, no other maintenance is required, no grazing by domestic livestock or harvesting of vegetation is allowed, and the site must remain in the CRP for at least ten years. Dianne Hall and Michael Willig (1994) have conducted field studies demonstrating that habitat created by the establishment of CRP results in an increase of species diversity in small mammals.

The Rolling Plains have also suffered from the over-pumping of the Ogallala Aquifer that has reduced flows in the Canadian River. Exotic tree species have impacted native riparian habitat, and there has been a loss of grassland habitat as a result of agricultural practices. The elimination of fire and impact of over-grazing has resulted in the growth and spread of brush (cedar, mesquite, scrub oak, and prickly pear) across the entire region, and this has severely impacted the native prairies and watersheds.

### The Cross Timbers

As its name depicts, and as Bailey's description implies, the Cross Timbers is a rolling to hilly region where prairies and timber intermingle. About 75 percent of the land area is today used as range and pasture, having been altered by plowing and overgrazing. Past mismanagement and cultivation have caused the uplands in this vegetative region to be invaded by shrubby vegetation along with weedy annual and perennial grasses. Grazing, farming, and other disturbances have altered the grassland vegetation so that little remains of the original Cross Timbers prairie (Bolen, 1998). There are many impoundments on the rivers that traverse this region, and this has resulted in a loss of riparian habitat.

Richard Francaviglia (2000) has published an extensive account of the natural and cultural history of the Cross Timbers. Before modern settlement, early explorers characterized the region as a "forest of cast iron" in reference to its nearly impenetrable forest of stunted oak trees. Since then large cities have grown up on the eastern boundary of the region in Dallas, Fort Worth, Arlington, and Waco, and the population pressure and associated development increased steadily throughout the twentieth century. Variations in the Cross Timbers vegetation are the result of both natural and cultural conditions—with people being significant agents who have wielded fire, axes, plows, and bulldozers in transforming the vegetation at both local and regional levels. The Cross Timbers have survived into the twenty-first century as discontinuous patches of forests—from copses or mottes of but a few trees to sections of hundreds of acres or more. These exist in an extremely complex pattern as they are interspersed with farms, pastures, and urban developments.

### The Blacklands

The Blackland Prairie has elements of both the tall-grass and coastal prairies and some unique elements of its own. However, because of precipitation and soil moisture retention characteristics, the prairie takes on a lowland grassland appearance even on well-drained upland. About 98 percent of the Blackland Prairie was cultivated to produce cotton, sorghum, corn, wheat, and forages during the latter part of the nineteenth century and the first part of the twentieth century. Since the 1950s, pasture and forage crops for livestock production have increased, and now only about 50 percent of the area is used as cropland. About 25 percent of the area is tame pasture and the remaining area is used as rangeland. As a result of cultivation, overgrazing, and other imprudent land-use practices, there are few if any remnants of climax vegetation in the region. Small remnants of native vegetation remain for grazing or for native hay production (Sharpless and Yelderman, 1993). The majority of the remaining prairielands are in Lamar County or northeastern Texas. Another center of remnant prairies is located around Temple and Waco in Bell and McLennan counties. Virtually nothing remains in the southwestern region of the Blacklands between the Colorado and San Antonio Rivers in the vicinity of Austin and San Antonio.

The Blacklands originally had numerous wooded belts along the streams that traversed the region. Settlements spread rapidly as farmers discovered the productive possibilities of the black prairie soils. Early immigrants from Germany and Czechoslovakia settled entire communities and made the Blacklands the foremost cotton-producing region of the state. So valuable was the land for farming that the row crops were usually planted to the immediate roadsides, and only the most necessary fences were built. Wooded and brush-covered bottomlands were cleared to the stream banks. The agricultural activity of this region was largely responsible for the growth of some of Texas's largest cities, including Dallas, Fort Worth, Waco, Temple, Austin, and San Antonio. Most of the Blackland region no longer provides suitable habitat for a diversity of wildlife.

## The Post Oak Belt

This region is best described as an ecotone between the eastern deciduous forest and the tall-grass prairie. The area supports a stunted, open forest dotted with small tall-grass prairies. There is a distinctive lowland forest habitat in the Post Oak region that is limited to the floodplains of the major streams. Heavy human use has severely impacted the entire region. The land is used primarily for farming and ranching. Much of the region is still in native or improved pastures, although small farms are common. Improved pastures are commonly seeded to bermudagrass, dallisgrass, vaseygrass, carpetgrass, and clovers. About 50 percent of the total area has been cleared, and about one-half of the cleared areas are planted with crops. Clearing of the wooded areas creates extensive edges that are further emphasized by the practice of clearing fairly small, irregular areas.

The phenomenon of land fragmentation is well demonstrated by changes in the Post Oak belt. Fragmentation of lands north and west of the Houston metropolitan area has resulted in long-term declines in the wildlife resources of the region.

## The Pineywoods

The Pineywoods have been severely impacted by human activity during the twentieth century. Early in the century, the largest oilfields in the state were located here. But lumbering was the main form of land use. Practically all the virgin pine timberland has been cut over and is now producing a second or third crop of timber. Over-cutting was widespread over much of the region as was the uncontrolled burning of pine woodlands. Small farming enterprises are scattered throughout the region, although most of the farms are comparatively small. For much of the twentieth century, hog farming was very popular in this region. Over-stocking, particularly with hogs, has been detrimental to range and forest management in the region. In many places, hogs became free ranging and severely damaged longleaf pine seedlings. Many of the streams and rivers have been dammed which has flooded much of the hardwood bottomland habitat. Joe Truett and Dan Lay (1984) have written a thorough and dramatic account of the natural history of the East Texas Pineywoods.

The status of longleaf pine forests in the southeastern United States, including East Texas, is a matter of serious concern to ecologists and conservationists. Once widespread, with an estimated 60–70 million acres present, longleaf pine communities today cover no more than 4 million acres. The demise of the longleaf communities can be attributed to overharvesting for wood products, problems associated with thousands of free-ranging hogs which annually uproot tens of thousands of seedlings, and fire suppression which allows for the invasion of oak forests (Bolen, 1998).

**The Barrier Islands**

More than two-thirds of the 365 miles of Texas Gulf shoreline is composed of six major barrier islands, including from north to south, Galveston, Matagorda, San Jose, Mustang, Padre, and South Padre Islands. The islands can be divided into three geographic groups based on the physical characteristics of the coastline. The first group includes only Galveston Island which is separated from the next island group by approximately 90 miles. The second group, or the Matagorda complex, includes Matagorda and San Jose Islands, which are occasionally joined at very low tide. These are separated from the third group by Aransas Pass, one of the most durable passes along the Texas coast. The third group, or the Padre complex, includes Mustang, Padre, and South Padre Islands. Padre and South Padres Islands were one island until 1957 when Mansfield Channel was dredged, and Mustang Is-

land has enjoyed frequent connections with Padre Island during its history. The three island groups each border the mainland adjacent to a different biotic province (Dice, 1943; Blair, 1950). Galveston Island is adjacent to the Austroriparian province; the Matagorda complex is adjacent to the Texan province; and the Padre complex is adjacent to the Tamaulipan province.

From the Gulf to the bay side, the habitat types on each barrier island grade from open, sandy beach to the dune ridge, then to coastal prairie dotted with freshwater to brackish ponds and marshes, and finally to salt marsh. The plant species within these habitats are similar from island to island, which is not surprising because the plants must be adapted to a lack of freshwater and have a tolerance of highly saline conditions.

The islands vary considerably in the extent of human impact. Galveston Island has the longest history of human impact, with the first permanent settlement founded in 1839. In contrast, Matagorda and San Jose Islands have received very little recent human impact, with only a handful of permanent residents located on Matagorda Island. San Jose Island is under private ownership and is managed as pastureland. Mustang Island has a small port, Port Aransas, founded in the 1850s. The remainder of the island is used mostly as pasture, with intervening housing developments, although not to the extent on Galveston Island. Most of Padre Island is protected as Padre Island National Seashore, with a small amount of human habitation at the northern end of the island. South Padre Island has a high level of tourist development at its southern end. This island had no protected land until the spring of 2000, when the Nature Conservancy of Texas purchased 24,500 acres.

Hice and Schmidly (1999, 2000) have provided detailed accounts of the mammals of coastal Texas, including a comparison between mainland and barrier island faunas. Their data show that the barrier islands of Texas have a depauperate mammalian fauna when compared to the fauna of the Texas coast. A number of factors have influenced this, including hurricane events, size of the island, mainland species pool for the island to draw on, and the degree of isolation of the island from the mainland.

# Twentieth-Century Changes in Texas Mammal Fauna

As the natural habitats of Texas were being obliterated or altered by the farming, ranching, and timbering practices of its ever-growing population during the twentieth century, the wildlife resources of the state suffered greatly. This chapter chronicles the changes in the Texas mammal fauna after the period of the biological survey up to the end of the century. Also included is a brief description about the development of the science of mammalogy in the state.

On a macroscale the diversity of mammals changed substantially during the twentieth century. There has been a substantial turnover in species composition, involving both a loss and gain in species since 1900. A significant number of mammals are now extinct and a growing number of species are regarded as endangered and threatened. Almost 35 percent of the mammal species (50 out of 144 species) either have become extinct or had subspecies or metapopulations become extinct, or they are rare and appear to face some sort of problem that potentially threatens their existence. In actuality the number of species in this situation may be much higher than this estimate would suggest. This is because we have not been able to do enough monitoring of populations to obtain usable information on population trends for most species of mammals.

Among the most significant trends during the century, the following are particularly important and worthy of discussion:

- Proliferation of extinctions
- Declines in geographic distribution and population abundance
- Range expansions and regional faunal changes
- Documentation of additional faunal elements and discovery of cryptic species
- Growth in the number of threatened, endangered, and rare species
- Introductions of nonindigenous species

## Proliferation of Extinctions

Species extinctions increased dramatically during the twentieth century. When Bailey published his work in 1905, the only extirpated mammals were bison (*Bos bison*) and elk (*Cervus elaphus merriami*), although other species, such as the beaver (*Castor canadensis*), black bear (*Ursus americanus*), spotted cats (ocelot, *Leopardus pardalis;* jaguarundi, *Herpailurus yagouaroundi;* and jaguar, *Panthera* onca), pronghorn (*Antilocapra americana*), and bighorn sheep (*Ovis canadensis*), were markedly reduced in distribution or in numbers. During the course of the twentieth century, the grizzly bear (*Ursus arctos*), gray wolf (*Canis lupus*), red wolf (*Canis rufus*), black-footed ferret (*Mustela nigripes*), jaguar, margay (*Leopardus wiedii*), and the bighorn sheep all joined the list of extirpated species. Populations of at least three of these extinct species have been reintroduced, although the subspecies introduced are not the ones that were native to the state.

The nine species that became extinct were all large, herbivorous or predatory species. This same pattern has been observed time and time again throughout the globe—large-bodied, wide-ranging species with complex social systems are highly vulnerable to extinction. A variety of factors can cause extinction, but in the case of these species, exploitation and habitat alteration by humans probably had more to do with their disappearance than any other single factor. Over-hunting definitely seems to have caused the disappearance of the grizzly, elk, and bison. Predator control activities probably had much to do with the extirpation of the gray wolf and the jaguar.

The tremendous herds of bison that were so conspicuous a feature of the plains and prairies in the mid 1800s were eliminated intentionally by the Anglo settlers. For all practical purposes they were gone before Bailey and the federal agents roamed the state. When protection of the bison was under consideration by the Texas Legislature after the Civil War, Gen. Phil Sheridan opposed it. He won his point by convincing the legislators that the sooner the bison were eliminated, the sooner the Native Americans who depended on them for food and clothing would be starved into submission. Sure enough, before 1900 the bison passed into oblivion and the remaining Native Americans were relocated. The big slaughter of bison took

place in the 1870s (Fig. 124). From Fort Griffin (Shackelford County) in the winter of 1877–78 more than 1,500 outfits killed in excess of 100,000 animals in the months of December and January alone (Davis, 1961). Hundreds of thousands of carcasses were strewn over the landscape. The last verified report of wild bison was from the northwestern part of the Panhandle (Dallam County) in 1889 (Jones, J. K. Jr. et al., 1988).

Though no longer wide-ranging, bison herds prevail on many national and state sanctuaries in the west. In Texas, bison are kept in captivity on many farms and ranches, and a herd of thirty-five head was established in 1997 on a three hundred-acre enclosure located at Caprock Canyons State Park in the Panhandle. The long-range goal at Caprock Canyons State Park is to purchase additional land and establish a true free-ranging herd of bison in their historical area of greatest abundance in the state.

The situation with wolves and coyotes (genus *Canis*) is especially interesting. At the end of the nineteenth century, gray wolves (*C. lupus*) occupied the western part and red wolves (*C. rufus*) (Fig. 125) the central and eastern parts of the state. Coyotes (*C. latrans*) occurred statewide but they were less abundant than today. With the onset of massive land clearing, coyotes increased in numbers and began to hybridize with red wolves. Wolves began to decline statewide. By the 1940s gray wolves had been all but eliminated in Texas, and when red wolf numbers began to decline as a result of predator control activities, coyotes moved in from the west to fill the vacant predatory niche. The two canines, being closely related and genetically similar, began to interbreed, and the remnant red wolf populations gradually declined. The last pure group of the Texas subspecies (*C. r. rufus*), found along the Gulf Coast south of Houston, seems to have been genetically swamped by 1970 (Paradiso, 1965, 1968; Paradiso and Nowak, 1972). The Central

Fig. 124. A pile of more than 40,000 bison hides awaiting shipment from Dodge City, Kansas, 1874. Bison, once numerous over the plains and prairies of Texas, were eliminated by 1889. Courtesy Kansas State Historical Society

Fig. 125. Texas red wolf (at the National Zoo), 1939. Courtesy National Archives, 22-WB-73-B57021

Texas subspecies (C. r. gregori) survived for a few more years in extreme southeast Texas and southern Louisiana but it subsequently disappeared in the wild (McCarley and Carley, 1979). A few dozen individuals were brought into captivity before the complete spread of the hybridization process, however, and only these captive individuals and their progeny have kept the subspecies gregori off the extinct list. Using the progeny of this captive stock, translocations back into native range began in 1987, when wolves raised in captivity were released on Alligator River National Wildlife Refuge in northeastern North Carolina. The current free-ranging wolf population consists of approximately eighty wolves roaming over approximately one million acres, and there are plans to establish two other populations, but Texas is not included among the list of southwestern states scheduled to receive reintroduced red wolves. One of the key issues that will determine the success of these introductions will be the success of efforts to eliminate hybridization with coyotes which caused much of the decline of red wolves in the first place.

Associated with the vast herds of bison that once roamed the plains of western Texas were considerable numbers of gray or lobo wolves which preyed on them. This predator-prey relationship between wolves and bison had existed more or less in balance for eons until the arrival of the white man who destroyed the bison and populated the ranges with cattle. Deprived of their natural prey, the lobos turned their attention to livestock and thereby incurred the wrath of the ranchers. The long-drawn battle between ranchers and lobo wolves during the next half-century was more or less a draw until the advent of World War I when the great demand for increased cattle production to supply meat for our armed forces led the federal government to back the ranchers with "government trappers." This action quickly led to the extermination of gray wolves in Texas and surrounding states, al-

though they still occur in northern Mexico in small numbers. Ironically, following the resignation of C. Hart Merriam as director, it was the U.S. Bureau of Biological Survey that employed and supported the federal trappers (Fig. 126).

The last gray wolves known to have been taken in Texas were two killed in December of 1970 in Brewster County (Scudday, 1972). It is possible that a few individuals still cross over into the Trans-Pecos region from Mexico, but the species is endangered there, too. Gray wolves have been reintroduced into Arizona and New Mexico and there has been some discussion of reintroducing them to Big Bend National Park as well, but any action on that proposal is years away and is likely to be strongly questioned by representatives of the livestock industry.

The grizzly or brown bear (Ursus arctos) probably occurred sparingly in western Texas from the Panhandle to the Trans-Pecos up until the days of early exploration of the region (Jones, 1993). However, as described in the first chapter of this book, only one specimen from the Davis Mountains has ever been recorded in Texas. The grizzly bear is regarded as threatened throughout its former range in the continental United States and in Mexico.

There have been no confirmed reports of black-footed ferrets (Mustela nigripes) (Fig. 127) since 1963 (Campbell, 1995), and it is possible that the species disappeared from the Texas scene before 1920 (Davis, 1961). Its historic range included roughly the northwestern third of the state in the Panhandle, much of the Trans-Pecos, and a considerable part of the Rolling Plains. This distribution corresponded with that of the ferret's principal prey, the black-tailed prairie dog. The decline of the black-footed ferret has been attributed to conversion of prairie habitat to agriculture and systematic efforts over the past one hundred years to eradicate prairie dogs. Ferrets were uninten-

Fig. 126. Wolves and coyotes killed by government agents on C. T. Mitchell Ranch, near Marfa, Presidio County, 1929. Courtesy National Archives, 22-WB-50-B4102M

Fig. 127. Black-footed ferret (at Crow Indian Reservation, Montana), 1927. Courtesy National Archives, 22-WB-59-B3480M

tional victims of prairie dog eradication efforts, and their numbers dwindled as prairie dog towns were plowed under and prairie dogs were poisoned (Thorne and Williams, 1988). It is believed that most existing prairie dog colonies are either too small or isolated from one another to support black-footed ferrets. However, the larger prairie dog colonies in the northern Panhandle may still provide suitable habitat to support reintroduced populations of these endangered mammals (Campbell, 1995).

The distribution of the jaguar (*Panthera onca*) once extended well into Central Texas, including much of the Edwards Plateau, as well as along the southern and southeastern parts of the state (Figs. 128, 129). There are many records and sightings that date from the late 1800s and early 1900s, and this large cat actually was regarded as common in some areas. The last documented record from the state was in the early 1950s (Tewes, 1990). This species is regarded as endangered throughout its relatively broad range in Central and South America. A recent assessment of the jaguar's current distribution (Swank and Teer, 1989) places the northernmost limit of established populations in central Mexico. While a few animals still may stray into the United States, there is no evidence that habitat in the southwest is crucial for survival of the species (Rabinowitz, 1999).

It is interesting that Bailey made no mention of the possible occurrence of the margay (*Leopardus wiedii cooperi*) in Texas. This species is known on the basis of a specimen taken near Eagle Pass in the 1850s, but this specimen was originally recorded in Spencer Fullerton Baird's 1859 account of *North American Mammals* as an ocelot. Ned Hollister, who was one of the federal agents assisting Bailey, later, in 1914, identified this specimen as a margay (Hollister, 1914). Some people have speculated the Eagle Pass margay was actually a pet brought to the border and sold. Whether this is

true or not is difficult to determine, but it is certain that margays no longer occur in Texas. This small spotted cat is regarded as endangered throughout the remainder of its range.

Bighorn sheep (*Ovis canadensis mexicana*) were still wide-ranging over many parts of the Trans-Pecos during the time of the biological survey. However, despite a ban against hunting them in 1903, they steadily declined in numbers and distribution. The primary cause of the decline appears to have been the introductions of large numbers of domestic sheep and goats. The mountain sheep competed directly with the domestic sheep and goats for food, were subjected to heavy losses from domestic sheep diseases, and were limited in their movements by net wire fences. William B. Davis (1939) summarized everything that was known about the distribution, sightings, and natural history of the species up to that time. By 1945, the total estimated population was less than a hundred and all of them were concentrated in the Beach, Baylor, and Sierra Diablo Mountains north of Van Horn (Davis, 1961). By 1961, their numbers had dwindled to some twenty-five to thirty individuals. However, even unmolested, the total Texas population probably was never greater than four hundred to five hundred individuals because suitable habitat was limited to a few isolated mountain ranges (Davis, 1961).

Following extinction, reintroductions in the Trans-Pecos area, not always of individuals representing the native subspecies, have been successful and bighorn sheep now occur in several mountainous areas of this region. The Texas Parks and Wildlife Department (TPWD) established an enclosed pasture for propagating mountain sheep (*Ovis canadensis mexicana* and *O. c. nelsoni*) on the Black Gap Wildlife Management Area in the late 1950s (Cook, 1991). Since that time, brood pastures have been established at two other locations. Since the 1980s, wild sheep have been released

Fig. 128. A jaguar taken near Goldthwaite, Mills County, 1903. (See Chapter 2, pages 165–66 of *Biological Survey of Texas.*) Courtesy Rollin Baker

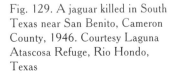

Fig. 129. A jaguar killed in South Texas near San Benito, Cameron County, 1946. Courtesy Laguna Atascosa Refuge, Rio Hondo, Texas

Fig. 130. Old antlers of Merriam's elk, photographed at a ranch in the Sacramento Mountains, New Mexico, 1903. Courtesy National Archives, 22-WB-57-B5519

in the Van Horn Mountains, Sierra Diablo Mountains, Elephant Mountain Wildlife Management Area, Baylor Mountains, and the Beach Mountains. The total population in January, 2001, was 381 individuals (Andrew Sansom, Texas Parks and Wildlife Department, personal communication).

The wapiti or elk once ranged over parts of northern and western Texas, although there seem to be no actual specimens to document its modern occurrence there (Jones, 1993) other than pre-historical archeological evidence (Pfau, 1994; Shaffer et al., 1995). These elk were originally assigned to the species *Cervus merriami*, Merriam's elk, which was later reduced to a subspecies of the more wide-ranging American elk, *Cervus elaphus* (Fig. 130). Merriam's elk resembled the American elk, but it was paler and more reddish in color, with a more massive skull and more erect antlers. It once roamed in the Guadalupe Mountains and perhaps other forested areas in West Texas, but it appears to have been killed off there before 1900. The elk currently occupying the Guadalupe Mountains are descendents of forty-four animals of another subspecies, *C. e. nelsoni*, that were released in McKittrick Canyon in 1928 by Judge J. C. Hunter. These elk increased at a maximum rate of 10 percent a year to a peak population size of approximately 350 in the mid 1960s. A severe reduction in population size commenced thereafter with only 108 individuals reported in a 1976–78 census and a further decrease to fifty-eight in 1983. The reason for this population decline is unclear (McAlpine, 1990). More recently, elk have been introduced into suitable habitat in the Wylie, Glass, Eagle, and Davis Mountains. The total number of free-ranging elk in the Trans-Pecos was estimated in 1995 at 330 individuals. In that year, elk were delisted as a game animal.

In addition to the nine extinct species, at least five subspecies have become extinct during the twentieth century. These include the Presidio mole (*Scalopus aquaticus texanus*), the Big Thicket hog-nosed skunk (*Conepatus mesoleucus telmalestes*), the Louisiana black bear (*Ursus americanus luteolus*), the Louisiana vole (*Microtus ochrogaster ludovicianus*), and Bailey's pocket gopher (*Thomomys bottae baileyi*).

William Lloyd, one of the federal agents, obtained the only specimen of the Presidio mole, *Scalopus aquaticus texanus*, in 1887 from Presidio County, which at that time consisted of the present West Texas counties of Presidio, Jeff Davis, and Brewster. No other specimen of mole has been observed, reported, or documented anywhere in West Texas. Rollin Baker (1951) trapped a new species of mole, *S. montanus* (now considered to be a subspecies of *S. aquaticus;* Yates and Schmidly, 1977) in the Sierra del Carmen, Coahuila, Mexico, just south of the Big Bend region. He hypothesized that *S. a. texanus* could have been trapped at high elevations in old Presidio County as well as near the river. However, given the extensive collecting in this region during the twentieth century without uncovering the Presidio mole, it seems likely this taxon is now extinct.

In his 1905 publication, Vernon Bailey described the Big Thicket population of the hog-nosed skunk as a distinct subspecies, *Conepatus mesoleucus telmalestes*, noting it was the most common skunk that he and the federal agents trapped in that area. No other specimens of this skunk were obtained or reported until March 5, 1960, when Gerald Raun and B. J. Wilks (1961) picked up a specimen dead on the road in Waller County. W. B. Davis (1945b) had assumed that the Big Thicket population had

been wiped out, but Howard McCarley (1959) believed that *Conepatus* was extant although rare in some sections of the area. From 1977 to 1982, while conducting five years of continuous fieldwork in Big Thicket National Preserve, I did not find any evidence of this skunk anywhere in the region (Schmidly, 1983). Since it has been four decades since anyone has made a confirmed sighting of the Big Thicket hog-nosed skunk, I presume that it is now extinct. The reason for its disappearance remains a complete mystery.

Historically, the Louisiana black bear (*Ursus americanus luteolus*) had a distribution that included the coastal plain of southern Mississippi, Louisiana, and East Texas (Hall, 1981). The lower portion of the Big Thicket area was apparently their last stronghold (Truett and Lay, 1984). Bailey already regarded them as rare at the beginning of the twentieth century. They were eliminated over most of the region during the period from 1850 to 1910 by hog raisers who felt that the bears were a threat to their free-ranging razorbacks. The big slaughter began about 1883 when two men in Liberty County alone killed 182 bears in a two-year period. Bailey became acquainted with one of them, Ab Carter, who told him his story (see Chapter 1).

Almost all the bears were gone by 1940, except for a few confirmed sightings in the Big Thicket of Hardin County and the dense woodlands of Matagorda County (Anonymous, 1945). The last confirmed kill was in the late 1950s near Livingston in Polk County (Fleming, 1980). Since then, TPWD has been recording and investigating sightings and mortalities. From 1993 through 1997, fifteen reliable sightings were recorded in counties bordering Louisiana, Arkansas, and Oklahoma (Cox, 1996; Garner and Willis, 1998). However, there is no evidence of a resident, breeding population, and the Texas sightings are considered transient, mainly consisting of young males seeking home territories (Cox, 1996).

The Louisiana black bear was listed as threatened because of similarity of appearance in the 1992 listing of threatened and endangered species in the *Federal Register*. The great amount of potential habitat remaining in the Big Thicket, and the fact there are scattered populations of the animals comparatively close to the Texas border, suggest it may be possible for viable populations to repopulate or be reintroduced into this region (Wooding et al., 1994). However, with 90 percent of the forested habitat in the region in private ownership, private landowners will be key to the success of any restoration effort.

The Louisiana vole (*Microtus ochrogaster ludovicianus*) is known on the basis of a single specimen secured by Ned Hollister in the coastal prairie region of Sour Lake on July 16, 1902. Numerous attempts during the twentieth century to collect this species by professional mammalogists have been unsuccessful, and it is now thought to be extinct throughout its range in both Texas and Louisiana.

C. Hart Merriam described *Thomomys baileyi* in 1901 on the basis of specimens collected by Bailey at Sierra Blanca in Hudspeth County (Merriam, 1901). Subsequently, E. A. Goldman (1938), another biological survey scientist, described a second race of *baileyi*, *T. b. spatiosus*, from Alpine and Paisano in Brewster County. In 1966, Syd Anderson synonymized *T. baileyi* with the more wide-ranging species, *T. bottae* (Anderson, 1966). Subsequent attempts by mammalogists, including myself, to collect gophers which fit the description of *baileyi* have failed. It now appears that *baileyi* is extinct, having been replaced ecologically by another pocket gopher, *Cratogeomys castanops*.

## Declines in Geographic Distribution and Population Abundance

A notable number of Texas mammals, including species of all sizes and life history traits, have undergone drastic range reductions and today occupy a mere scant portion of their former range.

The pronghorn antelope (*Antilocapra americana*) once occurred over the western two-thirds of Texas. The great herds that once roamed the Trans-Pecos and Panhandle regions were reduced to a mere handful by the time Bailey and the federal agents completed their work in Texas. Bailey counted only thirty-two pronghorns in a ninety-five-mile railroad journey from Canyon, Texas, to Portales, New Mexico. In South Texas, he encountered a few west of Alice, and small bands roamed near Cotulla and Rock Springs. But antelope had disappeared from the vicinities of Alpine and Marfa and from the outwash plains of the Davis Mountains. A 1924 survey of pronghorns showed a statewide population of only 2,407. The decline was associated with overgrazing of grasslands by domestic livestock, uncontrolled hunting, and extensive cultivation of prairie habitat. The pronghorn is now restricted to isolated patches of suitable habitat from the Panhandle to the Trans-Pecos (see Map 10, Chapter 3). It is a desirable game species, but despite extensive management efforts, including restocking programs begun in the 1940s and continuing even today, pronghorn numbers appear to be declining. The statewide population estimate in 1997 was thirteen thousand with about 70 percent of the population in the Trans-Pecos and 30 percent in the High Plains and Rolling Plains. Their decline now appears to be associated with drought and predation as well as the "hand of man" in the form of fencing and land use.

Fig. 131. Poisoning crew and dead prairie dogs, Means Brothers Ranch, Jeff Davis County, 1936. Courtesy National Archives, 22-WB-65-B43487

No Texas mammal has suffered more from population decline this century than has the black-tailed prairie dog, *Cynomys ludovicianus.* This highly gregarious rodent creates colonies or "towns" that can range anywhere from one to one thousand acres. Once widespread throughout the Great Plains states, prairie dog colonies are now in decline. It has been estimated that in the early 1900s, prairie dog colonies covered 100 to 250 million acres throughout North America. The largest expanse of prairie dog colonies occurred in Texas where their distribution covered one-third of the entire state or approximately 90,000 square miles (Map 26). In the 1890s, Vernon Bailey estimated that more than 800 million prairie dogs inhabited an area of 90,000 square miles in the western part of the state and that they were consuming as much range vegetation as would 3 million cattle. One 25,000 square-mile area just east of the Staked Plains from San Angelo to Clarendon was described as one continuous "dog" town with approximately 400 million inhabitants! Such concentrations were a heavy drain on range vegetation, and ranchers enlisted the federal government to combat them. Using mainly strychnine-treated grain, the ranchers, along with government rodent control specialists (employed by the U.S. Biological Survey), poisoned millions of prairie dogs (Fig. 131). By 1960 the once overwhelming populations had been reduced to scattered, small colonies (Davis, 1961).

Today, it is estimated that 98 percent of the population has been lost, and that only three hundred thousand prairie dogs remain in Texas (Long, 1998). These gloomy predictions may even overestimate the size of the population be-

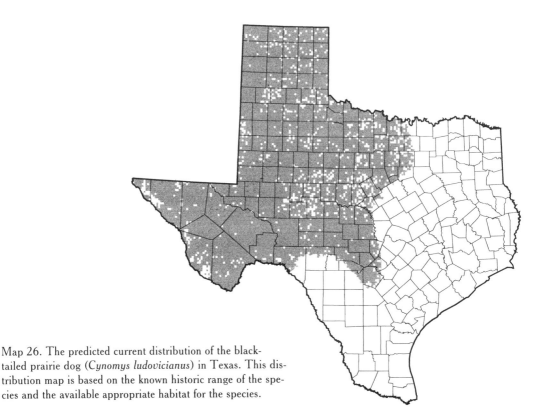

Map 26. The predicted current distribution of the black-tailed prairie dog (*Cynomys ludovicianus*) in Texas. This distribution map is based on the known historic range of the species and the available appropriate habitat for the species.

cause most surviving colonies are fragmented and cover less than fifty acres. Records indicate that prairie dog habitat declined 61 percent just in the last two decades of the twentieth century. At this rate of decline and habitat fragmentation, prairie dog eradication could occur during the first half of the twenty-first century. For this reason, the National Wildlife Federation has petitioned the U.S. Fish and Wildlife Service to list the prairie dog as a threatened species with all the rights and privileges thereof.

Such a listing would have been considered ludicrous at the beginning of the twentieth century. The *Austin Daily Statesman*, on August 8, 1899, published the following quote about prairie dogs: "During the recent session of the legislature, the western members tried to secure an appropriations bill to kill the millions of prairie dogs that are infesting and laying waste all over the Panhandle. They failed, so now W. L. Grogan of Sweetwater was in Austin yester-

day and stated that the people out on the plain have rigged up big mouse traps with long projecting noses which they sink in the holes of the prairie dogs leaving the trap above ground. The trap holds up to 10 prairie dogs. Thousands are being caught. The war waged on prairie dogs is proving effective."

Another interesting case is that of the muskrat, *Ondatra zibethicus*. In some regions of the state, muskrat populations appear to have declined or even disappeared, whereas in other regions they have invaded and increased in abundance. Bailey and the other field agents found them to be abundant at the beginning of the century in the Canadian River drainage. Frank Blair in 1954 reported a dense population in the tule marshes of Moore and Bugby Creeks in Hutchinson County. J. Knox Jones, Jr., Clyde Jones, and associates (1988), while conducting an extensive survey of the mammals of the northern Texas Panhandle during the 1980s,

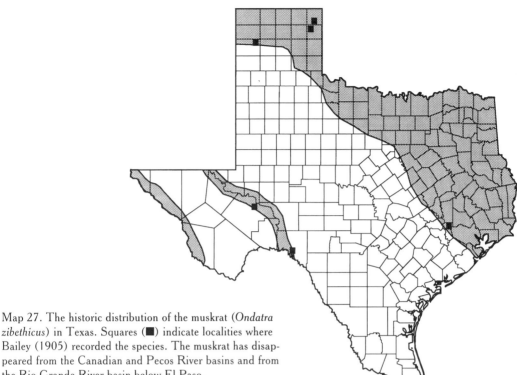

Map 27. The historic distribution of the muskrat (*Ondatra zibethicus*) in Texas. Squares (■) indicate localities where Bailey (1905) recorded the species. The muskrat has disappeared from the Canadian and Pecos River basins and from the Rio Grande River basin below El Paso.

did not find any evidence of muskrats at the sites where they have been previously reported. According to Clyde Jones (personal communication), most of the creeks are now dry and the tule marshes are greatly reduced in scope. Fred Stangl and his associates reported finding the bones of a muskrat in the regurgitated pellets of a great-horned owl near a stream in the vicinity of Clarendon in Donley County (Stangl et al., 1989). This is encouraging and suggests a few muskrats may still remain in the Panhandle.

During the time of the biological survey, muskrats occurred in numerous areas of the Trans-Pecos, along both the Pecos River and the Rio Grande and at springs such as those at Fort Stockton and Balmorhea. As human population and irrigation wells increased, many of the springs of the Pecos River drainage were destroyed. As the springs dried up, muskrat populations died out. Thus, today the drainage ditches near El Paso represent the last strong-

hold of *Ondatra zibethicus ripensis* in the Trans-Pecos. Interestingly, the federal agents who collected at El Paso during the survey did not collect or observe muskrats there, suggesting their occurrence in this region may be a recent event (Map 27).

Remarkably, neither Bailey nor the other field agents collected any muskrat along the upper Texas coast which is the region of the species' greatest abundance today. The only mention of muskrat is an account from Waller County by J. H. Gaut who reported them from the Brazos River and its tributaries. Previously, John James Audubon had reported them on Galveston Island in 1824 (Geiser, 1930). Del Weniger (1997) noted that none of the early explorers reported muskrats from the Texas coast, and they were certainly not common there during the biological survey. However, by 1936 muskrats produced 54 percent of the fur trapping income for Jefferson, Chambers, and Orange Counties (Lay and O'Neil, 1942). Bailey and his co-workers collected extensively in Jefferson County but never reported trapping or seeing muskrats. The most likely explanation for these observations is that the 1900 and 1915 hurricanes, which covered much of the prairies and marshes of the upper Texas coast, decimated muskrat populations and it took them almost three decades to fully recover.

Historically, mountain lions (*Puma concolor*) occurred virtually throughout the state. Years of predator control efforts by livestock producers, however, forced the remaining mountain lions into the more remote, thinly populated areas. Today, the largest mountain lion populations are in the desert mountain ranges of the Trans-Pecos, especially in the Big Bend region, and in the dense brushlands of the Rio Grande Plain. Also, reports of these large cats are still common in parts of the Edwards Plateau and even in the Big Thicket. Predator control efforts have slowed since about 1970 and lion populations appear to be stabilizing. An increasing number of encounters between people and mountain lions has been reported in Big Bend National Park in the decade of the 1990s. Another indication of increasing population is the dramatic rise in the number of lions taken by the Texas Wildlife Damage Management Service since the 1980s (Fig. 132).

Texas is the only state with a resident lion population that does not regulate taking of the mountain lion. Current management practices are controversial and relate to whether or not the species should be listed as nongame in an effort to regulate harvest within the state. Presently, the species is classified by TPWD as a predator, thus allowing unregulated trapping, killing, and transporting of mountain lions. Two main issues of concern are uncertainty about the population size because their low density and elusive behavior render censusing difficult, and the fact there is no evidence the populations are panmictic. Christopher Walker and associates examined genetic variation at ten micro-satellite loci from samples obtained in South and West Texas. They found less genetic variation than previously reported for the species in other parts of its range, and they found evidence for genetic subdivision with reduced gene flow between the two samples. Their data suggest that mountain lions should be partitioned into at least two management units (Walker et al., 2000).

Although still regarded by many as unwanted predators, mountain lions have begun in recent years to receive some recognition for their ecological, aesthetic, and sporting value. Efforts by concerned private citizens and environmental groups may someday result in their being recognized as a game animal, hunted in season and under license.

## Range Expansions and Regional Faunal Changes

Since the beginning of the twentieth century, a number of mammals have expanded their ranges in Texas. Notable examples include the armadillo (*Dasypus novemcinctus*), the northern pygmy mouse (*Baiomys taylori*), and the porcupine (*Erethizon dorsatum*). At the time that Bailey and the federal agents roamed the state, all these species had restricted distribu-

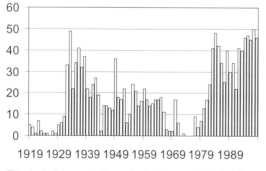

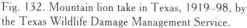

Fig. 132. Mountain lion take in Texas, 1919–98, by the Texas Wildlife Damage Management Service.

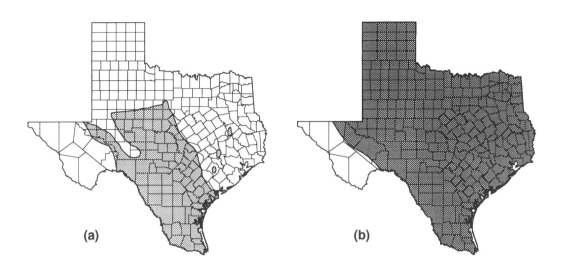

**(a)**  **(b)**

Map 28. The historic (a) and current (b) distribution of the nine-banded armadillo (*Dasypus novemcinctus*) in Texas.

tions, whereas today they are much more wide ranging and common.

Bailey mapped the distributional limits of the armadillo as between the Colorado and Guadalupe Rivers with extralimital records from Colorado, Grimes, and Houston Counties. By 1914 the armadillo had crossed the Brazos River and moved to the Trinity River and along the coast had already reached the Louisiana line in Orange County. The northward and eastward range expansions continued over the next forty years, and by 1954 it was known from everywhere except Red River and Lamar Counties in extreme northeastern Texas. By 1958, it was known from these latter two counties, and today is abundant everywhere in the region (Map 28).

Apparently, pioneering was most successful in riparian habitat, and invasion was especially rapid parallel to rivers, which served as dispersal conduits. Average invasion rates have been calculated as from 2 to 6 miles per year in the absence of obvious physical or climatic barriers. Possible reasons for the armadillo's northward expansion since the nineteenth cen-

tury include progressive climatic change, encroaching human civilization, overgrazing, and decimation of large carnivores (Cleveland, 1970; Humphrey, 1974).

The northern pygmy mouse (*Baiomys taylori*) represents another example of a southern species, characteristic of the tropical lowlands of Mexico, which has expanded its range northward and westward. The federal agents indicated it was restricted to the coastal and southern mesquite-chaparral regions. Since the early twentieth century, the species has consistently expanded northward and westward by invading the oak-hickory association, the Blackland Prairies, the Cross-Timbers, the Rolling Plains, and most recently the High Plains (see Map 14, Chapter 3). These mice have a preference for grassy areas, and they are commonly found in old fields, pastures, and along railroad and highway rights-of-way, which in conjunction with increasingly mild winters, may explain their rapid spread (Cleveland, 1986; Diersing and Diersing, 1979; Hollander et al., 1987; Jones and Manning, 1989; Choate et al., 1990).

The porcupine (*Erethizon dorsatum*) represents another example of a mammal that has expanded its range in Texas during the twentieth century. It is largely an inhabitant of forested areas in the west and prefers rocky areas, ridges, and slopes. Porcupines wander about a great deal and may be found irregularly in areas that appear wholly unsuited to them. Bailey and the federal agents recorded them only in one county in the Panhandle and in Jeff Davis and Brewster Counties in the western part of the state (see Map 19, Chapter 3). Today, they occur east to Bosque County and appear to be expanding southward. None of the early explorers or naturalists, until the report of Bailey, documented the porcupine's occurrence. Weniger (1997) apparently was not aware of Bailey's observations when he wrote: "The earliest record of porcupines here seems to be those reported from the Davis Mountains of the Big Bend in 1940." Weniger speculates that the spread of porcupines may have been facilitated by the practice of deicing highways with salt. The "salt drive" of these animals has been well documented, and salt availability is a limiting factor where they live and a clue to much of their behavior.

Documentation of range expansions has been very prevalent for bats in recent decades. Three species, the eastern pipistrelle (*Pipistrellus subflavus*), the evening bat (*Nycticeius humeralis*), and the Seminole bat (*Lasiurus seminolus*), previously thought to be confined to the eastern half of the state (Schmidly, 1983), have now been collected in far western Texas (Dowler et al., 1992; Brant and Dowler, 2000; Dowler et al., 1999; Yancey et al., 1995b) (Map 29). These examples suggest the Rio Grande may be serving as a dispersal corridor for eastern species of mammals to gradually expand their ranges westward during the last decade (Schmidly and Jones, 2000).

Unfortunately, not much is known about micro-scale changes in diversity such as reductions or expansions of geographic ranges, changes in species abundance and community structure, and extinctions of local populations and subspecies. But from the evidence at hand, it seems obvious that the faunal composition in several areas of the state changed during the twentieth century.

This is especially true on the High Plains, or Llano Estacado, and the northern Texas Panhandle. Bailey and the federal agents worked in these regions at the end of the nineteenth century when most of this country was composed of large ranches with little human settlement. Today, this region, and especially the Llano Estacado, has been converted to farmland for crop production. Larry Choate (1997) documented the mammal fauna of the Llano Estacado, and J. Knox Jones Jr. and associates (1988) did likewise for the northern Panhandle. Comparing their results with those of Bailey and the federal agents reveals some interesting differences. Several species, including the least shrew (*Cryptotis parva*), the western harvest mouse (*Reithrodontomys megalotis*), and the Plains harvest mouse (*Reithrodontomys montanus*), which are common in this region today were never trapped or sighted by Bailey or his coworkers. It is highly unlikely, given the prowess of the federal agents as field collectors, that they would have failed to collect these small mammals had they occurred in the region. Therefore, it is tempting to speculate the occurrence of these species on the High Plains and Panhandle is a phenomenon that has occurred this century, perhaps as an artifact of human intervention in the form of hauling hay from the central regions of the state to feed livestock in these areas during periods of drought.

There are other interesting examples of species being transplanted by humans from one region of the state to another, resulting in viable, breeding populations outside of a species' normal geographic range. One of the best cases of this involves tree squirrels of the genus *Sciurus*.

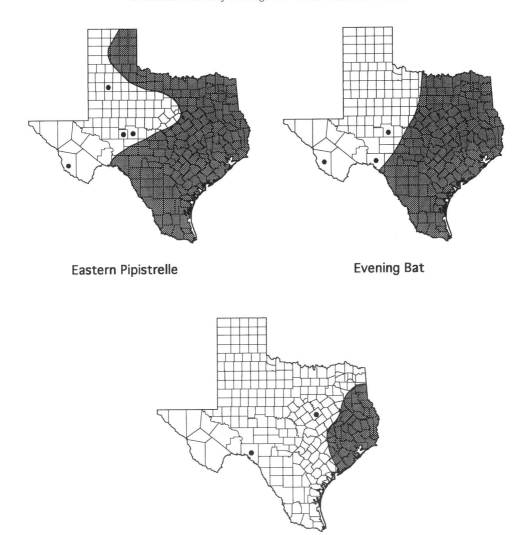

Eastern Pipistrelle      Evening Bat

Seminole Bat

Map 29. The current distribution of the eastern pipistrelle (*Pipistrellus subflavus*), evening bat (*Nycticeius humeralis*), and Seminole bat (*Lasiurus seminolus*) in Texas. Circles (●) indicate recent county records for each species in Texas.

Bailey and the federal agents mapped the distribution of the gray squirrel, *Sciurus carolinensis*, as occurring no further west than the eastern edge of the Balcones Escarpment. Gray squirrels have been introduced in many places outside of their natural range. A thriving population in the city of Lubbock was established in the 1970s, more than four hundred miles from the species' normal range.

Interestingly, the biological survey field agents did not document the occurrence of fox squirrels (*Sciurus niger*) in the Panhandle. Mammalogists from Texas Tech University found them to be common in the deciduous riparian vegetation, mostly cottonwoods, along the Canadian and its major tributaries (Jones, J. K., Jr., et al., 1988). Given the extensive amount of fieldwork the federal agents conducted in this region, it is not likely they would have overlooked the occurrence of fox squirrels. This would suggest that fox squirrels occupied this region sometime this century, dispersing along the Red River drainage system. The best fox squirrel habitat is mature oak-hickory woodland broken into small, irregularly shaped tracts and connected by strips of woodland. In the eastern part of their range, they occur primarily in the upland regions, whereas in the western part of the state they are restricted more or less to river valleys which support various fruit and nut trees. Also, there is good evidence that they have been introduced in several places on the Llano Estacado (Frey and Campbell, 1997).

### Documentation of Additional Faunal Elements and Discovery of Cryptic Species

Even though Bailey and the federal agents did a thorough job of documenting the mammal fauna, mammalogists working in the state throughout the twentieth century have continued to document additional species and subspecies, and they have altered the taxonomy of mammals based on new information about the status of populations, subspecies, and species. Such taxonomic changes undoubtedly will continue as more is learned about the genetic relationships of mammalian populations.

Twenty-four other species of mammals that have been documented since the biological survey include:

Order Insectivora
  Family Soricidae
    *Blarina hylophaga*, Elliot's short-tailed shrew

Order Chiroptera
  Family Phyllostomidae
    *Leptonycteris nivalis*, Mexican long-nosed bat
    *Choeronycteris mexicana*, Mexican long-tongued bat

    *Diphylla ecaudata*, hairy-legged vampire bat
  Family Vespertilionidae
    *Myotis lucifugus*, little brown myotis
    *Myotis austroriparius*, southeastern myotis
    *Myotis ciliolabrum*, western small-footed myotis
    *Myotis septentrionalis*, northern myotis
    *Myotis thysanodes*, fringed myotis
    *Myotis volans*, long-legged myotis
    *Lasionycteris noctivagans*, silver-haired bat
    *Lasiurus blossevillii*, western red bat
    *Lasiurus ega*, southern yellow bat
    *Lasiurus xanthinus*, western yellow bat
    *Euderma maculatum*, spotted bat
    *Plecotus rafinesquii*, Rafinesque's big-eared bat
  Family Molossidae
    *Nyctinomops femorosaccus*, pocketed free-tailed bat
    *Nyctinomops macrotis*, big free-tailed bat

Order Rodentia
  Family Geomyidae
    *Geomys knoxjonesi*, Jones' pocket gopher
  Family Muridae
    *Peromyscus nasutus*, northern rock mouse
    *Peromyscus truei*, pinon mouse
    *Ochrotomys nuttalli*, golden mouse
    *Sigmodon fulviventer*, tawny-bellied cotton rat

Order Carnivora
  Family Mephitidae
    *Mephitis macroura*, hooded skunk

(Note: this list does not include species or subspecies that have undergone taxonomic reassignment and are now referred to by different scientific names.)

Of these twenty-four species, almost two-thirds are bats. Bats were undoubtedly the least understood group of mammals at the time of the biological survey. Only seventeen taxa were included in the survey publication. Today, we know of thirty-three species that occur in the state. The primary reason bats were so little understood was the difficulty in obtaining specimens. Historically, the only methods available for capturing bats were shooting them with shotguns in the early evening and hand-capturing them in their daytime hiding places. These time-consuming and uncertain methods obtained only a fraction of the total number of species of bats occurring in an area. In 1937, A. E. Borell, while studying mammals in the Big Bend region, developed a method of capturing bats by stringing fine wire across a water tank frequented by bats coming to drink after dark (Borell, 1937). The bats would hit the wires and drop into the water, and they could then be collected when they swam to the side of the tank. This method was more effective and economical than shooting and allowed bats to be banded and released unharmed if desired. Slow-flying species, such as *Antrozous* and *Pipistrellus*, often avoided the wires, however, and the technique could be used only on relatively small, man-made water tanks.

In 1954, Walter Dalquest, a mammalogist at Midwestern State University in Wichita Falls, published a technique for capturing bats using Japanese silk "mist nets" (Dalquest, 1954). The use of this technique would soon revolutionize the study of bats and today it is still the most effective method available for capturing bats. The mist nets are most commonly strung across ponds after dark but can also be set among bushes or trees or across the openings of caves or other roost sites to capture bats as they leave their roosts in the evening. Mist nets offer the following advantages to the collector: bats can be taken in large numbers in them, species otherwise difficult to collect are easily

obtained, and common forms can be released alive.

Probably the most remarkable discovery of a new species of mammal during the twentieth century was the documentation of a third species of cotton rat (*Sigmodon fulviventer*, the tawny-bellied cotton rat) from near Fort Davis in Jeff Davis County in the spring of 1991 (Stangl, 1992a, b). Previously known only from southeastern Arizona and southwestern New Mexico, this isolated population represented not only a new species of mammal for the state, but Stangl described it as a new subspecies, *S. f. dalquesti*, named after his mentor, Walter Dalquest.

The extent of the tawny-bellied cotton rat's range and relative abundance remain unknown. The population was documented from an area where many mammalogists and their students previously had conducted extensive field work, documenting on numerous occasions two other species of cotton rats, the hispid cotton rat (*Sigmodon hispidus*) and the yellow-nosed cotton rat (*S. ochrognathus*). Recent attempts to collect *S. f. dalquesti* at its type locality have proven unsuccessful, and the status of this taxon remains an enigma.

Mammalogists documented other new taxa of bats and rodents during the latter half of the twentieth century. The first occurrence of the western yellow bat (*Lasiurus xanthinus*) in Texas was documented in the 1990s. Specimens were obtained in the Chisos Mountains of Big Bend National Park (Higginbotham, et al., 1999), Black Gap Wildlife Management Area (Bradley et al., 1999a), and the Davis Mountains near Ft. Davis (Jones et al., 1999b), places where many mammalogists had previously collected bats without finding this species (Map 30).

An example of the discovery of a subspecies new to the Texas fauna involves the prairie vole, *Microtus ochrogaster taylori*, which was discovered in two counties (Hansford and Lips-

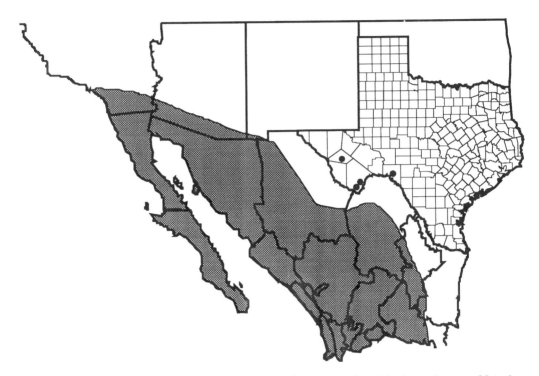

Map 30. The current distributioon of the western yellow bat (*Lasiurus xanthinus*) in the southwestern United States and northern Mexico. Circles (●) indicate recent records of the species from Texas.

comb) in the northern Panhandle along the Oklahoma border. This discovery was made by J. Knox Jones Jr. and Clyde Jones in 1988. The only other record of this species was of another subspecies, *M. o. ludovicianus*, recorded from the Big Thicket region by Bailey and his co-workers. A. H. Howell, one of the leading federal agents with the biological survey, worked extensively in Lipscomb County in 1903, collecting twenty species of small mammals, none of which was a vole. So the occurrence of *M. o. taylori* in Texas probably represents another invasion during the twentieth century.

Another trend in the twentieth century has been the dramatic shift in the philosophy for classifying mammals for the purpose of taxonomic designation. Vernon Bailey and his mentor, C. Hart Merriam, were restricted to a morphological concept of species and subspecies.

According to their logic, if specimens representing two populations could not be distinguished morphologically, then they would not be regarded as taxonomically distinct. If the specimens were different, depending on the degree of difference, then they would be classified as either subspecies or species.

As the biological species concept, dominated by the recognition of geographically variable, polytypic species, slowly began to take hold in the twentieth century, many of the species recognized by Merriam and Bailey were "lumped" into single wide-ranging species. With the advent of modern techniques of genetics and molecular biology in the latter three decades of the century, new tools have become available to measure genetic (and evolutionary) relatedness among populations. These techniques allow scientists to study chromosomes and the sequence of genes in animals. Likewise, new sophisticated techniques of statistics have allowed for more refined assessments of morphology among populations of mammals.

Using these new techniques, we have learned of many situations where populations have diverged substantially in their chromosomes and genes but have undergone little, if any, morphological change. These populations are referred to as cryptic species, meaning they cannot easily be differentiated on the basis of observed morphological characteristics, although they are genetically distinct and reproductively isolated, thus meeting the basic requirement for biological species distinctness. To the contrary, other cases have been described where populations very different from one another morphologically (different enough to be called separate species) are in fact almost identical genetically and thus are fully capable of interbreeding and producing viable offspring. Modern taxonomists typically arrange these populations as different subspecies of the same species.

The best example of cryptic species is represented by the pocket gophers of the genus *Geomys*. Bailey recognized nine taxa of *Geomys* in Texas, including five species and four subspecies, all on the basis of morphological distinctness. As the biological species concept slowly began to take hold in the twentieth century, all but two of the taxa recognized by Bailey (*G. personatus* and *G. arenarius*) were lumped into one wide-ranging species, named *G. bursarius*, which was distributed over most of the Great Plains and south-central United States, including almost all of Texas.

Recent studies by specialists trained in cytological and molecular taxonomy, however, have revealed the existence of five species of pocket gophers ranging over what was formerly considered the range of *G. bursarius*. These species (*G. bursarius*, *G. attwateri*, *G. breviceps*, *G. knoxjonesi*, and *G. texensis*) are considered cryptic species, meaning they cannot be easily

differentiated on the basis of observed morphological characteristics although they are genetically distinct and reproductively isolated. Although all the species appear to be allopatric in range (Baker and Genoways, 1975; Bohlin and Zimmerman, 1982; Elrod et al., 1996; Honeycutt and Schmidly, 1979; Jones et al., 1995; Tucker and Schmidly, 1981; Dowler, 1989), karyotypic, electrophoretic, and mitochondrial DNA data are required to confidently distinguish questionable specimens.

The five species formerly lumped under the name *G. bursarius*, together with *G. personatus* and *G. arenarius*, bring the number of species of *Geomys* in Texas to seven (Map 31). Similar instances of such cryptic species have now been discovered in several other groups of rodents, including deer mice (genus *Peromyscus*; Schmidly, 1973b), grasshopper mice (genus *Onychomys*; Hinesley, 1979), pocket mice (genus *Chaetodipus*; genus *Perognathus*; Lee and Engstrom, 1991; and Lee et al., 1996) and kangaroo rats (genus *Dipodomys*; Schmidly and Hendricks, 1976), as well shrews of the genus *Blarina* (Baumgardner et al., 1992). These types of discoveries, resulting from taxonomic revisions, account for much of the change in the taxonomy and classification of mammals during the twentieth century.

One of the best examples where new taxonomic approaches have resulted in a combining of species formerly considered to be distinct and separate involves the case of the arid-land foxes of the genus *Vulpes*. For most of this century, arid-land foxes have been regarded as comprising two similar but separate species, the swift fox (*Vulpes veloxs*) and the kit fox (*Vulpes macrotis*). This was the arrangement used by Bailey. However, in a recent taxonomic study of these foxes using advanced morphometric and protein-electrophoretic methods, Dragoo and colleagues (1990) concluded that these taxa are not sufficiently distinct to warrant separate species status. Thus, the two foxes are

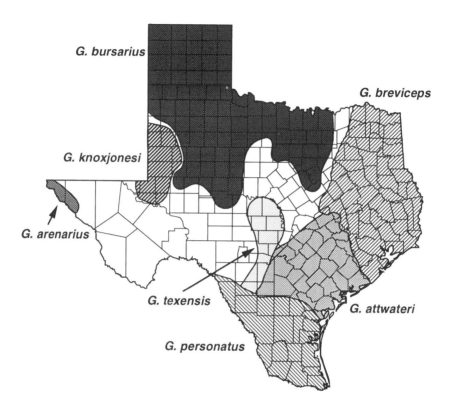

Map 31. The current distribution of the seven species of pocket gophers (genus *Geomys*) in Texas

now grouped into a single species, *Vulpes velox*, comprising two subspecies, *V. v. velox* from the Panhandle and adjacent areas and *V. v. macrotis* from the Trans-Pecos.

### Growth in the Number of Threatened, Endangered, and Rare Species

Several land mammals are viewed as having some sort of biological problem that threatens or potentially threatens their existence. These are species that, in the opinion of biologists and conservation groups, currently face or likely will face serious conservation problems in the future.

Many of the species in jeopardy share life history attributes that make them especially vulnerable to local extinction events. Some species, such as bats, have low reproductive rates, which means they are slow to recover from pop-

ulation declines either by catastrophic events or by habitat destruction. Others, such as many of the carnivores and larger herbivores, are large in body size and have an extensive home range, which coupled with low population densities and their trophic level, make them highly vulnerable to human disturbance. And many have confined geographic ranges, limited to a handful of places, which make them highly vulnerable to local extinction events.

Another category of vulnerability includes those species dependent on some highly specialized but scarce resource. The organism may be a masterpiece of adaptation but vulnerable because of one requirement within its habitat that must be met. An example would be the Mexican free-tailed bat, *Tadarida brasiliensis*. This species is highly mobile and can range widely in its feeding but is absolutely dependent on caves or other suitable roosts with the appropriate temperature and humidity for passing the day and rearing its young. Natural caves were the original source of refugia. If, for some reason, caves become unavailable to these bats, such as through commercial exploitation and mining, then the species would most likely become extinct.

State and federal agencies as well as private organizations have developed lists of rare and endangered mammals. The U.S. Fish and Wildlife Service (USFWS) publishes a list of endangered and threatened species which includes mammals listed in these categories in the federal register, and the Texas Parks and Wildlife Department (TPWD) has a list of protected nongame wildlife. These are the official lists governed by federal and state law, statutes, and regulations. A discussion of pertinent laws protecting these species, and the mammals included on these various listings, is provided later in this chapter.

Private organizations that maintain lists include the Texas Organization for Endangered Species (TOES), which considers species of plants and animals as endangered, threatened, or on their "watch list," the latter encouraging surveillance from year to year. Also, the Nature Conservancy of Texas actively evaluates and updates the Texas Natural Heritage Program database which includes a status list of rare Texas plants and animals. More than four hundred plant and animal species are listed on a "special species list" to indicate a need to assess their tenuous biological status.

Scientific documentation about the conservation status of mammals started early in the twentieth century and increased dramatically during the final decades of the millenium. Vernon Bailey was the first to draw serious attention to the plight of certain species and the need for immediate action. This was followed in 1917 by a paper written by H. P. Attwater, from Houston, a contemporary naturalist of

Bailey, who argued for the need to take action to prevent the further decimation of the fauna. In the closing paragraph of his paper, Attwater wrote: "I have no personal interests to serve, no 'axe to grind,' and I concede the right of any one to disagree with me, but I am absolutely certain that Texas people are making a great mistake in permitting the wanton and reckless destruction of valuable and useful wild life and that the future interests of the State demand that it be put a stop to, before it is too late" (Attwater, 1917).

Glover Allen (1942) drew continent-wide attention to the problem of extinct and vanishing mammals in the western hemisphere. His list of species and subspecies of concern included eighteen taxa from Texas. In the late 1940s and throughout the 1950s, a series of articles appeared in the *Texas Game and Fish* magazine about the declining status of many mammals (Burr, 1949a, b, c; Baughman, 1951; Slaughter, 1960), and Rollin Baker (1956) called attention to some of the most serious problems in East Texas.

Following the passage of the Endangered Species Act, written accounts about the status of mammals began to proliferate. Kaye Culbertson (1974) performed a status evaluation of Texas mammals, focusing on those species that required immediate attention. Rollin Baker (1977) and James Findley and William Caire (1977) prepared lists of rare, endangered, and poorly known species from the Chihuahuan Desert region, including Texas, and John Rappole and Alan Tipton (1987) prepared a summary of information on the small, terrestrial mammals that had been identified as potentially declining, threatened, or endangered. The latter authors surveyed mammalogists to determine their list. J. Knox Jones Jr. (1993) provided a synopsis of threatened and endangered species law and published a list of taxa warranting conservation concern. Finally, Linda Campbell (1995) discussed the life history and management of all the endangered and threatened vertebrates in Texas, including mammals on the federal and state lists.

The legal protection of plants and animals considered to be endangered or threatened was not an issue during the time of Bailey and the federal agents. The concept of federal and state laws to protect wildlife was just taking root at the beginning of the twentieth century (see Jones, 1993, for a thorough discussion). The first significant step in federal wildlife law was the Lacey Act of 1900 that prohibited interstate transportation of "any wild animals or birds" killed in violation of state law. At that time most of the laws in effect had to do with the protection of game animals.

One of the earliest efforts to give legal protection to non-game animals occurred in 1917. In that year, the Texas legislature passed a general law (H.B. No. 40) making it a misdemeanor to kill or injure bats because of their perceived value in controlling malarial mosquitoes (Schmidly, 1991). A provision of this law (Section I, Article 887a) stated, "If any person shall willfully kill or in any manner injure any winged quadruped known as the common bat, he shall be deemed guilty of a misdemeanor and upon conviction shall be fined a sum of not less than five ($5.00) dollars nor more than fifteen ($15.00) dollars."

It was only in the latter half of the twentieth century that federal and state laws were developed to protect nongame animal species, including invertebrates and also plants. The first federal legislation in this area was the Endangered Species Preservation Act of 1966, replaced soon thereafter by the Endangered Species Act of 1969 and culminating in congressional passage of the Endangered Species Act of 1973 (ESA) which was subsequently reauthorized in 1988 and amended in 1992 and 1996 (*Federal Register* 59 (219): 58982 et seq., 15 Nov. 1994; and FR 59 (219): 38983).

The ESA is the centerpiece of federal efforts to conserve biological diversity (NRC, 1995). Its aim is to prevent the extinction of plant and animal species by regulating a wide range of activities affecting plants and animals designated as endangered or threatened. By definition, an *endangered species* is an animal or plant listed by regulation as being in danger of extinction. A *threatened species* is any animal or plant that is likely to become endangered within the foreseeable future. A species must be listed in the *Federal Register* as endangered or threatened for the provisions of the act to apply. Any species or subspecies of plant or animal may be eligible for protection, including species found outside the United States. Distinct populations of vertebrate animals also may be protected under the act. Enforcement of the ESA falls under the authority of the U.S. Fish and Wildlife Service (USFWS).

The ESA prohibits the following activities involving endangered species: importing into or exporting from the United States; taking (includes harassing, harming, pursuing, hunting, shooting, wounding, trapping, killing, capturing, or collecting) within the United States and its territorial seas; taking on the high seas; possessing, selling, delivering, carrying, transporting, or shipping any such species unlawfully taken within the United States or on the high seas; delivering, receiving, carrying, transporting, or shipping in interstate or foreign commerce in the course of a commercial activity; and selling or offering for sale in interstate or foreign commerce. The ESA also provides for protection of *critical habitat* (habitat required for the survival and recovery of the species) and the creation of a *recovery plan* for each listed species.

The ESA provides for listing plant and animal species into the following categories: listed endangered species, listed threatened species, proposed endangered species, proposed threatened species, candidate species (category 1

—awaiting listing), and delisted species (species removed from endangered or threatened list because of extinction, taxonomic change, or because of abundance). Proposed species are those species for which a proposed rule to list as endangered or threatened has been published in the *Federal Register*. Candidate species are those species for which the USFWS has on file sufficient information on biological vulnerability and threats to support issuance of a proposed rule to list but issuance of the proposed rule is precluded. In earlier versions of the ESA, candidate species were classified into two categories: Category 1 species qualified for listing based on available data, and Category 2 species required additional information as to their status. The 1996 Act, as amended, dissolved Category 2, categorizing all of those taxa as Candidate Species.

According to the USFWS, Texas ranks sixth in the nation in terms of the number of endangered species living within its borders (see www.fws.gov/r9endspp/endspp.html). Seventy-two plants and animals protected under the ESA have been recorded from Texas, a number that reflects the state's large size, diverse array of habitats, and growing development pressures. The USFWS is required by law to assess periodically the status of America's endangered species and to report its findings to Congress. The most recent report, compiled in 1994, provided data on thirty-seven of Texas's forty-five listed animals and all twenty-seven of its listed plants (USFWS. 1994. Report to Congress. Recovery Program, Endangered and Threatened Species). According to this report, 39 percent of the endangered species found in Texas are still declining, only 24 percent are judged to be improving or stable, and for the remaining 37 percent the Service lacks the resources to determine how they are faring.

In 1973 the Texas legislature authorized the Texas Parks and Wildlife Department (TPWD) to establish a list of endangered animals in the state. Endangered species are those species that the executive director of TPWD has named as being "threatened with statewide extinction." Threatened species are those species that the TPWD Commission has determined are likely to become endangered in the future. Laws and regulations pertaining to endangered or threatened species are contained in Chapters 67 and 68 of the Texas Parks and Wildlife Department Code and Sections 65.171-65.184 of Title 31 of the Texas Administrative Code (T.A.C.). In 1988 the Texas legislature authorized TPWD to establish a list of threatened and endangered plant species for the state. Laws and regulations pertaining to endangered or threatened plant species are contained in Chapter 88 of the TPWD Code and Sections 69.01-69.14 of the T.A.C.

TPWD regulations prohibit the taking, possession, transportation, or sale of any of the animal or plant species designated by state law as endangered or threatened without the issuance of a permit. Listing and recovery of endangered species in Texas are coordinated by the Wildlife Diversity Branch in the Wildlife Division of TPWD. Currently, TPWD lists thirty-two terrestrial Texas vertebrates as endangered and seventy as threatened. No summary of the status of these species has been done.

Mammals included in the federal and state lists are distributed throughout the state. There is no obvious geographic pattern or concentration of occurrence of these species, suggesting that the conservation pressures impacting our rare and endangered resource are statewide and not just regional or local in nature. This conclusion is further substantiated by the work of Guy Cameron and his students (1997) who tracked the status of 409 rare plant and animal species on the Texas Parks and Wildlife Special Species List. Using the ninety-one plant communities recognized for Texas (see Diamond et al., 1987), these investigators assigned species to those plant communities in which they occurred. They found that rare mammals occurred in fifty-four of the ninety-one plant communities in Texas. The largest number of rare mammal species in a plant community was twelve, contained in the Lechuguila-Sotol plant community, followed by eleven in the Gray Oak-Oak and Pinyon Oak-Oak communities, and ten in the Cottonwood-Willow community; the least was one species contained in thirteen plant communities. Thirteen plant communities contained state or federal endangered species. These results demonstrate that no single habitat can be targeted for conservation of rare mammals in Texas.

## Mammals Endangered in Texas

Five extant taxa of land mammals currently are considered as endangered in Texas. Three of these, *Leptonycteris nivalis*, *Leopardus pardalis*, and *Herpaliurus yagouaroundi*, appear on both state and federal lists, whereas the black bear (*Ursus americanus*) and the white-nosed coati or coatimundi (*Nasua narica*) are listed as endangered by TPWD. Another four species (red wolf, gray wolf, black-footed ferret, and jaguar) are listed as endangered by both USFWS and TPWD, although they are now extinct as discussed earlier in this chapter.

*Leptonycteris nivalis*, the Mexican long-nosed bat, is a colonial, cave-dwelling bat that usually inhabits deep caverns. It was first discovered in the United States in 1937 in a cave in the Chisos Mountains of Big Bend National Park (Borell and Bryant, 1942). Even today, aside from a few records of foraging individuals, the only known colony of these bats in the United States is from the large cave on Mt. Emory in the Park and from the Chinati Mountains in Presidio County (Schmidly, 1991). Yearly estimates of population size at the Big Bend colony range from zero to as many as 10,650 individuals (Easterla, 1972). Reasons for these fluctuations are unknown, but some scientists believe that the colony forms in years

when overpopulation or low food supply in Mexico forces the bats to move northward. However, even considering natural fluctuations and different methods of estimating numbers, there still appears to be a downward trend in the numbers of bats at the Big Bend colony, and population declines also have been documented in Mexico (Campbell, 1995). For these reasons, the USFWS added this bat, along with its closely related congener, *Leptonycteris curasoae*, to the federal endangered species list in 1988 (Shull, 1988). Long-nosed bats are nectar-feeding species that utilize the pollen and insects from night-blooming century plants (*Agave* sp.). There are concerns about the loss of their habitat in Mexico and the destruction of caves throughout their range (Wilson, 1985).

A few black bears of the subspecies *Ursus americanus amblyceps* still were to be found in the Hill Country as late as 1902, and remnant breeding populations hung on in the woodlands of the isolated mountains in the Trans-Pecos (Davis and Guadalupe Mountains) until the middle part of the century. Many biologists thought bears were gone forever, but the last decade of the twentieth century witnessed the natural restoration of black bear populations as a result of the coalescing of biogeographic, ecological, and sociological factors. The presence of bears in adjacent but geographically isolated mountain ranges in northern Mexico facilitated the colonization of populations. In Coahuila, Mexico, just across the border from Texas, black bear populations have increased from previously endangered levels to one of the highest densities in North America because of landowner initiatives and encouragement from the Mexican government. Bear populations are now spilling over into the Big Bend region and other areas of West and southwest Texas. This case is worth noting because natural recolonization of historical range by large carnivores is uncommon in today's world of habitat fragmentation, disturbance, and destruction. Bear sight-

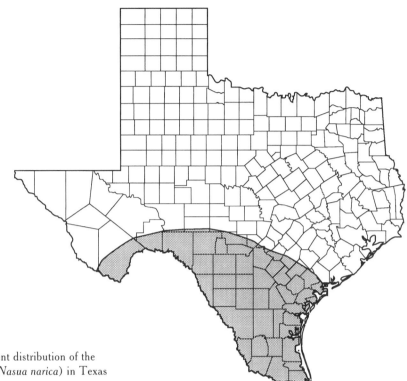

Map 32. The current distribution of the
white-nosed coati (*Nasua narica*) in Texas

ings especially increased in the Chisos Mountains of Big Bend National Park (BBNP), reaching levels of 21 in 1988, 29 in 1989, and 60 in 1990, including 11 sightings of female with young. These sightings suggest that the core of a breeding population now exists in the Chisos and Guadalupe Mountains and, coupled with other recent sightings in the Davis and Glass Mountains, as well as the far western reaches of the Edwards Plateau around Comstock in Val Verde County, may signal the return of permanent black bear populations to west Texas (Hellgren, 1993; McClinton et al., 1992; Cox, 1996).

*Nasua narica molaris*, the white-nosed coati, is the subspecies of coati that occurs in the extreme southern and southwestern areas of the state (Map 32). Because of its erratic distribution and destruction of most of its habitat, the coati was listed as endangered by the TPWD in 1987, and it is on the TOES watch list. It

evidently has not been listed as endangered by the USFWS because of the relatively good populations extant in southeastern Arizona. It is widespread in Mexico and Middle America. Little is known about the life history or abundance of the coati, and this species definitely is in need of serious study. Most of the Texas sightings of coatis have been from the southernmost portion of the state along the Rio Grande (Tabor, 1940; Kaufman et al., 1976; Davis and Schmidly, 1994). Specimens and/or sightings have been recorded in the following areas: Aransas Wildlife Refuge, Aransas County (Halloren, 1961); Dead Horse Mountains, Brewster County (Taber, 1940); Brownsville, Cameron County (Bailey, 1905); Eagle Pass, Maverick County (Taber, 1940); Rio Frio, Real County (Hall, 1981); Kerr and Uvalde Counties (Davis and Schmidly, 1994); and Laredo, Webb County (two specimens in the Philadelphia Academy of Sciences). These re-

Fig. 133. Ocelot, taken on Sauz Ranch, Cameron County, 1924. Courtesy National Archives, 22-WB-64-B26609

cords cover a time frame of almost a hundred years, from 1877 to 1966 (Henke and Young, 1997). The most recent records are of two sightings, possibly of the same individual, in Victoria County in 1994 and 1995 (Henke and Young, 1997). Coatis could be seriously impacted by the degradation and loss of much of the riparian woodland habitat in South and West Texas (Rappole and Tipton, 1987). These animals require a sizeable area of habitat to maintain a viable population.

*Leopardus pardalis*, the ocelot, was still common during the time of the biological survey, but predator control and habitat destruction have greatly reduced its range and numbers (Fig. 133). The ocelot is listed as endangered on both the TPWD and federal lists and by the Convention on International Trade of Endangered Species (CITES). Although still abun-

dant in parts of Mexico, Central America, and South America, within the United States the current ocelot population consists of 80–120 individuals confined to two isolated populations restricted to several small patches of suitable habitat in three or four counties in the Lower Rio Grande Valley (Tewes and Everett, 1986). Modifications of the landscape during the twentieth century, as a result of mechanical farming and brush eradication, have fragmented the ocelot's range, reduced its numbers, and presumably established barriers to dispersal between South Texas populations and the larger, more continuously distributed populations in northern Mexico. Michael Tewes, together with his students and collaborators of the Caesar Kleberg Wildlife Research Institute in Kingsville, Texas, has been studying the ecology and conservation of ocelots. They have documented aspects of its biology and natural history, and they have developed a habitat conservation plan to preserve this species (Tewes and Miller, 1987; Navarro et al., 1993; Young and Tewes, 1994; Tewes et al., 1995; Anderson et al., 1997; Shindle and Tewes, 1998; Tewes and Blanton, 1998; Hewitt et al., 1998; Walker, 1997). The ocelot is considered endangered throughout its entire range and habitat restoration will be important in enhancing its recovery.

Rodney Honeycutt and his students at Texas A&M University have been studying the genetic structure of the remaining ocelot populations using nuclear and mitochondrial DNA markers. Their data from the two populations— Willacy County and Laguna Atascosa National Wildlife Refuge (LANWR)—reveal that genetic variation in these populations is significantly less than seen in Mexico, and the distribution of genetic markers suggest no recent gene flow among these populations and those in northern Mexico. Genetic estimates of effective population size varied from eight to twenty-one individuals at LANWR and between 58 and 142 individuals in Willacy County. Future management and conservation strategies to ensure the survival of ocelots will have to include plans for offsetting the erosion of genetic variation in isolated populations.

*Herpailurus yagouaroundi*, the jaguarundi, apparently was still present over much of the Rio Grande Valley of South Texas at the time of the biological survey (Fig. 134). It was never as widely distributed as the ocelot but shares the latter's predilection for brushy country (Jones, 1993). The rarest of all the native cats, jaguarundis are now thought to be represented in the lower Rio Grande Valley by no more than fifteen individuals (Tewes, 1990). With numbers so low, it is doubtful it will survive. The last specimen taken was a road-killed individual found near Brownsville in 1986 (Tewes, 1990). As with the jaguar and ocelot, predator control and habitat destruction took their toll

Fig. 134. Jaguarundi, found dead on a highway near Harlingen, Cameron County. Courtesy Laguna Atascosa National Wildlife Refuge

on this species. The clearing of brushlands in the Rio Grande Valley destroyed its habitat, and only habitat restoration and reintroductions can save this species from extinction.

Conservation of remaining habitat, and maintenance or creation of new brush tracts, are necessary for survival of ocelot and jaguarundi populations (Tewes and Schmidly, 1987). The USFWS, TPWD, and the Nature Conservancy of Texas have been working for several years in a cooperative effort to restore habitat in the Rio Grande Valley.

### Mammals Threatened in Texas

Six species of mammals (three bats and three rodents) are regarded as threatened by the TPWD. The grizzly bear is listed as threatened by the USFWS, but it is now extinct in Texas as discussed earlier in this chapter.

*Lasiurus ega*, the southern yellow bat, is a neotropical species that reaches the United States in southern Texas where it has been recorded in Cameron, Kleberg, and Nueces Counties. These bats are associated with trees which can provide them with daytime roosting sites. In the vicinity of Brownsville, numbers of them inhabit a natural grove of palm trees (*Sabal mexicana*), and they appear to be a permanent resident of that area (Baker et al., 1971). This bat is listed by TPWD as threatened and as a watch-list species by TOES, primarily because of low population size and concerns about its habitat.

*Euderma maculatum*, the spotted bat, although unmistakable in appearance, is one of the least understood of American bats, primarily because of its relative scarcity, at least in mammal collections. There have been scattered records of this bat throughout the western United States dating back to 1891, but it has been taken with regularity only in California, Arizona, New Mexico, southern Utah, and southern Colorado. It was first found in Texas by David Easterla in 1967 in Big Bend National Park (Easterla, 1970). No one else has collected any specimens of the species in the state, and this infrequency of capture has caused much confusion and speculation regarding its status. It is listed as threatened by TPWD and as a watch-list species by TOES.

*Plecotus rafinesquii*, Rafinesque's big-eared bat, occurs throughout the southeast United States, reaching the westernmost portion of its range in the pine-oak and longleaf pine vegetational regions of East Texas. It was first recorded in 1965 (Michael and Birch, 1967), and it remains one of the rarest species of bats today, having been recorded from only fifteen counties. Its favored roosting sites include partially lighted, unoccupied buildings and other man-made structures such as wells and cisterns. It is listed as threatened by both TPWD and TOES.

*Dipodomys elator*, the Texas kangaroo rat, was obtained by the federal agents in Clay County. The species occurs in a band just south of the Red River from Motley County in the west to Montague County in the east but with substantial populations apparently only in Hardeman, Wichita, and Wilbarger Counties (Martin and Matocha, 1972; Dalquest and Horner 1984; Jones and Bogan, 1986; Jones, C. et al., 1988). Its historic range may have included southwestern Oklahoma but the species probably no longer occurs there (Moss and Melhop-Cifelli, 1990). Because of its restricted geographic range and habitat alteration from agricultural practices, the Texas kangaroo rat is protected by TPWD as a threatened species. The USFWS has taken a somewhat more cautious view of the status, all the while seeking additional information on *D. elator*. Several state- and federally sponsored studies have been completed in recent years (see, for example, Jones, C. et al., 1988). Heavily grazed rangeland and the eroded sides of well-worn rangeland roadways provide optimum habitat, much as overgrazing and trampling by bison may have done in the past (Stangl et al., 1992). Where it occurs the rodent is often common, even abundant, and certainly occupies its habitats to the limits imposed by food and other factors (Dalquest and Horner, 1984). Its limited geographic range, land-use practices within its range, and its selection of rather specific habitat—short grasses associated with mesquite on clay or sandy loam soils—are thought to contribute to its vulnerability (Stangl et al., 1992).

*Oryzomys couesi aquaticus*, Coues' rice rat, occurs in the United States only in two counties (Cameron and Hidalgo) in extreme South Texas. This is a common small mammal from Mexico southward to Panama, where it is in absolutely no danger. Whether it should be listed is problematic, although it could be threatened by habitat loss. The resaca environment is declining, largely because of drainage for irrigated agriculture. Resacas bordered by cattail-bulrush marsh and subtropical woodlands, the preferred habitat of this rat, are essentially confined to the Cameron-Hidalgo County region.

*Peromyscus truei comanche*, the Palo Duro mouse, was described as a separate species by Frank Blair (Blair, 1943). The species has had a varied taxonomic history, shifting between species and subspecies status. The latest taxonomic arrangement, based on a composite of morphological and genetic characters, arranges it as a distinct subspecies of the wide-ranging species, *Peromyscus truei* (Schmidly, 1973b). Its geographic range, which is completely isolated from the other populations of *P. truei*, encompasses three counties—Armstrong, Briscoe, and Randall—in Palo Duro Canyon State Park and Caprock Canyons State Park (Yancey et al., 1996). There it occupies high rocky ledges clothed with juniper along the break of the Llano Estacado. Taking into account the numerous side canyons, indentations, and contours along the edge of the Llano, this mouse must have at least a hundred miles of more or less continuous distribution. Because of its limited distribution, the Palo Duro mouse presently is regarded as threatened by TPWD, as a watch-list species by TOES, and as a former candidate for Category 2 listing by the USFWS. At this time, there appear to be no significant threats to its specific habitat. Moreover, there are two state parks within the geographic range to serve as refugia (Yancey et al., 1996).

Actually, another subspecies of the pinon mouse, *Peromyscus truei truei*, also occurs in Texas and is much rarer than *P. t. comanche*. It is known by only four specimens from Guadalupe Mountains National Park and five from along the northern edge of the Llano Estacado, just inside Texas from New Mexico in Deaf Smith County. To be consistent, all known populations of *P. truei* in Texas should be regarded as threatened (Jones, 1993).

**Mammals Listed as Candidate Species**

Three extant taxa of Texas mammals have been considered candidates for listing as endangered or threatened on the federal list. They are the Davis Mountains cottontail (*Sylvilagus robustus*), the eastern hog-nosed skunk (*Conepatus leuconotus texensis*), and the swift fox (*Vulpes velox*).

*Sylvilagus robustus*, the Davis Mountains cottontail, has a restricted distribution in the central core of mountains in Trans-Pecos Texas. This species was recently elevated to the status of a distinct species by Luis Ruedas (1998; see Chapter 3 for a discussion), previously having been considered as a subspecies of the wide-ranging species, *S. floridanus*. There is also one isolated population in the Sierra de la Madera in Coahuila, Mexico. This rabbit was listed by the USFWS as a candidate taxa in 1994 for inclusion in a forthcoming list of endangered and threatened taxa. Ruedas (1998) has recommended state listing for this species as well as redbook listing as endangered by the International Union for the Conservation of Nature (IUCN) pending the completion of more detailed studies that need to be undertaken of the biology of *S. robustus*, including assessment of population status and life history parameters, long-term ecological studies, and population genetic analyses.

The eastern hog-nosed skunk, *Conepatus leuconotus texensis*, which occurs in the brush country of South Texas and along the coastal lowlands of the state, was classified as a Category 1 candidate in the 1994 annual notice of review but was removed from that status in the 1996 list. The federal agents found the coastal populations of *C. leuconotus* to be relatively common during the time of the biological survey. By the end of the twentieth century, the coastal population had declined dramatically and very few specimens have been collected the latter half of the century. Out of 27,446 steel trap-days from a study of predator control in Kleberg County over a two-year period, Sam Beasom (1974) captured only two eastern hog-nosed skunks. There is no known explanation for a decline in their populations. The western species, *Conepatus mesoleucus mearnsi*, appears to be holding its own in Central and West Texas.

*Vulpes velox*, the swift fox, is listed as a candidate species on the 1996 federal endangered species list, and together with its closely related form, the kit fox (*Vulpes macrotis*), is listed as a watch-list species by TOES. The candidate listing means the USFWS has on file sufficient information on biological vulnerability to list it as endangered or threatened, but proposed rules have not yet been issued because this action has been precluded by other listing activities. Both of these foxes are notoriously susceptible to trapping and poisoning. Consequently, they have been greatly reduced or entirely eliminated in areas of their range where predator control campaigns have been carried out.

## Mammals Possibly Threatened or Endangered

There are several species of terrestrial mammals, or populations thereof, in Texas that may well warrant protection in the future. Certainly their situation bears watching; in some cases, considerable additional data are needed to establish the facts necessary to arrive at a meaningful and biologically defensible position as to their status.

Elliot's short-tailed shrew, *Blarina hylophaga*, has a disjunct distribution in Texas, having been recorded in Montague County on the Red River, in Bastrop County in the central part of the state, and in Aransas County along the lower Texas Coast. The only place where the species has been taken in any numbers is in Aransas County (Schmidly and

Brown, 1979), and that population has been described as a distinct subspecies, *B. h. plumbea* (George et al., 1981). The Aransas County population occupies the oak mottes at Aransas County Wildlife Refuge. A number of management proposals have been implemented for this habitat, including burning, clearing, and grazing, but the potential effects of these activities on the shrew are unknown.

*Myotis austroriparius*, the southeastern myotis, is listed as a watch-list species by TOES, although it is not on the TPWD or the federal list. It was first recorded in Texas in Bowie County in 1962 (Packard, 1966). In 1991, Schmidly noted nine county records. Now this species is known from twenty-two counties and the range line has been extended to the west by a hundred miles (Walker et al., 1996). Low population density has been the main concern about this bat, which roosts in live, hollow, bottomland hardwood trees in close proximity to slow moving rivers and man-made structures such as abandoned houses and culverts. Recent information suggests this species is not as rare as previously thought and probably should not be included on any species list of special concern.

Two other bats of the genus *Myotis*—*lucifugus* and *septentrionalis*—are known from Texas each by a single specimen, the former from Ft. Hancock in Hudspeth County in the early 1900s and the latter from Winter Haven, Dimmit County, in 1942 (Schmidly, 1991). Probably these represent wanderers and neither species now is a part of the permanent Texas fauna. Similarly, the Mexican long-tongued bat (*Choeronycteris mexicana*) is known only from photographs of a single individual and observations of several others at Santa Ana National Wildlife Refuge in the lower Rio Grande Valley. Recently, a specimen was obtained in Brownsville, Cameron County (Steve A. Smith, personal communication). It is not possible to determine if these are accidental occurrences or if there is a tenuous, seasonal population of this pollen- and nectar-feeding species in southernmost Texas. Of certain accidental occurrence is the one specimen of hairy-legged vampire bat (*Diphylla ecaudata*) found in a partially inundated railway tunnel in Val Verde County in 1967.

There are two bats of the genus *Lasiurus*—*blossevilli* and *xanthinus*—that have only recently been recorded in Trans-Pecos Texas and that seemingly are very rare. There is one record of *L. blossevilli*, the western red bat, from the Sierra Vieja in Presidio County (Genoways and Baker, 1988). The eastern red bat, *L. borealis*, is much more common, having been recorded in the Davis Mountains as well as the Sierra Vieja (Jones and Bradley, 1999). The western yellow bat, *L. xanthinus*, which was known from Mexico and extreme southwestern New Mexico, southern Arizona and southern California, has been reported recently from the Big Bend region in Brewster County (Higginbotham et al., 1999; Bradley et al., in press); the Davis Mountains, Jeff Davis County (Jones et al., 1999); and near Langtry, Val Verde County (Weyandt et al., in press). The total number of specimens obtained is only eight. *L. xanthinus* was recently elevated to a separate species by Robert Baker and colleagues (1988), who found the eastern (*L. ega*) and western (*L. xanthinus*) populations to be specifically distinct on the basis of chromosomal distinctions and electrophoretic data. These findings were confirmed by the work of John Morales and John Bickham (1995) using molecular data.

The large mastiff bat, *Eumops perotis*, has a restricted distribution along part of the southern border of the state and is recorded from few localities (Schmidly, 1991). It requires clefts in high, rocky cliffs as roosting sites. The pocketed free-tailed bat, *Nyctinomops femorosaccus*, requires similar habitats and has an even more restricted known range in Texas (southern Big

Bend region). Another free-tailed species (*N. macrotis*), although widespread as a transient, is a rare resident of the southwestern part of the state.

*Tamias canipes*, the gray-footed chipmunk, is known from the Guadalupe Mountains and Sierra Diablo in West Texas (Davis and Schmidly, 1994) and from three areas in New Mexico (Findley et al., 1975). It is restricted to the forests of pine, oak, and fir found at the highest elevations in Texas (1,800–2,500 m). Though the animal is common and presumably well protected in Guadalupe Mountains National Park, there are questions concerning its well-being elsewhere within its restricted range.

Texas is home to nine species and more than thirty subspecies of pocket gophers, belonging to the genera *Thomomys*, *Geomys*, and *Cratogeomys*. Several of these taxa have highly localized ranges and could be vulnerable to localized extinction events. Obvious examples include *Thomomys bottae limpiae* and *T. b. texensis*, two subspecies which occupy confined ranges in the Davis Mountains, the former at lower elevations and the latter at elevations above 5,000 feet (Blair, 1939; Davis, 1940a). Both subspecies have undergone range depletions, apparently as a result of competition with *Cratogeomys castanops* (Reichman and Baker, 1972). In fact, one of these races, *limpiae*, has not been found at its type locality since 1968. The replacement of *T. bottae* populations by *C. castanops* in the southwest has been noted by several authors during the twentieth century (Nelson and Goldman, 1934; Davis, 1940; Baker, 1953). This phenomenon could be considered as strictly "natural," one that normally occurs in the evolution and replacement of species over geological time. The problem, however, is complicated by the fact that overgrazing, which has taken place in the Davis Mountains since the 1870s, changes the environment causing dramatic plant community changes, increased runoff, and ultimately, more xeric conditions (Reichman and Baker, 1972). These xeric conditions, in turn, favor *Cratogeomys* over *Thomomys*.

Two subspecies of the Texas pocket gopher, *Geomys personatus*, also bear watching. *G. p. maritimus* is known only from its type locality which is at Flour Bluff, near Corpus Christi (Williams and Genoways, 1981). Since the only locality is within the greater Corpus Christi metropolitan area, it obviously could be threatened by urbanization. *G. p. streckeri* is another subspecies which is known only from its type locality at Carizzo Springs in Dimmit County (Williams and Genoways, 1981). Neither of these subspecies appears on any official rare or threatened listing of mammals.

*Geomys attwateri*, Attwater's pocket gopher, occurs in the south-central part of eastern Texas, from Milam County southward to Matagorda and San Patricio Counties and southwestward to Atascosa County. This species still appears to be locally common, although it is absent from some places where it was previously present.

*Ondatra zibethicus ripensis*, the Pecos River muskrat, occurred in numerous areas of the Trans-Pecos, along both the Pecos River and the Rio Grande and at springs such as those at Ft. Stockton and Balmorhea during the time of the biological survey. As human population and irrigation wells increased, many of the springs of the Pecos River drainage were destroyed. As the springs dried up, the population of muskrats they supported died out. Thus, today the drainage ditches near El Paso represent the last stronghold of *Ondatra zibethicus ripensis* in the Trans-Pecos. This taxon is listed as endangered by TOES.

The rock mouse, *Peromyscus nasutus*, which occupies a few mountainous habitats in the southern and western Trans-Pecos (Franklin, Guadalupe, Davis, Chinati, and Chisos Mountains) is another poorly known species which might be mentioned. These mice have been documented in small numbers from the mesic canyons associated with the forested woodlands of the largest mountain ranges in the Trans-Pecos. Its status bears watching in the future.

*Lontra canadensis*, the northern river otter, is presently known from the major watersheds in the eastern one-fourth of the state. It has been extirpated from the Panhandle, north-central, and southern portions of Texas and is listed as threatened by TOES but does not appear on the TPWD or federal lists. Habitat destruction, trapping pressure, and drowning in fish traps are considered to be threats to this species in Texas. Although their range is now restricted, recent sightings in much of its remaining suitable habitat (Jackson et al., 1998) suggests river otters may be increasing in abundance. Apparently, the reestablishment and abundance of beaver and the improved habitat diversity and productivity associated with beaver activity have benefited the otter. Human-induced changes in habitat, such as impoundments, canals, levees, and so forth are also providing improved conditions for the otter.

The hooded skunk, *Mephitis macroura*, was not documented in Texas by Bailey and the federal agents. The first Texas specimens were reported from Fort Stockton, Pecos County, in 1925 (Patton, 1974) and from near Mount Livermore, Jeff Davis County, in 1940 (Blair, 1940). A few other records have been reported since, but this is the rarest skunk in West Texas having been documented from Presidio, Brewster, Jeff Davis, Pecos, Reeves, and Ward Counties (Patton, 1974). Robert Patton, who was my first Ph.D. student at Texas A&M, conducted an ecological study of skunks near Balmorhea, Texas, and he reported sighting a few hooded skunks in the vicinity of Balmorhea Lake Dam in the early 1970s. However, Clyde Jones (personal communication) told me he has not seen a single hooded skunk in fifteen years of field work within its range in Texas. Reasons for its decline are unknown at this time, but this is clearly a species that warrants watching in the twenty-first century.

Another example of mammals that are possibly threatened or endangered involves the two species of spotted skunks in the state, *Spilogale gracilis* in the Trans-Pecos and adjacent regions and *S. putorius* in the east and north (Jones, 1993). Once relatively common, these two species now are rare in some areas and their current status in the state is unknown. The genus is in need of detailed study. Because these small skunks consume many insects, some believe populations (particularly those of *putorius*) were decimated by widespread use of chlorinated hydrocarbon insecticides, with the deadly effect passed (and concentrated) up the food chain.

Introductions of Nonindigenous Species

Throughout this century a number of lesser visible but nevertheless devastating species have been introduced into the state, including exotic mammals (rodents and ungulates), birds (starlings), fish (grass carp), and insects (Africanized honeybees and red imported fire ants). The character and composition of the fauna have changed substantially as a result of these biological invaders.

The red imported fire ant, *Solenopsis invicta*, was introduced into the United States through the port of Mobile, Alabama, in the early 1930s. Despite intensive control efforts, the species has infested much of the United States, including most of Texas. There have been numerous reports of the red imported fire ant causing damage to reptiles, birds, and mammals in Texas (Allen et al., 1994; Drecs, 1994; Wilson and Silvy, 1988). These ants have been shon to alter habitat use and to reduce the carrying capacity of the habitat for some small mammal species (Smith et al., 1990). Many conservationists believe that in

time, *S. invicta* will wreck havoc on Texas wildlife.

A particularly scary incident of a biological invasion occurred in 1993 when a brown tree snake (*Bioga irregularis*) was found in crated household goods shipped from Guam to Ingleside Naval Station near Corpus Christi (McCoid et al., 1994). Fortunately the snake was killed before it escaped into the wild but this incident illustrates how easy it can be for animals to become introduced outside of their native range. The brown tree snake, a New Guinea native, has caused significant economic, biological, and human safety problems wherever it has been introduced in the South Pacific islands, causing the extirpation of nine of Guam's eleven native birds and threatening the entire native forest-dwelling avifauna on many islands. This is not a species we would ever want to have introduced into Texas.

Nonindigenous mammals, which were hardly ever encountered by Bailey and the federal agents, now openly range over much of the state. Early explorers and settlers brought Old World rats (genus *Rattus*) and mice (genus *Mus*) to the United States. By the time Bailey worked in Texas, Old World rats and mice were already established in every city and town in the state as well as occurring in the feral state. But this was just about the extent of introduced mammals. Since 1900, the number of mammals introduced has increased at a staggering rate.

As Bailey noted, red foxes (*Vulpes vulpes*) were not native to Texas or anywhere else in the United States. It is generally agreed that the species was introduced from England by a group of Maryland planters in 1730 for the purpose of providing the sport of fox hunting in that colony. Whether any of the descendents of those first individuals ever reached Texas is not known (Weniger, 1997). Texas got its own infusion of the species later, when at least 145 individuals were released in the central and eastern parts of the state in the 1890s (Doughty, 1983). As Bailey comments, they quickly became locally common. Today, red foxes occur throughout eastern and North-Central Texas, as far west as the Panhandle and central Trans-Pecos, but they do not seem to be abundant anywhere. Highest densities occur in the Pineywoods region.

The next major mammalian introduction involved the nutria, *Myocastor coypus*, a native rat of South America, which was introduced into the southeastern United States in 1938 in the vicinity of Avery Island, Louisiana. Since the early 1940s, the nutria has spread throughout the southeastern United States and eastern Texas, often to the detriment of the native muskrat, *Ondatra zibethicus*, which occupies much the same habitat. Nutrias were widely introduced as a "cure-all" for ponds choked with vegetation. They do reduce many kinds of aquatic plants, but they will not eat "moss" (algae) and many of the submerged plants. The trouble is that once established in a lake, their high reproductive capacity soon results in overpopulation. They become so numerous that the available food supply will not satisfy them, and then trouble begins. The animals move into places where they are not wanted or where they destroy vegetation that is valuable for such wildlife as waterfowl and muskrats. Currently, nutria populations are moderately high and on the increase. The nutria has continued to expand its range and probably will spread throughout the state. Recently, specimens have been reported from Val Verde and Terrell counties, indicating that the species is finally reaching the Trans-Pecos (Hollander et al., 1992).

Feral hogs (*Sus scrofa*) are descended from introductions of European wild hogs for sporting purposes and from escaped domestic swine that established feral populations. Bailey and federal agents encountered them only in a few regions of the state, but they have now spread to

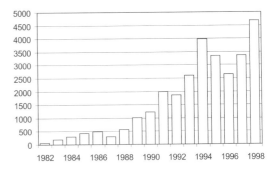

Fig. 135. Feral hog take, 1982–98, by the Texas Wildlife Damage Management Service.

200 of the 254 counties and there are thought to be in excess of 1 million feral hogs now living in Texas. The records of the Texas Wildlife Damage Management Service indicate a dramatic rise in the number of feral hogs taken since 1980 (Fig. 135). Because they are highly prolific breeders and are capable of incredible population explosions—three or four piglets in every litter and about 1-1.5 litters a year—and adaptable, feral hogs pose a danger to other wildlife and birds. Where the range of the feral pig overlaps that of the collared peccary (*Pecari tajacu*) in the thornscrub savannah of South Texas, there is some indication the two species may compete to the detriment of the native peccary. Wild swine alter their diet during drought or seasonal challenges, and in many cases, these food choices overlap with those of native species. Feral pigs disturb (root up) the ground and vegetation when feeding on plant roots and soil invertebrates, and pig-rooting reduces the number of plant species in an area. Besides their growing population, wild hogs also pose another serious problem—disease spread. They play a major role in the transmission of such diseases as brucellosis, pseudo-rabies, and swine fever. Slowing the population explosion of these animals can be achieved only through hunting, dying through natural causes, or trapping and removal of the pigs.

Likewise, domesticated species of mammals (cats and dogs), while not technically "alien," often become feral and free ranging and thereby become a serious threat to native wildlife. Feral cats prey on ground-nesting birds, songbirds in trees, and small mammals, and feral dogs are known to run down deer and livestock.

Amazingly, the most recent example, and perhaps the most dangerous, of an exotic mammal introduced in Texas involves a group of Old World monkeys called Japanese snow monkeys or macaques (*Macaca fuscata*) that have escaped captivity and established a free-living population in the vicinity of Dilley in Frio County about seventy-five miles southwest of San Antonio. The monkeys are descendents of an original group imported from Japan's snow-covered Areshiyama pine forest to a ranch near Laredo in 1972 (Racine, 2000). Later they were transported to an enclosure in the vicinity of Dilley. They have adapted well to the climate of south Texas and now have established a free-ranging, breeding population. Unfortunately, efforts to completely enclose them have failed and many individuals escape on a regular basis. The introduction of free-ranging primates on rangeland in Texas represents one of the most irresponsible acts of species introduction in the history of the state because wild monkeys pose a potential health hazard to people and our native wildlife.

## The Special Case of "Texotics"

Texas has the most widespread and abundant populations of nonindigenous ungulates within the United States (Teer et al., 1993) (Fig. 136a–d). The number of species and their populations has proliferated since their first known introduction on the King Ranch in southern Texas in the late 1920s (Jackson, 1964). Landowner and hunter interest in stocking exotic game have grown rapidly in recent years because of the potential economic return to landowners, the aesthetic value of the animals, and the demand for recreational harvest opportunities for these species (Demarais et al., 1998).

TPWD developed a statewide survey instrument beginning in 1963 and continues to document the status of exotic populations. Results of the 1963 through 1988 surveys were summarized by Elizabeth Mungall and Bill Sheffield (1994). During this time, the exotic population in Texas grew from about 14,000 animals of thirteen species to more than 164,000 animals and sixty-seven species. Based on the total estimate of exotic animals, this represents an average increase of 57 percent between sampling intervals during this period.

The 1994 TPWD survey (Traweek, 1995) produced an estimate of about 195,000 exotic animals and seventy-one species, which amounted to a 19 percent increase during the six-year interval after 1988, which is well below the average increase found from previous surveys. The estimated population of free-ranging exotics in 1994 was about 77,000 (39 percent of total) with 50 percent in the Edwards Plateau and 42 percent in the South Texas Plains, respectively (Traweek, 1995). The number of free-ranging exotics reported in the 1994 survey is about 4.5 percent greater than the approximately 74,000 free-ranging exotics in the 1988 survey.

Among the numerous exotic ungulates, six species have large enough populations in a free-living condition so that they must now be considered permanent additions to our mammal fauna. These are:

*Cervus axis*, the axis deer, a native of India introduced into Texas in 1932 and now occurring in a number of counties in the central and southern part of the state, with more than fifteen thousand free-living individuals;

*Cervus dama*, fallow deer, a native of Iran and North Africa, now with more than ten thousand

Fig. 136. Some exotic ungulates now free-ranging and common in Texas: (a) axis deer, (b) aoudad, (c) nilgai, and (d) blackbuck. a, b, and c. Courtesy Texas Parks and Wildlife Department. d. Courtesy John and Gloria Tveten

a.

b.

c.

d.

individuals, about one-third outside of confinement, mostly on the Edwards Plateau and adjacent areas;

*Cervus nippon*, sika deer, in the central part of the state with more than 5,500 individuals, about half of which are free ranging;

*Boselaphus tragocamelus*, the nilgai, a native of India and Pakistan with more than fifteen thousand animals now free-living in South-Central and southern Texas;

*Ammotragus lervia*, Barbary sheep or aoudad, a native of North Africa first introduced into the Panhandle in 1957 and now existing along much of the eastern edge of the Llano Estacado, in the rough country of Trans-Pecos and on parts of the Edwards Plateau, with a total population thought to exceed five thousand; and

*Antilope cervicapra*, the blackbuck, a native of India and Pakistan, with approximately twenty thousand individuals now living in the wild but with relatively few found outside controlled areas.

Ranching of exotics has become a significant source of revenue for landowners, but there is considerable concern among game biologists and mammalogists about the long-term impacts of these introduced animals on native wildlife. This controversy pits the private sector, eager to diversify its agricultural base, against traditional sportsmen and government agencies, worried about impacts of such activities on indigenous free-ranging wildlife, particularly ungulates (white-tailed deer) and their habitat (Demarais et al., 1990).

Some of the issues that concern conservationists and wildlife professionals about wildlife ranching and farming include disease-related interactions between commercial livestock and native cervids, competitive interactions between native and exotic big game, and potential consequences of interbreeding between native and exotic big game, which could alter the genetic make-up of affected populations (Samuel and Demarais, 1993). There are also indications that high densities of exotic ungulates, combined with overgrazing by native deer and livestock, may severely impact rare native plants. Bob O'Kennon, a rancher in Gillespie County in the Hill Country, established a fifteen-acre native-plant sanctuary on his ranch by installing fencing to keep out both exotic and native ungulates. In an eighteen-month period following establishment of the enclosure, he recorded thirty species of plants that previously had not been recorded in the county (*Austin American-Statesman*, Sunday, May 7, 1989).

There is fairly conclusive evidence of displacement of native ungulates by nonindigenous species (Demarais et al., 1998). Research at the Kerr Wildlife Management Area conducted by TPWD biologists has shown that sika deer and axis deer displaced white-tailed deer within experimental ninety-six-acre enclosures (Harmel, 1980). The most often cited mechanisms underlying potential competition are dietary overlap and competition for limited forage resources (Demarais et al., 1998). The theory is that sika and axis deer out-compete white-tailed deer because they compete directly for the forages most needed by whitetails, and they also do well on lower-quality forage that cannot sustain whitetails (Feldhamer and Armstrong, 1993).

Variation in reproductive characteristics of the three species of deer may also explain some of the competitive differences (Demarais et al., 1998). Whitetail females typically produce two fetuses with peak fawning in June of each year; sika and axis deer produce only one fawn and fawning season peaks during May. The effect of earlier fawning dates and producing only one fawn improves the recruitment rate for sika and axis deer over white-tailed deer.

On some ranches, exotics have displaced white-tailed deer (Butts, 1979), and the potential exists for a more widespread displacement in areas where deer-proof fences do not confine them. Certainly, exotics are here to stay, but their presence challenges Texas's wildlife managers to minimize habitat degradation, disease, competition, and possibly hybridization with native wildlife while at the same time retaining the economic and aesthetic attraction of such introductions. These are issues that have emerged in the latter half of the twentieth century, but they loom even larger for the twenty-first century.

## An Overall Status Summary of Mammals in Texas

As we look back at the twentieth century and prepare for the twenty-first, many issues will continue to influence the status of our fauna. The impact of over-exploitation, largely through over-harvesting and unregulated hunting, severely impacted wildlife at the beginning of the twentieth century. As we look to the next millenium, loss of habitat, landscape fragmentation, and the commercialization of wildlife undoubtedly will impact our landscapes, habitats, fauna, and flora.

The great diversity of forms and the fact that for most species there are no ongoing, standardized inventories makes it difficult to predict trends in mammal populations and species in the state. Using the best data available, as well as the opinion of many professional mammalogists and conservationists, the following summary assesses the current status of the major groups of mammals as the twenty-first century begins.

### Small Mammals and Armadillos

Long-term monitoring of small mammal populations, including shrews, moles, most rodents, armadillos, and bats, has not been done, primarily because these mammals are inconspicuous and mostly nocturnal. The effort needed to obtain reliable estimates of population trends would be extraordinarily costly.

Thus, quantitative assessments of population changes have been made for only a few species, and these based on occasional and geographically restricted studies. Nonetheless, the patterns that do emerge suggest that habitat alterations can have negative impact on populations of many species, as well as positive impact in some cases, such as the initiation of the Conservation Reserve Program.

For these reasons, it is difficult to predict to what extent conservation problems exist for most species of small mammals. For certain, we should be concerned about the status of our unique species. Each of them lives in pitifully small and easily altered habitats, and their status should be monitored carefully. Six species of mammals (one rabbit and five rodents) have most, or all, of their known geographic range confined to the mainland part of the state. For these species, Texas is the key to their survival. They are: the Davis Mountains cottontail (*Sylvilagus robustus*), Attwater's pocket gopher (*Geomys attwateri*), the Texas pocket gopher (*Geomys personatus*), the Llano pocket gopher (*Geomys texensis*), the Texas kangaroo rat (*Dipodomys elator*), and the Gulf Coast kangaroo rat (*Dipodomys compactus*).

In addition, the entire U.S. distribution of another six species of mammals (two bats, two rodents, and two carnivores) is confined to Texas. All these are tropically distributed types that are common over much of Mexico and reach their northern distributional limits in Texas, where they are typically restricted to a few counties along the Texas-Mexico border. These mammals include: the hairy-legged vampire bat (*Diphylla ecaudata*), the southern yellow bat (*Lasiurus ega*), the Mexican spiny pocket mouse (*Liomys irroratus*), the Coues' rice rat (*Oryzomys couesi*), the eastern hog-nosed skunk (*Conepatus leuconotus*), and the yaguarundi (*Herpailurus yagouaroundi*).

There are 229 described subspecies of mammals in Texas, and fifty-five species (about 38 percent of the total) are represented by more than one subspecies. Twenty-nine subspecies of Texas mammals are endemic and confined in distribution to the state. This diversity suggests that Texas harbors tremendous genetic and morphological variability in its mammal fauna.

Recently, concerns have been expressed about possible alarming declines in armadillo populations in many places in Texas. In 1999, Rollin Baker, a retired mammalogist living in Eagle Lake, undertook a survey of professional mammalogists in Texas and found that almost all agreed that armadillos are rare at best when compared with populations five years ago. Baker (personal communication) concludes that armadillo numbers along the Texas coast are truly down, and he suggests this may correlate with a dramatic upsurge in the past decade of feral hogs which may feed on newborn armadillos. The trouble with population declines is that rarely does anyone—even trained observers—notice them until the creatures involved are practically gone.

Thirty-three species of bats occur in Texas, including all but ten of the species and more than 50 percent of the subspecies in the United States. Throughout the southwest and Mexico, there is evidence that many bat populations are declining. The life history strategy of bats, which features low fecundity, specialized roosting requirements, and (in most cases) insectivorous habits, makes them especially vulnerable to environmental threats resulting from pesticide use, habitat destruction, and roost disturbance. There is unequivocal evidence that high levels of the pesticide DDT played a major role in the decline of bat populations in the southwest.

Texas has a large number of extensive caves that may harbor as many as 500 million bats, primarily comprising only two species (Brazilian free-tailed bats, *Tadarida brasiliensis*, and the cave myotis, *Myotis velifer*). Bats are major predators of night-flying insects, especially moths that produce the larvae of many agricul-tural pests. The bats in these caves are estimated to consume more than 6 million pounds of insects nightly. Bracken Cave, located near New Braunfels along the southeastern edge of the Hill Country, is the world's largest bat colony, serving as a nursery colony for adult female free-tailed bats and their young and housing perhaps as many as 20 to 40 million bats during the summer. Likewise, the largest urban colony of bats in North America is located at the Congress Avenue Bridge in Austin. This colony, which numbers about 2.5 million bats in the summer, has become one of the major tourist attractions in that city. The Big Bend region supports the greatest local diversity of bats of any region in the United States. More than twenty species, including some of the rarest and most unusual North American bats, occur in this area.

As many as twelve species of Texas bats—about one-third the total number of species in the state—appear on some sort of endangered, threatened, or rare species watch-list. One group of bats, in particular, that bears watching is the tree bats of the genus *Lasiurus*, of which there are seven species in Texas. *L. borealis*, *L. seminolus*, and *L. intermedius* are year-round residents in the eastern part of the state, and *L. borealis* also occurs, although not nearly as common, in western Texas. *L. cinereus* is a migratory species that is statewide in distribution. The other three species, *L. ega*, *L. blossevilli*, and *L. xanthinus*, have confined distributions in south (*ega*) and western Texas (*blossevilli* and *xanthinus*). None of the three is common where they occur in the state.

Texas is extremely fortunate that the major organization devoted to the conservation of bats, Bat Conservation International (BCI), is located in Austin. BCI has made substantial contributions to the scientific understanding and public appreciation of bats. As an example, BCI has convinced the Texas Department of Transportation to design more bat-friendly bridges that potentially will accommodate millions of new bats.

### Carnivores and Furbearers

This category includes both the small and large carnivores and the major group of Texas animals harvested for direct commercial use and sale of hides and pelts. Nuisance animal control also has a major influence on furbearer management and covers a wide range of issues, from coyote predation on livestock to damage to property or health concerns and safety in urban and suburban areas. Several social issues have impacts on furbearer management. One of these is opposition to trapping, based on reservations about steel leg-hold traps or animal-rights objections to killing furbearers to produce clothing.

Carnivores come in a wide variety of shapes and sizes, ranging from small weasels to large bears, and they too constitute a major component of the Texas mammal fauna. They are the major predators of other mammals, including domestic livestock, which has put them in conflict with humans and has led to massive campaigns to eradicate populations. Carnivores are highly important members of ecological communities. They control pests, such as rodents, and even consume large quantities of insects.

Because of the interplay of trophic level, life history strategy, and size, terrestrial carnivores also are extremely vulnerable to extinction. Within the last century, we have lost the red wolf, gray wolf, and jaguar from our fauna as well as most of our black bear populations. Many other species, such as the ocelot and jaguarundi, are now included on threatened and endangered species lists, and several other species in Texas (coati and eastern hog-nosed skunk) appear to be in serious jeopardy. Some species, such as the raccoon, opossum, gray fox, and striped skunk, have adapted well to urbanization and seem to be increasing in numbers and distribution in this state.

At the beginning of the twentieth century, most predator control efforts in Texas involved farmers and ranchers shooting, trapping, or poisoning predators (primarily coyotes and wolves) to protect their livestock (primarily sheep and goats). Many landowners paid bounties to "professional coyote killers" for each coyote, wolf, or other large predator killed. Beginning in 1915, the federal government became directly involved in predator-control activities with the establishment of the Predator and Rodent Control branch of the Bureau of the Biological Survey. This department is now known as the Animal Damage Control Program of the U.S. Department of Agriculture.

The cooperative Texas Animal Damage Control Program, and its predecessors, became involved in providing predatory animal control services for the next eighty years. The primary function of this cooperative wildlife damage management agency, which comprise the USDA Animal Damage Control Program, the Texas Animal Damage Control Service of the Texas A&M University System, and the Texas Animal Damage Control Association, is to conduct direct control operations for the protection of sheep and goats from depredation by coyotes and other predators (Nunley, 1995).

Organized predator control was begun on the Edwards Plateau, the largest area of sheep concentration, in the early 1900s. By the 1920s, many of the inner Edwards Plateau counties were almost free of coyotes and wolves and, by the 1950s, these predators were thought to be extirpated from most of the region. After a coyote population irruption in the early 1960s, coyotes began to reestablish themselves on the periphery of the Plateau. This encroachment process accelerated through the 1980s and 1990s, and coyotes have now become more common across the entire state (Nunley, 1995). Coyote reestablishment resulted from changing land use, away from sheep and goat production, and from banning toxicant controls, such as strychnine and Compound 1080 (sodium monofluroacetate), by the EPA in 1972 (Nunley, 1995). Despite intensive control efforts, coyotes remain common and widespread and their continued success is assured.

Historically, widespread poisoning and trapping for predators resulted in the destruction of many non-target animals and ultimately contributed to the extirpation of the gray wolf and red wolf. Today, control efforts result in the removal of thousands of predators in Texas each year, but the techniques used are safer—fewer non-target animals are lost—and often the offending individuals can be selectively taken.

The harvest of furbearing mammals fluctuated dramatically throughout the twentieth century. Texas law requires that a "trapper" (one who takes a fur-bearing mammal or the pelt of such an animal) must possess a trapping license. The trapping season for most species opens on December 1 and closes on January 31, lasting only two months. Fur prices are not static from season to season. They fluctuate according to supply and demand, and during periods of high demand a substantial crop of fur-bearing mammals is harvested each year in Texas. For example, the increase in prices paid for raw furs during the 1970s produced a 665 percent increase in licenses sold to trappers. Tabulations from a trapper survey revealed that more than 2.5 million furbearers were harvested, producing an income in excess of $30 million. During this period the average price paid for furs of most species increased substantially. For some species, the value of their fur tripled over this nine-year period. The bobcat possessed the most valuable pelt, followed by the otter and red fox. Other valuable furbearers were the gray fox, coyote, and raccoon. The mushrooming of license purchases caused concern over the possible adverse effects of increased harvest pressure on furbearers.

Special concern developed about the harvest of bobcat during the 1970s because of federal export restrictions from the 1973 Convention on International Trade in Endangered Species of Wild Fauna and Flora (CITES). After a 1977 ban on international trade of various species of endangered spotted cats, the value and demand for the fur of native cats, such as the bobcat, greatly increased. From 1976 to 1982, bobcat pelts in Texas sold for an average of $67.50, and approximately 97,000 bobcats were harvested. For the 1992–93 season, bobcat pelts were worth an average of $25.75 and the annual harvest declined to 4,657.

TPWD began collecting data on annual bobcat harvests in 1976 and Robert Bluett and associates analyzed the geographic distribution of the harvests from 1978–86 (Bluett et al., 1989). They found that 54 percent of the bobcats harvested in Texas during this period were taken in the Trans-Pecos, on the South Texas Plains, and on the Edwards Plateau. Regional harvest densities (number of bobcats harvested per 100 square kilometers) during this period were greatest in the Pineywoods, Cross Timbers and Prairies, and South Texas Plains. It was concluded that populations might have been over-harvested in some local areas and that the illegal transport of pelts from Mexico to Texas might have contributed to high harvest densities in some border counties.

Overall, there appear to be good reasons to be very concerned about three groups of furbearers in the state—skunks, mink, and weasels. Populations of several species of skunks, with the exception of the striped skunk (Mephitis mephitis), appear to be in decline. Hog-nosed skunks (genus Conepatus) have disappeared from the Big Thicket and South Texas plains and hooded skunks (Mephitis macroura) have not been sighted in West Texas in almost two decades. Even both species of spotted skunks (genus Spilogale) appear to be

Fig. 137. Rabbit harvest from a drive at Wall, Tom Green County, 1921. Courtesy National Archives, 22-WB-66-23707

declining. Populations of all our species of skunks bear watching as we enter the twenty-first century. As our natural waters have declined throughout the twentieth century, so have populations of mink and weasels which depend on this type of habitat.

## Game Mammals

Species in the category of big game include the white-tailed deer, mule deer, pronghorn, elk, peccary, aoudad sheep, and desert bighorn sheep. Squirrels, rabbits and hares, and beaver constitute the small game species. Both big and small game mammals have been under intense anthropogenic pressure throughout the latter half of the nineteenth and early part of the twentieth centuries.

By the early 1900s, overexploitation resulting from unregulated market hunting had become a serious threat to wildlife (Fig. 137). Trapping and unrestricted killing decimated many game species. Today, hunting of game species is an important management tool regulated by state law, and the revenue from hunting has become an effective market incentive for landowners to manage for wildlife habitat.

The restoration of populations of large game mammals and other species of special public interest has been a major component of conservation strategy in Texas. There are also some excellent examples of native species and subspecies substantially reduced in numbers by over-hunting and over-trapping but which have subsequently recovered over most of their range as a result of hunting regulations and restocking or other restoration efforts. Probably the most notable examples in Texas of successful restocking programs involve the white-tailed deer (*Odocoileus virginianus*), beaver (*Castor canadensis*), pronghorn (*Antilocapra americana*), and bighorn (*Ovis canadensis*). The situation of the latter two species has been discussed previously.

Native deer were virtually eliminated in Texas by the end of the nineteenth century because of indiscriminate slaughter by commercial meat and hide hunters (see Doughty, 1983, for a detailed discussion). TPWD developed a program to successfully restock deer from central or southern Texas into other regions of the state during the 1930s, 1940s, and 1950s. By the late 1950s and early 1960s deer populations had peaked in many areas and habitat decline because of excessive deer numbers began to occur. During the 1960s, cattle numbers increased dramatically and much native pasture was converted to coastal bermudagrass and other forages that are poor deer food. In addition, the brush on many abandoned farmlands had grown beyond the reach of deer. These factors led to a decline in deer numbers in many areas by the 1970s. Improved habitat management efforts and protection by private landowners, however, prevented a serious decline in deer numbers and deer are now common in most areas of the state. In fact, the white-tailed deer is today the most numerous and economically important big game animal in Texas. The 1997 population estimate was 3,359,000 deer, and 371,000 deer were harvested.

Population restoration involves more than returning extirpated fauna to their former range. Biological and law enforcement concerns must be part of a holistic approach that enhances the success of these increasingly popular efforts, and in Texas it is necessary to achieve the cooperation of private landowners. From a popula-

tion standpoint, it is better to emphasize the recovery of endemic stocks, as a result of protective legislation and habitat management, rather than supplementing populations with nonnative individuals. Conservation management initiatives seeking to restore threatened, endangered, or depleted populations should consider the degree to which reintroductions can contribute to the longevity of the population and potentially alter the population's gene pool. For example, Darrell Ellsworth and associates found that while restocking of white-tailed deer in the southeastern United States may have affected local genetic stocks in some instances, by and large it contributed insignificantly to the genetic composition of extant populations. These authors suggest that despite massive (and expensive) restocking efforts, the abundance of white-tailed deer today is primarily attributable to the recovery of native herds (Ellsworth et al., 1994).

As far as other big game mammals are concerned, their status can be summarized as follows. Native populations of elk and desert bighorns are now extinct in Texas, but TPWD has successfully reestablished populations in remote areas of western Texas. The aoudad is an introduced species which has increased in number in Palo Duro Canyon and several West Texas mountain ranges. Pronghorns suffered a severe population decline earlier in this century but then increased as efforts were made to reestablish the species on vacant historic habitat, and now appears to be in decline again. The white-tailed deer is being successfully managed in all the ecological regions of Texas. The population seems to be stable and healthy and even increasing in some regions of the state. Mule deer populations are considerably lower and of more concern than those of white-tailed deer. There are some indications that hybridization or replacement by white-tailed deer, or both, are occurring in some regions. The overall range of the peccary in Texas has declined substantially, although populations of the species still thrive along the Rio Grande, on adjacent areas of brush country, and in the Big Bend region.

Information on long-term population trends of small game mammals, including beaver, squirrels, rabbits, and hares is not available, but rabbit habitat, especially that of the swamp rabbit, is being lost as a result of changing land use, clear cutting, and overgrazing. There is also concern about the Davis Mountains cottontail because of its small range and apparently low numbers in the isolated mountains of West Texas. Two species of squirrels occur in Texas and they are quite popular with hunters. The most serious conservation problem appears to be with the gray or "cat" squirrel, the habitat of which is being severely reduced as a result of reservoir construction, clear cutting, agriculture, and urbanization.

Because of the high commercial value of their pelts, beaver (*Castor canadensis*) figured prominently in the early exploration and settlement of western North America, including Texas. Thousands of their pelts were harvested annually, and by the 1850s beaver were reduced to very low population numbers over a considerable part of Texas. However, these animals were able to survive on the remote streams of the upper and western Hill Country, along the Devil's River, along the edge of the Panhandle, and around El Paso (Weniger, 1997). By the early 1900s, the federal agents found them to be increasing in numbers and shortly thereafter strict harvest regulations were imposed and restocking of depleted populations became common practice. Today, beaver are found over much of the state where suitable aquatic habitat prevails, and their populations appear to be increasing.

## Growth in Wildlife Commercialization

Hunting on both private and public lands this century has trended toward commercial or fee-hunting in which those who own or manage the land receive compensation for their efforts (Teer et al., 1993). Commercial lease hunting has produced many positive benefits for wildlife conservation in Texas. Leasing of private land for hunting of white-tailed deer and numerous other game species has become a widespread and profitable practice for many landowners throughout the state. In 1991, private landowners received an estimated income from hunting leases of $163 million. The 1996 survey of hunting, fishing, and wildlife-associated recreation reported that 4.7 million Texas residents engaged in fishing, hunting, or wildlife-watching activities and that state residents and non-residents spent $6.5 billion on wildlife-associated recreation (U.S. Dept. Interior, 1998). Of the total, $1.4 billion was spent for hunting. By profiting from the resource, landowners have instituted habitat-management programs that benefit a wide variety of species. Also, the sale of hunting licenses by TPWD has resulted in the availability of public funds to support management programs for game animals.

In spite of these positive benefits, a few wildlife conservationists (Geist, 1988) have argued for a complete ban on any wildlife commercialization and have attacked the Texas system of game ranching and hunt-leasing on the basis of philosophical grounds. Among the drawbacks of game ranching and market hunting, mention has been made about its impact on predators, which are not compatible with this practice, and the reliance on exotics that potentially could threaten native ungulates (Geist, 1988). There is also the biopolitical and social issue of how to provide access to public resources in a system that is privately controlled. Paid hunting excludes many with low incomes, particularly ethnic minorities. Many wildlife professionals are concerned about the long-term erosion of public support for wildlife conservation and management in such a scenario. Game ranching did not exist at the beginning of the twentieth century. It grew as an enterprise the latter half of the century as demand for hunting opportunities increased and private landowners developed a need for income diversification. Although it is certainly here to stay and seems to be working well, it is an issue that bears watching as we seek to manage wildlife resources in the twenty-first century.

A recent survey by Jester et al. (1990) evaluated the commercial use of nongame species which prior to that time had been overlooked and virtually unknown. This report, although inconclusive in terms of the information available, documented several instances of unregulated commercial use of many terrestrial wildlife species. The major demand exists in the rattlesnake market, pet industry, food industry, apparel and decoration industry, oriental folk medicine market, and various opportunistic markets. The pet industry utilizes more species of nongame species than all the other industries combined. Reptiles, amphibians, mammals, and birds are all utilized by this trade along with songbirds, game birds, and game animals. The food, apparel, and decoration markets utilize selected species, primarily reptiles and mammals. The oriental folk medicine market utilizes venomous snakes and their parts. The opportunistic markets specialize in the use of live coyotes, cougars, jackrabbits, and feral pigeons.

The survey by Jester et al. (1990) suggests that the trade in nongame wildlife may be substantial. Markets for nongame wildlife and wildlife products are diverse, and the economic magnitude of this trade cannot be dismissed as inconsequential. Such commercial trade results in a few people realizing profits without returning anything back to the resource which is the property of all citizens. Until 1999, the only re-

quirement to collect and commercialize nongame wildlife was a hunting license. However, the 76th Legislature adopted a new section of the Parks and Wildlife Code, Chapter 67, which provides the commission with authority to establish any limits on the take, possession, propagation, transportation, importation, exportation, sale, or offering for sale of nongame fish or wildlife and establishes the requirement of a permit for the collection and sale of nongame wildlife. Perhaps, this will control any potential problems with commercialization that could endanger nongame wildlife and at the same time provide some funding to provide management of these species.

Another aspect on the negative side of wildlife commercialization has been the growing international traffic in illegal wildlife trade that has become one of the most serious conservation issues in the world. As an example, the illegal trade of cat skins has been a major factor in the decline of those species in South America (Mares and Ojeda, 1984).

## The Development of Mammalogy in Texas

During the time that Bailey and the federal agents worked in Texas there were no professionally trained mammalogists living in the state. A number of private citizens called themselves amateur naturalists and they collaborated with the federal agents. Probably the closest person to a so-called expert would have been H. P. Attwater from San Antonio. Attwater made extensive collections in the regions about San Antonio and Aransas Pass and discovered a number of new forms (including Attwater's prairie chicken) that were described by J. A. Allen in the bulletin of the American Museum of Natural History. He also collaborated and worked with the agents.

Vernon Bailey's 1905 publication was the first comprehensive study of mammals in the state and set the stage for further studies of their distribution, taxonomy, and natural history. It would not be until 1926 that an updated checklist would be published by John K. Strecker, curator of the museum at Baylor University (Strecker, 1926). The progress of mammalogy in Texas was slow for the first three decades of the twentieth century, and it was not until the decade of the great depression that the science started in earnest again. During the latter half of the twentieth century, the science of mammalogy exploded in Texas as a major field of research and education. A detailed account of this history, including the significant events and the many individuals who made significant contributions to it, is beyond the scope of this book, but highlights of the subject can be found in several sources (Baker, 1995; McCarley, 1986; Schmidly and Dixon, 1998; Birney and Choate, 1994; and Jones, 1991).

Among the most significant developments, the following are especially noteworthy:

- The establishment of the Cooperative Wildlife Research Unit at Texas A&M University in 1935, under the leadership of Walter P. Taylor, which was the first organized research unit to study wildlife management in the state.

- The establishment of the Department of Fish and Game (now the Department of Wildlife and Fisheries Sciences) at Texas A&M University in 1937 which, under the direction of William B. Davis, began to train graduate and undergraduate students in mammalogy and started the Texas Cooperative Wildlife Collections, the first major collection of mammals in the state.

- The publication of *The Mammals of Texas* in 1947 by Walter Taylor and William B. Davis, the first comprehensive survey of Texas mammals since Bailey's 1905 publication. This publication has now been revised three times by William B. Davis (1960, 1966, and 1974) and once by Davis and Schmidly (1994). If anyone has earned the title of the "father of mammalogy" in Texas, it would

Fig. 138. William B. Davis, 1939. Courtesy National Archives, 22-WB-51-B57328a

have to be William B. "Doc" Davis (Fig. 138).

- The establishment of the Museum and the Natural Science Research Laboratory at Texas Tech University in 1971. Texas Tech has now become the leading center for the study of mammals in the state, and it houses the state's largest scientific collection of mammals. The Occasional Papers and the Special Publications of the Museum, all produced at Texas Tech, have become the leading publication outlets for mammalian natural history studies. As of 1999, more than 225 scientific papers on mammalogy have been published in these two outlets. The leaders in the establishment of this program were Robert L. Packard, Robert J. Baker, J. Knox Jones Jr., Clyde Jones, Robert Bradley, and Dilford Carter.

- In 1990, the reopening of the Texas Cooperative Fish and Wildlife Research Unit at Texas Tech University. In 1993 this lab affiliated with the nation-wide Gap Analysis program. Gap Analysis was begun by the USFWS in 1989 as a protocol to identify geographic areas with important wildlife and habitat attributes in need of protection. Using geographic information system technology, a statewide database has been developed that represents vegetation communities, terrestrial vertebrate distributions, and boundaries of federal and state conservation areas. GAP is intended to provide resource managers with the most advanced and comprehensive tools to prioritize land use and conservation decisions.

- The establishment of the marine mammal stranding network and the research and graduate education program at Texas A&M University at Galveston. This is the largest academic research program in the world devoted to the study of whales, dolphins, and manatees. The Stranding Network, established in 1974, has collected information on more than a thousand marine mammals that have washed ashore on Texas beaches during the last three decades of the century. The key people who helped establish the marine mammal program in Galveston were William Merrill, David Schmidly, Bernd Würsig, Bill Evans, Randy Davis, and Graham Worthy.

With the explosion of trained scientific talent in mammalogy, including both terrestrial and marine forms, academic institutions across the state began to hire mammalogists and make the subject an important area of research and education. Almost every university in Texas, both public and private, has at one time or another employed a mammalogist and offered an academic course on the subject. More recently, mammalogists have been employed by state and federal governmental agencies responsible for natural resource management in the state (for example, the Texas Parks and Wildlife Department, the U.S. Fish and Wildlife Service, and the National Park Service) as well as many non-governmental organizations (for example, the Nature Conservancy of Texas, Bat Conservation International, and so forth).

The literature about mammalogy in Texas has grown exponentially throughout the twentieth century. Several thousand scientific papers have been published about Texas mammals by students and professionals working in the state. A comprehensive list of these papers was compiled by Jerry Raun in 1962, and the list has been updated every subsequent decade (Raun, 1962; Jones and Homan, 1976; Jones et al., 1985; Swepston and Thompson, 1986).

The twentieth century also witnessed the growth of collections of mammals in Texas. The major collections, with more than seventy thousand specimens, are located at Texas Tech and Texas A&M. Collections of more than ten thousand specimens are housed at Midwestern

Fig. 139. First meeting of the Texas Society of Mammalogists, 1981. Author standing in middle of front row wearing the hat.

State University and Angelo State University. A complete list of Texas mammal collections may be found in Hafner et al. (1997).

The crowning achievement in the growth of mammalogy in Texas was the establishment of a separate scientific society, the Texas Society of Mammalogists (TSM), in 1981 (Fig. 139). Texas is the only state in the United States with a state scientific society devoted to mammalogy, and there are more professional mammalogists living in Texas than any other state in the United States.

The mission of TSM, as stated in its constitution, is to "promote the study of mammals, living and fossil" in Texas. Beginning in 1983, TSM has held an annual meeting in February of every year at the site of Texas Tech University's Junction Campus in Kimble County. Mammalogists and students from throughout the state convene and present papers and hold discussions about the biology and conservation of Texas mammals. The membership of the Texas Society of Mammalogists now numbers approximately 240.

Clearly, Bailey and the federal agents planted a seed that would grow into a major scientific field of study. They probably had no idea this would happen, but it is almost certain they would be pleased with the outcome. The scope of the science of mammalogy and the scientific talent available in the state will be crucial to our ability to wisely manage and conserve mammalian species and communities in the twenty-first century.

# 7

# A Look to the Twenty-first Century

## Challenges for Wildlife Conservation in Texas

The twentieth century has proven as significant for changes made by humans in the landscape—its soils, waters, atmosphere, climate, habitats, and wildlife—as for its technological advancements. The risks as we progress through the twenty-first century are not just with extinction or restriction of wildlife species; there are serious economic ramifications associated with the continued loss of wildlife diversity. As species disappear, human capacity to maintain and enhance agricultural, forest, and rangeland productivity decreases. And with the degradation of ecosystems, valuable services that natural and seminatural systems provide are lost (Western and Pearl, 1989).

It seems inevitable that the twenty-first century will be as different from the twentieth century as the latter was from the nineteenth century, perhaps more so given the accelerating pace of change in lifestyle and technology. The next hundred years will likely decide the future of wildlife in Texas and other states. The decision will be made, directly or indirectly, as to how much and what kind of nature survives. It also seems evident that changes leading into this century are likely to substantially alter wildlife management and make it, and other types of management, increasingly complex in terms of both the clientele served and the socioeconomic and political environment in which management will occur.

Conservation pressures in the twenty-first century will come from a variety of sources. Habitat loss and degradation, over-harvesting, introduction of exotic species, pollution, and other causes will continue to take a significant toll. Global warming or climatic change could exacerbate the loss and degradation of biodiversity by increasing the rate of species extinction, changing population sizes and species distributions, modifying the composition of habitats and ecosystems, and altering their geographic extent.

Essentially the problem involves proliferating human land uses that are powerfully changing the form and shape of the landscape. This results in insufficient habitat for many species or situations in which habitats are isolated in separate pieces too small or too unstable to sustain viable populations of species and thus biological diversity. The study of biogeography reveals that species richness is a function of land area. All environmental variables being equal, the greater the area, the more species it supports. Thus, as habitats are fragmented and isolated into small islands, they lose the capacity to support wildlife diversity.

### New Perspectives in Conservation

As we enter the new century and this era of heightened public concern, the science of conservation has matured and gained universal recognition. American conservation began as an essentially moral movement and has, ever since, centered around several ethical foci that have produced conflict and disagreement. The most celebrated conflict has been the dichotomy between the so-called conservationists and preservationists. A conservationist advocates the wise use of a resource or the productive potential of a resource-generating system, with the goal of maintaining its future availability or productivity. A preservationist, on the other hand, advocates the protection of an ecosystem or a species, to the extent possible, from the disruptions attendant on it from human use.

Conservation and preservation are very different activities, which result from varied and complex motives. Conservationists typically adopt either a utilitarian or land-stewardship ethic about resources which argues that natural resources exist for the use of humans and that we have an obligation to improve on the natural condition and to pursue the sustainable exploitation of resources for the economic benefit of humans. The land stewardship perspective, which was so eloquently stated by Aldo Leopold (1933a, 1933b, 1939, 1947; Tanner, 1987), recognizes the complexity and integrated processes in nature, argues that those who live on the land should protect what they know and love, advocates a scientific basis for maintaining a sustainable harvest, and maintains that it is the responsibility of the individual, not government, to do right by the land.

The more conservative view of natural resource management has advocated the practice/science of making land produce valuable products (wildlife, rangeland, timber, or recreation). This perspective advocates direct or indirect management of resources through manipulation to produce or favor certain targeted goals (Bailey, 1984). Management, in this sense, is on a sustainable-yield basis so that the resource may be periodically harvested without reducing the base stock. The primary target of conventional resource management is economically important products, and the primary aim is to achieve economic benefit or some other desired outcome of benefit to people (Gilbert and Dodds, 1987).

More toward the preservationist viewpoint are the conservation biologists, many of whom advocate a "biophilia" perspective (Wilson, 1984; Wilson and Peter, 1988) that assumes that all living things have intrinsic value (biodiversity), and there is a scientific basis for maintaining biological diversity with the government in a major role. The goal of conservation biology, a term coined by population biologist and geneticist Michael Soule (Soule, 1986, 1987; Soule and Wilcox, 1980; Soule and Kohm, 1989), is to provide the principles and tools for preserving biological diversity, especially perturbed species, communities, and ecosystems. It is a crisis-oriented discipline concerned with the long-term viability of whole systems.

Several new perspectives have been proposed within the scientific community as effective solutions to the conservation/development dilemma at scales ranging from local situations to regional approaches to new thinking about development at both the national and international levels. The new approaches have been described under several labels, including conservation and sustainable development (Clark and Munn, 1986; Tolba, 1987); sustainable ecosystem conservation and management (Hunter, 1990); and holistic resource management (Savory, 1988). Each of these approaches, which fit together in a logical sequence, is built around the principle of sustainability and sustainable use of resources. None of them totally embraces the preservationist perspective, although elements of land acquisition and stewardship, which could include preservation, are advocated. Their goal is to make conservation as large and multi-faceted as the forces that are destroying biological diversity and diminishing human prospects. All consider place and process as well as economic, social, and environmental changes. All are concerned with management and maintenance of diversity at three levels: at the species level, at the level of ecological communities and natural ecological processes, and at the level of human uses of the natural system. The stress is on management that will foster stewardship, multiple values, and the sustainability of all the values and uses of healthy ecosystems, as well as being responsive to people's expectations.

The primary distinction between these various perspectives is the scale of application. They all stress a holistic approach, which has gained acceptance as the only way to go in conservation, and each stresses some aspect of social systems and cultural values. It is now widely accepted that conservation is not possible in a vacuum outside of the human dimension. Conservation biology offers new scientific understandings, particularly in genetics and evolutionary biology, to improve the theoretical framework of conservation. Bioreserves and ecosystem conservation stress regional development that is compatible with local ecosystem processes. Conservation and sustainable development teaches us that conservation is inextricably linked to national economies, policies, and government regulation. Holistic resource management focuses on an integrated land use approach that uses ecological principles to balance agricultural and natural resource production at the enterprise level in consideration of appropriate landowner goals. Sustainable ecosystem management advocates

that conservation on public lands must encompass the full range of services, values, uses, diversity, and continuity of ecological systems.

## Challenges for Managing Wildlife Diversity

Conservation management is about knowing when and how to intercede as the case for doing so becomes more compelling. Thinking in terms of long-term conservation of wildlife diversity in Texas, there are a number of crucial challenges that must be addressed in this new century.

### Find a Common Ground for Managing Wildlife Diversity

The real problem in resource conservation throughout the world involves proliferating populations and associated land conversion that is powerfully changing the form and shape of the landscape. People now constitute a pressure on the global environment that is evident everywhere. There are no longer any truly pristine environments or unoccupied frontiers because virtually every square centimeter of the earth's surface is affected by the activities of human beings. In many places the only way to restore the productivity of our land is through active management or ecological restoration.

Given this understanding, it is surprising to find strong elements within our society opposed to the concept of wildlife management. We are being challenged by "interest-group myopia" and our inability to find a common acceptable ground for managing natural resources. Strong positions have been staked out on the extremes of the spectrum of approaches to conservation, and it has become difficult to find a common ground where the majority of people can seek compromise for the common good. Advocacy groups have taken over and polarized the debate because no one has offered society an acceptable alternative to their winner-take-all strategies. Wildlife professionals, who have devoted their careers to the management and conservation of wildlife resources, must take the lead in creating this common ground.

To develop scientifically sound and socially acceptable wildlife conservation, we must actively work to help people understand the necessity of blending appropriate models of conservation with their respective values and aim for a sustainable stage of overall resource management. To do this we must build long-range thinking and planning into conservation and find ways for diverse groups to network and explore new collaborative ventures that bring separate approaches together in a complementary way.

The early part of the 1990s was a particularly contentious time in Texas conservation circles. The perceived threat of the application of the Endangered Species Act (ESA) convinced many private landowners that their property rights were under threat and that the government, both at the state and federal level, could not be trusted on conservation matters. Consequently, a conflict developed among private landowners, private wildlife managers, and professional wildlife scientists associated with government agencies (state and federal), non-governmental organizations, and universities. At the heart of the conflict was the government and its representatives, who were charged with protecting the people's resources, and the private sector, who felt those efforts were threatening their private property rights. The conflict has diminished somewhat as we enter the twenty-first century but it has not been completely resolved. We still need more positive examples of private landowners, government agencies and biologists, and non-governmental organizations (the Nature Conservancy) working together to find positive solutions to complex conservation issues without compromising private property rights. A few examples of projects are described below.

## Priority Setting Without Data: The Case for Monitoring

A major problem with wildlife management today is that we are often forced to act on the basis of incomplete information, or in some cases, no information at all. In setting priorities for conservation it is not uncommon to rely on "expert opinion" or models built around assumptions. This gives the pretence, and the false security, of an objective system when in fact much of the process is subjective. If we are to conserve wildlife diversity in Texas, we must have an adequate foundation of knowledge on which to base management decisions.

Clearly, what is needed to retard the events that could transpire in this new century is information on the status of vertebrate species and monitoring systems to provide an indication when a species appears to be in some danger (NRC, 1993; Kim and Knutson, 1986). Only if we know there is a problem can we attempt to develop a solution. The solutions we effect will be dependent on how much we know about natural history.

It has been almost a hundred years since the last biological survey of Texas (published in 1905), and this did not include fishes or the state's vast and important invertebrate fauna. A well-planned and carefully executed follow-up survey would provide the kind of baseline data necessary to assess wildlife population trends and habitat conditions. It also would contribute much life-history knowledge about the lesser-known components of our fauna. Texas has the resources within its university faculty, state biologists, and scientists who work for private organizations to develop a database network and coordinated approach to conduct biological surveys that would assess the status of wildlife populations.

## Recognize the Changing Nature of Our Clientele

The Texas public is showing an increasing interest and commitment to conservation more so than ever before. A 2000 public opinion survey of Texans revealed some startling results, including that 97 percent stated it was either very important (79 percent) or somewhat important (18 percent) that natural areas exist in Texas for enjoying and experiencing nature; 94 percent felt it was either very important (73 percent) or somewhat important (21 percent) that fish and wildlife populations are being properly managed and conserved in Texas; 94 percent felt it was either very important (69 percent) or somewhat important (25 percent) that ecologically important habitats and lands in Texas are being protected and preserved; and a staggering 100 percent felt it was either very important (93 percent) or somewhat important (7 percent) that Texas's water resources are safe and well protected (Duda, 2000). The public's concern for the plight of our wildlife diversity is reflected in the growing number of private conservation groups, environmental groups, and scientific societies concerned about wildlife and other natural resources.

At the same time, societal values regarding wildlife resources have adjusted in the past few decades, reflecting more concern for wildlife watching, for threatened and endangered species, and for shrinking global biodiversity. Today in Texas, 76 percent of state residents participate in some form of wildlife watching, compared to 53 percent in fishing and 18 percent in hunting (USDI/USDC, 1998). The 1996 survey revealed that state residents and nonresidents spent $6.5 billion on wildlife-associated recreation in Texas (USDI/USDC, 1998).

One of our greatest challenges will be to solicit the monetary and political support of the growing number of non-consumptive users to support the management and conservation of our wildlife resources on public and private land. We must recognize that our clientele are no longer just hunters. Certainly, we must work to increase the understanding of hunting as a viable method of wildlife conservation, but we must broaden our approach to include opportunities for the non-consumptive enjoyment of wildlife.

One area that holds much promise is wildlife-related tourism, or nature tourism, which increased by 63 percent from 1980 to 1990 and is now the fastest growing sector in the travel industry (Texas Audubon Society, 1997). It has been estimated that 18 million Texans participate in nature tourism and that they expend $1.4 billion of economic activity per year in wildlife viewing alone. Nowhere is nature tourism more evident in Texas than in the Lower Rio Grande Valley, which has the richest biodiversity of birds of any place in the United States. This region is a major attraction for birdwatchers, and the total economic contribution for avitourists to the region exceeds $100 million annually. Wildlife tourism engenders strong public support for conservation; it educates hundreds of thousands of people about the value and importance of biological diversity; and it generates funds for local conservation efforts and state government.

## Avoid Single Species Approaches

For most of the twentieth century, wildlife management tended to focus almost exclusively on one element of the wildlife fauna—game species (deer, quail, dove, turkey, and so forth). Most of our monetary resources and time have been spent on attempting to manage lands for these species almost to the total exclusion of nongame species. During the last two decades of the twentieth century we saw the public develop a growing commitment to the protection of endangered species. The endangered species issue is now confronting us in every region of Texas, and is only likely to get worse in the new century. During the 1990s, Travis County alone spent more than $150 million to protect two species of birds and several species of invertebrates. Among many citizens, there is a growing fear that the ESA could seriously jeopardize private property rights.

A quarter-century has passed since President Richard Nixon signed the ESA into law to protect rare plants and animals on the edge of extinction. Although the ESA has clearly helped to preserve the natural diversity of wildlife in the United States, it has had a checkered history in Texas, coming under strong criticism by many landowner associations and citizens concerned with the protection of private property rights. Despite good intentions, many citizens believe the act suffers from a heavy-handed environmentalism that focuses on imposition of big government to punish landowners and bottleneck important projects, thereby stifling economic growth and development.

Unfortunately, much of the federal government's focus on endangered species has been to protect them with little or no consideration for the impact on private landowners. The ESA is entirely punitive in nature, and it has no mechanism to encourage or reward those landowners who might wish to restore or enhance the habitats of endangered species on their property (Wilcove et al., 1996). Section 9 of the ESA prohibits citizens from "taking" any threatened or endangered species on their private property, and more than half of the listed endangered species have at least 80 percent of their habitat on private land (Innes, 1999). For the act to work in Texas, where more than 96 percent of the land is in private property, most people believe it will have to encourage more creative and less punitive solutions and find ways to create safe harbor provisions for landowners. Finally, it should be clear that the destruction of vast natural areas and the degradation of the environment that threatens all species in-

cluding our own require more than this one act to correct.

Jason Shogren and John Tschirhart (1999) have eloquently summarized the current status of the ESA as follows: "Broader scope and unfunded mandates fan the flame of controversy because the ESA epitomizes the classic quandary of diffuse benefits and concentrated costs. The benefits of protecting endangered species accrue to the entire nation, while a sizeable share of costs fall on private landowners. . . . No one sees a quick end to the ESA controversy. At the end of the day, society is left with difficult economic choices—choices that affect and are affected by biological needs and political realities. Working through this tangle requires more explicit attention as to how economic incentives affect all sides of the debate."

There is evidence that species can be recovered without adversely impacting the ability of private landowners to use their land, and where incentives have been tried they have proven to be remarkably successful. Many landowners are capable of helping endangered species by restoring or enhancing habitat on their land but are unwilling to do so from the fear of new restrictions. They are afraid that if they take actions that attract new endangered species to their land or increase the populations of endangered species that are already there, their "reward" for doing so will be more regulatory restrictions on the use of their property.

With the right tools, however, private landowners have demonstrated their willingness to develop wildlife habitat and protect species. The Environmental Defense Fund helped develop a solution to this problem that the USFWS adopted in April, 1995, under the name of "safe harbor." The safe harbor policy assures landowners that if they undertake actions that are beneficial to endangered species, they will not incur added regulatory burdens as a result of their good deeds. In other words, participants who improve their property for the benefit of endangered species retain the right to undo those voluntary improvements should they wish to make some other use of their land in the future (Earley, 1996).

Texas leads the nation in the creative use of safe harbor agreements (Fialka, 1998). More than a million acres of privately owned ranch land has been enrolled in a safe harbor program that aims to restore the endangered northern aplomado falcon in South Texas. About 16,500 acres of grassland have been enrolled in a safe harbor program for the Attwater's prairie chicken. A similar program has now been approved for the red-cockaded woodpecker in East Texas. In short, some of America's rarest birds are gaining a new lease on life as a result of safe harbor programs.

Environmental monitoring and single-species approaches can help divert problems before species become extinct, but this is a labor-intensive and extremely expensive solution. The least expensive solution is to manage at the ecosystem level, thereby attempting to conserve through time an entire assemblage of species. In a state like Texas, with its enormous biological diversity, this is really the only long-term approach that is feasible. We do not have the financial or human resources or the time to take a single-species approach toward managing our wildlife resources. We must develop a broader management approach that will consider ecosystems and landscapes and all biological resources instead of a limited subset of species and their habitats.

## Focus on Sustainable Resource Systems and Ecosystem Management

To succeed, resource management must be considered in the context of an ecosystem, where resource development, conservation, and protection are considered simultaneously (Western and Pearl, 1989). Competition for resources must give way to cooperative management strategies, where conservation and resource management are linked in sustainable resource systems. Such an approach affords the opportunity to focus on processes through which ecological and human communities are linked, such as the flow of water through a regional watershed, the nutrient cycles that help sustain productive soils, and the seasonal patterns of reproduction and regeneration that characterize the ecological community. We must go beyond a focus on just resources and yields to include the full range of services, values, uses, diversity, and continuity of ecological services.

The concept of sustainable ecosystems management is rapidly gaining acceptance as an appropriate basis for managing public lands in the United States, but we know very little about how to adapt it to private lands. The likelihood that it might work in a state like Texas should be pursued because it provides a conceptual basis for mixing economic, social, and ecological theory with the application of human, biological, and financial resources to manage resources at the land-enterprise scale.

## Strengthen Scientific Research Capability

Science has an essential, invaluable role in resource management: to provide basic knowledge, to yield objective and unambiguous information on what is possible, to help develop sound strategies to meet goals, and to show the costs and consequences of alternative strategies. Doing this requires a judicious mix of science and technology development that ranges from the most basic to the most applied. But we must remember that public policy and direction in a democratic society ultimately come from a political process that weighs scientific information with other considerations. For most of the twentieth century, science had too little to do with decision-making on conservation issues. Most of that was played out through the media and in the courtroom.

The demand will increase for expert opinion on how to manage wildlife resources that will be increasingly used by people. Therefore, not only is more research necessary, but also more effective ways to transfer this information to people and policymakers is required.

The only groups of wildlife species for which sufficient information or resources exist to effectively manage them at the present time are the commercially important species, primarily the game species and some of the large charismatic species. Game species, which constitute a small percentage of the Texas wildlife fauna, have historically received the primary attention of hunters, landowners, and professional wildlife managers. For most nongame species, the information base and the resources have been lacking to acquire the information needed for effective long-term management, although public concern for these species has increased substantially in the past two decades.

More effort is needed to develop the basic knowledge and tools that are the scientific foundation for managing wildlife. Wildlife research must improve in quality and at the same time broaden its scope if societal issues are to be addressed adequately. Essentially all the major scientific challenges require changes in the way researchers organize themselves as well as improvements in technology. It will be necessary to enhance and promote interdisciplinary research to provide new technology and different research approaches. As wildlife issues become more complex, the need for interdisciplinary research will become even greater.

A major opportunity to increase interdisciplinary research will be in the interaction of traditional wildlife biology with biotechnology and molecular biology. As species become more endangered and ecosystems more impoverished by habitat fragmentation, pollution, and other human impacts, methods to keep species artificially, to maintain and boost their reproduction, and eventually to return them to the wild will play a larger role in conservation. The field of ex situ care is growing with the involvement of zoos and zoo-parks (Oldfield, 1989). Techniques include capture, translocation, selective breeding, artificial rearing, genetic management, and disease treatment. The development of biotechnology in the last decade has provided many new tools to use in these efforts. Genetic mapping, protein assembly, cryobiology, nutrition, and reproductive manipulation (including artificial insemination and embryo transfer) potentially have great applications to wildlife management.

Another important area of research in need of strengthening is in the area of human-wildlife interactions. The needs of people drive the use and the misuse of wildlife resources. Our efforts to understand how people think about and act on wildlife resources have been minimal, and yet most controversies and shortages ultimately arise from human activity. Cooperative efforts between natural and social scientists in wildlife traditionally have been low, but the opportunity to increase knowledge and solve problems in this area is great.

A number of authors (Baker et al., 1998; Parker et al., 1998; Bisby, 2000; and Edwards et al., 2000) have advocated the use of the new area of bioinformatics to provide a more appropriate scientific framework for understanding biocomplexity. By using technology in communications, computers, remote sensing, and instantaneous analysis, these authors argue for the utility of a specimen-based geographic-information approach to synthesize historical and contemporary information about living things across interdisciplinary lines. The data sets on which bioinformatics are based can help us understand, recognize, and address such crucial issues as environmental quality, biodiversity, habitat composition, resource allocation, and sustainable development opportunities.

## Make Conservation Education a Priority for the Public

So what if we have the foresight, knowledge, and techniques to conserve wildlife diversity? Whether we act, and how, will depend on factors such as policies, education, socioeconomics, recreation interests, and planning capabilities. Broad-based conservation education programs, designed to diffuse conservation information to the public, are the most important of these considerations (Adams and Thomas, 1986). Without understanding of the need for action, and without commitment to that action, citizens will not contribute to the effort, nor will they cooperate with those so engaged.

With 80 percent of the population now concentrated in cities and towns, Texas has become an urbanized state. As Texas continues to urbanize, it is imperative that resource managers do a better job of educating urban audiences relative to proper wildlife conservation. Most of our citizens are not involved in day-to-day management of natural resources and are unaware of the technology being used, or available, for managing those resources on a sustainable basis. As the urban public assumes a more active role in public policy decision-making, it is critical to the natural resource base and the state's economy that educational programs be designed and supported that address scientific management for continued environmental quality and the necessary flow of goods that must come from our lands and waters. People must learn what it takes to produce the things they desire and at what costs and consequences. We need to understand more about how people get their information and form their opinions. Unfortunately, more people today are getting their information about conservation and resource issues from what they see and hear on television and read in the news media.

People can be educated to understand what the continuation—or destruction—of wildlife means to their future and that of their descendents, and they may be persuaded to act on their resulting concern in ways respectful to the diversity of life and to their own cultural values. However, to be effective, we must reach beyond our traditional clientele—the hunters and landowners—to include all segments of society.

We must also reach beyond the traditional commodity-oriented values to address the entire spectrum of values that society places on wildlife resources. Unless we broaden our clientele base, the public confidence to gain the political power and resources to conserve wildlife diversity will not be forthcoming. One of the most critical educational challenges in Texas will involve engaging minorities about conservation issues. Projections for Texas suggest that the population of the state in the year 2030 will be about 36 percent Anglo, 10 percent African American, 46 percent Hispanic, and 8 percent from other ethnic groups. In 1990, the breakdown was 60 percent Anglo, 12 percent African American, 26 percent Hispanic, and 2 percent from other groups (*Texas Outdoors: A Vision for the Future*, 1998).

The Texas Environmental Education Fund Board was created by the 76th Legislature (S.B. 1746) with appointees named by the governor in November, 1999. This board is charged with finding donated financial resources for environmental education. This represents a major partnership opportunity for the public and private sector in Texas to work together and be certain our citizens are well informed about natural resource and conservation issues. Funding from such a program could help to increase the number of nature centers in urban areas to provide environmental outreach activities to youth and adult groups where it is most needed.

## Increase Participation of Private Landowners

With almost 97 percent of Texas in private lands, it will not be possible to conserve wildlife diversity in Texas without the support and participation of landowners. The future of most wildlife habitat is in private hands. Because owning land is expensive, this creates an inseparable linkage between conservation and economics (Guynn and Steinbach, 1987). Therefore, we must find ways to encourage and not discourage the participation of private landowners in wildlife management. Landowners also represent an important link in rural-urban relationships in Texas. It has been estimated that as many as seventy-five thousand urban Texans own at least a hundred acres of land in a rural county. These absentee landowners are often innovative in their approach to land management, and they represent a new audience for wildlife managers.

Numerous factors, such as loss of open space, urban growth, fragmentation as a result of estate taxes, and loss of land productivity, are threatening the state's most prime habitat. With traditional agriculture declining, landowners have diversified and increased economic returns by converting land from agriculture to wildlife production. This trend can be expected to continue with increased emphasis on the commercialization of wildlife. Exotic game ranching, deer farming, lease hunting, and various forms of ecotourism, which create markets for wildlife and outdoor recreation, have become popular among landowners. When managed successfully on an acceptable ecological basis, wildlife ranching fulfills a vital role in the conservation of natural resources for the direct benefit of future generations and at the same time yields a sustained crop for the landowner (White, 1986).

Several state and federal agencies, as well as private organizations, offer incentive programs that provide technical or cost-share assistance to private landowners for voluntarily enrolling environmentally sensitive land or wildlife habitat in conservation programs to protect or enhance natural resources. Programs or incentives for private land conservation in Texas include:

*Landowner Incentive Program (LIP)*. This program, offered by the Texas Parks and Wildlife Department (TPWD), offers financial assistance to private landowners wishing to restore or enhance habitat for endangered, threatened, or selected rare species of plants or animals and rare habitats. Private landowners in the LIP enter into short-term conservation agreements for habitat improvements or protection that commonly span five years or less. As of 2000, LIP is assisting landowners to enhance or restore more than forty thousand acres of rare species habitat in sixty-two Texas counties.

*Texas Parks and Wildlife Department-Assisted Wildlife Management Plans (WMPs)*. TPWD offers free technical assistance regarding wildlife management activities to private landowners to help improve wildlife habitat for native Texas species. Under this program, TPWD staff help landowners prepare a wildlife management plan that states wildlife management goals, identifies key habitat resources, and prescribes habitat management practices to help reach the identified goals. By 2000 TPWD had assisted landowners with 2,727 WMPs covering approximately 11.5 million acres in two hundred Texas counties.

*Wildlife Management Use Property Tax Appraisal (WMU)*. In 1995, Texas voters approved an amendment to Article 8, Section 1-d-1 of the Texas Constitution that made wildlife management a qualified use for open-space property tax appraisal. This designation allows qualified land under active wildlife management to be appraised at its prior agricultural value. As of 1999, almost 178,000 acres distributed over forty-eight Texas counties were appraised for wildlife management use.

*Texas Prairie Wetlands Project*. This program, started 1993, is funded by Ducks Unlimited, TPWD, the Natural Resource Conservation Service (NRCS), and the USFWS. It provides technical and financial assistance to private landowners in twenty-eight Texas counties for the restoration and enhancement of Gulf Coast wetlands for the benefit of waterfowl and other coastal species. As of 2000, more than eighteen thousand acres of Texas coastal wetlands, from twenty-one of the twenty-eight counties, were enrolled in the program.

*Partners for Fish and Wildlife.* This is a voluntary technical and financial assistance program administered by the USFWS. Technical assistance is provided to restore important fish and wildlife habitat for federal trust species, including migratory birds, threatened and endangered species, and various forms of marine life. As of 2000, about seventy-three thousand acres in seventy-five Texas counties were enrolled in this program.

*Wildlife Habitat Incentive Program (WHIP).* This program is available through the NRCS to provide technical assistance and cost-share payments for private landowners to improve fish and wildlife habitat. Participants enter into a five year agreement and prepare and implement a wildlife habitat development plan. As of 2000, about eighty-one thousand acres, distributed over sixty-four Texas counties, were actively enrolled in the WHIP.

*Conservation Reserve Program (CRP).* This is a voluntary program established in 1985 offering financial assistance to farmers to establish approved cover on highly erodible cropland or pastureland. As of 2000, more than 3.9 million acres, distributed over 169 Texas counties, were actively enrolled in the CRP. Most CRP contracts typically span ten to fifteen years.

*Wetlands Reserve Program (WRP).* This program, first offered to Texas landowners in 1994, provides financial assistance and/or compensation for the restoration and protection of drained wetlands used for agricultural purposes. Under the program, permanent conservation easements, thirty-year conservation easements, or ten-year cost-share agreements for restoration activities are established between the NRCS and private landowners. The WRP currently includes almost thirty-six thousand acres spread over eighteen counties.

Other tools that are gaining popularity among landowners as we enter the twenty-first century include land trusts and conservation easements. Today in Texas there are thirty-four land conservation organizations commonly called land trusts. A land trust is a local, regional, or national nonprofit organization that protects land for its natural, recreational, scenic, historic, or productive value. Land trusts work with willing landowners to help them meet their long-term land conservation objectives by accepting donated properties and easements or by purchasing land and easements for conservation purposes. A total of 307,717 acres are conserved by non-profit land trusts in Texas, protecting 499 sites in ninety-five Texas counties, according to the 2000 survey by the Texas Land Trust Council.

A conservation easement is a legal agreement a property owner makes to restrict the type and amount of development that may take place on his or her property (Francell, 1998). Each easement's restrictions are tailored to the particular property and to the interests of the individual owner. People grant conservation easements to protect their land from inappropriate development while retaining private ownership. By granting an easement in perpetuity, the owner may be assured that the resource values of his or her property will be protected indefinitely, no matter who the future owners are. Easements include covenants or restrictions that limit subdivision, define building, prohibit destructive practices, and foster appropriate resource management (The Nature Conservancy, 1999). Granting an easement can also yield tax savings. The Nature Conservancy of Texas has used the easement concept to work with private landowners to protect more than ninety-five thousand acres at thirty-two different sites in Texas (Robert Potts, personal communication). These easements include covenants and restrictions to limit development and protect unique habitat, rare species, open space, and scenic landscapes.

Collectively the various programs described previously provide some sort of wildlife management to almost 16 million acres of land in Texas. Given that agriculture is the prevalent land use on approximately 136 million acres of Texas's lands, representing about 81 percent of the state's total land area, almost 12 percent of the state's available acreage is under some form of wildlife management.

## Expand Protected Area Acquisition and Management

As we think about managing wildlife diversity in the future, it is clear that we must give greater attention to increasing protected areas, or lands set aside exclusively or primarily to conserve wildlife. During the time of the biological survey, there were no parks or preserves in Texas. Today, there are hundreds of resource-based parks and preserves in the state managed by state and federal agencies, as well as numerous local parks managed by cities, counties, and river authorities for purposes of outdoor recreation (Table 4). The combined acreage of all these areas is 4,175,018 acres, or about 2.5 percent of the state's total area. This percentage is less than half the percentage of the total land area on the globe set aside in protected areas. In other words, Texas has a smaller percentage of its land devoted to protected areas than is found across the entire globe.

Parks and preserves serve as living laboratories for education and scientific investigation, and places for outdoor recreation activity. They also serve to protect natural diversity, although their capacity for preservation is limited by a number of factors, including the size of the protected area, their geographic distribution, the system and area configuration, the amount and kind of site development, management objectives and practices, and outside environmental influences (Carls, 1984). A study of the fourteen largest national parks in western North America concluded that none of them was large enough to retain an intact mammalian fauna (Newmark, 1987), and no protected area in

Texas is as large as the smallest of the fourteen parks used in that study.

Our parks and preserves are scattered throughout the state, although the geographical distribution is far from proportional (Map 33). The heaviest concentration of areas is found in the Trans-Pecos, Pineywoods, Gulf Coast, and South Texas Plains regions. The many sites in the Trans-Pecos clearly indicate the bias for siting parks and preserves in areas of scenic and more "spectacular" natural history. Concentrations in the eastern and southern part of the state reflect the great public demand for outdoor recreation in centers of population. The Rolling Plains and High Plains natural regions tend to be underrepresented by parks and preserves. These areas are generally more remote from centers of population, and they lack the scenic qualities usually favored for park development. Most conspicuous by absence from the system are protected areas of native grassland and prairie.

Although they represent only a small part of the Texas landscape, these parks and preserves, and the federal, state, and private entities that oversee them, play increasingly vital roles in the conservation of biodiversity in Texas. For some regions, such as the Rio Grande Valley, they are what are left of the native habitats. Clearly, there is a need for more parks and preserves and additions to existing areas to protect rare or unique natural resources and to better represent the natural regions of the state. Given their concerns about conservation and scenic beauty, Bailey and the federal agents, if they were alive today, surely would endorse such a strategy for the twenty-first century.

The notion of completely isolated conservation areas is untenable in the long term. An important component in identifying areas for conservation priority is to consider the corridors between conservation areas—the kinds of transfers that currently take place and that previously took place. Attention to planning and

Table 4. Parks, forests, and refuges in Texas

| | Area (acres) |
|---|---:|
| **Federal Lands** | |
| U.S. Forest Service | 755,396 |
| Bureau of Reclamation | 10,510 |
| National Park Service | 1,183,090 |
| U.S. Fish and Wildlife Service | 456,984 |
| U.S. Army Corps of Engineers | 469,754 |
| Subtotal Federal Lands | 2,875,734 |
| **State Lands** | |
| Texas Parks and Wildlife | |
| Recreation Areas | 242,459 |
| Natural Areas | 383,034 |
| Historic Sites | 8,162 |
| Wildlife Management Areas | 411,151 |
| Subtotal Texas Parks and Wildlife | 1,044,806 |
| Texas Forest Service | 8,386 |
| Subtotal State Lands | 1,053,192 |
| **Local Parks** | |
| Cities and Counties | 230,920 |
| River Authorities | 15,172 |
| Subtotal Local Parks | 246,092 |
| TOTAL Parks, Forests, and Refuges | 4,175,018 |
| Total area of Texas | 167,624,960 |
| Percent Parks, Forests, and Refuges | 2.5 |

management of the areas between conservation reserves must become an important priority for future reserves. Our goal should be to expand protected areas to include a cross-section of all major ecosystems in the state and to link them via conservation corridors so they are more effective (Adams and Dove, 1989).

## Promote Regionally Based Conservation Planning

There is a growing consensus that conservation is best practiced at the regional level where it can be integrated with local customs, values, and land uses and where people can have a vested interest and become a direct participant in the decision-making process. In the future, we must begin to effectively plan for various land uses within the dynamics of landscapes.

Most regional landscapes include a matrix of semi-natural habitats that surround natural reserves and support some sort of land use (Packard and Schmidly, 1991). These buffer areas are ideal for conservation-based rural development where products and services can be

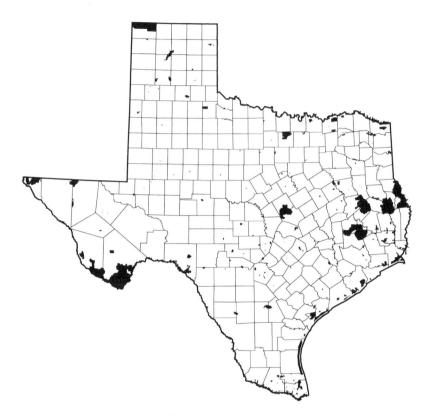

Map 33. Protected federal and state lands in Texas

produced from the land without destroying the long-term sustainability of the resource base. This is where holistic resource management can be practiced on private lands and sustainable ecosystem management on public lands. Most landscapes also contain highly developed and managed lands that have long since been converted from their original condition to agricultural or industrial purposes. However, by practicing restoration ecology and wise land management these areas have much to contribute toward conserving our natural resources. Finally, it must be remembered that large urban centers are now a major part of our landscapes. Most of the people are concentrated in these areas, and this is where much of the political clout resides relative to decision-making on environmental issues.

Developing regional conservation approaches requires multidisciplinary and interdisciplinary teams working together to create conservation plans. Coordination and control points must be spelled out clearly in the action plan so that the multidisciplinary aspects of the environmental problem-solving process move holistically toward an effective solution of the management problem. Professionals, especially naturalists and ecologists, and private organizations have an important role to play, especially in helping to overcome obstacles to cooperation imposed by conflicting political interests, official ideology, and bureaucratic inertia.

Three scientifically based strategies are essential to making regional conservation projects a reality. First, it is necessary to identify and locate the species and communities most in peril.

Second, efforts must be made to carefully define a "portfolio" of the most important places to protect. And third, we must learn how these ecosystems function and this knowledge must be used to develop and carry out long-term conservation strategies. Added to this must be efforts to build long-lasting and positive relationships with both public and private partners. Conservation projects are much more effective when they are locally based and involve private landowners.

Diamond et al. (1997) used the Texas Natural Heritage Program's biological and conservation database to analyze the geographic distribution of populations of rare taxa of plants and animals and the rare or unique plant communities in Texas. Their results show that the Trans-Pecos region of western Texas and the Edwards Plateau of Central Texas contain the highest density of rare plant and animals in the state. Other regions with a high density of rare species include the Blackland Prairies, the southeastern Gulf coastal prairies and woods, and the South Texas brush country. These areas are all worthy of developing regional conservation plans, and significant efforts already are underway in the Trans-Pecos and Hill Country regions.

There is a relatively large expanse of public lands along the front range of mountains of the Trans-Pecos, beginning with Big Bend National Park, Big Bend Ranch State Park, Black Gap Wildlife Management Area along the border and extending to the Chinati Mountains, Elephant Mountain Wildlife Management Area to the north, and Guadalupe Mountains National Park along the Texas–New Mexico border. With the exception of the Davis Mountains, this constitutes a virtual continuous corridor along the front range from Mexico to New Mexico. The conservation potential of this vast corridor, given the large number of rare plants and animals in this region, is immense.

The Nature Conservancy of Texas has put together an initiative in the Davis Mountains, in the central part of the front range, which is one of the most ambitious conservation projects ever attempted in Texas. The Conservancy purchased through a private land sale thirty-two thousand acres of the historic "U Up U Down" McIvor Ranch in the Davis Mountains in 1998. In a unique strategy involving private buyers and project fundraising, the Conservancy retained ownership of a twelve thousand-acre core nature preserve on the property but sold the remaining twenty thousand acres to private conservation buyers who were willing to make a binding commitment to conservation in the form of an easement. The Conservancy maintains conservation easements on the portions of the ranch that have been sold to private buyers, which restrict the property from subdivision and development. Since its inception, the Davis Mountains Ranch Preserve has now grown to encompass more than seventy-three thousand acres. This project is a success story of keeping large tracts of habitat intact while at the same time preserving the region's ranching heritage as well as its natural beauty and ecological value.

The species and communities of the Hill Country are facing increasing levels of habitat destruction, fragmentation, and isolation. Thus, this area is most deserving of conservation attention from a regional perspective since it contains few public lands and is important for both plants and animals (Diamond et al., 1997). Again, the Nature Conservancy of Texas has been involved and become a catalyst for seeking solutions. In partnership with other nongovernmental and government entities, it has been actively involved in the development of the Balcones Canyonlands Habitat Conservation Plan in western Travis County, one of the most ambitious habitat conservation plans ever developed (Pease and Grzybowski, 1991). At the heart of the plan is the ecological protection of the Hill Country, and its numerous endangered species, while maintaining long-term economic viability of the region. The plan encompassed political, legal, economic, and biological considerations.

Texas's newest State Natural Area, Government Canyon, lies sixteen miles from the city of San Antonio. It was created by a complex series of steps that required considerable cooperation among public and private groups, including the TPWD, Edwards Underground Water District, San Antonio Water System, the Nature Conservancy of Texas, and the Trust for Public Lands. This partnership established one of the largest urban-area parks in the nation, while at the same time fulfilling three conservation goals (protecting a major watershed, establishing a recreation area easily accessible by an urban population, and embodying the partnership of state agencies and private entities).

A good example of how state and federal government and private landowners can work together at the local level to protect endangered species is the Central Texas Private Lands Trapping (CTPLT) Initiative which is coordinated by TPWD and sanctioned by the USFWS, the main agency responsible for enforcing the federal Endangered Species Act. The idea was developed by the Central Texas Cattlemen's Association and includes as other partners the U.S. Army, the U.S. Department of Agriculture/Wildlife Services, the Texas Farm Bureau, the Texas Wildlife Association, and the Environmental Defense Fund. The program operates under a concept of the Endangered Species Act, known as safe harbor, which makes sure cooperating landowners are excluded from the act's restrictions in return for their cooperation and assistance. The CTPLT initiative involves more than thirty landowners around Fort Hood near Killeen who are helping two endangered songbirds (the black-capped vireo and the golden-checked warbler) by putting out traps on their land to remove brown-headed cowbirds that parasitize nests of the endangered birds. The cattlemen were looking for a way to be permitted to continue grazing on Fort Hood on a year-round basis. The USFWS wanted grazing restricted in or near endangered species habitat during the nesting season. Common ground was reached when the cattlemen volunteered to take the lead in enlisting support and coordinating a massive effort to place traps on private land around the perimeter of Ft. Hood. TPWD agreed to furnish materials for traps, and Wildlife Services hired a trapper.

This kind of buy-in by private landowners is essential to make rare species conservation possible. Community-based incentives are the key to solutions that work for local communities, and this kind of partnering among stakeholders with markedly different viewpoints and objectives marks a breakthrough for conservation. We will need more examples of this kind of cooperation and partnering in the future if we are to make rare species conservation possible.

## The Special Challenges of Land Fragmentation and Water

As mentioned in Chapter 5, land fragmentation and the misuse of water already had become the dominant conservation issues by the end of the twentieth century, and they will continue to be important challenges in this century as well. Texas is no longer a state where economy and culture are defined primarily by the land. With the continuing influx of new residents and a population increasingly shifting to cities and their suburbs, Texas has become a primarily urban society. Many landowners whose families have lived on the land for generations have come under tremendous pressures to sell their farms and ranches for development. As a result, Texas, like other states across the country, is in jeopardy of losing its legacy of families who live and work on the land—the traditional stewards of our natural heritage.

The fragmentation of large family-owned farms and ranches poses perhaps the greatest single threat to our wildlife because it places once plentiful habitat for native plants and animals increasingly at risk. For this reason, it is crucial to find ways to keep large continuous tracts of land together and to find ways for all landowners, including absentee landowners, to participate in conservation. To do this will require that we create incentives, like purchase of development rights programs, that will allow landowners to sell the development rights to their land by granting conservation easements to a government entity or nongovernmental conservation organization, yet retain all other rights of ownership, including the right to continue ranching, farming, hunting, and fishing.

Management of water will be the single most critical conservation issue in Texas in the twenty-first century. Water is the limiting factor for all aquatic life, plants, and wildlife. Rivers link our land and water ecosystems. With Texas's population expected to double in the first thirty years of the twenty-first century, there is an urgent need to maintain sufficient water for adequate flows to rivers, lakes, and estuaries to maintain the fish and wildlife that depend on them. Historically, the allocation of water rights in Texas has not taken into account the needs of the state's ecosystems. The state's current water statutes and regulations require that environmental needs be considered in the overall picture, but they do not assure minimal instream flows to sustain the health of rivers and estuaries. As Texas attempts to meet increased water needs, it must not impair the ecological health of these ecosystems, which form the natural infrastructure of our state.

### The Possible Impact of Climate Change

Global warming is predicted as a direct result of rising levels of greenhouse gases in the atmosphere and reduction of the ozone layer. Models developed by scientists predict that global mean surface air temperature will increase and that rainfall patterns will change, although there is no agreement on the precise distribution or magnitude of these changes. Because climate has a large impact on biological processes, rearrangement of existing biological communities is expected on a regional scale as individual animal or plant species respond to climate change (Scheel et al., 1996).

Two major climate models predict that temperatures will increase by 3-4° C in Texas relative to current conditions. One model predicts that Texas will be both warmer and wetter than the current climate, whereas the other predicts the state will be warmer and somewhat drier (Cameron and Scheel, 1993).

A northwest to southeast gradient of freeze-days and a west to east gradient of increasing soil moisture, both of which influence species distribution, represent two major influences of climate on regional vegetation in Texas (Owen and Schmidly, 1986). With the higher temperatures expected from climate change, evapotranspiration rates would increase and critical values of soil moisture would shift to the east along this gradient. Packard and Cook (1995) have hypothesized in such a scenario that the natural areas least likely to change location in Texas are the Edwards Plateau, the Trans-Pecos, and the High Plains, whereas those most like to shift to the northeast, possibly even out of the state, are the Pineywoods and Central Texas Prairies.

Because of their body size, morphology, and ecology, mammals would not be expected to react as a group to environmental shifts such as global climate change. Guy Cameron and his students at the University of Houston studied the predicted impact of climate change on Texas mammals, using insectivores, lagomorphs, bats, and rodents as representative groups (Cameron and Steel, 1993; Scheel et al., 1996; Cameron et al., 1997; and Cameron and Scheel, 2000). Their results indicate that under conditions of global warming all warm temperate vegetation will be lost from Texas and replaced either with tropical forests or subtropical forest, tropical dry forest, steppe, or desert scrub, depending on the climate model used.

In their analyses, the effects of climate change on individual species varied by taxa, geographic locality, and climatic scenario, but, in general, predicted mammalian responses involved movement and changes in the geographic extent of species' ranges. The magnitude of the responses was not the same for species in the four groups of mammals studied. The findings of Cameron and his students suggest that rodents would be more adaptable to changes in vegetation associations because their ranges would increase to accommodate new habitats, and consequently, they would be less affected by global climate change than lagomorphs, insectivores, or bats.

Two rodents, *Oryzomys cousei* and *Microtus mexicanus*, are the only species currently found in Texas that are not predicted to occur in the state under the conditions of global climate change. These species occupy restricted ranges at the southern and mountainous northwestern edges of the state, respectively, in habitats that were not predicted to occur after climate change. Therefore, assuming these predictions prove correct, it does not appear that predicted climate change, by itself, will present a grave threat to the species richness of mammals in Texas. In fact, species richness could increase substantially through the expansion of species ranges from within Texas and into Texas from Mexico.

## Conclusions

Early settlers in Texas found the country well populated with wildlife. Interestingly enough, deer were less abundant than now, but the plains supported huge herds of bison and pronghorn. Tall-grass prairies teemed with prairie chickens. The wooded areas supported large populations of wild turkeys, black bears, mink, and beaver. These animals served those early settlers mainly as a seemingly inexhaustible source of food and clothing. As the human population grew, lands in the eastern section of the state were cleared, plowed, and planted to crops. Thousands of livestock, mainly cattle, were brought in to stock the open ranges of the west, and later barbed-wire fences were built. All these events altered the original balance between wildlife and its habitat. This adjustment between wildlife and natural vegetation on the one hand and human use of the land on the other progressed steadily throughout the twentieth century, and it will continue. Only the highly adaptable species of wildlife are likely to survive; those that cannot adjust to changing conditions will be doomed unless we strengthen our commitment to conservation and improve the way in which we manage our landscapes.

Conserving wildlife, which recognizes neither ownership nor boundaries, calls for good science, first-rate technology, excellent management, and a broad constituency willing to make some concessions to save it. To maintain wildlife diversity in the next century will require financing, public support, and, above all, the integrated management skills that even the most sophisticated high-tech farming systems lack. And farm production systems pale in complexity compared to the natural systems we must preserve, repair, and reconstruct. The challenge is daunting. We face a monumental task, far beyond our existing capabilities. But now is the time to look ahead, coordinate and plan, before our options are further narrowed.

With that in mind, then-governor George W. Bush established in 2000 the Governor's Task Force on Conservation with the following charge:

- examine the impact of fragmentation on lands in Texas and the wildlife habitat located therein;
- make recommendations as to appropriate incentives and tools available to assist landowners in more effectively conserving and managing lands in their stewardship;
- make recommendations as to how all Texans may benefit from the many forms of economic activity associated with natural resources, including hunting, fishing, other forms of outdoor recreation, and nature tourism; and
- provide specific recommendations as to how the state, in partnership with other government entities, private landowners, and community-based groups can better meet the conservation and outdoor recreation needs of the state in the future.

I had the pleasure of serving as one of the thirteen task force members, including participation on the report drafting subcommittee. The task force issued its final report, "Taking Care of Texas: A Report from the Governor's Task Force in Conservation," in November of 2000 with three categories of primary recommendations: 1) private lands: incentives, partnerships, and stewardship; 2) public lands: planning, repairing, developing, and meeting future needs; and 3) water: assuring, protecting, and managing for conservation. The recommendations in the report are intended to serve as practical objectives and strategies for the state's leaders to ensure the future of our cultural, historical, and natural resources by using sound science, good planning, responsible management, assessment measures, respect for landowners, local participation, and economic incentives to bolster the protection of our unique landscapes, wildlife, and water.

In a parallel and complementary effort, the Texas Parks and Wildlife Department contracted with Texas Tech University in 2000 to conduct a study, "Texas Parks and Wildlife for the 21st Century." The objectives of the study

were to 1) conduct a major public opinion survey of Texans to gain a better understanding of their values and attitudes toward natural and cultural resources and outdoor recreation in Texas; 2) inventory current holdings of public lands for conservation and outdoor recreation purposes; and 3) conduct a needs assessment of future requirements for public land to ensure that historical, cultural, and natural resources will be adequately provided, maintained, and conserved for future generations of Texans. The public opinion part of the study revealed overwhelming support on the part of Texans (in excess of 90 percent of the sampled population) to conserve water and wildlife as well as to protect and preserve ecologically important habitats and lands in Texas (Duda, 2000). The needs and supply analysis reveal that Texas has fallen far short of its 1963 goal of 45 acres of publicly owned state parks per 1000 residents. Currently, the state has about 31.5 acres of state parks per 1,000 people, and 20.4 acres of wildlife management area per 1,000 residents for a combined total of 51.9 acres of combined parks and wildlife land per 1,000 people (Loomis Austin, Inc., 2000a, b, c). A professional needs conference conducted in 2000 recommended that Texas should have 55 acres of parks and wildlife preserve land per 1000 people which would place the state in the 75th percentile among all states (Loomis Austin, Inc., 2000c).

Texas faces a daunting challenge to conserve its natural resources, especially its wildlife diversity. For conservation to be successful, it is imperative that disparate groups (landowners, private conservation organizations, commodity groups, and state and federal agencies) begin to communicate, build trust, and find consensus solutions that satisfy the goals of society. To avoid repeating past mistakes we must understand what has happened to our fauna and flora. Conservationists working in Texas are fortunate to have a baseline inventory that provides a detailed and scientifically accurate description of the entire state. This archival information base can be exceptionally useful as we develop and implement future management strategies for our wildlife resources. It represents one of the key information sources necessary for the kind of planning, partnership, and management necessary to allow future generations to enjoy the great outdoors and the natural resources that are part of our heritage as Texans.

# Afterword

Field work by Vernon Bailey and his associates resulted in the publication of the *Biological Survey of Texas* in 1905. This milestone event provided baseline data for beginning to understand the diversity of habitats, natural history in general, and mammals in particular that occur in the state. The diversity of mammals in Texas reflects the variety of major biotic areas, including the southern Great Plains, Rocky Mountains, deciduous forests, pine woods, coastal plains and marshes, and the Chihuahuan Desert, plus other major features such as the Llano Estacado, the Edwards Plateau, and several major river systems. You could say that "east meets west" and "north meets south" in Texas.

Since the work of Vernon Bailey, a considerable amount of effort has been expended on the study of mammals in Texas. However, details of the current numbers and distributions of mammals, as well as relationships among and between the mammals in an area, are imperfectly known. For numerous reasons (climatic cycles, changes in land use, changes in supplies of surface and ground water, and other human impacts), landscapes and corresponding patterns of distribution, diversity, and relationships of mammals in Texas currently are in a dynamic state of change. Significant new findings are being reported with increasing frequency.

David Schmidly has placed in modern perspective a century of change in Texas natural history, through detailed review of archival materials and extensive personal experience. This work is another milestone for those working to understand the current state of the mammals of Texas and adjacent areas.

Clyde Jones
Paul Whitfield Horn Professor of
Biological Sciences
Texas Tech University

# Appendix

## Scientific and Common Names of Animals and Plants

Scientific names from the *Biological Survey of Texas* are listed along with the current taxonomic and common names for each taxon.

### Mammals

| Old Name | Current Name | Common Name |
|---|---|---|
| *Ammospermophilus* | *Ammosphermophilus* | |
| *Ammospermophilus interpres* | *Ammospermophilus interpres* | Texas Antelope Squirrel |
| *Antilocapra* | *Antilocapra* | |
| *Antilocapra americana* | *Antilocapra americana* | Pronghorn |
| *Antrozous* | *Antrozous* | |
| *Antrozous pallidus* | *Antrozous pallidus* | Pallid Bat |
| *Bassariscus* | *Bassariscus* | |
| *Bassariscus astutus* | *Bassariscus astutus* | Ringtail |
| *Bassariscus astutus flavus* | *Bassariscus astutus flavus* | Ringtail |
| *Bison* | *Bos* | |
| *Bison bison* | *Bos bison* | Bison |
| *Blarina* | *Blarina/Cryptotis* | |
| *Blarina berlandieri* | *Cryptotis parva* | Least Shrew |
| *Blarina brevicauda carolinensis* | *Blarina carolinensis* | Southern Short-tailed Shrew |
| *Blarina parva* | *Cryptotis parva* | Least Shrew |
| *Canis* | *Canis* | |
| *Canis ater* | *Canis lupus* | Gray Wolf |
| *Canis estor* | *Canis latrans mearnsi* | Coyote |
| *Canis frustor* | *Canis latrans frustror* | Coyote |
| *Canis griseus* | *Canis lupus griseoalbus* | Gray Wolf |
| *Canis mearnsi* | *Canis latrans mearnsi* | Coyote |
| *Canis microdon* | *Canis latrans microdon* | Coyote |
| *Canis nebracensis* | *Canis latrans latrans* | Coyote |
| *Canis nebracensis texensis* | *Canis latrans texensis* | Coyote |
| *Canis rufus* | *Canis rufus* | Red Wolf |

| | | |
|---|---|---|
| *Castor* | *Castor* | |
| *Castor canadensis frondator* | *Castor canadensis frondator* | American Beaver |
| *Castor canadensis texensis* | *Castor canadensis texensis* | American Beaver |
| *Cervus* | *Cervus* | |
| *Cervus canadensis* | *Cervus elaphus canadensis* | Elk |
| *Cervus merriami* | *Cervus elaphus merriami* | Elk |
| *Citellus* | *Spermophilus* | |
| *Citellus mexicanus parvidens* | *Spermophilus mexicanus parvidens* | Mexican Ground Squirrel |
| *Citellus spilosoma annectens* | *Spermophilus spilosoma annectens* | Spotted Ground Squirrel |
| *Citellus spilosoma arens* | *Spermophilus spilosoma canescens* | Spotted Ground Squirrel |
| *Citellus spilosoma major* | *Spermophilus spilosoma marginatus* | Spotted Ground Squirrel |
| *Citellus spilosoma marginatus* | *Spermophilus spilosoma marginatus* | Spotted Ground Squirrel |
| *Citellus tridecemlineatus pallidus* | *Spermophilus tridecemlineatus pallidus* | Thirteen-lined Ground Squirrel |
| *Citellus tridecemlineatus texensis* | *Spermophilus tridecemlineatus texensis* | Thirteen-lined Ground Squirrel |
| *Citellus variegatus* | *Spermophilus variegatus* | Rock Squirrel |
| *Citellus variegatus buckleyi* | *Spermophilus variegatus buckleyi* | Rock Squirrel |
| *Citellus variegatus couchi* | *Spermophilus variegatus couchii* | Rock Squirrel |
| *Citellus variegatus grammurus* | *Spermophilus variegatus grammurus* | Rock Squirrel |
| *Conepatus* | *Conepatus* | |
| *Conepatus leuconotus* | *Conepatus leuconotus* | Eastern Hog-nosed Skunk |
| *Conepatus leuconotus texensis* | *Conepatus leuconotus texensis* | Eastern Hog-nosed Skunk |
| *Conepatus mesoleucus* | *Conepatus mesoleucus* | Common Hog-nosed Skunk |
| *Conepatus mesoleucus mearnsi* | *Conepatus mesoleucus mearnsi* | Common Hog-nosed Skunk |
| *Conepatus mesoleucus telmalestes* | *Conepatus mesoleucus telmalestes* | Common Hog-nosed Skunk |
| *Corynorhinus* | *Plecotus* | |
| *Corynorhinus macrotis* | *Plecotus rafinesquii macrotis* | Rafinesque's Big-eared Bat |
| *Corynorhinus macrotis pallescens* | *Plecotus townsendii pallescens* | Townsend's Big-eared Bat |
| *Cratogeomys* | *Cratogeomys* | |
| *Cratogeomys castanops* | *Cratogeomys castanops* | Yellow-faced Pocket Gopher |
| *Cynomys* | *Cynomys* | |
| *Cynomys ludovicianus* | *Cynomys ludovicianus* | Black-tailed Prairie Dog |
| *Dasypterus* | *Lasiurus* | |
| *Dasypterus intermedius* | *Lasiurus intermedius* | Northern Yellow Bat |
| *Dasypus* | *Dasypus* | |
| *Dasypus novemcinctus mexicanus* | *Dasypus novemcinctus mexicanus* | Nine-banded Armadillo |
| *Didelphis* | *Didelphis* | |
| *Didelphis marsupialis texensis* | *Didelphis virginiana californica* | Virginia Opossum |
| *Didelphis virginiana* | *Didelphis virginiana* | Virginia Opossum |
| *Didelphis virginiana pigra* | *Didelphis virginiana pigra* | Virginia Opossum |
| *Dipodomys* | *Dipodomys* | |
| *Dipodomys elator* | *Dipodomys elator* | Texas Kangaroo Rat |
| *Dipodomys merriami* | *Dipodomys merriami* | Merriam's Kangaroo Rat |
| *Dipodomys merriami ambiguus* | *Dipodomys merriami ambiguus* | Merriam's Kangaroo Rat |
| *Dipodomys spectabilis* | *Dipodomys spectabilis* | Banner-tailed Kangaroo Rat |
| *Dipodomys spectabilis baileyi* | *Dipodomys spectabilis baileyi* | Banner-tailed Kangaroo Rat |
| *Erethizon* | *Erethizon* | |
| *Erethizon epixanthum* | *Erethizon dorsatum epixanthum* | Porcupine |
| *Eutamias* | *Tamias* | |
| *Eutamias cinereicollis canipes* | *Tamias canipes canipes* | Gray-footed Chipmunk |

| | | |
|---|---|---|
| *Felis* | *Herpailurus, Leopardus, Panthera, Puma* | |
| *Felis apache* | *Herpailurus yagouaroundi cacomitli* | Jaguarundi |
| *Felis cacomitli* | *Herpailurus yagouaroundi cacomitli* | Jaguarundi |
| *Felis coryi* | *Puma concolor coryi* | Mountain Lion |
| *Felis couguar* | *Puma concolor couguar* | Mountain Lion |
| *Felis eyra* | *Herpailurus yagouaroundi cacomitli* | Jaguarundi |
| *Felis hippolestes* | *Puma concolor hippolestes* | Mountain Lion |
| *Felis hippolestes aztecus* | *Puma concolor azteca* | Mountain Lion |
| *Felis onca* | *Panthera onca* | Jaguar |
| *Felis onca hernandezi* | *Panthera onca hernandezi* | Jaguar |
| *Felis pardalis* | *Leopardus pardalis* | Ocelot |
| *Felis pardalis limitis* | *Leopardus pardalis albescens* | Ocelot |
| *Felis yaguarundi* | *Herpailurus yagouaroundi* | Jaguarundi |
| *Fiber* | *Ondatra* | |
| *Fiber zibethicus* | *Ondatra zibethicus* | Muskrat |
| *Fiber zibethicus ripensis* | *Ondatra zibethicus ripensis* | Muskrat |
| *Geomys* | *Geomys* | |
| *Geomys arenarius* | *Geomys arenarius* | Desert Pocket Gopher |
| *Geomys breviceps* | *Geomys breviceps* | Baird's Pocket Gopher |
| *Geomys breviceps attwateri* | *Geomys attwateri* | Attwater's Pocket Gopher |
| *Geomys breviceps llanensis* | *Geomys texensis* | Llano Pocket Gopher |
| *Geomys breviceps sagittalis* | *Geomys breviceps sagittalis* | Baird's Pocket Gopher |
| *Geomys lutescens* | *Geomys bursarius lutescens* | Plains Pocket Gopher |
| *Geomys personatus* | *Geomys personatus* | Texas Pocket Gopher |
| *Geomys personatus fallax* | *Geomys personatus fallax* | Texas Pocket Gopher |
| *Geomys texensis* | *Geomys texensis* | Llano Pocket Gopher |
| *Heteromys* | *Liomys* | |
| *Heteromys alleni* | *Liomys irroratus alleni* | Mexican Spiny Pocket Mouse |
| *Lasiurus* | *Lasiurus* | |
| *Lasiurus borealis* | *Lasiurus borealis* | Eastern Red Bat |
| *Lasiurus borealis seminolus* | *Lasiurus seminolus* | Seminole Bat |
| *Lasiurus cinereus* | *Lasiurus cinereus* | Hoary Bat |
| *Lepus* | *Lepus/Sylvilagus* | |
| *Lepus aquaticus* | *Sylvilagus aquaticus* | Swamp Rabbit |
| *Lepus aquaticus attwateri* | *Sylvilagus aquaticus* | Swamp Rabbit |
| *Lepus arizonae* | *Sylvilagus audubonii* | Desert Cottontail |
| *Lepus arizonae baileyi* | *Sylvilagus audubonii baileyi* | Desert Cottontail |
| *Lepus arizonae minor* | *Sylvilagus audubonii minor* | Desert Cottontail |
| *Lepus floridanus alacer* | *Sylvilagus floridanus alacer* | Eastern Cottontail |
| *Lepus floridanus caniclunis* | *Sylvilagus floridanus chapmani* | Eastern Cottontail |
| *Lepus floridanus chapmani* | *Sylvilagus floridanus chapmani* | Eastern Cottontail |
| *Lepus merriami* | *Lepus californicus merriami* | Black-tailed Jackrabbit |
| *Lepus pinetus* | *Sylvilagus floridanus* | Eastern Cottontail |
| *Lepus pinetus robustus* | *Sylvilagus robustus* | Davis Mountains cottontail |
| *Lepus simplicicanus* | *Sylvilagus floridanus chapmani* | Eastern Cottontail |
| *Lepus texianus* | *Lepus californicus texianus* | Black-tailed Jackrabbit |
| *Lepus texianus griseus* | *Lepus californicus texianus* | Black-tailed Jackrabbit |
| *Lepus texianus melanotis* | *Lepus californicus melanotis* | Black-tailed Jackrabbit |
| *Liomys* | *Liomys* | |
| *Liomys texensis* | *Liomys irroratus texensis* | Mexican Spiny Pocket Mouse |
| *Lutra* | *Lontra* | |
| *Lutra canadensis* | *Lontra canadensis* | River Otter |
| *Lutra canadensis vaga* | *Lontra canadensis lataxina* | River Otter |

| | | |
|---|---|---|
| *Lutreola* | *Mustela* | |
| *Lutreola lutreocephala* | *Mustela vison* | Mink |
| *Lynx* | *Lynx* | |
| *Lynx baileyi* | *Lynx rufus baileyi* | Bobcat |
| *Lynx rufus* | *Lynx rufus* | Bobcat |
| *Lynx rufus texensis* | *Lynx rufus texensis* | Bobcat |
| *Mephitis* | *Mephitis* | |
| *Mephitis mesomelas* | *Mephitis mephitis mesomelas* | Striped Skunk |
| *Mephitis mesomelas varians* | *Mephitis mephitis varians* | Striped Skunk |
| *Microtus* | *Microtus* | |
| *Microtus ludovicianus* | *Microtus ochrogaster* | Prairie Vole |
| *Microtus mexicanus* | *Microtus mexicanus* | Mexican Vole |
| *Microtus mexicanus guadalupensis* | *Microtus mexicanus guadalupensis* | Mexican Vole |
| *Microtus pinetorum* | *Microtus pinetorum* | Woodland Vole |
| *Microtus pinetorum auricularis* | *Microtus pinetorum auricularis* | Woodland Vole |
| *Mormoops* | *Mormoops* | |
| *Mormoops megalophylla* | *Mormoops megalophylla* | Ghost-faced Bat |
| *Mormoops megalophylla senicula* | *Mormoops megalophylla megalophylla* | Ghost-faced Bat |
| *Mus* | *Mus/Rattus* | |
| *Mus alexandrinus* | *Rattus rattus* | Black Rat |
| *Mus musculus* | *Mus musculus* | House Mouse |
| *Mus norvegicus* | *Rattus norvegicus* | Norway Rat |
| *Mus rattus* | *Rattus rattus* | Black Rat |
| *Myotis* | *Myotis* | |
| *Myotis californicus* | *Myotis californicus* | California Myotis |
| *Myotis incautus* | *Myotis velifer incautus* | Cave Myotis |
| *Myotis velifer* | *Myotis velifer* | Cave Myotis |
| *Myotis yumanensis* | *Myotis yumanensis* | Yuma Myotis |
| *Nasua* | *Nasua* | |
| *Nasua narica* | *Nasua narica* | White-nosed Coati |
| *Nasua narica yucatanica* | *Nasua narica yucatanica* | White-nosed Coati |
| *Neotoma* | *Neotoma* | |
| *Neotoma albigula* | *Neotoma leucodon* | White-throated Woodrat |
| *Neotoma floridana* | *Neotoma floridana* | Eastern Woodrat |
| *Neotoma floridana attwateri* | *Neotoma floridana attwateri* | Eastern Woodrat |
| *Neotoma floridana baileyi* | *Neotoma floridana baileyi* | Eastern Woodrat |
| *Neotoma floridana rubida* | *Neotoma floridana rubida* | Eastern Woodrat |
| *Neotoma mexicana* | *Neotoma mexicana* | Mexican Woodrat |
| *Neotoma micropus* | *Neotoma micropus* | Southern Plains Woodrat |
| *Notiosorex* | *Notiosorex* | |
| *Notiosorex crawfordi* | *Notiosorex crawfordi* | Desert Shrew |
| *Nycticeius* | *Nycticeius* | |
| *Nycticeius humeralis* | *Nycticeius humeralis* | Evening Bat |
| *Nyctinomus* | *Tadarida* | |
| *Nyctinomus mexicanus* | *Tadarida brasiliensis* | Brazilian Free-tailed Bat |
| *Odocoileus* | *Odocoileus* | |
| *Odocoileus canus* | *Odocoileus hemionus crooki* | Mule Deer |
| *Odocoileus couesi* | *Odocoileus virginianus couesi* | White-tailed Deer |
| *Odocoileus hemionus* | *Odocoileus hemionus* | Mule Deer |
| *Odocoileus hemionus canus* | *Odocoileus hemionus crooki* | Mule Deer |
| *Odocoileus louisianae* | *Odocoileus virginianus* | White-tailed Deer |
| *Odocoileus virginianus* | *Odocoileus virginianus* | White-tailed Deer |
| *Odocoileus virginianus macrourus* | *Odocoileus virginianus macroura* | White-tailed Deer |
| *Odocoileus virginianus texanus* | *Odocoileus virginianus texana* | White-tailed Deer |

| | | |
|---|---|---|
| *Onychomys* | *Onychomys* | |
| *Onychomys leucogaster* | *Onychomys leucogaster* | Northern Grasshopper Mouse |
| *Onychomys leucogaster pallescens* | *Onychomys leucogaster pallescens* | Northern Grasshopper Mouse |
| *Onychomys longipes* | *Onychomys leucogaster longipes* | Northern Grasshopper Mouse |
| *Onychomys torridus* | *Onychomys arenicola* | Mearns' Grasshopper Mouse |
| *Onychomys torridus arenicola* | *Onychomys arenicola* | Mearns' Grasshopper Mouse |
| *Oryzomys* | *Oryzomys* | |
| *Oryzomys aquaticus* | *Oryzomys couesi* | Coues' Rice Rat |
| *Oryzomys palustris* | *Oryzomys palustris* | Marsh Rice Rat |
| *Oryzomys palustris texensis* | *Oryzomys palustris texensis* | Marsh Rice Rat |
| *Ovis* | *Ovis* | |
| *Ovis mexicanus* | *Ovis canadensis* | Mountain Sheep |
| *Perodipus* | *Dipodomys* | |
| *Perodipus compactus* | *Dipodomys compactus* | Gulf Coast Kangaroo Rat |
| *Perodipus montanus richardsoni* | *Dipodomys ordii richardsoni* | Ord's Kangaroo Rat |
| *Perodipus ordii* | *Dipodomys ordii* | Ord's Kangaroo Rat |
| *Perodipus sennetti* | *Dipodomys compactus sennetti* | Gulf Coast Kangaroo Rat |
| *Perognathus* | *Perognathus/Chaetodipus* | |
| *Perognathus flavescens copei* | *Perognathus flavescens copei* | Plains Pocket Mouse |
| *Perognathus flavus* | *Perognathus flavus* | Silky Pocket Mouse |
| *Perognathus hispidus* | *Chaetodipus hispidus* | Hispid Pocket Mouse |
| *Perognathus hispidus paradoxus* | *Chaetodipus hispidus paradoxus* | Hispid Pocket Mouse |
| *Perognathus hispidus spilotus* | *Chaetodipus hispidus spilotis* | Hispid Pocket Mouse |
| *Perognathus intermedius* | *Chaetodipus intermedius* | Rock Pocket Mouse |
| *Perognathus merriami* | *Perognathus merriami* | Merriam's Pocket Mouse |
| *Perognathus merriami gilvus* | *Perognathus merriami gilvus* | Merriam's Pocket Mouse |
| *Perognathus nelsoni* | *Chaetodipus nelsoni* | Nelson's Pocket Mouse |
| *Perognathus nelsoni canescens* | *Chaetodipus nelsoni canescens* | Nelson's Pocket Mouse |
| *Perognathus penicillatus* | *Chaetodipus eremicus* | Chihuahuan Desert Pocket Mouse |
| *Perognathus penicillatus eremicus* | *Chaetodipus eremicus* | Chihuahuan Desert Pocket Mouse |
| *Peromyscus* | *Peromyscus/Baiomys* | |
| *Peromyscus attwateri* | *Peromyscus attwateri* | Texas Mouse |
| *Peromyscus boylei* | *Peromyscus boylii* | Brush Mouse |
| *Peromyscus boylei laceyi* | *Peromyscus attwateri* | Texas Mouse |
| *Peromyscus boylei penicillatus* | *Peromyscus nasutus penicillatus* | Northern Rock Mouse |
| *Peromyscus boylei rowleyi* | *Peromyscus boylii rowleyi* | Brush Mouse |
| *Peromyscus canus* | *Peromyscus leucopus texanus* | White-footed Mouse |
| *Peromyscus eremicus* | *Peromyscus eremicus* | Cactus Mouse |
| *Peromyscus eremicus arenarius* | *Peromyscus eremicus eremicus* | Cactus Mouse |
| *Peromyscus gossypinus* | *Peromyscus gossypinus* | Cotton Mouse |
| *Peromyscus laceyi* | *Peromyscus attwateri* | Texas Mouse |
| *Peromyscus leucopus* | *Peromyscus leucopus* | White-footed Mouse |
| *Peromyscus leucopus mearnsi* | *Peromyscus leucopus texanus* | White-footed Mouse |
| *Peromyscus leucopus texanus* | *Peromyscus leucopus texanus* | White-footed Mouse |
| *Peromyscus michiganensis pallescens* | *Peromyscus maniculatus pallescens* | Deer Mouse |
| *Peromyscus rowleyi* | *Peromyscus boylii rowleyi* | Brush Mouse |
| *Peromyscus sonoriensis* | *Peromyscus maniculatus* | Deer Mouse |
| *Peromyscus sonoriensis blandus* | *Peromyscus maniculatus blandus* | Deer Mouse |
| *Peromyscus taylori* | *Baiomys taylori* | Northern Pygmy Mouse |
| *Peromyscus taylori subater* | *Baiomys taylori subater* | Northern Pygmy Mouse |
| *Peromyscus tornillo* | *Peromyscus leucopus tornillo* | White-footed Mouse |

| | | |
|---|---|---|
| *Pipistrellus* | *Pipistrellus* | |
| *Pipistrellus hesperus* | *Pipistrellus hesperus* | Western Pipistrelle |
| *Pipistrellus subflavus* | *Pipistrellus subflavus* | Eastern Pipistrelle |
| *Procyon* | *Procyon* | |
| *Procyon elucus* | *Procyon lotor elucus* | Raccoon |
| *Procyon lotor* | *Procyon lotor* | Raccoon |
| *Procyon lotor hernandezi* | *Procyon lotor hernandezii* | Raccoon |
| *Procyon lotor mexicanus* | *Procyon lotor mexicanus* | Raccoon |
| *Promops* | *Eumops* | |
| *Promops californicus* | *Eumops perotis californicus* | Western Mastiff Bat |
| *Putorius* | *Mustela* | |
| *Putorius frenatus* | *Mustela frenata* | Long-tailed Weasel |
| *Putorius frenatus neomexicanus* | *Mustela frenata neomexicana* | Long-tailed Weasel |
| *Putorius nigripes* | *Mustela nigripes* | Black-footed Ferret |
| *Rattus* | *Rattus* | |
| *Reithrodontomys* | *Reithrodontomys* | |
| *Reithrodontomys aurantius* | *Reithrodontomys fulvescens aurantius* | Fulvous Harvest Mouse |
| *Reithrodontomys griseus* | *Reithrodontomys montanus griseus* | Plains Harvest Mouse |
| *Reithrodontomys intermedius* | *Reithrodontomys fulvescens intermedius* | Fulvous Harvest Mouse |
| *Reithrodontomys laceyi* | *Reithrodontomys fulvescens laceyi* | Fulvous Harvest Mouse |
| *Reithrodontomys megalotis* | *Reithrodontomys megalotis* | Western Harvest Mouse |
| *Reithrodontomys merriami* | *Reithrodontomys humulis merriami* | Eastern Harvest Mouse |
| *Scalopus* | *Scalopus* | |
| *Scalopus aquaticus* | *Scalopus aquaticus* | Eastern Mole |
| *Scalopus aquaticus intermedius* | *Scalopus aquaticus aereus* | Eastern Mole |
| *Scalopus aquaticus texanus* | *Scalopus aquaticus texanus* | Eastern Mole |
| *Sciuropterus* | *Glaucomys* | |
| *Sciuropterus volans querceti* | *Glaucomys volans querceti* | Southern Flying Squirrel |
| *Sciurus* | *Sciurus/Tamiasciurus* | |
| *Sciurus carolinensis* | *Sciurus carolinensis* | Eastern Gray Squirrel |
| *Sciurus fremonti* | *Tamiasciurus hudsonicus* | Red Squirrel |
| *Sciurus fremonti lychnuchus* | *Tamiasciurus hudsonicus lychnuchus* | Red Squirrel |
| *Sciurus ludovicianus* | *Sciurus niger ludovicianus* | Eastern Fox Squirrel |
| *Sciurus ludovicianus limitis* | *Sciurus niger limitis* | Eastern Fox Squirrel |
| *Sciurus rufiventer* | *Sciurus niger rufiventer* | Eastern Fox Squirrel |
| *Sciurus texianus* | *Sciurus niger ludovicianus* | Eastern Fox Squirrel |
| *Sigmodon* | *Sigmodon* | |
| *Sigmodon hispidus* | *Sigmodon hispidus* | Hispid Cotton Rat |
| *Sigmodon hispidus berlandieri* | *Sigmodon hispidus berlandieri* | Hispid Cotton Rat |
| *Sigmodon hispidus pallidus* | *Sigmodon hispidus berlandieri* | Hispid Cotton Rat |
| *Sigmodon hispidus texianus* | *Sigmodon hispidus texianus* | Hispid Cotton Rat |
| *Sigmodon ochrognathus* | *Sigmodon ochrognathus* | Yellow-nosed Cotton Rat |
| *Sorex* | *Sorex* | |
| *Sorex personatus* | *Sorex cinereus* | Masked Shrew |
| *Spilogale* | *Spilogale* | |
| *Spilogale indianola* | *Spilogale putorius interrupta* | Eastern Spotted Skunk |
| *Spilogale interrupta* | *Spilogale putorius interrupta* | Eastern Spotted Skunk |
| *Spilogale leucoparia* | *Spilogale gracilis leucoparia* | Western Spotted Skunk |
| *Tatu* | *Dasypus* | |
| *Tatu novemcinctum mexicanum* | *Dasypus novemcinctus mexicanus* | Nine-banded Armadillo |
| *Tatu novemcinctum texanum* | *Dasypus novemcinctus mexicanus* | Nine-banded Armadillo |

| | | |
|---|---|---|
| *Tatusia* | *Dasypus* | |
| *Tatusia mexicana* | *Dasypus novemcintus mexicanus* | Nine-banded Armadillo |
| *Taxidea* | *Taxidea* | |
| *Taxidea taxus berlandieri* | *Taxidea taxus berlandieri* | Badger |
| *Tayassu* | *Pecari* | |
| *Tayassu angulatum* | *Pecari tajacu* | Collared Peccary |
| *Thomomys* | *Thomomys* | |
| *Thomomys aureus lachuguilla* | *Thomomys bottae lachuguilla* | Botta's Pocket Gopher |
| *Thomomys baileyi* | *Thomomys bottae baileyi* | Botta's Pocket Gopher |
| *Thomomys fulvus* | *Thomomys bottae* | Botta's Pocket Gopher |
| *Thomomys fulvus texensis* | *Thomomys bottae texensis* | Botta's Pocket Gopher |
| *Thomomys perditus* | *Thomomys bottae perditus* | Botta's Pocket Gopher |
| *Urocyon* | *Urocyon* | |
| *Urocyon cinereoargenteus floridanus* | *Urocyon cinereoargenteus floridanus* | Gray Fox |
| *Urocyon cinereoargenteus ocythous* | *Urocyon cinereoargenteus ocythous* | Gray Fox |
| *Urocyon cinereoargenteus scotti* | *Urocyon cinereoargenteus scotti* | Gray Fox |
| *Urocyon cinereoargenteus texensis* | *Urocyon cinereoargenteus scotti* | Gray Fox |
| *Ursus* | *Ursus* | |
| *Ursus americanus* | *Ursus americanus* | Black Bear |
| *Ursus americanus amblyceps* | *Ursus americanus amblyceps* | Black Bear |
| *Ursus horribilis horriaeus* | *Ursus arctos* | Grizzly Bear |
| *Ursus luteolus* | *Ursus americanus luteolus* | Black Bear |
| *Vespertilio* | *Eptesicus* | |
| *Vespertilio fuscus* | *Eptesicus fuscus* | Big Brown Bat |
| *Vulpes* | *Vulpes* | |
| *Vulpes fulvus* | *Vulpes vulpes* | Red Fox |
| *Vulpes macrotis neomexicanus* | *Vulpes velox macrotis* | Swift or Kit Fox |
| *Vulpes velox* | *Vulpes velox velox* | Swift or Kit Fox |

## Birds

| Old Name | Current Name | Common Name |
|----------|--------------|-------------|
| *Accipiter* | *Accipiter* | |
| *Accipiter cooperi* | *Accipiter cooperii* | Cooper's Hawk |
| *Aeronautes* | *Aeronautes* | |
| *Aeronautes melanoleucus* | *Aeronautes saxatalis* | White-throated Swift |
| *Agelaius* | *Agelaius* | |
| *Agelaius phoeniceus* | *Agelaius phoeniceus* | Red-winged Blackbird |
| *Agelaius phoeniceus floridanus* | *Agelaius phoeniceus* | Red-winged Blackbird |
| *Agelaius phoeniceus richmondi* | *Agelaius phoeniceus* | Red-winged Blackbird |
| *Agelaius phoeniceus sonorensis* | *Agelaius phoeniceus* | Red-winged Blackbird |
| *Aimophila* | *Aimophila* | |
| *Aimophila ruficeps eremoeca* | *Aimophila ruficeps* | Rufous-crowned Sparrow |
| *Aimophila ruficeps scotti* | *Aimophila ruficeps* | Rufous-crowned Sparrow |
| *Ajaia* | *Ajaia* | |
| *Ajaia ajaja* | *Ajaia ajaja* | Roseate Spoonbill |
| *Amazilis* | *Amazilia* | |
| *Amazilis cerviniventris* | *Amazilia yucatanensis* | Buff-bellied Hummingbird |
| *Amazilis cerviniventris chalconota* | *Amazilia yucatanensis* | Buff-bellied Hummingbird |
| *Amazilis tzacatl* | *Amazilia tzacatl* | Rufous-tailed Hummingbird |
| *Ammodramus* | *Ammodramus* | |
| *Ammodramus maritimus sennetti* | *Ammodramus maritimus* | Seaside Sparrow |
| *Ampelis* | *Bombycilla* | |
| *Ampelis cedrorum* | *Bombycilla cedrorum* | Cedar Waxwing |
| *Amphispiza* | *Amphispiza* | |
| *Amphispiza bilineata* | *Amphispiza bilineata* | Black-throated Sparrow |
| *Amphispiza bilineata deserticola* | *Amphispiza bilineata* | Black-throated Sparrow |
| *Antrostomus* | *Caprimulgus* | |
| *Antrostomus carolinensis* | *Caprimulgus carolinensis* | Chuck-will's-widow |
| *Antrostomus macromystax* | *Caprimulgus vociferus* | Whip-poor-will |
| *Aphelocoma* | *Aphelocoma* | |
| *Aphelocoma couchi* | *Aphelocoma ultramarina* | Mexican Jay |
| *Aphelocoma cyanotis* | *Aphelocoma californica* | Western Scrub Jay |
| *Aphelocoma sieberi couchi* | *Aphelocoma ultramarina* | Mexican Jay |
| *Aphelocoma texana* | *Aphelocoma californica* | Western Scrub Jay |
| *Aphelocoma woodhouseii* | *Aphelocoma californica* | Western Scrub Jay |
| *Arremonops* | *Arremonops* | |
| *Arremonops rufivirgatus* | *Arremonops rufivirgatus* | Olive Sparrow |
| *Astragalinus* | *Carduelis* | |
| *Astragalinus psaltria* | *Carduelis psaltria* | Lesser Goldfinch |
| *Auriparus* | *Auriparus* | |
| *Auriparus flaviceps* | *Auriparus flaviceps* | Verdin |
| *Baeolophus* | *Baeolophus* | |
| *Baeolophus atricristatus* | *Baeolophus bicolor* | Tufted Titmouse |
| *Baeolophus bicolor* | *Baeolophus bicolor* | Tufted Titmouse |
| *Baeolophus inornatus griseus* | *Baeolophus ridgwayi* | Juniper Titmouse |
| *Bubo* | *Bubo* | |
| *Bubo virginianus* | *Bubo virginianus* | Great Horned Owl |
| *Bubo virginianus pallescens* | *Bubo virginianus* | Great Horned Owl |
| *Bubo virginianus subarcticus* | *Bubo virginianus* | Great Horned Owl |

| | | |
|---|---|---|
| *Buteo* | *Buteo* | |
| *Buteo abbreviatus* | *Buteo albonotatus* | Zone-tailed Hawk |
| *Buteo albicaudatus sennetti* | *Buteo albicaudatus* | White-tailed Hawk |
| *Buteo borealis calurus* | *Buteo jamaicensis* | Red-tailed Hawk |
| *Buteo lineatus* | *Buteo lineatus* | Red-shouldered Hawk |
| *Buteo swainsoni* | *Buteo swainsoni* | Swainson's Hawk |
| *Callipepla* | *Callipepla* | |
| *Callipepla squamata* | *Callipepla squamata* | Scaled Quail |
| *Callipepla squamata castanogastris* | *Callipepla squamata* | Scaled Quail |
| *Calothorax* | *Calothorax* | |
| *Calothorax lucifer* | *Calothorax lucifer* | Lucifer Hummingbird |
| *Campephilus* | *Campephilus* | |
| *Campephilus principalis* | *Campephilus principalis* | Ivory-billed Woodpecker |
| *Cardinalis* | *Cardinalis* | |
| *Cardinalis cardinalis* | *Cardinalis cardinalis* | Northern Cardinal |
| *Cardinalis cardinalis canicaudus* | *Cardinalis cardinalis* | Northern Cardinal |
| *Carpodacus* | *Carpodacus* | |
| *Carpodacus mexicanus frontalis* | *Carpodacus mexicanus* | House Finch |
| *Catherpes* | *Catherpes* | |
| *Catherpes mexicanus albifrons* | *Catherpes mexicanus* | Canyon Wren |
| *Centurus* | *Melanerpes* | |
| *Centurus aurifrons* | *Melanerpes aurifrons* | Golden-fronted Woodpecker |
| *Centurus carolinus* | *Melanerpes carolinus* | Red-bellied Woodpecker |
| *Ceophloeus* | *Dryocopus* | |
| *Ceophloeus pileatus* | *Dryocopus pileatus* | Pileated Woodpecker |
| *Ceryle* | *Chloroceryle* | |
| *Ceryle* | *Ceryle* | |
| *Ceryle americana septentrionalis* | *Chloroceryle americana* | Green Kingfisher |
| *Ceryle torquata* | *Ceryle torquata* | Ringed Kingfisher |
| *Chordeiles* | *Chordeiles* | |
| *Chordeiles acutipennis texensis* | *Chordeiles acutipennis* | Lesser Nighthawk |
| *Chordeiles virginianus* | *Chordeiles minor* | Common Nighthawk |
| *Chordeiles virginianus chapmani* | *Chordeiles minor* | Common Nighthawk |
| *Chordeiles virginianus henryi* | *Chordeiles minor* | Common Nighthawk |
| *Coccyzus* | *Coccyzus* | |
| *Coccyzus americanus* | *Coccyzus americanus* | Yellow-billed Cuckoo |
| *Coeligena* | *Lampornis* | |
| *Coeligena clemenciae* | *Lampornis clemenciae* | Blue-throated Hummingbird |
| *Colaptes* | *Colaptes* | |
| *Colaptes auratus* | *Colaptes auratus* | Northern Flicker |
| *Colaptes cafer collaris* | *Colaptes auratus* | Northern Flicker |
| *Colinus* | *Colinus* | |
| *Colinus virginianus* | *Colinus virginianus* | Northern Bobwhite |
| *Colinus virginianus texanus* | *Colinus virginianus* | Northern Bobwhite |
| *Columba* | *Columba* | |
| *Columba fasciata* | *Columba fasciata* | Band-tailed Pigeon |
| *Columba flavirostris* | *Columba flavirostris* | Red-billed Pigeon |
| *Columbigallina* | *Columbina* | |
| *Columbigallina passerina pallescens* | *Columbina passerina* | Common Ground Dove |
| *Columbus* | *Tachybaptus* | |
| *Columbus dominicus brachypterus* | *Tachybaptus dominicus* | Least Grebe |
| *Contopus* | *Contopus* | |
| *Contopus richardsoni* | *Contopus virens* | Eastern Wood Pewee |
| *Contopus virens* | *Contopus virens* | Eastern Wood Pewee |

| | | |
|---|---|---|
| *Coturniculus* | *Ammodramus* | |
| *Coturniculus savannarum bimaculatus* | *Ammodramus savannarum* | Grasshopper Sparrow |
| *Corvus* | *Corvus* | |
| *Corvus corax sinuatus* | *Corvus corax* | Common Raven |
| *Corvus cryptoleucus* | *Corvus cryptoleucus* | Chihuahuan Raven |
| *Crotophaga* | *Crotophaga* | |
| *Crotophaga sulcirostris* | *Crotophaga sulcirostris* | Groove-billed Ani |
| *Cyanocephalus* | *Gymnorhinus* | |
| *Cyanocephalus cyanocephalus* | *Gymnorhinus cyanocephalus* | Pinyon Jay |
| *Cyanocitta* | *Cyanocitta* | |
| *Cyanocitta cristata* | *Cyanocitta cristata* | Blue Jay |
| *Cyanocitta stelleri diademata* | *Cyanocitta stelleri* | Steller's Jay |
| *Cyanospiza* | *Passerina* | |
| *Cyanospiza amoena* | *Passerina amoena* | Lazuli Bunting |
| *Cyanospiza cyanea* | *Passerina cyanea* | Indigo Bunting |
| *Cyanospiza versicolor* | *Passerina versicolor* | Varied Bunting |
| *Cyrtonyx* | *Cyrtonyx* | |
| *Cyrtonyx montezumae mearnsi* | *Cyrtonyx montezumae* | Montezuma Quail |
| *Dendrocygna* | *Dendrocygna* | |
| *Dendrocygna autumnalis* | *Dendrocygna autumnalis* | Black-bellied Whistling Duck |
| *Dendroica* | *Dendroica* | |
| *Dendroica aestiva sonorana* | *Dendroica petechia* | Yellow Warbler |
| *Dendroica auduboni* | *Dendroica coronata* | Yellow-rumped Warbler |
| *Dendroica chrysoparia* | *Dendroica chrysoparia* | Golden-cheeked Warbler |
| *Dendroica dominica albilora* | *Dendroica dominica* | Yellow-throated Warbler |
| *Dendroica graciae* | *Dendroica graciae* | Grace's Warbler |
| *Dendroica vigorsi* | *Dendroica pinus* | Pine Warbler |
| *Dryobates* | *Picoides* | |
| *Dryobates borealis* | *Picoides borealis* | Red-cockaded Woodpecker |
| *Dryobates pubescens* | *Picoides pubescens* | Downy Woodpecker |
| *Dryobates scalaris bairdi* | *Picoides scalaris* | Ladder-backed Woodpecker |
| *Dryobates villosus auduboni* | *Picoides villosus* | Hairy Woodpecker |
| *Dryobates villosus hyloscopus* | *Picoides villosus* | Hairy Woodpecker |
| *Elanoides* | *Elanoides* | |
| *Elanoides forficatus* | *Elanoides forficatus* | American Swallow-tailed Kite |
| *Elanus* | *Elanus* | |
| *Elanus leucurus* | *Elanus leucurus* | White-tailed Kite |
| *Empidonax* | *Empidonax* | |
| *Empidonax difficilis* | *Empidonax occidentalis* | Cordilleran Flycatcher |
| *Empidonax virescens* | *Empidonax virescens* | Acadian Flycatcher |
| *Falco* | *Falco* | |
| *Falco fusco-caerulescens* | *Falco femoralis* | Aplomado Falcon |
| *Falco mexicanus* | *Falco mexicanus* | Prairie Falcon |
| *Falco sparverius* | *Falco sparverius* | American Kestrel |
| *Falco sparverius phaloena* | *Falco sparverius* | American Kestrel |
| *Florida* | *Egretta* | |
| *Florida caerulea* | *Egretta caerulea* | Little Blue Heron |
| *Fregata* | *Fregata* | |
| *Fregata aquila* | *Fregata magnificens* | Magnificent Frigatebird |
| *Galeoscoptes* | *Dumatella* | |
| *Galeoscoptes carolinensis* | *Dumatella carolinensis* | Gray Catbird |
| *Geococcyx* | *Geococcyx* | |
| *Geococcyx californianus* | *Geococcyx californianus* | Greater Roadrunner |

| | | |
|---|---|---|
| *Geothlypis* | *Oporornis* | |
| *Geothlypis* | *Geothlypis* | |
| *Geothlypis formosa* | *Oporornis formosus* | Kentucky Warbler |
| *Geothlypis poliocephala* | *Geothlypis poliocephala* | Gray-crowned Yellowthroat |
| *Geothlypis trichas brachidactyla* | *Geothlypis trichas* | Common Yellowthroat |
| *Glaucidium* | *Glaucidium* | |
| *Glaucidium phalaenoides* | *Glaucidium brasilianum* | Ferruginous Pygmy-owl |
| *Guara* | *Eudocimus* | |
| *Guara alba* | *Eudocimus albus* | White Ibis |
| *Guiraca* | *Guiraca* | |
| *Guiraca caerulea* | *Guiraca caerulea* | Blue Grosbeak |
| *Guiraca caerulea lazula* | *Guiraca caerulea* | Blue Grosbeak |
| *Heleodytes* | *Campylorhynchus* | |
| *Heleodytes brunneicapillus couesi* | *Campylorhynchus brunneicapillus* | Cactus Wren |
| *Helminthophila* | *Vermivora* | |
| *Helminthophila celata orestera* | *Vermivora celata* | Orange-crowned Warbler |
| *Hydranassa* | *Egretta* | |
| *Hydranassa tricolor ruficollis* | *Egretta tricolor* | Tricolored Heron |
| *Hylocichla* | *Catharus* | |
| *Hylocichla* | *Hylocichla* | |
| *Hylocichla guttata auduboni* | *Catharus guttatus* | Hermit Thrush |
| *Hylocichla mustelina* | *Hylocichla mustelina* | Wood Thrush |
| *Icteria* | *Icteria* | |
| *Icteria virens* | *Icteria virens* | Yellow-breasted Chat |
| *Icteria virens longicauda* | *Icteria virens* | Yellow-breasted Chat |
| *Icterus* | *Icterus* | |
| *Icterus auduboni* | *Icterus graduacauda* | Audubon's Oriole |
| *Icterus bullocki* | *Icterus bullockii* | Bullock's Oriole |
| *Icterus cucullatus sennetti* | *Icterus cucullatus* | Hooded Oriole |
| *Icterus galbula* | *Icterus galbula* | Baltimore Oriole |
| *Icterus parisorum* | *Icterus parisorum* | Scott's Oriole |
| *Jacana* | *Jacana* | |
| *Jacana spinosa* | *Jacana spinosa* | Northern Jacana |
| *Junco* | *Junco* | |
| *Junco dorsalis* | *Junco hyemalis* | Dark-eyed Junco |
| *Lanius* | *Lanius* | |
| *Lanius ludovicianus excubitorides* | *Lanius ludovicianus* | Loggerhead Shrike |
| *Leptotila* | *Leptotila* | |
| *Leptotila fulviventris brachyptera* | *Leptotila verreauxi* | White-tipped Dove |
| *Lophortyx* | *Callipepla* | |
| *Lophortyx gambeli* | *Callipepla gambelii* | Gambel's Quail |
| *Loxia* | *Loxia* | |
| *Loxia curvirostra stricklandi* | *Loxia curvirostra* | Red Crossbill |
| *Megaquiscalus* | *Quiscalus* | |
| *Megaquiscalus major* | *Quiscalus major* | Boat-tailed Grackle |
| *Megaquiscalus major macrourus* | *Quiscalus mexicanus* | Great-tailed Grackle |
| *Megascops* | *Otus* | |
| *Megascops asio* | *Otus asio* | Eastern Screech Owl |
| *Megascops asio mccalli* | *Otus asio* | Eastern Screech Owl |
| *Megascops flammeolus* | *Otus flammeolus* | Flammulated Owl |
| *Melanerpes* | *Melanerpes* | |
| *Melanerpes erythrocephalus* | *Melanerpes erythrocephalus* | Red-headed Woodpecker |
| *Melanerpes formicivorus* | *Melanerpes formicivorus* | Acorn Woodpecker |

| | | |
|---|---|---|
| *Meleagris* | *Meleagris* | |
| *Meleagris gallopavo intermedia* | *Meleagris gallopavo* | Wild Turkey |
| *Meleagris gallopavo merriami* | *Meleagris gallopavo* | Wild Turkey |
| *Meleagris gallopavo silvestris* | *Meleagris gallopavo* | Wild Turkey |
| *Melopelia* | *Zenaida* | |
| *Melopelia leucoptera* | *Zenaida asiatica* | White-winged Dove |
| *Merula* | *Turdus* | |
| *Merula migratoria* | *Turdus migratorius* | American Robin |
| *Micropallas* | *Micrathene* | |
| *Micropallas whitneyi* | *Micrathene whitneyi* | Elf Owl |
| *Mimus* | *Mimus* | |
| *Mimus polyglottos* | *Mimus polyglottos* | Northern Mockingbird |
| *Mimus polyglottos leucopterus* | *Mimus polyglottos* | Northern Mockingbird |
| *Mniotilta* | *Mniotilta* | |
| *Mniotilta varia* | *Mniotilta varia* | Black-and-white Warbler |
| *Molothrus* | *Molothrus* | |
| *Molothrus ater obscurus* | *Molothrus ater* | Brown-headed Cowbird |
| *Mycteria* | *Mycteria* | |
| *Mycteria americana* | *Mycteria americana* | Wood Stork |
| *Myiarchus* | *Myiarchus* | |
| *Myiarchus cinerascens* | *Myiarchus cinerascens* | Ash-throated Flycatcher |
| *Myiarchus crinitus* | *Myiarchus crinitus* | Great Crested Flycatcher |
| *Myiarchus mexicanus* | *Myiarchus tyrannulus* | Brown-crested Flycatcher |
| *Nomonyx* | *Nomonyx* | |
| *Nomonyx dominicus* | *Nomonyx dominica* | Masked Duck |
| *Numenius* | *Numenius* | |
| *Numenius longirostris* | *Numenius americanus* | Long-billed Curlew |
| *Nuttallornis* | *Contopus* | |
| *Nuttallornis borealis* | *Contopus cooperi* | Olive-sided Flycatcher |
| *Nyctidromus* | *Nyctidromus* | |
| *Nyctidromus albicollis merrilli* | *Nyctidromus albicollis* | Pauraque |
| *Oreospiza* | *Pipilo* | |
| *Oreospiza chlorura* | *Pipilo chlorurus* | Green-tailed Towhee |
| *Ornithion* | *Camptostoma* | |
| *Ornithion imberbe* | *Camptostoma imberbe* | Northern Beardless-Tyrannulet |
| *Ortalis* | *Ortalis* | |
| *Ortalis vetula mccalli* | *Ortalis vetula* | Plain Chachalaca |
| *Otocoris* | *Eremophila* | |
| *Otocoris alpestris giraudi* | *Eremophila alpestris* | Horned Lark |
| *Otocoris alpestris leucolaema* | *Eremophila alpestris* | Horned Lark |
| *Parabuteo* | *Parabuteo* | |
| *Parabuteo unicinctus harrisi* | *Parabuteo unicinctus* | Harris' Hawk |
| *Parus* | *Poecile* | |
| *Parus carolinensis agilis* | *Poecile carolinensis* | Carolina Chickadee |
| *Parus gambeli* | *Poecile gambeli* | Mountain Chickadee |
| *Peucaea* | *Aimophila* | |
| *Peucaea aestivalis bachmani* | *Aimophila aestivalis* | Bachman's Sparrow |
| *Peucaea cassini* | *Aimophila cassinii* | Cassin's Sparrow |
| *Phainopepla* | *Phainopepla* | |
| *Phainopepla nitens* | *Phainopepla nitens* | Phainopepla |
| *Phalacrocorax* | *Phalacrocorax* | |
| *Phalacrocorax vigua mexicanus* | *Phalacrocorax brasilianus* | Neotropic Cormorant |
| *Phalaenoptilus* | *Phalaenoptilus* | |
| *Phalaenoptilus nuttallii* | *Phalaenoptilus nuttalli* | Common Poorwill |

| | | |
|---|---|---|
| *Pipilo* | *Pipilo* | |
| *Pipilo fuscus mesoleucus* | *Pipilo fuscus* | Canyon Towhee |
| *Pipilo maculatus megalonyx* | *Pipilo erythrophthalmus* | Eastern Towhee |
| *Piranga* | *Piranga* | |
| *Piranga hepatica* | *Piranga flava* | Hepatic Tanager |
| *Piranga ludoviciana* | *Piranga ludoviciana* | Western Tanager |
| *Piranga rubra cooperi* | *Piranga rubra* | Summer Tanager |
| *Pitangus* | *Pitangus* | |
| *Pitangus derbianus* | *Pitangus sulphuratus* | Great Kiskadee |
| *Podasocys* | *Charadrius* | |
| *Podasocys montanus* | *Charadrius montanus* | Mountain Plover |
| *Polioptila* | *Polioptila* | |
| *Polioptila caerulea* | *Polioptila caerulea* | Blue-gray Gnatcatcher |
| *Polioptila caerulea obscura* | *Polioptila caerulea* | Blue-gray Gnatcatcher |
| *Polioptila plumbea* | *Polioptila plumbea* | Tropical Gnatcatcher |
| *Polyborus* | *Caracara* | |
| *Polyborus cheriway* | *Caracara plancus* | Crested Caracara |
| *Pooecetes* | *Pooecetes* | |
| *Pooecetes confinis* | *Pooecetes gramineus* | Vesper Sparrow |
| *Protonotaria* | *Protonotaria* | |
| *Protonotaria citrea* | *Protonotaria citrea* | Prothonotary Warbler |
| *Psaltriparus* | *Psaltriparus* | |
| *Psaltriparus lloydi* | *Psaltriparus minimus* | Bushtit |
| *Psaltriparus melanotis lloydi* | *Psaltriparus minimus* | Bushtit |
| *Psaltriparus plumbeus* | *Psaltriparus minimus* | Bushtit |
| *Pyrocephalus* | *Pyrocephalus* | |
| *Pyrocephalus rubineus mexicanus* | *Pyrocephalus rubinus* | Vermilion Flycatcher |
| *Pyrrhuloxia* | *Cardinalis* | |
| *Pyrrhuloxia sinuata* | *Cardinalis sinuatus* | Pyrrhuloxia |
| *Pyrrhuloxia sinuata texana* | *Cardinalis sinuatus* | Pyrrhuloxia |
| *Quiscalus* | *Quiscalus* | |
| *Quiscalus quiscula aeneus* | *Quiscalus quiscula* | Common Grackle |
| *Salpinctes* | *Salpinctes* | |
| *Salpinctes obsoletus* | *Salpinctes obsoletus* | Rock Wren |
| *Sayornis* | *Sayornis* | |
| *Sayornis nigricans* | *Sayornis nigricans* | Black Phoebe |
| *Sayornis saya* | *Sayornis saya* | Say's Phoebe |
| *Scardafella* | *Columbina* | |
| *Scardafella inca* | *Columbina inca* | Inca Dove |
| *Selasphorus* | *Selasphorus* | |
| *Selasphorus platycercus* | *Selasphorus platycercus* | Broad-tailed Hummingbird |
| *Selasphorus rufus* | *Selasphorus rufus* | Rufous Hummingbird |
| *Sialia* | *Sialia* | |
| *Sialia mexicana bairdi* | *Sialia mexicana* | Western Bluebird |
| *Sialia sialis* | *Sialia sialis* | Eastern Bluebird |
| *Sitta* | *Sitta* | |
| *Sitta carolinensis* | *Sitta carolinensis* | White-breasted Nuthatch |
| *Sitta carolinensis nelsoni* | *Sitta carolinensis* | White-breasted Nuthatch |
| *Sitta pusilla* | *Sitta pusilla* | Brown-headed Nuthatch |
| *Sitta pygmaea* | *Sitta pygmaea* | Pygmy Nuthatch |
| *Speotyto* | *Athene* | |
| *Speotyto cunicularia hypogaea* | *Athene cunicularia* | Burrowing Owl |
| *Spizella* | *Spizella* | |
| *Spizella pusilla* | *Spizella pusilla* | Field Sparrow |
| *Spizella socialis* | *Spizella passerina* | Chipping Sparrow |

| | | |
|---|---|---|
| *Spizella socialis arizonae* | *Spizella passerina* | Chipping Sparrow |
| *Sporophila* | *Sporophila* | |
| *Sporophila morelleti* | *Sporophila torqueola* | White-collared Seedeater |
| *Sturnella* | *Sturnella* | |
| *Sturnella magna hoopesi* | *Sturnella magna* | Eastern Meadowlark |
| *Sturnella magna neglecta* | *Sturnella neglecta* | Western Meadowlark |
| *Syrnium* | *Strix* | |
| *Syrnium occidentale* | *Strix occidentalis* | Spotted Owl |
| *Syrnium varium helveolum* | *Strix varia* | Barred Owl |
| *Tangavius* | *Molothrus* | |
| *Tangavius aeneus involucratus* | *Molothrus aeneus* | Bronzed Cowbird |
| *Thryomanes* | *Thryomanes* | |
| *Thryomanes bewickii bairdi* | *Thryomanes bewickii* | Bewick's Wren |
| *Thryomanes bewickii cryptus* | *Thryomanes bewickii* | Bewick's Wren |
| *Thryomanes bewickii leucogaster* | *Thryomanes bewickii* | Bewick's Wren |
| *Thryothorus* | *Thryothorus* | |
| *Thryothorus ludovicianus* | *Thryothorus ludovicianus* | Carolina Wren |
| *Toxostoma* | *Toxostoma* | |
| *Toxostoma curvirostre* | *Toxostoma curvirostre* | Curve-billed Thrasher |
| *Toxostoma longirostre sennetti* | *Toxostoma longirostre* | Long-billed Thrasher |
| *Trochilus* | *Archilochus* | |
| *Trochilus alexandri* | *Archilochus alexandri* | Black-chinned Hummingbird |
| *Trochilus colubris* | *Archilochus colubris* | Ruby-throated Hummingbird |
| *Troglodytes* | *Troglodytes* | |
| *Troglodytes aedon aztecus* | *Troglodytes aedon* | House Wren |
| *Tympanuchus* | *Tympanuchus* | |
| *Tympanuchus americanus* | *Tympanuchus cupido* | Greater Prairie Chicken |
| *Tympanuchus americanus attwateri* | *Tympanuchus cupido attwateri* | Attwater's Prairie Chicken |
| *Tyrannus* | *Tyrannus* | |
| *Tyrannus melancholicus couchii* | *Tyrannus couchii* | Couch's Kingbird |
| *Tyrannus tyrannus* | *Tyrannus tyrannus* | Eastern Kingbird |
| *Tyrannus verticalis* | *Tyrannus verticalis* | Western Kingbird |
| *Tyrannus vociferans* | *Tyrannus vociferans* | Cassin's Kingbird |
| *Urubitinga* | *Buteogallus* | |
| *Urubitinga anthracina* | *Buteogallus anthracinus* | Common Black-hawk |
| *Vireo* | *Vireo* | |
| *Vireo atricapillus* | *Vireo atricapillus* | Black-capped Vireo |
| *Vireo bellii arizonae* | *Vireo bellii* | Bell's Vireo |
| *Vireo bellii medius* | *Vireo bellii* | Bell's Vireo |
| *Vireo flavifrons* | *Vireo flavifrons* | Yellow-throated Vireo |
| *Vireo flavoviridis* | *Vireo flavoviridis* | Yellow-green Vireo |
| *Vireo gilvus swainsoni* | *Vireo gilvus* | Warbling Vireo |
| *Vireo huttoni stephensi* | *Vireo huttoni* | Hutton's Vireo |
| *Vireo noveboracensis* | *Vireo griseus* | White-eyed Vireo |
| *Vireo noveboracensis micrus* | *Vireo griseus* | White-eyed Vireo |
| *Vireo olivaceus* | *Vireo olivaceus* | Red-eyed Vireo |
| *Vireo solitarius plumbeus* | *Vireo plumbeus* | Plumbeous Vireo |
| *Vireo stephensi* | *Vireo huttoni* | Hutton's Vireo |
| *Wilsonia* | *Wilsonia* | |
| *Wilsonia mitrata* | *Wilsonia citrina* | Hooded Warbler |
| *Wilsonia pusilla pileolata* | *Wilsonia pusilla* | Wilson's Warbler |
| *Xanthoura* | *Cyanocorax* | |
| *Xanthoura luxuosa glaucescens* | *Cyanocorax yncas* | Green Jay |
| *Zamelodia* | *Pheucticus* | |
| *Zamelodia melanocephala* | *Pheucticus melanocephelus* | Black-headed Grosbeak |

## Reptiles

| Old Name | Current Name | Common Name |
|---|---|---|
| *Agkistrodon* | *Agkistrodon* | |
| *Agkistrodon contortrix* | *Agkistrodon contortrix* | Copperhead |
| *Agkistrodon piscivorus* | *Agkistrodon piscivorus* | Cottonmouth |
| *Anolis* | *Anolis* | |
| *Anolis carolinensis* | *Anolis carolinensis* | Green Anole |
| *Bascanion* | *Masticophis* | |
| *Bascanion flagellum* | *Masticophis flagellum* | Coachwhip |
| *Bascanion ornatum* | *Masticophis taeniatus* | Striped Whip Snake |
| *Callopeltis* | *Elaphe* | |
| *Callopeltis obsoletus* | *Elaphe obsoleta* | Texas Rat Snake |
| *Chionactis* | *Sonora* | |
| *Chionactis episcopus isozonus* | *Sonora semiannulata* | Ground Snake |
| *Cnemidophorus* | *Cnemidophorus* | |
| *Cnemidophorus gularis* | *Cnemidophorus gularis* | Texas Spotted Whiptail |
| *Cnemidophorus perplexus* | *Cnemidophorus neomexicanus* | New Mexico Whiptail |
| *Cnemidophorus sexlineatus* | *Cnemidophorus sexlineatus* | Six-lined Racerunner |
| *Cnemidophorus tessellatus* | *Cnemidophorus tessellatus* | Colorado Checkered Whiptail |
| *Coleonyx* | *Coleonyx* | |
| *Coleonyx brevis* | *Coleonyx brevis* | Texas Banded Gecko |
| *Crotalus* | *Crotalus* | |
| *Crotalus atrox* | *Crotalus atrox* | Western Diamondback Rattlesnake |
| *Crotalus confluentis* | *Crotalus viridis* | Prairie Rattlesnake |
| *Crotalus horridus* | *Crotalus horridus* | Timber Rattlesnake |
| *Crotalus lepidus* | *Crotalus lepidus* | Rock Rattlesnake |
| *Crotalus molossus* | *Crotalus molossus* | Black-tailed Rattlesnake |
| *Crotaphytus* | *Crotaphytus* | |
| *Crotaphytus collaris* | *Crotaphytus collaris* | Collared Lizard |
| *Crotaphytus collaris baileyi* | *Crotaphytus collaris baileyi* | |
| *Crotaphytus reticulatus* | *Crotaphytus reticulatus* | Reticulate Collared Lizard |
| *Crotaphytus wislizenii* | *Gambelia wislizeni* | Leopard Lizard |
| *Diadophis* | *Diadophis* | |
| *Diadophis regalis* | *Diadophis punctatus regalis* | Regal Ringneck Snake |
| *Drymarchon* | *Drymarchon* | |
| *Drymarchon corais melanurus* | *Drymarchon corais erebennus* | Texas Indigo Snake |
| *Drymobius* | *Drymobius* | |
| *Drymobius margaritiferus* | *Drymobius margaritiferus* | Speckled Racer |
| *Elaps* | *Micrurus* | |
| *Elaps fulvius* | *Micrurus fulvius* | Coral Snake |
| *Eumeces* | *Eumeces* | |
| *Eumeces brevilineatus* | *Eumeces tetragrammus brevilineatus* | Four-lined Skink |
| *Eumeces guttulatus* | *Eumeces obsoletus* | Great Plains Skink |
| *Eumeces obsoletus* | *Eumeces obsoletus* | Great Plains Skink |
| *Eumeces quinquelineatus* | *Eumeces fasciatus* | Five-lined Skink |
| *Eutainia* | *Thamnophis* | |
| *Eutainia cyrtopsis* | *Thamnophis cyrtopsis* | Black-necked Garter Snake |
| *Eutainia elegans marciana* | *Thamnophis marcianus* | Checkered Garter Snake |
| *Eutainia proxima* | *Thamnophis proximus* | Western Ribbon Snake |
| *Gerrhonotus* | *Gerrhonotus* | |
| *Gerrhonotus liocephalus infernalis* | *Gerrhonotus infernalis* | Texas Alligator Lizard |

| | | |
|---|---|---|
| *Heterodon* | *Heterodon* | |
| *Heterodon nasicus* | *Heterodon nasicus* | Western Hog-nosed Snake |
| *Heterodon platirhinos* | *Heterodon platirhinos* | Eastern Hog-nosed Snake |
| *Holbrookia* | *Holbrookia* | |
| *Holbrookia maculata* | *Holbrookia maculata* | Lesser Earless Lizard |
| *Holbrookia maculata lacerata* | *Holbrookia lacerata* | Spot-tailed Earless Lizard |
| *Holbrookia propinqua* | *Holbrookia propinqua* | Keeled Earless Lizard |
| *Holbrookia texana* | *Cophosaurus texanus* | Greater Earless Lizard |
| *Lampropeltis* | *Lampropeltis* | |
| *Lampropeltis getula holbrooki* | *Lampropeltis getula hobrooki* | Speckled Kingsnake |
| *Leiolopisma* | *Scincella* | |
| *Leiolopisma laterale* | *Scincella lateralis* | Ground Skink |
| *Liopeltis* | *Liochlorophis* | |
| *Liopeltis vernalis* | *Liochlorophis vernalis* | Smooth Green Snake |
| *Natrix* | *Nerodia* | |
| *Natrix clarkii* | *Nerodia clarki* | Salt Marsh Snake |
| *Natrix fasciata transversa* | *Nerodia erythrogaster transversa* | Blotched Water Snake |
| *Opheodrys* | *Opheodrys* | |
| *Opheodrys aestivus* | *Opheodrys aestivus* | Rough Green Snake |
| *Ophisaurus* | *Ophisaurus* | |
| *Ophisaurus ventralis* | *Ophisaurus attenuatus* | Western Slender Glass Lizard |
| | | |
| *Phrynosoma* | *Phrynosoma* | |
| *Phrynosoma cornutum* | *Phrynosoma cornutum* | Texas Horned Lizard |
| *Phrynosoma hernandesi* | *Phrynosoma hernandesi* | Short-horned Lizard |
| *Phrynosoma modestum* | *Phrynosoma modestum* | Roundtail Horned Lizard |
| *Pituophis* | *Pituophis* | |
| *Pituophis sayi* | *Pituophis catenifer* | Bullsnake |
| *Rhinocheilus* | *Rhinocheilus* | |
| *Rhinocheilus lecontei* | *Rhinocheilus lecontei* | Long-nosed Snake |
| *Sceloporus* | *Sceloporus* | |
| *Sceloporus clarkii* | *Sceloporus olivaceus* | Texas Spiny Lizard |
| *Sceloporus consobrinus* | *Sceloporus undulatus* | Eastern Fence Lizard |
| *Sceloporus dispar* | *Sceloporus grammicus* | Mesquite Lizard |
| *Sceloporus merriami* | *Sceloporus merriami* | Canyon Lizard |
| *Sceloporus spinosus floridanus* | *Sceloporus olivaceus* | Texas Spiny Lizard |
| *Sceloporus torquatus poinsettii* | *Sceloporus poinsetti poinsetti* | Crevice Spiny Lizard |
| *Sistrurus* | *Sistrurus* | |
| *Sistrurus catenatus* | *Sistrurus catenatus* | Massasauga |
| *Sistrurus catenatus consors* | *Sistrurus catenatus edwardsi* | Desert Massasauga |
| *Storeria* | *Storeria* | |
| *Storeria dekayi* | *Storeria dekayi* | Brown Snake |
| *Tantilla* | *Tantilla* | |
| *Tantilla gracilis* | *Tantilla gracilis* | Flatheaded Snake |
| *Tropidoclonion* | *Tropidoclonion* | |
| *Tropidoclonion lineatum* | *Tropidoclonion lineatum* | Lined Snake |
| *Uta* | *Urosaurus* | |
| *Uta* | *Uta* | |
| *Uta ornata* | *Urosaurus ornatus* | Tree Lizard |
| *Uta stansburiana* | *Uta stansburiana* | Side-blotched Lizard |

## Plants

| Old Name | Current Name | Common Name |
| --- | --- | --- |
| *Acacia* | *Acacia* | |
| *Acacia amentacea* | *Acacia rigidula* | Blackbrush Acacia |
| *Acacia berlandieri* | *Acacia berlandieri* | Guajillo |
| *Acacia constricta* | *Acacia constricta* | Mescat Acacia |
| *Acacia roemeriana* | *Acacia roemeriana* | Roemer Acacia |
| *Acacia schottii* | *Acacia schottii* | Schott Acacia |
| *Acacia tortuosa* | *Acacia schaffneri bravoensis* | Twisted Acacia |
| *Acacia wrightii* | *Acacia greggii wrightii* | Wright Acacia |
| *Acer* | *Acer* | |
| *Acer drummondi* | *Acer rubrum* | Red Maple |
| *Acer grandidentatum* | *Acer grandidentatum* | Bigtooth Maple |
| *Acer rubrum* | *Acer rubrum* | Red Maple |
| *Acuan* | *Desmanthus* | |
| *Acuan illinoensis* | *Desmanthus illinoiensis* | Illinois Bundleflower |
| *Adelia* | *Forestieria* | |
| *Adelia angustifolia* | *Forestieria angustifolia* | Narrowleaf Forestiera |
| *Adelia neomexicana* | *Forestieria pubescens* | Elbowbush |
| *Adolphia* | *Adolphia* | |
| *Adolphia infesta* | *Adolphia infesta* | Texas Adolphia |
| *Agave* | *Agave* | |
| *Agave applanata* | *Agave havardiana* | Havard Agave |
| *Agave lecheguilla* | *Agave lechuguilla* | Lechuguilla |
| *Agave wislizeni* | *Agave havardiana* | Havard Agave |
| *Aloysia* | *Aloysia* | |
| *Aloysia ligustrina* | *Aloysia gratissima* | Whitebrush |
| *Amelanchier* | *Amelanchier* | |
| *Amelanchier alnifolia* | *Amelanchier utahensis* | Serviceberry |
| *Amorpha* | *Amorpha* | |
| *Amorpha canescens* | *Amorpha canescens* | Leadplant |
| *Amyris* | *Helietta* | |
| *Amyris parvifolia* | *Helietta parvifolia* | Barreta |
| *Aralia* | *Aralia* | |
| *Aralia spinosa* | *Aralia spinosa* | Devil's-walking-stick |
| *Arbutus* | *Arbutus* | |
| *Arbutus xalapensis* | *Arbutus xalapensis* | Texas Madrone |
| *Artemisia* | *Artemisia* | |
| *Artemisia filifolia* | *Artemisia filifolia* | Sand Sagewort |
| *Arundinaria* | *Arundinaria* | |
| *Arundinaria macrosperma* | *Arundinaria gigantea* | Giant Cane |
| *Asclepias* | *Asclepias* | |
| *Asclepias latifolia* | *Asclepias latifolia* | Broadleaf Milkweed |
| *Asclepias speciosa* | *Asclepias speciosa* | Showy Milkweed |
| *Asclepias tuberosa* | *Asclepias tuberosa* | Butterfly Milkweed |
| *Ascyrum* | *Hypericum* | |
| *Asimina* | *Asimina* | |
| *Asimina triloba* | *Asimina triloba* | Common Pawpaw |
| *Astragalus* | *Astragalus* | |
| *Astragalus bisulcatus* | *Astragalus bisulcatus* | Locoweed |
| *Astragalus caryocarpus* | *Astragalus crassicarpus* | Groundplum |
| *Astragalus molissimus* | *Astragalus mollissimus* | Wooly Locoweed |

| | | |
|---|---|---|
| *Azalea* | *Rhododendron* | |
| *Baccharis* | *Baccharis* | |
| *Baccharis glutinosa* | *Baccharis salicifolia* | Seepwillow |
| *Baccharis salicina* | *Baccharis salicina* | Willow Baccharis |
| *Baptisia* | *Baptisia* | |
| *Berberis* | *Mahonia* | |
| *Berberis repens* | *Mahonia repens* | Creeping Barberry |
| *Berberis trifoliata* | *Mahonia trifoliolata* | Agarito |
| *Bernardia* | *Bernardia* | |
| *Bernardia myricaefolia* | *Bernardia myricifolia* | Brush Myrtlecroton |
| *Betula* | *Betula* | |
| *Betula nigra* | *Betula nigra* | River Birch |
| *Bignonia* | *Bignonia* | |
| *Bignonia crucigera* | *Bignonia capreolata* | Crossvine |
| *Bradleia* | *Wisteria* | |
| *Brayodendron* | *Diospyros* | |
| *Brayodendron texanum* | *Diospyros texana* | Texas Persimmon |
| *Cactus* | *Escobaria* | |
| *Cactus* | *Mammillaria* | |
| *Cactus heyderi* | *Mammillaria heyderi* | Flattened Mamillaria |
| *Cactus missouriensis* | *Escobaria missouriensis* | Fox-tail Cactus |
| *Callicarpa* | *Callicarpa* | |
| *Callicarpa americana* | *Callicarpa americana* | American Beautyberry |
| *Callirhoe* | *Callirhoe* | |
| *Campsis* | *Campsis* | |
| *Campsis radicans* | *Campsis radicans* | Common Trumpet-creeper |
| *Carpinus* | *Carpinus* | |
| *Carpinus carolinana* | *Carpinus caroliniana* | American Hornbeam |
| *Castalia* | *Nymphaea* | |
| *Castalia elegans* | *Nymphaea elegans* | Senorita Waterlily |
| *Castanea* | *Castanea* | |
| *Castanea pumila* | *Castanea pumila* | Ashe Chestnut |
| *Castela* | *Castela* | |
| *Castela nicholsonii* | *Castela erecta* | Allthorn |
| *Ceanothus* | *Ceanothus* | |
| *Ceanothus greggii* | *Ceanothus greggii* | Desert Ceanothus |
| *Celtis* | *Celtis* | |
| *Celtis helleri* | *Celtis lindheimeri* | Palo Blanco |
| *Celtis mississippiensis* | *Celtis laevigata* | Sugar Hackberry |
| *Celtis reticulata* | *Celtis laevigata reticulata* | Netleaf Hackberry |
| *Cephalanthus* | *Cephalanthus* | |
| *Cephalanthus occidentalis* | *Cephalanthus occidentalis* | Common Buttonbush |
| *Cercidium* | *Parkinsonia* | |
| *Cercidium floridanum* | *Parkinsonia texana macra* | Border Paloverde |
| *Cercidium texanum* | *Parkinsonia texana texana* | Texas Paloverde |
| *Cercis* | *Cercis* | |
| *Cercis occidentalis* | *Cercis canadensis* | Redbud |
| *Cercocarpus* | *Cercocarpus* | |
| *Cercocarpus parvifolius* | *Cercocarpus montanus* | True Mountain Mahogany |
| *Cereus* | *Echinocereus* | |
| *Cereus enneacanthus* | *Echinocereus enneacanthus* | Pitaya |
| *Cereus paucispinus* | *Echinocereus triglochidiatus* | Claret-cup Echinocereus |
| *Cereus stramineus* | *Echinocereus enneacathus* | Pitaya |

| | | |
|---|---|---|
| *Chilopsis* | *Chilopsis* | |
| *Chilopsis linearis* | *Chilopsis linearis* | Desert Willow |
| *Condalia* | *Condalia* | |
| *Condalia obovata* | *Condalia hookeri* | Brasil |
| *Condalia spathulata* | *Condalia spathulata* | Knifeleaf Condalia |
| *Coreopsis* | *Coreopsis* | |
| *Covillea* | *Larrea* | |
| *Covillea tridentata* | *Larrea tridentata* | Creosotebush |
| *Crataegus* | *Crataegus* | |
| *Crataegus spathulata* | *Crataegus spathulata* | Littlehip Hawthorne |
| *Crataegus texana* | *Crataegus texana* | Texas Hawthorne |
| *Croton* | *Croton* | |
| *Croton torreyanus* | *Croton incanus* | Torrey Croton |
| *Cupressus* | *Cupressus* | |
| *Cupressus arizonica* | *Cupressus arizonica* | Arizona Cypress |
| *Cynoxlylon* | *Cornus* | |
| *Cynoxlylon floridum* | *Cornus florida* | Flowering Dogwood |
| *Cyrilla* | *Cyrilla* | |
| *Cyrilla racemiflora* | *Cyrilla racemiflora* | Swamp Cyrilla |
| *Dasylirion* | *Dasylirion* | |
| *Dasylirion texanum* | *Dasylirion texanum* | Texas Sotol |
| *Daubentonia* | *Sesbania* | |
| *Daubentonia longifolia* | *Sesbania drummondii* | Drummond Sesbania |
| *Dendropogon* | *Tillandsia* | |
| *Dendropogon usneoides* | *Tillandsia usneoides* | Spanish Moss |
| *Diospyros* | *Diospyros* | |
| *Diospyros virginiana* | *Diospyros virginiana* | Common Persimmon |
| *Echinocactus* | *Mammillaria* | |
| *Echinocactus* | *Ferocactus* | |
| *Echinocactus* | *Echinocactus* | |
| *Echinocactus hamatocanthus* | *Ferocactus hamatacanthus* | Turk's Head |
| *Echinocactus horizonthalonius* | *Echinocactus horizonthalonius* | Devilshead Cactus |
| *Echinocactus wislizeni* | *Ferocactus wislizeni* | Southwestern Barrel Cactus |
| *Echinocactus wrighti* | *Mammillaria wrightii* | Wright's Mamillaria |
| *Ehretia* | *Ehretia* | |
| *Ehretia eliptica* | *Ehretia anacua* | Anacua |
| *Ephedra* | *Ephedra* | |
| *Ephedra antisyphilitica* | *Ephedra antisyphilitica* | Vine Ephedra |
| *Ephedra trifurcata* | *Ephedra trifurca* | Longleaf Ephedra |
| *Euphorbia* | *Euphorbia* | |
| *Euphorbia antisyphilitica* | *Euphorbia antisyphilitica* | Candelilla |
| *Eustoma* | *Eustoma* | |
| *Eysenhardtia* | *Eysenhardtia* | |
| *Eysenhardtia amorphoides* | *Eysenhardtia texana* | Kidneywood |
| *Fagara* | *Zanthoxylum* | |
| *Fagara clavaherculis* | *Zanthoxylum clava-herculis* | Hercules Club |
| *Fallugia* | *Fallugia* | |
| *Fallugia paradoxa* | *Fallugia paradoxa* | Apache Plume |
| *Flourensia* | *Flourensia* | |
| *Flourensia cernua* | *Flourensia cernua* | Tarbush |
| *Fouquiera* | *Fouquieria* | |
| *Fouquiera splendens* | *Fouquieria splendens* | Ocotillo |
| *Fraxinus* | *Fraxinus* | |
| *Fraxinus greggii* | *Fraxinus greggii* | Gregg Ash |

| | | |
|---|---|---|
| *Garrya* | *Garrya* | |
| *Garrya lindheimeri* | *Garrya ovata lindheimeri* | Lindheimer Silktassel |
| *Garrya wrightii* | *Garrya wrightii* | Wright's Silktassel |
| *Gelsemium* | *Gelsemium* | |
| *Gelsemium sempervirens* | *Gelsemium sempervirens* | Carolina Jessamine |
| *Gleditsia* | *Gleditsia* | |
| *Gleditsia aquatica* | *Gleditsia aquatica* | Water Honey Locust |
| *Gleditsia triacanthos* | *Gleditsia triacanthos* | Common Honey Locust |
| *Goniostachyum* | *Lantana* | |
| *Grindelia* | *Grindelia* | |
| *Gutierrezia* | *Gutierrezia* | |
| *Gutierrezia sarothrae* | *Gutierrezia sarothrae* | Broom Snakeweed |
| *Hamamelis* | *Hamamelis* | |
| *Hamamelis virginiana* | *Hamamelis virginiana* | Common Witchhazel |
| *Hartmannia* | *Oenothera* | |
| *Hechtia* | *Hechtia* | |
| *Hechtia texensis* | *Hechtia texensis* | Texas False Agave |
| *Helianthus* | *Helianthus* | |
| *Helianthus annuus* | *Helianthus annuus* | Common Sunflower |
| *Helianthus petiolaris* | *Helianthus petiolaris* | Prairie Sunflower |
| *Hesperaloe* | *Hesperaloe* | |
| *Hesperaloe parviflora* | *Hesperaloe parviflora* | Red Hesperaloe |
| *Hicoria* | *Carya* | |
| *Hicoria alba* | *Carya alba* | Mockernut Hickory |
| *Hicoria aquatica* | *Carya aquatica* | Water Hickory |
| *Hicoria glabra* | *Carya glabra* | Swamp Hickory |
| *Hicoria ovata* | *Carya ovata* | Shagbark Hickory |
| *Hoffmanseggia* | *Caesalpinia* | |
| *Hoffmanseggia jamesi* | *Caesalpinia jamesii* | James Rushpea |
| *Hymenocallis* | *Hymenocallis* | |
| *Ibervillea* | *Ibervillea* | |
| *Ibervillea lindheimeri* | *Ibervillea lindheimeri* | Lindheimer Globeberry |
| *Ilex* | *Ilex* | |
| *Ilex decidua* | *Ilex decidua* | Possum-haw |
| *Ilex lucida* | *Ilex coriacea* | Baygall Holly |
| *Ilex opaca* | *Ilex opaca* | American Holly |
| *Ilex vomitoria* | *Ilex vomitoria* | Yaupon |
| *Inodes* | *Sabal* | |
| *Inodes texana* | *Sabal mexicana* | Texas Palmetto |
| *Ipomea* | *Ipomea* | |
| *Ipomea leptophylla* | *Ipomoea leptophylla* | Bush Morningglory |
| *Jatropha* | *Jatropha* | |
| *Jatropha macrorhiza* | *Jatropha macrorhiza* | Bigroot Nettle Spurge |
| *Jatropha multifida* | *Jatropha multifida* | Coralbush |
| *Juglans* | *Juglans* | |
| *Juglans nigra* | *Juglans nigra* | Black Walnut |
| *Juglans rupestris* | *Juglans microcarpa* | Little Walnut |
| *Juniperus* | *Juniperus* | |
| *Juniperus flaccida* | *Juniperus flaccida* | Weeping Juniper |
| *Juniperus monosperma* | *Juniperus monosperma* | One-seeded Juniper |
| *Juniperus pachyphloea* | *Juniperus deppeana* | Alligator Juniper |
| *Juniperus sabinoides* | *Juniperus ashei* | Ashe Juniper |
| *Juniperus virginiana* | *Juniperus virginiana* | Eastern Red Cedar |

| | | |
|---|---|---|
| *Karwinskia* | *Karwinskia* | |
| *Karwinskia humboldtiana* | *Karwinskia humboldtiana* | Coyotillo |
| *Koeberlinia* | *Koeberlinia* | |
| *Koeberlinia spinosa* | *Koeberlinia spinosa* | Allthorn |
| *Krameria* | *Krameria* | |
| *Krameria canescens* | *Krameria grayi* | White Ratany |
| *Laciniaria* | *Liatris* | |
| *Laciniaria punctata* | *Liatris punctata* | Dotted Gayfeather |
| *Lantana* | *Lantana* | |
| *Lantana camara* | *Lantana camara* | West Indian Lantana |
| *Leitneria* | *Leitneria* | |
| *Leitneria floridana* | *Leitneria floridana* | Corkwood |
| *Leucaena* | *Leucaena* | |
| *Leucaena retusa* | *Leucaena retusa* | Littleleaf Leadtree |
| *Leucophyllum* | *Leucophyllum* | |
| *Leucophyllum minus* | *Leucophyllum minus* | Big Bend Silverleaf |
| *Leucophyllum texanum* | *Leucophyllum frutescens* | Ceniza |
| *Linum* | *Linum* | |
| *Linum perenne* | *Linum lewisii* | Lewis Flax |
| *Linum rigidum* | *Linum rigidum* | Stiffstem Flax |
| *Lippia* | *Aloysia* | |
| *Liquidambar* | *Liquidambar* | |
| *Liquidambar styraciflua* | *Liquidambar styraciflua* | Sweetgum |
| *Lycium* | *Lycium* | |
| *Lycium berlandieri* | *Lycium berlandieri* | Berlandier Wolfberry |
| *Lycium pallidum* | *Lycium pallidum* | Pale Wolfberry |
| *Magnolia* | *Magnolia* | |
| *Magnolia foetida* | *Magnolia grandiflora* | Southern Magnolia |
| *Magnolia virginiana* | *Magnolia virginiana* | Southern Sweetbay |
| *Malpighia* | *Malpighia* | |
| *Malpighia glabra* | *Malpighia glabra* | Wild Crape-myrtle |
| *Manfreda* | *Manfreda* | |
| *Manfreda maculosa* | *Manfreda maculosa* | Spotted Manfreda |
| *Mentzelia* | *Mentzelia* | |
| *Mentzelia nuda* | *Mentzelia nuda* | Bractless Mentzelia |
| *Meriolix* | *Calylophus* | |
| *Meriolix intermedia* | *Calylophus serrulatus* | Yellow Evening Primrose |
| *Mimosa* | *Mimosa* | |
| *Mimosa biuncifera* | *Mimosa aculeaticarpa* | Catclaw |
| *Mimosa borealis* | *Mimosa borealis* | Fragrant Mimosa |
| *Mimosa emoryana* | *Mimosa emoryana* | Emory Mimosa |
| *Mimosa fragrans* | *Mimosa borealis* | Fragrant Mimosa |
| *Mimosa lindheimeri* | *Mimosa aculeaticarpa* | Catclaw |
| *Mitchella* | *Mitchella* | |
| *Mitchella repens* | *Mitchella repens* | Partridgeberry |
| *Momesia* | *Celtis* | |
| *Momesia pallida* | *Celtis pallida* | Spiny Hackberry |
| *Monarda* | *Monarda* | |
| *Morella* | *Morella* | |
| *Morella cerifera* | *Morella cerifera* | Southern Wax-Myrtle |
| *Morella crispa* | *Morella cerifera* | Southern Wax-Myrtle |
| *Morus* | *Morus* | |
| *Morus microphylla* | *Morus microphylla* | Texas Mulberry |
| *Morus rubra* | *Morus rubra* | Red Mulberry |

| | | |
|---|---|---|
| *Mozinna* | *Jatropha* | |
| *Mozinna spathulata* | *Jatropha dioica dioica* | Leatherstem |
| *Nicotiana* | *Nicotiana* | |
| *Nicotiana glauca* | *Nicotiana glauca* | Tree Tobacco |
| *Nolina* | *Nolina* | |
| *Nolina microcarpa* | *Nolina microcarpa* | Small-seed Nolina |
| *Nolina texana* | *Nolina texana* | Sacahuista |
| *Nyssa* | *Nyssa* | |
| *Nyssa aquatica* | *Nyssa aquatica* | Water Tupelo |
| *Nyssa sylvatica* | *Nyssa sylvatica* | Black Tupelo |
| *Oenothera* | *Oenothera* | |
| *Oenothera* | *Calylophus* | |
| *Opuntia* | *Opuntia* | |
| *Opuntia cymochila* | *Opuntia macrorhiza* | Grassland Pricklypear |
| *Opuntia davisi* | *Opuntia tunicata davisii* | Jeff Davis Cholla |
| *Opuntia engelmanni* | *Opuntia engelmannii* | Engelmann Pricklypear |
| *Opuntia leptocaulis* | *Opuntia leptocaulis* | Pencil Cholla |
| *Opuntia lindheimeri* | *Opuntia engelmannii lindheimeri* | Texas Pricklypear |
| *Opuntia macrorhiza* | *Opuntia macrorhiza* | Grassland Pricklypear |
| *Ostrya* | *Ostrya* | |
| *Ostrya baileyi* | *Ostrya knowltonii* | Western Hop Hornbeam |
| *Ostrya virginiana* | *Ostrya virginiana* | Eastern Hop Hornbeam |
| *Oxalis* | *Oxalis* | |
| *Oxalis violacea* | *Oxalis violacea* | Violet Woodsorrel |
| *Parkinsonia* | *Parkinsonia* | |
| *Parkinsonia aculeata* | *Parkinsonia aculeata* | Retama |
| *Parosela* | *Dalea* | |
| *Parosela aurea* | *Dalea aurea* | Golden Dalea |
| *Parosela enneandra* | *Dalea enneandra* | Bigtop Dalea |
| *Parosela formosa* | *Dalea formosa* | Feather Dalea |
| *Parosela frutescens* | *Dalea frutescens* | Black Dalea |
| *Passiflora* | *Passiflora* | |
| *Passiflora incarnata* | *Passiflora incarnata* | Maypop Passion Flower |
| *Persea* | *Persea* | |
| *Persea borbonia* | *Persea borbonia* | Red Bay |
| *Petalostemon* | *Dalea* | |
| *Petalostemon purpureus* | *Dalea purpurea purpurea* | Purple Prairie Clover |
| *Philadelphus* | *Philadelphus* | |
| *Philadelphus microphyllus* | *Philadelphus microphyllus* | Littleleaf Mockorange |
| *Pinus* | *Pinus* | |
| *Pinus cembroides* | *Pinus cembroides* | Mexican Pinyon |
| *Pinus echinata* | *Pinus echinata* | Shortleaf Pine |
| *Pinus edulis* | *Pinus edulis* | Pinyon Pine |
| *Pinus flexilis* | *Pinus strobiformis* | Southwestern White Pine |
| *Pinus palustris* | *Pinus palustris* | Longleaf Pine |
| *Pinus ponderosa* | *Pinus ponderosa* | Ponderosa Pine |
| *Pinus taeda* | *Pinus taeda* | Loblolly Pine |
| *Pistacia* | *Pistacia* | |
| *Pistacia mexicana* | *Pistacia mexicana* | Mexican Pistachio |
| *Pistacia vera* | *Pistacia vera* | Pistachio |
| *Platanus* | *Platanus* | |
| *Platanus occidentalis* | *Plantanus occidentalis* | American Sycamore |
| *Polygala* | *Polygala* | |
| *Polygala alba* | *Polygala alba* | White Milkwort |

| | | |
|---|---|---|
| *Populus* | *Populus* | |
| *Populus deltoides* | *Populus deltoides* | Eastern Cottonwood |
| *Populus tremuloides* | *Populus tremuloides* | Quaking Aspen |
| *Porlieria* | *Guajacum* | |
| *Porlieria angustifolia* | *Guajacum angustifolium* | Guayacan |
| *Prosopis* | *Prosopis* | |
| *Prosopis juliflora* | *Prosopis glandulosa* | Honey Mesquite |
| *Prosopis pubescens* | *Prosopis pubescens* | Screwbean |
| *Prunus* | *Prunus* | |
| *Prunus serotina* | *Prunus serotina* | Black Cherry |
| *Prunus serotina acutifolia* | *Prunus serotina* | Black Cherry |
| *Pseudotsuga* | *Pseudotsuga* | |
| *Pseudotsuga mucronata* | *Pseudotsuga menziesii* | Douglasfir |
| *Psoralea* | *Psoralidium* | |
| *Psoralea* | *Pediomelum* | |
| *Psoralea* | *Dalea* | |
| *Psoralea digitata* | *Pediomelum digitatum* | Palmleaf Scurfpea |
| *Psoralea linearifolia* | *Psoralidium linearifolium* | Slimleaf Scurfpea |
| *Quercus* | *Quercus* | |
| *Quercus acuminata* | *Quercus muhlenbergii* | Chinkapin Oak |
| *Quercus alba* | *Quercus alba* | White Oak |
| *Quercus digitata* | *Quercus falcata* | Southern Red Oak |
| *Quercus emoryi* | *Quercus emoryi* | Emory Oak |
| *Quercus fendleri* | *Quercus pauciloba* | Wavyleaf Oak |
| *Quercus grisea* | *Quercus grisea* | Gray Oak |
| *Quercus leucophylla* | *Quercus falcata* | Southern Red Oak |
| *Quercus lyrata* | *Quercus lyrata* | Overcup Oak |
| *Quercus macrocarpa* | *Quercus macrocarpa* | Bur Oak |
| *Quercus marylandica* | *Quercus marilandica* | Blackjack Oak |
| *Quercus minor* | *Quercus stellata* | Post Oak |
| *Quercus nigra* | *Quercus nigra* | Water Oak |
| *Quercus novomexicana* | *Quercus gambelii* | Gambel Oak |
| *Quercus phellos* | *Quercus phellos* | Willow Oak |
| *Quercus rubra* | *Quercus buckleyi* | Spanish Oak |
| *Quercus texana* | *Quercus texana* | Texas Red Oak |
| *Quercus undulata* | *Quercus pauciloba* | Wavyleaf Oak |
| *Quercus virginiana* | *Quercus virginiana* | Live Oak |
| *Ratibida* | *Ratibida* | |
| *Ratibida columnaris* | *Ratibida columnifera* | Upright Prairie Coneflower |
| *Rhamnus* | *Frangula* | |
| *Rhamnus caroliniana* | *Frangula caroliniana* | Carolina Buckthorn |
| *Rhamnus purshiana* | *Frangula betulaefolia* | Birchleaf Buckthorn |
| *Rhus* | *Toxicodendron* | |
| *Rhus* | *Pistacia* | |
| *Rhus mexicana* | *Pistacia mexicana* | Mexican Pistachio |
| *Rhus radicans* | *Toxicodendron radicans* | Poison-ivy |
| *Robinia* | *Robinia* | |
| *Robinia neomexicana* | *Robinia neomexicana* | New Mexico Locust |
| *Rubus* | *Rubus* | |
| *Rubus procumbens* | *Rubus canadensis* | Smooth Blackberry |
| *Rubus trivialis* | *Rubus riograndis* | Rio Grande Dewberry |
| *Sabal* | *Sabal* | |
| *Sabal adiantinum* | *Sabal minor* | Dwarf Palmetto |

| | | |
|---|---|---|
| *Salix* | *Salix* | |
| *Salix nigra* | *Salix nigra* | Black Willow |
| *Samuela* | *Yucca* | |
| *Samuela carnerosana* | *Yucca faxoniana* | Spanish Dagger |
| *Samuela faxoniana* | *Yucca faxoniana* | Spanish Dagger |
| *Sassafras* | *Sassafras* | |
| *Sassafras sassafras* | *Sassafras albidum* | Sassafras |
| *Schmaltzia* | *Rhus* | |
| *Schmaltzia* | *Pistacia* | |
| *Schmaltzia copallina* | *Rhus copallinum* | Flameleaf Sumac |
| *Schmaltzia lanceolata* | *Rhus lanceolata* | Prairie Sumac |
| *Schmaltzia mexicana* | *Pistacia mexicana* | Mexican Pistachio |
| *Schmaltzia microphylla* | *Rhus microphylla* | Littleleaf Sumac |
| *Schmaltzia trilobata* | *Rhus aromatica* | Fragrant Sumac |
| *Schmaltzia virens* | *Rhus virens* | Evergreen Sumac |
| *Sesbania* | *Sesbania* | |
| *Sesbania cavanillesii* | *Sesbania drummondii* | Drummond Sesbania |
| *Smilax* | *Smilax* | |
| *Smilax laurifolia* | *Smilax laurifolia* | Laurel Greenbrier |
| *Smilax pumila* | *Smilax pumila* | Sarsaparilla Vine |
| *Smilax renifolia* | *Smilax renifolia* | Kidneyleaf Greenbrier |
| *Solanum* | *Solanum* | |
| *Solanum triquetrum* | *Solanum triquetrum* | Texas Nightshade |
| *Solanum tuberosum boreale* | *Solanum tuberosum* | Potato |
| *Sophora* | *Sophora* | |
| *Sophora secundiflora* | *Sophora secondiflora* | Mescal Bean |
| *Sphagnum* | *Sphagnum* | |
| *Symphoricarpos* | *Symphoricarpos* | |
| *Symphoricarpos longiflorus* | *Symphoricarpos longiflorus* | Long-flower Snowberry |
| *Taxodium* | *Taxodium* | |
| *Taxodium distichum* | *Taxodium distichum* | Baldcypress |
| *Tecoma* | *Tecoma* | |
| *Tecoma stans* | *Tecoma stans* | Yellow Trumpetbush |
| *Tilia* | *Tilia* | |
| *Tilia leptophylla* | *Tilia americana* | American Basswood |
| *Tillandsia* | *Tillandsia* | |
| *Tillandsia baileyi* | *Tillandsia baileyi* | Bailey Ballmoss |
| *Tillandsia recurvata* | *Tillandsia recurvata* | Small Ballmoss |
| *Toxylon* | *Maclura* | |
| *Toxylon pomiferum* | *Maclura pomifera* | Osage Orange |
| *Ulmus* | *Ulmus* | |
| *Ulmus alata* | *Ulmus alata* | Winged Elm |
| *Ulmus americana* | *Ulmus americana* | American Elm |
| *Ulmus fulva* | *Ulmus rubra* | Slippery Elm |
| *Vaccinium* | *Vaccinium* | |
| *Vachellia* | *Acacia* | |
| *Vachellia farnesiana* | *Acacia smallii* | Huisache |
| *Verbena* | *Verbena* | |
| *Verbena stricta* | *Verbena stricta* | Wooly Vervain |
| *Viburnum* | *Viburnum* | |
| *Viburnum molle* | *Viburnum molle* | Softleaf Arrow-wood |
| *Viburnum nudum* | *Viburnum nudum* | Possumhaw Viburnum |
| *Viburnum rufotomentosum* | *Viburnum rufidulum* | Downy Viburnum |

*Vitis*
*Yucca*
  *Yucca arkansana*
  *Yucca baccata*
  *Yucca glauca*
  *Yucca louisianensis*
  *Yucca macrocarpa*
  *Yucca radiosa*
  *Yucca rostrata*
  *Yucca rupicola*
  *Yucca stricta*
  *Yucca treculeana*
*Zizyphus*
  *Zizyphus lyciodes*
  *Zizyphus obtusifolia*

*Vitis*
*Yucca*
  *Yucca arkansana*          Arkansas Yucca
  *Yucca baccata*            Datil Yucca
  *Yucca glauca*             Narrowleaf Yucca
  *Yucca louisianensis*      Louisiana Yucca
  *Yucca torreyi*            Torrey Yucca
  *Yucca elata*              Soaptree Yucca
  *Yucca thompsoniana*       Thompson Yucca
  *Yucca rupicola*           Texas Yucca
  *Yucca glauca*             Narrowleaf Yucca
  *Yucca treculeana*         Trecul Yucca
*Ziziphus*
  *Ziziphus obtusifolia*     Lotebush
  *Ziziphus obtusifolia*     Lotebush

# Literature Cited and References

Adams, C. E., and J. K. Thomas. 1986. Wildlife education: present status and future needs. *Wildl. Soc. Bull.* 14:479–86.

Adams, L. W., and L. E. Dove. 1989. *Wildlife reserves and corridors in the urban environment: a guide to ecological landscape planning and resource conservation.* Columbia, Md.: Natl. Inst. for Urban Wildl. 91 pp.

Allen, C. R., S. Demarais, and R. S. Lutz. 1994. Red imported fire ant impact on wildlife: an overview. *Tex. J. Sci.* 46:52–59.

Allen, G. M. 1942. *Extinct and vanishing mammals of the Western Hemisphere.* Lancaster, Pa.: Intelligencer Printing Co.

Allen, J. A. 1891. Notes on new or little known North American mammals, based on recent additions to the collection of mammals in the American Museum of Natural History. *Bull. Amer. Mus. Nat. Hist.* 3:263–310.

———. 1892. Description of a new species of *Perognathus* from southeastern Texas. *Bull. Amer. Mus. Nat. Hist.* 4:45–50.

———. 1894. On the mammals of Aransas County, Texas, with descriptions of new forms of *Lepus* and *Oryzomys. Bull. Amer. Mus. Nat. Hist.* 6:165–98.

———. 1896. On mammals collected in Bexar County and vicinity, Texas, by Mr. H. P. Attwater, with field notes by the collector. *Bull. Amer. Mus. Nat. Hist.* 8:47–80.

American Rivers. 2000. Web site, www.amrivers.org/mer00rio.html.

Anderson, G. L., M. Bray, D. Griffin, P. K. McDowell, W. Swanson, and M. E. Tewes. 1997. Using remote sensing and GIS to map vegetation and determine ocelot habitat. Pp. 451–59 in *Proc. Sixteenth Biennial Workshop and Color Photography in Resource Assessment.* Bethesda, Md.: Amer. Soc. Photography and Remote Sensing.

Anderson, S. 1966. Taxonomy of gophers, especially *Thomomys,* in Chihuahua, Mexico. *Syst. Zool.* 15:187–98.

Anonymous. 1945. *Principal game birds and mammals of Texas, their distribution and management.* Austin: Press of Von Boeckmann-Jones Co., 149 pp.

Attwater, H. P. 1917. The disappearance of wildlife. *Bull. Scientific Soc. San Antonio.* 1(3):47–60.

Baccus, J. T., and M. W. Wallace. 1997. Distribution and habitat affinity of the swamp rabbit (*Sylvilagus aquaticus:* Lagomorpha: Leporidae) on the Edwards Plateau of Texas. *Occas. Papers Mus. Texas Tech Univ.* 167:1–13.

Bailey, J. A. 1984. *Principles of wildlife management.* New York: John Wiley and Sons. 373 pp.

Bailey, V. 1900. Revision of American voles of the genus *Microtus. North Amer. Fauna.* 17:1–88.

———. 1902. Seven new mammals from western Texas. *Proc. Biol. Soc. Washington.* 15:117–20.

———. 1905. Biological survey of Texas. *North Amer. Fauna.* 25:1–222.

———. 1906. A new white-footed mouse from Texas. *Proc. Biol. Soc. Washington.* 19:57–58.

———. 1913a. Life zones and crop zones of New Mexico. *North Amer. Fauna.* 35:1–100.

———. 1913b. Two new subspecies of North American beavers. *Proc. Biol. Soc. Washington.* 26:191–94.

———. 1915. Revision of the pocket gophers of the genus *Thomomys. North Amer. Fauna.* 39:1–136.

———. 1926. A biological survey of North Dakota. Part I, Physiography and life zones. Part II, The mammals. *North Amer. Fauna.* 49:1–226.

———. 1932. Mammals of New Mexico. *N. Amer. Fauna.* 53:1–412.

Baird, S. F. 1859. *Mammals of North America.* Philadelphia: Lippincott Pub. 1974. Reprint, New York: Arno Press. Various pagings.

Baker, R. H. 1951. Two new moles (genus *Scalopus*) from Mexico and Texas. *Publ. Univ. Kansas Mus. Nat. Hist.* 5:17–24.

———. 1953. The pocket gophers (genus *Thomomys*) of Coahuila, Mexico. *Univ. Kansas Publ. Mus. Nat. Hist.* 5:499–514.

———. 1956. Remarks on the former distribution of animals in eastern Texas. *Texas J. Sci.* 3:356–59.

———. 1988. Future prospects for the depletion of mammalian populations in the Chihuahuan Desert region. Pp. 71–79 in *Third Symposium on Resources of the Chihuahuan Desert Region*. Edited by A. M. Powell, R. R. Hollander, J. C. Barlow, W. B. McGillivray, D. J. Schmidly. Alpine, Tex.: Chihuahuan Desert Research Institute.

———. 1995. Texas wildlife conservation–historical notes. *East Texas Historical Journal.* 33:59–72.

———. 1977. Mammals of the Chihuahuan Desert region—future prospects. Pp. 221–25 in *Symposium on the biological resources of the Chihuahuan Desert region*. Edited by R. H. Waner and D. H. Riskind. Washington, D.C.: Natl. Park Serv., Trans. Proc. Ser. 3.

Baker, R. H., and B. P. Glass. 1951. The taxonomic status of the pocket gophers, *Geomys bursarius* and *Geomys breviceps*. *Proc. Biol. Soc. Washington.* 64:55–58.

Baker, R. J., S. K. Davis, R. D. Bradley, M. J. Hamilton, and R. A. Van Den Bussche. 1989. Ribosomal-DNA, mitochondrial-DNA, chromosomal, and allozymic studies of a contact zone in the pocket gopher, *Geomys*. *Evolution.* 43:63–75.

Baker, R. J., and H. H. Genoways. 1975. A new subspecies of *Geomys bursarius* (Mammalia: Geomyidae) from Texas and New Mexico. *Occas. Papers Mus. Texas Tech Univ.* 29:1–18.

Baker, R. J., T. Mollhagen, and G. Lopez. 1971. Notes on *Lasiurus ega*. *J. Mamm.* 52:849–52.

Baker, R. J., J. C. Patton, H. H. Genoways, and J. W. Bickham. 1988. Genetic studies of *Lasiurus* (Chiroptera: Vespertilionidae). *Occas. Papers Mus. Texas Tech Univ.* 117:1–5.

Baker, R. J., C. J. Phillips, R. D. Bradley, J. Burns, D. Cooke, G. F. Edson, D. R. Haragan, C. Jones, R. R. Monk, J. T. Montford, D. J. Schmidly, and N. C. Parker. 1998. Bioinformatics, museums, and society: integrating biological data for knowledge-based systems. *Occas. Papers Mus. Texas Tech Univ.* 187:i+1–4.

Baker, R. J., L. W. Robbins, F. B. Stangl Jr., and E. C. Birney. 1983. Chromosomal evidence for a major subdivision in *Peromyscus leucopus*. *J. Mamm.* 64:356–59.

Ballinger, S. W., L. H. Blankenship, J. W. Bickham, and S. M. Carr. 1992. Allozyme and mitochondrial DNA analysis of a hybrid zone between white-tailed deer and mule deer (*Odocoileus*) in west Texas. *Biochemical Genetics.* 30:1–11.

Bartlett, R. C. 1995. *Saving the best of Texas: a partnership approach to conservation.* Austin: Univ. Texas Press. 221 pp.

Baughman, J. L. 1951. Texas natural history—one hundred years ago. *Texas Game and Fish.* 9(9):14–16; 9(10):18–21; 9(11):6–9.

Baumgardner, G. D., N. O. Dronen, and D. J. Schmidly. 1992. Distributional status of short-tailed shrews (genus *Blarina*) in Texas. *Southwestern Nat.* 37:326–30.

Baumgardner, G. D., and D. J. Schmidly. 1981. Systematics of the southern races of two species of kangaroo rats (*Dipodomys compactus* and *D. ordii*). *Occas. Papers Mus. Texas Tech Univ.* 73:1–27.

Beasom, S. L. 1974. Selectivity of predator control techniques in South Texas. *J. Wildl. Manage.* 38:837–44.

Benson, D. L., and F. R. Gehlbach. 1979. Ecological and taxonomic notes on the rice rat (*Oryzomys couesi*) in Texas. *J. Mamm.* 60:225–28.

Birney, E. C. 1973. Systematics of three species of woodrats (genus *Neotoma*) in central North America. *Misc. Publ. Mus. Nat. Hist. Univ. Kansas.* 58:1–173.

Birney, E. C., and J. R. Choate, eds. 1994. Seventy-five years of mammalogy (1919–1994). *Spec. Publ. Amer. Soc. Mammalogists.* 11:1–433.

Bisby, F. A. 2000. The quiet revolution: biodiversity informatics and the internet. *Science.* 289:2309–11.

Blair, W. F. 1939. New mammals from Texas and Oklahoma, with remarks on the status of *Thomomys texensis* Bailey. *Occas. Papers. Univ. Mich. Mus. Zool.* 403:1–7.

———. Blair, W. F. 1940. A contribution to the ecology and faunal relationships of the mammals of the Davis Mountain region, southwestern Texas. *Misc. Publ. Univ. Michigan Mus. Zool.* 46:1–39.

———. 1943. Biological and morphological distinctness of a previously undescribed species of the *Peromyscus truei* group from Texas. *Cont. Lab. Vert. Biol. Univ. Michigan.* 24:1–8.

———. 1950. The biotic provinces of Texas. *Tex. J. Sci.* 2:93–117.

———. 1954a. A melanistic race of the white-throated packrat (*Neotoma albigula*) in Texas. *J. Mamm.* 35:239–42.

——. 1954b. Mammals of the Mesquite Plains Biotic District in Texas and Oklahoma, and speciation in the central grasslands. *Tex. J. Sci.* 6:235–64.

Block, S. G., and E. G. Zimmerman. 1991. Allozymic variation and systematics of plains pocket gophers (*Geomys*) in south-central Texas. *Southwestern Nat.* 36:29–36.

Bluett, R. D., M. E. Tewes, and B. C. Thompson. 1989. Geographic distribution of commercial bobcat harvests in Texas, 1978–1986. *Tex. J. Sci.* 41:379–86.

Bogan, M. A. 1998. Changing landscapes of the middle Rio Grande. Pp. 562–63 in *Status and Trends of the Nation's Biological Resources*. Vol. 2. Edited by M. J. Mac, P. A. Opler, C. E. Puckett Haecker, and P. D. Doran. Reston, Va.: U.S. Dept. of Interior, U.S. Geol. Survey. 964 pp.

Bohlin, R. G., and E. G. Zimmerman. 1982. Genic differentiation of the chromosomal races of the *Geomys bursarius* complex. *J. Mamm.* 63:218–28.

Bolen, E. 1998. *Ecology of North America*. New York: John Wiley and Sons, Inc. 448 pp.

Borell, A. E. 1937. A new method of collecting bats. *J. Mamm.* 18:478–80.

Borell, A. E., and M. D. Bryant. 1942. Mammals of the Big Bend area of Texas. *Univ. California Publ. Zool.*, 48:1–62.

Box, T. W. 1990. Rangelands. Pp. 101–20 in *Natural Resources for the 21st Century*. Edited by R. N. Sampson and D. Hair. Covelo, Calif.: Island Press. 349 pp.

Boyd, R. A., R. C. Dowler, and T. C. Maxwell. 1997. The mammals of Tom Green County, Texas. *Occas. Papers Mus. Texas Tech Univ.* 169:1–27.

Bradley, R. D., D. S. Carroll, M. L. Clary, C. W. Edwards, I. Tiemann-Boege, M. J. Hamilton, R. A. Van Den Bussche, and C. Jones. 1999a. Comments on some small mammals from the Big Bend and Trans-Pecos regions of Texas. *Occas. Papers Mus. Texas Tech Univ.* 193:1–6.

Bradley, R. D., S. K. Davis, and R. J. Baker. 1991. Genetic control of premating-isolating behavior: Kaneshiro's hypothesis and asymmetrical sexual selection in pocket gophers. *J. Heredity.* 82:192–96.

Bradley, R. D., D. J. Schmidly, and C. Jones. 1999b. The northern rock mouse, *Peromyscus nasutus* (Mammalia: Rodentia), from the Davis Mountains, Texas. *Occas. Papers Mus. Texas Tech Univ.* 190:1–3.

Brant, J. G., and R. C. Dowler. 2000. A survey of the mammalian fauna of Devils River State Natural Area, Val Verde County, Texas. 18th Annual Meeting, Texas Soc. Mammalogists. Abstract.

Bray, W. L. 1906. Distribution and adaptation of the vegetation of Texas. Univ. of Texas Press, *Bull. No. 42, Sci. Series No.* 10:1–108.

Brune, G. 1975. Major and historical springs of Texas. *Texas Water Development Board, Report.* 189:1–94.

Bryant, M. D. 1945. Phylogeny of the Nearctic Sciuridae. *Amer. Midl. Nat.* 33:257–390.

Burr, J. G. 1949a. Conservation of Texas wildlife began almost a century ago. *Texas Game and Fish.* 7(10):5, 24–25.

——. 1949b. Game abundant when Mearns made survey. *Texas Game and Fish.* 7(12):9, 26.

——. 1949c. Texas teemed with all kinds of wildlife a century ago. *Texas Game and Fish.* 7(11):11, 29–30.

Butts, G. L. 1979. The status of exotic big game in Texas. *Rangelands.* 1:152–53.

Cameron, G. N., and D. Scheel. 1993. A GIS model of the effects of global climate change on mammals. *Geocarto. International.* 4:19–32.

——. 2001. Getting warmer: effect of global climate change on distribution of rodents in Texas. *J. Mamm.* 82:652–80.

Cameron, G. N., J. O. Seamon, and D. Scheel. 1997. Environmental change and mammalian richness: impact on preserve design and management in east Texas. *Tex. J. Sci.* 49(3) Supplement:155–80.

Cameron, G. N., J. M. Williams, and J. A. Robinson. 1997. Analysis of rare resources in Texas: implications for management. Final report submitted to Endangered Resources Branch, Resource Protection Division, Texas Parks and Wildlife Department, Austin. 242 pp. June 15, 1997.

Cameron, J. 1974. *The Bureau of Biological Survey: its history, activities, and organization*. New York: Arno Press. 339 pp.

Campbell, L. 1995. *Endangered and threatened animals of Texas, their life history and management*. Austin: Texas Parks and Wildl. Press. 130 pp.

Carleton, M. D. 1989. Systematics and evolution. Pp. 7–141 in *Advances in the study of Peromyscus* (Rodentia). Edited by G. L. Kirkland, Jr., and J. N. Layne. Lubbock: Texas Tech Univ. Press. 367 pp.

Carls, E. G. 1984. Texas natural diversity: the role of parks and reserves. Pp. 51–60 in *Protection of Texas natural diversity: an introduction for natural resource planners and managers*. College Station: Texas Agr. Exp. Sta., MP-1557. 60 pp.

Carr, S. M., S. W. Ballenger, J. N. Derr, L. H. Blankenship, and J. W. Bickham. 1986. Mitochondrial

DNA analysis of hybridization between sympatric white-tailed deer and mule deer in West Texas. *Proc. Nat. Acad. Sci.* 83:9576–80.

Casto, S. D. 1992. Texan contributors to the Mississippi Valley Migration Study of 1884–1885. *Bull. Texas Ornith. Soc.* 25(2):51–63.

———. 1999. Attwater, Henry Philemon. In *The Handbook of Texas Online*, www.tsha.utexas.edu.

Cathey, J. C., J. W. Bickham, and J. C. Patton. 1998. Introgressive hybridization and nonconcordant evolutionary history of maternal and paternal lineages in North American deer. *Evolution.* 52:1224–29.

Chapman, D. C., D. M. Papoulias, and C. P. Onuf. 1998. Environmental change in south Texas. Pp. 268–72, 314 in *Status and Trends of the Nation's Biological Resources.* Vol. 1. Edited by M. J. Mac, P. A. Opler, C. E. Puckett Haecker, and P. D. Doran. Reston, Va.: U.S. Dept. of Interior, U.S. Geol. Survey.

Choate, L. L. 1997. The mammals of the Llano Estacado. *Spec. Publ. Mus. Texas Tech Univ.* 40:1–240.

Choate, L. L., J. K. Jones Jr., R. W. Manning, and C. Jones. 1990. Westward ho: Continued dispersal of the pygmy mouse, *Baiomys taylori,* on the Llano Estacado and in adjacent areas of Texas. *Occas. Papers Mus. Texas Tech Univ.* 134:1–8.

Choate, L. L., and F. C. Killebrew. 1991. Distributional records of the California myotis and the prairie vole in the Texas Panhandle. *Tex. J. Sci.* 43:214–15.

Clark, W. C., and R. E. Munn, eds. 1986. *Sustainable development of the biosphere.* Cambridge: Cambridge Univ. Press. 491 pp.

Cleveland, A. G. 1970. The current geographic distribution of the armadillo in the United States. *Tex. J. Sci.* 22:90–92.

———. 1977. First South Texas records of *Pappogeomys castanops. Tex. J. Sci.* 29:299.

———. 1986. First record of *Baiomys taylori* north of the Red River. *Southwestern Nat.* 31:547.

Conway, W. C., L. M. Smith, R. E. Sosebee, and J. F. Bergan. 1999. Total nonstructural carbohydrate trends in Chinese tallow roots. *J. Range Manage.* 52:539–42.

Cook, R. L. 1991. A historical review of reports, field notes, and correspondence on the Desert Bighorn Sheep in Texas. Spec. Report, Desert Bighorn Sheep Advisory Committee, Texas Parks and Wildl. Dept., Austin. 68 pp.

Cox, J. 1996. Bears at our borders. *Texas Parks and Wildlife.* 54(6):48–52.

Culbertson, K. F. 1974. Rare, endangered, and peripheral mammals of Texas. Unpubl. manuscript thesis, Texas A&M Univ., College Station, Texas.

Dalquest, W. W. 1954. Netting bats in tropical Mexico. *Trans. Kansas Acad. Sci.* 57:1–10.

Dalquest, W. W., and N. V. Horner. 1984. *Mammals of north-central Texas.* Wichita Falls, Tex.: Midwestern Univ. Press. 261 pp., 72 pls.

Davis, W. B. 1939. The bighorn sheep of Texas. *J. Mamm.* 20:440–55.

———. 1940a. A new *Thomomys* from Texas. *J. Mamm.* 21:204–205.

———. 1940b. Mammals of the Guadalupe Mountains of western Texas. *Occas. Papers Mus. Zool. Louisiana State Univ.* 7:69–84.

———. 1942. The systematic status of four kangaroo rats. *J. Mamm.* 23:328–33.

———. 1945a. Identity of the central Texas bear. *J. Mamm.* 26:434.

———. 1945b. Texas skunks. *Texas Game and Fish.* 9:18–21, 31.

———. 1960. The mammals of Texas. *Bull. 41.* Texas Parks and Wildlife Dept., Austin. 252 pp.

———. 1961. Vanished: a commentary on the extinct and threatened mammals of Texas. *Texas Game and Fish.* December, 15–22.

———. 1966. The mammals of Texas. *Bull. 41.* Texas Parks and Wildlife Dept., Austin. 267 pp.

———. 1974. The mammals of Texas. *Bull. 41.* Texas Parks and Wildlife Dept., Austin. 294 pp.

Davis, W. B., and H. K. Buecher. 1946. Pocket gophers (*Thomomys*) of the Davis Mountains, Texas. *J. Mamm.* 27:265–70.

Davis, W. B., and J. L. Robertson, Jr. 1944. The mammals of Culberson County, Texas. *J. Mamm.* 25:254–73.

Davis, W. B., and D. J. Schmidly. 1994. *The mammals of Texas.* Austin: Texas Parks and Wildlife Press. 338 pp.

Demarais, S., J. T. Baccus, and M. S. Traweek, Jr. 1998. Nonindigenous ungulates in Texas: long-term population trends and possible competitive mechanisms. *Trans. North Amer. Wildl. and Natur. Resour. Conf.* 63:49–55.

Demarais, S., D. A. Osborn, and J. J. Jackley. 1990. Exotic big game: a controversial resource. *Rangelands.* 12:121–25.

Diamond, D. D., D. H. Riskind, and S. C. Orzell. 1987. A framework for plant community classification and conservation in Texas. *Tex. J. Sci.* 39:203–21.

Diamond, D. D., C. D. True, and K. He. 1997. Regional priorities for conservation of rare species in Texas. *Southwestern Nat.* 42:400–408.

Dice, L. R. 1943. *The biotic provinces of North America.* Ann Arbor: Univ. Michigan Press. 78 pp.

Diersing, V. E. 1976. An analysis of *Peromyscus difficilis* from the Mexican-United States boundary area. *Proc. Biol. Soc. Washington.* 89:451–66.

Diersing, V. E., and J. E. Diersing. 1979. Additional records of *Baiomys taylori* (Thomas) in Texas. *Southwestern Nat.* 24:707–708.

Diersing, V. E., and D. F. Hoffmeister. 1974. The rock mouse, *Peromyscus difficilis*, in western Texas. *Southwestern Nat.* 19:213–23.

Dixon, J. R. 2000. *Amphibians and reptiles of Texas.* College Station: Texas A&M Univ. Press. 421 pp.

Doughty, R. W. 1983. *Wildlife and man in Texas.* College Station: Texas A&M Univ. Press. 246 pp.

Dowler, R. C. 1989. Cytogenetic studies of three chromosomal races of pocket gophers (*Geomys bursarius* complex) at hybrid zones. *J. Mamm.* 70:253–66.

Dowler, R. C., R. C. Dawkins, and T. C. Maxwell. 1999. Range extensions for the evening bat (*Nycticeius humeralis*) in West Texas. *Tex. J. Sci.* 51:193–95.

Dowler, R. C., T. C. Maxwell, and D. S. Marsh. 1992. Noteworthy records of bats from Texas. *Tex. J. Sci.* 44:121–23.

Dragoo, J. W., R. D. Bradley, R. L. Honeycutt, and J. W. Templeton. 1993. Phylogenetic relationships among the skunks: a molecular perspective. *J. Mammalian Evol.* 1:255–67.

Dragoo, J. W., J. R. Choate, T. L. Yates, and T. P. O'Farrell. 1990. Evolutionary and taxonomic relationships among North American arid-land foxes. *J. Mamm.* 71:318–32.

Drecs, B. M. 1994. Red imported fire ant predation on nestlings of colonial waterbirds. *Southwestern Entomologist.* 19:355–59.

Duda, M. 2000. Texans' attitudes toward natural and cultural resources and outdoor recreation in Texas, completed as part of the Texas Parks and Wildlife for the 21st Century. Prepared for Texas Tech University, Texas Cooperative Fish and Wildlife Research Unit, Lubbock, Texas. Prepared by Responsive Management Inc., Va. 37 pp.

Duncan, K. W., S. D. Schemnitz, Z. N. Homesley, and M. Cardenas. 1999. Evolution of salt cedar management, Pecos River, New Mexico. Pp. 63–68 in *Fourth Symposium on Resources of the Chihuahuan Desert region, United States and Mexico, 30 September–1 October 1993.* Edited by J. C. Barlow and D. J. Miller. Fort Davis, Tex.: Chihuahuan Desert Res. Inst. 109 pp.

Earley, L. S. 1996. Safe harbor in the sandhills. *Wildlife in North Carolina.* October:11–15.

Easterla, D. A. 1970. First records of the spotted bat in Texas and notes on its natural history. *Am. Midl. Nat.* 83:306–308.

———. 1972. Status of *Leptonycteris nivalis* (Phyllostomatidae) in Big Bend National Park, Texas. *Southwestern Nat.* 17:287–92.

Edwards, C. W., C. F. Fulhorst, and R. D. Bradley. 2001. Molecular phylogenetics of the *Neotoma albigula* species group: further evidence of a paraphyletic assemblage. *J. Mamm.* 82(2): 267–79.

Edwards, J. L, M. A. Lane, and E. S. Nielsen. 2000. Interoperability of biodiversity databases: biodiversity information on every desktop. *Science.* 289:2312–14.

Ellis, D., and J. L. Schuster. 1968. Juniper age and distribution on an isolated butte in Garza County, Texas. *Southwest. Nat.* 13:343–48.

Ellsworth, D. L., R. L. Honeycutt, N. J. Silvy, M. H. Smith, J. W. Bickham, and W. D. Klimstra. 1994. White-tailed deer restoration to the southeastern United States: evaluating genetic variation. *J. Wildl. Manage.* 58(4):686–97.

Elrod, D. A., G. A. Heidt, D. M. A. Elrod, M. Birdsong, and E. G. Zimmerman. 1996. A second species of pocket gopher in Arkansas. *Southwestern Nat.* 41:395–98.

Feldhamer, G. A., and W. E. Armstrong. 1993. Interspecific competition between four exotic species and native artiodactyls in the United States. *Trans. North Amer. Wildl. and Natur. Resour. Conf.* 58:468–78.

Fialka, J. J. 1998. Endangered Species Act, itself endangered, may have found the political backing to survive. *Wall Street Journal.* March 2, p. A20.

Findley, J. S. 1987. *The natural history of New Mexico mammals.* Albuquerque: Univ. New Mexico Press. 164 pp.

Findley, J. S., and W. Caire. 1977. The status of mammals in the northern region of the Chihuahuan Desert. Pp. 127–39 in *Symposium on the biological resources of the Chihuahuan Desert region.* Edited by R. H. Waner and D. H. Riskind. Washington, D.C.: Natl. Park Serv., Trans. Proc. Ser. 3.

Findley, J. S., A. H. Harris, D. E. Wilson, and C. Jones. 1975. *Mammals of New Mexico.* Albuquerque: Univ. New Mexico Press. 360 pp.

Fleming, K. M. 1980. Texas bear hunting a thing of the past. *Texas Parks and Wildlife.* 38(5):12–15.

Francaviglia, R. V. 2000. *The cast iron forest: a natural and cultural history of the North American Cross Timbers.* Austin: Univ. of Texas Press. 276 pp.

Francell, J. 1998. Conservation easements: a guide for Texas landowners. Booklet, Texas Parks and Wildlife Department, Austin. 33pp.

Frey, J. K, and M. L. Campbell. 1997. Introduced populations of fox squirrel (*Sciurus niger*) in the Trans-Pecos and Llano Estacado regions of New Mexico and Texas. *Southwestern Nat.* 42:356–58.

Frey, T. C., and J. K. Frey. 2000. Railroads: an alternative mechanism for mesquite invasion in the southwest. Southwestern Association of Naturalists, 47th Annual Meeting, April 20–22, 2000, Abstract.

Gardner, A. L. 1973. The systematics of the genus *Didelphis* (Marsupialia: Didelphidae) in North and Middle America. *Special Pub. The Mus., Texas Tech Univ.* 4:1–81.

Garner, N. P., and S. E. Willis. 1998. Suitability of habitats in east Texas for black bears. Eleventh International Conf. on Bear Research and Management. Unpubl. paper, Gatlinburg, Tenn.

Gehlbach, F. R. 1981. *Mountain Islands and Desert Seas: a natural history of the U.S. Mexican borderlands.* College Station: Texas A&M Univ. Press. 298 pp.

Geiser, S. W. 1930. Naturalists of the frontier. VIII. Audubon in Texas. *Southwest Review.* pp. 108–35.

———. 1956. William Lloyd, British-American natural-history collector in Texas. *Field and Laboratory.* 24(4):116–22.

Geist, V. 1988. How markets in wildlife meat and parts, and the sale of hunting privileges, jeopardize wildlife conservation. *Conservation Biol.* 2:15–27.

Genoways, H. H., and R. J. Baker, eds. 1979. Biological investigations in the Guadalupe Mountains National Park, Texas. *Proc. and Trans. Series, Natl. Park Serv.* 4:1–442.

Genoways, H. H., and R. J. Baker. 1988. *Lasiurus blossevilli* (Chiroptera: Vespertilionidae) in Texas. *Tex. J. Sci.* 40:111–13.

Genoways, H. H., R. J. Baker, and J. E. Cornely. 1979. Mammals of the Guadalupe Mountains National Park, Texas. Pp. 271–332, in *Biological Investigations in the Guadalupe Mountains National Park, Texas.* Edited by H. H. Genoways and R. J. Baker. Washington, D.C. Proc. Trans. Ser., Nat. Park Service. 4:xviii+1–442.

George, S. B., J. R. Choate, and H. H. Genoways. 1981. Distribution and taxonomic status of *Blarina hylophaga* Elliot (Insectivora: Soricidae). *Ann. Carnegie Mus.* 50:493–513.

Gilbert, F. F., and D. G. Dodds. 1987. *The philosophy and practice of wildlife management.* Malabar, Fla.: R. E. Krieger Publishing Co. 279 pp.

Goetze, J. R. 1998. The mammals of the Edwards Plateau, Texas. *Spec. Publ. Mus., Texas Tech Univ.* 41:1–263.

Goldman, E. A. 1923. Three new kangaroo rats of the genus *Dipodomys. Proc. Biol. Soc. Washington.* 36:139–42.

———. 1938. Six new rodents from Coahuila and Texas and notes on the status of several described forms. *Proc. Biol. Soc. Washington.* 51:55–61.

Grinnell, J. 1919. Four new kangaroo rats from west-central California. *Proc. Biol. Soc. Washington.* 32:203–206.

Guynn, D. E., and D. W. Steinbach. 1987. Wildlife values in Texas. Chapter 10 in *Valuing wildlife economic and social perspectives.* Edited by D. J. Decker and G. R. Goft. Boulder: Westview Press. 424 pp.

Hafner, J. C., and M. S. Hafner. 1983. Evolutionary relationships of heteromyid rodents. *Great Basin Nat. Mem.* 7:3–29.

Hafner, M. S., W. L. Gannon, J. Salazar-Bravo, and S. T. Alvarez-Castaneda. 1997. *Mammal collections in the western hemisphere: a survey and directory of existing collections.* Lawrence, Kans.: Amer. Soc. Mammalogists, Allen Press. 93 pp.

Haines, H. 1963. Geographical extent and duration of the cotton rat, *Sigmodon hispidus,* 1958–1960 fluctuation in Texas. *Ecology.* 44:771–72.

———. 1971. Characteristics of a cotton rat (*Sigmodon hispidus*) population cycle. *Tex. J. Sci.* 23:3–27.

Hall, D. L., and M. R. Willig. 1994. Mammalian species composition, diversity, and succession in Conservation Reserve Program grasslands. *Southwestern Nat.* 39:1–10.

Hall, E. R. 1951a. American weasels. *Univ. Kansas Publ., Mus. Nat. Hist.* 4:1–466.

———. 1951b. A synopsis of North American Lagomorpha. *Univ. Kansas Publ., Mus. Nat. Hist.* 5:119–202.

———. 1981. *The mammals of North America.* 2d ed. New York: John Wiley and Sons. 1:xv+1–600+90 and 2:vi+1–1181+90.

Halloran, A. F. 1961. The carnivores and ungulates of the Aransas National Wildlife Refuge, Texas. *Southwestern Nat.* 6:21–26.

Harmel, D. E. 1980. The influence of exotic artiodactyls on white-tailed deer production and survival. Perform. Rept. Job No. 20, Fed. Aid Proj. No. W-109-R-3, Texas Parks and Wildlife Dept., Austin. 14 pp.

Harris, D. R. 1966. Recent plant invasions in the arid and semi-arid southwest of the United States. *Annals of Assoc. of Amer. Geog.* 56:408–22.

Hatch, S. L., K. N. Gandhi, and L. E. Brown. 1990. *Checklist of the vascular plants of Texas.* Texas Agric. Exp. Station, College Station, Tex. 158 pp.

Heaney, M. R., E. J. Cook, and R. L. Manning. 1998. Noteworthy record of the yellow-nosed cotton rat (*Sigmodon ochrognathus*) from Trans-Pecos Texas. *Tex. J. Sci.* 50:347–49.

Hellgren, E. 1993. Status, distribution, and summer food habits of black bears in Big Bend National Park. *Southwestern Nat.* 38:77–79.

Henderson, W. C., and E. A. Preble. 1935. Fiftieth anniversary notes: work and workers of the first twenty-five years. *The Survey.* 16(4–6):59–65. Bureau of Biological Survey, Washington, D.C.

Henke, S. E., and J. G. Young. 1997. First sight records of a white-nosed coati in Texas in nearly thirty years. *Texas J. Agric. Nat. Res.* 10:51–53.

Hewitt, D. G., A. Cain, N. Tuovila, D. B. Shindle, and M. E. Tewes. 1998. Impacts of an expanded highway on ocelot and bobcats in southern Texas and their preferences for highway crossings. Pp. 126–34 in *Proc. International Conf. Wildlife Ecology and Transportation.* Edited by G. L. Evink, P. Garrett, D. Zeigler, and J. Berry. FL-ER-69-98, Florida Department of Transportation, Tallahassee, Fla. 263 pp.

Hice, C., and D. J. Schmidly. 1999. The non-volant mammals of the Galveston Bay region, Texas. *Occas. Papers Mus., Texas Tech Univ.* 194:1–23.

———. 2002. The mammals of coastal Texas: a comparison between mainland and barrier island faunas. *Southwestern Nat.* In press.

Higginbotham, J. L., L. K. Ammerman, and M. T. Dixon. 1999. First record of *Lasiurus xanthinus* (Chiroptera: Vespertilionidae) in Texas. *Southwestern Naturalist.* 44(3):343–47.

Hinesley, L. 1979. Systematics and distribution of two chromosome forms in the southern grasshopper mouse, genus *Onychomys. J. Mamm.* 60:117–28.

Hobbs, R. J., D. A. Saunders, and A. R. Main. 1993. Conservation management in fragmented systems. Pp. 279–96 in *Reintegrating fragmented landscapes: towards sustainable production and nature conservation.* Edited by R. J. Hobbs and D. A. Saunders. New York: Springer Verlag.

Hollander, R. R. 1990. Biosystematics of the yellow-faced pocket gopher, *Cratogeomys castanops* (Rodentia: Geomyidae) in the United States. *Spec. Publ. Mus., Texas Tech Univ.* 33:1–62.

Hollander, R. R., and K. M. Hogan. 1992. Occurrence of the opossum, *Didelphis virginiana* Kerr, in the Trans-Pecos of Texas. *Tex. J. Sci.* 44:127–28.

Hollander, R. R., J. K. Jones, Jr., R. W. Manning, and C. Jones. 1987. Noteworthy records of mammals from the Texas panhandle. *Tex. J. Sci.* 39:97–102.

Hollander, R. R., R. N. Robertson, and R. J. Kinncan. 1992. First records of the nutria, *Myocastor coypus*, in the Trans-Pecos region of Texas. *Tex. J. Sci.* 44:119.

Hollister, N. 1913. A systematic account of the grasshopper mice. *Proc. U.S. Natl. Mus.* 47:427–89.

Hollister, N. 1914. The spotted tiger cat in Texas. *Proc. Biol. Soc. Washington.* 27:219.

Honeycutt, R. L., and D. J. Schmidly. 1979. Chromosomal and morphological variation in the plains pocket gopher, *Geomys bursarius*, in Texas and adjacent states. *Occas. Papers Mus., Texas Tech Univ.* 58:1054.

Horner, P., and R. Maxey. 1998. East Texas rare bat survey: 1997. Unpubl. report, Texas Parks and Wildl. Dept., Austin, 14 pp.

Howell, A. H. 1910. Notes on mammals of the Middle Mississippi Valley, with description of a new woodrat. *Proc. Biol. Soc. Washington.* 23:23–33.

———. 1914. Revision of the American harvest mice (genus *Reithrodontomys*). *North Amer. Fauna.* 36:1–97.

———. 1915. Description of a new genus and seven new races of flying squirrels. *Proc. Biol. Soc. Washington.* 28:109–14.

———. 1918. Revision of the American flying squirrels. *N. Amer. Fauna.* 44:1–64.

Hume, E. E. 1942. Basil Hicks Dutcher (1871–1922). Pp. 105–29 in *Ornithologists of the United States Army Medical Corps.* Baltimore: John Hopkins Press.

Humphrey, S. R. 1974. Zoogeography of the nine-banded armadillo (*Dasypus novemcinctus*) in the United States. *Bioscience.* 24:457–62.

Hunter, M. L., Jr. 1990. *Wildlife, forests, and forestry. Principles of managing forests for biological diversity.* Englewood Cliffs, N.J.: Prentice-Hall. 370 pp.

Innes, R. 1999. Taking and endangered species protection. *Choices.* (3rd Quarter):10–16.

Jackson, A. W. 1964. Texotics. *Texas Game and Fish.* 23:7–11.

Jackson, M. A., D. Fertl, and J. F. Bergan. 1998. Recent records of the river otter (*Lutra canadensis*) along the Texas Gulf Coast. *Tex. J. Sci.* 50:243–47.

Jahrsdoerfer, S. E., and D. M. Leslie, Jr. 1988. Tamaulipan brushland of the Lower Rio Grande Valley of South Texas: description, human impacts, and management options. Biological Report No. 88(36), U.S. Fish and Wildl. Serv., Washington, D.C. 63 pp.

Jester, S. L., C. E. Adams, and J. K. Thomas. 1990. *Commercial trade in Texas nongame wildlife.* Texas Agric. Exp. Sta., Texas A&M Univ. System, College Station. 22 pp.

Jones, C., and M. A. Bogen. 1986. Status report: *Dipodomys elator* Merriam, 1894. Office Endangered Species, U.S. Fish Wildl. Serv., Albuquerque, New Mexico. 32 pp.

Jones, C., M. A. Bogen, and L. M. Monnt. 1988. Status of the Texas kangaroo rat (*Dipodomys elator*). *Tex. J. Sci.* 40:249–58.

Jones, C., and R. D. Bradley. 1999. Notes on red bats, *Lasiurus* (Chiroptera: Vespertilionidae), of the Davis Mountains and vicinity, Texas. *Tex. J. Sci.* 51:1–3.

Jones, C., L. Hedges, and K. Bryan. 1999. The western yellow bat, *Lasiurus xanthinus* (Chiroptera: Vespertilionidae) from the Davis Mountains, Texas. *Tex. J. Sci.* 51:267–69.

Jones, J. K. Jr. 1991. Genealogy of twentieth-century systematic mammalogists in North America: the descendents of Joseph Grinnell. Pp. 48–55 in *Latin American mammalogy: history, biodiversity, and conservation.* Edited by M. A. Mares and D. J. Schmidly. Norman: Univ. Okla. Press. 468 pp.

———. 1993. The concept of threatened and endangered species as applied to Texas mammals. *Tex. J. Sci.* 45:115–28.

Jones, J. K. Jr., R. D. Bradley, and R. J. Baker. 1995. Hybrid pocket gophers and some thoughts on the relationship of natural hybrids to the rules of nomenclature and the Endangered Species Act. *J. Mamm.* 76:43–49.

Jones, J. K. Jr., and J. A. Homan. 1976. Contributions to a bibliography of Recent Texas mammals, 1961–1970. *Occas. Papers Mus., Texas Tech Univ.* 41:1–21.

Jones, J. K. Jr., and C. Jones. 1992. Revised checklist of Recent land mammals of Texas, with annotations. *Tex. J. Sci.* 44:53–74.

Jones, J. K. Jr., and M. R. Lee. 1962. Three species of mammals from western Texas. *Southwestern Nat.* 7:77–78.

Jones, J. K. Jr., and R. W. Manning. 1989. The northern pygmy mouse, *Baiomys taylori*, on the Texas Llano Estacado. *Tex. J. Sci.* 41:110.

Jones, J. K. Jr., R. W. Manning, C. Jones, and R. R. Hollander. 1988. Mammals of the northern Texas Panhandle. *Occas. Pap. Mus., Texas Tech Univ.* 126:1–54.

Jones, J. K. Jr., C. J. Young, and D. J. Schmidly. 1985. Contributions to a bibliography of Recent Texas mammals, 1971–1980. *Occas. Papers Mus., Texas Tech Univ.* 95:1–44.

Judd, F. D. 1970. Geographic variation in the deer mouse, *Peromyscus maniculatus*, on the Llano Estacado. *Southwestern Nat.* 14:261–82.

Kaufman, J. H., D. V. Lanning, and S. E. Poole. 1976. Current status and distribution of the coati in the United States. *J. Mamm.* 57:609–11.

Kellogg, R. 1946. A century of progress in Smithsonian biology. *Science.* 104:132–41.

Kendeigh, S. C. 1932. A study of Merriam's temperature laws. *Wilson Bull.* 44:129–43.

Kim, K. C., and L. Knutson. 1986. Foundations for a national biological survey. Association of Systematics Collections, Museum of Natural History, Univ. Kansas, Lawrence. 215 pp.

Kofalk, H. 1989. *No woman tenderfoot: Florence Merriam Bailey, pioneer naturalist.* College Station: Texas A&M Univ. Press. 225 pp.

Kofalk, H. (with E. Hone). Unpubl. manuscript. My game is mice: Vernon Bailey and a lifetime in the field.

Krausman, P. R., D. J. Schmidly, and E. D. Ables. 1978. Comments on the taxonomic status, distribution, and habitat of the Carmen Mountains white-tailed deer (*Odocoileus virginianus caminis*) in Trans-Pecos Texas. *Southwestern Nat.* 23:577–90.

Lay, D. W., and T. O'Neil. 1942. Muskrats on the Texas coast. *J. Wildl. Manage.* 6:301–11.

Lee, T. E., Jr., B. R. Riddle, and P. L. Lee. 1996. Speciation in the desert pocket mouse (*Chaetodipus penicillatus* Woodhouse). *J. Mamm.* 77:58–68.

Lee, T. J., and M. D. Engstrom. 1991. Genetic variation in the silky pocket mouse (*Perognathus flavus*) in Texas and New Mexico. *J. Mamm.* 72:273–85.

Lehman, V. W. 1969. *Forgotten legions.* El Paso: Texas Western Press. 226 pp.

Leonard, R. I., J. H. Everitt, and F. W. Judd. 1991. Woody plants of the Lower Rio Grande Valley, Texas. Misc. Pub. 7, Texas Memorial Mus., Univ. Texas at Austin. 179 pp.

Leopold, A. 1933a. The conservation ethic. *J. Forestry.* 31:634–43.

———. 1933b. *Game management.* New York: Charles Scriber's Sons. 1948. 481 pp.

———. 1939. A biotic view of land. *J. Forestry.* 37:727–30.

———. 1947. The ecological conscience. *Bull. Garden Club America.* (September):45–53.

Levenson, H., R. S. Hoffmann, C. F. Nadler, L. Deutsch, and S. D. Freeman. 1985. Systematics of the Holarctic chipmunks (*Tamias*). *J. Mamm.* 66:219–42.

Lidicker, W. Z. Jr. 1960. An analysis of intraspecific variation in the kangaroo rat *Dipodomys merriami. Univ. California Publ. Zool.* 67:125–218.

*Life* Magazine. 1952. Man vs. mesquite. Edition of 18 August.

Long, M. E. 1998. The vanishing prairie dog. *Natl. Geog.* 193:116–31.

Loomis Austin, Inc. 2000a. Inventory of conservation and recreation land in Texas: a report on the supply of natural resource areas, recreation areas, and historic and cultural resources, completed as part of the Texas Parks and Wildlife for the 21st Century. Prepared for Texas Tech University, Texas Cooperative Fish and Wildlife Research Unit, Lubbock, Texas. Prepared by Loomis Austin, Inc., Austin, Texas with the assistance of Glenrose Engineering, Capitol Environmental Services and the Texas Land Trust Council. LAI project no. 000304. 19 pp. + tables (138 pp.) + appendix (8 pp.).

———. 2000b. Directions in land conservation and historic preservation: a report on the nationwide strategies and trends in natural and cultural resource protection, completed as part of the Texas Parks and Wildlife for the 21st Century. Prepared for Texas Tech University, Texas Cooperative Fish and Wildlife Research Unit, Lubbock, Texas. Prepared by Loomis Austin, Inc. and Capitol Environmental Services, Austin, Texas. LAI project no. 000304. 34 pp. + 1 p. appendix.

———. 2000c. Proceedings of the professional needs analysis conference, completed as part of the Texas Parks and Wildlife for the 21st Century. Prepared for Texas Tech University, Texas Cooperative Fish and Wildlife Research Unit, Lubbock, Texas. LAI project no. 000304. 25 pp. + 55 p. appendix.

Loomis, J. A. 1982. *Texas ranchman: the memoirs of John A. Loomis.* Chadron, Nebr.: Fur Press.

Luo, H. R., L. M. Smith, B. L. Allen, and D. A. Haukos. 1997. Effects of sedimentation on playa wetland volume. *Ecological Applications.* 7(1):247–52.

Malin, J. C. 1953. Soil, animal, and plant relations of the grassland, historically reconsidered. *Sci. Monthly.* 76:207–20.

Manning, R. W., and C. Jones. 1998. Annotated checklist of Recent land mammals of Texas, 1998. *Occas. Papers Mus., Texas Tech Univ.* 182:1–19.

Manning, R. W., F. D. Yancey, II, and C. Jones. 1996. Nongeographic variation and natural history of two sympatric species of pocket mice, *Chaetodipus nelsoni* and *C. eremicus,* from Brewster County, Texas. Pp. 191–95 in *Contributions in mammalogy: a memorial volume honoring Dr. J. Knox Jones, Jr.* Edited by H. H. Genoways and R. J. Baker. Lubbock: Mus. Texas Tech Univ. 315 pp.

Mares, M. A., and R. A. Ojeda. 1984. Faunal commercialization and conservation in South America. *BioScience.* 34:580–84.

Martin, R. E., and K. G. Matocha. 1972. Distributional status of the kangaroo rat, *Dipodomys elator. J. Mamm.* 53:873–77.

Maxwell, T. C. 1979a. Avifauna of the Concho Valley of west-central Texas with special reference to historical change. Unpubl. Ph.D. diss., Texas A&M Univ., College Station. 321 pp.

———. 1979b. Three men in Texas ornithology. *Bull. Texas Ornith. Soc.* 12:2–7.

McAlpine, S. 1990. Continued decline of elk populations within Guadalupe Mountains National Park, Texas. *Southwestern Nat.* 35:362–63.

McCarley, H. 1959. The mammals of eastern Texas. *Tex. J. Sci.* 11:385–426.

———. 1986. Ecology. Pp. 227–42 in *One-hundred years of science and technology in Texas.* Edited by L. J. Klosterman, L. S. Swenson, Jr., and S. Rose. Houston: Rice Univ. Press. 391 pp.

McCarley, H., and C. J. Carley. 1979. Recent changes in distribution and status of wild red wolves (*Canis rufus*). Endangered Species Report No. 4, U.S. Fish and Wildlife Service, Albuquerque, New Mexico. 38 pp.

McClinton, S. F., P. L. McClinton, and J. V. Richerson. 1992. Food habits of black bears in Big Bend National Park. *Southwestern Nat.* 37:433–35.

McCoid, M. J., T. H. Fritts, and E. W. Campbell, III. 1994. A brown tree snake (Colubridae: *Boiga irregularis*) sighting in Texas. *Tex. J. Sci.* 46:365–68.

Mead, R. A. 1968a. Reproduction in eastern forms of the spotted skunk (genus *Spilogale*). *J. Zool.* (London). 156:119–36.

———. 1968b. Reproduction in western forms of the spotted skunk (genus *Spilogale*). *J. Mamm.* 49:373–90.

Mearns, E. A. 1896. Preliminary diagnosis of new mammals from the Mexican border of the United States. *Proc. U.S. Nat. Mus.* 19:137–40.

————. 1898. Descriptions of three new forms of pocket mice from the Mexican border of the United States. *Bull. Amer. Mus. Nat. Hist.* 10:299–302.

————. 1907. Mammals of the Mexican Boundary of the United States. *Bull. 56.* U.S. Natl. Mus., Washington, D.C. 530 pp.

Merriam, C. H. 1889. Descriptions of two new species and one new subspecies of grasshopper mouse. *North Amer. Fauna.* 2:1–6.

————. 1890a. Descriptions of twenty-six new species of North American mammals. *North Amer. Fauna.* 4:1–34.

————. 1890b. Results of a biological survey of the San Francisco Mountain region and desert of the Little Colorado, Arizona. *North Amer. Fauna.* 3:1–126.

————. 1893. Descriptions of eight new ground squirrels of the genera *Spermophilus* and *Tamias* from California, Texas, and Mexico. *Proc. Biol. Soc. Washington.* 8:129–38.

————. 1894. Laws of temperature control of the geographic distribution of terrestrial animals and plants. *Nat. Geog. Mag.* 6:229–38.

————. 1895. Monographic revision of the pocket gophers, family Geomyidae (exclusive of the species of *Thomomys*). *North Amer. Fauna.* 8:1–258.

————. 1898a. Descriptions of six new ground squirrels from the western United States. *Proc. Biol. Soc. Washington.* 12:69–71.

————. 1898b. Life zones and crop zones of the United States. Bull. 10, Biol. Survey, U.S. Dept. Agric., 79 pp.

————. 1901. Description of twenty-three new pocket gophers of the genus *Thomomys*. *Proc. Biol. Soc. Washington.* 14:107–17.

Michael, E. D., and J. B. Birch. 1967. First Texas record of *Plecotus rafinesquii*. *J. Mamm.* 48:672.

Miller, G. S., Jr. 1929. Mammalogy and the Smithsonian Institution. Smithsonian Report 2995:391–411.

Miller, G. S., Jr., and R. Kellogg. 1955. List of North American Recent mammals. *U.S. Natl. Mus. Bull.* 205:1–954.

Morales, J. C., and J. W. Bickham. 1995. Molecular systematics of the genus *Lasiurus* (Chiroptera: Vespertilionidae) based on restriction site maps of the mitochondrial ribosomal genes. *J. Mamm.* 76:730–49.

Moss, S. P., and P. Mehlhop-Cifelli. 1990. Status of the kangaroo rat, *Dipodomys elator* (Heteromyidae), in Oklahoma. *Southwestern Nat.* 35:356–58.

Mungall, E. C., and W. J. Sheffield. 1994. *Exotics on the open range*. College Station: Texas A&M Univ. Press. 265 pp.

Nadler, C. F., R. S. Hoffman, J. H. Honacki, and D. Pozin. 1977. Chromosomal evolution in chipmunks, with special emphasis on A and B karyotypes of the subgenus *Neotamias*. *Am. Midl. Nat.* 98:343–53.

National Agricultural Statistics Service. 1999. *1997 Census of Agriculture, Texas State and County Data.* Washington, D.C.: U.S. Dept. Agric. 1130 pp.

National Research Council (NRC). 1993. *A biological survey for the nation*. Washington, D.C.: National Academy Press. 205 pp.

————. 1995. *Science and the Endangered Species Act*. Washington, D.C.: National Academy Press. 271 pp.

Nature Conservancy, The. 1999. A landowner's guide to conservation options. Pamphlet. Arlington, Va. 28 pp.

Navarro, D. L., J. H. Rappole, and M. E. Tewes. 1993. Distribution of the endangered ocelot (*Felis pardalis*) in Texas and northeastern Mexico. Pp. 157–69 in *Avances en el estudio de los mamiferos de Mexico*. Edited by R. A. Madellin and G. Ceballos. Asociacion Mexicana de Mastozoologia, Publicaciones Especiales Volume 1, A. D. Mexico, D. F.

Nelson, E. W., and E. A. Goldman. 1934. Pocket gophers of the genus *Thomomys* of the Mexican mainland and bordering territory. *J. Mamm.* 15:105–24.

Nelson, K., R. J. Baker, and R. L. Honeycutt. 1987. Mitochondrial DNA and protein differentiation between hybridizing cytotypes of the white-footed mouse, *Peromyscus leucopus*. *Evolution.* 41:864–72.

Newmark, W. D. 1987. A land-bridge island perspective on mammalian extinctions in western North American parks. *Nature.* 325:430–32.

Noss, R. F., E. T. LaRoe III, and J. M. Scott. 1995. *Endangered ecosystems of the United States: a preliminary assessment of loss and degradation*. National Biological Service Biological Report 28. 58 pp.

Nunley, G. L. 1995. The re-establishment of the coyote in the Edwards Plateau of Texas. Pp. 55–64 in *Symposium Proceedings, Coyotes in the southwest: a compendium of our knowledge*. Edited by D. Rollins, C. Richardson, T. Blankenship, K. Canon, and S. Henke. Austin: Texas Parks and Wildlife Department. 180 pp.

Oberholser, H. C. 1974. *The bird life of Texas*. 2 vols. Austin: Univ. Texas Press. 1069 pp.

Oldfield, M. L. 1989. *The value of conserving genetic resources*. Sunderland, Mass.: Sinauer Associates, Inc. 379 pp.

Osgood, W. H. 1900. Revision of the pocket mice of the genus *Perognathus*. *North Amer. Fauna*. 18:1–72.

———. 1909. Revision of the mice of the American genus *Peromyscus*. *North Amer. Fauna*. 28:1–285.

———. 1925. Ned Hollister. *J. Mamm*. 6:1–12.

———. 1943. Clinton Hart Merriam (1855–1942). *J. Mamm*. 24:421–36.

Osterkamp, W. R., and W. W. Wood. 1987. Playa-lake basins on the Southern High Plains of Texas and New Mexico: I. Hydraulic, geomorphic, and geological development for their development. *Geological Society of America, Bulletin*. 99:215–23.

Owen, J. G., and D. J. Schmidly. 1986. Environmental variables of biological importance in Texas. *Tex. J. Sci*. 38:99–119.

Packard, J., and T. Cook. 1995. Effects of climate change on biodiversity and landscape linkages in Texas. Pp. 322–36 in *The changing climate of Texas: predictability and implications for the future*. Edited by J. Norwine, J. R. Giardino, G. R. North, and J. B. Valdes. College Station: GeoBooks, Texas A&M Univ. 348 pp.

Packard, J. M., and D. J. Schmidly. 1991. Graduate training integrating conservation and sustainable development: a role for mammalogists at North American universities. Pp. 392–415 in *Latin American mammalogy: history, biodiversity, and conservation*. Edited by M. A. Mares and D. J. Schmidly. Norman: Univ. Okla. Press. 468 pp.

Packard, R. L. 1960. Speciation and evolution of the pygmy mice, genus *Baiomys*. *Univ. Kansas Publ. Mus. Nat. Hist*. 9:579–670.

———. 1966. *Myotis austroriparius* in Texas. *J. Mamm*. 47:128.

Palmer, T. S., and others. 1954. Biographies of members of the American Ornithologists' Union, reprinted from "The Auk," 1884–1954. Baltimore: Lord Baltimore Press. 630 pp.

Paradiso, J. L. 1965. Recent records of red wolves from the Gulf Coast of Texas. *Southwestern Nat*. 10:318–19.

———. 1968. Canids recently collected in East Texas, with comments on the taxonomy of the red wolf. *Am. Midl. Nat*. 80:529–34.

Paradiso, J. L., and R. M. Nowak. 1972. A report on the taxonomic status and distribution of the red wolf. *Spec. Sci. Report*. 145:1–36, U.S. Dept. Int., Fish and Wildlife Serv.

Parker, N. C., R. D. Bradley, J. Burns, G. F. Edson, D. R. Haragan, C. Jones, R. R. Monk, J. T. Montford, C. J. Phillips, D. J. Schmidly, and R. J. Baker. 1998. Bioinformatics: a multi-disciplinary approach for the life sciences. *Occas. Papers Mus., Texas Tech Univ*. 186:i+1–8.

Patton, R. F. 1974. Ecological and behavioral relationships of the skunks of Trans-Pecos Texas. Ph.D. diss., Texas A&M Univ., College Station. 199 pp.

Pease, C. M., and J. A. Grzybowski. 1991. Protection of biodiversity in Texas. *Cons. Bio*. 5:7–8.

Peck, R. M. 1982. *A celebration of birds: the life and art of Louis Agassiz Fuertes*. New York: Walker and Co. 178 pp.

Pemberton, E. F., and R. J. Baker. 1978. Studies of a contact zone between chromosomally characterized populations of *Geomys bursarius*. *J. Mamm*. 59:233–42.

Pfau, R. S. 1994. First record of a native American elk (*Cervus elaphus*) from Texas. *Tex. J. Sci*. 46:189–90.

Pitts, R. M., Y. Lou, J. W. Bickham, and G. C. Ellis. 1999. Range extension for *Geomys breviceps* and *Geomys texensis* (Rodentia: Geomyidae) in Texas. *Tex. J. Sci*. 51:191–93.

Poole, A. J., and V. S. Schantz. 1942. Catalog of the type specimens of mammals in the United States National Museum, including the Biological Surveys collection. *U.S. Natl. Mus. Bull*. 178:1–705.

Rabinowitz, A. R. 1999. The present status of jaguars (*Panthera onca*) in the southwestern United States. *Southwestern Nat*. 44:96–100.

Racine, M. 2000. Hey, hey it's the monkeys. Pp. 8–13 in *Texas: Houston Chronicle Magazine*. May 28, 2000.

Rappole, J. H., C. E. Russell, J. R. Norwine, and T. E. Fulbright. 1986. Anthropogenic pressures and impacts on marginal, neotropical, semiarid ecosystems: the case of south Texas. *Sci. Total Env*. 55:91–99.

Rappole, J. H., and A. R. Tipton. 1987. An assessment of potentially endangered mammals of Texas. Unpubl. Final Rep. (Coop. Agreement #14-16-0002-86-927) to U.S. Fish and Wildlife Service, Office of Endangered Species, Albuquerque, New Mexico. 167 pp.

Raun, G. G. 1962. A bibliography of the Recent mammals of Texas. *Bull. Texas Mem. Mus*. 3:1–81.

Raun, G. G., and B. J. Wilks. 1961. Noteworthy records of the hog-nosed skunk (*Conepatus*) from Texas. *Tex. J. Sci*. 13:204–205.

Reichman, O. J., and R. J. Baker. 1972. Distribution and movements of two species of pocket gophers (Geomyidae) in an area of sympatry in the Davis Mountains, Texas. *J. Mamm.* 53:21–23.

Riddle, B. R., D. J. Hafner, and L. F. Alexander. 2000. Phylogeny and systematics of the *Peromyscus eremicus* species group and the historical biogeography of North American warm regional deserts. *Mol. Phylo. and Evol.* 17 (2): 145–60.

Rogers, D. S., and D. J. Schmidly. 1981. Geographic variation in the white-throated woodrat (*Neotoma albigula*) from New Mexico, Texas, and northern Mexico. *Southwestern Nat.* 26:167–81.

Rosenfeld, D. 2000. Suppression of rain and snow by urban and industrial air pollution. *Science.* 287:1793–96.

Ruedas, L. A. 1998. Systematics of *Sylvilagus* Gray, 1867 (Lagomorpha: Leporidae) from southwestern North America. *J. Mamm.* 79:1355–78.

Russel, R. J. 1953. Mammals from Cooke County, Texas. *Tex. J. Sci.* 5:454–64.

Samuel, W. M., and S. Demarais. 1993. Conservation challenges concerning wildlife farming and ranching in North America. *Trans. North Amer. Wildl. and Natur. Resour. Conf.* 58:445–47.

Sansom, A. 1995. *Texas lost: vanishing heritage.* Parks and Wildl. Found. of Texas, Inc., Dallas. 135 pp.

Saunders, D. A., R. J. Hobbs, and C. R. Margules. 1991. Biological consequences of ecosystem fragmentation: a review. *Cons. Bio.* 5:18–32.

Savory, A. 1988. *Holistic resource management.* Covelo, Calif.: Island Press. 564 pp.

Scheel, D., T. L. S. Vincent, and G. N. Cameron. 1996. Global warming and the species richness of bats in Texas. *Cons. Biol.* 10:452–64.

Schmidly, D. J. 1973a. Geographic variation and taxonomy of *Peromyscus boylii* from Mexico and the southern United States. *J. Mamm.* 54:111–30.

———. 1973b. The systematic status of *Peromycus comanche. Southwestern Nat.* 18:269–78.

———. 1977. *The mammals of Trans-Pecos Texas.* College Station: Texas A&M Univ. Press. 225 pp.

———. 1983. *Texas mammals east of the Balcones Fault Zone.* College Station: Texas A&M Univ. Press. 400 pp.

———. 1984a. Texas mammals: diversity and geographic distribution. Pp. 13-25 in *Protection of Texas natural diversity: an introduction for natural resource planners and managers.* College Station: Texas Agr. Exp. Sta., MP-1557. 60 pp.

———. 1984b. The furbearers of Texas. *Texas Parks and Wildl. Dept. Bull.* 7000-111:1–55.

———. 1991. *The bats of Texas.* College Station: Texas A&M Univ. Press. 188 pp.

———. 1998. Texas natural history: a century of change. Pp. 264–67, 314 in *Status and Trends of the Nation's Biological Resources.* Vol. 1. Edited by M. J. Mac, P. A. Opler, C. E. Puckett Haecker, and P. D. Doran. Reston, Va.: U.S. Dept. of Interior, U.S. Geol. Survey. 964 pp.

Schmidly, D. J., and W. A. Brown. 1979. Systematics of short-tailed shrews (genus *Blarina*) in Texas. *Southwestern Nat.* 24:39–48.

Schmidly, D. J., and J. R. Dixon. 1998. William B. "Doc" Davis: 1902-1995. *J. Mamm.* 79:1076–83.

Schmidly, D. J., and F. S. Hendricks. 1976. Systematics of the southern races of Ord's kangaroo rat, *Dipodomys ordii. Bull. Southern Calif. Acac. Sci.* 75:225–37.

Schmidly, D. J., and C. Jones. 2000. 20th century changes in mammals and mammalian habitats along the Rio Grande/Rio Bravo from Fort Quitman to Amistad. Proc. Rio Grande/Rio Bravo Binational Symposium: Fort Quitman to Amistad Reservoir, June 14, 2000, Ciudad Juarez, Mexico.

Schmidly, D. J., and J. A. Read. 1986. Cranial variation in the bobcat (*Felis rufus*) from Texas and surrounding states. *Occas. Papers Mus., Texas Tech Univ.* 101:1–39.

Scudday, J. F. 1972. Two recent records of gray wolves in west Texas. *J. Mamm.* 53:598.

Shaffer, B. S., B. C. Yates, and B. W. Baker. 1995. An additional record of the native American elk (*Cervus elaphus*) from north Texas. *Tex. J. Sci.* 47:159–60.

Sharpless, M. R., and J. C. Yelderman, Jr. 1993. *The Texas Blackland Prairie land, history, and culture.* Waco: Baylor Univ. 369 pp.

Shelford, V. E. 1932. Life zones, modern ecology, and the failure of temperature summing. *Wilson Bull.* 44:144–57.

———. 1945. The relative merits of the life zone and biome concepts. *Wilson Bull.* 57:248–52.

Shindle, D. B., and M. E. Tewes. 1998. Woody species composition of habitats used by ocelots (*Leopardus pardalis*) in the Tamaulipan biotic province. *Southwestern Nat.* 43:273–79.

Shogren, J. F., and J. Tschirhart. 1999. The Endangered Species Act at twenty-five. *Choices.* (3rd Quarter):4–9.

Shull, A. J. 1988. Endangered and threatened wildlife and plants; determination of endangered status for two long-nosed bats. *Federal Register.* 53:38456–60.

Slaughter, B. 1960. Vanquished lords. *Texas Game and Fish.* 18(1):24–25.

Smith, H. N., and C. A. Rechenthin. 1964. *Grassland restoration: the Texas brush problem.* Temple, Tex.: Soil Cons. Serv., U.S. Dept. Agric.

Smith, T., S. A. Smith, and D. J. Schmidly. 1990. Impact of fire ant (*Solenopsis invicta*) density on northern pygmy mice (*Baiomys taylori*). *Southwestern Nat.* 35:158–62.

Smolen, M. J., R. M. Pitts, and J. W. Bickham. 1993. A new subspecies of pocket gopher (*Geomys*) from Texas (Mammalia: Rodentia: Geomyidae). *Proc. Biol. Soc. Washington.* 106:5–23.

Solow, A. R., and S. Polasky. 1999. The Endangered Species Act as a tool to conserve biological diversity. *Choices.* (3rd Quarter):17–23.

Soule, M. E. 1985. What is conservation biology? *Bioscience.* 35:727–34.

———, ed. 1986. *Conservation biology: the science of scarcity and diversity.* Sunderland, Mass.: Sinauer Associates, Inc. 584 pp.

———, ed. 1987. *Viable populations for conservation.* Cambridge, N.Y.: Cambridge Univ. Press. 189 pp.

Soule, M. E., E. Bolger, A. Alberts, J. Wright, M. Sorice, and S. Hill. 1988. Reconstructed dynamics of rapid extinctions of chaparral-requiring birds in urban habitat islands. *Cons. Biol.* 2:75–92.

Soule, M. E., and K. A. Kohm. 1989. *Research priorities for conservation biology.* Covelo, Calif.: Island Press. 97 pp.

Soule, M. E., and L. S. Mills. 1998. No need to isolate genetics. *Science.* 282:1658–59.

Soule, M. E., and B. A. Wilcox, eds. 1980. *Conservation biology: an evolutionary-ecological perspective.* Sunderland, Mass.: Sinauer Associates, Inc. 395 pp.

Stangl, F. B. Jr. 1986. Aspects of a contact zone between two chromosomal races of *Peromyscus leucopus* (Rodentia: Cricetidae). *J. Mamm.* 67:465–73.

———. 1992a. A new subspecies of the tawny-bellied cotton rat, *Sigmodon fulviventer*, from Trans-Pecos Texas. *Occas. Papers Mus., Texas Tech Univ.* 145:1–4.

———. 1992b. First record of *Sigmodon fulviventer* in Texas: natural history and cytogenetic observations. *Southwestern Nat.* 37:213–14.

Stangl, F. B. Jr., and R. J. Baker. 1984. A chromosomal subdivision in *Peromyscus leucopus:* Implications for the subspecies concept as applied to mammals. Pp. 139–45 in *Festschrift for Walter W. Dalquest in honor of his sixty-sixth birthday.* Edited by N.

V. Horner. Wichita Falls, Tex.: Dept. Biol., Midwestern State Univ.

Stangl, F. B. Jr. and C. B. Carr. 1997. Status of *Blarina hylophaga* (Insectivora: Soricidae) in north Texas and southern Oklahoma. *Tex. J. Sci.* 49:159–62.

Stangl, F. B. Jr., S. Kasper, and T. S. Schafer. 1989. Noteworthy range extensions and marginal distributional records for five species of Texas mammals. *Tex. J. Sci.* 41:436–37.

Stangl, F. B. Jr., T. S. Schafer, J. R. Goetze, and W. Pinchak. 1992. Opportunistic use of modified and disturbed habitat by the Texas kangaroo rat (*Dipodomys elator*). *Texas J. Sci.* 44:25–35.

Steinhart, P. 1994. *Two Eagles/Dos Aguillas: the natural world of the United States-Mexico borderlands.* Berkeley: Univ. Calif. Press. 201 pp.

Sterling, Keir B. 1974. *Last of the naturalists: the career of C. Hart Merriam.* New York: Arno Press. 478 pp.

———. 1978. Naturalists of the Southwest at the turn of the century. *Environmental Review.* 3:20–33.

———. 1989. Builders of the U.S. Biological Survey, 1885–1930. *J. Forest History.* 33:180–87.

Strecker, J. K. 1926. A check-list of the mammals of Texas, exclusive of the Sirenia and Cetacea. *Baylor Bull.* 29(3):1–48.

———. 1929. Notes on the Texas cotton and Attwater wood rats in Texas. *J. Mamm.* 10:216–20.

Swank, W. G., and J. G. Teer. 1989. Status of the jaguar—1987. *Oryx.* 23:14–21.

Swepston, D. A., and B. C. Thompson. 1986. *Texas furbearer bibliography 1851–1985.* Fed. Aid Proj. W-117R. Tex. Parks and Wildl. Dept, Austin. 114 pp.

Tabor, F. W. 1940. Range of the coati in the United States. *J. Mamm.* 21:11–14.

Tanner, T., ed. 1987. *Aldo Leopold: the man and his legacy.* Ankeny, Iowa: Soil Cons. Soc. Amer. 175 pp.

Taylor, W. P., and W. B. Davis. 1947. The mammals of Texas. Bull. 27,Game, Fish, and Oyster Comm., Austin, Tex. 79 pp.

Teer, J. G., L. A. Renecker, and R. J. Hudson. 1993. Overview of wildlife farming and ranching in North America. *Trans. North Amer. Wildl. and Natur. Resour. Conf.* 58:448–59.

Tewes, M. E. 1990. Cat country. *Texas Parks and Wildlife.* 48:4–11.

Tewes, M. E., and D. R. Blanton. 1998. Potential impacts of international bridges on ocelots and jaguarundis along the Rio Grande Wildlife Corridor. Pp. 135–39 in *Proc. International Conf. Wildlife Ecology and Transportation.* Edited by

G. L. Evink, P. Garrett, D. Zeigler, and J. Berry. FL-ER-69-98, Florida Department of Transportation, Tallahassee, Fla. 263 pp.

Tewes, M. E., and D. D. Everett. 1986. Status and distribution of the endangered ocelot and jaguarundi in Texas. Pp. 147–58 in *Cats of the world: biology, conservation, and management*. Edited by S. D. Miller and D. D. Everett. Washington, D.C.: National Wildlife Federation. 501 pp.

Tewes, M. E., L. L. Laack, and A. Caso. 1995. Corridor management for ocelots in the southern United States and northern Mexico. Pp. 444–46 in *Integrating people and wildlife for a sustainable future*. Edited by J. A. Bissonette and P. R. Krausman. Bethesda, Md.: The Wildlife Society.

Tewes, M. E., and S. D. Miller. 1987. Future research for the endangered ocelot population of the United States. Pp. 164–66 in *Proc. 3rd Southeastern Nongame and Endangered Wildlife Symposium*. Edited by R. R. Odom, K. A. Riddleberger, and J. C. Ozier. Athens, Ga.: Georgia Dept. Nat. Resources. 253 pp.

Tewes, M. E., and D. J. Schmidly. 1987. The neotropical felids: jaguar, ocelot, margay, and jaguarundi. Pp. 703–705 in *Wild furbearer management and conservation in North America*. Edited by M. Novak, J. Baker, M. E. Obbard and B. Mulloch. Ontario: Ministry of Natural Resources.

*Texas Almanac for 1873 and emigrant's guide to Texas*. 1873. Richardson and Co., Galveston, Texas.

*Texas Almanac and State Industrial Guide*. 1904. A. H. Belo Corp., Dallas, Texas.

*Texas Almanac and State Industrial Guide*. 1926. A. H. Belo Corp., Dallas, Texas.

Texas Audubon Society. 1997. *Facts about Texas' birds, wildlife and habitat: a Texas briefing guide for policy makers*. Texas Audubon Society, Austin.

*Texas Environmental Almanac* (2d Edition). 2000. Compiled by M. Sanger and C. Reed, Texas Center for Policy Studies. Austin: Univ. Texas Press. 387 pp.

Texas Outdoors: A Vision for the Future. 1998. A report to the Texas Parks and Wildlife Department, prepared by Texas A&M University Agriculture Program, Institute of Renewable Natural Resources. 34 pp.

Texas Parks and Wildlife Department (TPWD). 1988. The Texas Wetlands Plan Addendum to the 1985 Texas Outdoor Recreation Plan. Austin: Texas Parks and Wildl. Dept. 35 pp.

Thorne, E. T., and E. S. Williams. 1988. Disease and endangered species: the black-footed ferret as a recent example. *Conservation Biology*. 2:66–74.

Tiner, R. W., Jr. 1984. *Wetlands of the United States: current status and recent trends*. Washington, D.C.: U.S. Dept. of the Interior, Fish and Wildl. Serv. Natl. Wetlands Inventory. 59 pp.

Tolba, M. K. 1987. *Sustainable development: constraints and opportunistics*. London: Butterworths. 221 pp.

Traweek, M. S. 1995. *Statewide census of exotic big game animals*. Prog. Rept., Fed. Aid Proj. W-127-R-3 No. 21, Texas Parks and Wildl. Dept., Austin.

Truett, J. C., and D. W. Lay. 1984. *Land of bears and honey*. Austin: Univ. Texas Press. 176 pp.

Tucker, P. K., and D. J. Schmidly. 1981. Studies of a contact zone among three chromosome races of *Geomys bursarius* in east Texas. *J. Mamm.* 62:258–72.

U.S. Census Bureau. 2001. Website, quickfacts.census.gov/qfd/states/48000.html.

U.S. Department of the Interior, Fish and Wildlife Service, and U.S. Department of Commerce, Bureau of the Census (USDI/USDC). 1998. *National survey of fishing, hunting, and wildlife-associated recreation, 1996*. 47 pp.

Van Gelder, R. G. 1959. A taxonomic revision of the spotted skunks (genus *Spilogale*). *Bull. Amer. Mus. Nat. Hist.* 117:233–392.

Walker, C. W. 1997. Patterns of genetic variation of ocelot (*Leopardus pardalis*) populations for South Texas and northern Mexico. Unpubl. Ph.D. diss., Texas A&M Univ., College Station. 117pp.

Walker, C. W., L. A. Harveson, M. T. Pittman, M. E. Tewes, and R. L. Honeycutt. 2000. Microsatellite variation in two populations of mountain lions (*Puma concolor*) in Texas. *Southwestern Nat.* 45:196–203.

Walker, W. W., J. K. Sandel, R. L. Honeycutt, and C. Adams. 1996. Winter utilization of box culverts by Vespertilionid bats in southeast Texas. *Tex. J. Sci.* 48:166–68.

Walpole, D. K., S. K. Davis, and I. F. Greenbaum. 1997. Variation in mitochondrial DNA in populations of *Peromyscus eremicus* from the Chihuahuan and Sonoran deserts. *J. Mamm.* 78:397–404.

Weniger, D. 1984. *The explorers' Texas: the lands and waters*. Vol. 1. Austin: Eakin Press. 224 pp.

———. 1997. *The explorers' Texas: the animals they found*. Vol. 2. Austin: Eakin Press. 200 pp.

Western, D., and M. Pearl. 1989. *Conservation for the twenty-first century*. New York: Oxford Univ. Press. 365 pp.

Weyandt, S., T. E. Lee, and J. C. Patton. 2001. Noteworthy record of the western yellow bat, *Lasiurus xanthinus* (Chiroptera: Vespertilionidae) and a report on the bats of Eagle Nest Canyon, Val Verde County, Texas. *Tex. J. Sci.* 53:289–92.

White, P. S., S. P. Wilds, and G. A. Thunhorst. 1998. Southeast. Pp. 255–307 in *Status and Trends of the Nation's Biological Resources.* Vol. 1. Edited by M. J. Mac, P. A. Opler, C. E. Puckett Haecker, and P. D. Doran. Reston, Va.: U.S. Dept. of Interior, U.S. Geol. Survey. 964 pp.

White, R. J. 1986. *Big game ranching in the United States.* Mesilla, N.M.: Wild Sheep and Goat International. 355 pp.

Wilcove, D. S., M. J. Bean, R. Bonnie, and M. McMillan. 1996. *Rebuilding the Ark: toward a more effective Endangered Species Act for private land.* Washington, D.C.: Environmental Defense Fund.

Wilkins, K. T., and D. J. Schmidly. 1979. Identification and distribution of three species of pocket mice (genus *Perognathus*) in Trans-Pecos Texas. *Southwestern Nat.* 24:17–32.

Wilkins, N., R. D. Brown, R. J. Conner, J. Engle, C. Gilliland, A. Hays, R. D. Slack, and D. W. Steinbach. 2000. Fragmented lands: changing land ownership in Texas. Brochure, The Agriculture Program, Texas A&M Agricultural Communications, College Station. 8 pp.

Williams, D. F. 1978. Systematics and ecogeographic variation of the Apache pocket mouse (Rodentia: Heteromyidae). *Bull. Carnegie Mus. Nat. Hist.* 10:1–57.

Williams, S. L., and H. H. Genoways. 1981. Systematic review of the Texas pocket gopher, *Geomys personatus* (Mammalia: Rodentia). *Ann. Carnegie Mus., Carnegie Mus. Nat. Hist.* 50:435–73.

Wilson, D. E. 1973. The systematic status of *Perognathus merriami* Allen. *Proc. Biol. Soc. Washington.* 86:175–92.

———. 1985. Status report: *Leptonycteris nivalis* (Sassure), Mexican long-nosed bat. Unpubl. report prepared for Office of Endangered Species, U.S. Fish and Wildl. Serv. 33 pp.

Wilson, D. E., and J. F. Eisenberg. 1990. Origin and applications of mammalogy in North America. Pp. 1–35 in *Current mammalogy.* Vol. 2, Edited by H. H. Genoways. New York: Plenum Publishing Corporation.

Wilson, D. E., and N. J. Silvy. 1988. Impact of the imported fire ant on birds. Pp. 70–74 in *Proceedings*

*of the governor's conference. The red imported fire ant: assessment and recommendations.* Edited by J. Teer. Austin: Sportsmen Conservationists of Texas.

Wilson, E. O. 1984. *Biophilia: the human bond with other species.* Cambridge, Mass.: Harvard Univ. Press. 157 pp.

Wilson, E. O., and F. M. Peter, eds. 1988. *Biodiversity.* Washington, D.C.: National Academy Press. 521 pp.

Wolff, S. E. 1948. *An evaluation of some weedy Texas junipers.* Fort Worth: Soil Cons. Service.

Wooding, J. B., J. A. Cox, and M. R. Pelton. 1994. Distribution of black bears in the southeastern coastal plain. *Proc. Annu. Conf. Southeastern Assoc. Fish and Wildl. Agencies.* 48:270–75.

Yancey, F. D. II. 1997. The mammals of Big Bend Ranch State Park, Texas. *Spec. Publ. Mus., Texas Tech Univ.* 39:1–210.

Yancey, F. D. II, and C. Jones. 1996. Notes on three species of small mammals from Big Bend region of Texas. *Tex. J. Sci.* 48:247–50.

———. 1997. Dispersal of two species of harvest mice (*Reithrodontomys*) between the High Plains and Rolling Plains of Texas. *Occas. Papers Mus., Texas Tech Univ.* 166:1–5.

Yancey, F. D. II, C. Jones, and J. R. Goetze. 1995a. Notes on harvest mice (*Reithrodontomys*) of the Big Bend region of Texas. *Tex. J. Sci.* 47:263–68.

Yancey, F. D. II, C. Jones, and R. W. Manning. 1995b. The eastern pipistrelle, *Pipistrellus subflavus* (Chiroptera: Vespertilionidae) from the Big Bend region of Texas. *Tex. J. Sci.* 47:229–31.

Yancey, F. D. II, R. W. Manning, and C. Jones. 1996. Distribution, natural history, and status of the Palo Duro mouse, *Peromyscus truei comanche*, in Texas. *Tex. J. Sci.* 48:3–12.

Yates, T. L., and D. J. Schmidly. 1977. Systematics of *Scalopus aquaticus* (Linnaeus) in Texas and adjacent states. *Occas. Papers Mus., Texas Tech Univ.* 45:1–46.

Young, J. H., and M. E. Tewes. 1994. Evaluation of techniques for initial restoration of ocelot habitat. *Proc. Ann. Conf. Southeastern Assoc. Fish and Wildl. Agen.* 48:336–42.

Zahniser, H. 1942. Vernon Orlando Bailey, 1864–1942. *Science,* 96:6–7.

# Index

Please note that all species are indexed by their current scientific names. Page numbers of photographs are in **bold**.